A HISTORY OF
AIR WARFARE

EDITED BY

JOHN ANDREAS OLSEN

Potomac Books, Inc.
Washington, D.C.

Library of Congress Cataloging-in-Publication Data
A history of air warfare / edited by John Andreas Olsen. — 1st ed.
  p. cm.
 Includes bibliographical references and index.
 ISBN 978-1-59797-440-0 (hardcover : alk. paper) — ISBN 978-1-59797-433-2 (pbk. : alk. paper)
 1. Air warfare—History. 2. Air power—History. I. Olsen, John Andreas, 1968–

 UG625.H57 2009
 358.4'1409—dc22

                                                                    2009036637

Printed in the United States of America on acid-free paper that meets the American National Standards Institute Z39-48 Standard.

Potomac Books, Inc.
22841 Quicksilver Drive
Dulles, Virginia 20166

First Edition

10 9 8 7 6 5 4 3

A HISTORY OF
AIR WARFARE

ALSO BY JOHN ANDREAS OLSEN

Strategic Air Power in Desert Storm
John Warden and the Renaissance of American Air Power

CONTENTS

Acknowledgments vii

List of Abbreviations ix

Introduction xiii

PART I: 1914–1945 1

1 The First World War, 1914–1919, *John H. Morrow Jr.* 3

2 The Air War in Europe, 1939–1945, *Richard Overy* 27

3 The Air War in the Pacific, 1941–1945, *Richard R. Muller* 53

PART II: 1945–1990 81

4 The Air War in Korea, 1950–1953, *Alan Stephens* 85

5 Operations over North Vietnam, 1965–1973, *Wayne Thompson* 107

6 Air Superiority in the Israel-Arab Wars, 1967–1982, *Shmuel L. Gordon* 127

7 Air Power and the Falklands, 1982, *Lawrence Freedman* 157

PART III: 1990–2000 175

8 Operation Desert Storm, 1991, *John Andreas Olsen* 177

9 Operation Deliberate Force, 1995, *Robert C. Owen* 201

10 Operation Allied Force, 1999, *Tony Mason* 225

PART IV: 2000–2006 253

11 Operation Enduring Freedom, 2001, *Benjamin S. Lambeth* 255

12 Operation Iraqi Freedom, 2003, *Williamson Murray* 279

13 The Second Lebanon War, 2006, *Itai Brun* 297

PART V: PERSPECTIVES   325
14   Air Power in Small Wars: 1913 to the Present, *James S. Corum*   327
15   The Rise and Fall of Air Power, *Martin van Creveld*   351
16   Air and Space Power: Climbing and Accelerating, *Richard P. Hallion* 371

Notes   395
Selected Bibliography   441
Index   453
Biographical Notes   481

ACKNOWLEDGMENTS

IN THE SUMMER OF 2008, I was appointed visiting professor at the Swedish National Defence College's Department of Military Studies. In addition to teaching responsibilities, the college gave me the specific challenge of compiling a one-volume history of air warfare. The task was to produce a book that would appeal to military professionals; to scholars and specialists in the field of military studies; to general readers interested in air power history, theory, doctrine, and strategy; and to faculty and students at both military and civilian colleges and universities.

In an attempt to meet those objectives, I approached some of the world's leading air warfare experts with a request to describe and analyze various campaigns in which air power has played a significant role, from the First World War to the second Lebanon war. The authors of this volume were chosen for their insight into air warfare and its history, their critical approach to the utility of air power, and their ability to present their analysis in a concise and readable fashion. I am most grateful to the authors for their contributions, their team spirit, and their appreciation of the very real difficulties of deadlines and editing that beset a project with as many authors as there are chapters.

I am naturally grateful to the Swedish National Defence College for having initiated and financed this project. In addition, I am much obliged to Sitakumari for providing the photographs and to Simon Moores for his editorial support. I would also like to thank a long-standing friend, H. P. Willmott, for advice and encouragement, and I am deeply grateful to Margaret S. MacDonald for her generous help in finalizing the manuscript. Finally, I have worked with Potomac Books previously, and again its team has been professional in its commitment to see manuscripts turned into books: I would especially like to thank John Church, Elizabeth Demers, Sam Dorrance, Julie Kimmel, and Lisa Yambrick.

ABBREVIATIONS

AAA	antiaircraft artillery
ABCCC	airborne command and control center
ACTS	Air Corps Tactical School
AD	air defense
AEW	airborne early warning
AFSOUTH	Allied Forces Southern Europe
AirSols	Air Solomons
AOR	area of responsibility
ATGM	antitank guided missile
ATO	air tasking order
AWACS	Airborne Warning and Control System
BEF	British Expeditionary Force
C^2	command and control
C^3I	command, control, communications, and intelligence
C^4I	command, control, communications, computers, and intelligence
CAOC	Combined Air Operations Center
CAS	close air support
CBI	China-Burma-India
CENTPAC	Central Pacific
CJTF	Combined Joint Task Force
CSIS	Center for Strategic and International Studies
DMPI	desired mean point of impact
EAF	Egyptian Air Force
EBO	effects-based operations
ECM	electronic countermeasures

EDT	Eastern Daylight Time
ELN	*Ejército de Liberación Nacional*
ETAC	enlisted tactical air controller
FAC–A	forward air controller–airborne
FARC	*Fuerzas Armadas Revolucionarias de Colombia*
FEAF	Far East Air Forces
FLN	*Front de Libération Nationale*
FRY	Former Republic of Yugoslavia
GPS	Global Positioning System
GQG	*Grand Quartier Général*, or French high command
HARM	high-speed antiradiation missile
IADS	integrated air defense system
IAF	Israeli Air Force
IDF	Israel Defense Forces
IED	improvised explosive device
IJN	Imperial Japanese Navy
ISR	intelligence, surveillance, and reconnaissance
JDAM	joint direct attack munition
JFACC	joint force air component commander
JNA	*Jugoslovenska Narodna Armija*, or Yugoslav People's Army
KARI	integrated air defense system (Iraq)
KEZ	Kosovo Engagement Zone
KLA	Kosovo Liberation Army
KTO	Kuwaiti theater of operations
KVM	Kosovo Verification Monitor
LDK	League for a Democratic Kosovo
LZ	landing zone
MANPADS	man-portable air defense system
MAW	Marine Aircraft Wing
NAC	North Atlantic Council
NASM	National Air and Space Museum
NATO	North Atlantic Treaty Organization
NBC	nuclear, biological, and chemical
NKAF	North Korean Air Force
OAS	offensive air strike
OHL	*Oberste Heeresleitung*, or German high command
OIF	Operation Iraqi Freedom

OODA	observe, orient, decide, and act
OPLAN	operational plan
OSCE	Organization for Security and Cooperation in Europe
OSRD	Office of Scientific Research and Development
PGM	precision-guided munition
PLA	People's Liberation Army
PLAAF	People's Liberation Army Air Force
PLO	Palestine Liberation Organization
RAAF	Royal Australian Air Force
RADREL	radio relay
RAF	Royal Air Force
RAFM	Royal Air Force Museum
RFC	Royal Flying Corps
RHAF	Royal Hellenic Air Force
RNAS	Royal Naval Air Service
ROE	rules of engagement
RPV	remotely piloted vehicle
RRF	Rapid Reaction Force
RS	*Republika Srpska*
RSK	*Republika Srpska Krajina*
RV i PVO	*Ratno Vazduhoplovstvo i Protiv Vazdusna Odbrana* (FRY air force and air defense)
RWR	radar warning receivers
SAASS	School of Advanced Air and Space Studies (USAF)
SAC	Strategic Air Command
SAF	Syrian Air Force
SAM	surface-to-air missile
SAS	Special Air Service
SEAD	suppression of enemy air defenses
SOF	special operations forces
SPIN	special instruction
SSM	surface-to-surface missile
SWPAC	Southwest Pacific
TLAM	Tomahawk land attack missile
TP	Trenchard Papers
UAV	unmanned aerial vehicle
UCAV	unmanned combat aerial vehicle

UN	United Nations
UNC	United Nations Command
UNPROFOR	United Nations Protection Force
UNSCR	United Nations Security Council Resolution
USAAF	U.S. Army Air Forces
USAF	U.S. Air Force
USAFE	U.S. Air Forces in Europe
USCENTCOM	U.S. Central Command
USEUCOM	U.S. European Command
USMC	U.S. Marine Corps
USN	U.S. Navy
VJ Day	Victory over Japan Day
VNAF	South Vietnamese Air Force
ZOA	zone of action

INTRODUCTION

HISTORY: AN ARGUMENT WITHOUT END

HISTORY CONTRIBUTES TO KNOWLEDGE, but how can students of warfare best increase their knowledge of military history and military campaigns? To answer this question, Sir Michael Howard, one of the twentieth century's most distinguished military historians, offered students three general "rules of study."[1]

First, the student must focus on *width*: that is, study the way in which warfare has developed over time to determine the elements that remain constant and those that change. An appreciation of recurring themes in warfare—such as command in war, principles of war, and logistics—demands the kind of perspective that only extensive reading can provide. By approaching a subject in breadth, the student should recognize how different developments relate to each other, and perhaps identify links that are not apparent at first sight.

The second general rule is to study in *depth*. The student who seeks to improve professional insight needs to study individual wars, campaigns, and battles in detail and to explore specific issues meticulously. The student must consult different expert sources and obtain several interpretations in order to understand the background of a given event, identify its unique features, and assess what characteristics it had in common with other events.

Third, the student must examine military history in *context*. Wars, campaigns, and battles can best be understood if one also understands the nature of the societies and combat forces involved on both sides. The real causes of victory and defeat usually lie far away from the theater of operations, in the realms of political, economic, social, and industrial factors. Without some knowledge of the broader background to military operations, the student may reach the wrong conclusions; in this way, history can lend itself to abuse and become useless or even counterproductive.

Professor Howard concluded,

Pursued in this manner, in width, in depth and in context, the study of military history should not only enable the civilian to understand the nature of war and its part in shaping society, but also directly improve the officer's competence in his profession. But it must never be forgotten that the true use of history, military or civil, is, as Jacob Burckhardt once said, not to make men clever for next time; it is to make them wise forever.[2]

In addition to following these rules of study, the student of warfare should bear in mind the words of Dutch professor Pieter Geyl, who, more than five decades ago, taught us that history is "an argument without end."[3] In essence, there is always room for new, and even conflicting, interpretations of events and the connections among them. Reaching objective and dispassionate conclusions on cause and effect might well be an illusory goal because at the heart of interpretation lies subjectivity. There is invariably a difference between what actually happened in the past and what a historian *says* happened in the past, in part because all events are unique in terms of time, space, and content, and in part because every historian is certain to have preconceived notions, whether or not he or she is fully aware of them.

Inevitably, every historian seeks answers to certain questions. Equally inevitably, every historian makes certain choices in selecting data, prioritizing sources, and interpreting them. In all of this, a strong element of subjectivity is unavoidable.[4] Subjectivity is natural—perhaps even desirable, as it includes passion and creativity, and thus makes for interesting reading. The danger arises when a historian combines preconceptions or bias with bad methodology, or even worse, when prejudice results in systematic attempts at falsification, tampering with facts, and arguments based on a very selective reading of events. Almost all historical accounts include some level of misdirection.

Military history offers an excellent illustration of H. L. Mencken's famous observation that "there is always an easy solution for every human problem—neat, plausible, and wrong."[5] In the study of history, there is no such thing as the definitive truth: there are too many variables, too many unknowns, too many uncertainties, and too many hidden agendas. Certainty in history "is beyond the grasp of the human mind."[6] Those who read about war must seek variety and acknowledge inconclusiveness in the sources they consult. Warfare cannot be understood without taking those elements into account. Accepting the possibility of alternative explanations is especially important in military studies, where lives ultimately may be at stake if decisions are based on misinterpretations of history. Students must accept that insight comes from listening to new arguments, challenging accepted truths, questioning their own convictions, and uncovering bias.

One of the main lessons of the modern era is just how complex warfare has become: how many uncertainties are involved, and how many potential lessons can be drawn from a given conflict. Military professionals must recognize the pitfalls of assuming immediate relevance and the inherent dangers of seeking to draw upon the lessons of the past without knowing how the present relates to the future. Who would have thought in July 1990 that a massive military campaign would take place in the Persian Gulf a few months later? Who would have thought on September 10, 2001, that Western forces would find themselves extensively involved in Afghanistan and Iraq? Although the study of military history is crucial in terms of causes, conduct, and consequences, planners must still assume some degree of unpredictability. History is indicative, not prescriptive: it is likely that something unlikely will happen.

Nevertheless, only by studying history can one begin to acquire a basis for appreciating the present. This means recognizing how and why the international community, individual states, societies, industry, business, and the military services developed as they did, and how they arrived at their present form. This is an immense and frustrating task and one, moreover, made no easier by the reality that an individual who seeks proper understanding will be beset by those who want answers in two sentences.[7]

THE "ICARUS SYNDROME"

Armed forces and their military institutions tend to concern themselves more with warfighting capabilities, such as weapon systems, high technology, and firepower, than with the study of history. Consequently, when examining the enemy, they often concentrate on numeric orders of battle and the comparative performance of military equipment, rather than on exploring the complexities inherent in the nature of war. The focus on military tools rather than objectives seems both to stem from and encourage a belief that the right technological edge can allow the warrior to disregard the very characteristics of war and the enemy.

Air forces in particular confront an institutional challenge. Airmen are trained to get "bombs on target," and to do so effectively they must think in terms of improving the accuracy and destructive power of those bombs and the speed, range, instrumentation, and maneuverability of aircraft. In a 1994 book, analyst Carl Builder coined the term "Icarus syndrome" to describe how the U.S. Air Force had come to view the airplane as both end and means, contending that

> Air power theory, valid or not, was like the wax that held together the feathers in the wings of Icarus. When the wax melted from the heat of the Sun, the

fabric of the wings disintegrated and Icarus fell to his death. When the Air Force
leadership abandoned the institution's single unifying theory in favor of the
diverse interests of its factions, they allowed the wax to melt.[8]

Perhaps for this reason, of all the military services, air forces, although brilliant at
tactics, are probably the least intellectual, insisting as they so often do on technological
answers to very complex problems. Moreover, individual airmen who break away
from this path and decide to study the history of air warfare concern themselves
mostly with targeting because they were raised in a culture that thinks in prescriptive
and scientific terms.[9] This preoccupation with mechanistic, linear, and formulistic
thinking has prevented airmen and air forces from fully exploiting the nature of air
warfare and its objectives. Given such an environment, most studies of air warfare
reflect a belief in the existence of general formulations, universal models, and clear
links between cause and effect.

ABOUT THIS BOOK

A History of Air Warfare is intended as an introductory text for students of air warfare
who wish to expand their horizons by following the advice of Sir Michael Howard: to
combine studies in width, in depth, and in context. The book provides an overview
of air power—specifically its effectiveness, utility, and applicability—through critical
examinations of the most important campaigns in which air power played a significant
role, from the First World War to the second Lebanon war.

The book is organized chronologically, with sixteen chapters divided among
five parts. The first part deals with air power in the First and Second World Wars,
considering the latter in both the European and the Pacific theaters. Part 2 examines
various air campaigns during the Cold War period, starting with Korea and Vietnam
and ending with the Middle East and the Falklands. The third part focuses on the
liberation of Kuwait in 1991 and the air campaigns in the Balkans throughout the
1990s. The fourth part explores three recent military confrontations in Afghanistan,
Iraq, and Lebanon. The last part offers wider perspectives by focusing on air and
space power in both unconventional and conventional warfare from 1913 to the
present, and includes some speculation about the future.

While the book is intended as a cohesive whole, each chapter can be read in
isolation. Each author was asked to include a factual narrative of the given case study,
such as a brief background, objectives (declared or not), dates, dramatis personae,
and orders of battle. Next, authors were asked to provide interpretations of the
conduct of operations and the political and military outcomes. The chapters focus

primarily on the strategic and operational levels of war rather than the tactical and technological, and the discussion of each conflict deals with the interplay between politics and military operations proper. The authors have also sought to present the strategy and concept of operations for forces on both sides of the conflict. The resulting examination reveals both the strengths and the weaknesses of air power.

A History of Air Warfare steps back from immediate experience and presents an independent view of events. In the future, others will revise the accounts and conclusions set forth in these pages—because history is and should remain "an argument without end."

PART I: 1914–1945

INTRODUCTION

FROM ITS INCEPTION, manned flight opened the window to a new arena of warfare. In 1908, as the airship and the airplane emerged from their earliest stages of development, European military establishments were already on the verge of accepting powered flight. The years 1909 to 1914 witnessed the transformation of airships and airplanes into embryonic instruments of modern warfare. In chapter 1, John H. Morrow Jr. examines the use of airplanes in the First World War, suggesting that four powers merit special attention in the early evolution of military aviation: England, France, and Germany in general, and Italy for its early focus on strategic bombardment in particular. In August 1914, the European powers went to war with rudimentary air services and nascent aviation industries. The rigid airship, exemplified by Germany's gigantic Zeppelins, initially appeared a likely vehicle for aerial bombardment, but wartime events revealed it to be expensive and vulnerable. Instead, the small, fragile airplane quickly proved itself as a means of reconnaissance and artillery spotting in 1914, and by 1918 its missions had expanded to include aerial fighting, ground attack, and tactical and ultimately strategic bombing. Morrow describes how air forces, and consequently the aviation industry, increased rapidly in size and sophistication as aviation technology evolved to meet the demands of the Great War.

Before 1939, many nations shared a fear that the next war would be decided quickly by air attacks on home populations with weapons of mass destruction, but as Richard Overy explains in chapter 2, the Second World War in Europe took a very different form. Overy argues that aerial bombardment, performed in conjunction with operations by ground and naval forces to defeat enemy armed forces, remained the central function of air power and one of the most important explanations for German victories from 1939 to 1941 and Allied victories from 1942 to 1945. The chapter also explores the war's two major independent bombing campaigns—the

German Blitz of Britain in 1940 and 1941, and the Anglo-American bombing campaigns against Germany, Italy, and areas of German-occupied Europe—neither of which achieved their aim of breaking the population's morale. Still, in the Allied case, the development of an effective concept of operational air war became an essential ingredient for victory in Western and Southern Europe. The long, drawn-out Allied bombing campaigns succeeded in distorting German strategy and inhibiting war production by denying important military resources to German forces at the front, and the Allies' numerical advantages in aircraft eventually proved decisive. Overy concludes that the combatants exhibited important differences in the priority they gave to aircraft production, the integration of the air force into planning and decision-making processes, and the political acceptance of air power at the highest level, all of which shaped the eventual outcome of the air war.

Air power dominated events in the Pacific theater to an even greater extent than it did in Europe. Richard Muller shows in chapter 3 that the vastness of the battlespace compelled both the United States and Japan, the major belligerents, to rely extensively on land- and carrier-based aviation to achieve their objectives. The Imperial Japanese Navy developed a first-rate carrier force, capable of executing powerful and flexible mobile strikes across great distances. The United States also developed a capable naval air arm and a strategy for war in the Pacific, while its Army Air Corps focused primarily on preparing for war in Europe against Nazi Germany. In the six months that followed Japan's devastating air-sea assault on Pearl Harbor, which quickly secured vital resource zones and a formidable defensive perimeter and temporarily eliminated the U.S. Pacific Fleet, U.S. forces could fight only a valiant rearguard action. Muller argues that the dramatic U.S. victory at Midway and the hard-fought but even more significant victory at Guadalcanal turned the tide in the Pacific. However, the Japanese military remained powerful and benefited from good interior lines and strong defensive outposts. Air power provided a means of first outflanking these defenses and eventually bringing the Japanese home islands under direct air attack. Muller shows how U.S. Army Air Forces units in the Southwest Pacific helped make General Douglas MacArthur's island-hopping campaign possible, while Navy carrier task forces blazed a trail across the Central Pacific to the Philippines. Only then could B–29 Superfortress bombers based in the Marianas lay waste to Japan's cities in a devastating and controversial firebombing campaign and, ultimately, usher in the atomic age.

1

THE FIRST WORLD WAR, 1914–1919

John H. Morrow Jr.

FROM THE ORIGINS OF MILITARY AVIATION TO AUGUST 1914

FLIGHT OFFERED THE PROSPECT of a new arena of warfare from its inception, and the military's adoption and use of captive observation balloons in the latter half of the nineteenth century paved the way for its later acceptance of powered flight at the turn of the twentieth century. In 1883, one year before the invention of the dirigible, Albert Robida's book *War in the Twentieth Century*[1] envisaged a sudden crushing air strike, while Ivan S. Bloch's 1898 treatise on warfare[2] predicted bombardment from airships in the near future. By the end of the nineteenth century, balloon flight had prompted the foundation of civilian aviation societies and small military aviation units and established certain expectations for military powered flight.

The invention and evolution of more reliable and efficient high-speed gasoline engines in the 1880s and 1890s made powered flight a definite possibility by the turn of the twentieth century. European armies acquired their first airships in the years 1906 to 1908; the French army bought the Lebaudy brothers' nonrigid dirigibles, and the German army acquired Count Ferdinand von Zeppelin's gigantic rigid dirigibles. Noted Englishmen such as press magnate Alfred Harmsworth, Lord Northcliffe, and the Honorable Sir Charles Rolls of Rolls-Royce recognized, in Northcliffe's words, that "England was no longer an island."[3] H. G. Wells's *The War in the Air*, published in 1908,[4] dramatically portrayed the destruction of cities and, ultimately, of civilization by gigantic airships and airplanes in a future aerial conflict. Such dire expectations notwithstanding, airships and airplanes had not emerged from the experimental stage by the end of 1908, and their military effectiveness remained questionable.

At this crucial juncture, the airplane burst upon the scene in European aviation. In January 1908, Frenchman Henri Farman took off in a Voisin biplane under the plane's own power to fly the first officially monitored closed-circuit kilometer. On October 30, he made the first cross-country flight, some 27–30 kilometers from Bouy to Reims. French and German military observers considered these two achievements signals of the birth of aviation practical for military use. While they acknowledged the Wright Brothers' astounding duration record of two hours and twenty minutes aloft, their airplane required a launching apparatus and had flown only over a maneuver field and not over varied terrain.

Even in these early days of aviation, international jurists deemed its destructive potential significant enough to attempt to delineate the ramifications of aerial warfare for international law. They disagreed on the legitimate uses of aviation for warfare— some were willing to allow aerial bombing but not fighting, while others would permit reconnaissance, communications, and exploration but not bombing. Peace conferences at The Hague in 1899 and 1907 included discussions of air warfare. In 1899, the dirigible's potential as a bomber led to five-year prohibitions against the discharge of projectiles and explosives from balloons and against the bombing of undefended towns and cities. Yet in the absence of effective and proven bombers, the French, German, and Russian representatives would not foreclose the use of new weapons in warfare. In 1907, the Hague conferees agreed only not to bomb undefended towns and villages. The closer the aerial weapon came to being useful, the closer international jurists edged toward acknowledging its legitimacy as a weapon. In 1908, such reliability and usefulness still lay in the future, as the suitability of the infant airship and airplane for military use remained more a matter of conjecture than proven fact. Yet by 1909, aeronautics stood on the verge of acceptance by military establishments; the years 1909 to 1914 would witness its transformation into an embryonic instrument of modern warfare.

In 1909, French achievements—Louis Blériot's crossing of the English Channel in July and the Reims aviation week in August—stimulated aviation development and military interest everywhere. The French army bought its first airplanes after Reims and determined during maneuvers in September 1910 that airplanes served effectively for reconnaissance and liaison. The fall maneuvers of 1911 demonstrated that airplanes could locate an enemy's exact location at sixty kilometers, which prompted army officers to contemplate air-to-air combat and bombing masses of troops on the ground. In the *Revue générale de l'aéronautique militaire* in 1911, Belgian officer Lieutenant Poutrin suggested that the aerial bombardment of urban centers and government capitals could disorganize a nation's life and weaken its morale.[5]

While the French concentrated on airplanes, the Germans divided their resources between airplanes and airships, the former for tactical reconnaissance and the latter for strategic reconnaissance and possibly bombing. The German War Ministry regarded airships as a symbol of German aerial superiority and a political and military means of exerting pressure on foreign countries, and consequently was reluctant to admit their repeated failures (airships lacked reliability, particularly in bad weather). Ironically, across the English Channel, R. P. Hearne's book *Aerial Warfare*, published in 1909, proclaimed that everything was at the mercy of the Zeppelin, raids by which would destroy morale and disable military forces. By 1911, all the European powers were engaged in the development of military aviation at the same time that some observers calculated that the very fear of air war would lead to dissolution of armies and navies, and aerial warfare would be so gruesome that war would die "of its own excesses."[6]

In fact, once the Moroccan Crisis of 1911 prompted expectations of European war, armies began studying and testing aircraft armed with machine guns and cannon and equipped to drop shells and fléchettes—six-inch metal darts in canisters. The Michelin brothers launched an annual bombing competition in 1912 and published brochures that advocated bombing troops and supplies beyond the range of artillery. Despite such initiatives, the French army went to war in 1914 with 141 airplanes intended for reconnaissance, not combat.

In contrast, German General Staff Chief Helmuth von Moltke desired to have as many airships as possible operational for a future war and held exaggerated notions of the Zeppelin's "first-strike capability." On December 24, 1912, he informed the War Ministry that

> in the newest Z-ships we possess a weapon that is far superior to all similar ones of our opponents and that cannot be imitated in the foreseeable future if we work energetically to perfect it. Its speediest development as a weapon is required to enable us at the beginning of a war to strike a first and telling blow whose practical and moral effect could be quite extraordinary.[7]

German aviation journals echoed von Moltke's sentiments, anticipating pinpoint and unstoppable Zeppelin attacks on enemy targets in the dead of night.[8] German war plans in 1913 placed dirigibles under the control of the overall high command and individual army commands for strategic reconnaissance and bombing missions, although the dirigibles performed only one bombing trial before the war and the army had only seven of the monsters in the summer of 1914. The German army did have 245 airplanes for tactical reconnaissance, communications, and artillery spotting.

Britain, lagging behind both France and Germany in its development of aerial machines, did enjoy in Winston Churchill, First Lord of the Admiralty, a staunch supporter of aviation. The darling of the British aviation press, Churchill, dubbed the "fairy godfather" of naval aviation in January 1914, proclaimed that aviation's "great driving power is derived from its military aspect and utility" and that the "Navy and the Army . . . must be the main propulsive force of aviation in this country."[9] Both the navy and army agreed that the airplane's primary mission would be reconnaissance, although the navy's aviators yearned for a fighting aircraft as well.

In Italy, the visionary army major Giulio Douhet predicted aviation would become the decisive element of modern warfare and supported aircraft designer Gianni Caproni's efforts to design and build a fleet of multiengine bombers for tactical and strategic missions. Every European power, facing the likelihood of war by 1914, had an army air service, with a smaller naval service if its navy was large enough to require reconnaissance craft. Yet four powers merit attention in the evolution of military aviation: England, France, and Germany in general, and Italy in particular for its early focus on strategic bombardment. Clearly, doctrine often did not necessarily accord with the technological and industrial state of aviation, as inflated German expectations of the dirigible illustrated. On the whole, however, a limited doctrine restricting the aircraft's use to reconnaissance and communications accorded well with the state of aviation prior to the outbreak of war.

AUGUST TO DECEMBER 1914: AN INSTRUMENT OF WAR

Starting with the Battle of the Marne in September 1914, French reconnaissance planes played a key role in detecting the German army's turn to the northeast of Paris, thus enabling the French and British to strike the Germans in the flank. At the tactical level, some artillery commanders used aerial observation planes to direct artillery bombardments of enemy targets, and the aircrews used the occasion to drop 90-millimeter (mm) shells and fléchettes on the enemy.

In November, the French high command (*Grand Quartier Général*, or GQG) began to consider the strategic bombardment of German industrial centers. As early as August 2, War Minister Paul Painlevé and industrialists such as the Michelin brothers and aircraft builder Paul Schmitt had expressed interest in bombing Essen, the center of the Krupp Works in the Ruhr valley—a task beyond the capacity of the tiny air arm. On November 23, however, GQG formed four squadrons of Voisin biplanes into the First Bombardment Group of eighteen planes under Commandant de Göys. This force struck the railway station at Freiburg on December 4 and was drawing up a list of important and vulnerable targets by the end of the year.

The German high command (*Oberste Heeresleitung*, or OHL) used four Zeppelins in August and September for reconnaissance and bombing missions against cities such as Antwerp, Zeebrugge, Dunkirk, Calais, and Lille. All four airships were destroyed by enemy action (the last was destroyed during a British bombing attack on its shed in Düsseldorf on October 8). By the end of the year, the army had given up on the airship, but German naval airship commander Peter Strasser remained determined to strike at England despite having no suitable ships.

German airplanes performed such critical reconnaissance on the Western and Eastern fronts—particularly in the east at Tannenberg, where Russian cavalry out-numbered German—that by the end of August, the airplane had developed from "a supplementary means of information relied upon principally for confirmation" to "the principal means of operational reconnaissance—an important factor in forming army commanders' decisions."[10] At the end of August, in two separate incidents, German pilots dropped a bomb on Paris and then a note advising Parisians that "the German army stands before the gates of Paris. You have no choice but to surrender."[11] Perhaps these feats should count as early, if unsuccessful, uses of the airplane for psychological warfare.

German parliamentary deputies reflected a sentiment in military, diplomatic, and business circles that favored "breaking British resistance" through aerial bombing. In late August, the German minister in Stockholm, Franz von Reichenau, hoped "with all his heart" that "Germany would send airships and aircraft cruising regularly over England dropping bombs" until "the vulgar huckster souls" of those "cowardly assassins" would forget "even how to do sums." Walther Rathenau also advocated "systematically working on the nerves of the English towns through an overwhelming air force."[12] The German high command did form a bombing corps under a fanciful and intentionally deceptive name, the Carrier Pigeon Unit Ostende. However, as the Germans never captured Calais, their bombers could not reach England and thus had to content themselves with raids on Dunkirk and French harbors and railroad junctions.

The British Royal Flying Corps (RFC) won the praise of British Expeditionary Force (BEF) commander General John French on September 7 for its "admirable work" in providing him with "the most complete and accurate information, which has been of incalculable value in the conduct of operations."[13] The Royal Naval Air Service (RNAS), stuck with the unwelcome task of home defense even though the British navy's precedence over the army endowed the naval air service with nearly equal strength to its military counterpart, interpreted its home defense mission aggressively and struck Zeppelin sheds in Germany.

Such offensive efforts notwithstanding, aerial reconnaissance constituted the airman's essential contribution to warfare in 1914, although further advances in photography and wireless telegraphy would be required to make the airplane a truly efficient instrument of observation. Yet even in its embryonic state, the airplane forced armies to conceal their activity more extensively. A French artilleryman, pointing to a German aircraft over Péronne road near Albert early in October, commented to a British reporter, "There is that wretched bird which haunts us."[14] In 1914, the bird of war had spread its wings, casting its shadow over the battlefields of Europe. In 1915, it would grow fierce talons, to become a bird of prey, and the skies, like the Earth and seas below, would become an arena of mortal combat.

1915: THE AIR WEAPON

In 1915, particularly the latter half, observation, pursuit, and bombing became distinct specialties. Aviation arms concentrated on reconnaissance and artillery spotting, both of which improved markedly, while pursuit aviation and aerial combat, despite significant strides, remained less developed.

The French GQG focused on aerial bombardment in an effort to carry the war to the enemy. In 1915, and again in 1918, GQG concentrated on the development of French bomber forces, emphasizing bombers and more powerful aircraft engines. Aware that the war was becoming a conflict of matériel, GQG selected industrial targets for a strategic bombing campaign intended to shorten the war. The sturdy Voisin pusher biplanes that the French employed in 1915 could carry 40-kilogram 155mm artillery shells, and from May through September the French bombed such western German cities as Ludwigshafen (where the Badische Anilin Company produced explosives and poison gas), Karlsruhe, Trier, and Saarbrücken.

Early in June, GQG had proposed an air arm of fifty squadrons (five hundred bombers) to attack Essen, the home of the Krupp Works, but doing so would require more powerful bombers and thus more powerful engines. In July and again in September, the French parliament's aviation commissions demanded the bombardment of German industrial centers and the construction of large, long-range bombers for the mission. Even university professor A. Le Châtelier wrote the government advocating an aviation arm of one thousand planes, each capable of carrying a three-hundred- to four-hundred-kilogram bomb load to attack German communications, stations, and supply and munitions depots in the Rhine region around the clock.[15]

By July, however, German armed aircraft, including the new Fokker monoplane fighter, were taking higher tolls on the slow and vulnerable Voisin and Farman biplanes, although the French bombers now flew in groups in V formation for defense. GQG responded by using the bombers increasingly on night raids as extra-long-range artillery against military targets directly behind the front. However, night operations sacrificed speed for heavier bomb loads, complicated navigation, and decreased the precision and intensity of the raids. GQG consequently renounced its hopes for strategic aviation because of the cost, matériel deficiencies, and awareness that Paris would become Germany's prime target for reprisal raids in any strategic air war.

In the winter of 1914–1915, the German army and navy jockeyed to undertake strategic attacks on England with dirigibles. The navy claimed that the effect that bombing London would have on British morale could diminish British determination to prosecute the war. Two German dirigibles did bomb the British coast in January 1915, but Kaiser Wilhelm initially forbade attacks on London out of concern for opinion in neutral countries, particularly the United States. Late in April, the Kaiser reversed himself and consented to raids to demoralize the population, damage war production, and divert British airplanes to home defense.

Throughout the year, the Zeppelins grew larger and more powerful, approaching six hundred feet in length, with a volume of more than one million cubic feet, a speed of fifty miles per hour, and a bomb load of over two tons. The loss of two army airships, one of which had staged the first bombing raid on London the night of May 31–June 1, prompted the army to transfer its Zeppelins to the less heavily defended Eastern front. The navy remained determined to use airships to scout for the fleet and bomb England, and its Zeppelins bombed London in August, September, and October. In 1915, raiding Zeppelins dropped 1,900 bombs totaling just over 36 tons, killing 277, wounding 645, and causing an estimated damage of £870,000. The onset of winter halted the raids, but the navy prepared to continue its campaign in 1916, as British airplanes were unable to intercept the fast-climbing airships.

In 1915, the British Expeditionary Force's RFC concentrated on tactical aviation, artillery spotting and reconnaissance, and aerial fighting, while the RNAS continued its bombing raids on German targets in Belgium, particularly Zeppelin bases. Members of the government and Parliament, increasingly dissatisfied with the air war effort, contemplated devastating aerial attacks on Germany. At a meeting of the war council on February 24, 1915, one member advocated an air attack to distribute a "blight" on Germany's next grain crop, while another preferred to burn the crop using thousands of little discs of gun cotton. Winston Churchill preferred burning, while David Lloyd George, then minister of munitions, averred that the blight "did not poison, but merely deteriorated the crop." Prime Minister Herbert Balfour resolved to resort to such measures only under extreme provocation.[16]

In a manifesto published in the *Daily Express*, H. G. Wells demanded a fleet of ten thousand airplanes with reserves and personnel; he argued that two thousand planes, even if half were lost, could demolish Essen more cheaply than the cost of the Battle of Neuve Chapelle or a battleship. Parliament member William Joynson-Hicks took up the cudgels for a ten-thousand- or even twenty-thousand-plane force to end the war with reprisal bombing of Germany. The extent to which such preposterous proposals exceeded industrial capacity and technological capability indicates more than a touch of hysteria in the face of Zeppelin raids, but a more reasonable demand that emerged from the debate focused on the formation of an air ministry or air department.[17]

Ironically, only Italy, a small air power in comparison to the others, began the war with a plane expressly designed as a bomber: the Caproni Ca1, which the supreme command used for long-range reconnaissance and for bombing railroad junctions and stations. Behind the front, however, Giulio Douhet's superiors had removed him from command of the Italian aviation battalion for exceeding his authority in authorizing the Caproni bombers in the first place. In July 1915, Douhet, undaunted, was sowing the seeds of strategic bombing doctrine by advocating the formation of a huge group of heavy airplanes for strategic operations against enemy military and industrial centers, railroad junctions, arsenals, and ports.[18]

In 1915, air arms became more sophisticated, performing specialized functions at the front and adapting existing or developing new models to perform these missions. Bombardment and pursuit, the aircraft's new roles, prompted the adaptation of suitable types—light craft for fighting and heavier ones for bombing—but in general, the absence of powerful aircraft engines enabling large planes to carry defensive armament and greater bomb loads over longer distances limited bomber development. Yet during that year, all the eminent issues of strategic bombardment appeared—daylight versus night bombing and attendant matters of accuracy and aircraft type, around-the-clock bombing, appropriate target selection—that would continue through the Second World War and even today.

At the front, the beginning of fighter, or pursuit, aviation also was a major development in 1915. The appearance of the Fokker *Eindecker*, a monoplane with a machine gun synchronized to fire forward through the propeller arc, signaled the beginning of the race for aerial mastery. By the end of 1915, an effective fighting machine required speed and maneuverability as well as fixed forward-firing machine guns. The early pursuit pilots on all sides—Frenchmen Roland Garros and Georges Guynemer, Germans Max Immelman and Oswald Boelcke, and Englishman George Lanoe Hawker—evolved fighting tactics to maximize their chances of becoming aerial predators without falling prey to the enemy. They even recommended technical improvements to fighter aircraft. Their efforts would make the skies over Europe's battlefields far more dangerous in 1916.

1916: A WATERSHED YEAR

The great land battles of Verdun and the Somme on the Western front in 1916 signaled the first major struggles for aerial control over the battlefield, as fighter or pursuit aviation became necessary to prevent enemy aerial observation and protect one's own vulnerable observation planes over and behind the lines. Here again, the fundamental factors of fighter escort of reconnaissance and bombing airplanes arose— close protection of one's own planes or constant sector patrols to sweep the skies clear of enemy planes. Verdun demonstrated that aerial mastery over and behind the battle lines was essential to the progress of the land battle and required the concentration of fighter forces to achieve it. On the other hand, aerial control remained transitory and incomplete, depending upon the shifting concentration of force at points of penetration of airspace over the battlefield, and it was thus practically impossible for either side to attain absolute security.

By October 1916, French tactical bombing in daylight over enemy lines would practically cease because of the heavy casualties German fighters exacted. To that point, GQG had targeted German industrial centers—first chemical and powder plants and metallurgical shops, and then munitions and armaments plants— within a three-hundred-kilometer radius of the French bombardment groups' base at Malzéville near Nancy. Raids struck railroad stations, blast furnaces, and even airfields, but the losses on raids, even those escorted by French fighters, became too prohibitive and forced a shift exclusively to night attacks. In December 1916, GQG's new bombardment program limited targets to those within 160 kilometers of Nancy, in particular the metallurgical shops of the Saar–Luxembourg–Lorraine region, as the French bombers' performance in fact barely enabled them to reach those targets.

Behind the front, a triangular struggle over control of aviation production programs among GQG, the War Ministry, and parliamentary aviation subcommittees continued, as French aviation lurched from crisis to crisis and program to program in the political arena. At least in the procurement realm, French military administrators rationalized the research and procurement offices in their attempt to improve aircraft types and manufacture.

In 1916, French observation squadrons, like their bomber counterparts, suffered from the use of outmoded, outclassed, and thus highly vulnerable airplanes. One Voisin squadron, acknowledging the speed of its planes, chose a snail as its emblem. Farmans were fragile and burned easily because of the gas tank's location directly above the hot engine.[19] These numerous army corps squadrons bore the brunt of the mounting losses the expanding French air service experienced in 1916.

French fighter aviation initially excelled in 1916, as pursuit groups formed featuring such aces as Georges Guynemer and Charles Nungesser flying light, maneuverable Nieuport biplanes armed with a Lewis machine gun attached to the top wing that fired over the propeller arc. Yet as of midsummer 1916, the Nieuport could barely hold its own against the new German Albatros fighters, and as the year drew to a close the French air arm had a desperate need for modern airplanes. Fortunately, although it had taken a year, two French manufacturers had designed such planes— Louis Béchereau's SPAD fighter powered by the revolutionary Hispano-Suiza 150-horsepower (hp) V-8 watercooled engine, and Louis Breguet's reconnaissance/ tactical bomber framed of duralumin and steel tubes for lightness and strength. The SPAD 7 and 13 versions, with ever-higher-horsepower Hispano-Suiza engines, would drive French fighter aviation through the end of the war, while the Breguet 14s, powered by Renault 300-hp engines, would spearhead the resurgence of French tactical bombardment in 1918.

As French fighter aviation excelled, particularly in the first half of 1916, its opponent, the German fighter arm, desperately needed a new fighter airplane to replace its obsolescent Fokker monoplanes, which the Nieuports easily outclassed. Max Immelmann fell to his death in combat, and Germany's remaining star pilot, Oswald Boelcke, was withdrawn from the front to preserve German morale. Boelcke took the occasion to draw up the "Dicta Boelcke," guidelines for aerial fighting that still apply today: seek the advantage before attacking; attack from the rear, if possible with the sun at one's back (thus the Allied dictum of two world wars, "Beware the Hun in the sun"); carry through an attack keeping the opponent in sight and firing only at close range; if attacked from above, turn and meet the adversary; and never forget the line of retreat over enemy territory.[20]

If Verdun had been difficult for the German air service, the opening of the Battle of the Somme brought disaster, as the British and French air services outnumbered the German by a three-to-one ratio. In mid-September, however, Oswald Boelcke returned to the front with new fighter units equipped with the new Albatros D1 twin-gun fighter, a sleek, sturdy, and powerful killer that wrested aerial supremacy from the British and French. Although Boelcke, with forty kills to his credit, fell to his death on October 28 after a collision with a comrade, he bequeathed to Germany his dicta and his most adept pupil, Manfred Freiherr von Richthofen.

The Germans now concentrated their strength on the Somme front and reorganized the air service during the summer and fall to reflect the increased importance and specialization of function of the aerial units. Fighter units became a new elite. Flight units divided into two types of maneuverable two-seat single-engine biplanes, one equipped with special cameras for long-range reconnaissance, and the other designated for artillery observation. The latter type, embryonic ground support squadrons (*Schutzstaffeln*) of light, well-armed planes, flown by ground attack fliers, protected observation planes and conducted ground attacks in offensive or defensive roles. Last, a few bomber units under the OHL were now equipped with twin-engine Gotha bombers for longer range striking power.

On October 8, 1916, the German high commanders, Paul von Hindenburg and his chief quartermaster, Erich Ludendorff, established a Commanding General of the Air Forces (*Kommandierender General der Luftstreitkräfte*, or *Kogenluft*) directly subordinate to them. The next month, the aviation staff officers assigned to German army commands became aviation commanders with the authority to employ their units tactically. A cavalry general, Ernst von Hoeppner, became *Kogenluft*, but the key to the future of German aviation lay with his subordinates, his chief of staff, Colonel Hermann von der Lieth-Thomsen, and the procurement chief, Major Wilhelm Siegert, who had guided the rise of German aviation since early 1915 as chief and deputy chief of field aviation. The elevation of the air forces in the German command hierarchy coincided with the proclamation of the Hindenburg Program, which decreed total mobilization in an all-out effort to win the war. Thomsen requested and received from Ludendorff special status for aviation procurement in Germany's total mobilization. Thomsen and Siegert reorganized the aviation procurement bureaucracy by placing construction inspectorates at all aircraft factories to monitor manufacture as the army prepared to face the increasing war of attrition over the Western front. Army aviation had clearly assumed a position of major importance in the German military hierarchy, and Thomsen moved rapidly to abandon army Zeppelin operations because of their high costs and negligible results.

The German navy, on the other hand, increased its Zeppelin raids on England during 1916, employing gargantuan airships nearly 650 feet long with a gas volume of nearly 2 million cubic feet and capable of carrying a bomb load of some 5 tons at 60 miles per hour. The naval airship commander, Capt. Peter Strasser, set out to destroy England, to deprive it "of the means of existence through increasingly extensive destruction of cities, factory complexes, dockyards . . . railways, etc."[21] Yet by the late summer of 1916, the Zeppelin could no longer elude more powerful British fighters equipped with explosive and incendiary bullets, and the increasing losses of Zeppelins indicated that its time as a bomber had passed, although Strasser was determined to preserve it. Now the Zeppelin's major duty became scouting for the high seas fleet, which also acquired capable armed floatplanes, built by designer

Ernst Heinkel at the Hansa-Brandenburg Works, that would give the British a rude shock over the Flanders coast in 1917.

As England prepared to take the offensive in 1916, RFC commander General Hugh "Boom" Trenchard was initially concerned about inadequate aircraft and aircrew training. Nevertheless, the RFC quickly seized the initiative from the start of the Somme offensive on July 1 and dominated the skies over the battlefield, as Trenchard was determined to fight the Germans over their own territory. RFC pilots flew constantly on "contact" patrols to support infantry operations, on photographic observation missions to direct artillery fire, and on tactical bombing missions. These missions cost the British unparalleled casualties because of the poor performance of the RFC's obsolescent two-seat biplanes. Confronted with resurgent German fighter forces in the fall, Trenchard did not relent, instead hardening his determination to conduct a "relentless and incessant offensive" up to twenty miles behind German lines regardless of losses.[22] British aircrews found themselves caught in a vicious circle—equipped with inferior airplanes, they fell to German fighters so quickly that their replacements arrived at the front with increasingly inadequate training, which in turn rendered them even easier fodder for German fighter pilots.

The RNAS meanwhile pursued its bomber offensive against Zeppelin sheds and German airfields in the spring of 1916 using new Sopwith 1½ strutter two-seat biplanes, and by the fall it had placed one of its three wings of twenty-four aircraft at Luxeuil, near Nancy, where it conducted the first joint raid with the French against the Mauser factory at Oberndorf. Fall's foul weather soon ended further operations. In England, the Admiralty and War Office grappled over control of wartime aviation, particularly strategic bombing and the production of powerful aircraft engines for bombers, which the RNAS refused to relinquish to the RFC. Inadequate British aircraft and engine production forced a reliance on a hard-pressed French aviation industry, but developments toward the end of the year boded well for the future. Rolls-Royce was starting to hit its stride in delivering its superlative but highly complex combat engines, the 200-hp (later 275-hp) Falcon and the 275-hp (later 360-hp) Eagle for fighters and bombers, respectively. Britain's three most famous fighters, which would serve through the end of the war and beyond, appeared in the latter part of 1916—the Sopwith Camel, the SE–5, and the Bristol F–2 two-seat reconnaissance fighter. The first Dehavilland DH–4 single-engine day bombers and Handley-Page 0/100 twin-engine night bombers also appeared at year's end.

In 1916, Italy had the most operational multiengine bombers, as the Caproni factory delivered 136 trimotored bombers powered by increasingly powerful Fiat engines during the year. Raids of up to fifty-eight bombers struck Austro-Hungarian railway stations and even the city of Trieste. While strategic bomber aviation formed the centerpiece of the Italian aerial effort, its staunchest advocate, Giulio Douhet, left a memorandum criticizing the Italian war effort on a train and found himself duly sentenced to one year in prison in October. Ultimately, he would be exonerated in 1920.

The year 1916 became a watershed in the First World War, as Verdun and the Somme dashed both sides' hopes of imminent victory. These battles also marked the true beginning of aerial warfare, as the combatant powers committed to building and wielding larger air forces to attain aerial superiority. France's aircraft engine production far outdistanced that of Germany and England thanks to France's early mobilization of its automotive industry to manufacture aviation engines. The aerial policies of the major powers reflected these industrial realities and their basic military strategies. British and French air policy and overall military strategy were offensive, the British more relentlessly than the French. The Germans, in danger of being overwhelmed numerically on the Western front, reorganized and elevated their aviation forces in importance, husbanded their resources, fought defensively, and planned to concentrate their aviation forces to seek occasional mastery limited in time and space. In 1916, with the preeminence of fighter aviation, the air services provided the European combatants with their most revered heroes—aces such as Albert Ball, Oswald Boelcke, and Georges Guynemer—youth who epitomized the national willingness to sacrifice in the monstrous struggle on the Western front. The era of the individual ace would last into 1917, but individuals would soon find themselves submerged in the burgeoning aerial war of attrition, as the deployment of aviation forces in mass became indispensable to the conduct of war.

1917: AERIAL WAR OF ATTRITION

In early April 1917, French general Henri Nivelle launched an ill-fated assault on the Aisne River, at the Chemin des Dames, where the Germans had already withdrawn to their recently constructed Hindenburg Line. At GQG, Nivelle exhorted, "The aerial victory must precede the terrestrial victory of which it is both part and pawn. It is necessary to seek out the enemy over his own territory and destroy him."[23] The offensive, in the air and on land, turned into an abysmal failure, with high casualties and few results other than Nivelle's removal and the French army units' refusal to conduct any further absurd attacks.

General Henri Pétain succeeded Nivelle and promptly confined the army to limited offensives, husbanding his infantry while wearing down the German forces with superior artillery, aviation, and assault tanks. Pétain informed Minister of War

Paul Painlevé on May 28, "Aviation has assumed a capital importance; it has become one of the indispensable factors of success. . . . It is necessary to be master of the air. The obligation to seize aerial mastery will lead to veritable aerial battles."[24] By December 1917, Pétain sought certain aerial mastery in the new year by using the tactical bomber defensively, against the anticipated German offensive of 1918: "[I]n great mass, systematically, with continuity, on the enemy's rear along the front of attack, it is perfectly capable of paralyzing the offensive."[25] Furthermore, in an Allied offensive, he anticipated that his bombers could attack enemy lines of communication and prevent the Germans from massing their troops to block attacks.

French and German aviation commands concentrated their fighter forces in steadily larger formations, but the French fighter pilots, imbued with a sense of "knightly" individualism and independence that such aces as Guynemer, Nungesser, and René Fonck embodied, were reluctant to embrace the new massed tactics. Jean Villar's memoir, *Notes of a Lost Pilot*, lamented, "[T]he veterans want to hunt individually, through overconfidence and a desire to work on their own; the novices imitate them through vanity and ignorance. And both finish by being killed."[26]

At least French fighter pilots had the SPAD as a mount. Observation and bomber crews flew planes that were cannon fodder. GQG concentrated on battlefield aviation in 1917, but some bomber commanders yearned to strike Germany and regretted the feeble state of French strategic aviation. In April, Captain Kérillis longed for reprisal raids to "strike the morale of the enemy, to intimidate him." Kérillis believed that a fifty-plane raid on Munich "would have flung enough German entrails on the pavement of the city to give the torpedoers of the *Lusitania* and the arsonists of Reims pause for reflection."[27] Pétain did not consider German morale susceptible to reprisal raids and feared that such raids would degenerate into a cycle of atrocities. The French Air Staff, which understood that Kérillis's sanguine fantasies were out of the question, planned in 1917 and 1918 to concentrate on accessible and vulnerable targets within one hundred miles of Nancy while acknowledging that destruction of such targets would be "problematical."[28]

In the French political arena in early 1917, parliamentary deputies were concerned about an increasingly debilitating schism between GQG at the front and the War Ministry and politicians in the rear. Fortunately, in March, Painlevé appointed as undersecretary of aeronautics Daniel Vincent, a Radical Socialist, who had served as reporter of the aviation budget in Parliament and earlier as an observer in a Voisin squadron. Radical Socialist deputy J. L. Dumesnil, who succeeded Vincent as reporter of the aviation budget, would again succeed Vincent as undersecretary five months later and serve to the end of the war. These two men did much to improve aviation, as they struggled to mesh GQG's ever-escalating demands for airplanes with the matériel and manpower resources of the rear. Finally, the appointment of Georges Clemenceau as prime minister in mid-November meant that France had acquired a civilian dictator in the person of "The Tiger," who planned to control all such matters from above. Despite such political and bureaucratic instability during 1917, compounded by labor unrest in French industry, the French aircraft and engine factories increased production, aided by the procurement bureaucracy's decision to concentrate on the production of SPAD fighters and their Hispano-Suiza engines and Breguet bombers and their Renault engines. The results of their labor would become evident in 1918.

In 1917, the German air service, like the army, pursued a defensive strategy on the Western front. Fending off the French attack at the Chemin des Dames and the British attack at Arras, German fighters fought only over their own lines, while lone high-performance two-seat biplanes flew high-altitude photographic reconnaissance missions over enemy lines. The fighters' toll of British aircraft in April 1917 caused the month to be known as "Bloody April," as German fighter units led by Manfred von Richthofen and equipped with the superior Albatros D3 fighter ripped into British two-seaters over German airspace. By the summer, however, SPADs, SE5As, Sopwith Camels and Triplanes, and Bristol fighters easily outclassed the latest Albatros D5s, and not even the introduction of the first Fokker DR1 triplanes offset the Allied aerial superiority. Still, twenty thousand feet above the front, expert long-range reconnaissance crews flew their missions in their superb Rumpler C-type biplanes. They thus evaded British and French interceptors or, if the Germans chose to fight, held their own against even the newest Allied fighter planes.

Far below, at ground level, the battle of Arras also witnessed the debut of German "infantry-fliers," "battle-fliers," or, as these aviators preferred to be called, "stormfliers." Filling the ranks of the *Schutzstaffeln* formed in late 1916, the stormfliers—noncommissioned officers and soldiers, many of whom had served in the trenches—supported the infantry on offense and defense with machine guns, grenades, and fragmentation bombs. Mounted in small, strong, light, and highly maneuverable two-seat Halberstadt and Hannoverana biplanes, they ranged over the front at two thousand feet altitude, then descended to strafe enemy troops, batteries, strongpoints, and reserves from three hundred feet above the trenches, in the dead zone between the artillery fire of both sides. On days when heavy rain and low clouds grounded other aviators, these determined crews of anonymous aviators from the ranks flew under the low ceiling below three hundred feet over the *rue de merde*, or "shit street," as they called the front, to support their kin on the ground—the anonymous frontline infantry.[29] As the war continued, they also received AEG, Albatros, and Junkers armored infantry planes, the last of which was the first all-metal airplane. The Junkers J1 *Möbelwagen*, or "furniture van," was slow and ungainly, but impervious to machine gun fire from the ground.

In Germany's strategic air war against England, *Kogenluft* launched a bomber campaign named "Turk's Cross" with thirty-six Gotha twin-engine bombers and a few gigantic four- or five-engine R-planes (*Riesenflugzeuge*) in the late spring of 1917. By summer, losses over England or from crashes upon landing forced the bombers to strike at night, and *Kogenluft* decided to cut its losses and instead allocated precious materials to construction of fighters, not bombers. Naval airship commander Peter Strasser, however, persevered fanatically, lightening the giant Zeppelins to fly up to twenty thousand feet, where crews suffered from cold and oxygen deprivation, and unanticipated gale force winds scattered the airships all over Western Europe. At the end of 1917, Strasser was ordering even larger Zeppelins, thus expending Germany's scarce resources to wage a separate strategic campaign uncoordinated with the army. At least the navy seaplane fighter fleet, equipped with Hansa-Brandenburg two-seat twin-float monoplanes, regained command of the air from the English over the Flanders coast from Zeebrugge to Ostende.

In the German rear, with the new year came the understanding that the Hindenburg Program's total mobilization had only partially succeeded, as material and labor shortages prevented the aviation industry from meeting production goals, while the lapse in German fighter development invalidated their razor-thin qualitative superiority. Ludendorff planned a great German offensive to win the war in 1918, before the might of a mobilized United States fell upon Germany. To this end, on June 25, 1917, *Kogenluft* declared the America Program, primarily to double the number of fighter squadrons to eighty. Yet only a month later, the OHL warned that Germany's economic situation made complete fulfillment of the program doubtful. Shortages, strikes, and transportation delays plagued a German economy strained to the breaking point.

British fortunes during 1917 began with RFC commander Trenchard's determination to stage an increasingly vigorous offensive, thrusting patrols far behind enemy lines to raid supply depots and troop assembly points, a plan that culminated in "Bloody April." Although the RFC was taking a beating in the air, BEF commander General Douglas Haig acknowledged the efficiency of the RFC's artillery, photographic, and contact patrols and their importance to the land battle.[30] After suffering disturbingly high casualties during the summer and early fall, which elicited much criticism of the offensive policies on the part of airmen who flew the patrols, the RFC's superior fighter aircraft enabled its pilots to gain the advantage over their German opponents. Day bomber crews received the speedy DH4 bomber, deficient only in the location of its main fuel tanks between pilot and observer, which impaired communication.

England's circumstances in the tactical air war thus improved in 1917, but it lacked a strategic riposte to the German air assault on England that began in May. The Admiralty redirected the naval wing from ineffective strategic raids to assist the RFC on the front, yet many British officials, including Haig and Trenchard, persisted in overestimating the damage strategic raids inflicted upon German material and morale even at night, when crews had difficulty hitting targets smaller than a large town.[31] If the navy was relinquishing strategic bombing over land, its acquisition and modification of American Glenn Curtiss's large twin-engine flying boats enabled systematic antisubmarine patrols from naval air stations that covered some four thousand square miles of the North Sea.

In English politics, the German raids provoked an intense desire not merely for defense, but also for retaliation. The British war cabinet assigned South African soldier-statesman J. C. Smuts to assess the situation in two reports, the second of which, issued in August, advocated an independent unified air service to gain overwhelming aerial predominance to carry the war to Germany, strike its industrial centers and lines of communication, and win the war.[32] The Ministry of Munitions aviation and aircraft supply chief, William Weir, firmly believed that British industry could supply sufficient planes to equip a greatly expanded air force, and everyone was tired of the wasteful RFC–RNAS rivalry over industrial output. Unfortunately, Weir's enthusiasm outran his discretion, and no surplus of production materialized. In fact, British aircraft engine production failed miserably except for bright spots such as Rolls-Royce's superlative engines. The year ended with the matter of a unified air service unresolved.

In Italian aviation, the Caproni bombers continued to hold center stage, arranging wave attacks against enemy front and rear areas in support of infantry offensives during the battles along the Isonzo River. The collapse of the Italian front at Caporetto and retreat to the Piave River during the disastrous twelfth Battle of the Isonzo forced the bombers to undertake repeated ground attacks in the effort to stem the enemy tide. The Caproni works at Taliedo was building one biplane and one triplane bomber daily with completely standardized wing construction, while Fiat manufactured steadily more and more powerful engines. Giulio Douhet and Gianni Caproni were advocating an Allied fleet of strategic bombers. Writing from prison in June, Douhet called for Allied production of twenty thousand airplanes in order to bomb enemy cities.[33] He anticipated, incorrectly, that the United States, which had entered the war in April, would contribute twelve thousand aircraft. The potential industrial giant across the Atlantic was totally unprepared to serve as an arsenal of democracy and would in fact have to rely on its European allies to train and equip its aerial squadrons in 1918.

In 1917, the airplane rapidly evolved into a multifaceted weapon of war, undertaking missions from close air support to strategic bombing. The differing nature of the major air forces emerged clearly during the year. The RFC, relentlessly aggressive, carried the fight to the Germans regardless of circumstances, denigrating the significance of high losses while touting them as proof of the service's contribution to the war effort. It replaced its losses with men from the Dominions, took delivery of new fighter aircraft, surmounted the midyear crisis by fall, and plunged into 1918 anticipating an enhanced ability to bomb strategic targets in Germany with a unified air force. The French air service pursued a more circumspect offensive policy to conserve dwindling manpower, as its army confined itself to limited offensives after the debacle at Chemin des Dames. Pétain had taken a pragmatic approach to strategic bombing, prioritizing targets and assessing bombing effectiveness based on military results, not calculations of the effect on morale like the British. Now the French army was concentrating on the combination of the SPAD 13 pursuit plane and the Breguet 14 tactical bomber to regain French aerial ascendancy over the front in 1918. The German air service, like its army, fought a defensive war over the Western front, but the OHL also undertook a strategic air offensive against England along with its unrestricted submarine warfare in an attempt to drive England from the war.

By 1917, the British and German commands believed that ground attack aircraft proved a powerful weapon in battle. British fighter pilots assumed responsibility for ground attack, although they reviled the duty and engaged in random, uncoordinated, and individual strafing missions. In contrast, the Germans developed suitable airplanes for ground attack and manned them with former infantry who valued the task. The French did neither, and lagged far behind in ground attack operations. The airplane's heightened military importance and its expansion of military roles coincided with heightened aviation mobilization by all combatant powers in order to wage the bitter war of attrition. This rapid evolution of air power demonstrated the importance of aircraft engines, the heart of the airplane, and France displayed best the ability to manufacture high-powered aircraft engines in quantity.

In England and France, aviation mobilization occasioned much political strife. The English administration of aviation was as highly politicized and personalized as the French, but the former system was not wracked by ministerial instability as was the constantly shifting French government. Parliament played an important role in aviation in both countries, as representatives desired strategic air arms to bomb Germany. In France, where the army's control of aviation was a given, the deputies interpellated and intrigued to get their way, to no avail. In England, the air lobby pressed for an independent air force, to which the Lloyd George government agreed to resolve the army-navy conflict over aviation and to give the prime minister an independent ally in his struggle against the army and BEF commander Douglas Haig for control.

Compared to these complex situations, the authoritarian German system rendered the German military aviation bureaucracy a paragon of stability, as the same officers presided over the air service and aviation production from the beginning to the end of the war. In light of serious shortages of material and manpower in a blockaded country, such stability and unity was more imperative for Germany than for the Allied powers. Furthermore, the lack of coordination on the Western front between the English and French air forces enabled the German air service to survive despite the Allies' increasing numerical superiority. Yet Allied coordination would be necessary to bring American forces to bear against Germany as quickly as possible, and any joint strategic air offensive would necessitate inclusion of Italian planes and engines to attain as much aerial superiority over the Western front as possible. French military and political leaders, however, were not prepared to wage strategic air warfare, while the British cared little for inter-Allied strategic coordination. Under these circumstances, it remained to be seen how effective the Inter-Allied Aviation Committee, formed in November 1917 to meet monthly in Paris to discuss aviation production and supply, would be.

1918: TO THE BITTER END

As the year 1918 opened, French army commander Pétain, emphasizing the importance of concentrating aerial forces, planned to destroy enemy aviation to gain definitive aerial mastery over the battlefield and directly behind the front in tactical offensive operations. During the defensive struggle against the German March offensive, bomber and fighter aviation supported French ground forces in constant operations over the battle zone. In April and May, when French fighter protection waned, GQG formed the Aerial Division of all day bombers and half the fighters for tactical operations over enemy lines. Although the reluctance of French army commanders to liaise with the Aerial Division limited its effectiveness, it continued its offensives and formed the nucleus of American General Billy Mitchell's fourteen-hundred-plane strike force in the St. Mihiel offensive in the fall.

The Breguet 14 proved to be an outstanding tactical day bomber, high-altitude photographic reconnaissance plane for distances up to sixty miles behind the lines, and a sturdy artillery observation craft. The Breguet and Salmson 2A2 radial-engined biplane finally gave French army corps pilots a fighting chance against German fighters. Night bombers remained a weak link in French aviation throughout 1918, but the French had no further plans to conduct strategic bombing operations and instead struck at German railroad traffic in iron ore within forty-five miles of the front. The French army, preoccupied with the war at the front, opposed both strategic aviation and an autonomous air force. In May, long-range heavy bombers appeared last on Pétain's priorities for aircraft types.

In the rear, French politics and administration of French aviation stabilized considerably in 1918, as Prime Minister Clemenceau and Minister of Munitions Louis Loucheur supported GQG before the parliament as the high command continued to press for strategic air power. To the very end of the war, French parliamentary deputies harped on the absence of a strategic air arm, ignoring the facts that France possessed the world's largest air fleet on the Western front—four thousand planes and twenty-six hundred in reserve—and had produced more airplanes (fifty-two thousand) than either Britain (forty-three thousand) or Germany (forty-eight thousand), and more aircraft engines (eighty-eight thousand) than the other two powers (forty-one thousand each) combined.

The German air service began the March offensive effectively but then found itself increasingly overwhelmed by Allied numerical superiority in 1918. The German fighter squadrons, grouped into larger formations of some sixty airplanes labeled "circuses," took delivery of the superlative Fokker D7, whose BMW 185-hp high-compression engine and thick wing granted it superiority over all Allied challengers to the end of the war. Manfred von Richthofen, with eighty kills to his credit (making him the ace of aces of the First World War), fell in combat in April, thus meeting the fate that greeted practically all of his contemporary high scorers, with the exception of Frenchman René Fonck. The German air arm, short of experienced pilots and fuel, spent the last days of the war retreating from airfield to airfield, inexorably outnumbered by the Allies. The OHL relinquished its strategic bomber campaign in May to assign all bombers to tactical raids over the Western front. Aircraft and engine production flagged in the face of material and labor shortages, ensuring defeat in a war of attrition. Like army fighter forces, German naval fighter forces possessed superior airplanes in Heinkel's Hansa-Brandenburg floatplanes, but never enough to perform their various missions. By the end of the war, German frontline airplanes had declined from some 3,600 in January to 2,700, and the looming winter of 1918–

1919 would have brought all production to a crashing halt from coal, material, fuel, and food shortages.

The RFC confronted the German offensive initially at a disadvantage in March 1918, but despite heavy losses, which it could replace, the RFC had regained aerial ascendancy by the end of the month. With the British introduction of the tank in numbers in 1918, the army assigned aerial squadrons to the tank corps to develop aircraft-armor liaison and to neutralize German antitank artillery. Starting with an offensive against Amiens in early August, the British army, coordinating its tank, artillery, and airplane forces, advanced relentlessly for the rest of the war. From the beginning of 1918 to the Armistice, British fliers carried the war to the Germans in constant offensives over enemy territory. They paid for this dominance with high casualties until the very end; one fighter pilot calculated that a pilot's life in France during 1918 averaged less than six weeks, to be terminated by nerves, crashes, injury, capture, or death.

The tactical air war consumed the bulk of the air arm's attention and resources to the end of the war, although the creation in April 1918 of the Air Ministry, the Royal Air Force (RAF), and the Independent Bombing Force under Trenchard often receive disproportionate attention from historians because of the controversial and political nature of the new aviation establishment. In fact, Secretary of State for Air William Weir planned to build the Independent Bombing Force to conduct a massive aerial offensive against German cities, and in September he wrote Trenchard, "I would very much like it if you could start up a really big fire in one of the German towns. . . . The German is susceptible to bloodiness."[34] Meanwhile, Trenchard considered his command, the Independent Bombing Force, a "gigantic waste of effort and personnel" and proceeded to ignore directives from the Air Ministry to strike at chemical factories and iron- and steelworks in favor of striking at tactical targets such as airfields and railroads.[35] The sole achievement of the Independent Bombing Force was to divest naval aviation of its focus on strategic bombing and force the navy to concentrate on fleet and antisubmarine patrol duty. The Ministry of Munitions did succeed in mobilizing the aviation industry, which, with nearly 350,000 workers, was the world's largest at the end of the war. The RAF split its forces between the Western front and far-flung imperial bases stretching to the Middle East, and its long logistical "tail" meant that it was the world's largest air force in personnel at the end of the war.

Finally, Italian military and naval aviation dominated its Austro-Hungarian enemy in 1918. Giulio Douhet returned to aviation to serve as director of aviation in a general commissariat established in April 1918, but he retired from the army in

June at the age of forty-nine to write. Caproni manufactured 330 bombers in 1918, the last 290 powered by three 200-hp engines, or double the power of the early Capronis. Both the English and French rejected Caproni bombers for use on the Western front, and no Allied strategic bombing campaign ever occurred.

CONCLUSION

In August 1914, the European powers had gone to war with rudimentary air services and embryonic aviation industries. Once airplanes proved themselves as a means of reconnaissance and artillery spotting, air commanders required more of them to conduct effective aerial operations and prevent enemy aerial reconnaissance. The second aim led to armed aircraft and then the development of specialized pursuit, or fighter, aircraft. The battles of Verdun and the Somme forced the codification of aerial combat tactics and brought home the importance of mass. The size of the air services and aviation industries consequently spiraled rapidly upward. Airplanes became more specialized in function, although the basic wartime types remained the two-seat, single-engine, all-purpose biplane and the single-seat, single-engine, pursuit biplane. All the aviation commands contemplated strategic bombing to damage enemy production and morale, but the early aviation technology placed limits on size, speed, load, range, and accuracy of navigation and bombing that would not be overcome until the middle of the Second World War twenty-five years later.

Military aviation did not determine the outcome of World War I, but the airplane did establish its very real significance in support of the army on the battlefield. Control of the airspace over the battlefield became essential to victory in World War I, just as it would be twenty years later in the next world war. Strategic aviation in fact played little role in the 1914–1918 conflict, although it seemed to offer the key to victory in future wars. The fighter pilots and ground attack aircrews developed the basic techniques employed for the rest of the twentieth century, and many of those young airmen became the aerial commanders of the second Great War. In both strategy and tactics, the air war of 1914–1918 portended the larger aerial struggle of 1939–1945.

The war of the masses bequeathed to them a new individual hero: the aviator, in particular the fighter ace—honored as a demigod, object of a secular holy cult—whose fame and heroism were quantifiable in terms of his number of conquests, or "kills." The ancient warrior reappeared, now mounted in a lethal machine that elevated him above all earthly mortals, ready for repeated trials by combat on behalf of the honor and survival of his nation. This very circumstance prompted dispro-portionate attention to fighter aviation, when the lessons of the battlefields of 1914–1918 proved the worth of the airplane as a tactical weapon for observation, bombing, and strafing in the land battle. The fighter was necessary primarily to protect these other airplanes in the performance of their duties, but aerial fighting took on a life of its own, above the fray.

Theory and wishful thinking after the Great War focused on strategic aviation and nearly drove the lessons of tactical aerial importance and success from the minds of postwar observers. The more postwar aviation theorists speculated on the ability of strategic bombardment to force enemy capitulation by bombing cities, wrecking war industry and civilian morale, the less they seemed to remember the contributions of battlefield aviation. Giulio Douhet was the most eminent of these theorists. His work, *The Command of the Air*, encapsulated the claims for strategic air power—that striking directly at civilian centers with bombs or chemicals would bring states to their knees because civilians could not withstand such pounding—assertions that sprang less from the limited and inconclusive experience of 1914–1918 and more from inductive speculations and extrapolations. Sir William Weir's desire to "start up a really big fire in a German town" sowed the seed of RAF Bomber Command's devastating fire raids of 1943–1945, which cost Bomber Command and German civilians horrendous casualties without ending the war as the theorists had claimed. Victory in 1939–1945 in fact would require tactical air power to support ground and naval forces and the more precise targeting of key strategic industrial and transportation sites, which confirmed the actual experience of the air war of 1914–1918.

2

THE AIR WAR IN EUROPE, 1939–1945

Richard Overy

WHEN A SECOND MAJOR EUROPEAN war broke out in September 1939, there was a widespread popular expectation that it would be waged with ruthless disregard for the traditional conventions of warfare. At the heart of this fear was a belief that modern air power would be aimed at an enemy's home population, whose morale might crack completely under a hail of bombs, gas canisters, and biological weapons. These first "weapons of mass destruction" failed to materialize fully, but on the very first morning of the European war, September 3, an air raid alarm sounded in London, triggered by an aircraft mistakenly identified as hostile. This panic-driven reaction symbolized the conviction that the new war would be decided by air power, a view unthinkable only twenty-five years before, when in 1914 a few primitive biplanes launched the air power century.

In the twenty years between the First and Second World Wars, all the major European powers encouraged the development of technically advanced air forces while military thinkers grappled with the issues of how aircraft might be employed with maximum military utility. There was no consensus on the future of air power. In Germany, France, and the Soviet Union, each with a powerful army tradition, air power was regarded as something that would be exercised in conjunction with the ground forces to speed up the defeat of the enemy's army. This involved bombing at distances a few hundred kilometers behind the front at the most, but usually much closer to it. German air doctrine showed an awareness of the possibility of long-range bombing acting independently of the ground forces, but this was regarded as something to be done under provocation or for retaliation and not as an integral element in the exercise of what German airmen called "operational air war."[1] German theorists shared with their French counterparts the lesson of the Great War that air power had to be used first to achieve success at the fighting front, a view consistent with their geopolitical position.[2] They also regarded the use of aircraft alongside the main ground offensive as a strategic use of air power and did not subscribe to the view that such operations were merely tactical.[3] The Soviet case was similar, since any potential threat from the capitalist West was, it was thought, likely to come across the long Soviet frontier. It was therefore necessary to use all military force, aircraft included, in support of armies deployed at or near the frontier for launching offensive operations. The Soviet decision was also a product of geopolitical reality because current Soviet aircraft could reach none of the major cities of any potential enemy.

The exception to this rule was the Royal Air Force (RAF). In the closing months of the First World War, when the RAF was formed, British air leaders subscribed to the view that an independent bombing campaign directed at the vital centers of the enemy's war production and economic infrastructure—particularly if the bombing created widespread popular demoralization—might prompt a political upheaval and force Germany to sue for peace. The idea that morale was a vulnerable target has generally been ascribed to General (later Air Marshal) Hugh Trenchard, the chief of the air staff during the 1920s, who famously asserted that the effect on morale was twenty times greater than the effect of physical destruction, but ideas about the political dividend from long-range bombing were already current by 1918, promoted by the first RAF chief of staff, Frederick Sykes.[4] During the interwar years, RAF doctrine was divided between the desire to offer some effective form of defense of the home islands against air attack and the belief that the best form of defense was attack against the enemy homeland, either to act as a deterrent to further attacks or to provoke a crisis in the heart of the enemy war effort.

The contradiction represented by this strategic profile was never fully confronted during the interwar years. The RAF War Manual published in 1935 had as its first line the assertion that "the bomb is the chief weapon of an air force" and went on to describe a campaign against "the nerve centres, main arteries, heart and brain" of the enemy state in order to reduce "his power to continue the war."[5] This remained the central feature of RAF strategy through 1945 and the end of the European war. The force sustained the distinction between an independent bombing strategy, with its own strategic trajectory aimed at defeating the enemy nation rather than the enemy armed forces, and the tactical use of air power in support of ground campaigns on land and sea, for which the RAF remained poorly prepared and doctrinally deficient. Yet from 1936, with the advent of radar and fast monoplane fighters, greater emphasis was placed, at political insistence, on the possibilities of an active air defense whose purpose was also strategic rather than tactical, denying the enemy air force the possibility of attacking the home front in operations again independent of the army or navy.

These differences in strategic outlook determined the way the air war was to be fought in Europe between 1939 and 1945. With the exception of German air attacks against British cities in the autumn and winter of 1940–1941, for which the German air force had not been well prepared, the exercise of air power by the major continental European air forces was strategic in the narrower sense of supporting the main strategic aim of the armed forces in the destruction of enemy armed power. There was little preparation for the use of aircraft against shipping. The Italian navy made few provisions for fighting a modern air/sea war; Britain had a few aircraft carriers but little experience in how to use them; Germany had no aircraft carriers, and relations between the country's navy and air force were too poor to develop effective air-sea operational collaboration. Air power could be exercised over sea as long as there were airfields close enough to the coast to permit extensive oversea flights, but much of this was improvised in wartime when the war spread to the Mediterranean theater in June 1940 and German naval and air forces began the campaign against British Atlantic trade the same month.

The use of aircraft in conjunction with ground operations was thoroughly vindicated in the opening campaigns of the European war. The prevailing view that German success relied on overwhelming numerical superiority was certainly true in the case of the campaign against Poland, which began on September 1, 1939, when the 1,500 first-line aircraft of the German air force overwhelmed the 397 aircraft used by the Poles. But against Britain and France, who declared war against Germany on September 3, 1939, the balance of air resources was more even, with 2,741 first-line German combat aircraft (including 1,180 bombers and 970 single-seat fighters) pitted against more than 2,000 British and French first-line planes. The Western Allies also had much higher reserves, though of less advanced design.[6] The rapid success of German armies in the campaigns against the Netherlands, Belgium, and France was achieved largely thanks to German air superiority. The twenty-seven hundred aircraft assigned to the task by the German high command were all concentrated on the single aim of supporting the ground armies, which they did by a mixture of reconnaissance flights, fighter-to-fighter contests for air superiority, dive-bombing attacks on enemy strongpoints, and medium-bomber attacks on more distant targets of opportunity behind the enemy front line. They were organized in integrated air fleets, employing different types of aircraft but with centralized control, high mobility, and effective radio communication. The bulk of British aircraft, however, remained in Britain to defend against a possible German air assault, while French aircraft were distributed around mainland France and in North Africa to protect the more dispersed French war production and guard against the possibility of Italian intervention.[7] The Western

Allies failed completely to coordinate their two air forces or to concentrate their main air strength at the battlefront. As a result, they lost command of the air and the land campaign simultaneously.[8]

THE BATTLE OF BRITAIN AND THE BLITZ

The most significant air battle of the European war followed the defeat of France in June 1940. The Battle of Britain was regarded on the British side as a campaign to prevent a German invasion. As such, it involved not just Fighter Command but also extensive military preparations for the home-based army and the use of bomber aircraft to attack German-controlled ports and the shipping intended for Operation Sealion, the proposed German invasion of Britain authorized by Adolf Hitler on July 16, 1940. Both sides, however, recognized that air superiority would be essential for the complex combined operation planned by the German high command. The German air force commander in chief, Reich Marshal Hermann Göring, undertook to neutralize the RAF to the point where it could no longer intervene in the battle, at which stage German bombers would attempt to degrade the British military and economic structures in southern Britain to permit an invasion of the southern counties of Sussex and Kent.[9] Although the aerial Battle of Britain is usually dated from mid-July, the preliminary bombing began in June 1940, and there was almost continuous, if limited, air combat until the onset of the major air force assault against the RAF, which was scheduled to begin on "Eagle Day," August 13, 1940.

The Battle of Britain illuminated the difference in the strategic profiles of the two opposed air forces. The German air force, organized in Air Fleets Two and Three in northern France and Belgium, had not been prepared for an independent air assault carried out over enemy territory against strong active and passive defenses. Although the bomber force was capable of reaching a large part of the United Kingdom, it focused its attention on the port cities in the early stages of the campaign. The standard prewar bombers were slow and carried a light bomb load for urban targets. The fighter force had very limited range, extending to the southern counties of England and with an endurance time in combat of around thirty minutes. Some nine-tenths of Britain was beyond German single-seat fighter range.

On the British side, the battle was the kind of campaign for which extensive preparations had been made. The substantial fighter force was composed of Hawker Hurricane and Supermarine Spitfire fighters, both on the cutting edge of aviation technology; there was a well-organized observer and communications system in place in southern England; and above all, the development of radar meant that there would be limited, but in many cases sufficient, warning of approaching enemy aircraft.

There was also a contrast in production priorities and training. Overconfidence on the German side about the quality of aircraft and pilots was compounded with poor intelligence on British capabilities (supported by an unflattering assessment of RAF performance in the Battle of France). The German air force high command expected to eliminate the RAF as a threat in four days and believed that the pilots and planes on hand would be sufficient for the task. The German fighter force had 1,011 planes, 805 of them serviceable, on August 10, 1940. The RAF had 1,032 fighter aircraft on August 9, with 768 serviceable. In addition, there were 424 in store ready for operations the next day. Throughout the three months of the air battle, from August to October 1940, the number of trained pilots on hand for RAF Fighter Command exceeded the number of single-seat fighter pilots available on the German side.[10] British numbers remained roughly constant over the period of the battle (despite a marginally higher loss rate than the Germans), but by early September, with the battle at its height, German numbers fell to around 500 fighters and on October 1 fell for one day to only 275. The key to this difference lay in aircraft production. British industry was geared to produce fighters as a top priority. German industry produced a wide range of tactical aircraft and more medium bombers than fighters. In August and September 1940, the German aircraft industry produced 775 fighters, the British industry 1,900.[11]

The outcome was nevertheless not entirely preordained. German fighters were of high quality and the pilots well trained and experienced. They were also able to choose the point of engagement, while the defending air force had to anticipate enemy operations and engage in the space of the enemy's choosing. As a result, RAF Fighter Command suffered a marginally faster rate of loss than the German fighter arm, even though it had more substantial reserves and replacements. German advantages were nevertheless outweighed by some substantial disadvantages. German pilots were lost to the force once they were forced to bail out over enemy territory or crashed in the sea; German fighter aircraft had to protect the bombers and were less free to engage in direct fighter-to-fighter combat; and German air intelligence persistently overestimated the British loss rate and level of damage to the air force infrastructure. At the end of August, German air intelligence estimated that eight Fighter Command airfields had been rendered unusable (in fact, three were rendered briefly unusable and then reopened) and that Fighter Command was down to around 200 aircraft with no reserves (the true figure was 700 operational and 250 in store for immediate use).[12]

The miscalculation of the amount of damage inflicted convinced the German air commanders to shift strategies. In early September, Göring ordered a switch from attacks on the enemy air force—airfields and radar stations—to attacks on cities and communications. Heavy attacks were made on Bristol, Liverpool, Birmingham, and other industrial and port towns. On September 2, he ordered attacks on London to reduce military capability prior to launching Operation Sealion on September 15. On September 5, Hitler confirmed that the German air force should now attack London and other urban centers to degrade Britain's capacity to resist invasion.

This final decision has sometimes been presented as an improvised reaction to two British attacks on Berlin in the last week of August 1940, but this viewpoint is not convincing. The German air force had planned in advance of the August battle to knock out Fighter Command first and then begin a bombing campaign to prepare the way for the seaborne invasion. The shift to bombing was authorized in early September according to this original plan and had begun even before Hitler's formal directive on September 5. From September 7 on, continued and heavy daylight attacks were mounted against the British capital. They proved a disaster for the German air force because Fighter Command had not been eliminated. A high toll was taken of enemy bombers, even though a great many delivered their bomb load as directed. The attacks forced German fighters to engage in air combat at the very limit of their range, while the bombers were easy prey for the faster and heavily gunned British fighters. By the time the campaign petered out at the beginning of October, the German air force had lost 1,733 aircraft versus 915 for the RAF. By this time, Hitler had decided to postpone Sealion indefinitely. All preparations were scaled down after September 19. The failure to secure air supremacy was a central explanation for this decision, though not the only one. Despite extensive preparations and training, the German navy could not guarantee the success of a difficult cross-channel operation that would be under attack from British naval forces and by RAF Bomber Command.[13]

The third phase of the air assault on Britain was an attempt by the German air force to mount an independent strategic campaign to use demoralizing attacks on trade, shipping, industrial production, and communications to force Britain out of the war. This approach represented not only a clear break with German objectives of the summer and autumn of 1940, but also the onset of a campaign for which the air force had not been prepared. Moreover, there were no clearly defined objectives beyond the hope that Britain might sue for peace while German forces prepared for the campaign against the Soviet Union, finally decided by Hitler in November 1940 and authorized in the "Barbarossa" Directive 21 of December 18.

The new air strategy unfolded incrementally. On September 14, following suggestions from Admiral Erich Raeder, commander in chief of the German navy, about the necessity of maintaining air attacks on British trade regardless of the fate of Sealion, Hitler ordered a continuous bombardment of selected military and economic targets with an emphasis on port and shipping targets. On September 16, Göring ordered air force units to begin the new phase. It was to be conducted at night, using a system of radio beams to direct bombers to the targets and increasing the ratio of incendiary bombs carried to increase the prospects of inflicting extensive physical damage. Finally, in October 1940, the switch to regular night bombardment of major cities was made in the hope that the aerial blockade would bring a political dividend in the form of the collapse of Winston Churchill's government or a request for an armistice.[14]

The seven-month bombing campaign from October 1940 to the last major attack on London on May 10, 1941, has been neglected by historians of air power, who have tended to focus on the "Blitz" as a British event rather than a stage in the development of German air strategy. This was the only time that Hitler flirted with the ideas of "Douhetism": the belief that heavy attacks on an enemy's capital and major cities would rapidly provoke demoralization and the possibility that the enemy would abandon the war.[15] It is not clear how much confidence Hitler placed in the strategy, and after the failure of the Blitz to produce a satisfactory political outcome, he became permanently disillusioned with the idea of an independent air campaign. He had remarked to his headquarters staff late in 1939 that "the ruthless employment of the Luftwaffe against the heart of the British will-to-resist can and will follow at the given moment."[16] Yet when the German air force chief of staff, Hans Jeschonnek, asked for permission to bomb residential areas to create panic in September 1940, Hitler refused. In January 1941, he insisted that bombing had to have a purpose—in this case, the war against trade and industry—and told his staff that terror raids "have small value and accomplish little."[17] German bombing was not intended to be simply indiscriminate, although the extant technology, even with radio-beam navigation, was incapable of avoiding extensive civilian damage.

At least part of the motive for maintaining the attacks was to sustain the impression that Britain was Germany's main strategic concern, thus masking the shift in German military preparations to the Barbarossa campaign. On the other hand, continued German losses during the Blitz, many of them the result of accidents or poor weather conditions, eroded the force that would be needed for the campaigns in Russia. Over the course of the Blitz, 384 bombers were destroyed, 63.5 percent of them noncombat casualties.[18] The German air force fielded two hundred fewer bombers at the start of the Barbarossa campaign on June 22, 1941, than had been available on May 10, 1940.[19]

The German experience from October 1940 to May 1941 provided important lessons on the conduct of an independent bombing campaign (though the RAF learned few of them before beginning its own operations). The high losses from daylight raids forced the German air force to shift to night bombing, as the RAF had already done earlier in 1940. Losses from antiaircraft fire and the first nightfighter squadrons of the RAF were small in relation to the effort made, but German success rested on effective navigation, an advantage sustained until British scientific intelligence experts correctly interpreted the nature of the electronic beams and devised countermeasures in November 1940. This began a four-year electronic battle between the two sides to keep one step ahead in navigational and radar technology, an early ancestor of the electronic battlefields of the late twentieth and early twenty-first centuries.[20] The campaign also revealed the importance of carrying a mixed armament, combining high-explosive with incendiary bombs, as well as aerial mines, which had a powerful destructive effect; 4,729 of them were dropped between September 1940 and May 1941. The proportion of incendiaries used rose over the course of the attacks: between September and December 1940, incendiaries made up 6.2 percent of the bomb tonnage dropped; between January and May 1941, they made up 12.8 percent.[21]

A number of factors limited what the Blitz could achieve. In the first place, there was no clear pattern to the attacks, except for the continued assault on British trade and dock areas, which was designed to complement the growing submarine campaign. The absence of clear strategic objectives betrayed the improvised nature of the campaign and the political motives that sustained it. In addition, the operations were inhibited not only by poor weather but also by the relatively small bomb loads that the standard medium bombers—the Heinkel He–111, Dornier Do–17, and Junkers Ju–88—were capable of carrying. The He–111, with the largest bomb lift, could carry 5,512 pounds over a short range, but the later RAF Avro Lancaster could carry 22,000 pounds, and the U.S. Boeing B–17E more than 20,000 pounds. Between September 1940 and May 1941, the German air force dropped 45,969 tons of bombs on British targets. Prewar extrapolations had suggested that the British would find bombing on such a scale insupportable, but the damage was restricted in scope outside London and the major dock cities and had a limited effect on war potential. The level of casualties was high, partly because air raid precautions were not extensive enough (few deep shelters had been constructed), and partly because of the concentrations of population in the vicinity of the major dock areas in London, Liverpool, Southampton, Portsmouth, Plymouth, and Bristol. The toll of 41,987 dead and 49,405 injured over eight months represented a higher level of casualty per ton dropped than the RAF was able to inflict in the first year of attacks on German targets.[22]

What had been incalculable was the effect such attacks would have on civilian morale. Although there was evidence of panic, increased criminality, and defeatism in all bombed areas, urban populations did not collapse in the face of attack, despite the fact that the British had never experienced such high civilian casualties and massive urban destruction in modern history. It is open to debate whether a longer offensive might have eventually provoked a more serious social and political crisis, but by the time the Blitz ended, British air raid precautions and antiaircraft defenses were substantially improved from the opening of the bombing campaign, while much of the threatened population had been evacuated from the major cities.[23]

THE AIR WAR AT SEA

The RAF and the Royal Navy shared duties in the air war at sea, and it was fought in the English Channel, over the Atlantic, and throughout the Mediterranean basin over a four-year period. From early 1942 onward, it was also fought by the U.S. Navy against the German submarines and by shore-based army aircraft in North Africa. The antisubmarine campaign involved aircraft in a number of different roles. RAF Coastal Command conducted regular patrols through the English Channel and over submarine approach routes to the French Atlantic ports; the heavy bombers of Bomber Command pounded the submarine pens and German submarine production, though in both cases with slight effect; Royal Navy aircraft attacked Italian shipping in the Mediterranean and gave increasing levels of protection to shipping convoys in the Atlantic and the Mediterranean from fleet carriers or small escort carriers; RAF forces in North Africa bombed Axis shipping and ports or conducted patrols against enemy submarines. In all naval theaters, it took time to develop the forces and the necessary degree of collaboration between the services to achieve significant results. In the Mediterranean, over two-thirds of Italy's merchant marine was eventually sunk, with 37 percent of the losses attributed to aircraft.[24] The effect was to cripple Axis operations in North Africa by 1942 and to open the way to complete victory there in May 1943.

The Italian air force, originally organized for offensive operations in the Mediterranean theater, was composed predominantly of obsolescent aircraft and was too small to challenge Allied air power effectively. The number of combat aircraft available to the Italian air force declined from 1,780 in June 1940, when Italy declared war on Britain and the Commonwealth, to 1,493 in December 1941 and 860 in November 1942. When Italy surrendered in September 1943, there were only approximately two hundred modern aircraft left.[25]

The situation in the Atlantic became more dangerous once the submarine campaign reached its height. Sinkings in 1942 totaled 5.4 million tons, and British exports fell to one-third of their prewar level. Much of the damage to shipping was inflicted in the so-called Atlantic Gap beyond the range of existing long-range patrolling aircraft. The German navy attempt to get large vessels into the Atlantic to act as "merchant-raiders" in collaboration with submarines failed in 1941 with the sinking of the *Bismarck*, crippled by Royal Navy aircraft, while the early success of German long-range aircraft against shipping, particularly the Focke-Wulf 200 Kondor, was blunted by more active British air defense of the shipping lanes.[26]

The introduction of aircraft into the antisubmarine war suffered from the failure of both interservice and inter-Allied collaboration. In the United States, the U.S. Army Air Forces (USAAF), created in June 1941, wanted to control the operation of long-range bomber aircraft over the Atlantic and in spring 1942 formed the USAAF Anti-Submarine Command, denying command or control to the U.S. Navy. Only in June 1942 did the Army chief of staff, General George Marshall, insist that 187 long-range B–24 Liberators be released for the use of the Navy, which had already begun a program of escort-carrier construction so that aircraft could accompany the convoys directly.[27]

In Britain, the same problem arose in relations between the RAF and the Royal Navy. The navy enjoyed operational control over long-range aircraft (almost all of them converted heavy bombers) assigned to RAF Coastal Command for work over the Atlantic approaches. But in the spring of 1942 there were far too few of them, and Bomber Command resisted the allocation of more bombers to the naval war because of the demands of the bombing campaign against Germany. This argument, too, could be resolved only at the highest level. In August 1942, Prime Minister Winston Churchill established an Anti–U-Boat Warfare Committee that, with his backing, insisted that more long-range aircraft be converted to an antisubmarine role. The B–24 Liberators that were capable of covering the Atlantic Gap were made available only in March 1943, and by the summer there were 37 with Coastal Command and 209 serving with the U.S. Navy.[28]

The conduct of operations also caused friction between the Allies, since the U.S. Navy commander in chief, Admiral Ernest King, wanted to retain control of his part of the Atlantic war and opposed any suggestion of a unified command of the antisubmarine war. The first Liberators operating with Coastal Command were loaned by the USAAF, whose role King also distrusted.[29] In the end, the friction did not seriously jeopardize the Atlantic campaign, which finally turned in the Allies' favor in March 1943 thanks to a range of important tactical and operational innovations— the introduction of flexible naval "support groups" to attack the submarines around the convoys, the use of new centimetric radar (and in particular the new generation of air-to-surface-vessel equipment), searchlights fitted on all aircraft operating at night, and air attack on submarines in the Bay of Biscay as they entered or left their bases. Although the introduction of very-long-range aircraft did ensure that the German submarines could not easily return to the Atlantic, the battle was won before they were widely introduced. It is nevertheless evident that the battle could have been won sooner and at lower cost if the air effort had been properly appreciated and the resources made available.

THE AIR WAR ON THE EASTERN FRONT

While the German bombers kept up a relentless series of attacks in May 1941— including over seven hundred tons of bombs dropped on London on the night of May 10–11—the German air force prepared for the major campaign in the East. The war against the Soviet Union required the air force to conduct an operational air war alongside the ground offensive as it had in 1939 and 1940, using a combination of fighter activity to win air superiority over the front and fighter-bomber and medium-bomber attacks on the enemy air organization, battlefield targets, and rear areas of supply and reinforcement. On June 21, 1941, the German air force deployed 3,664 aircraft (2,815 combat-ready) for the invasion.[30] Opposing the Germans were an estimated ten thousand Soviet aircraft, with perhaps as many as eight thousand concentrated on the western frontier. Soviet aircraft were of mixed quality, many of them obsolete or obsolescent, but a new generation of high-quality fighters, the Yak–1, MiG–3, and LaGG–3, were appearing in small numbers, as was the Il–2 "shturmovik" fighter-bomber. Soviet air forces were organized not in air fleets but in units assigned to particular frontline army groups, with little flexibility in their deployment. There was no central control of air units that might move aircraft quickly to threatened sectors of the front.

The thinking of the Red Army was offensive, and too little attention had been paid to questions of air defense. When the forces of Germany and its cobelligerents attacked on June 22, 1941, Soviet air power temporarily crumbled, with more than seven thousand aircraft destroyed by early October 1941 and forward air bases and much of the air communications system lost.[31] By the end of December 1941, German sources calculated that Soviet losses totaled 20,392 aircraft (the true figure was even higher) against German losses of 2,505. Soviet air activity was concentrated on direct battlefield support consistent with the prevailing doctrinal emphasis on the destruction of enemy forces through offensive action, but poor tactical awareness and lack of combat experience contributed to very high loss rates: of 21,200 aircraft lost in 1941, 7,600 were noncombat losses.[32]

From that point on, the air battle on the Eastern front assumed a new character. The high losses inflicted on the Soviet air force in 1941 were not repeated, while the scale of the Eastern campaign produced a rising attrition of the German force, which was always smaller than its Soviet opponent. The failure to enlarge the force and the exceptionally wide front in Russia meant that the German air force was spread very thin. The operational air war launched in the summer of 1941 gave way to a situation in which the air force became "the flying artillery of the army," confined to battlefield interdiction and increasingly limited in its efforts to combat Soviet fighter aviation and to bomb more distant targets.[33] The demands made on the transport units to supply trapped pockets of German troops at Demyansk and other areas, most famously Stalingrad, eroded the capacity of the German air force to undertake extensive transport operations.

Moreover, unlike Soviet air forces, the German air force was compelled to keep a significant part of its establishment elsewhere, in Western and Southern Europe. On the eve of Barbarossa, there were approximately 1,800 aircraft in other theaters, including 861 in Air Fleet Three opposing the RAF and 423 aircraft in the Mediterranean and North African theaters.[34] By the autumn of 1943, some 60 percent of the fighter force was defending the German homeland; a year later, it was around 80 percent. These other fronts absorbed between one-third and one-half of German air strength over the period 1941 to 1944. Only a very large increase in aircraft output could have compensated for fighting air wars on three fronts, but in 1942, only 15,409 new aircraft were produced. In 1943, the number was 24,807, around two-thirds of the number produced by the Soviet Union alone, and a mere 16 percent of the total produced by the three major Allies.[35]

By contrast, the Soviet Union moved from static army-based aviation in 1941 to a flexible operational air war closely modeled on German practice. The principal organizer of this transition was a young air force lieutenant general, Alexander Novikov, whom Josef Stalin appointed Red Air Force commander in chief in April 1942.[36] The divisional air units were scrapped and instead grouped into air armies (the equivalent of the German air fleets) with mixed components of bombers, fighter-bombers, fighters, and reconnaissance aircraft. Each air army was attached to an army group, whose commander was responsible for the tactical deployment of air power. Each air army had a deputy chief of staff stationed at the front line to facilitate rapid communication between the shifting frontline situation and the air army central command. Novikov insisted on reforming the system of air control with centralized control centers and more extensive use of radio. In addition, the central Soviet headquarters maintained separate strategic forces, not directly under army group command. These consisted of tactical reserve corps of fighter-bombers, fighters, and medium bombers for use at critical points in the battle; by the end of the war, these reserve corps constituted some 43 percent of all available tactical forces.[37] There was also a long-range bomber force to be used for strategic tasks on or behind the battlefront as circumstances dictated, and finally a fighter defense force, similar to the fighter defense organization set up in Britain by 1940, used to defend Soviet cities from German bombers. A separate service maintenance command was also established to ensure that damaged aircraft were rapidly repaired and returned to battle—a factor of considerable importance given the difficulty experienced by both sides in maintaining satisfactory levels of serviceability in bad weather, far from major supply centers. The improvements in maintenance also relied on a new system of air bases, with small, often improvised fields near the front and a series of larger and better resourced bases at safer distances (forty to sixty kilometers) from the front line.

By force of circumstance, the Soviet armed forces constructed a flexible operational air force that was used to maximize the impact of the large ground armies in the major offensives conducted from 1943 onward. Aircraft were used principally to achieve temporary air superiority over the battlefield area through strikes against enemy airfields and fighter aircraft and secondly to provide massive aerial firepower in tactical attacks on or near the battlefront—the form of operational air warfare exploited by the German air force in 1939–1941. The first point at which these operational and command reforms were used with great effect was at Stalingrad, where Novikov organized an aerial blockade combining regular fighter interception of enemy combat and transport aircraft with heavy tactical bombing attacks on German airfields and troop concentrations. German Air Fleet Four was decimated during the siege at Stalingrad, with 488 aircraft destroyed or damaged beyond repair. Of the 624 aircraft remaining on the German southern front in Russia, only 240 were operational when Field Marshal Friedrich Paulus surrendered on January 31, 1943. The German effort to supply the Sixth Army from the air had also cost the German transport arm dearly: 266 Junkers Ju–52 transport aircraft were lost, one third of the force, while a further 222 bombers converted to a transport role were also destroyed.[38]

For the German air force in the East, the size of the front and the failure to expand aircraft production to match the scale of its demands made it difficult to maintain an effective operational air war. Although German pilots occasionally were able to win local air superiority when there were sufficient numbers of combat-worthy aircraft, most German aviation had to concentrate on supporting ground forces in the long retreat back to Germany in 1943–1945. German air attacks became brief spoiling missions rather than a systematic operational campaign. During the summer of 1943, the Red air force was able to deploy up to ten thousand frontline aircraft; the German air force had thirty-five hundred combat-ready aircraft on all fronts in the summer of 1943, but only eighteen hundred to two thousand on the entire Eastern front—including just six hundred fighter aircraft, most of which were deployed in unequal combat over the battlefield at Kursk in July 1943. In the opening phase of this battle, the German air force had only 700 fighters and fighter-bombers against 2,170 for the Red air force, which could also draw on substantial reserves positioned close behind the battle. In July and August, the German air fleets lost 1,272 aircraft around Kursk and in the retreat that followed. This high loss rate was largely owing to the inability of attenuated German air forces to prevent the enemy from operating heavy attacks against air bases and supply or from using its larger number of fighters to maintain local air superiority.[39]

The operational flexibility and concentration of force characteristic of the early years of German victories were lost in the face of a vastly larger force and high levels of force attrition. As a result of German weakness, Soviet loss rates fell from 34 percent of combat aircraft in 1942 to 14 percent in 1944, even though poor handling and training still resulted in very high noncombat losses.[40] Falling loss rates and high production meant that by January 1944, the Red air force had 13,500 combat aircraft; a year later, 15,500. The final major offensives into Central Europe involved army groups supported by up to eight thousand aircraft.[41] By that stage, additional German aircraft production (which reached 39,807 in 1944) was sucked into the major battles in the West and the defense of the Reich from bomb attack.

THE AIR WAR IN WESTERN EUROPE

The circumstances of war also contributed to the RAF's choice of air strategy from 1941 onward. But unlike the German experience, these circumstances compelled Britain to adopt an operationally diverse strategy while encouraging commitment of a large proportion of the British and Commonwealth war effort to aircraft production, pilot training, and air operations. The impossibility of launching a major land offensive on the Continent without major allies predisposed the British military leadership to adopt a strategy of long-range bombing against Axis military and economic targets and, indirectly, against the enemy's will to fight. The necessity of keeping open sea-lanes in the Atlantic and Mediterranean compelled greater attention to air power and the war at sea. The defense of Egypt against Italo-German attacks in 1941–1942 forced the RAF to learn to fight the kind of operational air war in support of ground offensives developed by the German air force (and subsequently imitated by all of Germany's major enemies). At the same time, the air defense of Britain was strengthened to ensure that if Germany won the war against the Soviet Union, renewed air attacks on Britain could be met by a more effective shield than had been available in 1940–1941. In the middle years of the war, the exercise of air power became the essential component of British strategy, as it was for U.S. forces arriving in Europe in 1942 following the Japanese attack on Pearl Harbor on December 7, 1941, and the German and Italian declaration of war on the United States four days later.

As in the air war at sea, there were also issues of service politics and inter-Allied collaboration to address in the development of an effective operational air power against Axis forces in North Africa in 1941–1943, in Italy during the invasion of 1943–1945, and in the campaign across France in 1944. During the desert campaigns of 1941–1942, the RAF and the Commonwealth air forces generally enjoyed numerical superiority over the combined Italian and German air forces but found it difficult to make that difference effective at the operational level. The British armies in North Africa expected close protection for their forces and would have preferred tactical control of air forces by the ground army. The RAF in the Middle East wanted to retain independence from the ground commanders but needed to establish a clear doctrine governing the way air operations could best serve the central strategic objective. This doctrine was worked out under the leadership of Air Marshal Arthur Tedder, commander in chief of RAF Middle East Command, one of the few senior airmen who understood the importance of winning air superiority rather than simply bombing the enemy. The new doctrine, like the reform instituted in the Soviet air force in 1942, relied on imitating German practice. Fighter squadrons were to be used to eliminate enemy air power and attack enemy air bases; bomber aircraft were used at night to attack enemy supplies and air bases, and by day or night against targets of opportunity such as supply depots, ports, and communications. Everything was coordinated by a centralized command and relied on establishing high levels of mobility, force maintenance, and intelligence. The emphasis was on a mixture of concentration and flexibility of effort. Air command was organized alongside the army, each headquarters having an air and army component, but the army generals could not compel ground support if other operations promised a more effective outcome. At ground level, special liaison units helped to feed vital information to the central air controller and air support units based on trucks armed with radio, and radar traveled with the moving front to provide up-to-the-minute information.[42]

This form of operational warfare could not guarantee that ground campaigns would succeed even with air superiority, as the disastrous retreat into Egypt in June

1942 demonstrated. But at the Second Battle of Alamein, the system proved its worth when 350 Axis aircraft, many short of fuel, were overwhelmed by more than 1,500 Allied aircraft stationed in the Middle East and Mediterranean, who fought a continuous and interdependent campaign against all elements of Axis supply, deployment, and battlefield forces. Even then, many of the lessons learned in Egypt had to be relearned by Allied forces as they pushed the Axis back into Tunisia, while the USAAF, arriving in Algeria and Morocco for Operation Torch, launched on November 8, 1942, began from the basis that the Army ground commanders had priority over air forces tied closely to particular Army divisions. The introduction of a more flexible air doctrine and the principle of command equivalence followed the appointment of Tedder to head the combined Mediterranean Air Command and of RAF Air Vice Marshal Arthur Coningham to command the North-West African Air Forces, but the U.S. Army still had the right under Field Manual 31–35 to order air units to support Army units on the battlefield. In July 1943, Field Manual 100–20 finally conceded that "land power and air power are co-equal," a concession that freed the American tactical air forces to fight an operational air war like the RAF.[43]

From mid-1943 until the end of the war, the tactical air forces of all three major Allies grew enormously in size and competence. They imposed on the German air force, fighting on its own after the surrender of Italy on September 8, 1943, a level of attrition that could not be reversed despite the large increase in German aircraft production in 1944. The disparity between the two sides is best illustrated by the figures available for the Normandy landings on June 6, 1944. The Allies had on hand 12,837 aircraft including a complement of 5,400 fighters. German Air Fleet Three in northern France had only 300 aircraft, and on June 6, only 170 were serviceable. Over the days that followed, 1,000 more German aircraft were flown into the region, but they were easily destroyed.

In addition, both the RAF and the USAAF in France could draw on a new generation of high-performance fighter-bombers (the aircraft the RAF crucially lacked for much of the early period of the war). The American P–38 Lightning and P–47 Thunderbolt and the British Hawker Typhoon were all capable of carrying rockets and bombs for attacks on battlefield targets. Recent research has suggested that their role as "tank-busting" aircraft has been exaggerated, but the psychological impact on ground forces that were almost wholly without effective air support was profound.[44] Almost all the senior German generals interrogated about the cause of the Allied victory in the West held the view that air power had been decisive. Hitler's chief of operations, Colonel General Alfred Jodl, told his American interrogator late in June 1945, "I would say in general that in the end the winning of complete air superiority in the whole area of the war has altogether decided the war."[45] Field Marshal Gerd von Rundstedt, German commander in chief in the West, explaining the German defeat after the war, also argued that "the root of the whole trouble was air power, air power."[46]

THE STRATEGIC AIR CAMPAIGNS

A principal reason why German air power evaporated was the distorting effect on German strategy and production of the cumulative impact of the RAF Bomber Command and U.S. bomber forces campaigns in Europe. These independent air campaigns, critical elements in Western air strategy, were sometimes constrained by, but never entirely subordinate to, the operations of the rest of the armed forces. Although both the British and the Americans viewed bombing as a campaign that could fatally weaken Axis forces at the front by sapping the supply of munitions, the assumption was that an enemy nation would be more likely to succumb if the armed forces in the field were simply bypassed and the "vital centers"—the economic and military structures on the home front and the morale of the enemy population—struck instead.

These views were fully developed in both air forces before 1939, and they rested on an assumption that the next war would be a total war in which the whole of the enemy state would be involved and therefore could legitimately be disabled.[47] In both cases, the aim was not to inflict indiscriminate destruction and killing but rather to find those objects or areas in an enemy's industrial and economic structure most susceptible to debilitating interruption. However, it was never intended that such attacks would not also have a profound social and political effect and weaken enemy resistance, perhaps to the point of collapse.[48] When both bomber forces began to plan seriously for a future campaign, they tried to identify which target systems would be most likely to yield rapid and significant dividends. The British Western Air Plans, drawn up in December 1937, identified attacks on production in the German Ruhr industrial region as vital and added attacks on other industrial areas, the capital city of Berlin, and German docks and trade.[49] Other target systems—oil, aircraft production, machinery, chemicals, and the power industry—were added by 1939. When U.S. Air Intelligence was asked to draft the air component of the Victory program drawn up in the summer of 1941 on President Franklin Roosevelt's orders, the group under Colonel Harold George identified a web of key industries and services whose disruption would fatally undermine the German war effort. Air War Plans Division Plan 1 (AWPD–1) listed nine core areas, including transport, aircraft industries, electricity generation, and chemicals; a further list produced on the orders of General Hap Arnold, chief of staff of the USAAF, added ten vital target systems.[50] AWPD–1 even suggested the precise number of bomber sorties, 66,045, thought necessary to achieve the primary objective.

Not only did no other major air force place such reliance on the impact of independent bombing, but the high aspirations of prewar planning were also shown to be almost entirely unrealistic. It was never possible to disrupt individual target systems completely, and it took so long to effect massive damage on German society that the country was invaded and occupied by ground armies while the bombers continued to hammer away at German cities. In the process, around 410,000 German civilians and between 60,000 to 70,000 foreign forced laborers, camp prisoners, and POWs were killed—an outcome that was never planned for since bombing was expected to yield much faster dividends. The two bomber forces also killed an estimated sixty thousand Italian civilians and sixty thousand to seventy thousand French, most of them as a result of efforts to liberate them from German rule between 1943 and 1945.[51] These paradoxes have helped to fuel the popular postwar perception that bombing was a wasted strategic effort and that the heavy cost to the German, Italian, and French populations was ethically insupportable.[52]

Of course, none of these outcomes could have been known with any certainty at the start of the campaigns, since almost no hard evidence was available that bombing had, or would have in the future, the effects described in the strategy. The evidence of the popular reaction to the Blitz and the limited damage that nine months of bombing did to Britain's productive war effort failed to undermine the expectations of the RAF or the political leadership about probable results. This was partly because the bombing campaigns were promoted not necessarily to produce clearly understood strategic goals but sometimes to serve political ends. Both Winston Churchill and Franklin Roosevelt played a central part in promoting and supporting the bombing campaigns and in allocating the generous productive capacity needed to sustain them. When Churchill became prime minister on May 10, 1940, the RAF was still restricted by a general ban introduced by Neville Chamberlain's government in 1939 that stated that no air attacks should be undertaken that risked inflicting civilian casualties. Only five days later, Churchill's war cabinet approved attacks on economic and military targets in German towns (in fact, Mönchengladbach had already been attacked on May 11)—not, as has often been argued, in reaction to the bombing of Rotterdam on May 15, which did not feature in the cabinet discussions, but as a desperate means to reduce pressure on British forces trapped in northeastern France.[53]

The subsequent directive nevertheless opened the way to a continuous campaign against German targets, and when Britain was expelled from continental Europe by June 1940, Churchill famously told Lord Beaverbrook, the minister of aircraft production, that only "an absolutely devastating, exterminating attack by very heavy bombers" would bring about Hitler's downfall.[54] At all the major points in 1940 and 1941 where decisions had to be made about bombing strategy, Churchill played an approving part, encouraged by his chief scientific adviser, Lord Cherwell. In July 1941, Churchill requested the RAF commander in chief to undertake the "devastation of German cities"; on July 9, Bomber Command was directed explicitly to attack urban industrial targets as a whole on nights when precise targets were not visible.[55]

For Churchill, and later for Roosevelt, there were also wider strategic considerations. It was considered important that Britain could demonstrate to the Empire, to the United States, and to occupied Europe that she was still a willing participant in the war; and in 1940, it was also important to sustain domestic war-willingness by the same route.[56] In July 1941, Churchill's enthusiasm for the indiscriminate bombing of Germany had to be set against his desire to show Stalin that Britain was keen to assist the Soviet war effort, and the same argument was used at the Moscow Conference with Stalin in mid-August 1942: that bombing could be regarded as a surrogate for a second front.

For Roosevelt, who shared Churchill's enthusiasm for a bombing strategy and who in the 1930s had helped to overcome Army hostility to a heavy-bomber program, the bombing campaign in Europe was also a way to show that the United States was serious about the war and to convince the home population, whose gaze was fixed on the harsh struggles in the South Pacific, that the war in Europe was a priority. When there was growing criticism of the slow progress of American attacks against Germany in late 1942, the Eighth Air Force commander, Major General Carl Spaatz, was redeployed to the Mediterranean and replaced by the commander of Eighth Bomber Command, Major General Ira Eaker. It was also hoped that bombing might indeed provoke a political reaction in Germany, a dividend that might mean a smaller land commitment and fewer casualties.[57] The Italian surrender in September 1943 was attributed partly to the effects of the bombing war, and it was hoped that the Italian people, prompted by the high losses from bombing, might help to overthrow German occupation of the north of the country in 1944 and 1945.[58]

There nevertheless remained for the first three years of the bombing campaign a wide gap between expectations and reality. Bomber Command had only a small number of aircraft capable of penetrating German airspace, while technical problems of navigation at night, in the face of heavy antiaircraft defenses and German counter-measures, meant that the great bulk of bombs were dropped in open country or on the wrong city.[59] The growing realization that Bomber Command could inflict little concentrated damage was revealed in a report drawn up by a member of the British cabinet secretariat, D. M. Butt, in August 1941. The Butt Report, based on photoreconnaissance evidence, concluded that only one-third of Bomber Command aircraft got within even five miles of the target.[60] Churchill, despite his instrumental view of bombing, became disillusioned with its results and paid less attention to the details of the campaign thereafter.

Bomber Command faced a temporary crisis from which it was rescued in February 1942 with the appointment of Air Chief Marshal Arthur Harris as commander in chief, a role he held until the end of the war. Harris, a career airman with much experience of air policing in areas of the British Empire and the Middle East, adopted a maximum view of bombing strategy. He was armed with a new directive, issued on February 14, 1942, shortly before he assumed command, that instructed the force to adopt as its primary mission an attack on the morale of the German home population in general, and industrial workers in particular.[61] He was also supplied by the Ministry of Economic Warfare with a list of one hundred German cities, each with a points rating according to its size and industrial importance, which he could choose to attack as and when opportunity arose. Over the next three years, and despite the regular temporary loss of a portion of his force to other purposes, Harris remorselessly set out to do what his instructions told him.[62] To demonstrate the change in strategy and command, he organized a raid on the city of Cologne on May 30, 1942, with "a thousand bombers," although only 868 reached and bombed the target.

Harris's appointment coincided with the arrival of the U.S. Eighth Air Force, which began training programs and base construction in the spring of 1942. The first operations were mounted in August against French targets, but the force still had only 119 operational bombers. The U.S. commanders preferred to fly by day and to rely on the large firepower of the Boeing B–17 bomber. They remained critical of British night bombing and planned their own operations on the basis of hitting specific, visible economic targets in as systematic a way as possible. This distinction between day and night operations prevented serious friction between the two Allies except at those times when the U.S. air forces (the Fifteenth Air Force joined in the attacks from 1943 on from Mediterranean bases) wanted to mount a coordinated effort against a particular target such as the German aviation industry or the oil sector.

The different modes of operation were confirmed after the Allied leaders met at Casablanca in January 1943. The Combined Bomber Offensive ordered USAAF operations by day, RAF operations by night, to be directed against five major target systems (submarine industry, aircraft industry, transport, oil production and refining, secondary manufacturing sectors) and to apply "continuous pressure on German morale."[63] The edict was confirmed in the "Pointblank Directive" in June 1943, which laid the basis for the bombing campaigns for the rest of the war. The major difference in strategic outlook between the two forces lay in the American realization, evident from the lessons of the Blitz, that the German air force was an intermediate target that would have to be neutralized or defeated in order to maximize what the bombing campaign could achieve.

The German air defense force was one of the major factors inhibiting the full development of the bombing campaign. The early RAF bombing attacks were expected to be dealt with by antiaircraft fire and a well-prepared emergency air raid precautions system.[64] As the attacks grew in intensity during 1941, a sophisticated system of air interception (generally known as the Kammhuber Line after the commander in chief of air defense, Lieutenant General Josef Kammhuber) based on radar and night fighters was developed across northern Germany. By 1943, 70 percent of German fighter and night fighter strength was concentrated in Germany and Western Europe. New detection instruments were devised against RAF nightflying bombers—first, the ultra-high-frequency radar called Lichtenstein and then, when that was jammed, by British scientific counterintelligence, a very-high-frequency version known as SN2. The German fighter force did what the RAF had done in the Battle of Britain, exacting an escalating toll against the large unescorted U.S. bomber streams that stretched across northern and central Germany, though generally without preventing the bombers from dropping their payload, however inaccurately. Both Allied bomber forces were compelled to adjust their tactics to take account of German defense and the difficulty of finding and hitting even close to the designated target in the face of unpredictable weather, heavy antiaircraft fire, and German deception operations.

The tactical performance of the bomber force was enhanced by improved aluminized explosive, new navigational aids—the radio navigation system Gee, introduced in 1942, and the air-to-ground radar, known as H2S—and the introduction of special groups (Pathfinders in the RAF) to precede the bombers and to illuminate or indicate the target area clearly. The capability of the force was crudely demonstrated in Operation Gomorrah when the German port of Hamburg was subjected to four British and two American raids between July 24 and August 2, 1943. The raid of July 27–28 caused a firestorm that killed an estimated forty thousand people and destroyed twenty-two square kilometers of the city. Even this raid could not prevent the city from returning to 80 percent of its wartime output within a few months.[65]

Once Hitler had reluctantly accepted the need during 1943 to divert resources to combating the bombing, the balance between attacking force and air defense began to move in Germany's favor. The RAF launched the Battle of Berlin in the autumn of 1943, but loss rates rose to 14 percent of the attacking force destroyed or seriously damaged. The last raid, on March 24, 1944, cost 10 percent of the force destroyed, and a further raid on Nuremberg on March 30 saw the destruction of 11 percent. Harris admitted to the Air Ministry in London that these loss rates could not be sustained for long. The U.S. Eighth Air Force also suffered debilitating losses in the autumn of 1943, most famously during a raid on October 14, 1943, against the ball-bearing plants at Schweinfurt, which cost 60 bombers destroyed and 138 damaged out of a force of 300.[66] The USAAF then suspended further deep raids into Germany.

The solution was to find ways of contesting German air forces over German territory, the problem that had faced the German air force over Britain in 1940. During the winter of 1943–1944, the Eighth Air Force planned a concentrated assault on German aircraft production (Operation Argument), which took place in the weeks starting February 20, 1944. The 3,800 bombers of the U.S. Eighth and Fifteenth Air Forces and 2,351 RAF bombers dropped 20,000 tons of munitions on the German aircraft production sector, delaying two months of fighter production and forcing the dispersal of much German production underground or to more distant sites.

The most significant aspect of the operation was the use of large numbers of long-range fighter aircraft converted for the purpose of contesting German air superiority in German airspace. The search for a means of bringing direct pressure on the German defense force began in the autumn of 1943, but the solution proved deceptively easy. The standard U.S. fighter aircraft, the P–38 Lightning and P–47 Thunderbolt, were fitted with extra fuel tanks when they were ferried to the Air Force. It was found that they could also fight very effectively with the extra load of fuel and could fly two thousand miles instead of five hundred. The most successful adaptation was the P–51 Mustang, produced for the RAF in American factories with a Rolls-Royce Merlin engine. Extra fuel tanks extended its range to eighteen hundred miles, fully armed and with little loss of performance. A crash production program began, and the first aircraft flew on a raid to Kiel in December 1943. In March 1944, Mustangs accompanied bombers all the way to Berlin and back.

The high performance and large numbers of American fighter aircraft turned the tide of the air war over Germany. German monthly fighter losses rose from 30.3

percent in January 1944 to 56.4 percent in March.[67] This rate of attrition could not be sustained, and despite high fighter output, the loss of pilots and degradation of training owing to fuel shortages reduced the ability of the German air force to contest the bombing campaign effectively. In the last year of the war, Allied air forces dropped 1.18 million tons of munitions on Germany and German-occupied Europe, or 83 percent of the tonnage dropped throughout the war. The neutralization of the German air force opened the way for the remorseless destruction of much of urban Germany and its communications, fuel supply, and infrastructure from the summer of 1944 onward. Historians have recently demonstrated that during the latter stages of the war, American bombers engaged increasingly in blind bombing through clouds and haze, achieving in effect a form of area bombing not very different from that of RAF Bomber Command. Between September and December 1944, 52.9 percent of bomb tonnage was delivered by blind bombing.[68]

The effects of the bombing campaign have been widely debated. A recent study has suggested that the last stages of the campaign yielded what economists call *diminishing returns*—that the cost of the campaign in its last year produced a proportionately smaller effect per bomb dropped than earlier in the war. There is little argument that the final stages of the bombing war, including the destruction of Dresden on February 13–14, 1945, did represent a form of "overkill" with few direct strategic benefits and an excessive level of casualty for an increasingly defenseless civilian population.[69] There has also been much argument over whether German war production was seriously affected, since in 1944 German industry produced three times as many weapons as in 1941.

The question is really one of what might have been. Here there are two central considerations. First, the German war economy from 1942 onward was capable of producing a great deal more than it did. The physical damage to plants, forced dispersal, the loss of hours caused by air raid alarms, and the diversion of more than 2 million people, 55,000 antiaircraft guns, 20 percent of all ammunition, and extensive electrical, optical, and radar production to the defense effort inhibited substantially what the German economy, if entirely free of bombing, might have been capable of producing.[70]

Second, the bombing offensives distorted German air strategy entirely and undermined the capacity of the army to fight effectively at the major European fronts. The diversion of fighter defense aircraft to Germany reduced the aircraft available to support ground forces. In January 1944, for example, 68 percent of German fighters were defending the homeland and only 17 percent were in the East. The emphasis on defense also degraded aircraft output: in 1942, over 50 percent of combat aircraft produced were bombers, which played a central role in operational air warfare; by 1944, only 18 percent of combat aircraft were bombers, denying the German army the means to disrupt enemy supply lines and troop concentrations effectively. For much of the last two years of the war, the German army was forced to fight with a shrinking number of aircraft and a consequent rise in attrition rates. Without the impact on production and the distorting effects on German strategy, German frontline troops might have had as much as 50 percent more weaponry and supplies, and it would have taken a larger and more costly ground campaign to dislodge them.

The answer to whether morale was undermined by bombing is in some respects self-evident. The bombed populations in Italy and Germany were deeply demoralized and profoundly affected by intense bombardment. But the expected political dividend, which was the implied goal of the Combined Offensive assault on morale, did not merely fail to materialize, but in fact accrued to the German leadership: heavy bombing provoked an apathy and resignation that permitted the regime to continue to impose high demands on the population without provoking much overt political dissent.[71] The "nation" in that sense was not a target that could be defeated until the armed forces of the enemy had been compelled to surrender.

CONCLUSION

The air war that materialized between 1939 and 1945 was not the war that had been popularly expected. No "knockout blow" from the air against the civilian home front materialized in the early weeks of the war, and even after four years of heavy bombing, German society continued to fight until the armed forces had to accept defeat. Yet the role of air power in the war was undoubtedly of great importance. In any balanced explanation, air power made the difference in a great many different campaigns.

Once the historical emphasis is shifted from the major bombing campaigns, it is evident that the development of operational air warfare for land or sea campaigns was the most significant contribution aircraft could make to the conduct of war. The neglect in many general accounts of the air war of the development of tactical air power by the British Commonwealth air forces and the U.S. Army and Navy has obscured the extent to which the campaigns in North Africa, Italy, France, and Eastern Europe relied on extensive and effectively deployed battlefront air forces. The winning of air superiority, from the Battle of France in May–June 1940 to the conquest of Germany in January–May 1945, gave a degree of strategic flexibility in the conduct of operations denied to the loser. It was here that the numerically largest effort was made, even by Britain and the United States. What distinguished the air strategy of the Western Allies from that of Germany or the Soviet Union was the recognition that air power is indivisible, with one form of air strategy supporting the others. Hence, while Germany and the Soviet Union concentrated on operational air warfare in collaboration with frontline armies, Britain and the United States also developed long-range bombing, air-sea cooperation, and an effective air supply system.

These different choices also reflected differing historical circumstances. The war Germany was forced to fight from 1941 onward narrowed strategic options, as it also did for the Soviet Union. Long-range bombing was neglected and air defense had to be constructed in the face of a deteriorating strategic situation on all fronts. Britain and the United States opted for the exercise of air power in all its ramifications because neither was directly threatened with invasion after 1941 and both had powerful political motives to avoid building a large infantry army if air power could achieve as much. The eventual cost of 120,000 airmen and 21,000 bombers spread over five years of war was low in comparison to the annual losses of the other combatants. Air power reflected too the scientific, technical, and manufacturing capabilities of the two democracies, which were exploited at the expense of devoting greater resources to creating a very large infantry army.

The success of Allied air power also depended on other factors, the most important of which was the contrast in numbers. German and Italian aircraft production was never equal to the scale of the strategic task. Although efforts were made to expand German output, many factors, including the later impact of bombing, inhibited higher levels of output. In both cases, the attrition cycle caused by an imbalance of numbers could not be reversed, creating accelerating loss rates in the last years of the war, however high the quality of German aircraft.

Second, there were differences in the way the air forces were integrated into the overall command structure. In Germany, they were closely controlled by Hitler's supreme headquarters, where there was no equivalent of a general staff committee to which air commanders could make reasoned arguments and expect clear decisions. In the Soviet Union, Britain, and the United States, the air force commanders were closely integrated into the overall military committee system and could argue as equals against the interests of other services. In the West, this also involved the combined chiefs of staff, where top-level decisions were taken together with army, navy, and air force representatives.

Third, there was a contrast in political receptivity. Churchill and Roosevelt were air power enthusiasts and accepted a high level of commitment to its exploitation and supply. Hitler was much more attracted to an army view of warfare and became progressively disillusioned with air power. By 1944, he threatened to disband the air force, replace it with antiaircraft defenses, and trust instead in new weapons of vengeance (the V1 flying bomb, the V2 rocket). Although there were many arguments on the Allied side over strategic options for the use of air power, or the command of particular air forces, there was a general acceptance at the highest level that war conducted on such a geographical scale and waged with such intensity required a consistent commitment to air power in all its many manifestations.

3

THE AIR WAR IN THE PACIFIC, 1941–1945
Richard R. Muller

A BLUE, GREEN, AND ORANGE AIR WAR

THE AIR WAR IN THE PACIFIC from December 7, 1941, to September 2, 1945, was a global endeavor.[1] The size of the theater exceeded that of the European theater of operations, even if the Eastern front, North Africa, and the Mediterranean are included. In terms of primitive operating conditions, climatic extremes, and logistical difficulties, it was perhaps the toughest air force operating environment of the Second World War.[2] Despite the many obstacles and challenges, air power in its many forms came to dominate events in the Pacific to an even greater extent than in Europe.

It was an air war fought primarily between the United States and Japan. In the Southwest Pacific, Australian and New Zealand air units made a major contribution, while Britain's Royal Air Force waged a determined and costly campaign in Burma, and her carriers joined the U.S. Pacific Fleet in the final year of the war. Air forces of the colonial powers fought courageously in obsolete aircraft against the Japanese advance in 1941–1942, and Chinese and Filipino airmen also played their part. But only the United States had the industrial and demographic power to make a major effort in both Europe and the Pacific simultaneously, and to make sustained efforts in the four major subtheaters that made up the vast Pacific.

The roots of conflict in the Pacific stretch back to the nineteenth century, but the proximate cause was Japanese growth and expansionism. A latecomer to both industrialization and imperialism, Japan sought to increase its regional power at the expense of China, Russia, and the colonial powers in the Far East. Militarization of Japanese society and a domination of foreign policy by the army led to hostilities in Manchuria in 1931 and to open war with China in 1937.

China was "the army's war." The navy had a somewhat different outlook but felt obligated to participate in the undertaking, which, despite impressive Japanese operational victories, degenerated into stalemate. The war brought Japan into conflict with both the Soviet Union and the Western powers, and ultimately the United States. The Soviets handed the Japanese a telling defeat in border clashes in Manchuria in 1939, which may have dissuaded their leaders from further action against the Soviet Union.

Japanese strategic planning envisioned the establishment of a "Greater East Asia Co-Prosperity Sphere." Japan would expand into the oil-rich Southern Resource Zone (especially Singapore and the Netherlands East Indies), driving out the fading colonial powers and establishing itself as a regional hegemon. German successes in Europe against those colonial powers emboldened Japan. It concluded the Tripartite Pact, a defensive alliance with Nazi Germany and fascist Italy, in September 1940. The three Axis powers would be allies only in name; there was never any serious effort to coordinate global strategy, even when obvious opportunities presented themselves.

Japan's actions put it on a collision course with not only the colonial powers, but also the United States. Popular opinion in the United States was firmly with China, which had resisted Japanese aggression and brutality with great courage. The Roosevelt administration sought to check that aggression using diplomatic and economic tools, such as an embargo on aviation gasoline, lend-lease aid to China, and establishment of an American Volunteer Group, the famed Flying Tigers. War with Japan would of necessity take a backseat to war in Europe against Nazi Germany, which was seen as a more dangerous enemy on land and at sea.

A comprehensive U.S. oil embargo in July 1941 accelerated events. Prior to this decision, the Japanese army and navy commands were divided as to the necessity of war with the United States; some believed that the United States might acquiesce to Japanese expansion. Now, it seemed that Japan's economic position was in jeopardy. The commander of the Japanese Combined Fleet, Admiral Isoroku Yamamoto, argued that any war with the United States had to begin with a strike against its Pacific Fleet at Pearl Harbor. This would clear the way for the advance southward into the rich resource zone and enable Yamamoto to, as he promised, "run wild."

Historian Richard J. Overy divides the air war in the Pacific into three broad phases: a successful Japanese offensive, spearheaded by carrier and land-based air power; an Allied "defensive-offensive," in which the Allies first blunted the Japanese advance, then began to apply pressure at key points, gradually bringing the home islands within range; and the strategic bombing offensive, during which the Japanese homeland was attacked directly with long-range aircraft.[3] The enormous battlespace of the Pacific was partitioned into a number of subtheaters. The blue-water Central Pacific (CENTPAC) was dominated by the U.S. Navy, as its prewar "Orange" war plan envisioned; the green jungles of New Guinea in the Southwest Pacific (SWPAC) were the responsibility of U.S. Army and Australian forces under General Douglas MacArthur, while U.S. Navy and Marine units predominated in the adjoining South Pacific. Operations on the Asian mainland were under the China-Burma-India (CBI) theater, a combined command.

THE AIR POWER BALANCE

The air arms that fought the Pacific war were the products of rapid interwar development. Each developed capabilities and technology appropriate to its national context and strategy, service culture and aspirations, and theoretical mind-set. The U.S. air power that eventually met the Japanese in combat represented the thinking of three services—the U.S. Army Air Corps (later U.S. Army Air Forces [USAAF]), the U.S. Navy (USN), and the U.S. Marine Corps (USMC). All of these services could be considered "air-minded" in that they believed that aviation would play a central role in future conflicts. Each had a very different vision of the form that contribution would take.

American airmen, like most Army officers, saw that aviation was an indispensable part of modern combined arms. Air superiority, observation, interdiction of enemy supply lines, and direct intervention in ground operations had proved their worth. Yet some airmen believed that the airplane had the potential to dominate or bypass surface forces. Decades earlier, Brigadier General William "Billy" Mitchell maintained that bomber aircraft rendered even the most modern naval vessels obsolete and "proved" his case with demonstrations against warships off the Virginia coast in 1921. Mitchell argued that long-range bombers could do a better and more cost-effective job of protecting the United States and its overseas territories than could the Navy. With characteristic hyperbole, Mitchell wrote that "a thousand airplanes could be built for the price of one battleship."[4]

Mitchell faded from the scene after his 1925 court-martial brought on by his intemperate denunciations of the War and Navy departments. Yet others carried on, with somewhat less drama and controversy, the idea that aviation might play a greater role in a future war. The 1931 MacArthur–Pratt agreement secured for the Air Corps a role in coastal defense, while the establishment of General Headquarters Air Force in 1935 created a semi-independent combat air force headquarters. A compelling vision of independent air warfare waged by long-range bombers against the industrial heart of an enemy nation animated the Air Corps in the 1930s. Though air power advocates in a number of nations entertained similar ideas, a group of dedicated faculty at the Air Corps Tactical School (ACTS) at Maxwell Field, Alabama, raised them to an art and a science. Modern states depended on a complex "industrial web," which contained a small number of vital chokepoints that could be identified through careful analysis. Fleets of self-defending heavy bombers, the ACTS bomber mafia believed, could reach these key targets and destroy them through precision bombardment. Other voices, such as Claire Chennault, who argued that modern pursuit aircraft could threaten the bomber, or George Kenney, who maintained that attack aviation had a major role to play, were silenced or marginalized.[5]

On the eve of war, the Air Corps was gearing up to wage a strategic air offensive against the Axis. A farsighted if untried doctrine was in place, and remarkable aircraft—the Boeing B–17 Flying Fortress and Consolidated B–24 Liberator heavy bombers—were in production to make it a reality. Yet the focus on strategic bombardment came at a price. Attack or Army support aviation atrophied during the 1930s. The pursuit planes then in service—the Curtiss P–36 Mohawk and P–40 Warhawk, and the Bell P–39 Airacobra, were inferior to frontline Axis fighters. The best fighter aircraft in the USAAF's inventory at the time, the twin-engine, twin-boom Lockheed P–38 Lightning, was slated for Europe, for the U.S. air arm's main focus was on the coming war against Nazi Germany. The Air War Plans Division's requirements plan (AWPD–1) noted, almost as an afterthought, that the USAAF's mission included the need "to conduct effective air operations in connection with hemispheric defense and a strategic defensive in the Far East."[6]

Therefore, the Army's air arm found itself ill equipped to face the challenges of a war in the Pacific. Impressive as they were in terms of early 1940s technology, the B–17 and B–24 did not possess the range to strike Japan from friendly territory. Very-long-range bomber prototypes (the Boeing XB–15 and Douglas XB–19) had flown in the late 1930s and early 1940s but had proved unsatisfactory, and their successors were years away from service.[7] Despite the confidence of USAAF planners, who sent a handful of B–17s to the Philippines, or of Chief of Staff General George C. Marshall, who spoke of setting the "paper cities of Japan" afire, high-altitude daylight bombardment had little to contribute in the early phases of the war against Japan. Nor was the Army's air arm much able to assist in other ways. Its fighters were decidedly inferior to those of the opposition, and its light and medium bombardment forces, such as they were, lacked the equipment, training, or doctrine to effectively engage surface forces on land or at sea. In any case, most of the first-line equipment was slated for Europe.

Fortunately for the Allies, the U.S. Navy was in a somewhat better position. The service had begun the twentieth century steeped in the influence of naval theorist Alfred Thayer Mahan, what historian Ronald Spector famously called "the classic brew of imperialism and saltwater."[8] Mahan argued that national greatness came to those nations that were not only favored by geography and culture, but that also assiduously developed sea power. Command of the sea, he insisted, was best seized by ships of the line waging a decisive battle against an opposing fleet. Commerce raiding, or *guerre de course*, was the refuge of second-rate sea powers.

Some argue that Mahan's influence was an intellectual straitjacket. Yet it was this emphasis on the decisive naval clash between great sea powers that led the USN to focus for decades on a coming war with Japan and to rigorously evolve the plan for that war, color-coded War Plan Orange. Unlike the Army and its Air Corps, the Navy's senior leadership had thought extensively about war with Japan. Generations of officers at the Naval War College wargamed successive iterations of the plan, which were constantly updated as technology evolved and geopolitical realities altered.[9]

For all the talk about "battleship admirals" keeping the "brown shoe" aviators down, naval aviation enjoyed a fairly strong position, allowing for the strictures of interwar budget cutbacks. Mitchell's 1921 battleship bombing tests helped spur the creation of the Navy's Bureau of Aeronautics. The bureau's first chief, Rear Admiral William A. Moffett, served for twelve years at the head of the bureau, and his impact on the future of naval aviation is considerable.[10] To be sure, not every innovation he championed bore fruit. Moffett believed that rigid airships, with their tremendous endurance, could serve as "the eyes of the fleet." Even after the loss of the USS *Shenandoah* in a thunderstorm in 1925, Moffett persisted. Two giant rigid airships, the *Akron* and the *Macon*, were laid down. Exercises with the fleet indicated that the airships held promise, although they were often misused for tactical scouting, when strategic reconnaissance would have been more appropriate. Both airships were lost at sea in storms, the *Akron* in 1933 and the *Macon* in 1935. The *Akron* crash was especially costly, with heavy loss of life, including Admiral Moffett himself. Shortly thereafter, his successor, Admiral Ernest J. King, shelved further development of rigid airships; only small, nonrigid blimps had a future in the Navy.

Moffett's advocacy of long-range patrol aircraft and carrier aviation was on much sounder technological and doctrinal footing. Both of these capabilities could enhance the operations of the traditional battle line. Few senior officers, even the most ossified "mossback admirals," doubted the value of aircraft for scouting and screening the fleet. The question was, could they do much more than play an auxiliary role?

One means of answering this question during peacetime was with the regular Fleet Problems. There were twenty-one of these major exercises held from 1923 to 1940.[11] They enabled officers to think through the implications of new technology and concepts, including aviation, submarines, and amphibious operations. Many questions of carrier operations were worked out in the years before the war. By Fleet

Problem XVIII in 1937, full-scale task force operations were included. Recently qualified aviators William F. "Bull" Halsey and Ernest J. King were among the air commanders that year.[12] In no small measure because of the experience gained in the Fleet Problems during the course of the 1930s, the navy's carrier force evolved from "Eyes of the Fleet," to a vital defensive and supporting role, to a potentially formidable striking force in its own right.

Improvements in technology accompanied and spurred the development process. The Navy's first carrier, the USS *Langley* (CV–1), was converted from a collier in 1922. Displacing only 12,700 tons, she carried 34 aircraft and had a maximum speed of only 15 knots. As useful as she was for training and concept development, *Langley* was only a stopgap. The USN's first true carriers were the USS *Lexington* and USS *Saratoga*. These began life as battle cruisers, canceled after the 1922 Washington Conference limited capital ship strength in the major navies. Converted into carriers, they displaced 43,000 tons and carried 63 modern aircraft at 33 knots—fast enough to keep up with any ship in the fleet.[13] The next generation of flattops was the *Yorktown* class, including the USS *Enterprise* and USS *Hornet*, the three "ships that held the line" during the dark days of the early Pacific war.[14]

The evolution of aircraft types also reflected the Navy's changing view of how aviation contributed to naval strategy. The late 1930s saw a shift from biplanes to all-metal monoplanes. The poor Brewster F2A Buffalo and the better Grumman F4F Wildcat served as first-generation monoplane fighters in Navy and Marine squadrons. Offensive action was the job of torpedo- and dive-bombers. Torpedo attacks were hampered by inadequate torpedoes and the obsolescent Douglas torpedo bomber Devastator. The Navy did have a first-rate scout- and dive-bomber in the SBD Dauntless, which served throughout the war. The Bureau of Aeronautics also developed large flying boats (notably the famed PBY Catalina) for long-range reconnaissance and antisubmarine warfare.[15]

The Navy was still in the midst of developing attack tactics, involving complex coordination between fighters, torpedo planes, scouts, and dive-bombers, when war came. During its early months, innovative tactics developed by young fighter leaders Jimmy Thach and Jimmy Flatley helped offset the superiority of the Japanese Zero. Flatley's unofficial manual "Combat Doctrine," as well as aerial maneuvers such as the "Thach Weave," gave U.S. naval pilots a fighting chance against the best of the Imperial Japanese Navy (IJN).[16]

The relative newness of aviation meant that few senior leaders were airmen. The service took a farsighted step by requiring all commanders of aircraft carriers to qualify as aviators.[17] These "latecomer" aviators, King and Halsey among them, would bridge the gap until career aviators such as Marc Mitscher attained the necessary seniority. In historian Clark Reynolds's words, an "Air Navy" was being forged. From the powerful fleet carriers to the humble catapult seaplanes on the decks of cruisers and battleships, this was a service that thought—and would fight—in three dimensions.

The Marine Corps also valued its aviation component, but its small size and narrow mission focus shaped its aviation forces and doctrine accordingly. During the interwar era, the Marines emphasized two main missions: waging "small wars" and undertaking amphibious landings against defended shores. In the former, aviation could serve as a means of observation, transportation, or in direct support of combat operations.[18] As war with Japan loomed, the latter, more complex mission assumed greater prominence. Marine forces were integrated into War Plan Orange as a means of seizing advanced bases from the Japanese, and Marine air power would support these landings with direct and indirect air support, operating either from carriers or forward airfields. One pioneer Marine aviator summed up the service's mind-set: "Marine aviation is not being developed as a separate branch of the service that considers itself too good to do anything else. Unlike the army air service, we do not aspire to be separate from the line or to be considered as anything but regular marines."[19]

In Imperial Japan, the United States faced a formidable adversary that also took aviation seriously.[20] Japanese military aviation got its start with the arrival of foreign training missions; the French assisted the army, the British the navy. The division between army and naval aviation eventually became a serious drain on Japanese industry and resources. Of the two services, it was the navy that developed the more effective, balanced, and technically advanced air arm. Japan's navy was essentially Mahanian in outlook, and its senior leadership believed that aviation would support the battle line. Air power advocates in the navy, Yamamoto among them, argued that air power would dominate the battleship, whose future value was merely "symbolic."[21] The debate was never fully resolved; not only did Japan develop a daunting carrier striking arm, but it also invested in the largest battleships ever constructed.

The Japanese naval air arm by the late 1930s evolved into a formidable force. Its doctrine and supporting tactics enabled it to function not only as a powerful weapon in fleet actions, but also in support of amphibious operations. The navy also developed a land-based striking arm; long-range bombers would cooperate with the carrier forces and operate independently from shore bases. Japan's advanced aviation technology was symbolized by the remarkable Mitsubishi A6M Zero fighter. In terms of maneuverability and range, it was superior to all other land- and sea-based fighters in theater in 1941–1942. Japan's offensive strike aircraft were also capable.

The Nakajima B5N Kate was the finest torpedo plane in the world, carried the best torpedoes, and could also operate as a high-level bomber. The Aichi D3A Val dive-bomber was a potent ship killer despite its anachronistic fixed landing gear. Land-based attack planes (the G4M Betty) gave the navy long-range strike capability, while its long-range flying boats were among the best patrol planes in existence.[22] Western complacency helped to increase the Japanese technical edge; many intelligence estimates dismissed Japanese technology as inferior knock-offs of Western designs and disparaged the quality of Japanese aviators as poor.[23]

Yet this powerful front line concealed critical weaknesses. The force was focused almost entirely on the offensive; there was a corresponding neglect of fleet defense, antisubmarine warfare, and commerce protection.[24] The Japanese flight-training regimen, especially for naval aviators, was one of the most demanding in the world. Fighter ace Saburo Sakai recalled that more than half his class at the Naval Fliers School was expelled during the course of their training, many for the most minor infractions.[25] Such a program certainly produced top-notch pilots, yet with its draconian washout rate, it was completely unsuited to producing the number of trained pilots demanded by modern combat. One German historian criticized the Luftwaffe leadership for adopting a "preindustrial" approach to warfare in its championing of martial virtues above mundane yet essential functions such as intelligence, logistics, and training;[26] the observation applies equally well to the IJN. This training system was ill equipped to provide replacements following the loss of the initial cadre. Meanwhile, at Pensacola, thousands of U.S. Navy aviators were being readied for the battles ahead.

Japanese army aviation, prominent in the campaign against China, proved poorly adapted to the war in the Pacific. Army aircraft, such as the Ki–43 Oscar fighter, were generally inferior to their navy counterparts. While the United States could afford to develop separate Army and naval air arms, Japan could not. One scholar has gone so far as to assert, "The waste and inefficiency created by this duplication of effort . . . were major contributing factors in Japan's defeat."[27]

THE JAPANESE MARCH OF CONQUEST: "RUNNING WILD"

Theory suddenly became practice on the morning of December 7, 1941, at the U.S. naval base at Pearl Harbor in the Hawaiian Islands.[28] Yamamoto and his air planners envisioned a surprise strike from a force of six carriers, the Kido Butai, commanded by Admiral Chuichi Nagumo. The task force launched two waves of 360 carrier planes, the first wave lifting off from the flight decks in the predawn darkness. The strike found a base that, despite intelligence indications of Japanese moves in the Pacific and a general war warning, was on a peacetime footing. The cumulative effect of mistaken assumptions, complacency, poor liaison and communications, and human error left the base poorly prepared to face the attack.[29] Such preparations that had been taken were to forestall sabotage; aircraft were grouped in the center of the airfields where they could be more easily guarded. Long-range reconnaissance patrols were curtailed in favor of training routines.

The IJN scored an undeniable tactical success. The Pacific Fleet battle line was devastated, with four of eight battleships sunk or crippled. Nearly three hundred aircraft were put out of action, and U.S. forces suffered over three thousand casualties. The battleship USS *Arizona* was struck by an armor-piercing bomb that penetrated her forward magazine, killing more than twelve hundred of her crew in an instant. The airfields were heavily damaged. All this was accomplished for the loss of twenty-nine aircraft and a handful of midget submarines. But the precious aircraft carriers were not in port. The dry dock and the oil tank farm were undamaged. Many of the sunken or damaged ships returned to service after a Herculean salvage operation. The raid galvanized U.S. public opinion; isolationism vanished almost overnight. The idea that Pearl Harbor forced the U.S. Navy to abandon its battleship-centric worldview and concentrate on carriers is an oversimplification, if not completely erroneous; carriers were to be an important part of the service's effort even prior to Pearl Harbor. The disaster did bring a formidable leadership team to the fore: Admiral Ernest J. King and Admiral Chester A. Nimitz took over as commander in chief, U.S. Fleet, and commander in chief, Pacific Fleet, respectively. And the strike precipitated Adolf Hitler's declaration of war on the United States four days later, which altered the strategic balance of the global war.

Yet the raid met the immediate Japanese objectives—to remove the U.S. Pacific Fleet from the chessboard for six months—and they made full use of it. What followed was an almost unbroken string of Japanese air-land-sea victories. Hours after Pearl Harbor, U.S. air forces in the Philippines were destroyed on the ground at Clark Field. While it is tempting to blame MacArthur for the disaster, the entire U.S. air deployment to the islands was ill conceived. The infrastructure to support the B–17s was not in place, no early warning system had been developed, and confusion and operational and tactical mistakes that day did the rest.[30] The Japanese quickly gained air superiority, and the Philippines were overrun after a heroic defense.

The Japanese march of conquest was impressive in both its scope and its tactical brilliance. British naval power off Malaya was wiped out when "Force Z," the *Prince of Wales* and *Repulse*, ventured within range of Japanese land-based air power without fighter protection. Malaya, Singapore, Java, and Wake Island fell. The Zero fighter seemed to sweep all before it, inflicting a latter-day "Fokker Scourge" on the demoralized Allies. One historian noted, "The Japanese carrier force . . . launched a series of offensive operations that were unrivalled in their speed, force and technical excellence until the American fast carrier operations of 1944–45."[31] The Japanese offensive, including the seizing of the Southern Resource Zone, was in some ways even more impressive than the German conquest of Poland, Scandinavia, and Western Europe.

Air power proved to be one of the few ways for the U.S. Navy to hit back. It undertook a series of wide-ranging carrier raids, hoping to divert Japanese attention without undue risk with strikes against the Gilberts, the Marshalls, Wake, and Lae and Salamaua on New Guinea. Army long-range aviation struck the new Japanese base at Rabaul on New Britain. The damage inflicted was minor, but the raid served to raise Allied spirits and give personnel and units valuable experience.

Most famous among these rearguard actions was the Doolittle raid on Tokyo. The operation had a complex pedigree. Roosevelt badly wanted to strike Japan, largely as a means of bolstering home front morale after months of bad news. The idea of using Army medium bombers launched from a carrier originated with King's staff but found ready favor with USAAF chief General Henry H. "Hap" Arnold.[32] A task force built around the carriers *Hornet* and *Enterprise* would steam to within five hundred miles of Japan. After executing a night attack on Japan, the force would continue to China. Commanding the raiding force was Lieutenant Colonel James H. "Jimmy" Doolittle, an Air Corps reservist, Massachusetts Institute of Technology graduate, engineer, and prewar record-setting test pilot, who had been handpicked by Arnold. Doolittle oversaw the selection of the volunteer crews and their hurried training in short-field takeoffs.

On April 15, 1942, the *Hornet* was docked at Alameda Naval Air Station, and sixteen B–25 Mitchell medium bombers were loaded onto her flight deck. The *Hornet* rendezvoused with Halsey and the *Enterprise* in mid-ocean. The planners hoped to launch the strike during the late afternoon of April 18, which would bring the targets within a five-hundred-mile range and put the bombers over their objectives in darkness. After Japanese picket boats spotted the carriers shortly after dawn on the eighteenth, the planners had no choice: rather than further risk the task force, the strike would have to launch from a range of nearly 650 miles, with little chance of a safe landing in China. Doolittle himself took off in the lead bomber. The other fifteen planes followed him and set off individually for the mainland.

Despite the warning, the raid achieved tactical surprise. Doolittle's bombers dropped high-explosive and incendiary bombs on Tokyo, as well as on Kobe, Yokohama, and Nagoya. Physical damage to the targets was minimal, and the raid costly; the entire strike force was lost (although seventy-one of the eighty airmen survived), and the tactic was never attempted again. Moreover, the Japanese army wreaked cruel revenge on the Chinese civilian population suspected of aiding the fliers.

Nonetheless, the raid was a dramatic propaganda coup for the United States. Roosevelt told reporters that the aircraft came from a "secret base at Shangri-La." What was hoped to have been at best a small morale boost instead had far-reaching effects. That American bombers had struck Tokyo was a profound shock to the Japanese military leadership that sparked a reevaluation of its defensive perimeter. Few air operations of such small size have had such impact.

THE TIDE TURNS: CORAL SEA, MIDWAY, AND GUADALCANAL

In the wake of its stunning success in the first months of the war, the Japanese leadership debated how to proceed. Ultimately, the decision was made to launch an assault on Port Moresby, the last Allied foothold on New Guinea and the gateway to Australia, and to establish an air base on Tulagi. The IJN dispatched an invasion force from Truk into the Coral Sea. Commander Joseph Rochefort's brilliant code breakers at Pearl Harbor had cracked the Japanese naval code JN–25 and learned the details of the Japanese assault, named Operation MO. A task force including USS *Yorktown* and USS *Lexington* under Vice Admiral Frank Jack Fletcher was sent to intercept.

The resulting Battle of the Coral Sea demonstrated that, tactically, both sides had much learning to do. The opening engagements on May 7 were characterized by mutual failures to locate and correctly identify the enemy's main force. The Japanese sank the fleet oiler *Neosho* and the destroyer *Sims*, while U.S. planes sank the light carrier *Shoho*. On May 8, the main carrier forces finally clashed. The Japanese fleet carrier *Shokaku* was badly damaged, while her sister ship *Zuikaku*'s air group suffered heavy aircraft and crew losses. The *Lexington* received damage but was thought to be out of danger (flight operations had resumed). However, poor damage control procedures failed to contain the onboard fires, and the "Lady Lex" was wracked by internal explosions. She was successfully abandoned and dispatched by one of her own destroyers. One of her crew admitted, "I couldn't watch her go, and men who had been with her since she was commissioned in '27 stood with tears streaming."[33] *Yorktown* took a single bomb hit, which caused serious damage. Notably, Coral Sea was the first major naval action in which the opposing surface fleets never caught sight of one another—all of the contact was through aircraft.

Despite not being a well-fought battle in the traditional sense, the case can be made that Coral Sea was the decisive battle of the early Pacific war. The invasion of Port Moresby was called off. *Shokaku* and *Zuikaku* would miss the Battle of Midway, where their presence might have been critical. For the first time, a major Japanese offensive effort had been turned back, and Japanese forces were critically weakened for the battle to follow.

Had Coral Sea turned out differently, it is difficult to see how the U.S. Navy could have won at Midway the following month.[34] The Doolittle raid gave Yamamoto the ammunition to extend the outer defense perimeter to include Midway and at the same time draw the U.S. carriers into a decisive battle. Yamamoto's plan, Operation MI, has come under heavy criticism from both participants and historians. It was overly complex and divided the available carrier power, including a diversionary and subsidiary operation to the Aleutians. This ensured that the forces that met off Midway were at rough parity.

Rochefort's code breakers gave Nimitz much valuable information regarding Japanese intentions, but the correct judgment of the commanders on the scene would still be vital. Nimitz husbanded his limited carrier forces under Admirals Fletcher and Raymond Spruance. The *Yorktown* was repaired and readied for action in a feat of shipyard heroics. Nimitz gave careful guidance to his commanders: "You will be governed by the principle of calculated risk . . . the avoidance of exposure of your force to attack by superior enemy forces without good prospect of inflicting, as a result of such exposure, greater damage on the enemy."[35]

The dramatic sea-air battle opened on the morning of June 4, 1942. The Japanese task force launched a strike against Midway that inflicted some damage but did not render the base inoperable. Scout planes from both sides groped to locate the opposing task forces. The Japanese search plan was totally inadequate given the magnitude of the task, and the United States was able to strike first. High-altitude bomb runs by USAAF B–17s failed to score any hits. Strikes from Midway by dive- and torpedo-bombers were beaten back with heavy losses to the attackers, and the torpedo-bomber groups from the U.S. carriers were virtually annihilated as they attempted to penetrate the Kido Butai's fighter cover. A late report from one of his scout planes finally alerted Nagumo to the presence of the American carriers, and he ordered his aircraft rearmed and refueled for a strike. Before this rearmament was complete, and with most of his aircraft still below decks, the delayed appearance of the dive-bombers from *Yorktown* and *Enterprise* transformed the battle in spectacular fashion.

Diving out of the sun in what one participant recalled as a "beautiful silver waterfall," the Dauntlesses lined up on three Japanese carriers.[36] Within a matter of minutes, the flagship *Akagi*, the *Kaga*, and the *Soryu* were ablaze. Later that day, *Hiryu* drew blood on the *Yorktown*, first damaging her with a dive-bombing attack and finally crippling her with a torpedo-plane strike. (She was finished off by a Japanese submarine on the afternoon of June 6 and sank the following day.) *Hiryu* was already gone; a U.S. riposte set her ablaze late in the afternoon of June 4, and she sank the following morning.

To be sure, there were mistakes on both sides. *Hornet's* air group was largely a nonparticipant in the battle, with the heroic exception of her torpedo squadron. Her dive-bombers failed to find the Japanese task force, and the bulk of her fighters ditched in the sea after running out of fuel. Her air group commander later admitted he had made a faulty "estimate of the situation."[37] The use of B–17s against Japanese warships had been a failure, despite the official historians' attempt to put the best possible gloss on the action by judging it merely "inconclusive."[38] Yet the Japanese errors—primarily the failure to concentrate the IJN's carrier power—were far greater, and the U.S. intelligence advantage conferred by Rochefort's analysts, coupled with Spruance's and Fletcher's cool leadership and the heroism of the American pilots, won out.

By any measure, Midway was a terrible defeat for the IJN. Four carriers and hundreds of officers and men were gone, including Rear Admiral Tamon Yamaguchi, the skilled and aggressive Carrier Division 2 commander who chose to go down with *Hiryu*. Every plane in the task force was lost, and 110 airmen were killed.[39] The magnitude of the defeat was carefully hidden from the Japanese people. The IJN even lied to itself—two of the sunken carriers remained on official naval strength lists.[40]

The victory at Midway accelerated the U.S. transition to the offensive in the Pacific. The Japanese had begun construction of an airfield on the island of Guadalcanal in the Solomons, which the United States was determined to prevent (underscoring yet again the importance of key air bases in the Pacific). On August 7, 1942, Operation Watchtower, the landing on Guadalcanal, began.[41] The early departure of the U.S. carrier forces left the Marine landing force in a precarious position, and its first priority was to finish the airstrip. The Marine engineers accomplished this feat in a matter of days; the strip was christened Henderson Field in honor of a Marine Corps aviator killed at Midway. The Japanese conducted long-range air strikes on Guadalcanal from Rabaul and reinforced their combat troops on the island by running fast escorted convoys, the "Tokyo Express," under cover of darkness. For the next six months, a grim sea-air-land battle raged on and around Guadalcanal. The perimeter of Henderson Field was just about the only place in the war where a Marine might be bombed from high altitude, strafed by a Zero, shelled by both "Pistol Pete" in the jungle and Japanese battleships, and menaced by a Japanese infantry assault, and all in the course of a single day.

Marine air power came of age in the expeditionary environment of Cactus, the code name for Guadalcanal.[42] Brigadier General Roy S. Geiger, a pioneer Marine aviator who commanded First Marine Air Wing, arrived on the island on September 3. He brought with him reinforcements and a flair for organization, as well as inspired combat leadership. Upon hearing a young pilot complaining about the poor condition of the runway, Geiger went without a word to a dive-bomber, took off, dropped a bomb, and returned to base.[43]

The naval battles off Guadalcanal demonstrated that the IJN still packed a punch. The disaster off Savo Island in August was one of the worst defeats in U.S. Navy history. During the Battle of the Santa Cruz Islands in October, Japanese carrier planes sank the *Hornet* and badly damaged the *Enterprise*. But the American efforts gradually reduced Japan's ability to reinforce its garrison, and by February 1943, Halsey received a report that "Tokyo Express no longer has terminus on Guadalcanal."[44] Before it was over, the prewar "treaty navies" of both combatants largely destroyed each other—not for nothing did the body of water off the northwest coast of the island become known as "Ironbottom Sound."

The campaign was the true turning point of the Pacific war. Japanese naval air forces began a precipitous decline—the cumulative effect of losses at Coral Sea, Midway, and the Solomons destroyed the elite cadre of Sea Eagles with which the Kido Butai so confidently began the war. The training establishment was unable to make good the losses. Zero pilot Sakai recalled, "I know that the forty-five pilots expelled from my own student class . . . were superior to those men who completed wartime training."[45] The American forces absorbed the hard lessons taught by the campaign.[46] From 1943 on, the United States had a firm upper hand. The reversal of fortune was accomplished without a huge influx of new production—that was still to come.

AIR POWER IN THE GREEN WAR: THE SOUTHWEST PACIFIC

Some have argued, then and now, that the SWPAC theater was an unnecessary diversion from the main focus of the Central Pacific effort against Japan, and that the theater in fact existed only because of Douglas MacArthur's vanity and desire for prestige. Others maintain that the complementary thrust through the Southwest Pacific greatly complicated Japanese defensive problems and robbed Japan of the ability to exploit its interior lines.

MacArthur arrived in Australia in March 1942 very dissatisfied with the operations of his air force, and he poured out a catalog of criticisms to his newly arrived air commander, General George C. Kenney.[47] A key to Kenney's eventual success was the remarkable partnership he forged with MacArthur through a combination of being conciliatory, talking tough, and delivering results. Moreover, Kenney had been the ACTS attack aviation instructor from 1927 to 1930 and had an excellent grasp of the essentials of tactical aviation. "I was the papa of attack aviation," he recalled. "I wrote the textbooks on it, taught it, and developed its tactics."[48] He had more to offer MacArthur than many of his peers.

First, he had to neutralize MacArthur's powerful chief of staff, General Richard Sutherland: "I told him that I was running the Air Force because I was the most competent airman in the Pacific and that, if that statement was not true, I recommended that he find someone that was more competent and put him in charge."[49] Kenney also drew a tiny pencil dot on a piece of paper, telling Sutherland that the dot represented Sutherland's knowledge of air power, while the vast whiteness of the paper encompassed Kenney's grasp of the subject.[50] Kenney trimmed the dead wood at Fifth Air Force, sending many officers home, revising maintenance procedures, and jettisoning cumbersome regulations and paperwork. Most importantly, Kenney's forces began to prove themselves in combat.

During the campaign to reduce the Japanese position at Buna from November 1942 to January 1943, Kenney demonstrated his air power "formula." His fighters would first establish air superiority over the battle zone and then erect an "air blockade" to check Japanese attempts to reinforce. His bombers would relentlessly "hammer" the enemy's forces, while providing close air support to Allied ground forces. Finally, he would set up forward air bases, get them operational, and extend the "bomber line" out toward the next objective.[51]

Kenney's Fifth Air Force employed an effective combination of specialized aircraft and munitions and innovative tactics. For antishipping strikes, his technicians converted B–25 bombers into gunships mounting up to twelve forward-firing .50-caliber guns. Some carried a 75-millimeter howitzer. His airmen developed "skip-bombing" techniques and dropped a type of deadly parachute fragmentation bomb Kenney had developed before the war. In common with other backwater theaters in World War II, tactical aviation thrived in the Southwest Pacific because of its remoteness, the lack of strategic targets, and freedom from regulations and higher headquarters oversight.

Kenney's weapons and techniques proved their worth in the March 1943 Battle of the Bismarck Sea. A Japanese resupply convoy of eight large transport ships and eight escorting destroyers en route from Rabaul to New Guinea was relentlessly attacked by a mixed force of skip-bombing B–25s and Australian Beaufighters. All the transports and six of the escorts went to the bottom. Aircraft and patrol torpedo boats strafed survivors and life rafts. In a testament to the harsh feelings that predominated during the war years, Kenney noted that "to the American and the Australian, the Nips were just vermin to be exterminated."[52]

Air power advocates frequently cite Bismarck Sea as an example of air power winning an independent victory over surface forces. A broad view of the campaign reveals that the success was only a part of an impressive combined arms victory, won by a balanced force.[53]

The Japanese sought to stop the hemorrhaging in April 1943 by striking Allied air bases in New Guinea and the Solomons—the "I Operation." Yamamoto launched some three hundred aircraft in a series of futile raids.[54] On an inspection trip to Bougainville to congratulate his pilots on their efforts, the admiral was shot down and killed by a flight of P–38s on April 18, 1943. A bitter dispute ensued over taking credit for downing Yamamoto's bomber, but the achievement belonged to the code breakers and mission planners who ensured a flight of P–38s turned up in just the right spot. In any case, Yamamoto was past his prime; his days of victory were behind him.

One last major operation took place before events moved away from the Southwest Pacific—Operation Cartwheel, the isolation of Rabaul. Capturing or neutralizing the powerful Japanese base on New Britain was a priority for both MacArthur and Halsey. Ultimately, it was decided to employ the "indirect approach"—bypassing Rabaul rather than seizing it. Thus began the dramatic "island-hopping" campaign, with the U.S. Navy driving up the Solomons, and MacArthur's U.S. and Australian forces proceeding along the New Guinea coast. Both drives were supported by increasingly effective air power—most notably Kenney's Fifth Air Force and Halsey's hard-hitting joint and combined air component, Air Solomons (AirSols). AirSols, the successor to the Cactus Air Force, contained units from the USAAF, U.S. Navy and Marine Corps, and Royal New Zealand Air Force, with a rotating command. From April 1943 to June 1944, this air task force compiled an admirable combat record, most notably in the preparation and execution of the assault on Bougainville. The official Navy historian praised AirSols as "one of the world's finest, with a matchless *esprit de corps*."[55]

The theater became a graveyard for Japanese air power. Rabaul was ultimately isolated and left to wither on the vine. And the war moved on.

RETURN TO WAR PLAN ORANGE: ON THE OFFENSIVE IN CENTPAC

The U.S. Navy senior leadership never abandoned its vision of the "Orange" thrust across the Central Pacific—engaging and destroying the Japanese fleet and besieging the home islands. By the fall of 1943, it was possible to open up CENTPAC. The days of the prewar "treaty navy" were over, and the power of U.S. industry and technological superiority was beginning to show. From late 1943 to the end of the war, the Navy would wage its war with fast carrier task forces, equipped with the new *Essex*-class carriers. These powerful ships carried ninety-one aircraft and had the latest radar sets and command and control facilities. They also possessed lavish antiaircraft armament, with improved gun directors and deadly proximity fuses. As a hedge against any delay in the arrival of the *Essex* carriers, the shipyards produced a class of *Independence*-class light carriers, constructed on the hulls of fast light cruisers and carrying thirty aircraft. To relieve the fast carriers of the need to accompany convoys or provide air support to amphibious landings, mass-produced escort carriers, sometimes referred to as "baby flattops" or "Kaiser coffins" (after the famed shipbuilder Henry J. Kaiser), also appeared and did yeoman's service.

Numbers were not everything in the Pacific campaign, but the U.S. Navy certainly had them. Seventeen *Essex*-class flattops were commissioned prior to VJ Day, with others in the wings. When the nine *Independence*-class carriers and the nearly ninety escort carriers were factored in, the late-war navy was completely transformed both qualitatively and quantitatively. A new generation of naval aircraft filled the flight decks: the Grumman F6F Hellcat, the Curtiss SB2C Helldiver, and the Grumman TBF Avenger torpedo bomber. The Vought F4U Corsair, a superior fighter aircraft, proved ill suited to carrier operations and was used extensively by Marine units.

The U.S. Navy did perhaps the best public relations job of any service. Central to this effort were the activities of Captain Edward Steichen and his team of award-winning photographers. The "air navy" figured prominently in their work, and one of their most striking images was titled *Murderer's Row* (a nod to the 1927 New York Yankees world championship baseball team, without a weak hitter in the lineup). The photo of six identically dazzle-painted *Essex*-class flattops was a powerful image of U.S. industrial and naval might.[56]

The IJN simply could not match this output. Only fifteen new carriers joined the fleet during the course of the war, and many of those were small escort carriers or stopgap conversions from merchant ships. The aircraft situation was a little better. In 1943, two new carrier types, the Nakajima B6N Jill torpedo-plane and the Yokosuka D4Y Judy dive-bomber, appeared. Both were first-rate aircraft (the latter was the fastest carrier dive-bomber of the war), yet lack of sufficiently trained crews reduced their effectiveness. A new air superiority fighter was slower in coming. Like the old warhorse the Messerschmitt Bf 109, the Mitsubishi A6M Zero soldiered on, despite the fact that the Allies had long since taken its measure. Not until mid-1944 was the successor naval fighter, the Kawanishi N1K2J George, available in any numbers.

The Central Pacific drive opened with the assaults on Makin and Tarawa in November 1943. The Tarawa operation did not go well, but the lessons—involving naval gunfire and air support, and ship-to-shore movement—were quickly learned. Dramatic improvements were evident in the subsequent Marshall Islands operations. Preparations for the invasion of Eniwetok demonstrated the striking power of the new carrier forces. Blocking the assault was the Japanese naval and air stronghold on Truk. Mitscher assembled fifteen carriers and launched a series of thirty separate raids on the base, completely neutralizing it.[57]

Spearheading Nimitz's Central Pacific drive was the Third/Fifth Fleet, a single force with alternating commanders and staff. The force was designated Fifth Fleet when Spruance was in command; when he and his staff were planning future operations, Halsey stepped in as Third Fleet commander. Even more importantly, this was "a completely air oriented naval force," with career naval aviators such as Mitscher serving either as task force commanders or chiefs of staff.[58]

By the summer of 1944, U.S. naval aviation was near the peak of its power. Its operational concepts, tactics, leadership, and technology were all at very high levels of development and effectiveness. Nimitz's force was capable of executing an air-sea concept of operations that dwarfed even the most optimistic prewar visions.

The superiority of this force was again demonstrated during the Marianas operations. Nimitz and his commanders believed that the Saipan landing, which began on June 15, 1944, would elicit a strong Japanese response. The IJN leadership obliged, ordering Operation A, a combined attack by Admiral Jisaburo Ozawa's newly established carrier force and air units based on the Marianas. Many of Ozawa's pilots were as new as his carriers; some had only two months' training. The resulting Battle of the Philippine Sea, June 19–20, 1944, was a rout. Known to American airmen as the "Marianas Turkey Shoot," the battle cost the Japanese 218 aircraft against U.S. losses of only 29. The massacre marked the virtual end of the IJN's air arm, even if the empty carrier force survived the day.

The main purpose of seizing the islands of Guam, Tinian, and Saipan was simple: to acquire B–29 bases and thereby bring the Japanese home islands under siege. The Air Staff's munitions requirements plan AWPD–42 predicted, "Considering the great distances involved, it is apparent that the majority of the bombing effort (against Japan) must be carried out by long range bombers (B–29 type). These will not be available in quantity until late in 1944."[59] The stage was set for one of the most destructive and controversial air campaigns in history.

THE WAR IN ASIA
Although the Central, Southwest, and South Pacific theaters were the focus of aerial

action during the Pacific war, air action of note occurred in other, more peripheral areas. Some of these were truly footnotes, such as the air-naval-land war in the Aleutians in 1942–1943. Of much greater importance was the air war on the Asian mainland, known in Allied parlance as the China-Burma-India theater. Although the linchpin of Japanese strategy in the 1930s, and still the location of its strongest single land army, China had receded in importance as the war developed in the Central and Southwest Pacific. Difficulties in coordinating with the Allies, and especially Chiang Kai-Shek's corrupt and increasingly ineffective regime, also caused the theater to decline in importance in the eyes of some American strategists.

Nevertheless, there were a number of air power-related developments in the CBI that are worth a brief examination. Command relationships were every bit as problematic as those between MacArthur and Nimitz, and even the vastness of the theater could not prevent friction among the senior American Army commander, General "Vinegar Joe" Stillwell; the theater commander, Admiral Lord Louis Mountbatten; and the airmen. First and foremost of these was Major General Claire Chennault of the Fourteenth Air Force, who had won fame with his American Volunteer Group in early 1942 and who wielded considerable clout on air matters in the theater.

Perhaps the most significant air operation in the theater was not even waged by a combatant force, but rather by the India-China Wing of the Air Transport Command. Japanese success in Burma had cut land access between India and China, which necessitated that transport planes keep the theater supplied via a dangerous 550-mile air route across the Himalayas. This route was soon known as the "Hump." It also acquired the less lighthearted nickname "the Aluminum Trail," as its path was marked by the crumpled wreckage of transport planes. It is no exaggeration to say that the airlift sustained the war in China, although it also occasioned bitter battles between Chennault and the ground commanders for control of the supply flow. Since 1942, Chennault had maintained that even a modest reinforcement of his air units would produce a major victory. In this he was incorrect, but his political influence with Chiang and Roosevelt meant that he had to be tolerated. Although the Fourteenth Air Force performed well, its actions were never decisive.

The lasting significance of the "Hump" may have been the lessons it taught about the fundamentals of successful air logistics operations. Although the lift increased its monthly tonnage from a dismal fifteen hundred tons in January 1943 to over nine thousand tons by the end of that year, the real dramatic increase came in August 1944 with the arrival of Brigadier General William H. Tunner. A career airlifter in a service dominated by bomber and fighter pilots, Tunner applied what he termed "businesslike methods" to the airlift, increasing monthly tonnage to a high of seventy-two-thousand tons, with a significant decline in the accident rate. Tunner would later apply the lessons learned in CBI when he ran the famed Berlin Airlift in 1948–1949, using many of the same methods.[60]

The air war in Burma was undeniably a backwater for both sides. Yet a number of air operations featured novel or tactically significant developments. Perhaps the most noteworthy of these were the operations of the First Air Commandos. The unit, often considered the forerunner of modern U.S. Air Force Special Operations, specialized in conducting and sustaining operations behind the Japanese lines. In March 1944, the unit executed Operation Thursday, an "aerial invasion of Burma." Its gliders not only transported nine thousand of General Orde Wingate's Chindits to four landing zones deep in Japanese territory, but also kept them supplied and supported for several months of operations. Also in Burma, Royal Air Force units helped win the battles of Imphal and Kohima, April–July 1944, through effective close air support and aerial resupply, helping to inflict what a British army commander called "the greatest defeat in the history of the Japanese army."[61]

THE ENDGAME

By the autumn of 1944, the Imperial Japanese air arms were dying on the vine, along with the rest of the Japanese war machine. One Japanese admiral recalled that, in attacks against Halsey's Third Fleet during mid-October, "our fighters were but so many eggs thrown at the stone wall of the invincible enemy formations."[62] On October 20, 1944, MacArthur's forces landed on Leyte, fulfilling the general's promise to return to the Philippines. The land campaign in the Philippines was among the most destructive of the entire war, with artillery and close air support on a scale rivaling that seen on European battlefields.

The invasion of the islands also triggered the last great sea battle in the Pacific war—indeed, in history—as the Japanese fleet sallied for a final decisive battle. The "battle" was actually a series of loosely coordinated actions, but the centerpiece was an attempt by Admiral Takeo Kurita's battleship force to annihilate the U.S. landing force off Samar. A decoy force of empty aircraft carriers under Ozawa was intended to draw off Halsey's powerful task force, leaving the landing force exposed. Halsey, believing that Ozawa's carriers were the real center of gravity, took off north in pursuit, in what has been derisively labeled "The Battle of Bull's Run." All that stood between Kurita's battle force and the landings was a handful of escort carriers and destroyers of Admiral Clifton Sprague's Task Unit 77.4.3 off Samar. In an improbable display of heroism, the carriers and destroyers engaged Kurita's much more powerful force until it inexplicably turned away. In many ways, this great clash at sea was an anachronism.[63] Yet it remains as a cautionary tale—it showed that the IJN, technically outclassed and without air power, was still capable of endangering a much stronger adversary that possessed all the advantages of intelligence, technology, and numbers.

Shortly after the Battle of Leyte Gulf, the Japanese naval leadership unleashed one of the most extraordinary weapons in the history of air warfare, the *tokko* (Special Attack) forces, commonly referred to as the "kamikaze" or "divine wind," a reference to the providential storm that scattered a Mongol invasion force threatening Japan in 1281. As early as the war with China in the late 1930s, individual Japanese pilots had sacrificed themselves by diving into enemy targets. With Japan's military position becoming more desperate, Admiral Takijiro Onishi recommended institutionalizing the practice by forming the Special Attack Corps.[64]

Motivation for joining varied widely. Some signed up out of youthful idealism or a simple sense of duty; others felt peer pressure, especially when entire units "volunteered" for the program. New recruits underwent a minimalist training program and often flew obsolescent aircraft. Specially designed suicide planes, including the "Ohka" flying bomb, were later employed. Most of these half-trained pilots failed to penetrate the screens of U.S. fighters and storms of antiaircraft fire protecting the task forces. Yet enough of them got through to sink or damage hundreds of U.S. ships, including the escort carrier USS *St. Lo*. Nimitz later admitted that the kamikaze campaign took him by surprise. There is also no doubting the psychological effect they had on U.S. sailors as they closed in on the Japanese home islands. James J. Fahey, a young sailor on the light cruiser USS *Montpelier*, recalled, "Before the attack started we did not know that they were suicide planes, with no intention of returning to their base. . . . These suicide or kamikaze pilots wanted to destroy us, our ships, and themselves. You do not discourage the Japs, they never give up, you have to kill them."[65]

THE INCENDIARY CAMPAIGN

The Boeing B–29 "Superfortress" was one of the biggest industrial projects of the entire war.[66] Everything about it—its pressurized cabin, remote-controlled gun turrets, powerful Wright Cyclone R–3350 engines, range and altitude performance— set it apart from other Second World War bombers. As were many new designs, it was plagued by teething troubles, especially engine fires. Reports from the training units showed evidence of desperation, including a suggestion that a method of jettisoning burning engines be devised.[67] The aircraft represented much more than a technological leap forward. For Arnold and the other USAAF leaders, this was the chance to achieve "victory through air power"—to bring the Japanese home islands under sustained strategic attack. The aircraft was deemed much too important to go to the theater commanders; Kenney's request for B–29s at SWPAC was brushed aside. A unique bomber demanded a unique organization to employ it; the Twentieth Air Force was created (with two Bomber Commands), and it reported directly to Arnold.[68]

Operations out of China by the XX Bomber Command, code-named Operation Matterhorn, began in June 1944. The logistical obstacles were formidable. The Hump airlift, impressive as it was, proved incapable of getting sufficient quantities of aviation gasoline to the bases, and airfield construction and the B–29's technical problems added to the difficulties. The impatient Arnold fired the XX's commander after barely a month, replacing him with Major General Curtis E. LeMay, a no-nonsense combat leader who had proved himself over Europe during the Eighth Air Force's daylight offensive. Even LeMay could not turn things around, and B–29 operations from China never fulfilled Arnold's hopes. Fortunately, the seizure of the Marianas offered an alternative.

Major General Haywood S. Hansell, one of the brains behind the ACTS precision daylight bombardment theory of the 1930s, commanded XXI Bomber Command operating out of the Marianas. He oversaw the development of the massive base complex on Saipan, Tinian, and Guam. Raids from the Marianas started in November 1944 but still did not meet expectations. Hansell attempted to conduct a high-altitude precision daylight campaign against the Japanese aircraft industry, but poorly trained crews, technical problems, and the unexpected jet stream over Japan reduced bombing accuracy and drove up the accident rate. After barely two months, Arnold, quite ready to fire even old and trusted subordinates if they did not deliver the goods, lost confidence in Hansell and brought in the hard-charging LeMay to replace him.

The change of command is often viewed as a clash between different bombing philosophies—daylight precision strikes on individual factories versus night incendiary area raids. Certainly Hansell's postwar memoirs supported this interpretation. Yet initially, LeMay adhered to the same targeting and tactical philosophy as Hansell, with only slightly better results. The difference between the two was as much a matter of leadership style as of doctrine. LeMay overhauled training and maintenance, increasing mission-ready rates.[69] When the daylight raids were not succeeding, LeMay was quick to try other tactics. His willingness to undertake low-level fire raids on Japanese cities revolutionized B–29 operations out of the Marianas.

As LeMay readied his revised offensive, U.S. forces moved to take the tiny island of Iwo Jima in February 1945. Among the many arguments for the operation were air power considerations: the island could serve as a base for P–51 escort fighters, and an emergency airstrip for B–29s returning from raids over Japan. Capturing the island would also eliminate an air base the Japanese were using to raid the B–29 base complex in the Marianas.[70]

Iwo was a desperate fight. The Japanese garrison employed ingenious new defensive tactics, setting up interlocking fields of fire from deeply dug-in and secure positions. Even 1945-era close air support, honed to a fine edge in the previous years of island fighting, proved of very limited effectiveness. The cost to the Marines taking the island, and to the Japanese defenders, was staggering. For years after the battle, many believed that emergency landings by crippled B–29s saved thousands of bomber crewmen, offering some compensation for the sacrifices of the nearly six thousand Marines killed in action. Some 2,251 B–29s landed on Iwo, and USAAF sources, both during and after the war, implied that "a large number" of the 24,761 men on board would have been lost. Yet the figures included all landings, for any reason, and many of the landings were not of an emergency nature.[71] In any case, it is hard to disagree with Nimitz's observation that on Iwo "uncommon valor was a common virtue."

LeMay's hard-driving leadership and revised tactics soon paid huge dividends. There was no need to gain air superiority over Japan. The Japanese home defenses lacked command and control, radar, and interceptors capable of effectively engaging the bombers, especially at night. Attempts to acquire German radar, jet aircraft, and engine technology came to naught, although some equipment and technical drawings came in by U-boat through the blockade. The first large-scale application of LeMay's new tactics was Operation Meetinghouse, the dreadful March 9–10, 1945, Tokyo fire raid. Three hundred and twenty-five B–29s, loaded with the new M–69 napalm incendiary, attacked the capital. Updrafts of hot air from the blazing capital buffeted the bombers, and the smell of burning flesh permeated the cockpits. Upward of 100,000 people perished in the attack, and sixteen square miles of the city were completely burned out.[72]

And the drumbeat of urban fire raids continued. The main industrial centers of Nagoya, Osaka, and Kobe were raided in rapid succession. A notorious graphic developed for USAAF chief Arnold compared the percentage of devastation to U.S. cities of comparable size. Kobe was Baltimore; Osaka, Chicago; and Tokyo, New York.[73] The firebombing campaign killed more than 300,000 civilians and in many ways was the apogee of total war. In his postwar memoir, LeMay offered the following rationale for the attacks:

We were going after military targets. No point in slaughtering civilians for the mere sake of slaughter. Of course, there is a pretty thin veneer in Japan, but the veneer was there. It was their system of dispersal of industry. All you had to do was visit one of those targets after we'd roasted it, and see the ruins of a multitude of tiny houses, with a drill press sticking up through the wreckage of every home. The entire population got into the act and worked to make those airplanes or munitions of war . . . men, women, children. We knew we were going to kill a lot of women and kids when we burned the town. Had to be done.[74]

The effectiveness and morality of the B–29 campaign remain subjects for debate. Impressive as the percentage of destruction of the Japanese industrial base undoubtedly was, much of that plant was virtually idled by both the U.S. submarine campaign and the intensive B–29 aerial mining campaign of Japanese coastal waters, Operation Starvation. The fire raids brought home to the Japanese leadership and population the precarious position in which Japan found herself. One noted scholar of the Pacific war commented on the impact on the emperor, who toured his shattered capital shortly after LeMay's bombers had done their work: "There is reason to believe that what the shaken, ashen-faced monarch saw at firsthand intensified his determination to bring the war to an end as soon as possible."[75] Yet as even participants at the time acknowledged, it was a grisly business.

In the meantime, the advance toward the home islands continued. U.S. forces landed on Okinawa on April 1, 1945. The conventional Japanese air force had all but disappeared, but the ships off Okinawa, and especially the tenacious destroyers on picket duty, "the fleet that came to stay," were subjected to the most intensive kamikaze attacks of the entire war—1,162 in the month of April alone.[76] The destroyer USS *Laffey* faced twenty-two separate attacks by suicide planes in the space of eighty minutes; six were direct hits.[77] In the fight for the island, U.S. aircraft flew combat air patrol and provided close air support, but the soldiers and Marines were in such close contact with Japanese forces that close air support was often impracticable; the positions had to be taken with "blowtorch and corkscrew."[78]

Okinawa suggested that the invasion of the home islands, code-named Olympic, would be an even more savage fight. Yet events would rapidly overtake the planning. On August 6, 1945, Colonel Paul Tibbets, commander of the 509th Composite Group, flying a bomber named *Enola Gay* after his mother, dropped a single bomb on the city of Hiroshima. The city was eradicated, and at least eighty thousand people lost their lives in the immediate attack. Japanese radio informed the stunned population,

"It is believed that a new type of bomb was used."[79] Physical and psychological effects plagued the survivors for decades.

A new type of bomb, indeed. The weapon carried by the *Enola Gay* was the product of the largest military-scientific-engineering project in U.S. history. Since 1942, U.S. and émigré scientists, under the direction of Major General Leslie Groves, had been working on the Manhattan Project, the development of fission weapons using isotopes of uranium and plutonium. Originally, the project was designed to checkmate a German attempt to build a similar device; with the German surrender, the project forged on to completion.

The Japanese war council voted to continue hostilities after Hiroshima, and three days later, a second B–29 named *Bockscar* dropped another bomb, "Fat Man," on Nagasaki. The council was deadlocked, but this time the emperor intervened to bring the war to an end. After an attempted coup by a group of officers, the Japanese asked for terms.

The use of such terrible weapons, with the heavy loss of civilian life, has naturally occasioned intense debate regarding the military necessity and morality of employing the bombs, or whether there were alternatives to their use. Some scholars have argued that the weapons were unleashed as a means of intimidating the Soviets, and as such were the opening shots of the Cold War rather than the final act of the Second World War. These are important questions, but the balance of evidence suggests that the bombs were used primarily to bring the war to a close as quickly as possible. The debate continues to this day.[80]

The last major air operation of the war was staged as a show of force to deter any last-ditch Japanese resistance and for its tremendous public relations value. Above the surrender ceremonies aboard the battleship USS *Missouri* in Tokyo Bay on September 2, 1945, hundreds of Navy carrier planes, as well as formations of over four hundred B–29s, slowly circled.[81]

SUMMING UP

Without a doubt, the role of air power in the defeat of Imperial Japan was central. Beyond this general premise, however, the exact mechanism by which air power, broadly defined, contributed to the Allied victory was complex. Former Japanese premier General Hideki Tojo told MacArthur that "the three principal factors that defeated Japan were the indirect approach of the latter's island-hopping campaign, the independent and persistent operations of the fast carrier task forces, and the submarine campaign against Japanese merchant shipping."[82] This last may have been the single most decisive campaign of the Pacific war. In the words of one historian, "In its far-reaching and continuous influence on the course of the war, and its role in undermining, then ruining, the Japanese war economy, the submarine campaign bore some resemblance to the lengthy strategic bombing campaign against Germany."[83] The influx of raw materials to Japanese factories, and the distribution of finished goods throughout the shrinking empire, had slowed to a trickle by the time the B–29 raids attacked Japanese industrial centers directly.

Air power played a major role in two of the three factors cited by Tojo. Air power—including Kenney's Fifth Air Force, AirSols, the USN carrier strike forces, and USMC aviation—made the island-hopping campaign in the South and Southwest Pacific possible. And the fast carrier task forces, "the air navy," enabled the United States to strike the Japanese across the length and breadth of their defense perimeter, negating the advantage of interior lines. With a battle fleet's punch and aviation's range, they were the most flexible and versatile weapons in the Allied arsenal.

Tojo might also have indulged in a bit of self-critique, for a catalogue of Japanese errors contributed materially to the outcome. These crossed the spectrum from the grand strategic to the tactical and were magnified by a military culture of self-deception. Japanese air planners forged an impressive naval air strike weapon, but it was a "brittle aerial rapier."[84] A training philosophy more suited to producing individual samurai, a logistical system that relied on baskets and hand tools to construct airfields, and a research and development program that failed to produce a second generation of combat aircraft in a timely fashion represent the other side of the coin. The force that destroyed the U.S. Pacific Fleet at Pearl Harbor and "ran wild" through the southern seas was ill equipped to deal with the U.S. submarine menace or to turn back the B–29 offensive.

The victorious air arms drew their own conclusions from the Pacific war. The USAAF's official historians, in introducing their seven-volume work, suggested that "the special character of the air force" was shaped by the quest for independence, a doctrine of strategic bombing, and a bomber to execute that doctrine.[85] The development of the B–29 and its use against the Japanese home islands, albeit in a modified form, must be seen as the culmination of this prewar vision. The Twentieth Air Force, beholden to the Air Staff and not to any theater commander, seemed to be the pattern for the future. The postwar U.S. Strategic Bombing Survey seemed to validate this belief:

> Based on a detailed investigation of all the facts, and supported by the testimony of surviving Japanese leaders, it is the Survey's opinion that certainly prior to 31 December 1945, and in all probability prior to 1 November 1945, Japan would have surrendered even if the atomic bombs had not been dropped, even

if Russia had not entered the war, and even if no invasion had been planned or contemplated.[86]

The emphasis on the final months of the war tended to push other USAAF accomplishments into the shadows. The legacies of Kenney's campaign in the Southwest Pacific, of air mobility in China-Burma-India, or of the unconventional success of the Air Commandos in Burma were muted. Tactical aviation faded from the U.S. Air Force's "skill set" in the postwar years, leaving the air arm dangerously ill equipped for postwar limited conflicts such as those that broke out on the Korean Peninsula in June 1950.

The U.S. Navy took away a different set of lessons. To the admirals, the carrier task force, alongside the submarine, had been the decisive weapon. The mobility and flexibility of the carriers destroyed the Japanese fleet and cleared the path to Japan. Its forces demonstrated an unmatched ability to achieve strategic, operational, and tactical effects. And the Marines also took heed of the war's lessons. The experience of Guadalcanal, where the Corps fought some of its most defining battles, led the postwar service to seek to maintain and control its own air support, independent of carrier air, which, in the memories of many senior marines, had left them "holding the hot potato" during Watchtower.

The war certainly left a powerful legacy of combined arms effectiveness, what today is called jointness. But it also left a bitter and lingering memory of interservice rivalry. Competing and apparently incompatible visions of how World War II in the Pacific was brought to a victorious conclusion, between fast carriers and huge bombers, set the stage for the 1949 "Revolt of the Admirals" and the B–36 controversy. At the dawn of the atomic age, there would be turbulent times ahead.

PART II: 1945–1990

INTRODUCTION

THE KOREAN WAR BEGAN in June 1950 along the country's dividing line, the thirty-eighth parallel. For the next year, the competing armies took turns forcing each other to the peninsula's geographic extremities, with the United Nations Command (UNC) almost pushed off the southern tip in August 1950 before a reversal of fortune saw the communists driven back to the northern border with China. By June 1951, the two armies were back where they had started, on either side of the thirty-eighth parallel, where they remained in a stalemate for two years until a cease-fire was negotiated. By contrast, the war in the air demonstrated its innate flexibility of maneuver as it continually swept along the length and breadth of Korea. In chapter 4, Alan Stephens suggests that in the brief interval since 1945, airmen had forgotten many of the lessons they had learned the hard way during World War II. Having to relearn them proved a costly and bitter experience. Like their armies, the UNC's air forces could not secure victory in Korea. Nevertheless, despite serious command and control problems and a number of operational shortcomings, air power came to represent the UNC's greatest comparative advantage. Stephens concludes that air power saved the UNC from disaster on several occasions, most notably at Pusan, where control of the air, close attack, and air maneuver were all that prevented the communists from driving the UNC into the sea. In a war in which those fighting on the ground seemed to run out of ideas, air operations made the difference between defeat and an acceptable political outcome.

In examining air operations over North Vietnam, Wayne Thompson tells "a tale of air power badly used." Despite years of American intervention, involving more than half a million soldiers and the heaviest aerial bombardment in history, communist North Vietnam eventually conquered South Vietnam. Chapter 5 focuses on the bombing of North Vietnam—the failure of the long Rolling Thunder campaign of

1965–1968 and the comparative (though limited) success of the two Linebacker campaigns in 1972. Thompson explains why Rolling Thunder has become a model for how *not* to wage an air campaign. Fearing a possible war with China, President Lyndon Johnson placed crippling constraints on U.S. operations, permitting fighter aircraft to bomb only a few targets at a time, starting with the least important. His successor, Richard Nixon, negotiated with the Chinese and the Russians while launching a more robust air campaign to counter North Vietnam's 1972 invasion of South Vietnam. In Linebacker, for the first time, North Vietnam's ports were mined and laser-guided bombs enabled efficient destruction of bridges. When negotiations with North Vietnam stalled in December 1972, Nixon at last used two hundred B–52 bombers to attack targets near Hanoi in Linebacker II. While Rolling Thunder and the initial Linebacker campaign had sought to interdict forces and supplies heading for South Vietnam, Nixon intended Linebacker II to intimidate the North Vietnamese leadership and reassure the South Vietnamese leadership. Even though the Linebacker campaigns achieved sufficient success to revive negotiations and enabled the United States to exit the war, American air power shared the blame for America's defeat in Vietnam.

Chapter 6 takes a closer look at the struggle for air superiority in four Israel-Arab wars: the Six Days War in 1967, the War of Attrition in 1969–1970, the Yom Kippur War in 1973, and the first Lebanon war in 1982. Shmuel Gordon offers a comparative study by examining these four campaigns in light of developments in strategy, operational planning, and technology, while acknowledging that in each conflict, both sides acted as proxies for the superpowers. The author begins with the formative years of the Israeli Air Force before turning to the conflict of 1967 and then examines what became a continuous, drawn-out confrontation in 1970 between Israel and Egypt, with both the United States and the Soviet Union as players. He analyzes and reveals new facts about the intensive battles at the outbreak of the 1973 war before describing the contest between the Israeli and Syrian air forces in 1982. Gordon compares the dynamic interplay between aircraft and surface-to-air missiles, the development of air-to-air battles, and the close relationship between politics and air power as the preferred instrument of force.

In chapter 7, Lawrence Freedman argues that air power played a key role in the Falklands campaign of 1982, although both sides experienced practical limits on deployment. Sea Harriers proved highly effective for the British, but only a limited number could be transported on the two available carriers, while the Falklands were at the limit of the range for Argentine aircraft. Thus, neither side could establish command of the air. To create the conditions for a successful amphibious landing, the British strategy depended on reducing the Argentine naval and air threat. After a torpedo from a nuclear submarine sank Argentina's old cruiser, the *General Belgrano*, the Argentine navy stayed back. The British demonstrated their advantage in air-to-air combat in early engagements, after which Argentina held its air force in reserve until the landing took place. Through special forces operations and the use of long-range Vulcan bombers, the British made it difficult for Argentine aircraft to operate effectively from the Falklands, but they could do little to prevent the waves of attacks unleashed against British ships once the landing was under way. Argentine pilots showed great bravery as they sustained heavy losses (albeit not as heavy as the British later claimed) and caused considerable damage to the Royal Navy, but in the end they could not prevent the movement of men and matériel ashore.

4

THE AIR WAR IN KOREA, 1950–1953

Alan Stephens

AT THE END OF WORLD WAR II, the Korean Peninsula was divided at the thirty-eighth parallel, with the Soviet Union exercising authority over the North and the United States over the South. Tensions between the two superpowers and their proxies, the nominally communist North Korea and the nominally democratic South Korea, ensured that nationwide elections leading to unification never eventuated. Emboldened by Mao Zedong's victory in China's civil war in October 1949, and encouraged by Joseph Stalin in Moscow, on Sunday, June 25, 1950, North Korean forces launched a series of attacks against the South, including aerial bombing strikes against the undefended capital of Seoul.

As the North Korean army poured across the demarcation line, the United Nations Security Council passed a resolution condemning the invasion and authorizing a military response. Eventually, twenty-two nations led by the United States combined to form the United Nations Command (UNC), which fought the communists for the next three years. Air power played an intriguing role in the struggle.

Within a year, the war on the ground had reached a geographic stalemate, with the two armies entrenched on either side of the thirty-eighth parallel—a standoff that lasted until a cease-fire was negotiated in July 1953. By contrast, the war in the air demonstrated innate flexibility of maneuver as it constantly swept along the Korean Peninsula and occasionally into China.

Air power in Korea was dominated by the United States in general and the U.S. Air Force (USAF) in particular, which explains the focus of this chapter. UNC air forces flew a total of 1,040,708 sorties during the war, of which the USAF accounted for 720,980—that is, almost 70 percent.[1] Those sorties covered the full range of air power capabilities, from strategic strike to control of the air, interdiction, close attack, reconnaissance, and airlift. The UNC's opponents from China's People's Liberation

Army Air Force (PLAAF) in turn flew 26,491 sorties over Korea, almost all of which were air-to-air combat.[2]

THE NUCLEAR SPECTER

The use of air power during the Korean War can be understood only in context, and superseding all other contextual considerations in the 1950s was the nuclear standoff between the United States and the Soviet Union. American B–29 Superfortresses had dropped two atomic bombs on Japan in August 1945 to end World War II, while the Soviet Union had tested its first atomic weapon in August 1949. The beginning of the nuclear era symbolized the beginning of the fifty-year Cold War between the East and the West.

With their threat of utter devastation, atomic bombs changed everything. As the American strategist Bernard Brodie famously wrote in 1946, "Thus far the chief purpose of our military establishment has been to win wars. From now on, its chief purpose must be to avert them. It can have almost no other useful purpose."[3] Plainly, nuclear weapons did not avert war in Korea, but they did exert a powerful implicit constraint on the scale and nature of the hostilities. A brutal conflict in North Asia was bad enough; no one wanted it to escalate into a nuclear-fueled third world war.

The advent of nuclear weapons had three significant consequences for air power. The first was the continuing rise of air forces as the dominant form of military power. Until intercontinental ballistic missiles began to enter operational service in 1959, manned aircraft were the only means of delivering nuclear weapons. Thus, air forces, and in particular their bomber fleets and senior pilots, assumed preeminence in military planning—a situation that in turn influenced strategies, priorities, and institutional attitudes. That preeminence was especially pronounced in the United States, where the USAF had been established as a separate service in 1947 with a leadership group determined to justify its independence and to demonstrate the service's capacity to dominate the battlefield.[4] Long-range bombers armed with atomic bombs gave them the capability they needed to pursue both objectives.

The second consequence was incorporated within the concept of "mutual assured destruction," more commonly known by the apt acronym MAD. As Brodie had pointed out, total war between the superpowers would now lead to an apocalypse. However, as long as the protagonists were rational—and despite the sometimes disturbing behavior that both the United States and the Soviet Union engaged in throughout the Cold War—the prospect of mutual destruction would deter them from initiating a nuclear exchange. Armed confrontation was still likely, however, and this led to the third consequence: the notion of deterrence within war. Although this sophisticated interpretation of deterrence was not formally articulated until after the Korean War, it was implicitly observed during the conflict. What it meant in practice was that the superpowers might still engage each other militarily, but they would do so indirectly through proxies and would observe self-imposed limits. Those limits might or might not be defined, but could mean the exclusion of certain weapons and targets, a ceiling on the level of force applied, and the observance of strict geographic boundaries. All of these unspoken proscriptions affected the employment of air power in Korea.

The concept of deterrence within war also affirmed the continuing relevance of conventional (nonnuclear) weapons and theater-level war, the future of which some analysts had questioned following the nuclear strikes on Japan.

A final comment on the politics of the Korean War is necessary. The United States went to war in Korea more for psychological than for geostrategic reasons. President Harry S. Truman's administration had decided that the United States's post–World War II priorities were to secure Western Europe from the Soviet Union and to establish Japan as the West's new bulwark against communism in the Far East. That is not to suggest that the Americans were indifferent to the possibility of losing South Korea, but simply that there were more important geostrategic challenges. Most officials in Washington saw communism as a monolithic entity controlled by Stalin and the Kremlin. Their concern, therefore, was less about what might happen in Korea than about the world. In other words, America's rationale for going to war in North Asia arose more from the perceived need to oppose communism at every turn than from any imperative to defend South Korea. This interpretation of world affairs also influenced the application of force in Korea.

COMMAND AND CONTROL CONFUSION

At the end of the Second World War, air power was acknowledged as the preeminent expression of military force; as the Royal Australian Navy concluded in its postwar report, "the master weapon of World War II has been the aeroplane." Each of the main air roles had made a major contribution to the Allies' victory. Control of the air had become the sine qua non for combat success on the surface, having underwritten the Soviet advance into eastern Germany, the Allied advance through Western Europe, and the U.S. "island-hopping" campaign in the Pacific. The defeat of the U-boats in the Battle of the Atlantic was attributable in equal parts to Allied air and naval forces. Across all theaters, aerial surveillance and reconnaissance had given the Allies a battle-winning intelligence edge. The Combined Bomber Offensive had eventually brought the Nazi war economy to its knees, and the atomic attacks against Japan had literally ended the war. Technological developments such as jet engines, swept wings, airborne radar, advanced weapons, and electronic navigation aids promised an even more potent future.

By 1950, advanced air forces were reequipping themselves with transonic jet fighters (which almost invariably had some residual ground attack capability to complement their primary task of control of the air), long-range bombers, and heavy airlifters. In the USAF, for example, piston-engine F–51 Mustangs were being replaced by jet F–80s and F–84s, and the supersonic swept-wing F–86 Sabre was about to enter service; the B–29 Superfortresses and the B–36 Peacemaker would soon be complemented by the near-revolutionary B–47 Stratojet bomber; and the twin-engine C–47 airlifter had been superseded by the four-engine C–54.

Doctrinally, however, progress had been problematic. American and British air force commanders tended to focus on the war they thought they would have to fight, or that they perhaps would have preferred to fight—namely, a massive confrontation with the Soviet Union on the plains of Western Europe. Insufficient thought had been given to the demands of mounting campaigns in places such as North Asia, with their associated range of vexing limitations. Priority in training and force structuring accordingly went to "strategic" fighter and bomber units, while skills in tasks that apparently seemed less "air force," such as close air attack, were allowed to degrade.[5]

The senior USAF entity in North Asia was the Far East Air Forces (FEAF), with responsibility for a vast area stretching from the Philippines across to Japan and Korea and into the Pacific. Overall, the command, led by General George E. Stratemeyer, was in poor condition. FEAF's primary task was air defense. Little attention was paid to other roles, including air-to-ground operations; most units were under strength; and many facilities were substandard. Perhaps even more damning, there was no formal process for planning and coordinating joint operations, nor was this most complex of staff skills practiced.[6] Institutional shortcomings flowed through to the Fifth Air Force, which was to become FEAF's (and therefore the UNC's) main combat air command during the war.

Complementing the USAF (which itself was supplemented by air force contributions from a number of allied countries)[7] were the U.S. First Marine Air Wing and U.S. Navy air groups, which were embarked on aircraft carriers and were under the separate command of U.S. Naval Forces Far East. Two carrier stations were established—one to the west of the Korean Peninsula in the Yellow Sea and one to the east in the Sea of Japan.[8]

The division of air power between air forces, navies, marines, and armies was a persistent problem for the UNC. Unity of command existed only at the very highest level, in the office of the commander in chief, UNC, the imperious General Douglas MacArthur.[9] As soon as decision making moved to a lower level, the process was riven by competing priorities and biases. Furthermore, MacArthur's headquarters was dominated by Army officers with little, if any, understanding of air operations. The situation was untenable to the extent that the official Air Force history later blamed the "fantastically confused command system in the Far East" for the UNC's inability to bring "the full force of air power" to bear against hostile target systems in Korea,[10] but it was allowed to continue.

Matters were made worse in the early stages of the war by the lack of readiness of the UNC's major land forces, those of South Korea and the United States. Only days after the fighting started, the South Korean army was in full retreat, and reinforcements were either in short supply or unready for combat. The U.S. Army was also struggling. America's military strength had been slashed after World War II, and the units that were rushed to the front in Korea had grown soft from their undemanding occupation duties in Japan. According to General Omar Bradley, the U.S. Army "could not fight its way out of a paper bag."[11] The penalty for this negligence was a UNC army incapable of standing firm against the charging North Koreans. Joint command problems notwithstanding, it therefore fell largely to air power to halt the communist advance.

General Stratemeyer defined three main tasks for his air forces: achieve and maintain air superiority, provide close attack for land forces, and isolate the battlefield.[12] As the essential precondition for all other actions, control of the air was the priority. This was quickly achieved against the largely ineffectual North Korean Air Force (NKAF), which was poorly trained and equipped with obsolescent Chinese and Soviet aircraft. Consistent with classical air power doctrine, most of the NKAF was destroyed on the ground.

Eliminating the NKAF was the necessary starting point for the UNC's air campaign, but in itself it was insufficient to ensure air supremacy. Ground-based air defense systems remained a constant danger and ultimately accounted for 816 of the 1,041 UNC aircraft lost to enemy action.[13] Throughout the war, the fire from small arms, heavy machine guns, and antiaircraft batteries was often intense. As the loss rates show, close attack was a more dangerous mission for UNC pilots than air-to-air combat.

Still, the destruction of the NKAF eliminated any immediate possibility that the UNC's armies might be attacked from the skies. In addition, as long as UNC strike aircraft remained above the maximum altitude of ground fire, they could maneuver freely throughout Korea, which in turn meant that, unlike their beleaguered Army colleagues, they could go on the offensive.

VICTORY AT PUSAN

By August 1950, the UNC's armies had been forced back almost to the southern tip of the peninsula. Their commander, U.S. Army Lieutenant General Walton H. Walker, established his final defensive line behind the Naktong River, 150 kilometers from the town of Pusan. One more successful thrust by the communists would have driven the UNC out of Korea. In the event, Walker's "Pusan Perimeter" held and became famous as the line where the communists were first stopped and then driven back. As U.S. Army General Matthew Ridgway later reflected, the battle for the Pusan Perimeter was one of those occasions where air power saved the ground forces from disaster.[14]

It took the UNC some weeks to sort out its close air attack system. Shortcomings in command and control and operational readiness were exposed by a number of distressing "friendly fire" incidents in which pilots who sometimes were poorly trained and briefed unintentionally attacked their own soldiers, who themselves might have been in the wrong place or displaying incorrect identification markings. Repeating centuries of history, commanders once again had to learn on the job—that is, under fire—which they soon did, identifying problems and developing solutions. In addition to the difficulties associated with joint planning and processes, the performance of close attack aircraft required urgent attention.

The mainstay of the USAF's close attack force in theater was the Lockheed F–80 Shooting Star jet. However, circumstances had conspired against the F–80, which had been designed primarily as an interceptor. Many airfields in Korea were unsuitable for jet aircraft, which generally require longer and stronger sealed runways, while others that were suitable had been captured by the communists on their push south. Forced to fly from Japan, the F–80 lacked endurance and operational flexibility. Under the prevailing conditions, the ideal aircraft seemed to be the machine the F–80 had replaced in USAF frontline squadrons, the piston-engine F–51 Mustang. A robust, versatile fighter capable of operating from rough airstrips, armed with six .50-caliber machine guns and either two 227-kilogram bombs or napalm canisters or six 27-kilogram rockets, and having exceptional range and endurance, the Mustang had been one of the great combat aircraft of World War II.

When the communists crossed the thirty-eighth parallel, the only Mustangs ready for combat belonged to the Royal Australian Air Force's No. 77 Squadron, on duty with the occupation forces in Japan. It took the USAF until mid-July to deploy two squadrons of the vintage fighter to the theater and an additional month to reequip six F–80 squadrons with F–51s. In the meantime, during what was for the air forces essentially a ground attack campaign, No. 77 Squadron exerted an influence on the war out of all proportion to its modest size. The keys here were having both the right weapons system for the circumstances and pilots who specialized in air-to-ground operations.

During the weeks that the battle for the Pusan Perimeter was in the balance, UN close attack squadrons maintained a punishing routine. Squadrons based in Japan routinely scheduled predawn takeoffs for the front line, where pilots flew up to six missions a day. Refueling and rearming between sorties were carried out at forward airstrips constructed from pierced steel planking, just inside the perimeter. At the end of the day, usually after dark, the squadrons returned to Japan, where it was not uncommon for ground staff to work all night repairing battle-damaged aircraft for the next day's fighting. The pilots' growing skill in air-to-ground weapons application was crucial as they attacked enemy troop concentrations, motor vehicles, artillery, and armor with bombs, rockets, guns, and napalm, on occasions rolling onto a target almost as soon as they had taken off.

Flying conditions were exacting, as stifling summer heat could be accompanied by heavy rain and low clouds—hazards that were increased by mountainous terrain and inadequate radio navigation equipment. Pilots became adept at flying the length and breadth of the country solely by map reading and with limited radio communication. Targets had to be positively identified before an attack could be made, a difficult task made more so by ground fire and the smog and haze (or, in winter, whiteouts) that often reduced visibility to a few hundred meters. After five or more hours strapped into their aircraft under almost constant danger, pilots were exhausted when they landed in Japan.

The decisive air-land battle at Pusan was sustained by an airlift campaign that rushed reinforcements to the front line. Several aspects of this campaign are noteworthy. Most obvious, but often overlooked, was the need to establish control of the air. The airlift into the Pusan zone was typical of countless similar campaigns conducted over the decades, in which control of the air has underwritten battle-saving logistics missions. Second, by moving soldiers, weapons, and supplies to the battle, the airlift was acting as a *maneuver force* for the UNC's army. Such missions should be regarded as an integral component of a land force's overall maneuver capability; at no stage of the Korean War was the enemy able to call on air for that purpose.

The final aspect relates to equipment and planning and bears some similarity to the early close attack experience. Just as the USAF's jet fighters initially were unsuited to the prevailing conditions, so too were the four-engine C–54 transports to which planners originally assigned the mission of providing the airlift into Pusan. The mainstay of the Berlin Airlift only a year before, the C–54 could carry double the load of the C–47 it had superseded. But at thirty-three thousand kilograms, it was also double the weight. Within days of starting operations into Pusan, the C–54s were breaking up the only available runways. Repeating the Mustang experience, C–47s had to be rushed to Korea to take over the airlift. Additional delays were then incurred because planning based on larger loads and fewer sorties had become obsolete.

Before leaving Pusan, one last observation on close attack is warranted. The argument is sometimes made that because the Mustangs were so successful there, piston-engine aircraft should have been retained in the role throughout the war.[15] The Mustangs' success was, however, specific to the circumstances and cannot be translated into general terms. Even though some UN units (for example, the South African air force) continued to operate F–51s until 1953, the shift to jets was well advised once better airfields started to become available. Korea was a hostile environment for ground attack aircraft, with the dangers posed by widespread antiaircraft weapons intensified by demanding terrain and weather. Jets could climb more steeply than their piston-engine predecessors, which enabled them to cope better with terrain and weather. They were quieter and faster, which increased the chance of approaching a target undetected. And finally, the Mustang's liquid-cooled engine was extremely vulnerable to ground fire, with only one shot being needed to sever a coolant line and cause the engine to seize. In the month of April 1951 alone, the Americans lost thirty Mustangs to ground fire, a much higher loss ratio than that experienced by jet close attack aircraft. The UNC probably would have lost many more aircraft to ground fire had jets not been introduced. Better technology usually provides better outcomes.

POLITICAL AND MANEUVER WARFARE

Concurrent with his control of the air, close attack, and airlift operations at Pusan, General Stratemeyer initiated an interdiction campaign intended to isolate the battle-field. Whereas the purpose of close attack is to win the battle in progress, interdiction is intended to "win" the battle of the future. Interdiction missions therefore tend to focus on cutting the enemy's supply lines and impeding his ability to maneuver.

It follows from the objective of interdiction that the mission's effectiveness will be directly related to the status of the air-land battle in general and the enemy army in particular. If, for example, no fighting is taking place, the enemy will have much less need for reinforcement and resupply (ammunition, medical supplies, and so forth) than when a battle is in progress. Or if the enemy is fighting a guerrilla war and has relatively unsophisticated requirements, air interdiction is less likely to disrupt his ability to move and to fight. Conversely, a well-equipped, mechanized army engaged in battle generates a huge demand for resupply and consequently is vulnerable to air interdiction. As is invariably the case with any form of airstrike, the key to success is target selection.

Stratemeyer's interdiction planning had to address several contradictory factors. His objective was to cut the North Korean army's lines of communications, a task that proved much more difficult than first appreciated. While in no way a guerrilla force, the North Koreans were adept at making do with little, which reduced their logistics demands. Compared to an American division, which typically consumed up to five hundred tons of stores per day, the North Koreans (and Chinese) needed only sixty to seventy tons. Favored high-value targets of interdiction campaigns such as rear-area depots, bridges, and road and rail systems thus became dubious propositions. Stratemeyer's attention accordingly turned to the communists' means of transport, such as trucks and coolie labor, but these kinds of targets were both low value and difficult to find and hit. Finally, in the back of everyone's mind was the fear that China might enter the war, a possibility that became more likely once the UNC started to gain the upper hand at Pusan. Interdicting transportation focal points might have represented a poor return as far as operations against the North Korean army were concerned, but it was the obvious way of blocking any movement of Chinese troops down the peninsula. In short, UNC air campaign planners were confronted by conflicting considerations.

Stratemeyer's challenge was compounded by the difficulty of matching weapons systems to targets. Close attack aircraft almost invariably are developed from air superiority fighters, which have the necessary speed and maneuverability. As a result, however, they also have a limited capacity to carry weapons. As noted, fighters from the Korean era typically carried no more than two medium-weight (227 kilogram) bombs, or two napalm canisters, or about six rockets, complemented by either machine guns or cannons. While effective against an army on the move—troops, trucks, tanks, and artillery—none of those weapons is ideal for substantial road/rail bridges and similar infrastructure targets. Interdiction campaigns therefore are more often the province of medium and heavy bombers, which can carry heavier bombs and larger weapon loads. The tradeoff, of course, is that they are less maneuverable, a shortcoming that created problems in Korea.

Two of Stratemeyer's primary interdiction aircraft were the B–26 medium bomber and the B–29 heavy bomber, the former capable of carrying up to twenty-seven hundred kilograms of bombs, the latter nine thousand kilograms. Korea's sharply rising mountain ranges and often narrow valleys exposed the bombers' performance limitations and forced crews to operate from medium rather than low altitudes, as too did the need to stay above often intense antiaircraft fire. Bombing accuracy suffered accordingly. Another constraint arose from the crews' inexperience in night operations, a legacy of FEAF's peacetime training routines of the recent past. Nor was Stratemeyer's cause helped by MacArthur's headquarters, where Army officers with little knowledge of air warfare too often were guilty of poor target selection.[16] The upshot was that in its early phase, the UNC air interdiction campaign was of questionable value as it struggled for purpose and professionalism.

The reverse was true of air power at Pusan, where air superiority, close air attack, and maneuver (in the form of airlift) joined with reinforced UNC armies not merely to repulse the communists but to force them to retreat.

The successful defense of the Pusan Perimeter was accompanied by an adventurous amphibious landing conceived by General MacArthur and carried out at Inchon, some 240 kilometers to the communists' rear on the west coast, on September 15, 1950. Outflanked and with their supply lines vulnerable, the North Koreans now retreated up the peninsula as quickly as they had advanced down it. On October 7, forward elements of the UNC crossed the thirty-eighth parallel on their way north.

The charge north coincided with the start of Korea's brutal winter, with the debilitating heat, dust, and haze of summer being replaced by subzero temperatures, snow, and biting winds. Ground crews labored under the most demanding conditions. Aircraft frequently were parked in the open in two feet of snow. Ice had to be scraped off wings and windscreens before servicing could be started, and the extreme cold made it painful to touch metal surfaces. Despite the severe environment, aircraft were always available.

By late October 1950, MacArthur's spectacular tactics had taken his forces almost to the border between Korea and China, the Yalu River, and it seemed the war would soon be won. MacArthur's expectations of a quick victory were not, however, shared by all of his commanders, some of whom justifiably feared Chinese intervention. Chinese involvement had in fact been under way since halfway through October, when eighteen of Mao Zedong's divisions had crossed undetected into Korea. On November 1, UNC pilots attacked Chinese troops for the first time; on the same day, the appearance of PLAAF MiG–15 jet fighters over the Yalu provided another indication that the war had entered a new and more dangerous phase.

If the fighting had become more dangerous, so too had the politics, which, for the egotistic MacArthur, would soon be fatal. Making too many decisions from his remote headquarters in Japan, MacArthur was isolated from the realities of the battlefront. As UNC forces poured over the thirty-eighth parallel on their charge north, neither the Truman administration back in Washington nor MacArthur himself had clearly articulated a desired political end state. Throwing the communists out of South Korea was one thing; occupying North Korea and racing toward China with no indication of where the advance might end was something else altogether. President Truman and his advisers were keenly aware of the potential for the war to expand, but MacArthur was in no mood to rein in an action that, to him at least, seemed to be on the brink of dealing world communism a massive blow.

Despite the dispatch of increasingly concerned messages from Truman and the Joint Chiefs of Staff in Washington, MacArthur pressed on, using denial by omission or lofty disregard for his political and military superiors to pursue his own course. Somewhat nervously, Truman and the Joint Chiefs of Staff approved bombing attacks across the Yalu against Chinese supply depots and transportation systems.

An observation on MacArthur as an air commander is pertinent here. Few if any Army generals used air power better during World War II. Advised by one of the war's outstanding airmen, General George C. Kenney, MacArthur employed his airstrike forces to great effect; indeed, his so-called island-hopping campaign in the Pacific might more accurately be described as an "airfield-hopping" campaign, in which his ground forces progressively captured airfields from which devastating air attacks could be launched against increasingly isolated enemy outposts. As forward bases and airfields were either taken or bypassed, the perimeter of Japanese expansionism was rolled back, making defeat ever more likely. Circumstances in Korea were, however, entirely different. In the Pacific, MacArthur's bombing campaign had been directed against large ground installations and naval fleets, both ideal, high-value targets for air power. MacArthur consequently had acquired an exaggerated notion of what "strategic" air power could do, for which he was to pay a price when he tried the same approach in Korea against a different enemy with different vulnerabilities.[17]

MacArthur also had little appreciation of the quality of the Chinese army, which Mao Zedong and his lieutenants had built into a formidable force in the course of a savage twenty-five-year civil war. Among other things, the experience of having to cope with the near-continuous air superiority of their opponents, Chiang Kai-shek's Nationalists, had made the People's Liberation Army (PLA) adept at concealment from offensive air power. If aircraft were heard approaching, PLA units immediately would cease moving and seek cover. In addition, they were skilled at camouflage and maneuvering by night.

Matters quickly turned worse for the UNC early in November. Belatedly realizing the danger of the Chinese intervention, MacArthur ordered Stratemeyer to bomb seventeen key bridges across the Yalu in an attempt to stop more PLA troops from advancing into North Korea.[18] The decision was made against Stratemeyer's advice and revealed MacArthur's ignorance of the situation. Difficult terrain and heavy enemy antiaircraft fire compelled UNC strike aircraft to fly above fifty-five hundred meters' altitude, which considerably reduced their bombing accuracy. Although most bridges were hit and half were briefly made unusable, the damage was insufficient to stop the enemy's advance. Furthermore, the strikes provoked China, the last thing Truman wanted. More to the point, the campaign was futile because, as Stratemeyer had already told MacArthur, the Yalu was about to freeze over to such a depth that trucks and railway trains would be able to traverse its surface. MacArthur nevertheless clung to the hope that the strikes had isolated the battlefield, when they had done no such thing. A couple of weeks later, tens of thousands of Chinese soldiers surged across the Yalu in surface transport.

The revelation that UNC forces were now facing as many as half a million Chinese troops compelled a sober reevaluation of MacArthur's previously unrestrained optimism. Back in Washington, the Joint Chiefs of Staff feared that any extension of the war could cause so many casualties that the United States would be seriously weakened should a separate conflict break out with the real enemy, the Soviet Union; indeed, there were concerns that MacArthur's offensive might even precipitate Soviet military action in Europe.

That disturbing possibility was accompanied by reverses on the ground as Chinese troops gained the upper hand and started retaking territory. The battle at the Chongchon River in late November proved to be a turning point of the war, with MacArthur's headstrong tactics drawing his main U.S. formation, the Eighth Army, and its South Korean and other UN allies into one of the biggest ambushes in history. Outwitted and outflanked by the PLA, the Eighth Army's defeat at Chongchon came as a stunning blow and precipitated the longest retreat ever made by an American army. Events were just as bad to the east near the Chosin Reservoir, where a thirty-thousand-man force from the Marines and Army was surrounded by six Chinese divisions and sustained more than fifteen thousand casualties before breaking out of the encirclement. Close air attack was vital in covering the retreat from Chongchon and the escape from Chosin, as were "combat cargo" airdrop and airlift missions. Naval strike fighters played an important role in both actions because the UNC aircraft carriers were mobile airfields that could position themselves relatively close to the battlefields, thereby reducing response times.

So desperate had the situation become that MacArthur now canvassed the use of nuclear weapons, a prospect that alarmed his UNC allies. Truman and the Joint Chiefs of Staff considered the option but quickly concluded that the implicit limits that had been observed from the start should not be breached. They decided that they should do as little as possible to aggravate the situation and that the best outcome they could now expect was a negotiated settlement. When MacArthur publicly criticized Truman's management of the war, the president replaced him with General Matthew Ridgway. Ridgway's immediate challenges were to arrest the calamity on the ground and to fight the war within the tacit parameters set by the politicians—from both sides.

For the first half of 1951, fighting on the ground was typified by major offensives and alternating fortunes, as first one side and then the other gained or lost ground between the Yalu and the thirty-eighth parallel. By the middle of the year, the surface war had reached a territorial stalemate, with the thirty-eighth parallel once again becoming the dividing line between north and south. That was to remain the case for the next two years.

Responding to the static nature of the land war, from early 1951 onward the air interdiction campaign assumed a primarily defensive nature as UNC commanders tried to stem the movement of Chinese troops and supplies from Manchuria and North Korea south down the peninsula. The underlying logic of the campaign is instructive.

The revised interdiction campaign was eventually characterized by four distinct approaches to targeting, two of which were incorporated in Operation Strangle, one in Operation Saturate, and the last in Operation Spring Thaw. Strangle started in May 1951 with the objective of cutting the communists' most important road routes, while its second phase began in August and was directed against the enemy's railway system. Saturate began in March 1952 and concentrated on what were perceived to be vital short segments of railway track. The final approach, Spring Thaw, was applied in March 1953 and attempted to close transportation chokepoints before following up with intensive airstrikes against (supposedly) trapped enemy troops.

All four approaches fell short of expectations, for many of the same reasons that had blunted previous interdiction operations. The communists were adept at repairing damaged roads, bridges, and rail tracks; heavy antiaircraft fire made interdiction dangerous and bombing inaccurate; and unless the opposing armies were actually engaged in combat, the enemy reliance on resupply was relatively small.

Thus, while air interdiction imposed strict limits on the enemy army's ability to maneuver by day, the campaign struggled to have a significant effect on the war's outcome.

STRATEGIC AIR SUPERIORITY

The story with the crucial and intriguing campaign to control the air was very different. Although largely inept and obsolescent, in the first days of the war the

NKAF was able to take advantage of the element of surprise to attack several South Korean cities and air bases. However, once the UNC's air forces were mobilized, the NKAF was quickly destroyed. From that point, the communists rarely used offensive air power against surface targets. Lacking a strategic dimension—Mao Zedong neither understood nor valued air power—the PLAAF was incapable of mounting sustained strike, reconnaissance, and maneuver campaigns.[19] Like its Soviet mentor, the PLAAF was largely defensive in outlook. Thus, the one campaign it pursued with full vigor was air superiority, as a means to the end of protecting surface forces, infrastructure, and lines of communication.[20] By contrast, UNC fighter squadrons fought to provide their air, land, and sea forces with strategic freedom of action.

Despite those sharply differing defensive-offensive postures, within itself, the war in the air assumed a fascinating, wholly offensive nature. Korea was the first war in which pilots flying jets fought against each other. Aircraft such as the Me–262 and the Meteor had appeared in the final stages of World War II but had never clashed. The appearance over northwestern Korea of Chinese air force swept-wing, jet-powered MiG–15 fighters in November 1950 immediately changed that.

"Defense" may have been the objective of the communists' control of the air campaign, but their tactics often were exceedingly aggressive. Massed formations, or "trains," of MiG–15s on fighter sweeps would boldly seek out their UNC counterparts, looking to seize the initiative and achieve control of the air through attrition. The ensuing dogfights were reminiscent in their magnitude and violence of air combat over the Western front during the Great War. By early 1951, the area between the Yalu and Chongchon rivers had become a dangerous place for UNC aircraft, acquiring the sobriquet "MiG Alley."

As far as the UNC's surface forces were concerned, their air force's ability to win air superiority in MiG Alley on a daily basis was nothing more than a necessary precondition for the delivery of airstrike, reconnaissance, and maneuver missions. However, such were the intensity, magnitude, and sheer duration of the air war that, contrary to the contention that control of the air can only ever be a means to an end, at the psychological level at least, the campaign assumed something of a strategic meaning of its own.

Like every other air campaign, the keys to success over the Yalu were first-rate people, advanced technology (especially platforms, systems, and weapons), high-quality engineering support, and innovative research and development.

The MiG–15 was an excellent aircraft, its swept wings facilitating supersonic speed in a dive, and its light weight and robust engine enabling a rate of climb and service ceiling superior to the UNC's straight-wing F–80s, F–84s, F–94s, and Meteors.

Incidentally, the MiG–15's Soviet-built RD–45 turbojet engine was derived from the Rolls-Royce Nene, which the British government had sold to the Soviet Union at the beginning of the Cold War in 1946 in an act later described by one American historian as "utterly stupid—if not covertly treasonous."[21]

It quickly became apparent that the MiG–15 was superior to the USAF's straight-wing fighters, so the Americans rushed three squadrons of their newest fighter, the swept-wing F–86 Sabre, to the theater. The first F–86 sorties were flown on December 17, 1950, and the battle between the Sabre and the MiG–15 for the next two and a half years was one of the great rivalries in the history of air warfare.

Pilots from both sides benefited from certain advantages. The most useful was enjoyed by the communists and was a result of the UNC army's defeat at the Chinese border in November. The Truman administration's pragmatic decision that a negotiated settlement was now the best outcome the UNC could achieve had important implications for air operations. UNC commanders were forbidden to take the air war across the Yalu, a constraint that turned Manchuria, on the border with North Korea, into a sanctuary for the Chinese air force. Any time a PLAAF pilot felt he was losing control of an engagement, he could break contact and head for the safety of Manchuria, rarely more than fifteen minutes away. Compounding this tactical problem for UNC pilots was the comparatively distant location of their own airfields, often as far south as Seoul, with longer transit times meaning less fuel for combat.

As the communist pilots started to exploit their tactical edge and the number of MiG–15s grew, Stratemeyer's air forces could no longer guarantee air superiority over the North. At this stage, however, several advantages enjoyed by the UNC pilots started to come into play. Three were especially important, two technological and one human.

First, the F–86 had a radar-ranging gunsight, which automatically calculated the distance to a target and the lead angle, or deflection, the pilot needed to allow before firing his guns. This meant that the average pilot was more likely to be able to track and hit a moving target. By contrast, the MiG–15's gunsight required manual inputs, a serious distraction from the business of actually flying the fighter.[22] Second, while early models of the F–86 were fitted with manually operated flight controls, subsequent versions were hydraulically powered. Lighter to manipulate and quicker to respond, hydraulic controls gave F–86 pilots a vital split-second advantage in the deadly contest to maneuver into a position from which they could track, aim, fire, and kill.[23]

The UNC's final advantage was human. The experience of two world wars had graphically demonstrated that in air combat, there is no substitute for high-quality recruitment and training. By the end of World War II, for example, the German and Japanese air forces had unraveled because of their inability to sustain first-class training systems, not least because flight instructors had been diverted from training units to the front line. In Korea, the UNC fighter pilots generally were better trained than their opponents, many having graduated from advanced tactics and weapons schools. By contrast, the PLAAF's reliance on the stolid and sometimes capricious Soviet training system institutionalized operational deficiencies. The Soviets themselves (who flew covertly in the war from November 1950 onward) fared better, often because of previous combat experience.[24] Nevertheless, they too were generally inferior to their Western adversaries, and while there may be some doubt regarding the 10:1 kill ratio long asserted in USAF sources, there is no doubt that superior training produced a superior outcome.[25]

Jet technology notwithstanding, air combat tactics were little different from those of the world wars. Aircraft might have flown faster and higher and used more sky, but pilots still sought the advantages of position, height, and speed; and when in contact with the enemy, they still maneuvered fiercely to get behind their opponents and close enough to shoot them down with guns (air-to-air missiles did not enter service until the mid-1950s).

Apart from fighter sweeps, the most common mission for UNC pilots was bomber escort. Despite the UNC's qualitative edge, clashes were often desperate and violent, especially once the communist pilots started to become more aggressive and actively sought air superiority. In October 1951 alone, for example, UNC pilots reported more than twenty-five hundred sightings of MiG–15s, almost all of which were seeking combat.

Massed dogfights were the symbol of the fight to control the air, but a number of complementary activities were no less important to the battle's outcome. Both sides constructed effective integrated air defense systems, incorporating early warning and intercept radars, command and control networks, and ground-based weapons systems. Because of their defensive posture, the communists developed a particularly potent antiaircraft artillery capability that compelled the UNC's medium and heavy strike aircraft to operate from medium or high altitude, thus reducing their bombing accuracy.

Command and control philosophies represented another notable difference between the two air defense systems. Reflecting their doctrinaire ideological heritage, the communists determinedly centralized authority, preferring where possible to use ground-based controllers to direct fighter operations, an approach that tended to undermine their pilots' initiative. The UNC's American-derived system, by contrast, while also based on ground radars and fighter controllers, was far more flexible in its practices and encouraged independence, a philosophy that maximized its pilots' superior skills, not least in decision making.

While fighting on the surface had reached a territorial, even strategic, stalemate by mid-1951, the war in the air continued at a furious pace across a vast front. No more graphic illustration of this extraordinary dichotomy can be found than in the monthly statistics of aircraft loss rates. In the fight to control the air, UNC pilots achieved their highest kill rate for the war in June 1953, the last full month of fighting before a cease-fire took effect on July 17.[26] The record number of seventy-seven MiG–15s claimed as shot down typified the unyielding nature of the battle in MiG Alley, where air-to-air combat had assumed something of a strategic meaning in its own right.

"STRATEGIC" AIR PRESSURE

Notwithstanding the drama of the combat above the Yalu, the air war in itself was unlikely to realize the rapid strategic effect that has been one of the constants of air power theory. Attention therefore began to turn toward strategic bombing, for which politics almost inevitably set the scene.

Armistice talks had started in July 1951, but the intransigence of North Korea's Chinese and Soviet patrons had hampered progress. In mid-1952, General Otto P. Weyland (who had replaced General Stratemeyer as commander of FEAF in June 1951) launched an "air pressure" campaign against a series of presumed strategic targets in North Korea, with the aim of coercing the communists into negotiating seriously.

The targets were typical of "strategic" bombing campaigns and included the electric power grid, military command posts, and major infrastructure. Weyland's bombers quickly disabled some 90 percent of North Korea's power generation capacity, but fierce international protests against the bombing of alleged nonmilitary targets undermined the campaign's legitimacy.[27] Perhaps more to the point, the campaign did not put any pressure on either China or the Soviet Union, whose potential targets were protected by the war's implicit limitations. Furthermore, as the bombing of North Vietnam some fifteen years later was to confirm, it remains a moot point whether strikes against first-world targets such as electricity and infrastructure can generate a strategic effect in third-world countries.

Weyland gave the strategic bombing dice one last roll in April and May 1953 when he authorized a series of strikes against the system of dams that supplied irrigation water for North Korea's rice crops. In strictly professional terms, this was an impressive example of center-of-gravity analysis and effects-based targeting because, unlike electricity and infrastructure, rice was essential to North Korea's well-being; indeed, in a peasant-based economy, it was probably *the* essential item for daily life. The envisaged follow-on effect of destroying the rice crop seemed to have the potential to bring North Korea to its knees. But once again, the strikes created a storm of international outrage. Whether the campaign succeeded is uncertain: the USAF claimed it helped pressure the communists into accepting cease-fire terms in July; others believed it was immaterial to that decision. One of the skeptics was UNC commander General Matthew Ridgway, who regarded strategic bombing as a "sort of high-tech aspirin; it gave some immediate relief, but it did not cure the underlying problem."[28] (The same conclusion might have been drawn, of course, about the UNC army's inability to achieve its objectives on the ground.)

Given the UNC's supremacy in the air, it seems possible that a sustained bombing campaign against the irrigation system might have succeeded. However, like any form of military power, strategic bombing can be applied only in accordance with the prevailing political ethos, and in 1953 that ethos would not countenance an attempt to starve North Korea into submission.

KNOWLEDGE WARFARE

The strategic bombing campaign was, like every other UNC activity, largely dependent on good reconnaissance.[29] Because its air forces controlled the skies, the UNC enjoyed an immense reconnaissance—that is, an information—advantage in Korea. Plainly, that advantage did not translate into a war-winning edge; equally plainly, without the intelligence gathered by its air reconnaissance units, the UNC would have found the overall campaign even more difficult to plan and to prosecute than was already the case.

Reconnaissance in Korea began from precisely the same condition of neglect as did the other air roles; namely, much of the expertise that had been acquired at great cost during the Second World War had been lost and had to be regained the hard way. Two aspects of reconnaissance operations require comment. Technology in the form of platforms and sensors is the first; the management of information the second.

Air reconnaissance routinely involves the overflight of hostile territory by unarmed aircraft, which in turn indicates a requirement for platforms with a high degree of survivability. By the end of World War II, the Allies had adapted outstanding strike and fighter aircraft such as the Mosquito and the Spitfire for the role. Fast, high-altitude flight offered the best chance of staying beyond the reach of enemy air defenses, so every effort was made to extract the last ounce of performance. Aircraft skins were polished and rivets flush-mounted to reduce drag, engines were turbocharged to boost power, and surplus fittings were removed to reduce weight. So effective were those kinds of modifications that, ironically, piloting reconnaissance aircraft directly above Germany's most valuable targets became a relatively safe task.

Once the aircraft had been prepared, they had to be fitted with suitable sensors, which in the 1950s meant wet-film cameras. Camera focal length, shutter speed, magazine capacity, operating altitude, and the like all had to be matched to the platform and to the kinds of pictures required.

The second key aspect of reconnaissance is managing the product: that is, coordinating the collection of imagery with analysis and dissemination. Because photographic interpretation is a specialized, labor-intensive activity, and because aircraft can collect very large numbers of images in a very short time, analysis centers can easily be overwhelmed. Setting priorities and matching collection rates to interpretation resources are features of every successful reconnaissance program.

There is a tendency in air forces to allocate superseded strike and fighter aircraft to the reconnaissance role, and Korea was no exception. During the first year of the war, the UNC relied on an assortment of converted heavy bombers (RB–17s and RB–29s) and second-tier fighters (RF–80As and RF–51s), none of which was ideal. The lumbering bombers needed either benign operating conditions or a large escort of fighters, while the obsolescent fighters increasingly became untenable as the MiG–15 threat grew. Nor were the cameras always ideal. The RF–80 was not especially fast, but on photographic runs it sometimes had to be flown at reduced speed because of the technical limitations of its cameras, an operational mismatch that left pilots even more vulnerable. To be fair to the USAF, attempts were made to adapt the war's outstanding fighter, the F–86 Sabre, to the reconnaissance role, but problems with the camera fitment undermined the quality of its imagery. Still, the F–86 could at least operate around MiG Alley with minimal escort.[30]

By 1952, the UNC reconnaissance service was functioning reasonably efficiently, helped in part by the stalemate on the ground, which tended to reduce the urgency of the process. The Fifth Air Force was capable of providing the Eighth Army with some twenty-one hundred negatives a day, ostensibly an impressive number. However, the problem of matching collection rates with analysis capabilities then came into play, and because the Army routinely took more than a week to analyze and disseminate the product, the overall potential of air reconnaissance was diminished.

AIR POWER AND JOINT WARFARE

The final topic to emerge from the war in Korea is perhaps the most controversial, at least for airmen. Maneuver in the form of rotary-wing (helicopter) operations might be the context, but command and control in joint warfare is the issue.

The inexorable trend toward joint operations that gathered momentum during World War II and that continues today can be attributed solely to the rise of air power. In Korea, it was the U.S. Army that pushed the often-vexing question of air power in joint warfare to the forefront of the doctrine debate.

Once the UNC's land forces had become entrenched at their original starting point along the thirty-eighth parallel by mid-1951, the static nature of the fighting came to resemble World War I. Properly haunted by that specter and desperate to find a way out of their strategic immobility, U.S. Army generals increasingly saw an answer in helicopters.

The unique maneuver qualities of helicopters had become apparent in the final months of World War II. Now, in Korea, they seemed to offer a means of restoring balance to the contest between firepower and maneuver, which on the ground had become heavily biased in favor of the former. Impressed by the mobility conferred on ground forces by the small number of helicopters flown by U.S. Marines under his command, in November 1951 General Ridgway made an urgent request for four troop transport battalions, each comprising 280 helicopters, for the U.S. Army in Korea; simultaneously, he flagged a longer term need for every future American field army to incorporate ten such battalions, totaling 2,800 helicopters.[31]

Ridgway's attempt to introduce helicopters in such massive numbers was a legitimate response to a serious tactical problem. (Indeed, his assessment that the Army "vitally needed helicopters" for maneuver was to be given its full expression only a decade later, when the Army used them in the thousands during the disastrous war in Vietnam.) At the same time, however, the implied concept of operations threatened to exacerbate existing tensions in the joint command and control system.

In his end-of-war report, FEAF commander General Weyland identified three principles for the use of airlift, all of which would have been familiar to anyone with knowledge of air power doctrine. Weyland concluded that priorities should be set by the theater commander; individual services should not have exclusive access to any airlift capability; and assets should be concentrated to the maximum extent.[32] Exceptions to those principles had abounded in Korea, where each of the U.S. services (including the Marines) had operated its own airlift services, and unity of command was rarely observed.

The division of air power assets and command authority did not end with airlift. Throughout the war, Navy strike, reconnaissance, and air defense aircraft flying from carriers off the Korean coast were routinely tasked separately or were allocated for the sole use of specific units, and Marine aircraft were usually reserved for Marine operations. As noted previously, this disorderly arrangement prevented "the full force of air power" from being brought to bear against the enemy.

Korea marked the point at which the command and control of air assets became *the* central challenge for the effective conduct of joint warfare. Because neither the UNC nor the communists were wholly displeased with the stalemate on the ground—the situation was, after all, consonant with the politics of the conflict—any friction between the UNC's surface and air forces was of no real consequence, at least as far as the eventual outcome was concerned (noting that the availability or unavailability of air could be a matter of life or death for individuals). Ten years later in Vietnam, however, disagreements between the U.S. Army, Navy, and Air Force over the command of air assets were to assume major significance.

CONCLUSION

Clausewitz's famous stricture that "war is a mere continuation of policy by other means" was writ large in Korea. Above all else, Korea was a political war, fought essentially for ideological (as opposed to territorial or resource) reasons. Strategies were shaped by the protagonists' implicit acceptance of the concept of deterrence within war, which imposed strict limits on who could do what to whom, how, and where. The war ended when politics in the United States and the Soviet Union needed it to end, not because any military resolution had been reached.

By mid-1951, the war on the ground had degenerated into a series of unimaginative and unwinnable battles. Once that stalemate had been reached, it was the war in the air that provided the most interesting professional study. The results were, unsurprisingly, both good and bad.

In the five short years since World War II, many of the essential skills required for air campaigning had been lost and had to be regained the hard way. It was even more disappointing, therefore, that ten years later in Vietnam, many of the unambiguous signals transmitted from Korea were either misunderstood or ignored by the United States.

The introduction of swept-wing jet fighters and the widespread use of rotary-wing aircraft were the two most significant technological advances, although neither altered the fundamentals of air warfare. While the former was the more spectacular, the latter had profound implications for the command and control of air assets in joint warfare.

A series of interdiction campaigns struggled to generate a cumulative effect as UNC planners too often applied first-world values (in terms of target selection) to their third-world enemy. At the same time, the continual harassment from the sky made it extremely difficult for the enemy's armies to maneuver by day. Theater-wide reconnaissance and maneuver via airlift were two other capabilities UNC forces enjoyed that the communists did not.

Late in the war, the strategic bombing campaign against North Korea's irrigation system might have got the targeting right in a strictly military sense, but it got the politics wrong—the classic conundrum for such campaigns. By contrast, the UNC's victory on a daily basis in the first jet air war underpinned every other military action the command fought and assumed a strategic quality in its own right.

Like their armies, the UNC's air forces could not bring victory in Korea. Air did, however, save the UNC at least twice, probably more often, most notably at Pusan, where control of the air, close attack, and maneuver were all that prevented the communists from driving the UNC into the sea. In a war in which those fighting on the ground seemed to run out of ideas, air was the difference between defeat and an acceptable political outcome.

5
OPERATIONS OVER NORTH VIETNAM, 1965–1973

Wayne Thompson

THE AMERICAN AIR WAR in Southeast Asia was the most extravagant ever waged. The eight million tons of bombs dwarfed even the avalanche that flattened the cities of Germany and Japan in the Second World War. Yet Hanoi, communist North Vietnam's capital and principal city, emerged intact and triumphant. This is a tale of air power badly used, but from it sprang new technologies such as guided bombing that would make air power more useful elsewhere.[1]

Vietnamese communism's greatest advantage was its grip on nationalist sentiment. Ho Chi Minh and his comrades eliminated most of their Vietnamese nationalist rivals before driving the French from Vietnam, Laos, and Cambodia in mid-1954. A major exception was Ngo Dinh Diem, who survived in the United States and returned to take charge of the new government of South Vietnam. His Catholicism proved a handicap in a Buddhist country; his assassination (with American connivance) in 1963 led eventually to a government headed by General Nguyen Van Thieu and Air Marshal Nguyen Cao Ky, both veterans of the French colonial regime. South Vietnam and its American ally never moved to conquer North Vietnam. Only the communists strove to unify Vietnam.

America's Vietnam War began gradually, and gradualism became its defining attribute. The independence of South Vietnam from communist North Vietnam depended on a growing American military intervention. President Dwight Eisenhower sent a few hundred military advisers. President John Kennedy sent more than sixteen thousand and added aircraft. By 1962, American pilots in propeller-driven fighters were attacking communist forces in South Vietnam. North Vietnamese soldiers and supplies moved down the Ho Chi Minh Trail, an expanding network of paths and dirt roads through Laos into South Vietnam.

The U.S. Air Force chief of staff, General Curtis LeMay, argued that the best way to win the war was to bomb North Vietnam. He wanted to send the Air

Force's biggest bombers, B–52s, against targets throughout North Vietnam, but bad memories of Chinese intervention in the Korean War brought fear that dramatic action in North Vietnam might provoke a repetition. After Kennedy's assassination in 1963, President Lyndon Johnson laid the groundwork for LeMay's retirement in early 1965. Meanwhile, in August 1964, Johnson limited the initial American airstrikes on North Vietnam to a few Navy fighter sorties against coastal gunboat facilities in retaliation for North Vietnamese gunboat attacks (real and alleged) on Navy destroyers in the Gulf of Tonkin.[2] The U.S. Congress passed a resolution giving Johnson authority to take whatever actions he deemed necessary in Southeast Asia. Nevertheless, until he won the November 1964 presidential election, Johnson continued to promise that American boys would not fight a war in Vietnam.

ROLLING THUNDER

A few months after his victory over Barry Goldwater (a Republican senator and a major general in the Air Force Reserve), President Johnson authorized Rolling Thunder, a bombing campaign in North Vietnam that would prove to be too weak to discourage the communist leadership there. For years (March 1965 through October 1968), American fighter aircraft dropped bombs on North Vietnam almost every day. Johnson withheld the B–52s from North Vietnam for a year and then used them only near the borders with South Vietnam and Laos, far from North Vietnam's cities. He imposed numerous restrictions on the fighter aircraft that did the bulk of the bombing. He forbade attacking most leadership targets, and few targets of any kind were approved in or near Hanoi until mid-1966.

Since North Vietnam had little manufacturing and depended on imports of weapons, trucks, and oil from communist allies, Rolling Thunder was primarily an interdiction campaign. But it was an interdiction campaign from which Johnson subtracted key targets. He ruled out the mining or bombing of ports, including the principal port of Haiphong. Large portions of the critical rail links between China and Hanoi were also off limits much of the time. Added to those political limitations, the limited ability of fighter aircraft in the 1960s to bomb effectively at night or in bad weather meant that Rolling Thunder was mostly a daylight, fair weather interdiction campaign—not one likely to have much success.

Beginning very gradually with a few targets in the southern panhandle of North Vietnam, Rolling Thunder did permit Johnson to say that he had tried bombing before he sent American soldiers to die on the ground in South Vietnam. Thousands of American soldiers began to arrive in April 1965, and, by 1968, they exceeded half a million. During those three years, American troop increases in South

Vietnam were accompanied by very gradual increases in the severity of the bombing of North Vietnam.

President Johnson prided himself on personally picking targets that would not endanger civilians, North Vietnamese leaders, and Russians or Chinese. The Chinese presence was especially numerous along the railroads connecting China and Hanoi. Early in the war, these North Vietnamese railroads were the best transportation route connecting the southern coast of China and the mineral resources of China's land-locked Yunnan Province. More than 100,000 Chinese maintained those North Vietnamese railroads and defended them with antiaircraft guns. Chinese pilots had trained North Vietnamese pilots and were present on North Vietnamese air bases, as were Russians, who were also present as advisers at surface-to-air missile (SAM) sites. Johnson forbade attacks on most North Vietnamese air bases until 1967. Despite good intelligence on the development of SAM sites, Johnson prohibited attacking those sites until SAMs shot down American fighter aircraft in the summer of 1965.

The hesitant bombing of North Vietnam paused occasionally for a few days or a few weeks to entice the North Vietnamese government into negotiations. These peace overtures failed until early 1968, when communist insurgents throughout South Vietnam went on the offensive during Tet, the lunar New Year holiday. Although the insurgents were badly defeated by American ground and air forces, popular opinion in the United States turned against the war. On national television, President Johnson announced that he was cutting back the bombing of North Vietnam to the panhandle well south of Hanoi. The seriousness of this peace overture was underscored by Johnson's decision not to run for reelection. The North Vietnamese cooperated to the extent of agreeing to formal peace talks in Paris—talks that would continue for years while the war continued. In the fall of 1968, just before voters chose a Republican, Richard Nixon, as the next president, Johnson terminated Rolling Thunder. Most bombing ceased throughout North Vietnam not merely for days or weeks but for years, until full-scale bombing of North Vietnam resumed when the North invaded South Vietnam in 1972.

The changing bombing policy and changing leadership of the United States encountered a remarkable consistency in North Vietnam's policy and leadership. Le Duan (born in South Vietnam) and his principal ally, Le Duc Tho, had gained much of Ho Chi Minh's authority more than a decade before Ho died in 1969. General Vo Nguyen Giap, the longtime leader of North Vietnam's military, had to share command with General Nguyen Chi Thanh (also born in South Vietnam) until Thanh's death in the summer of 1967. For Le Duan and Nguyen Chi Thanh, victory in South Vietnam was the foremost objective, and the most important decision was when to make major moves in South Vietnam. North Vietnam would persist and (with air defense weapons supplied by the Russians and the Chinese) exact a high price from the American attackers.[3]

At its peak, Rolling Thunder was the work chiefly of Navy fighters flying from one or two carriers in the South China Sea and about two hundred Air Force fighters at four bases in Thailand and Da Nang Air Base in northern South Vietnam. More than four hundred other Air Force fighters in South Vietnam were almost entirely dedicated to supporting ground forces there. The territory of ally South Vietnam bore the brunt of American bombing—about five times the tonnage dropped on North Vietnam and twice the tonnage dropped on Laos.

Parts of North Vietnam, such as downtown Hanoi, could rarely be bombed at all. American aircrews were expected to know extensive and shifting rules of engagement that included zones where bombing was restricted or prohibited. Since the boundaries of restricted and prohibited zones often bore little relationship to geographical features, aircrews were sometimes at a loss to know whether a target of opportunity like a train or a truck convoy was legitimate. Early in the war, targets of opportunity could be struck only if they were south of an armed reconnaissance line that President Johnson permitted to move northward only very gradually. Finally, in the summer of 1966, most of North Vietnam was opened to armed reconnaissance with the principal exception of populated areas in general and three restricted zones in particular: a circular zone with a radius of thirty nautical miles around Hanoi, a circular zone with a radius of ten nautical miles around Haiphong, and a buffer zone along the Chinese border with a depth of twenty-five nautical miles in the east and thirty nautical miles in the west. In December 1966, President Johnson established within the restricted Hanoi zone a prohibited zone with a radius of ten nautical miles. American planes were not even to fly through the prohibited zone without the president's approval.

One of the best-known breaches of the rules of engagement occurred on June 2, 1967, when an Air Force F–105 strafed a Russian ship in the port of Cam Pha about forty miles north of Haiphong. Colonel Jack Broughton, acting wing commander at Takhli Air Base, Thailand, tried to save the pilot from punishment by exposing the incriminating gun camera film. Although Broughton's court-martial conviction was eventually set aside, the incident ended his Air Force career and began his writing career. The title of his first book, *Thud Ridge,* was a reference to a small range of mountains northwest of Hanoi.[4] The F–105s, nicknamed "Thuds," used "Thud Ridge" to mask their approach to Hanoi from North Vietnamese radar, but many F–105s were shot down near the ridge.

The Air Force used the F–105 Thunderchief single-seat, single-engine fighter as its principal bomber in North Vietnam. Designed for low-level penetration with a nuclear bomb, the "Thud" was converted to a less-than-agile conventional dive-bomber. The Air Force gave the job of protecting the F–105s from enemy MiG fighters to its version of the Navy's two-seat F–4 Phantom II. Both services employed the F–4 as a bomber and an air-to-air fighter, but during Rolling Thunder the Navy made heavier use of the older A–4 Skyhawks and F–8 Crusaders, the latter shooting down more North Vietnamese MiGs than did the Navy F–4s. The F–4 originally lacked a built-in gun, a defect that mounting an external gun pod did not entirely remedy. Not until 1968 did a new version of the F–4 with built-in gun become available. Even late in the war, however, F–4s continued to rely on undependable radar-guided Sparrow and heat-seeking Sidewinder missiles despite rules of engagement that required visual identification of enemy fighters before firing. Air Force pilots preferred these Navy-developed missiles to the inferior Falcons developed by their own service.

However undependable, air-to-air missiles were not much affected by weather that could cripple air-to-ground weapons. Political and military leaders could set rules of engagement and select targets, but uncontrollable weather determined much of the air war's rhythm. During the relatively sparse rains of the northeast monsoon from November to May, persistent cloud cover over North Vietnam interfered with bombing, while the roads dried in Laos and air power shifted its emphasis to interdict truck traffic there. During the remainder of the year, the heavy rains of the southwest monsoon turned Laotian roads to mud, but intermittently cleared the skies over targets in North Vietnam.

A service division of bombing overlaid the seasonal division. Air Force C–130 command and control aircraft helped to coordinate strikes by Air Force and Navy fighters in Laos, but those converted C–130 transports were too slow to survive over North Vietnam. There, command and control problems were alleviated by assigning geographical sectors called "route packages" to each service. The four Navy route packages ran along the coast, while two of the Air Force's three route packages required penetration deeper into North Vietnam; the third Air Force route package bordered South Vietnam and came within the purview of the U.S. Army general who was the joint commander in South Vietnam. Most famous and well defended were route packages 6A and 6B. The Air Force bombed targets in route package 6A around Hanoi, while the Navy's route package 6B included the principal port of Haiphong.

The route package system emerged from a complicated command structure for American forces in Southeast Asia. The commander in chief, Pacific, Admiral U. S.

Grant Sharp, controlled bombing operations in North Vietnam from his head-quarters in Hawaii, but he gave the Seventh Air Force commander (since mid-1966, Lieutenant General William "Spike" Momyer) in South Vietnam a fairly free hand there as well as in Laos and in the Air Force's North Vietnam route packages. General Momyer squeezed a degree of independence from being subordinate to both Army general William Westmoreland (the joint commander in South Vietnam) and Admiral Sharp. Although Westmoreland was in theory also subordinate to Sharp, the general in fact took orders directly from Washington. Air Force B–52 commanders in Asia looked to Strategic Air Command (SAC) headquarters in Omaha, Nebraska, for guidance and deferred more to Westmoreland than to Momyer, a fighter pilot.

Differences in chain of command amplified other service differences. Navy fighter pilots visited and revisited Southeast Asia as aircraft carrier schedules dictated. An Air Force fighter pilot might spend a year flying mostly in South Vietnam or a shorter time flying one hundred missions into North Vietnam interspersed with missions into Laos—after a year in Southeast Asia or one hundred missions into North Vietnam, he would not return to Southeast Asia unless he volunteered. On the other hand, Air Force B–52 crew members were obliged to take repeated six-month combat tours in Guam or Thailand.

In addition to B–52s, SAC also contributed air-refueling tankers. One of the characteristics of air warfare introduced during the Vietnam War was the routine use of air-refueling in combat operations. By the end of Rolling Thunder in 1968, ninety KC–135 air-refueling tankers made possible not only B–52 operations from Guam, but also fighter operations from Thailand. Since Navy carriers were closer to their targets, the more limited air-refueling needs of carrier aircraft could usually be handled by smaller onboard tankers. A dramatic exception occurred on May 31, 1967, when an Air Force KC–135 refueled a Navy KA–3 tanker while it was refueling a Navy F–8. Although they frequently saved fighters that were low on fuel, efficient employment of the tankers contributed to the predictable regularity of Air Force bombing operations in North Vietnam. Between the morning and afternoon strikes was a long pause while the tankers landed and refueled. North Vietnam's air defenses could concentrate their efforts accordingly.

Of the more than three thousand American planes lost in Southeast Asia, about a third went down in North Vietnam. While the U.S. loss rate throughout Southeast Asia was less than one per thousand attack sorties, the Air Force loss rate in route package 6A around Hanoi rose to more than twenty-five per thousand attack sorties in 1966. This, the worst air loss rate of the war, was but the latest spur for the Air Force to make tactical and technical changes.

North Vietnam's air defenses included about one hundred Russian SA–2 SAM launchers shifting in groups of six or less among scores of prepared sites. Even veterans of the Korean War or World War II had no experience contending with SAMs. The initial attack on two of the early sites proved disastrous. Following Washington's instructions, on July 27, 1965, fifty-four Air Force F–105s went in below five hundred feet. The missiles had been moved, and the sites had become flak traps. North Vietnamese guns shot down four F–105s, and two more collided. Thereafter, the Air Force relied on two other ways of dealing with SAMs. The first was to threaten immediate attack on any SAM site that turned on its radar. This threat could be carried out thanks to the Shrike radar-seeking missile developed by the Navy. The two-seat trainer version of the F–105 became a "Wild Weasel" with an electronic warfare officer in the backseat. A Wild Weasel and three accompanying F–105s composed an "Iron Hand" flight that could reinforce Shrikes with bombs. While few SAM sites were destroyed by Iron Hand, many sites turned off their radar.

The Air Force's second relatively successful method of coping with SAMs also followed in the Navy's wake. Navy fighters had considerable success with transmitters that deceived North Vietnamese radar about a fighter's exact location. Air Force B–52s and EB–66s carried bulky equipment to jam SAM radar and guidance signals. That was the EB–66's principal function, but the aircraft was too big and too slow to survive near Hanoi. In late 1966, the Air Force began to deploy jammers small enough to fit in a removable pod that could be carried externally by F–105s and F–4s.

One early success of the jamming pods (on January 2, 1967) had nothing to do with their ability to foil SAMs. Since the jammers were initially deployed on the F–105, their association with that aircraft was used to deceive North Vietnamese MiG fighters into attacking what they believed was a formation of F–105s when in fact the MiGs encountered F–4s carrying the jamming pods. Part of the ruse was to make the F–4s appear to be F–105s about to bomb the principal airfield at Phuc Yen northwest of Hanoi. Although President Johnson still forbade an attack on Phuc Yen, the MiG–21s there took the bait. Leading this unusual deception, called Bolo, was Colonel Robin Olds, a World War II ace who commanded the Eighth Tactical Fighter Wing at Ubon Air Base, Thailand. Olds himself claimed one of the seven MiG–21s believed to have been shot down that day.

When President Johnson finally allowed attacks on Phuc Yen, the Navy and Marines wanted to participate, even though the airfield was in the Air Force's route package 6A. In the initial strikes on October 24 and 25, 1967, the Navy lost three fighters, two to SAMs and one to flak, and the Air Force lost one to flak. Perhaps a dozen MiGs were damaged on the ground, and one was shot down by an Air

Force F–4 using a gun pod. On October 26, Air Force F–4s used missiles to shoot down three more MiGs. After the raids on Phuc Yen and other airfields in North Vietnam, most of the surviving MiGs (about one hundred) moved to airfields in China. Although that shift increased the temptation for American fighter pilots to fly into China, many fewer cross-border incidents occurred during the Vietnam War than during the Korean War. Most American pilots even obeyed the order not to enter the U.S. self-imposed buffer zone south of the border with China.

More often defied was guidance intended to get pilots to pull out of their dive-bombing runs above the effective range of North Vietnamese guns. Released too high, unguided bombs usually missed targets by a wide margin. Many fighters were shot down while diving too low. After Rolling Thunder, the Air Force's answer to this dilemma would be widespread use of laser-guided bombs that enabled accurate bombing from above ten thousand feet. Meanwhile, antiaircraft artillery continued to take a heavier toll on U.S. fighters than did MiGs or SAMs. Other than releasing bombs at higher altitude, the best remedy was using cluster bombs that could kill artillery crews or at least cause them to take cover.

Although it would fall behind the Air Force in using guided bombs, the Navy led the way in this technology (as in so many others) early in the war. The Navy's television-guided Walleye glide bomb overcame President Johnson's reluctance to bomb any targets in Hanoi. In May 1967, Navy A–4s used Walleyes to put the Hanoi thermal power plant out of commission. Five months later, a Walleye damaged the control tower at Phuc Yen airfield. The Walleye's one-thousand-pound warhead proved too light for North Vietnam's strongest bridge at Thanh Hoa, however, and the Walleye's television guidance was more expensive and less reliable in most circumstances than the Air Force's laser guidance system that became available in 1968.

The strength of the Thanh Hoa Bridge was a consequence of its destruction during the war for independence from the French, who had built the railroad linking Hanoi with Saigon one thousand miles to the south. About ninety miles from Hanoi, the railroad crossed the Ma River on the Thanh Hoa Bridge. Communist-led Vietnamese rebel soldiers destroyed the bridge by having two explosives-filled locomotives collide. Communist North Vietnam rebuilt the bridge so solidly that repeated strikes by Navy and Air Force fighter aircraft failed to dislodge it. One night in May 1966, an Air Force C–130 dropped five five-thousand-pound weapons upriver from the bridge; they were intended to float downstream and detonate when their sensors detected the bridge above them. The weapons produced no apparent damage; a second attempt the next night led to the loss of a C–130 with its crew of seven and an F–4 with its crew of two.

As strikes on the Thanh Hoa Bridge continued, the bigger Doumer Bridge across the Red River in Hanoi remained off limits to attack. President Johnson's reluctance to attack that bridge was finally overcome by pressure from Senate hawks. In August 1967, while Senator John Stennis (D–MS) was launching hearings to investigate Rolling Thunder's gradualism, President Johnson at last permitted the Doumer Bridge to be bombed. The railroads from China and from the port of Haiphong converged into one line before passing south over the Doumer Bridge into downtown Hanoi and to all points south. Although laser-guided bombs were not yet available, the Air Force enjoyed remarkable success in bombing North Vietnam's longest and most important bridge. One of the bridge's nineteen spans came down after F–105s struck it with three-thousand-pound bombs. Subsequent raids in October and December would bring down more spans.

The Doumer Bridge raids forced the North Vietnamese to ferry goods across the Red River, and supplies backed up at Yen Vien rail yard north of the river. President Johnson had permitted earlier raids on Yen Vien and then withdrawn the yard from the approved target list. When the yard was approved for attack again on August 21, 1967, Air Force fighters caught 150 railroad cars in the yard and destroyed most of them. These Doumer and Yen Vien strikes occurred at the peak of Rolling Thunder.

Only a year before, in mid-1966, President Johnson had begun to permit some strikes in the Hanoi area, but those strikes against oil tank farms had come too late—North Vietnam had already dispersed much of the fuel for its trucks in drums along roads throughout the country. Subsequent raids against North Vietnam's principal industrial facility, the Thai Nguyen ironworks north of Hanoi, curtailed North Vietnam's ability to manufacture its own fuel drums and river barges, but imported munitions and other supplies continued to move south through North Vietnam and Laos on thousands of trucks also imported from communist countries. The Tet uprising throughout South Vietnam in early 1968 and the simultaneous siege by North Vietnamese forces of the Marine base at Khe Sanh in northern South Vietnam were ample proof that American efforts to interdict North Vietnamese supply lines had been inadequate.

For five months before President Johnson's March 1968 cutback of Rolling Thunder operations, there was little bombing in the Hanoi-Haiphong region. The annual northeast monsoon blanketed the area in thick, low clouds. Since the Air Force's B–52s were forbidden to bomb there, the Navy's A–6s were the only night and bad-weather bombers available, and there were not enough of them. The Air Force built a radar control facility at Site 85 on a hill in northern Laos, too far from Hanoi to match the precision of ground radar-controlled bombing in South

Vietnam. Site 85 could control formation bombing of an area target. The major problem was that a tight formation would have to fly straight and level over a heavily defended target. On November 18, 1967, Colonel Edward Burdett, the F–105 wing commander at Korat Air Base, Thailand, led a dozen F–105s with bombs (escorted by a dozen more F–4s and F–105s) on a raid against Phuc Yen airfield. Burdett was shot down by a SAM and died in captivity. The loss of three F–105s to SAMs and one to a MiG caused the Air Force to reduce each radar-controlled raid in route package 6 to a single flight of four. In January, two North Vietnamese biplanes were shot down while attacking Site 85 (the first North Vietnamese air attack on a ground target). On March 11, 1968, communist forces took the site and killed or captured twelve Americans.[5]

President Johnson's March 31 cutback of Rolling Thunder operations meant that for the next seven months (until Rolling Thunder ended), the Air Force and Navy would concentrate their interdiction bombing on the southern panhandle of North Vietnam. The great barrier that needed to be overcome was darkness. The effectiveness of American air power during the day persuaded thousands of North Vietnamese trucks to move at night. In 1968, the best solution to this problem was being tested in Laos. The AC–130 gunship, a cargo aircraft with guns and sensors (including infrared) that could find trucks at night, would become the best truck hunter and killer of the war. But the AC–130 was too slow to survive the heavier air defenses of North Vietnam. There, the Navy and Marine night attack aircraft, the A–6, was more effective against fixed targets such as truck parks and storage depots than against moving trucks. The A–6's terrain-following radar permitted it to fly low at night, but it moved much faster than the AC–130 and lacked the gunship's sensors. Nevertheless, the A–6 was the envy of the Air Force, which hastened to get its new F–111 into combat in 1968—too soon. Three F–111s were lost (they apparently flew into the ground) before the surviving aircraft were withdrawn for further development.

The Air Force did have ground radar sites in South Vietnam that could control strikes in the southern panhandle of North Vietnam at night, but however accurate those strikes might be on a fixed target, moving trucks were not likely to be struck in that way. The best the Air Force could do in the panhandle of North Vietnam was to assign night operations to F–4 crews, who did nothing else. These "Night Owls" went out night after night and sometimes made themselves obvious targets for North Vietnamese artillery by using flares to see trucks.

Although the route package system usually separated Air Force and Navy operations in North Vietnam, the services sometimes cooperated in truly joint efforts. The biggest of these in 1968 was the bombardment of the Vinh Linh sector, including part of the so-called demilitarized zone separating North Vietnam from South Vietnam. On a twelve-by-twenty-mile area, ten thousand tons of munitions fell in early July—a ton a minute for a week. The bulk came from B–52s, but Air Force, Navy, and Marine fighter aircraft contributed, as did Army artillery from South Vietnam and naval gunfire from offshore. The purpose of the Vinh Linh bombardment was to silence North Vietnamese guns. Mobile field artillery fired into South Vietnam from more than four hundred prepared positions. The number of antiaircraft gun positions was even greater. Although the bombardment reduced artillery fire from the Vinh Linh sector for several weeks, photography could confirm the destruction of only two occupied field artillery positions and eleven occupied antiaircraft positions.

Vinh Linh was accustomed to bombardment. B–52s had cratered the landscape, and the remaining villagers had joined soldiers in underground supply depots. Three years and five months after Rolling Thunder came to an end on November 1, 1968, the demilitarized zone would become an entry point for North Vietnam's invasion of South Vietnam. Until then, the absence of bombing throughout North Vietnam facilitated military preparations, transportation, and life in general. Trucks could move in daylight again, and boats could move freely along the coast. Roads and railroads were repaired. New roads were built. Construction of an oil pipeline from the principal panhandle port of Vinh to Laos was already under way before the end of Rolling Thunder. A second pipeline from the coast to Laos would be built nearer South Vietnam. Subsequently, pipelines would reach to Haiphong and China. The pipelines would be far more efficient and far less vulnerable to bombing than trucks loaded with fuel drums. The communist leadership knew that the bombing of North Vietnam might resume, and some of the major targets of Rolling Thunder like the Thai Nguyen ironworks were not rebuilt. While what would be years of peace talks commenced in Paris, North Vietnam prepared to take South Vietnam.

LINEBACKER

North Vietnam waited until most American ground forces had left South Vietnam before invading on March 30, 1972. More than 100,000 North Vietnamese soldiers and hundreds of tanks moved into South Vietnam from across the demilitarized zone, from Laos, and from Cambodia. Yet with the help of American air power, South Vietnam was able to stop this invasion, if not expel it. Even when the American presence in South Vietnam had numbered half a million troops, their role had often been to draw the communist enemy out of hiding to be killed by artillery and bombing. Now, as conventional invaders, the communist forces were in the open— vulnerable to close air support in South Vietnam, vulnerable to air interdiction in North Vietnam.

At the outset of the invasion, the northeast monsoon was coming to an end and with it the dry weather conducive to truck traffic in Laos. Despite more than three years of emphasis on interdiction in Laos, North Vietnam had been able to mount its invasion partly from Laos and Cambodia. When Cambodia had been taken over in 1970 by a general friendly to the United States, he had closed the country's principal port to the communists. Henceforth, the Ho Chi Minh Trail road system in Laos had become even more essential to preparations for invasion. As the invasion consumed the munitions and supplies carefully hoarded in advance, however, replenishment would have to come through North Vietnam. A new, improved Rolling Thunder was required, and it was called Linebacker.

Linebacker differed from Rolling Thunder in important respects. President Nixon used air power more aggressively than his predecessor. Nixon's successful diplomacy made him far less fearful than Johnson that China or Russia would intervene more dangerously. At last, Navy aircraft were permitted to mine the North Vietnamese ports, a key development that increased the utility of bombing the railroads from China. The Air Force downed bridges on those railroads and throughout North Vietnam with laser-guided bombs. Finally, in a sequel called Linebacker II, Nixon sent two hundred B–52s against targets on the outskirts of Hanoi and Haiphong.

Rolling Thunder took more than three years at the beginning of America's Vietnam War. Linebacker and Linebacker II took less than a year at the end. But South Vietnam's war for survival continued after Linebacker II, and without American air power, South Vietnam fell to another North Vietnamese invasion in 1975.

As in 1968, the North Vietnamese communists attempted in 1972 to exploit the U.S. presidential election. Both times their offensives helped to elect Nixon, but two key aspects of the 1972 election were favorable to the communist cause. American voters indicated their fatigue with the war by handing control of Congress to Democrats hostile to further support of South Vietnam, and a break-in at Democratic national headquarters in the Watergate Building led to Nixon's resignation in 1974. When the North Vietnamese invaded South Vietnam again in 1975, Nixon's successor, Gerald Ford, could not persuade Congress to help South Vietnam with air power.

North Vietnam's 1972 invasion was premature. Nixon could still unleash massive air power. At the outset, the Air Force had only about two hundred fighter aircraft in Southeast Asia, a third as many as in Rolling Thunder. But the Air Force quickly deployed another 150 fighters and expanded the B–52 force in the area to 200, more than three times the Rolling Thunder B–52 contingent. The Navy also increased its presence from the two or three carriers of Rolling Thunder to four carriers. Both services sent a newer mix of aircraft. The Air Force had almost entirely replaced F–105s with F–4s, except in the Wild Weasel's anti-SAM role (and even in that role there were now some F–4s). Navy A–7s replaced A–4s, and F–8s had mostly given way to F–4s. Late in the year, the Air Force version of the Navy A–7 also joined the fight, and the Air Force's F–111 rebounded from its dismal debut in 1968 to be an effective night and all-weather bomber. Navy and Marine A–6s continued in that role throughout the year. Well before the end of 1972, the Air Force had moved all its fighter aircraft in South Vietnam to Thailand, and even the Marines had established an air base there for F–4s and A–6s. In contrast to Rolling Thunder, air operations launched from Thailand in 1972 were as likely to give close support to soldiers in South Vietnam as to strike interdiction targets in North Vietnam.

President Nixon had far more confidence in aircraft and bombs than he did in the leadership of the Department of Defense or the services. His relationships with the secretary of defense, generals, and admirals were as strained as President Johnson's had been. Johnson eventually pushed Secretary of Defense Robert McNamara out of office, after the latter soured on the war, but Nixon's secretary of defense, Melvin Laird, was an influential former congressman who could not be cast aside. A proponent of "Vietnamization" (that is, turning the war over to the South Vietnamese), Laird opposed the renewed bombing of North Vietnam and sought at least to moderate it. Nixon sometimes circumvented Laird and worked directly with the chairman of the Joint Chiefs of Staff, Admiral Thomas Moorer. Although Moorer's relationship with Nixon's national security adviser, Henry Kissinger, was troubled by evidence that Moorer had used his liaison officer to Kissinger as a spy at the White House, Moorer remained in an alternative chain of command that excluded not only Laird, but also the joint commander in South Vietnam, Army General Creighton Abrams. The number of U.S. Army soldiers in Vietnam was shrinking, and Nixon blamed Abrams for a failed 1971 South Vietnamese incursion into Laos.[6]

Nixon and Moorer dealt directly with the Seventh Air Force commander, General John Vogt, who had worked in the Pentagon with Moorer (and with Kissinger) as director of the joint staff until the invasion. The Seventh Air Force's change of command at so critical a time was, however, not the result of any dissatisfaction on Nixon's part with Vogt's predecessor, General John Lavelle. Nixon liked Lavelle's stretching the rules of engagement before the invasion to send raids into North Vietnam against trucks, SAM transporters, SAM sites, and airfields. Nixon had even told his ambassador to South Vietnam, Ellsworth Bunker, that SAM sites could be struck before they reacted to American planes.[7] Unfortunately, Lavelle's subordinates falsified reports of the small planned raids to make them fit "protective reaction" rules of engagement designed for the defense of reconnaissance aircraft. When an Air Force sergeant in Thailand complained to his senator about false reporting, the Air Force chief of staff, General John Ryan, recalled Lavelle and retired him. Nixon sympathized with Lavelle, but the president did not come to his defense then or during subsequent congressional hearings—even though Nixon had authorized much larger raids on North Vietnam in 1970–1971, and even though he had authorized a false reporting scheme for bombing North Vietnamese forces in Cambodia.

As much as any general, Lavelle experienced the bitter frustration of the Vietnam War. He had been instrumental in developing an elaborate network of acoustic and seismic sensors along the Ho Chi Minh Trail in Laos. Yet while he was in command of the air war in Laos, the North Vietnamese had successfully used those roads to bring tanks and other munitions to invasion launch positions. His command's new and unprecedented ability to drop laser-guided bombs had found few rewarding targets. It was perhaps his greatest misfortune that he just missed commanding the most satisfactory part of a very unsatisfactory war.

Linebacker picked up where Rolling Thunder left off and quickly moved beyond it. While the old route package system dividing Navy and Air Force responsibilities geographically was unchanged, most of the targets gradually authorized over the years of Rolling Thunder became available in a few weeks. The restricted zone limiting bombing near Hanoi shrank from thirty nautical miles to ten nautical miles. On the morning of May 9, Navy A–6s dropped mines into the channel connecting Haiphong harbor to the Tonkin Gulf. The next day, Air Force F–4s with laser-guided bombs began downing bridges on the railroads between China and Hanoi, and south of Hanoi as well. One of the first to have spans destroyed by laser-guided bombs was the Doumer Bridge in Hanoi. Then on May 13, the Thanh Hoa Bridge, which had withstood so many bombing raids in Rolling Thunder, was at last broken by laser-guided bombs.

Although the Air Force had thousands of laser-seeker guidance kits for its bombs, it had only six new laser designators that could be used in the well-defended area near Hanoi and Haiphong. Unlike older designators, the new ones could swivel and permit an F–4 to maneuver while keeping the laser beam on the target. General Vogt built his air campaign around the preservation of those precious laser designators, and at the end of Linebacker his command still had four of the original six. He made that possible by protecting laser designation F–4s with large formations of other aircraft. Eight strike F–4s (of which two carried laser designators) might be escorted by five times that many aircraft, including eight F–105 Wild Weasels and eight F–4s dropping chaff to interfere with radar tracking—a tactic little used since World War II.

The task of keeping more than one hundred bridges down required revisiting many, as the North Vietnamese repaired them and bypassed them with pontoon bridges. The bridge-bombing effort was most effective at stopping rail traffic. When trains were not moving, Linebacker did not have to bomb rolling stock and rail yards, tasks that had absorbed so many Rolling Thunder sorties. Although bombing bridges slowed truck traffic, thousands of trucks continued to roll south. Since the Navy flew its normal armed reconnaissance and "alpha strikes" (with formations usually about half the size of Air Force guided-bombing formations), it had many more sorties than the Air Force to go after trucks, truck parks, and storage depots.[8]

North Vietnamese trucks no longer had to carry so many fuel drums thanks to oil pipelines that were hard to bomb and easy to repair. Trucks carrying supplies to South Vietnam had always carried rice as well as munitions and fuel, but, in 1972, trucks also carried rice from China to North Vietnam because a typhoon in 1971 had breached the dikes of the Red River and reduced the rice harvest. North Vietnamese propaganda that Americans were threatening the food supply by bombing dikes betrayed fears of that tactic. During Rolling Thunder, the Air Force had studied the possibility of breaching earthen dikes with bombs and concluded that the bigger dikes were too hard to destroy and the smaller ones too easy to repair. Guided bombing made breaching dikes more feasible, but not even the Nixon administration was willing to tolerate the likely bad press (some of which came anyway).

Nixon's actions were often cautious. Most targets of any kind in downtown Hanoi were in effect off limits because Nixon gave Secretary of Defense Laird veto authority over them. Other than bridges, the principal targets for laser-guided bombs in North Vietnam were power plants, especially the new Lang Chi hydroelectric plant on the Red River seventy miles northwest of Hanoi. That plant could supply half of North Vietnam's electricity requirement. In this case, Nixon made the bold decision to attack the Lang Chi generators, even though they sat on top of the dam's spillway. The Seventh Air Force was told to destroy the generators and leave the dam intact. General Vogt visited Ubon Air Base in Thailand to make sure that the commander of the Eighth Tactical Fighter Wing, Colonel Carl Miller, and his aircrews understood the importance of sparing the dam. On June 10, their laser-guided bombs destroyed all three generators and left the dam standing.

Air Force laser-guided bombing in North Vietnam and South Vietnam was the work primarily of the Eighth Tactical Fighter Wing. During Rolling Thunder, the Eighth under Colonel Robin Olds had been best known for air-to-air operations, but that role had passed largely to the 432d Tactical Reconnaissance Wing at Udorn Air Base, Thailand. This wing would produce the only Air Force aces of the war, but the Navy achieved that honor first, on May 10, 1972, the war's most intense day of air-to-air fighting. Navy F–4s shot down seven MiG–17s and a MiG–21, all with Sidewinder heat-seeking missiles, while the Air Force shot down three MiG–21s with Sparrow radar-guided missiles. The Navy's first and only Vietnam air aces, pilot Lieutenant Randall Cunningham and backseat radar intercept officer Lieutenant (j.g.) William Driscoll, won their third, fourth, and fifth victories before being shot down by a SAM and rescued.[9]

American fighter pilots were still dealing with a small but growing North Vietnamese air force. By 1972, North Vietnam had over two hundred MiGs, about double their number during Rolling Thunder. MiG losses early in Linebacker reduced opportunities for shooting down more MiGs as the year wore on. Not until August 28 did F–4 pilot Captain Richard "Steve" Ritchie become the Air Force's first Vietnam ace, followed in September by his usual backseat weapons system officer, Captain Charles DeBellvue, whose six victory credits were the most awarded to any American during the war. Finally, on October 13, another weapons system officer, Jeffrey Feinstein, became the fifth and last ace of the war.

Giving a "backseater" (a Navy F–4 radar intercept officer or an Air Force F–4 weapons system officer) credit for a kill equal to that given his pilot did not sit well with all pilots. Some believed pilots Cunningham and Ritchie were the only real aces of the war, despite the fact that all their victories were achieved with missiles. Indeed, the Air Force aces had won all their victories with radar-guided Sparrow missiles, and it was the weapons system officer who had to lock the radar onto the MiG in each case. Feinstein was a particular problem for those wishing to discount the importance of the man in the backseat. Unlike Driscoll and DeBellvue, Feinstein was not associated with a single ace pilot. Feinstein was known for bringing victory to four pilots, none of them close to being an ace. For decades, an allegation circulated that in the case of one of the MiG victories claimed by Feinstein, he and his pilot had really shot down another F–4. Not until 2001 did an Air Force investigation disprove this allegation.[10]

More troubling to the Air Force in 1972 was the Navy's superior performance against MiGs. The Air Force's two-to-one kill ratio (forty-eight MiGs shot down versus twenty-four aircraft lost to MiGs) compared poorly with the Navy's six-to-one kill ratio (twenty-four MiGs shot down versus only four losses). Navy aircrews did have the advantage of operating near the coast and their radar ship, which was superior to the Air Force's EC–121 radar aircraft. The Air Force built an intelligence fusion center in Thailand, but Air Force aircrews thought it inferior to the fusion center on the Navy's radar ship. Air Force F–4 aircrews had the capability to locate MiGs beyond visual range by interrogating MiG identification transponders, but the rules of engagement still required visual identification before firing a missile. The major Navy advantage was probably better training at the service's Top Gun school in California. After the war, the Air Force would begin Red Flag exercises in Nevada to make training more realistic.[11]

Air-to-air combat in the Vietnam War was on a much smaller scale than it was in the Korean War, not to mention World War II, but the relative scarcity of aces did not make them bigger celebrities. Even within the Navy and the Air Force, less attention was paid to aces than to the more than five hundred Americans imprisoned in North Vietnam, most of them aviators who were shot down. The depth of concern led to a rescue attempt. In November 1970, U.S. Army soldiers in Air Force helicopters landed at Son Tay, west of Hanoi, but the prisoners who were being held there had been moved.[12]

While some fighter pilots were irked to see prisoners elevated above aces, the Red River Valley Fighter Pilots Association (pilots who had flown in route package 6 near Hanoi and Haiphong) held "practice reunions" in honor of the day when the prisoners would return. After their return, celebrity would continue for many. Four would receive the Medal of Honor for their service in the prison camps: Navy Commander James Stockdale and Air Force Major George "Bud" Day, who came home, and Air Force Captain Lance Sijan and Marine Captain Donald Cook, who did not. A fifth received the Medal of Honor for an action preceding captivity: Air Force Wild Weasel pilot Major Leo Thorsness. Twenty would become generals or admirals, and four would be elected to Congress, including Air Force Captain Douglas "Pete" Peterson (who would become the first U.S. ambassador to Hanoi in 1997) and Navy Lieutenant Commander John S. McCain III (whose father, Admiral John S. McCain Jr., was commander in chief, Pacific, during his son's imprisonment). The Nixon administration had used growing popular interest in the plight of the prisoners to bolster support for the war. Retrieving the prisoners became the most important war objective for many Americans.[13]

On October 23, 1972, when the North Vietnamese invasion had been halted and Kissinger thought he was close to a cease-fire agreement with the North Vietnamese, Nixon cut back the bombing of North Vietnam to the panhandle. With the arrival of the northeast monsoon, there would be little good bombing weather for six months. Following the bombing cutback and the election of a Congress hostile to funding the war, however, negotiations broke down. The South Vietnamese government resisted an agreement that would leave North Vietnamese forces in South Vietnam. The North Vietnamese also began to ask for more: linking North Vietnam's release of American prisoners of war to South Vietnam's release of communist prisoners;

banning American civilian technicians from South Vietnam (technicians necessary to maintain South Vietnam's aircraft); and weakening the definition of the demilitarized zone separating North Vietnam and South Vietnam.

Nixon broke the deadlock by sending B–52s against rail yards and other targets near Hanoi. This operation, called Linebacker II, lasted eleven nights from December 18 to December 30, excluding Christmas. While inadequate for precise bombing, the B–52's onboard radar system could not be defeated by darkness or bad weather. Rail yards were the principal targets, but Linebacker II was not an interdiction campaign. Linebacker II was intimidation. This was not a few fighter aircraft dropping a few tons of bombs in the Hanoi area from time to time as in Rolling Thunder or Linebacker, but rather more than two hundred B–52s dropping fifteen thousand tons of bombs in less than two weeks. Hanoi had seen nothing like the tonnage of bombs exploding close to the city each night, and Nixon did little to dissuade the American press from believing that the city was being destroyed. Since Nixon was already taking the political heat for Hanoi's destruction, there was reason for North Vietnam's leaders to fear that the B–52s might actually do so. Such fears were probably heightened by bombing errors that caused heavy damage to a residential street and a hospital. Altogether, some two thousand North Vietnamese died in Linebacker II.

The Air Force too paid in lives for Nixon's threat. North Vietnam's SA–2 SAMs eliminated fifteen B–52s. While five of those made it out of North Vietnam, twenty-seven crew members were presumed dead and thirty-four captured. The Air Force and the Navy lost eleven other aircraft with six aircrew killed and ten captured. Many B–52 crew members thought that the losses were excessive, and they blamed tactics prescribed by SAC headquarters in Omaha, Nebraska.[14]

Months earlier, SAC's initial experience in route package six had been reassuring. Nixon permitted eighteen B–52s to attack an oil tank farm in Haiphong before dawn on April 16. More than one hundred SAMs missed the B–52s, and the planes came home without a loss. That was the only B–52 strike in route package six before Linebacker II. After three B–52 losses on the first night of Linebacker II, there were none on the second night. Only on the third night, when six B–52s went down, was need to make changes obvious in Omaha.

The SAC commander, General John C. Meyer, had been a leading fighter ace in World War II, as had the more immediate boss of Linebacker II on Guam, Lieutenant General Gerald W. Johnson, commander of the Eighth Air Force. Johnson's principal subordinate in Thailand, Brigadier General Glenn Sullivan, had years of experience with B–52s and was relatively quick to advocate tactical changes. Meyer's first adaptation was to withdraw B–52Gs from bombing near Hanoi. Although newer and longer range than the B–52Ds, the B–52Gs carried fewer bombs and inferior electronic jamming equipment. Six of the nine B–52s lost on the first three nights of Linebacker II were B–52Gs.

The most important tactical change may have been to bring as many B–52s as possible over Hanoi in the shortest possible time. On each of the first three nights of Linebacker II, about a hundred B–52s had been divided into three waves arriving at four-hour intervals; each wave spent about thirty minutes within range of North Vietnamese missiles. Although six B–52s were lost on the third night, no single wave lost more than three. Before a wave passed beyond the range of any missile launcher, it was unlikely to fire more than one missile. When, on December 26, a single wave of more than one hundred B–52s bombed and left the target area in twenty minutes, the SAMs got just two B–52s. Through compression of three waves into one, SAC may have cut B–52 losses by as much as two-thirds.

SAC had made the original three-wave tactic even more vulnerable by sending each wave over the same route in cells of three B–52s—the same practice SAC had followed in South Vietnam, where communist air defenses were minimal. The route included a post-target turn into a headwind—a practice that carried over from preparing for nuclear strikes, when turning away from bomb detonation would be vital. The new compression tactics included a reduction in sharp post-target turns. Simultaneous streams of B–52s from different directions were separated by altitude. At the beginning of Linebacker II, SAC had been more concerned about its B–52s colliding with each other than about SAMs. The deadly success of the SAMs made compression tactics necessary.

An added advantage of a single wave per night was that Seventh Air Force F–4s could provide a chaff blanket for the single wave (but could not do so for three waves a night). Apparently less effective than the chaff blanket were the F–105 and F–4 Wild Weasels that sometimes received SAC plans too late for good coordination with the B–52s. Navy A–6s joined Air Force F–111s, F–4s, and B–52s in attacking SAM launch sites. Air Force A–7s bolstered the attack on SAM storage and assembly sites. Whether owing to these attacks or mostly to expenditure, the North Vietnamese seemed to run short of SAMs in the last two nights of Linebacker II.

North Vietnamese SAMs were more effective against the big, high-flying (above flak at more than thirty thousand feet), hard-to-maneuver B–52s than against fighter aircraft. North Vietnamese MiGs, on the other hand, were not effective at night, and raids on airfields by F–111s and B–52s may not have been necessary. At least the airfields were area targets reasonably well suited to B–52 bombing. Other targets such as the broadcast facility of Radio Hanoi were not suitable, and B–52s scattered bombs around the facility without effect. Finally, a break in the weather permitted F–4s with laser-guided bombs to destroy a transmitter, but they too were unsuccessful in keeping the propaganda broadcasts of Radio Hanoi off the air. An F–4 laser-guided strike on the Hanoi thermal power plant was more successful, and most of the lights in the city went out. One bomb failed to guide, however, and may have hit communist party headquarters. If so, that bomb was a harbinger of another role laser-guided bombs would play in future wars.[15]

Linebacker II did not require precise bombing. President Nixon wanted dramatic force to intimidate the North Vietnamese leaders and to reassure South Vietnamese leaders. In January 1973, the North Vietnamese leadership signed a cease-fire agreement not much different than the one they were ready to sign in October; the South Vietnamese government acquiesced, and in two months, nearly six hundred American prisoners of war came home. North Vietnam completed its conquest of South Vietnam two years later without opposition from American air power.

While casualty estimates vary, it is possible that more than 3 million Vietnamese soldiers and civilians on both sides were killed in the war, mostly in South Vietnam, but including perhaps 70,000 civilian deaths from bombing in North Vietnam; 58,000 Americans died, of whom about 1 percent died in North Vietnam. America's military commitment delayed for years the communist takeover of South Vietnam, Laos, and Cambodia, but that was all Americans had to show for so many lives and so much bombing.

The moral of this story is buried in an unanswerable question: how different would the war have been if, early in 1965, Navy aircraft had mined Haiphong and Air Force B–52s had bombed Hanoi? General LeMay, Admiral Sharp, General Momyer, and many other senior officers continued to think that the United States had missed the path to victory and instead adopted, in Admiral Sharp's words, a "strategy for defeat."[16] Younger officers, especially Air Force Major Mark Clodfelter, challenged their view that there could have been a strategy for victory. In his 1989 book, *The Limits of Air Power*, Clodfelter attacked the adherence of senior officers to strategic bombing in a "guerrilla war."[17] Both sides of this dispute could at least agree that the employment of laser-guided bombs to help thwart North Vietnam's conventional offensive in 1972 promised a brighter future for air power.

AIR SUPERIORITY IN THE ISRAEL-ARAB WARS, 1967–1982

Shmuel L. Gordon

⸺ How are the mighty fallen! The bow of Jonathan turned
not back, and the sword of Saul returned not empty.
They were swifter than eagles, they were stronger than lions.
How are the mighty fallen in the midst of the battle. ⸺

THE HOLY BIBLE, SAMUEL 2, CHAPTER 1

THE MOST IMPORTANT ROLE of air power in the course of its brief history has been achieving air superiority. That is one of the guiding principles of modern air forces and a key factor in the results of air campaigns and of entire wars. This chapter uses a methodology of comparative analysis of the developments and changes in successive campaigns for air superiority. It concentrates on the struggle for air superiority in four consecutive wars in the Middle East between Israel and its rivals in 1967–1982: the Six Days War, the War of Attrition, the Yom Kippur War, and the First Lebanon War. These wars were selected because numerous variables can be kept constant, such as geography, weather, political environment, and operational cultures. It focuses on the most vital battles in each war in order to derive meaningful conclusions.

Although the chapter incorporates Arab perceptions where possible, access to the archives of Egypt, Syria, and the other Arab states remains restricted. Consequently, data and interpretations are derived mainly from Western and Israeli documents and other sources. The sections on the War of Attrition and the Yom Kippur War are based on recent thorough and lengthy research.[1] The section on the First Lebanon War is drawn from an ongoing study that attempts to analyze the revolutions in technology and doctrines that followed the Yom Kippur War and have revived the ability of air power to gain freedom of action over the battlefield and beyond.[2]

FORMATIVE YEARS

Arab states and Israel have been in a state of war ever since Israel's birth in May 1948. This geostrategic environment has forced Israel to allocate a considerable share of its national budget and human resources to self-defense. Since its founding in 1948, the Israeli Air Force (IAF) has played an increasing role in the Israel Defense Forces (IDF).

The IAF was built on the basis of lessons learned by its commanders, who served in the Royal Air Force (RAF) during World War II. The roots of its strategy, doctrine, and war plans can be found in the doctrine and operations of the German air force (Luftwaffe) throughout the early years of the war.[3] Later on, the RAF and the U.S. Army Air Forces (USAAF) learned much from the Germans—for example, the loose flying formation in the tactical realm, the emphasis on airfield attacks, and the integration of air power into the ground campaign. Israeli pilots who had flown in the RAF inherited those concepts and adapted them to the IAF's unique situation and conditions.

Israel's perceptions regarding national security rested on a few basic assumptions. The main vulnerabilities were considered to be a relatively small population, a lack of strategic depth, a limited amount of natural resources, a lack of strategic early warning, and continuous and immediate threats to its existence. Israel's advantages included the high quality of its human resources, national cohesiveness, effective exploitation of its national power sources, and the support of Jewish people throughout the Western world.[4] Israel's strategy relied on existing buffer zones such as the Sinai Peninsula and the West Bank, military power for deterrence, capable early warning intelligence, rapid mobilization of reserves, decisive swift victory in the event of war, and preemptive attacks.

The IAF celebrated its birth in the middle of the War of Independence in 1948 by attacking armored Egyptian forces advancing toward Tel Aviv, the capital of the young state. A few months later, IAF pilots engaged in air combat against RAF pilots who took off from an Egyptian air base and shot down five of them without any losses.[5] Soon after, David Ben-Gurion, the legendary Israeli prime minister and defense minister, declared, "Our security depends on the air force. If it doesn't command the air, I am doubtful whether we will be able to mobilize our army; I am doubtful whether we will be able to fight. The first precondition is acquiring air superiority."[6] Ben-Gurion formulated the primary goals of the IAF: complete destruction of hostile air forces to achieve air superiority, support of ground and sea forces, and systematic destruction of strategic targets in enemy territory to degrade or destroy the enemy's capability and will to continue a war.[7] These roles have not changed significantly since then.[8]

The quantitative advantage of the Arab air forces was clear to the IAF planners. Thus, they developed a reasonable strategy to achieve air superiority by destroying the hostile air forces on the ground. The first operation order, *Zela*, was written in 1955, when Czechoslovakia signed a major agreement to equip the Egyptian Air Force (EAF) with hundreds of aircraft of various types and the army with hundreds of armored vehicles. *Zela*, the predecessor of *Moked*, the grand plan executed in the 1967 war, considered the EAF an especially severe threat that should be destroyed on the ground by a surprise attack.[9]

In 1956, Great Britain, France, and Israel initiated a joint campaign against Egypt to achieve different goals. At midnight on the day before the war broke out, General Abd El-Hakim Amar, the Egyptian minister of war, planned to fly back from Syria. An Israeli pilot scrambled to intercept his plane. His Meteor 13 NF closed in on General Amar's airplane and almost collided with it before shooting it down. The pilot recalled later, "We accomplished our mission in a frightening flight. Due to shortage of fuel the engines shut off immediately after touchdown. General Moshe Dayan, the IDF commander at the time, and General Dan Tolkowsky, the IAF commander, waited for us and told us that General Amar had decided to postpone his flight and sent his headquarters staff in the plane we shot down."[10] Amar lived another eleven years to witness the disastrous results of the 1967 war.

The RAF and the French air force gained air superiority over the battlefield. The IAF exploited it to concentrate on supporting IDF ground forces in their advance to the Suez Canal.[11]

An important Israeli conclusion from this conflict emphasized air and armored forces. Prior to the 1967 war, the IAF underwent a long process of modernizing its aircraft, logistics, early warning equipment, and operational doctrine. It purchased the best French technologies and weapons systems, and the embryonic Israeli defense industries developed essential technology such as electronic warfare systems.[12]

The IAF's operational culture rested on the conceptual foundation of an integrated campaign for air superiority.[13] General Moti Hod defined the most decisive factors as "simplicity in planning, high degree of discipline in executing operation orders by pilots, effective central C³I [command, control, communications, and intelligence], and accurate, timely intelligence."[14]

The first challenge the IAF encountered was an Egyptian initiative in February 1960 to deploy its forces close to the Israeli border. That event enabled the IAF to demonstrate its high degree of readiness and its deterrent effect against surprise threats, while ground forces required several days to deploy a few units along the border. The alarming incident, called *Rotem*, was considered a general rehearsal for dealing with the chain of events that led to the 1967 war.[15] It was followed by the surprise Egyptian deployment that triggered the Six Days War and by the surprise attack of the Yom Kippur War.[16]

During this period, the Soviet Union demonstrated its commitment to its proxies Egypt and Syria by supplying them with enormous numbers of aircraft, tanks, heavy artillery, surface-to-air missile (SAM) systems, other military systems, and logistics in case of war. This forever changed the geostrategic balance in the Middle East and shaped the IAF's dominant role in Israel's strategy for the Six Days War.

THE SIX DAYS WAR

Egypt, Syria, and Iraq identified themselves as allies of the Soviet Union and benefited from its unconditional political, military, and economic support.[17] Israeli policy also always emphasized the need to gain the support of a great power; thus, Israel had strengthened the close relations it had had with France since 1953. However, during the period of growing tension in May 1967, France withdrew its support as a result of the revolutionary shift in the policies of President Charles de Gaulle. Moreover, Israel failed to receive a formal commitment of assistance from the United States.

Ongoing hostilities on the Israeli-Syrian border throughout the 1960s did not change the nonviolent atmosphere on the Israeli-Egyptian border. Egypt was heavily involved in a conflict with Yemen, the buildup of its military power, and internal issues, and it was in Israel's national interest to avoid a conflict with two neighbors at the same time.[18] However, the growing intensity of the confrontations along the Syrian border ended with a series of air battles on April 7, 1967, in which six Syrian MiG–21s were shot down.[19] This demonstrated the IAF's preparedness and readiness as the drumbeat of the approaching war began to be heard. The IAF's operational culture awaited its second crucial ordeal.

Israel celebrated its nineteenth anniversary on May 14, 1967. Its national security assessment predicted that no war would break out for years to come. In the middle of the traditional parade in Jerusalem, the IDF commander, General Yitzhak Rabin, received a message that changed the history of the Middle East: the Egyptian army had crossed the Suez Canal and deployed in the Sinai Peninsula near the Israeli border. This strategic surprise to the Israeli leadership echoed that of 1960.[20] General Rabin stated, "The potential outcomes of the Egyptian surprise deployment are entirely dependent on the IAF readiness."[21] This failure of the Israeli intelligence community should be borne in mind when we deal with the surprise of the 1973 war.

At that time, Arab air forces enjoyed a significant quantitative advantage over the IAF. They were equipped with about six hundred fighters and bombers, twenty-seven SAM batteries, twenty-seven radars, and twenty-four airfields. The IAF arsenal included about one hundred modern fighters such as Mirages, Super Mystères, and Vautours, one hundred Mystères and Ouragans ("veterans" of the 1956 war), and a few dozen Fuga Magisters—vulnerable, slow, training planes, as well as five airfields, six radars, and four U.S.-made Hawk SAM batteries. The ratio of power in aircraft and pilots was three to one in favor of the Arabs; in SAM batteries, it was seven to one. These favorable ratios from the Arab point of view increased the impact of the unexpected results of the first day of the 1967 war (see table 6–1).

TABLE 6-1. BALANCE OF AIR FORCES IN THE SIX DAYS WAR

	Arab Air Forces	IAF	Force Ratio
Aircraft & bombers	594	203	2.9:1
Fighter pilots	715	235	3:1
SAM batteries	27	4	6.8:1
Radar sites	27	6	4.5:1
Airfields	24	5 ·	4.8:1
Runways	44	12	3.7:1

Note: The table refers to June 5, 1967, 0700. Note that only sixty Iraqi aircraft and bombers and sixty pilots assigned to the war and a few airfields were taken into account. Source: Abudi, *The IAF in the Six Days War*, taken from 6, 9, 15–17, 27, 30–32.

The quantities did not tell the entire story of the balance of power, however. The IAF emphasized power multipliers: mainly high-quality aircrews; an effective real-time C^3I network; high-quality, on-time operational planning; timely, accurate intelligence; and efficient logistics that enabled each serviceable aircraft to fly about four sorties a day. The three weeks between the first alert and the actual outbreak of war enabled the IAF to refine its plans, train its reserves, and prepare its aircraft.[22] By the time the war began, about 98 percent were armed and ready for takeoff, compared to the usual 60 percent.[23]

Within hours of the Egyptian deployment, the IAF announced a high alert, mobilized its reserves, initiated preparations for the predicted conflicts, and updated its primary war plan, *Moked*, to achieve air superiority. *Moked* had grown out of the IAF's operational culture, which emphasized quality over quantity, surprise, simplicity, concentration of forces, and swift offensive operations.[24] It preserved the principles and methods of its predecessor *Zela*. The process of developing, refining, and finalizing the "grand plan" had taken about seven years.[25] General Ezer Weizman, the IAF commander in 1958–1966, is considered the "father" of *Moked*. He encouraged the planners, allocated resources, increased training and exercises, and tried to prevent hostile intelligence organizations from discovering *Moked*'s existence so that planning could be completed.

Moked focused on destroying the enemy's air forces on the ground in a surprise attack, using all available aircraft. The surprise would rely on very low-level flights to avoid detection of the penetrating formations by early warning radar systems. The attackers would first destroy runways to prevent aircraft from taking off and then would strafe the hundreds of parked, defenseless fighters and bombers. Because the IAF lacked the aircrews and aircraft to attack all its targets at the same time, the first strike concentrated on the EAF's airfields and aircraft. Despite the vital need to disable early warning and control systems and threatening SAM batteries, these targets would be left to the subsequent waves so that the first wave could focus on its critical mission.

Moked seemed too ambitious for the tiny IAF:[26] planners assessed that it would take six to eight hours to execute the mission, with heavy losses of about 25 percent of the IAF fighters.[27] The risky plan assigned just twelve Mirages to defend the Israeli skies from possible counterattacks by the Syrian and Jordanian air forces as well as the EAF.[28]

The Arab air forces also prepared themselves for the coming war. Not surprisingly, the EAF developed war plans quite similar to the IAF's. Aware of the need for updated intelligence, the EAF carried out some successful reconnaissance flights over southern Israel that revealed the IDF's offensive deployment.[29] However, the Arab nations erred in their assessments of the IAF's capabilities and intentions, and the scenario for the first move. A lack of updated information and early warning, and a relatively low level of readiness meant that the EAF was far from prepared to implement its plans. The Syrian Air Force (SAF) commander, Hafez Assad (president of Syria during the 1973 and 1982 wars), had planned a very moderate operation owing to the SAF's small order of battle.

At the beginning of June, Moshe Dayan was appointed Israel's defense minister, and the IAF finished its preparations. Before dawn on June 5, IAF pilots awoke and were briefed on the decision to go to war. Their aircraft had been armed for days; all C³I posts were on alert. H-hour was set for 7:45 a.m., when the fog and haze over the Nile Delta airfields would evaporate and most high-ranking EAF officers would still be driving to their posts and could not be informed or given orders on how to respond.[30] First, a dozen Fuga trainers took off to simulate routine training activities. Immediately thereafter, all the serviceable IAF aircraft took off and flew southwest below Egyptian radar coverage, maintaining communication silence, heading almost directly to their various targets in order to save precious fuel.

The first wave achieved complete surprise and produced astonishing results. The pilots who climbed to higher altitudes saw lines and lines of MiGs, undefended, dispersed, and unaware of the approaching attack. After bombing the runways, the IAF aircraft strafed and destroyed the MiGs one by one. Each formation added to the growing number of burning aircraft on the ground. About 190 Egyptian aircraft were destroyed, among them most of the bombers, which were considered the highest priority targets. The IAF lost eight aircraft and ten pilots in this first wave, which included 180 sorties.

Because the EAF was still functional and other air forces had not yet reacted, another wave was executed against the EAF, while some sorties assisted the attacking ground forces. The second wave complemented the achievements of the first, but some tasks remained.

Since noon, the SAF, the Jordanian air force, and the Iraqi air force had penetrated Israeli borders about ten times. The IAF shifted some of its formations from Egypt to those air forces and attacked them using the same tactics, with similar success. That day, the IAF destroyed 402 Arab aircraft (see table 6–2). The IAF also suffered severe losses: twenty-one pilots (almost 9 percent of the fighter pilots) were killed, captured, or wounded, and twenty-eight aircraft (over 13 percent of the total force) were lost.[31] The IAF had accomplished its mission and gained substantial air superiority. But the war was not yet over.

The general conclusion drawn by most who have studied the Six Days War—that the IAF achieved victory in about three hours—is incorrect.[32] In fact, the last aircraft returned to base at 7:00 p.m., twelve hours after the first takeoff. The campaign

TABLE 6-2. LOSSES OF THE ARAB AIR FORCES IN OPERATION MOKED

	Total	Egypt	Syria	Jordan	Iraq	Lebanon
Aircraft & bombers	342	244	63	25	9	1
Cargo & helicopters	66	54	6	5	1	
Total losses	402	298	63	30	10	1
Radar sites	5+26*	5+26*				
SAM batteries	1+9*	1+9*				

* Captured
Source: Abudi, *The IAF in the Six Days War*, 6.

for air superiority continued throughout the day and did not complete the overall mission.[33] In other words, the IAF did not destroy the fleet of three Arab air forces in one brief attack.

Another conclusion—that the battle for air superiority included only attacks on airfields—is also erroneous. The struggle for air superiority shifted to air-to-air battles, which continued throughout the next few days. The severely damaged EAF scrambled frequently to defend its retreating ground forces. In spite of its inferior numbers, it fought bravely until the fifth day of the war, when the number of encounters dwindled and the total number of Arab sorties decreased to seventeen from more than ninety the day before.[34] At that point, Israel had achieved air superiority and victory on the ground in the Sinai Peninsula, the Golan Heights, and the West Bank.

Moreover, the Egyptian command, control, and early warning systems remained operational by the end of the first day and were effective in helping to intercept IAF aircraft. It therefore became necessary to eliminate them, and Israel succeeded in destroying or capturing most of the sites west of the Suez Canal.

The 1967 war was the first in the ongoing confrontation between aircraft and missiles. Egypt had purchased and deployed twenty-seven Soviet-made SA–2 batteries for the purpose of defending the Nile Delta, the Suez Canal, and the routes to the heartland. Air forces had no experience in suppressing SAM batteries, but the deployed SA–2 batteries threatened IAF operations and had marginally challenged its air superiority. Thus, following the airfield attacks, a battle against SAM batteries took place. The EAF deployed heavy antiaircraft guns around the SAM batteries for short-range defense, which caused the loss of two IAF aircraft. Nine SAM batteries were destroyed, and one battery was captured intact (see table 6–3).

TABLE 6-3. SORTIES FOR AIR SUPERIORITY MISSIONS IN THE SIX DAYS WAR

Mission Days	Airfield Attacks	Interception	SAM and Radar Attack Missions		Total
			Main	Secondary*	
First day	475		32	55	
Other days	16		36	24	
Total	491	554	68	79	1,113

*Secondary mission executed after the main mission.
Source: Abudi, *The IAF in the Six Days War*, 486.

The qualitative advantage of the IAF pilots has become legendary, but the results of this war should temper that judgment somewhat. Fifty-six Arab fighters and bombers (and three transport aircraft) were lost in air-to-air combat as opposed to eighteen Israeli planes.[35] The kill ratio of three to one (more than three Arabs for each Israeli) favored the IAF, but considering its expectations, such a ratio was somewhat disappointing.

The formidable success of the counter-airfield campaign has led historians and analysts to overlook the importance of the other vital missions for gaining air superiority, such as attacks on SAM batteries and C³I arrays, and air-to-air combat. Over one-half of the IAF's total sorties were assigned to air superiority missions—1,100 sorties, 560 of them air-to-air missions. The IAF suffered heavy losses in gaining air superiority: more than 11 percent of its fighter pilots were killed, wounded, or captured, and more than 12 percent of its aircraft were lost.[36] However, the victories in the air and on the ground and the declaration by IDF commander General Rabin that the astounding results of the IAF's operations had determined the fate of the war had a mitigating effect on those losses.[37]

The IAF operational culture created the abstract infrastructure of the integrated campaign for air superiority.[38] General Hod explained, "Most decisive factors defined: simplicity in planning, high degree of discipline in executing operation orders by pilots, effective central C³I, and accurate, updated intelligence."[39]

Studies and research have also misinterpreted the actions and significance of integrated Egyptian air defense systems, which revealed modern thinking and an unsuspected defensive strategy. Israel claimed that because the Egyptian army had crossed the canal in mid-May 1967 and Egyptian president Abdul Nasser intended to attack, Israel had to initiate a preemptive offensive because of its lack of strategic depth. Did the EAF deployment support this assumption? The answer is rather ambiguous. Most MiG–21 interceptors were deployed deep in the delta, at locations from which they could defend the Suez Canal and westward because of their short range. The SAM batteries, and most of the early warning radar systems, were also dispersed in the delta and near the Suez Canal and could not defend the ground forces in the Sinai Peninsula. Thus, the entire Egyptian deployment of air defense systems reveals a defensive strategy rather than an offensive one. Any Egyptian ground offensive would be executed under hostile skies and exposed to relentless IAF attacks. It seems that assumptions regarding Egyptian offensive intentions and capabilities require fresh and thorough analysis.[40]

The Six Days War is widely considered a swift, victorious war in which Israel destroyed the armies and air forces of the surrounding nations. It captured new territories, demonstrated its military power, gained U.S. support, and eliminated the main threats to its existence. The fragility of these results became apparent in only a few years.

THE WAR OF ATTRITION, 1969–1970

The Six Days War triggered military, social, and political crises in the Arab states.[41] It led to radical changes in their armed forces and strengthened their dependence on their patron, the Soviet Union, which rearmed Egypt and Syria with advanced military equipment within a few months and provided unwavering political support. The Soviet Union exploited the weaknesses of the defeated countries to increase its involvement in the Middle East. Its policy of restraint would change radically to become one of direct involvement to avoid the likelihood that its clients would suffer another defeat.

The United States also increased its involvement in the ongoing conflict by supporting Israel politically, militarily, and economically. Henry Kissinger, the national security adviser to President Richard Nixon, believed that Israel might play a key role in the "Nixon Doctrine," which sought to reduce direct U.S. military participation in regional conflicts.[42] Thus, the War of Attrition is often characterized as one between the proxies of the great powers who controlled and regulated the height of the flames and brought the conflict to an end when they realized the situation threatened the progress of détente.

Many studies deal with the background and various aspects of the War of Attrition.[43] Despite its victory in the 1967 war, the IAF found itself smaller and weaker than ever. The force had experienced its first technological revolution before the 1956 war, when France equipped Israel with aircraft and other modern systems, but most of its aircraft had become obsolete and were not suitable for another all-out war. As it happened, those aircraft played no role in the forthcoming air superiority campaign. Only sixty Mirages remained serviceable for the imminent long struggle for air superiority in the War of Attrition.[44] The United States acted quickly to make up for this shortage, and the IAF would embark on its second technological revolution when it replaced most of its French-made weapons systems with U.S. aircraft, helicopters, munitions, radars, and other equipment.

Egyptian president Nasser adopted the view that the strategy of all-out war should be changed, but that political achievements required military activity. Therefore, he implemented a strategy of attrition that could increase international pressure on Israel and would hit the Israelis where they were most vulnerable: inflicting human casualties.[45] His minister of war, General Mahmud Fauzi, summarized the goals of the

War of Attrition as killing as many Israeli soldiers as possible, acquiring operational experience, and initiating consecutive air battles with the IAF.[46] Had he foreseen the results of those encounters, he would probably have avoided them.

The Soviets agreed with Nasser's new strategy, and on March 3, 1969, Nasser declared that the cease-fire had ended. Egyptian artillery shelled the eastern bank of the Suez Canal around the clock. Soon after, Syria and the Palestinian terrorist organizations located in Jordan joined the war.

The IDF could find no effective response to the continuous, intense Egyptian bombardment, and the number of casualties grew daily. During this time, the IAF was busily incorporating U.S.-made Skyhawks, Phantoms, CH–53 cargo helicopters, missiles, radars, and various other weapons systems into its operational force. General Hod favored preparing for probable future wars over arming for involvement in such a limited conflict, but pressure from his superiors in the IDF and the government impelled him to take part in the battle.

The aerial War of Attrition formally began on July 20, 1969, and ended at midnight on August 8–9, 1970. Israel's first aerial attack struck Egyptian posts and artillery along the Suez Canal. Formations of interceptors defended the attacking aircraft. This was the first scene of a Greek tragedy that led to ruinous consequences for both sides.

In reality, the aerial war had begun about a month earlier. The first mission was to acquire freedom of action over the canal. The IAF had destroyed SAM sites that defended the Egyptian artillery and executed air combat to push MiG–21 patrols westward. After a month of strikes and dogfights, the IAF had achieved adequate air superiority and began relentless aerial bombardments of Egyptian ground forces. This pressure achieved marginal success in reducing the number of IDF casualties from the artillery shelling. Consequently, the Israeli government decided to escalate the fighting, following a plan for deep operations named *Priha*. First, the IAF destroyed most of the SAM sites that surrounded Cairo, shot down dozens of MiGs, and achieved limited air superiority over the Nile Delta up to Cairo, whose environs were attacked frequently.

Thus, Egypt found itself in a new crisis just two and a half years after the Six Days War. It had lost air superiority over essential territory, was exposed to IAF attacks anywhere, and could neither prevent them nor retaliate. However, the interim military success of *Priha's* deep operations did not meet the unofficial goal of Israeli prime minister Golda Meir, who had expected Nasser's resignation.[47] In fact, *Priha* brought about an unexpected, dangerous response. President Nasser, left with no alternatives, flew to Moscow on January 3, 1970, and begged the Kremlin leaders immediately to implement a well-prepared plan to deploy Soviet air defense forces in Egypt and to assume responsibility for defending the Egyptian skies.

In a few months, the Soviets covertly deployed a comprehensive air defense system. It consisted of dozens of SAM batteries, mostly SA–3s and their upgraded version, SA–2Es, seventy-two brand-new MiG–21s, some radar systems for early warning and control, a C³I network, and logistics. These forces were operated and commanded by Soviet manpower: pilots, SAM operators, controllers, technicians, and commanders, about fifteen thousand personnel in all.

The Soviets had devised a prudent, cautious strategy. At the beginning, they deployed SAM batteries around Cairo and deterred Israel from deep attacks. As they assumed greater responsibility for air defense of the delta, the Soviet forces gradually advanced to regain air superiority over the delta and the Suez Canal. At the same time, three Soviet interceptor squadrons were deployed at air bases south of Cairo and assumed responsibility for air defense of the southern flank of the SAM battery. They were ordered not to cross the canal under any circumstances.[48]

The IAF carefully assessed this unanticipated situation. Fighting against a super-power was risky, both militarily and politically. The Israeli government limited the IAF's role to retaining air superiority over the canal and about thirty kilometers west-ward to defend ground forces deployed along the east bank of the Suez Canal. A heated, continuous campaign had erupted between the advancing Soviet SAM array and the opposing IAF pilots. Both sides fought bravely and persistently, using every means at their disposal, and the mighty Soviet forces moved forward slowly but inexorably.

In the face of the Soviets' dominance in electronic warfare, neither Israel nor the United States had any countermeasures to protect the tiny fleet of Phantoms, the newcomers to the IAF. The United States, deeply involved in Vietnam at the time, had no wish for a direct confrontation with the Soviets but did provide Israel with technical advisers and sophisticated electronic systems, neither of which proved effective.

Strategists and historians broadly characterize the aerial War of Attrition as a conflict between SAM systems and aircraft, but the situation was far more con-voluted. Another campaign, attracting less notice but no less intensive, crucial, and imperative, occurred in the skies over both sides of the Suez Canal. Both air forces recognized the importance of air-to-air warfare. As noted earlier, the Egyptian minister of war considered it a means of restoring the confidence of his officers. On the other side, the IAF had emphasized air combat in its training and drills, built its C³I system to meet the unique requirements of that type of warfare, and relied on the lessons learned from the previous war and subsequent combat. Consequently, the IAF considered air combat a valuable means to gain air superiority over enemy territory.

As Soviet pilots began to patrol the southern flank of the SAM network, Israel decided to avoid engagements because of potential political implications and the risk of military escalation. Noting the withdrawal of the IAF's Mirages and Phantoms, the Soviet pilots and their commanders became bold and adventurous. One day, two Soviet pilots chasing a Skyhawk attack aircraft crossed the canal, launched an Atoll air-to-air missile, and slightly hit the plane. The Israeli government decided to meet the challenge and clarify its red lines.[49]

General Moti Hod, well known for his ability to organize air engagements and command them in real time, had learned the Soviets' flying routines, their reactions to IAF flights, and other potentially useful patterns. His staff then planned an operation that could serve as a model for the planning and execution of air battles. On July 30, 1970, he sent a seemingly innocent reconnaissance formation as bait deep into Egypt. Between sixteen and twenty Soviet MiG–21s scrambled toward the ostensibly helpless formation and flew into the trap of an IAF ambush. All of a sudden, Phantoms and Mirages appeared from different directions and engaged the MiGs. The reconnaissance aircraft—which in fact were interceptors—also turned on the MiGs. The Soviet pilots found themselves in an elaborate trap that led to five losses the most severe defeat inflicted on Soviet pilots since World War II. The leader of the bait formation, which suffered no losses, later wrote a detailed description of this historic encounter.[50]

That decisive air battle, from a tactical point of view, was not repeated because of Soviet and Israeli mutual interests and tacit agreement. Moscow, realizing that U.S. policy might change, persuaded President Nasser to accept a cease-fire. Defense Minister Dayan was deterred from further operations, and the Israeli government, recognizing the sensitivity of the political situation, avoided subsequent engagements with the Soviets.

Nevertheless, the fate of the integrated campaign had been decided elsewhere. Along the Suez Canal, IAF pilots were killed, wounded, or captured while trying to halt the eastward advance of Soviet SAM batteries. The IAF was left with no adequate operational or technological responses. President Richard Nixon, on whom Israel depended strongly in the face of the Soviet threat, compelled Israel to avoid an escalation that might force him to intervene actively in the heated conflict and to accept the offer of a cease-fire. At midnight on August 8–9, 1970, after 385 days of a relentless aerial war, the battles ended.[51]

In the course of the aerial War of Attrition, the IAF carried out a total of 12,500 sorties, 10,500 of them against Egypt. During the same period, the EAF executed only 540 sorties that crossed the Suez Canal. The IAF attacked about seven hundred air defense targets and lost eleven aircraft to SAMs and antiaircraft artillery (AAA).[52] The EAF lost nineteen aircraft to Israeli AAA and SAM batteries.[53]

The results of the aerial battles astonished both sides. Egypt lost seventy-three aircraft, whereas Israel lost only four.[54] The kill ratio in air combats had changed significantly since the 1967 war: it was now eighteen to one in favor of the IAF. No less impressive was another result: Egypt had received five hundred new aircraft after the 1967 war and lost ninety-two of them (over 18 percent) during the War of Attrition.[55] These results illuminate the tactical dimension of the air engagements, although the strategic consequences were rather different.

Some important lessons can be drawn from the War of Attrition. As is clear, it comprised two integrated campaigns for air superiority: the battle between the mighty Soviet-Egyptian SAM systems and the IAF aircraft, and, no less important, the air-to-air battles.

The critical factor in the outcome of the War of Attrition was the active involvement of the Soviet armed forces, which played a dominant role in the SAM systems campaign against IAF aircraft and constituted a plausible threat to Israel's existence. Before the Soviet Union deployed its forces in Egypt, the IAF had gained air superiority from the Suez Canal to Cairo. As the Soviets employed operational units, they slowly but surely regained air superiority over the delta, the canal, and beyond. For the first time in Israel's history, a cease-fire had become the only viable alternative.

Another lesson concerns the influence of the different strategies and technologies used by the rivals, which characterized the differences between the Warsaw Pact and the North Atlantic Treaty Organization (NATO) strategies. The Soviet Union had developed, produced, and deployed huge, modern, sophisticated SAM defenses, and its advanced electronic technology surpassed the U.S. countermeasures at the time. This Soviet defensive concept was to raise the question whether the Eastern Bloc in Europe and the Middle East had developed a defensive rather than an offensive concept of operations, contrary to NATO's annual strategic assessments.

The Western concept of air superiority was based mainly on using aircraft for offensive and defensive missions. However, the War of Attrition ended with undeniable results: the Soviet concept, technologies, and soldiers won the battle between aircraft and missiles, even though the United States assisted Israel with its most advanced electronic countermeasures (ECM).

The air-to-air campaign revealed several different shifts that can be captured in a few numbers. As noted, despite the destruction of a considerable part of the Arab air forces in the 1967 war, the kill ratio was only three to one in favor of the IAF. During the War of Attrition, this was multiplied by six. Most of the combat in both wars involved the same types of interceptors; only a few involved U.S.-made Phantoms, which were equal to the Mirage and MiG–21 in daylight combat. Equality in weapons systems implies that the operational culture and quality of pilots, commanders, and intelligence officers were the decisive factors of the growing IAF advantage, but this assumption must be thoroughly evaluated.

The cease-fire did not really end the war. Despite Israeli and U.S. expectations, the Soviet-Egyptian air defense forces completed their mission after the cease-fire and moved forward to the western edge of the Suez Canal. Within twenty-four hours, approximately fifty SAM batteries were dispersed there and gained air superiority about fifteen miles deep in the Sinai Peninsula. This "unfair" forward deployment shaped the partial victory of the integrated Soviet-Egyptian power and the circumstances surrounding the beginning of the next conflict—the Yom Kippur War.[56]

THE YOM KIPPUR WAR

The Yom Kippur War in October 1973 encompassed a series of operations to gain air superiority.[57] The most decisive battles, which are the focus of this section, transpired during the first two days following the Arab surprise offensive, from the outbreak of war on October 6 at 1:50 p.m. until the evening of October 7.

Several studies of the 1973 war were written before enough information had been disclosed by the belligerent nations and by the two great powers that manipulated their proxies before, during, and after the war.[58] Most of these studies did not thoroughly examine the air campaigns and did not reach conclusions useful to knowledgeable readers. Some of them concentrated on the battle between SAMs and aircraft, and neglected the other, no less important, clash in the air. This section attempts to present new data and insights, and evaluates the crucial influence of the decisions made regarding the battle for air superiority.

The war was intended to fulfill the limited political-strategic goals of President Anwar Sadat: to capture a thin strip of the eastern bank of the Suez Canal and to destroy the IDF's armored divisions by exploiting the advantage of air superiority over the canal.[59] As in previous conflicts, the Arab air forces enjoyed significant advantages in force ratio and the balance of power. They had three times more aircraft than the IAF, four times the helicopters, fifteen times the SAM batteries, and twenty-two times the radar sites (see table 6–4). Recognizing the limitations of the EAF vis-à-vis the IAF beyond the SAM umbrella, the EAF commander, General Hosni Mubarak (who later became president of Egypt), planned a classic surprise aerial attack. The

EAF's plan was based upon mass, surprise, and focused on essential military targets such as airfields, radars, intelligence sites, and SAM batteries. The SAF's plan was very limited but quite similar in timing, size, performance, and results.

TABLE 6-4. AIR FORCES IN THE YOM KIPPUR WAR

Systems	EAF, SAF, & Iraq	IAF	Force Ratio
Fighters & surveillance	1,410	390	3.6:1
Helicopters	320	70	4.6:1
SAM batteries	182	12	15.2:1
Cargo planes	85	46	1.8:1
Fighter pilots	735	650	1.1:1
Airfields	56	12	4.7:1
Shelters	780	400	1.95:1
Radar sites	445	20	22.2:1

Source: Most of the data appear in Haim Nadel, *Between Two Wars (1967–1973)* (Tel Aviv: Maarhot, 2006), attachment E, 290. For the data on the IAF aircraft and helicopters, see Head of Logistics Department IAF, *Data on Activities: The Yom Kippur War—The Logistics System* (Tel Aviv: IAF headquarters, 1974); for data on the SAM batteries, see Yossi Abudi, "Comparing Tagar and Dugman," *Essays Collection* 2 (The Fisher Institute for Air and Space Strategic Studies, October 2005), 8–9.

Countless memoirs and studies of the Yom Kippur War conclude that Egypt and Syria achieved a complete surprise attack, that Israel received only a few hours' early warning,[60] and that this was the main factor in the bloodshed inflicted on the IDF at the beginning of the war and thereafter.[61] Actually, the true story of the IAF was different. Its headquarters had begun intensive preparations ten days before war actually started on October 6. The IAF mobilized reserves, increased readiness, and updated operations orders. Exactly twenty-four hours before the war began, IAF commander General Beni Peled assembled his high-ranking officers for a decisive briefing. He overruled intelligence assessments, gave a strong warning that a war would break out the next day, and ordered that the IAF complete preparations for a preemptive strike on the Syrian SAM array in the Golan Heights.[62] On the morning of Yom Kippur, he estimated that hostilities would begin at 3:00 p.m.—three hours earlier than the intelligence predicted.[63] Thus, the IAF did receive timely warning that enabled it to prepare itself in advance, but because of last-minute changes of orders given by its commander, General Peled, it was definitely surprised when the war broke out an hour before General Peled had predicted.[64] General Shazly, the Egyptian army commander, recalled,

> The clocks on the wall of the operations room showed 1:50 p.m., the telephones on the command table rang as the air bases reported "ready for takeoff." I imagined seeing the aircraft move slowly from the darkness of their shelters to the light of the runways, bombs on their wings. Then, the roars of their engines as they accelerate on the runways. At 2:00 p.m. on the dot, 200 aircraft crossed the canal in low-level flight on their way to their targets, deep in Sinai.[65]

At the same time, a Syrian coordinated surprise attack swept the Golan Heights. Both attacks found the IAF unprepared because of last-minute wrong decisions. As a result, in the remaining three daylight hours, the IAF concentrated on defending the skies over the fronts and deep in Israel, attacking penetrating ground forces, and providing close air support (CAS) to outnumbered ground forces on the borders. However, the well-coordinated aerial surprise offensives of the EAF and the SAF caused only marginal damage to the IDF ground forces (damage that would be repaired during the coming night). The EAF targeted dozens of military objectives but succeeded in destroying only one radar site with a Kelt long-range antiradar missile (see table 6–5).

In contrast to the poor results of the aerial surprise attacks, the huge Egyptian and Syrian ground forces attained most of their goals. During the night and the following day, the Egyptian army crossed the Suez Canal, deployed five divisions on

TABLE 6-5. EAF AND SAF SORTIES ON OCTOBER 6, 1973

Mission	EAF	SAF	Total
Attack missions	134	85	219
Cross-border interceptions	70	104	174
Assault missions	48	11	59
Total that crossed the border	250	200	450
Air defense missions (estimate)	200	100	300
Total	450	300	750

Source: Yizhak Shteigman, *The IAF in the Defensive Phase: October 6–7 1973* (Tel Aviv: IAF headquarters, 1976), Logistics Department.

the eastern bank, and destroyed most of the IDF armored division that defended this front. At the same time, Syrian armored forces captured the southern flank of the Golan Heights, obliterating the defending force and threatening the Israeli heartland.

By the end of October 6, decision makers were divided in their assessments of the missions for the IAF on the next day. Defense Minister Dayan said, "Tomorrow, the IAF will face a grave and rigorous challenge. We need a lot of success in order to safely complete the battle of tomorrow."[66] The IDF commander, General David Elazar (Dado), commented optimistically, "That is the day for the IAF."[67]

Since the crossing of the canal was (erroneously) considered the most threatening attack, the IAF was ordered to destroy the Egyptian air defenses first. During the night, the IAF finished preparations for the next morning's operations. The dawn of October 7 saw Arab successes on the Sinai and the Golan Heights, which imposed constraints on the IAF. General Shazly concluded, "On the morning of the seventh the crossing of the canal proved victorious. The four Israeli brigades that defended the 'Bar-Lev Line' were actually destroyed. The enemy has lost its tactical armor units."[68] The commander of the IDF Southern Command, General Shmuel Gonen (Gorodish), a hero of the 1967 war, reported to General Elazar that only thirty to forty tanks remained intact.[69]

The IAF's primary goal remained gaining air superiority over the battlefields, while at the same time defending the homeland skies and providing CAS to the ground forces. Squadrons received their operations orders; aircraft were armed with bombs, missiles, and ECM; pilots were briefed; and C³I sites were updated. The IAF was ready for action, but again the leadership made the wrong decisions.

Before the war, the IAF had prepared several strategic and operational plans to eliminate SAM systems. Two of the plans, *Tagar* 4 and 5, focused on Egypt. One plan, to be activated in case of surprise, aimed at attacking the missile sites first, to achieve a decisive advantage immediately. The other, which considered AAA as the most serious threat to the penetrating aircraft, targeted this threat first and delayed attacking SAM sites until the second wave about four hours later. In addition, following IAF tradition, about half of the sorties were assigned to airfield attacks.[70]

Despite the desperate situation of the IDF ground forces on both fronts, the IAF headquarters adhered to the second plan and prioritized AAA and airfield targets in the first wave. No SAM sites were attacked on the morning of October 7. The Egyptian air defense commanders and operators could scarcely believe that a fleet of Israeli aircraft, flying in an apparently concentrated attack, did not drop any bombs on their vulnerable sites. This course of action did not represent a failure of the airmen or of the IAF doctrine or preparedness, but rather was caused by misguided, inexplicable decisions that prevented any possibility of success that day and delayed gaining air superiority over the Egyptian front for at least two weeks. Operation *Tagar* left the most important target—the SAM systems—intact, while enemy airfields and AAA suffered only marginal damage.[71]

Operation *Tagar* is considered a failure. The operation fostered deep disappointment among tactical- and operational-level officers alike. The decision by IAF headquarters to direct their forces at AAA and airfields prevented Israeli pilots from winning a battle for which they had been preparing for years.[72] This bad decision should shift analysis of the air campaign in a new direction: from the comparison between the technological capabilities of aircraft and missiles and the opposing doctrines toward the area of decision making.

The failure of Operation *Tagar* appears marginal compared to the unforgettable defeat that the IAF experienced a few hours later. By 1:00 a.m. on October 7, the situation on the Golan Heights had deteriorated. General Yzhak Hofi, the commander of the Northern Command, repeatedly sent urgent warnings. Early in the morning, Dayan flew to the battlefield to make his own assessment. Almost immediately, he witnessed the collapse of the southern sector close to his home village. He telephoned General Beni Peled personally and asked him to increase the CAS missions to the depleted forces. Books and articles report that the defense minister ordered the IAF commander to terminate Operation *Tagar* in the south immediately and to shift forces to attack the Syrian SAM systems, but recordings of this discussion make it obvious that Dayan demanded more CAS sorties and did not mention the counter-SAM *Tagar* operation. But the IAF attack aircraft were already directed to this mission. This information makes an important contribution to research and debate on Dayan's role and decisions during those days and is even more important in helping to comprehend the decision-making process regarding the next operation: *Dugman*.

General David Elazar, the IDF commander, recognized the strategic change in the situation and discussed the issue with General Peled soon afterward. Later that morning, he came to the IAF command cell a few minutes before H-hour of Operation *Tagar*, as more than one hundred aircraft hit their targets. After a brief consultation with Peled, he ordered the general to end the operations against the Egyptian air defense and airfields and to begin Operation *Dugman* against the Syrians' advance SAM systems, which had been deployed along the Syrian front. Neither staff work nor a situational assessment had been carried out prior to this decision; in fact, he made the decision far away from his staff and advisers, and the IAF commander ignored alternatives suggested by some of his senior officers.

Analysts as well as veterans often conclude that this decision was the primary reason for the next failure, but this conclusion is largely wrong. The failure resulted mainly from subsequent operational and tactical decisions. During the final phase of the War of Attrition, Soviet SA–3 batteries changed their positions under cover of darkness and deployed devastating ambushes against IAF attack formations. In addition, the Soviet Union had given Syria the most advanced mobile SA–6, which could change its position in a few minutes. The IAF learned this lesson and incorporated a new precondition for attack into its doctrine and operations orders: preliminary reconnaissance sorties to locate the recent positions of hostile batteries before executing any counter-SAM operations.[73]

Because of bad weather and other reasons, the results of early reconnaissance flights the previous day proved disappointing. The IAF concentrated on the Egyptian front, and therefore no reconnaissance missions were carried out on the morning of October 7 over the Syrian front. General Peled was informed that most of the SAM batteries had moved to new, unknown positions. Both doctrine and the limited updated intelligence of experienced operational planners required a preliminary reconnaissance mission before launching an attack.

However, owing to the revolutionary change in operational plans, that mission was not executed and the backbone of the IAF took off toward abandoned sites. The IAF had decided to strike the Syrian air defenses almost immediately despite General Elazar's permission to accomplish the required preparations for the complicated, hazardous Operation *Dugman*.

As the smoke and fire over the battlefield evaporated following this operation, results unexpected by either side were revealed. The shock for the IAF came from the failure to destroy the Syrian air defenses. Of the twenty-five sites attacked by the IAF, only one SAM battery was destroyed. Six Phantoms were shot down, ten others were heavily damaged, and eleven Israeli pilots were killed or captured.[74] However, this number of casualties had been expected. Strangely, no aircraft were lost or damaged by missiles; they were hit by AAA as they executed low-level flights to and from the targets in order to avoid missiles.

Those decisions—to attack too quickly, without necessary intelligence—coupled with others, determined the results of the air battles against the Syrian and Egyptian SAM systems. The Syrian SAM defense retained its advantage throughout the war. The Egyptians suffered heavy losses later in the war and lost air superiority over the battlefield after a brave, skillful campaign. The IAF's brief official history praised the effective fighting of the Syrian and Egyptian air defense forces at the outbreak of the 1973 war.[75] The failure of Operations *Tagar* and *Dugman* resulted mainly from bad decisions rather than from the new technological capabilities of air defense systems.[76]

General Ezer Weizman, former IAF commander and later president of Israel, declared, "The IAF did not overcome the Syrian and Egyptian SAM arrays on time. *The missile has bent the aircraft's wings* in this war. This fact should be analyzed very closely in order to deduce essential lessons."[77] His subsequent recommendations directed the IAF's policy toward the next conflict.

Despite this focus on missiles versus aircraft, the struggle for air superiority at the beginning of the war included another extensive campaign that most historians of the 1973 war tend to overlook: the battle in the air. Since the EAF and the SAF had learned the lessons of the 1967 war regarding the vulnerability of airfields and aircraft on the ground, they had built hundreds of aircraft shelters and multiplied their number of airfields and runways. The IAF's opportunity to repeat a blow similar to Operation *Moked* had vanished. Therefore, air battles became more significant in creating freedom of action on both fronts.

Weapons systems for air-to-air warfare had marginally improved since the War of Attrition. However, the advantage of the quality of Israel's human resources continued to improve. The IAF's advantage in previous wars had changed the Arab concept of operations. Generally speaking, the Arab air forces had preferred to preserve their air forces rather than risk them confronting the IAF.[78] Only once, during the surprise attack of the 1973 war, did they dare to use their air forces to attack dozens of IDF installations. The heavy losses and poor results of that offensive reinforced their previous conclusion.

Throughout the first thirty hours, the air forces reversed their roles in the 1967 war. The EAF and SAF took the initiative and attacked targets in the Sinai and the Golan Heights. The IAF reacted immediately and defensively despite the lack of tactical early warning. Seventy-six Arab aircraft and helicopters and two Kelt air-to-ground missiles were shot down, with no IAF losses to enemy aircraft.[79] Consequently, the Arab air forces ceased to play a significant offensive role in the war. Nevertheless, owing to the limited area controlled by surface-to-air defense and the IAF's relentless offensive strikes, the Arab armed forces had to employ their aircraft defensively, and they suffered hundreds of losses during the war.

The IDF, meanwhile, was caught by surprise: its reserves did not even mobilize until the war had broken out. Its regular forces did not deploy in time and suffered crucial losses. The critical situation on the ground forced the tiny IAF (three hundred serviceable aircraft) to divide its force among various vital missions (see table 6–6). Thus, it could not exploit the principle of concentration of forces. The IAF played a significant role in the ground battles mainly on the northern front; it succeeded in preventing airstrikes against both civilians and armed forces and in deterring hostile air forces from strategic strikes against the nation's centers of gravity.

TABLE 6-6. IAF SORTIES IN THE FIRST THIRTY HOURS OF THE YOM KIPPUR WAR

Targets	Against Egypt	Against Syria	Total	Percentage of the Total
SAMs & AAA	78	113	191	16.4
Airfields	47	-	47	4.0
Air defense	320	128	448	38.6
Total air superiority	445	241	686	59.0
Ground forces	340	129	469	40.4
Total	785	377	1,162	100.0
Percentage of the total	67.6	32.4	100	

Source: Yizhak Shteigman, *The IAF in the Defensive Phase: October 6–7 1973* (Tel Aviv: IAF headquarters, 1976), Logistics Department, 12–13.

The first phase of the war shaped the characteristics of the battles for air superiority throughout the Yom Kippur War. Neither the IAF's massive operations against the dense SAM arrays nor the Arab air forces' offensive operations have ever been repeated. The Syrian SAM systems' victory and the IAF's superiority in the aerial campaign became important lessons that Israel and Syria (as well as the United States and Soviet Union) learned and acted upon en route to the next conflict in 1982.

THE FIRST LEBANON WAR, 1982

Fewer than nine years elapsed between the Yom Kippur War and the Lebanon War. On June 9, 1982, after a few days of fighting, the IAF achieved revenge, delivering a comprehensive blow in retaliation for the well-remembered humiliating defeat by the Syrian air defense systems.[80]

For years, Palestinian terrorist organizations in Lebanon had used Soviet-made Katyushas and mines and carried out ambushes to terrorize Israeli civilians who lived along the peaceful Israel-Lebanon border. Since 1976, Syrian SAM systems had been deployed along the border with Lebanon and had created an umbrella under which the terrorist organizations could feel somewhat protected from aerial attacks. Israel used the IAF as its primary means of retaliation. In 1981, a cease-fire was declared, and the next year appeared to be calm and promising.

Throughout this period, the IAF controlled the Lebanese skies, apart from a strip close to the Syrian border. Random clashes between Syrian and Israeli interceptors

ended with the IAF having an undisputable advantage. In 1981, to assert its dominance over Lebanon, Syria deployed a few SA–6 batteries there, increasing the tension
in the region. At the very last minute, Israel halted an operation against those batteries
because of political reasons. The status quo over the Lebanese skies was maintained,
but both sides predicted a forthcoming confrontation.

Some strategic circumstances distinguish this conflict from the clash in 1973.
Israel had signed a peace agreement with Egypt, and Syria had been left alone against
the mighty IDF. The conflict was confined to Lebanese territory in order to control
the threat of all-out war. Both Israel and Syria meticulously kept their activities
within certain bounds because neither country wished to broaden the scope of the
limited conflict.

The great powers still supported their clients, but the qualitative military balance
had changed radically. The IAF received modern fighters: F–15s and F–16s equipped
with look-down shoot-down radars, and new air-to-air missiles. At the same time,
Israel revolutionized its military technology and developed important advanced
weapons systems and electronics that would prove decisive in the coming battle.
Israeli industry developed and produced ECM, decoys, unmanned aerial vehicles
(UAVs), and command, control, communications, computers, and intelligence (C⁴I)
systems, and had tailored them to the IAF's roles and missions. Nevertheless, the
IAF's most important advantage in countering SAM arrays relied on the revolutionary
development of standoff air-to-ground precision-guided munitions (PGMs) by the
Armament Development Authority. These weapons systems have completely changed
the aircraft–SAM balance ever since.[81]

The Syrian air defense forces, which had bathed in the glory of having thwarted
Operation *Dugman*, had not greatly improved their weapons systems, mainly
because the Soviet Union had lagged significantly behind the United States in this
area. However, the SAF had received MiG–23 swing-wing interception and attack
versions, MiG–25 high-altitude reconnaissance aircraft, the improved SA–6, and
new types of SA–8 and SA–9 short-range SAM systems.

The trigger for the 1982 war resembles the one for World War I: the Israeli
ambassador to Britain was shot by a Palestinian member of an obscure terrorist
organization.[82] The government of Israel decided to launch a large operation against
the terrorist organizations in Lebanon; the level of Syrian involvement in the assassination remained unclear.

In the days immediately before the war, Syria deployed a dense SAM array
in Lebanon that resembled the 1973 deployment. It included nineteen batteries,
fifteen of which were improved SA–6s. Since 1973, the SAF had tripled in size to
675 aircraft and 150 attack helicopters. The IAF, in addition to its technological

revolution, deployed 610 aircraft, but only 100 of them were suitable and serviceable for countering SAM systems, and only 90 for air-to-air combat. The rest consisted of old aircraft that were used almost solely for CAS missions or were unserviceable. In addition, the arsenal included twenty-seven attack helicopters.[83]

The Lebanon war broke out on June 5. From then on, the belligerents prepared themselves for an unavoidable confrontation for superiority in the skies of Lebanon. On the night of June 8, a few hours before the battle, Syria increased its SAM array in Lebanese territory by four SA–6 batteries and the IAF stepped up its efforts to locate them.

On June 9, at 2:00 p.m., the IAF launched Operation *Arzav*. Most descriptions of the battle are inaccurate or unreliable, but Syrian defense minister General Mustafa Tlas wrote a valuable, objective account in which he analyzed the IAF doctrine, tactics, and the phases of Operation *Arzav*:

> At 1:50 p.m., the Syrian radar array identified many hostile aircraft formations which concentrated in several areas in Lebanon. In addition, it located formations flying in the Mediterranean Sea west of Lebanese airspace. The enemy [IAF] initiated electronic jamming of all detection, early warning, and control systems of the Syrian air defense system. Some types of aircraft participated in performing this important mission. A Boeing 707, in collaboration with ground stations (primarily the station located on Mount Hermon), initiated active communication and radar jamming. Early warning Hawkeye E–2Cs carried out surveillance and air control missions. Skyhawk A–4s activated active and passive jamming. Unmanned aerial vehicles (UAVs) took part in reconnaissance, jamming, and communication missions, and were used as false targets for the first burst of the Syrian missiles. At 2:00 p.m., 20–24 Phantom F–4 aircraft launched air-to-ground missiles toward the Syrian SAM batteries from a long distance, more than 35 km [kilometers]. Long-range artillery and "Zeev" surface-to-surface rockets operated in conjunction [with the air attack]. These weapon systems aimed at radar stations and fire control centers of the SAM batteries. As a result of the centralized bombardment and the continuous electronic jamming, the capabilities of the SAM array were temporarily paralyzed. Fifteen minutes later, the main part of the enemy attack force of about forty aircraft penetrated the SAM deployment in the Bekaa Valley. It attacked SAM sites, headquarters, and other forces. They used "television" and high explosive bombs. This attack ended at 14:35. At the end of the attack, the enemy launched surveillance aircraft to measure results, the degree of the SAM batteries' operational capability, and the necessity to attack them again.[84]

This description is corroborated by General David Ivri, the IAF commander at the time, who described the clash from an Israeli point of view. He wrote that the operation was a concert rather than dozens of solos. He and his staff coordinated the attack force with various types of supporting aircraft and ground systems: electronic warfare planes, UAVs, helicopters, air refueling planes, and communication relays. The concert was conducted using the most advanced, real-time centralized C⁴I system available at the time. In fact, it was the first operational, real-time command and control system to rely on computers for battle management. In about two hours, the IAF destroyed fourteen SAM batteries and badly damaged the other five.[85]

Operation *Arzav* included only 125 attack sorties and 58 supporting sorties of various types (see table 6–7). An additional sixty attack sorties were canceled because the mission was accomplished earlier than expected.[86] These numbers reveal the effectiveness of the standoff PGM systems, as well as the need for a substantial number of supporting missions. In the course of the war, another ten SAM batteries were destroyed, among them the most modern SA–8 and SA–9 missiles.[87]

TABLE 6-7. ARZAV AND AIR-TO-AIR MISSIONS, 1400–1700, JUNE 9, 1982

	Counter-SAM	Interception	Support	Total Sorties	SAMs Destroyed	Aircraft Kills
Sorties	125	80	58	263	5+14*	28

* Damaged
Source: Abudi, *The Operations of the IAF in the "Peace of Galilee" War*, 354, 367.

Operation *Arzav* had tactical, strategic, political, and psychological implications and almost erased the dark shadow of the *Dugman* defeat. Since then, the widespread military belief that SAM systems would spell the end of the aircraft era has undergone a complete reversal, and the "wings of air power" have become stronger than ever. The success of Operation *Arzav* changed the superpowers' conventional military balance significantly in favor of the United States and increased the confidence of fighters, planners, and commanders in their ability to gain air superiority over the most sophisticated Soviet air defense systems. The longer range consequences of the operation were highlighted in a powerful way less than nine years later, when on January 17, 1991, the U.S. Air Force showed the dominant role it would play throughout the Persian Gulf War.

The success of Operation *Arzav* again overshadowed the battle in the air— another example of analysts' neglect of the IAF's repeated achievements in air-to-air warfare. The air battle lasted for six days, with its zenith occurring in parallel with Operation *Arzav*. The Syrian defense minister wrote that "about seventy Syrian aircraft were scrambled to defend the damaged SAM array. About ninety IAF aircraft joined the battle. It was the biggest air battle among advanced aircraft that has ever occurred."[88] General Ivri lifted the veil further on the dynamic air situation. He recalled that the SAF realized quickly that the SAM array was being destroyed and sent dozens of interceptors to disrupt the IAF's attacking force. Then, suddenly, they were engaged by F–15 and F–16 ambushes guided by the central command post. Syrian pilots and controllers, flying "blind" because of Israeli ECM and decoys, could not cope with the surrounding ambushes and suffered heavy losses.[89] Twenty-eight of the SAF interceptors that crossed the Lebanese border throughout that afternoon failed to return home, but the battle was not over yet. The brave Syrian pilots repeatedly engaged IAF formations despite their heavy losses. Sixty-five Syrian aircraft and helicopters were lost in the air battles before the cease-fire on June 11, compared to no IAF losses. This highlight of the IAF's centralized C⁴I system proved its ability to direct concerted and coordinated complex air operations in a tiny zone.

Victories are harder to explain than defeats. An obvious explanation emphasizes the technological revolution—in fact, two revolutions. First, Israeli industry countered SAMs with various developments in standoff PGM, ECM, and advanced C⁴I systems, which changed the aircraft–SAM balance entirely. A second revolution took place in U.S. development of aircraft, airborne radars, and air-to-air missiles, which utterly surpassed its Soviet contenders. Another explanation highlights the qualitative advantages of IAF pilots, its operational culture, and the human factors of command, control, and battle management.

Nevertheless, these explanations are only partial and fragmented. Syrian and Soviet analysts should have been familiar with the performance of the U.S.-made systems and should have understood the real Israeli-Syrian balance of power in the air. Previous air combat over Lebanese territory should have demonstrated the superiority of IAF pilots and aircraft, as well as the quality of the central C⁴I, which General Ivri has discussed in detail.[90] Cognition, psychology, and background also play a pivotal role in war, but it is difficult to measure the extent of that role accurately. It is hardly far-fetched to conclude that the IAF's operational culture and the different lessons that the SAF and the IAF drew from Operation *Dugman* in 1973 were decisive factors in Operation *Arzav*.

CONCLUSION: SWIFTER THAN EAGLES

A comprehensive analysis should consider these four wars as phases in the evolutionary progress of the struggle for air superiority. These campaigns incorporated both traditional characteristics and revolutionary features. They combined complementary elements to form a fascinating "orchestra." They represented the most technologically sophisticated battles in modern warfare at the time, although they also demonstrated the importance of the spirit and intelligence of the men who fought, commanded, planned, and integrated sophisticated weapons systems into a powerful war machine. These wars can teach some lessons for the future in various areas.

MISSILES AGAINST AIRCRAFT

The first area concerns trends in the confrontation between aircraft and missiles— between SAM systems and integrated aerial formations. Throughout this relatively short period in the history of war (1967–1982), the pendulum of superiority swung from one side to the other and back. The fledgling technological and operational SAM systems in 1967 did not play a significant role. But a few years later, in the War of Attrition, new SA–3 systems, manned by well-trained Soviet personnel, overcame the most advanced U.S. technology and most capable IAF pilots. This advantage persisted through the 1973 war, but it should be acknowledged that the IAF's aerial force was badly hampered by poor decisions by the high command.

Throughout the history of war, the balance of capabilities has always changed as a result of the historical process of challenge and response. Thus, it is no surprise that aircraft were victorious over missiles in 1982. The advantage may swing the other way in the future, depending on changes in the importance of air power in future conflicts.

AIR-TO-AIR WARFARE

The battles in the air between the belligerent aerial forces experienced momentous developments throughout the period. The 1967 war echoed another famous air battle, the Battle of Britain, in which the outcome depended mainly on the skills and quality of fighter pilots and leaders. Air Marshal Hugh Dowding and Air Vice Marshal Keith Park are forever remembered for their formidable near-real-time command and control throughout the battle.[91] Thanks to developments in radar, communications, electronic warfare, and integrated C[4]I systems, air battles became complicated and more intellectually demanding than ever. IAF commander General Hod, a genius at planning and executing encounters in the air, used these new systems effectively. Before the War of Attrition, he created a tactical doctrine that emphasized painstaking planning, initiative, avoidance of encounters in unfavorable situations, and the quality of pilots and formation leaders. In practical terms, he created conditions that significantly improved the ability of his pilots to shoot down their adversaries and fly home safely.

Table 6–8 illustrates the difficulty of performing quantitative analysis of air battles. In general, the IAF's advantage grew significantly over time. Its losses decreased, the kill ratio improved considerably, the number of kills increased slightly, and the average number of kills per day grew as well.

TABLE 6-8. COMPARISON OF AIR COMBAT RESULT

War	Duration of War (Days)	Kills	Average Kills per Day	IAF Losses	Kill Ratio
1967	6	56	9.3	18	1:3.1
Attrition	385	73	0.2	4	1:18.3
1973	1.25	76	60.8	0	76:-
1982	6	76	14.7	0	76:-
Average & Sum	13.25*	281	15.7*	22	1:12.8

* The War of Attrition is not included.
Source: Abudi, *The IAF in the Six Days War*; Schiftan, *Attrition*, 239; Shteigman, The *IAF in the Defensive Phase: October 6–7, 1973*; Abudi, *Operations of the IAF in the "Peace of Galilee" War.*

The outcomes of the defensive battle of the 1973 war are difficult to explain. They are better than those of the 1982 war, but the circumstances were worse. The IAF was surprised by the beginning of the 1973 war, and the rivals used similar aircraft, missiles, and C^{3}I systems. Conversely, in 1982, Israel enjoyed the advantage of initiative, and the IAF had acquired modern aircraft, missiles, and C^{4}I systems. However, the decisive technological advantage in the 1982 war did not improve results compared to the beginning of the Yom Kippur War. It appears that regardless of technological progress, the quality of the people flying the aircraft and operating the C^{4}I systems will remain the key factor in air battles for years to come.

THE FUTURE OF AIR POWER

Are we close to the end of the aircraft era? Throughout the history of air power, some analysts and policymakers have failed to recognize the essential requirement for air superiority to enable air power freedom of action and thereby dominate the battle on the ground. One notable advocate for this minority position was British minister of war Stanley Baldwin, who stated in 1932 that "bombers will always get through."

From time to time, analysts who have a limited understanding and knowledge of the characteristics, capabilities, technologies, advantages, and weaknesses of air power predict the end of it. A thorough discussion of this view is beyond the scope of this chapter; however, a few brief comments should be noted.

First, manned aircraft are not the only aerial platforms. UAVs have already replaced various aircraft missions, and the number of these platforms in modern air forces is growing. Nevertheless, it seems that they will be operated in tandem with manned aircraft for decades to come.

Second, air power has not lost its unmatched ability to project national power in short times and over long distances. It appears that national deterrence, coercive policy, and soft diplomacy, among other sources of national power, will continue to rely on military forces and air power in particular.

Third, surface-to-surface missiles (SSMs) and rockets have become major competitors that some believe may replace the aircraft's offensive roles and consequently reduce the importance of air power. However, this threat has existed for decades. The RAF encountered V–1s and V–2s many decades ago. The campaign to locate and destroy V–2 sites was repeated in the Gulf War, the second Lebanon war, and the war in Gaza. Several factors, such as cost-effectiveness, vulnerability, and limited capabilities, prevent SSMs from replacing air power. On the other hand, technological advances in counter-SSM weapons systems will reduce their effectiveness in the near future.

Finally, the new characteristics of modern wars enhance the roles of air power and emphasize its advantages. In Kosovo, Afghanistan, Iraq, southern Lebanon, and elsewhere, air power played a dominant role. Air superiority is essential for enabling aerial forces to locate and neutralize terrorist organizations, win asymmetric wars, and project military power swiftly and far away in limited conflicts. The history of confrontations between Israel and the Arab states should be comprehensively studied, not only in military academies, but also by policymakers, senior commanders, strategists, analysts, operational planners, and research and development engineers who prepare their nations to deter enemies, maintain peace, and win wars.

AIR POWER AND THE FALKLANDS, 1982

Lawrence Freedman

BACKGROUND

THE FALKLANDS CONFLICT OF 1982 between Britain and Argentina began with the Argentine invasion of the Falkland Islands on April 2 and ended with the surrender of Argentina's forces on June 14.[1] The origins of the conflict lay in a long-standing dispute over the sovereignty of the islands. From the Argentine perspective, there had been an illegal British takeover of the islands in January 1833. Ever since then, Argentine governments had engaged in a continuing struggle to regain territory that they believed to be rightfully part of Argentina for reasons of both geography and law. Relevant to the timing of the war was the fact that January 1983 would represent, from the Argentine point of view, the 150th anniversary of Britain's original aggression. The anniversary summed up the futility of past campaigns and of the reliance on diplomatic measures. From the perspective of the military junta in charge, the British had been procrastinating for over a dozen years of tedious and pointless negotiations. Now was the time to bring matters to a head.

In fact, while the British did not accept that any illegality had occurred and could claim unbroken occupation since 1833, they had no particular desire to hold on to the Falklands for any economic or strategic purposes. There was reluctance to spend more than was necessary subsidizing the feeble local economy and providing a degree of security in the face of the potentially overwhelming Argentine local military presence. There was also a full understanding of the irritation the colony caused in relations with Argentina in particular and Latin America in general. Successive governments would probably have been content to transfer sovereignty to Argentina were it not for the bitter opposition of the islanders. Although their numbers were small and declining, with barely eighteen hundred left in 1982, the British government had agreed in 1968 that their wishes were paramount when it came to any deals with Argentina. Perhaps it was the case that the true interests

157

of the islanders were at variance with their expressed wishes, given the declining population and miserable economic prospects, but Argentine pressure had been deeply counterproductive. In addition, the 1974 military coup had rendered the prospect of being part of the Argentine state extremely unattractive. At no point did the islanders wish for anything other than the constitutional status quo.

Although the occupation of the islands on April 2, 1982, was triggered by a crisis revolving around the separate island of South Georgia (also claimed by Argentina) and was improvised, it did reflect a deliberate policy agreed to in December 1981. The plan had been to generate a crisis later the following year by accusing Britain in the United Nations General Assembly of failing to keep to its promise of serious negotiations on sovereignty and then invading. However, during a curious episode involving the transport of workers by the Argentine navy to South Georgia to gather scrap metal from an old whaling station, the navy saw an opportunity to make its own direct challenge to British sovereignty, which soon got out of hand and created an early crisis that brought the invasion forward. This was not to the Argentine advantage. The British were in a far better position to respond in April 1982 than they would have been in October. The full effects of the cuts approved in the 1981 defense review had yet to be realized, and the Royal Navy was either back at port for Easter or on exercises close to Gibraltar. It was therefore possible for Britain to dispatch a credible naval task force to the South Atlantic almost immediately. In this, the British surprised themselves almost as much as their opponents. If Argentina had waited until the planned time to invade, Britain would have had far fewer military options.

The credibility of the task force depended on its incorporating all available firepower, including two aircraft carriers that carried both Sea Harriers and a range of helicopters. It also carried 3 Commando Brigade of the Royal Marines, reinforced by two battalions of paratroopers. So there was from the start some capacity for an amphibious landing and an understanding that the threat posed by Argentine air and sea power would need to be reduced before a landing could be attempted. But the speed with which the task force had been put together meant that the assets available to the commanders consisted of what was at hand and could be packed into the available storage. As it became more probable that a landing would be needed, more had to be supplied—more aircraft, more ships, and another brigade. As the task force set sail in early April, however, the general assumption was that a settlement would be negotiated before the crisis would lead to serious fighting. U.S. Secretary of State Alexander Haig offered himself as a mediator, and for much of April he shuttled between Buenos Aires and London trying to find the basis for a compromise. His efforts faltered on the basic problem of principle. Britain could make a number of concessions, notably in allowing Argentina some role in an interim administration, but could not agree that any negotiations on a long-term settlement must eventually lead to a transfer of sovereignty. Argentina could envisage withdrawing its occupation force, but it had to be sure that eventually there would be a transfer of sovereignty. Later efforts, notably one led by the secretary general of the United Nations, foundered on this point. It was the end of April before Haig was prepared to acknowledge failure and authorize a tilt to Britain.

By that point, the task force had arrived, and the start of May saw some intense fighting as the air forces and the navies of the two belligerents were tested in several short, sharp exchanges. With the sinking of the old cruiser, the ARA *General Belgrano*, by a torpedo from a nuclear submarine, the naval war was over almost as it began. Thereafter, the Argentine navy dared not venture out into the open seas. The British also gained the advantage in the air-to-air combat of May 1, but in this case the Argentines decided to conserve their air assets until the British attempted a full landing. There were a few exceptions to this policy. The most important one came on May 4, when HMS *Sheffield* was hit by an Exocet antiship missile launched from Argentine Super Étendard aircraft. This gave Argentina some confidence that it could disrupt British plans, while the British became aware that because Argentina was holding back the bulk of its aircraft, an amphibious landing was becoming an increasingly hazardous enterprise. When the landing came at San Carlos on May 21, it was a calculated risk. With great bravery, fliers from both the Argentine air force and navy hurled themselves at the elements of the task force supporting the landing force. The damage to British warships was severe and caused immense anxiety in London, but by May 26 the landing was largely complete and the Argentine assault had run out of aircraft and energy.

In the first serious land battle, the Second Battalion of the Parachute Regiment (Two Para) took on the Argentine garrisons at the settlements of Goose Green and Darwin. The British made life difficult for themselves by committing insufficient troops and equipment, but the eventual victory over a dogged defense established a psychological superiority. The greatest problem was getting the two brigades into position around the main Argentine garrison at the capital, Stanley. Because of insufficient helicopters, many members of the brigade had to walk. Others were brought round by sea, with the final elements caught by attack on two landing ships, *Sir Galahad* and *Sir Tristram*, on June 8. A sequence of tortuous moves was made to ferry Five Brigade from Goose Green to Bluff Cove. The last of these moves was being completed when Skyhawks came in and dropped three bombs on *Sir Galahad* and two on *Sir Tristram*. None exploded, but those on *Sir Galahad* caused fierce fires to break out. This caused forty-nine British deaths, largely of Welsh Guardsmen, delaying but not seriously disrupting the British move toward Stanley. There was a limited air role in the tough battles for the high ground around Stanley, leading up to the Argentine collapse and surrender on June 14.

THE BALANCE OF AIR POWER

Initially, twelve Sea Harriers were taken on HMS *Hermes* and eight on HMS *Invincible*. Eventually, another eight Sea Harriers were sent, plus ten Royal Air Force (RAF) GR–3 Harriers. The other available air power consisted of helicopters. During the course of the campaign, the Royal Navy deployed twenty-four Lynx, twenty-six Sea King Mark II, thirteen Sea King Mark IV, nine Sea King Mark V, two Wessex III, fifty-seven Wessex V, and twelve Wasps. The RAF contributed seven Chinooks and one Sea King. In addition, at Ascension Island, the midpoint between Britain and the South Atlantic that was used as a staging post, the RAF deployed a number of aircraft. There were twelve Nimrod aircraft used for sea surveillance and six Vulcans for long-range attack, supported by twenty-three Victor tankers. Hercules and VC–10 transport aircraft were used to get material to Ascension. Without the carriers and the availability of Ascension Island, the British position would have been virtually hopeless. The limiting factor on strategy and tactics during the campaign was always the risk that a carrier might be lost, at least until it was possible to establish a forward operating base on the Falklands after the landings in late May. This meant that as much as possible, the carriers had to keep out of the range of Argentine aircraft, and this in turn affected the amount of time that the Harriers could spend providing cover and engaging enemy aircraft.

Argentina had a much larger air inventory, but it was also operating at the limits of its range. One of its missed opportunities between its successful invasion and the arrival of the British task force was its failure to construct a temporary runway at Stanley Airport that could accommodate its more capable aircraft. Such construction was not beyond Argentina's capability. It had made some preparations. But there was a shift in logistical priorities after the junta decided to increase the size of the land force on the Falklands. This was an error in many respects as it created a supply problem that was never solved.

In the event, Argentina had only light aircraft, particularly Pucarás, on the Falklands. Their role in the fighting was marginal, and along with the Argentine helicopter fleet, most were caught on the ground. The backbone of Argentine air power was composed of Skyhawks and Daggers (the Israeli version of the Mirage V). For a variety of technical and operational reasons, not all of the inventory was available for combat. By the time the British arrived at the end of April, the spearhead of Argentine air power consisted of eighty-two aircraft—six Canberra B–62s, twenty-four Daggers, eight Mirage IIIs, fourteen Skyhawk A–4Cs, and eighteen A–4Cs, plus a further twelve Navy A–4Qs that could be operated either from the sole Argentine carrier, the ARA *25 de Mayo*, or the mainland. In addition, there were five French Super Étendards and five Exocet missiles. This was potentially the deadliest combination available to Argentina, and it tried to obtain extra missiles; however, France agreed to British requests to make sure no more reached Argentina. The Super Étendards could refuel in the air, and so could some Skyhawks, a feature underestimated by the British, but most Argentine aircraft, flying at least three hundred miles from their mainland bases, had only minutes over their targets.

This meant that while air power was crucial in deciding the course of the conflict, neither side could establish command of the air. Both struggled to reduce significantly the impact of enemy air power by means of sea-based or land-based air defenses. Only toward the end of the conflict, with the fighting around Stanley, did the exhausted and depleted Argentine air force become irrelevant. The central story of air power and the Falklands concerns Britain's determination to limit the risks its forces faced in the course of the amphibious landing. Before addressing that story, however, it is important to note the essential role of aircraft in the logistics efforts undertaken by both sides.

The British logistical effort at a strategic level was largely dependent on sea transport, but critical items were sent regularly by air, using the Ascension base as a staging post. For the RAF, this was the most intensive air transport effort since the Berlin Airlift. It was undertaken largely by the Hercules and VC–10 air transport force, with Belfast aircraft chartered for extra large loads. By the end of the campaign, there had been over forty Hercules supply drops around the Falklands, each involving a twenty-five-hour round-trip flight. Remarkably, less than 5 percent of tasks were delayed owing to aircraft being out of service. The distances had made air-to-air refueling essential. By employing all the available Victor forces, Hercules could be used to carry out airdrop sorties to the task force, deliver Harrier reinforcements directly to the carriers, support the Vulcan raids, and conduct isolated long-range reconnaissance missions.

Even after the runway at Stanley was damaged by a Vulcan raid on May 1, Argentina managed to maintain an air bridge to the Falklands. This required its transport aircraft to avoid Sea Harrier patrols and keep clear of the air defense missiles of British warships. None of the seventy-three sorties flown to the islands from May 1 to June 14 were shot down, although a number were deterred from completing their journeys. Five were aborted, and there are doubts about the success of others. Around 50 transports landed at Stanley during this period, carrying 854 passengers and some 505 tons of cargo. This amount was insufficient to keep the garrison supplied, and coupled with the greater hazards of moving materials by sea because of the submarine threat, it contributed to the strain placed on Argentine forces.

ATTEMPTED ATTRITION

As soon as the British task force arrived in the South Atlantic, it addressed the problem of preventing the Argentine navy and air force from interfering with either the imposition of a blockade or, more challenging, a landing. The Argentine surface fleet was not a major concern, other than the sea-launched version of Exocet that it carried. Of the Argentine navy's thirteen major surface units, most were elderly, although two British Type 42 and three French A69 frigates had recently entered service. Argentina had four submarines, two quite old (ex-U.S. *Guppy* class) and two quite new (German Type 209), that would pose a major and continuing challenge to Britain's antisubmarine capabilities. The surface fleet would be vulnerable to air attack. The most modern air defense system available was the Sea Dart, fitted on the Type 42 destroyers, but this system was well understood by the British, and the problems the Argentines had suffered were known. The best prospect the Argentine navy had of getting close to the task force was its single carrier, the ARA *25 de Mayo*. So the Argentine navy could hurt the task force, but only by taking substantial risks itself.

In the mid-April assessments prepared for the British war cabinet, the air threat was judged to be "only moderate. The Argentines will need luck on their side if they are to inflict substantial damage on the Task Force."[2] This assessment of the air threat was seriously contested at the time. It in part depended on assumptions about the conduct of the landing. There was, however, a simple calculation: the further east the landing, the more difficult it would be for the Argentine air force but also the easier it would be for the defending garrison; the further west the landing site, the more grave the air threat. There was also an assumption, which turned out to be erroneous, that Argentine commanders would commit aircraft to battle before a landing. By May 1, the British were less sanguine, and a three-pronged approach was developed to deal with the Argentine threat: take out the aircraft carrier; destroy the runway at Stanley airport; and draw out the Argentine air force by suggesting that a landing was imminent.

The first issue with regard to the aircraft carrier was changing the rules of engagement so that she could be attacked outside of the two-hundred-mile total exclusion zone imposed by Britain to prevent the resupply of Argentine forces on the Falklands.

While the potentially damaging political impact of a submarine-based attack on such a large and important target well away from the islands was appreciated, so was the threatening nature of the carrier at great distances once Skyhawks, and potentially Super Étendards, were on board. Once the rules had been changed, the next issue was whether the carrier could be found. In the event, it was not, to the point that its undetected presence at sea became a real concern to the task force during the course of May 1.

Whereas the carrier had eluded the nuclear submarines looking for it, the *General Belgrano* was detected. Admiral Sandy Woodward, in charge of the task force in the South Atlantic, was fearful that he might get caught in a pincer movement, so he sought and received a change in the rules of engagement that allowed the *Belgrano* to be attacked outside the exclusion zone. This was done on May 2, with the loss of 351 lives. The news rocked international opinion and led to soul-searching in Britain, but the net effect was the same as if the carrier had been struck. The Argentine navy became conscious of its vulnerability and barely ventured out thereafter.

The plan on May 1 had been to persuade the Argentine air force that the British were engaged in a major maneuver to establish a presence on the Falklands. They did this sufficiently well to trigger a wave of Argentine air attacks. Fortunately for the British, they were poorly planned and executed. Of fifty-six planned sorties, only thirty-five reached targets, and what they reached was irrelevant. The Mirage IIIs were an obvious disappointment, as were the Daggers and Canberras. Strategically, the result was even less satisfactory. British air superiority had been demonstrated so conclusively that, with a Canberra and two Mirages lost (one to friendly fire), the Argentine conclusion was not to put more aircraft at unnecessary risk until the British tried a proper landing.

The other part of the plan was to make it difficult for Argentine aircraft to use the various airstrips dotted around the islands, and in particular the runway at Stanley. This was both to ensure that the more high-performance aircraft could not operate from the Falklands and to make it harder for the Argentines to get in supplies. Attacks on the runway at Stanley represented a more challenging problem. The RAF had not envisaged carrying out offensive air operations in the South Atlantic, and when the task force was constituted, few of the roles that the RAF could play in its support were immediately apparent. Only Nimrod Maritime Patrol aircraft were initially seen as having an operational task, in addition to the transport aircraft required to supply the forward base at Ascension Island. The only way the RAF could mount attacks against targets thousands of miles away would be to involve its long-range Vulcan bomber force. This was a force at the end of its operational life:

the remaining squadrons were due to be phased out by June 30, 1982. It was also configured for nuclear operations. Using Vulcans therefore meant both working up a conventional bombing capability and reconnecting and providing the air-to-air refueling capability for the first time in twenty years.

There were a number of possible options for using Vulcans. Attacks on mainland airfields and ports were ruled out as being of questionable legality, as well as politically provocative and probably operationally doubtful, given the known difficulties of putting such facilities out of action with anything other than massive raids. They would also depend on the use of Chilean airfields, should the aircraft need to divert. At the same time, the air staff argued that it would do no harm if Argentina came to fear such attacks, as that would force it to retain aircraft in reserve for defending the mainland rather than defending the Falklands.

Planning soon focused on the airfield at Stanley, once it was concluded that there would be little risk of civilian casualties. The aircraft would be at risk from antiaircraft guns and surface-to-air missiles, but this risk could be reduced by surprise and by flying at night in probable bad weather. No Argentine air defense aircraft were deployed to Stanley. So the main challenge was to get a single Vulcan to the Falkland Islands from Ascension Island, 3,350 miles away. Outside of the RAF, the widely held view was that the Vulcan operation was an expensive and cumbersome effort to achieve an uncertain result. The main alternative, however, was to use Sea Harriers to attack the airfield. Their use would cause fewer presentational issues, and they would also be better placed to prevent the runway being repaired and the airfield reopened. But the Harriers already had more than enough to do and were not suited to attacking runways. Even so, Admiral Woodward was concerned that Harriers would still have to be put in harm's way to take photographs after the Vulcan attack for damage assessment purposes.

The operation was named Black Buck. Eleven tankers, two reserve tankers, the primary Vulcan, and a reserve, took off from Ascension during the night of April 30. The first Vulcan had to return because of a minor problem. The reserve Vulcan executed the mission, with, in all, eighteen Victor sorties flown in support. The attack was made at a height of eight thousand feet and a ground speed of three hundred knots. Twenty-one one-thousand-pound bombs at approximately forty-eight-yard spacing were delivered. This raid was followed up by attacks from nine Sea Harriers, while three attacked targets at Goose Green, including the local airstrip.

The hole in the middle of the runway was probably as much as could have been achieved, and it precluded Stanley's use by the more capable Argentine aircraft, Skyhawks and Super Étendards, although not by air transports. Later Black Buck raids did not add much to the initial achievement. Perhaps most importantly, this raid alerted Argentina to the potential vulnerability of mainland bases. This led to the redeployment of the Mirage III to the defense of the mainland bases and away from the support of offensive operations against the task force. The revelation of the Mirage III's vulnerability in air combat against Sea Harriers on May 1 also may have made this prudent. The Mirage was the Argentine air force's most recent acquisition, well armed and with an all-weather capability. The British had expected the Mirage III to escort Argentine air raids, flying high above them and adding to the risk facing the defending Sea Harriers. It was a relief that they stayed at home.

Much effort was put into locating and destroying shore radars using naval gunfire, Special Forces, and Vulcan raids with Shrike missiles, but none met with complete success. The radars remained a thorn in the side of British forces until the fall of Stanley, when it was discovered that they were mobile and frequently moved. A major factor throughout the month of May was the weather, which could never be entirely favorable to attacking forces. Heavy, low clouds and fog, frequently encountered at this time of the year, inhibited the task force's aim of attacking the airfield and airstrips and other military locations on the Falkland Islands. There were many days in the month when almost no flying was possible, and while this provided protection for the task group, it also provided cover for the Argentines to break the blockade by sea.

That Falklands-based aircraft were vulnerable was demonstrated by a Special Forces raid on May 15 that destroyed or put out of commission eleven Argentine aircraft (six Pucarás, four Mentors, and a Skyvan) based at Pebble Island. These posed a threat to British ships wanting to use the northern entrance to Falkland Sound. This left three Skyvan light transports, two Navy Tracker early warning aircraft, nine Pucarás, four Chinooks, three Pumas, and one Agusta 109 on the Falklands. There was no firm intelligence on the actual deployment of these remaining aircraft. The fixed-wing aircraft could be operated from any of four or perhaps as many as twenty of the small airstrips, while the helicopters, on which the Argentine forces relied so much for mobility, were expected to be dispersed away from the airstrips.

A Special Forces raid also seemed to be the only acceptable way of dealing with the mainland bases. The priority target had to be the Rio Grande airfield in Tierra del Fuego, where the Super Étendards were stationed. An operation was requested but soon became controversial even among the Special Air Service (SAS) because of the risks involved. It was difficult enough to imagine how men could get into the base to destroy the aircraft and even harder to work out how to extract them. Eventually, on May 17, an attempt was made to get a reconnaissance party close to the base, but bad weather forced the Sea King carrying the troops down in Chile well away from where it had hoped to be. When its burned-out helicopter was found, the crew had only a somewhat contrived cover story about engine failure. Discussions about a second try were continuing at the time of the Argentine surrender.

The major concerns revolved around the vulnerability of British ships, especially when supporting an amphibious landing. During the Cold War, the Royal Navy had put considerable effort into preparing to deal with submarines but less into preparing for air attack. Sea Dart air defense missiles were designed to deal with missile-carrying aircraft, probably Soviet Bears and Badgers, coming over the open seas rather than actions close to the shore. Sea Wolf, the point-defense missile, was still relatively new. The successful attack on HMS *Sheffield* on May 4 made the task force keenly aware that it could not expect everything to go its way after the successes of May 1.

It was hard to judge the strength of air defenses without much of an Argentine challenge, but the results from the only two bursts of air activity prior to the landing were not wholly encouraging. On May 9, after some naval gunfire against targets close to Stanley, Argentine Skyhawks and Daggers, with Learjets acting as pathfinders, made an appearance. They did not reach any targets, but neither did the British hit anything, despite firing Sea Darts. Two Skyhawks collided on their way home. Later, an Argentine Puma was caught by a single Sea Dart from HMS *Broadsword*. It was comforting to know that against a slow-moving target, clear of land, and not engaged in a direct attack on a defending ship, Sea Dart could work, but it would have to do far better. The second burst of activity, on May 12, was also triggered by intense naval gunfire from two warships, HMS *Brilliant* and HMS *Glasgow*. When the Argentine response came—from two groups of four Skyhawks—the ships were ready. But when the opportunity came to strike the first group, *Glasgow*'s Sea Dart failed and its guns misfired. By contrast, the shorter range Sea Wolf on *Brilliant* was effective, taking out two Skyhawks, while a third, taking evasive action, flew into the sea. A bomb from the fourth Skyhawk missed *Glasgow*. During the second raid, none of the systems on either ship worked, allowing four Skyhawks to release their one-thousand-pound bombs. One hit *Glasgow* but failed to explode.

On May 13, one RAF officer found it "profoundly disturbing that some 6 raids by the Argentines have resulted in the loss of one ship and severe damage to another and that, conversely, we have only succeeded in destroying 4 enemy aircraft. This is an extremely unfavorable ratio and does not augur well for the future." Another expressed concern that the capability of Argentine aircraft was being "underrated." The Argentine aircrew had already impressed with their "skill, determination and press-on spirit."[3] The air staff view was that if a mass attack of Argentine air and navy aircraft were mounted at the right moment, heavy damage would probably be inflicted on British forces.

There was a degree of denial about the potential inadequacies of the air defenses. A naval staff paper in London acknowledged problems but insisted that "sharp lessons have already been learned and there is no reason to doubt that these systems can cope adequately with the threats for which they were designed." This paper gave little sense of the difficulties that had already arisen with fusing and taking on multiple targets, and how these problems might get worse when ships were operating in a confined and busy area. The paper's readers were assured: those defects that had occurred should not recur.

THE BATTLE OF SAN CARLOS

As the task force prepared to land on the Falklands, there was growing confidence at all levels that the naval threat was under control, but the same could not be said about the air threat. Those in charge of the amphibious landing had assumed that air superiority was an essential precondition; it gradually dawned on them that no such assumption was being made in London. On May 6, Brigadier Julian Thompson, commanding 3 Brigade, told General Jeremy Moore, land forces commander: "Unpalatable though it may be, fact must be faced that amphibious operations cannot be successfully carried out in hostile air environment. This is not a new thought."[4] In London, the view was that having got the task force to the South Atlantic, it could not be readily withdrawn, and if that meant taking risks with the landing, then so be it. These risks could be mitigated by efforts to deceive the Argentines by landing in darkness and trying to get as much as possible loaded onto the beachhead before the Argentines realized what was happening. It would be possible to take out most of the Argentine aircraft based in the Falklands before the landing. The Sea Harriers would then make it difficult for the attacking Argentine aircraft, and after that the surface-to-air Rapier missiles should start to make a difference, provided they could get ashore quickly. But three of the original twenty Sea Harriers had been lost (two in a midair collision), and further potential losses of one aircraft per day were assumed. Fortunately, eight more were on their way, with six Harrier GR–3s due to arrive on the HMS *Atlantic Conveyor*. Even assuming that the Rapiers were in decent condition after their long journey and could get ashore, Thompson was not alone in doubting that the missiles could be decisive in turning away an Argentine air assault. He remained unconvinced that the conditions were appropriate for a landing. When Thompson raised the issue directly with Admiral John Fieldhouse, the task force commander, he was told that it was not his responsibility to weigh the risks of a landing. There were many considerations to be taken into account, of which the air threat was but one.

The balance of confidence favored Argentina, which felt well prepared for the coming battle. Its aircraft, deployed among the southern airfields, were well armed and had been practicing attacks against naval targets. Studies of the failure of the high-altitude attacks of May 1 concluded that incoming aircraft should fly low to avoid the Sea Harrier patrols and the ships' radars. By attacking in the late afternoon, they could come in from the west with the setting sun at their backs. The aim was to overwhelm the British defenses: all operations were to be carried out by a minimum of eight aircraft, arriving together. Yet there were limitations. Aircraft would still have to fly in daylight and at the limits of their range, although the A–4 was capable of aerial refueling. Intelligence was poor and command was divided. Attacks on ships were to be controlled from the mainland, while those on ground forces would be coordinated with the Southern Air Force, and the role of the garrison's commanders was confined to providing information on targets, leaving decisions on what to attack to the mainland. The air force focused on ships in the vicinity of the islands, the navy on a decisive Exocet strike against a carrier.

The British task force chose San Carlos as a landing site, with remarkably little controversy, because it reduced the threat from Argentine ground forces, submarines, and air-launched Exocet missiles. West Falkland was ruled out because it was closer to the Argentine mainland, and a second landing would be required when it became necessary to move across to the east. But San Carlos was still in range of land-based aircraft. As already noted, the Sea Dart and Sea Wolf had serious problems. Few vessels carried dedicated antiaircraft guns, although in the confines of San Carlos they would have been of more use than missiles. Sea Harriers armed with Sidewinder missiles would be extremely effective whenever they got enemy aircraft in view. But because of the need to keep the carriers out of harm's way, the aircraft were operating at the edge of their range, short on fuel, and thus pressed to get any engagements over quickly. They had to restrain themselves when tempted to chase too far from home. They achieved impressive sortie rates, but time was always short, and they were used best when a ship on the spot was able to task them.

The initial air activity on May 21 was to support the British landing. A pair of GR–3s from HMS *Hermes* successfully attacked a helicopter park at Mount Kent, destroying a Chinook and a Puma, thereby reducing the Argentine ability to move reinforcements to critical areas. Less successful were another pair directed against West Falkland: one had to return with a jammed undercarriage, and the other was shot down with a Blowpipe missile, providing Argentina with its only prisoner of war. SAS observers, watching six Pucarás preparing for takeoff at Goose Green, called in naval gunfire on the airfield. Only one aircraft got airborne, and it was later shot down by an SAS Stinger, although not before it had reported on the activity in San Carlos Water.

Now the Argentine command realized that something was happening at San Carlos. This was the moment for which the Argentine air force had been holding itself in readiness, and it was soon unleashed. Everything was to be thrown into the battle. For tactical and practical reasons, some sorties had to be aborted, but over the course of the day some forty-five reached the Falklands. In the first wave, the two most accessible targets, HMS *Antrim* and *Broadsword*, were hit. Both were left damaged, *Antrim* most seriously. Later, HMS *Argonaut* was spared after two bombs hit her but failed to explode. The frigate HMS *Ardent*, returning from naval gunfire duties, was found by chance by three Argentine navy A–4s and then caught by two bombs. *Ardent* had to be evacuated, and burnt alone before sinking. The Royal Navy had suffered, but it could have been worse. Argentina lost ten aircraft (five Daggers, three A–4Qs, and two A–4Cs), and a number of others were out of action until they could be repaired.

The attacking aircraft had flown without any escorts to protect them from the Sea Harriers, with no intelligence about the disposition of British ships and little time over the target. So the attacks had been opportunistic, by and large neglecting the most important targets—that is, the amphibious ships—and aiming for the frigates and destroyers. In addition, they had not addressed the more technical issue of bomb fusing. Because of the attack profiles, many bombs simply failed to explode. All this effort therefore made no difference to the actual landing and to the vital process of getting equipment and stores ashore. This was a major comfort to the British. The amphibious ships had been spared because of their judicious positioning and the readiness of the escorts to draw the attack.

After the challenges on the first day, the British decided to get as many of the amphibious ships as possible out of the range of Argentine aircraft for the second day. Although this would cause delays on the ground, the safest course was to keep them out of danger during daylight, allowing them to return in the evening, lest the Argentines awake to the advantages of attacking the ships unloading stores rather than the frigates and destroyers protecting them. There was little activity on May 22, but the Argentines came back again with full force the next day. The pattern was not very different from that of the first day: aircraft flying in at low level, facing a barrage of Rapier, Blowpipe, and small arms, and again concentrating on the most obvious rather than most important targets. This time, HMS *Antelope*, which had been with the task force for only twelve hours, was hit with two one-thousand-pound bombs in the course of its first encounter with the enemy. Although neither exploded immediately, one later did as an attempt was being made to defuse it, setting the ship on fire and leading to an order to abandon ship—just before magazine explosions began. The ship sank the next morning. From this point, the British determined not to talk publicly again about unexploded bombs so as not to encourage the enemy to address the problem. The basic problem with fusing the bombs was not easily soluble so long as the effort to survive air defenses made it impossible to fly at optimum altitudes.

On May 24, the Argentines tried a new strategy. The attack was to be concentrated into a half-hour period, with a change in direction and amphibious ships as targets. Although they hit three landing ships—*Sir Galahad*, *Sir Lancelot*, and *Sir Bedivere*—bombs failed to explode on the first two and passed through the third. HMS *Fearless* and *Sir Galahad* were strafed with cannon shells. The damage caused delay, but with each day more vital equipment and stores were getting ashore. The British remained anxious: the fleet was becoming depleted, and reinforcements, steaming in from Britain, were still a few days away. The hope was that the Argentine air capacity had also been depleted. The British consistently overestimated the effectiveness of the air defenses, believing that the Argentines had lost twice as many aircraft as was in fact the case. Any optimism was soon dashed on May 25.

The initial raids of that day saw Argentine aircraft losses without any successful attacks. At the center of the action were the Type 42 Destroyer HMS *Coventry* and the frigate *Broadsword*, acting in combination. With their position identified, three A–4Bs came in low to attack, achieving surprise. They were too low for *Coventry's* Sea Dart to work. A maneuver by *Coventry* made it impossible for *Broadsword's* Sea Wolf to hit incoming aircraft, and *Coventry* was caught on the port side with cannon fire and three bombs, at least two of which exploded. Seventeen men were killed outright, and two died later. With *Broadsword's* boats soon available, the ship was quickly evacuated.

While this loss was alarming, the second Argentine success of the day was far more harmful to the British campaign. The Argentines were determined to mark Argentine Navy Day with a successful attack on the British carriers, which were moving toward San Carlos with a number of escorts and amphibious ships, including the *Atlantic Conveyor*. This was a container ship that had been taken from trade for the duration of the conflict and was full of vital stores. The intention was to complete their transfer by helicopter that night before moving into San Carlos Water. This was assessed to be safer than being close to San Carlos in daylight and reflected a wider judgment that the Argentine focus was still on disrupting the beachhead. It also meant that Sea Harrier air patrols were focused on San Carlos. Two Super Étendards, with one Exocet each, flew from Rio Grande, refueled, and then flew 270 miles to reach their targets. Although the incoming attack was spotted only belatedly, the British soon used chaff. This was the best countermeasure to an Exocet attack and worked as well as hoped, except that having been diverted from their intended targets, the two missiles both found the *Atlantic Conveyor*, which lacked any defenses. The loss of three Chinooks and six Wessex helicopters—another Chinook and a Wessex were airborne at the time—was a severe blow. Also lost were a tented camp for forty-five hundred men, and runway and fueling equipment for the Harrier forward operating base.

While the loss of the *Atlantic Conveyor* complicated British plans, it was not quite the result intended by the Argentine navy, which was more interested in dealing a crippling blow to the task force than disrupting the landing. From their perspective, they had used up two Exocets in failing to get the carrier, and they now had only one of the missiles left. Efforts to obtain more from abroad had so far been unavailing. Despite this being one of their more effective days, the air force and naval air arm had both run out of time, targets, and steam. That evening, the Argentine commanders accepted that their battle must now move on to the next phase. Though the risks remained, this was the effective end of this stage of the battle.

It was also a moment of deep gloom for the task force, fully reflected in London: two ships lost, another damaged, a loss of helicopters that would cause real problems, and gaps continually being exposed in British defenses. If a future gap led to the loss of a carrier, then the whole campaign would be placed in jeopardy. Another day like this might make it necessary to conclude that the entire battle was being lost.

The gloom might have been even greater had the British appreciated the extent to which Argentine air losses at this point were being exaggerated. Because of the normal problems associated with the "fog of war," in particular optimistic claims from those operating the various surface-to-air missiles, the British thought that they had downed far more aircraft than was the case. While the British were estimating that twenty Skyhawks and seventeen Daggers had been lost since May 21, the actual numbers were half these totals—ten Skyhawks and nine Daggers. That was in addition to the six Skyhawks, one Dagger, two Mirage IIIs, and a Canberra lost before, so the actual number was only two-thirds of the British assessment of Argentine losses. In addition, eight Pucarás, four Mentors, one Aermacchi, and three light aircraft had been lost, excluding accidents. By this time, the British had lost five Harriers to accidents and enemy attack.

By the evening of May 26, with little activity that day and the landing work virtually complete, it dawned on the task force commanders that the worst might be over. There were only four ships to be protected on May 27, and that night no new ships were taken in for unloading. All the guns, vehicles, and the bulk of the immediate stores and ammunition were ashore, as were eleven Sea Kings, four Wessexes, and one Chinook. Progress had been made with constructing a forward operating base for Harriers. There were two Argentine raids, but they turned back when they realized that they faced Sea Harriers. The Argentine pilots, who had flown with great bravery, did not give up, but the number of sorties was declining, fewer reached the task force, and none were successful.

EVALUATION

In retrospect, victories often seem inevitable. British forces had some crucial advantages over their Argentine counterparts, including nuclear submarines and Sea Harriers. Their forces were better trained and better led. But they were operating a long way from home, against a capable and determined enemy. Those conducting the campaign never took victory for granted. If Argentina had managed to get a temporary runway for its best aircraft on the Falklands, worked out the problems with the fusing of its bombs, found a way to concentrate attacks on the amphibious forces after the landing, or managed to strike a carrier or a packed troop ship, or if the British had been unlucky with a major equipment failure or accidents, then the result could have been different.

Without naval air power, the campaign would have been unthinkable—a point not lost among those in the Royal Navy who had long sought to preserve some sort of fleet air arm in the face of Whitehall skepticism. In the event, the large flight deck of *Hermes* made all the difference. It could cope with up to twenty-one Harriers, nine Sea Kings, two Lynxes, and two Wessexes, compared with the ten Harriers, nine Sea Kings, and one Lynx on *Invincible*. With so few assets, each had to be worked extremely hard, maintained in test conditions, and used with versatility. On one occasion, *Hermes* was able to launch twelve Sea Harriers to attack Stanley and Goose Green and, one hour after their return, relaunch the same aircraft on air defense tasks.

Defensive systems against enemy air attack had been a major disappointment. Until 1978, HMS *Ark Royal* could have launched airborne early warning (AEW) aircraft, but these were no longer available. In a North Atlantic Treaty Organization setting, AEW could be provided by shore-based aircraft, but out at sea the lack was keenly felt. This allowed Super Étendards to penetrate Exocet missile launch range. It was fortunate for the British that the enemy had been unable to use electronic countermeasures. This gap was the more noticeable because of the inadequacies of most shipborne warning radars close to land.

The Sea Harrier aircraft performed exceptionally well, exceeding expectations. Nonetheless, their dominance in air-to-air combat was undoubtedly helped by the fact that they were attacking fighter-bombers, with minimum fuel, in daylight.

Of the missiles, it could be argued that the British Sea Dart had a strong tactical influence on the Argentine air operations, which was surprising as the Argentine experience with their own Sea Dart had hardly been satisfactory. Still, the missile's actual performance in terms of reaction times and its radar was disappointing. Sea Wolf had appeared more effective, but at this point the air defense system was installed on only a few warships. Initially, Rapier came out of the campaign with a strong reputation because of the number of claims of successful "kills"—a number that escalated from eight to fourteen after the conflict. Proponents claimed the missile had been proven in combat, yet after the war investigations revealed that its effectiveness had been greatly exaggerated, with only one certain success, two other probables, and two possibles. This was never fully acknowledged officially. The long sea voyage and the lack of second-line support had rendered the Rapier unreliable. It had also been hampered by the low altitude of enemy air attacks, often coming out through valleys shrouded in mist and in poor light.

Six British ships were lost, and eleven were damaged. If a further thirteen bombs that hit ships but failed to explode had detonated, the record would have been even grimmer. The losses of ships led to public debate about the "lack of survivability" of warships. Their loss, and the near loss of many more, was owing to an unfortunate combination of factors—the need to operate in range of the Argentine mainland against an opponent who understood the Royal Navy's defenses, the gaps in those defenses, and some characteristics of the ships that limited their ability to absorb damage. Whatever the problem of survivability, the ships did their job, which in the circumstances of the landing meant acting as bait. This meant that the damage to the amphibious force was far less severe, and only one civilian ship, *Atlantic Conveyor*, was lost, and that occurred because of the diversion of an Exocet. *Coventry* had been overwhelmed by numbers: the frigates were on duty in the narrow confines of Falkland Sound, unable to take advantage of their maneuverability and their weapons systems. If there were lessons for future ship design, they would lie in finding better ways to contain fire and smoke. Chaff decoys also showed their value and would be relatively easy to add to most ships, including otherwise unarmed Royal Fleet Auxiliaries.

Ground attack operations, particularly against the runways, had only moderate success. There was also a basic tactical lesson to be learned, in that two of the three

Harrier GR–3s shot down were lost while making multiple pass attacks. The risks of multiple passes were well known, and in these cases one was to help out Two Para and the other because of a direct order. All such risks could be reduced with good information about targets as well as the systems to destroy them. Out of this experience came a determination to acquire an effective airfield denial weapon.

The conflict also revealed a great deal about the demands of joint operations. At the top levels of command the Falklands campaign was led by admirals, from the chief of defense staff to the task force commander to the commander of the carrier battle group—the senior figure in the South Atlantic. By and large the command structures in the United Kingdom worked well, but those in the South Atlantic were strained. There was no RAF officer on Woodward's staff. Captain Middleton of *Hermes* performed the role of air adviser, but his relationship with Woodward was not good. A squadron leader was sent as a liaison officer but was outranked in any debate. The air operations room on *Hermes* was at full stretch defending the task force rather than mounting offensive air operations. There were no means for allocating the aircraft when faced with competing demands from Woodward, Middleton, and the land commanders, with whom communications were difficult.

There is often a rush to learn lessons from wars. In this case, the vulnerability of ships to air attack was one of the most noted. Yet the special conditions of the conflict made it impossible to draw general conclusions. Exocets, for example, gained a reputation for being unstoppable, yet it was clear that they could be diverted by the use of chaff. It was alarming that the defensive missiles did not work when conditions were less than optimal, but this did not preclude a better performance when conditions were closer to the optimum. Improved early warning and the introduction of high-quality antiaircraft guns were obvious remedies to the gaps in defenses.

The unusual circumstances of 1982 produced a one-off campaign, unlike any of the other wars of the time. It was about old-fashioned issues of territory and sovereignty, involved combat between regular forces rather than against and among civilians, and was never likely to be a walkover for either side. Logistical factors limited the ability of both sides to commit forces to fight, and it was Britain's ability to find creative solutions to these limitations that made a crucial difference. Air power was important, but neither side had sufficient aerial forces to make it decisive. The Royal Navy had a torrid time, losing a number of ships, but in the end it oversaw a successful amphibious landing.

PART III: 1990–2000

INTRODUCTION

PART 3 FOCUSES ON THE MAJOR military campaigns of the 1990s, beginning with the liberation of Kuwait in 1991. John Andreas Olsen argues in chapter 8 that the United States and its allies inaugurated a new era in the application of air power by paralyzing key parts of a modern state's political, economic, and military infrastructure without resorting to nuclear weapons or heavy bombers and without heavy losses among either the civilian population or the attacking forces. At the same time, the air forces of the U.S.-led coalition substantially reduced the enemy's land combat effectiveness prior to ground engagements. This achievement was enabled by technology, which both increased bombing accuracy and decreased the effectiveness of the Iraqi air defense system, and by a reexamination of traditional theories regarding strategic bombing and systematic attrition-style attacks on tanks, artillery, transportation vehicles, and supply lines. The combination of new technology, in the form of Tomahawk cruise missiles and F–117 stealth aircraft armed with precision weapons, and old technology, in the form of B–52s and their dumb bombs, simply overwhelmed the Iraqi state, society, and its armed forces at all levels of war: strategic, operational, and tactical. For the first time in history, air power was allowed to dominate a large-scale military campaign, and it proved itself beyond expectations.

In chapter 9, Robert C. Owen discusses the use of air power during Operation Deny Flight, the North Atlantic Treaty Organization's intervention in the Bosnian civil war, which raged from March 31, 1993, to December 20, 1995. Owen pays special attention to Operation Deliberate Force (August 28–September 14, 1995), the phase of Deny Flight during which NATO applied air power energetically, persistently, and effectively to force an end to the bloody conflict. During this phase, NATO and U.S. diplomats exploited air operations to compel all sides, particularly the Bosnian Serbs, to cease fighting and commit to negotiations. They accomplished these objectives despite rules of engagement that placed unprecedented restrictions on the freedom of NATO air leaders to control the timing, aim points, and weapons, and to determine acceptable levels of collateral damage. In the Bosnian operation, however, the military efficiency of the air campaign was less important than the need to preserve political unity among the allies, which, in turn, demanded careful limitation of collateral casualties and property damage. The differing strategic perspectives of the various participants in the intervention made such unity both essential and difficult to achieve. Thus, Owen contends that the specific circumstances of Deliberate Force reduced the importance of precision weapons in relation to the decisive importance of the campaign's mix of persistence, careful targeting, and aggressive diplomacy.

In 1999, NATO again elected to rely on air power to coerce Yugoslav president Slobodan Milosevic into stopping repression in the province of Kosovo. In fact, air power was the only coercive mechanism that NATO applied during Operation Allied Force. However, Milosevic's commitment to Kosovo was far greater than his interest in Bosnia had been, and on this occasion the alliance expressly refused to provide ground forces. Consequently, NATO's expectations of a swift concession were dashed. Instead, NATO had to increase aircraft numbers, sorties, and targets over a period of eleven weeks before Milosevic accepted its demands. Tony Mason shows in chapter 10 that NATO quickly took command of the air but never neutralized Yugoslav surface-to-air defenses. Although precision weapons struck static targets, rigorous rules of engagement and reluctance to take and create casualties and collateral damage greatly complicated attacks on the Serbian forces in Kosovo, which moved in small numbers and relied on deception and concealment among the population. Both sides exploited the media: images of NATO bombing errors were countered by pictures of thousands of Kosovar refugees. Milosevic capitulated only after his Russian supporters abandoned him, after he was indicted as a war criminal, after the citizens of Belgrade began to suffer from power outages and disruptions to their daily lives, and after NATO had begun to reconsider its decision not to deploy ground forces. The widespread use of unmanned aerial vehicles, satellites, all-weather navigation, and precision-guided, networked weapons delivery systems met asymmetric Serbian responses. For these reasons, Mason argues that Allied Force, rather than Desert Storm, set the agenda for twenty-first-century air power.

8

OPERATION DESERT STORM, 1991

John Andreas Olsen

OPERATION DESERT STORM, the U.S.-led military campaign designed to drive Iraqi forces from Kuwait, began in the early hours of January 17, 1991, and ended on February 28, when George H. W. Bush declared a cease-fire. In forty-two days of military action, Coalition ground forces experienced combat in only the last one hundred hours.

The ground campaign, with its wide and deep sweep into Iraq, combined with a shrewd, amphibious deception effort and careful logistical planning, constituted an impressive achievement. Yet in assessing the speed and scale of the victory, it is important to grasp that Coalition accomplishments were, in large measure, made possible by the comprehensive air offensive. The fighting on the ground unfolded without the fluctuating fortunes that normally mark major military campaigns because air operations, with more than 1,800 combat aircraft in action, roughly 110,000 flights recorded, and more than 90,000 tons of aerial ordnance delivered,[1] had decided the fate of the battle well before the ground offensive began. It was not the volume alone that proved devastating to the Iraqi regime and its armed forces, but also the unprecedented precision of the air campaign. Of all the weapons dropped or launched, an estimated 8 percent were precision guided. These weapons proved very effective and improved air power effectiveness considerably.[2]

This chapter examines what the Coalition accomplished at the operational level by focusing on the application of air power through the lens of five distinct types of air operations, or primary combat functions. The first, *control of the air*, ensured that air, sea, and ground operations could proceed at the place, intensity, and time of the Coalition's choosing without significant interference from Iraq's armed forces. The second, *strategic attack*, largely paralyzed the Iraqi command and control apparatus and the regime's ability to pursue its political and military goals. The third, *supply interdiction*, denied Iraqi soldiers efficient use of transportation links, halting timely delivery of food, water, and spare parts. Fourth, *direct force attack* destroyed large portions of Iraq's artillery, tanks, and armored personnel carriers in the field prior to engagements on the ground. Finally, air power filled its traditional role by providing *close air support* (CAS) to Coalition forces once the ground invasion began.[3] The chapter describes the direct and indirect effects of the air campaign and includes Iraqi perspectives on the "Mother of All Battles," as Saddam Hussein dubbed the 1991 war.[4]

THE INVASION OF KUWAIT

From the West's viewpoint, the crisis in the Gulf began on August 2, 1990, when Iraqi president Saddam Hussein ordered his elite military force to invade neighboring Kuwait. Iraq's stated objectives were to "occupy the city of Kuwait and other Kuwait cities" and to capture the ruling family as well as senior government officials.[5] The Republican Guard initiated the main effort by conducting a well-integrated and deliberate corps-level attack over multiple axes of advance. The attack was based on surprise, mass, and speed. An estimated 100,000 officers and men from the Republican Guard crossed the border with an array of tanks, artillery, and armored personnel carriers, supported by fighter-bombers, helicopters, special forces, and naval vessels.

Although the ground advance dominated the invasion, the attacking force included all of Iraq's military services. The Iraqi air force conducted reconnaissance missions and gained control of the air by attacking Kuwait's air defense system, aircraft, helicopters, and airfields. Helicopters from the army's aviation branch conducted a major airlift operation, flying from southern Iraq into several landing zones in Kuwait, and dropping special forces in downtown Kuwait City. The Iraqi navy, for its part, took control of Faylakah and other islands, naval bases, and Kuwaiti territorial waters. In less than forty-eight hours, Iraqi soldiers, airmen, and seamen controlled strategic positions throughout Kuwait, including its capital. The attack in force took the world by surprise.[6]

A long-standing and complex mix of grand strategies, conspiracy theories, regional animosities, and personal resentment underlay Saddam's decision to invade Kuwait. The immediate impetus for the invasion resulted from an economic crisis triggered by Iraq's pursuit of further political and military power, coupled with Saddam's belief that Iraq deserved more generous financial assistance, especially from its southern Gulf neighbors. Iraq had tried to maintain high levels of military spending despite having accumulated considerable debt from its war with Iran, but by 1989–1990 most creditors had become increasingly reluctant to provide new loans to Iraq or to forgive debts. At the same time, after eight years of war, the

Iraqi population sought an improved standard of living and became restive when the government failed to meet its expectations. Saddam found it deeply offensive that rather than being grateful to Iraq and to him personally for saving Kuwait from the Iranian mullahs, the emir of Kuwait lowered oil prices, thereby cutting into Iraq's oil revenues; refused to forgive Iraq its war debt; and turned down Iraq's request to buy or lease the islands of Warba and Bubiyan. The Iraqi leadership also accused Kuwait of using state-of-the-art drilling technology to tap into the underground reservoir of Iraqi oil in the Rumaylah field, further reducing Iraq's sources of income. Throughout the summer of 1990, Saddam proclaimed that he considered these actions tantamount to economic war and threatened that Iraq would take action if Kuwait did not agree to its demands.[7]

More prosaically, Saddam Hussein simply wanted to add Kuwait's fabulous wealth to the depleted Iraqi treasury and believed that nothing could prevent him from taking control of his small, poorly armed neighbor. Kuwait's armed forces consisted of 20,300 troops, 245 tanks, and 35 combat aircraft; Iraq outnumbered them 25 to 1 in tanks and 20 to 1 in combat aircraft. Thus, Saddam had little fear of serious resistance.

Iraq had long claimed that Kuwait had been a district governed by Basra during the Ottoman Empire and that the separate emirate was an artificial creation of the British, who sought to divide and control the Iraqi people. Saddam used this argument to characterize Iraq's takeover of Kuwait as an "internal matter," but he fully expected that the world would react negatively. Indeed, the United States responded immediately by condemning the invasion and freezing Iraqi assets. U.S. policy was motivated by a combination of ideology and realpolitik. The only remaining superpower could not stay passive when one sovereign state invaded another—a country whose independent status had been recognized by the United Nations (UN). Equally important, the United States viewed the invasion of Kuwait as a threat to oil fields in the region on which the United States and its allies depended. The UN Security Council also condemned the invasion within hours.

On August 8, President George H. W. Bush publicly outlined the U.S. position, stating both defensive and offensive objectives. The United States would defend Saudi Arabia against a possible invasion and would pursue four political objectives: to effect the immediate, complete, and unconditional withdrawal of all Iraqi forces from Kuwait; to restore Kuwait's legitimate government; to protect the lives of American citizens; and to promote the security and the stability of the Persian Gulf.[8] That afternoon, the first squadron of U.S. fighter-bombers arrived at Dhahran Air Base, marking the beginning of an American deployment that would include more than 500,000 men and women and several million tons of equipment and supplies.

The deployment was initially geared toward defending Saudi Arabia (Operation Desert Shield), but the Coalition soon started preparing for the offensive scenario (Operation Desert Storm).

While the United States took the lead in opposing the Iraqi occupation, the Bush administration worked with the UN and secured broad support for its undertakings. As the Iraqi occupation continued, the UN Security Council consecutively passed twelve resolutions, culminating on November 29, 1990, in the authorization for the American-led Coalition to use "all means necessary" if Iraqi forces did not leave Kuwait by January 15, 1991.

When it became obvious that Iraq would not comply with the UN resolutions, President Bush authorized Operation Desert Storm. The Bush administration had from the beginning defined two constraints that went hand in hand with the political objectives and were governed by the same combination of ideology and realpolitik. The first was to minimize U.S. and Coalition casualties and collateral damage resulting from military attacks, taking special precautions to avoid Iraqi civilian casualties. The administration believed that low casualties would be essential to securing and maintaining U.S. public support for the war. The second was to discourage Israel from undertaking any military action. With Egypt, Syria, and other Arab states declaring their commitment to the liberation of Kuwait, the cooperation between Christians and Muslims was in many ways unprecedented. Not only had Saudi Arabia invited military forces to the region, but it would also fund large parts of the participation of Coalition forces, make preexisting bases available, and ensure an abundance of fuel. U.S. policymakers recognized that it would be very difficult, if not impossible, to maintain a multinational coalition that relied on Arab support if Israel became a de facto member of the alliance.

Saddam Hussein could have averted a full-scale conflict if he had made political concessions early on and withdrawn his troops from Kuwait. Instead, his immediate response was to demonstrate his resolve by declaring complete annexation of Kuwait as Iraq's "nineteenth province." The weeks and months that followed witnessed an enormous military buildup: the Iraqis built "Fortress Kuwait," while the Coalition deployed more and more troops to the region. The Coalition's military preparations were coupled with diplomatic initiatives and economic sanctions. Meanwhile, the Iraqis showed little mercy toward occupied Kuwait,[9] and their brutality strengthened the Coalition's justification for action.

In hindsight, Saddam made several major miscalculations. The first was that his surprise attack caused the United States to become suspicious about his wider intentions—especially the possibility that he might order the Iraqi troops positioned on the Saudi-Kuwaiti border to advance into Saudi Arabia. Thus, when four days after the invasion Saddam promised the United States that he would not attack Saudi Arabia, he lacked credibility. Moreover, he had not foreseen that the Arab League, as well as the UN, would sharply condemn his actions. Most important, he had not predicted that King Fahd of Saudi Arabia would call upon the United States for help, he underestimated the U.S. administration's determination to see Kuwait liberated, and he failed to realize that the Soviet Union was no longer in a position to influence U.S. decision making.[10]

Nevertheless, Saddam did not view war as an instrument to be used only when all other options had been exhausted. Rather, he seems to have believed that this war would provide him a historic opportunity to unite the Arab peoples under his leadership and to deal with the conspiracies of his enemies—who included the Gulf states as well as the United States and Israel. Ideally, Iraq would retain Kuwait, or at least part of it; however, if that proved impossible, Iraq could avoid humiliation simply by putting up a fight. According to Saddam's calculations, if Iraq achieved even the appearance of a stalemate with the Coalition, he and his regime would reap enormous political dividends and prestige in the Arab world. Finally, even if Iraq suffered a military defeat, Saddam would ensure the survival of his regime. Thus, despite the unexpectedly large and determined forces mustering against him, Saddam resolved to stay in Kuwait and fight the "Mother of All Battles."

THE AIR CAMPAIGN: THE LIBERATION OF KUWAIT

Secretary of Defense Richard Cheney and his military commanders, Army Generals Colin Powell (the chairman of the Joint Chiefs of Staff) and Norman Schwarzkopf (the commander in chief of U.S. Central Command), defined their military goals according to the declared political objectives and the associated political constraints: to destroy Iraq's military capability to wage war; to gain and maintain air superiority; to cut Iraqi supply lines; to eliminate Iraq's nuclear, biological, and chemical (NBC) capability; to destroy the Republican Guard forces; and to facilitate the liberation of Kuwait City by Arab forces.[11] Having consulted various air power experts, General Schwarzkopf became convinced that air power could play an unprecedented role in preparing for the liberation by ensuring that bloodshed on the ground would be kept to a minimum. With a substantial leap of faith, Schwarzkopf moved beyond the traditional AirLand Battle doctrine, which saw air power as only a supporting rather than a dominant element of a military campaign. Schwarzkopf instead decided to give air power time to systematically decompose the Iraqi political-military apparatus by attacking high-value targets in downtown Baghdad, lines of communications throughout Iraq, as well as ground formations in occupied Kuwait.[12]

The conceptual framework for the offensive operation had been clearly defined and was in place only three weeks after the Iraqi invasion of Kuwait. On August 25, Schwarzkopf declared his intent:

> Initially execute deception operations to focus his [Saddam Hussein's] attention on defense and cause incorrect organization of forces. We will initially attack into Iraqi homeland using air power to decapitate his leadership, command and control, and eliminate his ability to reinforce Iraqi forces in Kuwait and Southern Iraq. We will then gain undisputed air superiority over Kuwait so that we can subsequently and selectively attack Iraqi ground forces with air power in order to reduce his combat power and destroy reinforcing units. Finally, we will fix Iraqi forces in place and destroy reinforcing units, attacks followed by armored force penetration and exploitation to seize key lines of communication nodes, which will put us in a position to interdict resupply and remaining reinforcements from Iraq and eliminate forces in Kuwait.[13]

Against this backdrop, Schwarzkopf defined a four-phased strategy: a strategic air campaign to establish air superiority over Iraq and incapacitate its regime; a subsequent air campaign to establish air superiority over Kuwait; a series of air strikes against Iraqi tanks, artillery, and troops in Kuwait; and, finally, a ground campaign that would secure the liberation of Kuwait.[14] While the different elements of the air campaign were to be executed concurrently, with various levels of effort, the final phase—the ground campaign—would not start until the fighting capacity of Iraqi formations had been reduced by 50 percent.

Saddam Hussein underestimated the military might and the technical superiority of his opponents. Still, he expected that the Coalition would open hostilities with an air campaign and was confident that the Iraqis could absorb such punishment and even succeed in shooting down several Coalition aircraft with its air defense system. He viewed the air campaign merely as a phase before the "real war." In anticipation of large-scale air attacks, he instructed his commanders to ensure "wide dispersion and large distances between different set of troops" and to combine the principle of dispersion with the extensive use of camouflage and decoys.[15] The initiatives generally focused on "force protection," were passive in nature, and included restrictions on using electronic communications. The Iraqi army's chief of staff later noted that Saddam gave the order "not [to] use the phones. . . . there were microwave phones and landlines, he prohibited us from using [them all], all messages were to be hand delivered through liaison officers."[16]

If a ground war occurred, Saddam's overall military strategy rested on inflicting high casualties as he was well aware that this was the Western world's most vulnerable point. Over time, he reasoned, Iraq would inflict higher losses than the Coalition could bear. Moreover, he viewed the Coalition as an ad hoc alliance and therefore an unstable one. Like the United States, he recognized that Arab nations would find it politically impossible to remain in an alliance that included Israel as an active member, and therefore he planned on attacks that would draw Israel into the conflict.

CONTROL OF THE AIR: SUPPRESSION OF THE IRAQI AIR DEFENSE SYSTEM

The responsibility for executing the Coalition air campaign fell on the shoulders of Schwarzkopf's air commander, Lieutenant General Charles A. Horner.[17] With aircraft from the United States and eleven other European and Arab countries,[18] his first operational task was to gain control of the air.

The Iraqi air force was considered the sixth largest in the world. It had a substantial number of attack helicopters and more than seven hundred combat aircraft, including the aging MiG–21 and the more capable MiG–23 and MiG–25. Most important, it had thirty-five MiG–29s and sixty-five French-built Mirage F–1Es, both high-technology air superiority fighters. These aircraft were supported by an infrastructure of twenty-four main operating bases, thirty dispersal bases, and more than six hundred hardened aircraft shelters, some of which were designed to survive a nuclear attack.

However, studies of the Iran-Iraq War indicated that Baghdad would depend mainly on its ground-based air defenses rather than fighter aircraft to deal with air attacks.[19] To gain and maintain air superiority, the Coalition set out to suppress Iraq's integrated air defense system and its radar-guided surface-to-air missiles (SAMs), destroy Iraqi combat aircraft, and render its airfields unusable.

The Iraqi air defense system, named KARI (Iraq spelled backward in French), included four sector operation centers, seventeen regional interception centers, and more than four hundred observation posts, most of them well protected by concrete and equipped with state-of-the-art technology. Although the air defenses were dispersed throughout the country, focusing on the defense of more than 200 national "headquarters and projects," of which 125 were military, the KARI system was set up primarily to deal with attacks from the east (Israel) and the west (Iran).[20]

KARI's command and control system was designed to track airborne threats and allocate particular tracks to either fighter aircraft or SAM batteries. The radar-guided SAMs included SA–2s, SA–3s, SA–6s, and the shorter range SA–8s and Rolands. These batteries were concentrated around major cities and significant military facilities, with the purpose of shooting down aircraft from medium and high altitudes. In addition, Iraq had a large number of antiaircraft artillery and a variety of infrared SAMs to protect point targets from low-altitude threats.

Coalition planners realized early on that KARI was the nervous system of Iraq's air defenses. Thus, the plan to suppress Iraq's radar-guided SAMs without risking numerous casualties to friendly forces was based on a three-track approach. The first track sought to damage and disable the command and control system, thereby preventing Iraqi commanders from coordinating a sustainable defense. This portion of the plan first became "visible" to the Iraqis through the impact of precision-guided bombs from stealthy F–117s and, shortly afterward, Tomahawk land attack missiles. It was heavily armed U.S. Army AH–64 Apache and MH–53 Pave Low helicopters, however, that first crossed into Iraqi airspace and destroyed a radar station guarding the approaches to Baghdad.

The second track focused on the active suppression of Iraq's radar-guided SAMs by using drones and high-speed antiradiation missiles (HARMs). The Coalition launched a series of BQM–74 drones in advance of suppression of enemy air defense (SEAD) packages. The drones looked like aircraft on Iraqi radar screens, and as the Iraqis activated their SAMs, they had to turn on their radars to fire. When the radars revealed their positions, HARMs from Wild Weasel F–4Gs and F/A–18s destroyed them to free the medium-altitude range for non-stealthy aircraft. In the first hours of the war, Coalition sensors logged nearly one hundred Iraqi air defense radar emissions—a number that dropped to fifteen shortly afterward and then became only "sporadic." The Coalition fired five hundred HARMs during the first twenty-four hours of the war, with the result that Iraqi air defense operators quickly realized that their best chance of survival lay in keeping their SAM batteries switched off.[21]

The third track followed up the initial weakening of the Iraqi air defenses with wide and deep attacks by a whole range of aircraft: A–10s, F–16s, F–111Es, F–111Fs, F–15s, GR–1s, F/A–18s, A–6Es, and B–52s. The plan was to ensure that the attacks were so intense that the Iraqis would be unable to defend themselves in a coordinated fashion and thus would be discouraged from further action.

By U.S. government estimates, the Coalition attacks effectively eliminated the Iraqi air defense system within the first hour of war: after the very first night of operations, individual air defense sectors were forced into autonomous mode, and KARI no longer functioned as an integrated system. The initial HARM attacks, combined with precision strikes from F–117s and Tomahawk cruise missiles, left much of KARI shattered, opening up the country so completely that within days, Coalition air-to-air tankers regularly operated in Iraqi airspace.[22] Simultaneously,

Coalition aircraft rendered several airfields inoperable and severely damaged others by dropping mines on runways and hitting maintenance and storage facilities. By preventing the Iraqis from taking to the skies, the Coalition also eliminated an especially feared possibility: that the Iraqis might use aircraft to deliver biological or chemical weapons.

After the first night of attacks, Saddam Hussein visited the air defense center in Baghdad to receive an update on unfolding events and provide guidance. His main purpose was not to assess the damage that the Coalition had inflicted but to prevent the Iraqi air defense commanders and Iraqi air force from overreacting. He reminded his forces that in the greater scheme of his strategy for a long campaign, their presence on the battlefield was more important than their military effectiveness. He then ordered them to reposition MiG–29s to air bases that had already been struck, assuming that the Coalition would focus on the undamaged airfields. He instructed the air defense commanders that rather than engage in intense and random firing, they should institute "disciplined shooting instructions because the enemy will try to force us to use our ammunition continuously."[23]

As for Saddam Hussein's "courageous air falcons," with few exceptions the Iraqi pilots did not fight after the first few days. The Iraqis flew slightly over one hundred air-to-air sorties in the first three days of the war—an unimpressive performance given the size of Iraq's air force.[24] Around midday on January 24, the Iraqi air force came close to completing its most daring and only significant strike mission of the war: two F–1s set out to attack the huge oil export terminal center at Ras Tanura, Saudi Arabia, but a Royal Saudi Air Force F–15C shot down both.[25] From the next day onward, the Iraqi air force registered fewer than five sorties a day, and even the best pilots stood little chance: nearly half of the thirty-three confirmed allied air-to-air kills were accomplished beyond visual range. Many Iraqi pilots never knew what hit them. Others were shot down shortly after takeoff; thus, Iraqi pilots soon became reluctant to fly at all. Just as the air defenders quickly learned that activating their radars meant inviting a deadly attack, the pilots concluded that flying meant dying.[26]

Iraqi records concede that after one week of Coalition bombing, "The enemy has achieved air superiority. . . . The Iraqi Air Force lost the ability to move between bases. . . . The air bases themselves were 'busy repairing the tarmacs and runways and deactivating the bombs.'"[27] The Iraqi air force commanders quickly realized that they could not dispute Coalition air superiority and thus sought to hide and protect Iraqi aircraft in hardened shelters rather than challenge the Coalition in the air. After four days of operations, Coalition aircraft began to destroy these shelters with precision-guided munitions. F–111Fs, capable of carrying four laser-guided bombs, served as the principal shelter-busters, delivering GBU–10s and GBU–24s. According to Iraqi reports, "The enemy was able to strike these bunkers, destroy them, and the aircraft inside them. While the battle was still going, orders were given to evacuate the [bunkers] of all the aircraft to outside the airbase into the surrounding area."[28] The "surrounding area" meant relocating aircraft to schools and mosques, as Saddam was certain that the Coalition would not attack civilian, historic, or religious sites. Aircraft were also camouflaged in palm groves, placed under tents "covered with a layer of mud to match the surrounding area,"[29] or buried in the sand. The overall effect was to render all the aircraft irrelevant by moving them away from operational airfields.

The decision to send first-line combat aircraft to sanctuary in Iran further illustrates Iraq's desperation.[30] Even before the war, Saddam had decided to send Iraq's largest aircraft, Soviet-made Ilyushin transporters, to Iran, and he had ordered the remaining transportation fleet hidden in "hills and valleys,"[31] but on January 26 he issued an order that the Iraqi air force fly its surviving combat aircraft to Iran. The memorandum directs that eighteen Mirages, nine Sukhois, and one Falcon–50 be "evacuated" to Iran; additional orders were issued over the next three weeks. Iraqi intelligence reports state that a total of 137 Iraqi aircraft and 11 captured Kuwaiti aircraft were sent to Iran before and during the war.[32] Saddam later explained that the decision to evacuate resulted from Coalition air superiority and the limited impact Iraqi planes had on the battle. Thus, for "safekeeping . . . the planes were sent to Iran until the appropriate time comes to use them against the enemy."[33]

Having suppressed the Iraqi air defense system and rendered the Iraqi air force largely inoperable, the Coalition had achieved the basis from which allied air commanders could mount systematic and sustained attacks from the medium-altitude environment of ten thousand to twelve thousand feet against any target in Iraq without major risk to Coalition aircraft and pilots.[34] On January 27, Schwarzkopf and Horner declared that the Coalition had secured air supremacy, as distinguished from air superiority, which it had seized in the first moments of the war. The declaration characterized the Iraqi air force as no longer combat-effective.[35]

Although the Iraqis had to accept that they would be bombed whenever and wherever the Coalition chose, they had one weapon that presented a major challenge to the Coalition: modified Scud missiles attached to mobile launchers that could reach any city in Israel. Before the war began, Saddam had decided that he could achieve three goals by attacking Israel: improve Iraqi morale; increase Iraq's and his own personal prestige in the Arab world; and force the Jewish state to retaliate by bombing Iraq, thereby driving the Arab states out of the Coalition.

As an immediate response to the Coalition's attack on Baghdad, Saddam Hussein ordered his missile commander to begin "striking targets inside the criminal Zionist entity with the heaviest fire possible." Probably aware of the warning issued by Secretary of State James Baker in early January that the United States would be willing to use unconventional weapons if the Iraqis used chemical or biological weapons, Saddam specified that "strikes must be carried out with 'ordinary' conventional ammunition for the missiles. The firing must continue until further notice."[36]

On January 18, Iraq launched eight missiles in quick succession at predesignated targets in Tel Aviv and Haifa. The Iraqi operational pattern of firing, moving, confirming new targets, reloading, and firing again from a position five to ten kilometers from the previous one became more efficient with every launch. However, the actual number of launches decreased thanks to a combination of Coalition efforts and Saddam's order to hold back to ensure that Iraq would not run out of missiles. Of the eighty-eight total Scud launches, thirty occurred during the first seven days of the war. January 25, when Iraq fired ten missiles at Israel and Saudi Arabia, saw the most launches. Over the last thirty days of the war, the Iraqis barely launched one missile per day on average.[37]

The United States assigned Patriot antiair missiles to counter these Scuds. Although after-action reports questioned the military effectiveness of these missiles, they contributed significantly to raising public morale in Israel and helped discourage Israel from undertaking military action. Yet while the Coalition succeeded in keeping Israel out of the war, the Scud attacks allowed Saddam Hussein to make a claim that gained the respect of many Arabs: Iraq was the only Arab state with the courage to attack deep into Jewish territory. According to Saddam, the Israelis "stood around with their hands positioned on their heads, and the missiles rained down on them."[38]

Operations intended to gain and maintain control of the air accounted for 14 percent of the Coalition's total air-to-ground strikes.[39] The Coalition launched 1,270 strikes against SAM batteries, 2,990 against airfields, and 1,460 against Scud launchers. An Iraqi after-action report shows that the Iraqis had assumed that the air attacks would be at low altitude, permitting destruction of Coalition aircraft. Iraq certainly had not anticipated the sheer mass of air power, or that the "interceptors would be neutralized in such a short period of time."[40]

STRATEGIC ATTACK: INCAPACITATING THE IRAQI REGIME

At the same time as the Coalition established air superiority, it also sought to paralyze the Iraqi leadership, degrade Iraq's military capabilities, and neutralize the collective will to fight.[41] This strategic portion of the air offensive emphasized concurrent and precise targeting of the regime itself. Rather than apply air power in a gradual fashion, it was designed as an all-out offensive. The underlying theory was that striking at the heart of the regime from the opening moment of the war would introduce so much friction into Iraq's political-military system that it would be unable to coordinate offensive and defensive responses effectively. Air attacks would simultaneously disrupt crucial communications nodes and electric power throughout the country. Additional strikes would disable facilities for the production and storage of refined petroleum products and advanced weapons facilities such as those related to Iraq's nuclear weapons program.

As noted, this concept represented a significant departure from the established military doctrine at the time, according to which air power could play only a supporting and secondary role to ground forces as soon as air superiority was achieved. It was also a departure from the type of strategic bombing associated with the Second World War: rather than target the population and industry per se, the new strategy was designed to incapacitate the leadership itself and to achieve functional disruption and dislocation rather than physical destruction. For this aspect of the campaign, the Coalition relied on precision-guided munitions and designated the F–117 twin engine strike aircraft rather than the traditional heavy bomber as the "strategic bomber" of choice.[42] With the exception of a few F–16 sorties, only the F–117 and Tomahawk cruise missiles were used against downtown Baghdad.

The leadership targets included presidential palaces and residences, national command and control bunkers, Ba'ath Party headquarters, secret police centers, and government ministries. The telecommunications category encompassed targets such as radio relay facilities, telephone exchanges, fiber-optic repeater stations, satellite receiving stations, and television and radio centers. The electricity category consisted primarily of power generation plants and transformer stations, while oil targets included refineries, fertilizer plants, and pumping stations. The air planners also listed "unconventional weapons" targets, such as nuclear research facilities, in addition to research and production facilities for chemical and biological weapons.

Interviews with Iraqi officers after Desert Storm suggest that the combination of stealth aircraft, precision-guided bombs, and cruise missiles never completely cut communications between Baghdad, Basra, and the military forces occupying Kuwait, despite 260 strikes against leadership facilities and 580 strikes against command, control, and communications sites.[43] Iraq had modern computerized equipment with high levels of redundancy between multiple landlines, fiber-optic cables, and microwave relays. Saddam Hussein also relied on face-to-face meetings with his staff, couriers on motorcycles, and predelegated orders.

In sum, aerial attacks on leadership and communications facilities caused the regime untold inconvenience, consumed resources of valuable spares, and demanded a high level of repair effort. The delays and uncertainties, combined with the overall damage caused by strategic bombing, compelled the Iraqi leadership to spend considerable time in improvised and for the most part ineffectual command centers. In addition to fearing for their personal safety, many Ba'ath Party members and government ministers were forced to relocate their headquarters to school buildings and to shift to less-than-reliable backup communications.[44] Saddam Hussein ordered his ministers and commanders to stay on the move, to change meeting places and locations for rest, to follow unpredictable schedules, and to travel incognito, in civilian dress. The Iraqi leader himself conducted meetings from a variety of locations and seldom slept in the same place more than a few times in a row; occasionally, he changed locations in the middle of the night.[45] Although the Coalition never succeeded killing the Iraqi leader or any of the key members of the regime, strikes on the command and control headquarters seem to have kept the Iraqi leadership under constant pressure.[46]

In addition, recognizing that Iraq could not preserve what it could not hide, the Iraqi president on January 22 ordered all government ministers to "break down any device, [or] machine into vital parts . . . and move them outside [of] the sites that the enemy might recognize through air photography."[47] He urged his ministers to disassemble whatever they could in order to "reassemble them intact once the war is over [and we are] crowned with a great victory."[48]

Coalition air planners believed that the loss of electric power would degrade Iraq's military capability as well as lower the morale of the Iraqi population, and hoped that the people would then put pressure on the Iraqi regime. The Coalition succeeded at reducing power output to about 55 percent during the opening hours of the war and 88 percent by February 9. Baghdad and the other major cities lacked electric lights throughout the war. Iraq's oil refining capability was reduced by 93 percent after one month of bombing, and the Coalition destroyed about 20 percent of the fuel and lubricants at refineries and major depots.[49] These attacks certainly worsened the situation of the leadership, but it is difficult to assess the impact of this effort alone.

The Coalition achieved only mixed success against targets related to weapons of mass destruction, although aircraft bombed production, storage, and research facilities deep within Iraq. Air strikes caused substantial damage to the *known* programs: of the eight nuclear targets listed by the air planners, the Coalition had destroyed five and damaged two by the end of the war. However, later investigations revealed that Iraq had more extensive nuclear programs than previously thought; the UN inspection team uncovered twenty-one facilities. Attacks on Iraq's chemical and biological production fared better, and the Coalition destroyed or heavily damaged 75 percent of the known facilities.

The failure to take out more of the research and production facilities reflected not a failure of air power, but rather inadequate intelligence. Air power is seldom more effective than the intelligence on which it relies for targeting.[50] As it happened, the Iraqis had anticipated some of these attacks: after-action reports show that some of the 970 strikes at NBC facilities amounted to precision bombing of empty buildings.[51]

Strategic attacks also had a tactical side effect. During Operation Desert Storm, the Ba'ath Party, despite its political commissars in the armed forces, failed to prevent an unprecedented level of troop desertion, and its grip on power loosened considerably. Approximately 20 percent of the troops were on leave at any given time, and few of those on leave when the bombing started returned to the theater, partly because they refused to and partly because the damaged infrastructure made it difficult to do even for those who wanted to fight.[52] The party could do little about this situation. Even the *Mukhabarat* (secret police) seemed more preoccupied with staying alive than with protecting the regime.

From the Coalition's perspective, the course of the strategic air campaign must be viewed in the framework of political constraints that demanded minimization of casualties. Pilots operating over downtown Baghdad went to extraordinary lengths to avoid collateral damage and thus stayed away from targets that would draw unfavorable media coverage. For example, the air planners were well aware that the Rasheed Hotel had a vast intelligence center in the basement, but it was never attacked. The planners also suspected that numerous bunkers and houses served as operational centers or residences for regime members, but they were very careful not to authorize attacks without confirmed reports of such uses.

The most unfortunate incident during the war was the attack on the al-Firdos command and communications bunker. Two F–117As dropped one bomb each on the bunker: one clipped the outside of the bunker; the other penetrated the bunker and exploded, killing between two hundred and three hundred women and children who had taken shelter on the upper floor. The attack drew much negative press, and on February 13, Schwarzkopf informed Horner that central Baghdad was "off limits." Although the prohibition was lifted on February 22, the last two weeks of strategic bombing were more notable for frustration than for results, since the air planners were denied the option of attacking vital targets in Baghdad.[53]

The strategic air campaign helped to meet the military objectives of Desert Storm, but it had limitations. Although the bombing of Baghdad seriously weakened the Iraqi regime, the planners had no real knowledge and even less understanding of the system that Saddam Hussein had put into place: the workings of the regime, the social fabric of the state, and the security system created to ensure his personal safety and authority. When considering the effectiveness of the strategic portion of the air campaign, one must also recall that for the last two-thirds of the Gulf War, the Coalition conducted the strategic air campaign at a minimum level.[54] Several hundred sorties were canceled because of difficult weather conditions, the Scud hunt required assets that could have been used against the leadership and its communication apparatus, and the priority given to targeting Iraqi ground forces resulted in the strategic air campaign receiving less emphasis than some of the air planners had hoped.

SUPPLY INTERDICTION: DEPRIVING IRAQI TROOPS OF FOOD AND WATER

After days of sustained and systematic attacks against the air defense system and strategic targets in Baghdad, the situation steadily worsened for the Iraqi state, population, and military as the air offensive broadened to include attacks on supply routes, bridges, railroad yards, various military production and storage facilities, and water distribution centers. By depriving the Iraqi army of food and water, ammunition, petroleum, oil, lubricants, and other essential supplies, the Coalition expected to weaken the Iraqi soldiers' ability to resist the ground offensive.[55] General Powell declared on January 23 that "our strategy to go after this army is very, very simple. First, we're going to cut it off, and then we're going to kill it."[56]

Powell's statement referred to air interdiction of the highways and rail lines on which troops and material moved between central Iraq and the Kuwaiti theater of operations (KTO).[57] Bridges became a key target set to "isolate the theater." General Schwarzkopf ordered strikes against certain bridges early in the air campaign, not only to stop the flow of supplies and movement of forces into the theater, but also to interrupt the retreat of the elite Republican Guard forces out of it.[58] Bridges also represented attractive targets because there were relatively few of them, and they were easy to locate, vulnerable to attack, hard to repair, and frequently difficult for the Iraqis to bypass. Moreover, the Iraqis had no real countermeasures to many of these attacks and failed to restore any of the major bridges during the war. By the end of the war, 37 of 126 highway bridges and all 9 railroad bridges south of Baghdad were no longer usable; another 9 highway bridges were severely damaged but passable.[59] Of fifty-four fixed bridges across the two rivers, forty were unusable, ten were damaged, and four had purposely been left undamaged. Thirty-two pontoon bridges constructed to circumvent the effects of the bridge attacks were also destroyed.[60] This in turn prevented a speedy retreat of the Iraqi army's armored and mechanized units,[61] although much of the Republican Guard did manage to escape.

Supply interdiction quickly achieved its intended purpose of degrading the position of the Iraqi military in Kuwait. Essential commodities failed to reach deployed troops in quantities sufficient to maintain their combat capability. The Iraqi truck fleet was large enough to resupply the Kuwaiti theater despite air attacks on convoys and vehicle parks, but the attacks caused considerable distribution problems even from nearby sources. The bombing greatly complicated the transport of supplies from dumps in Kuwait to Iraq's unit logistics center and troops in the field by targeting supply convoys and even individual trucks.[62] Prisoners of war cited food shortages and scarcity in drinking water as a leading reason for low morale in their units.[63] Some forces were virtually on the brink of starvation and dehydration, and the shortage of supplies in general was a major reason why several battalions surrendered after only minimal resistance.[64] Several Iraqi generals captured during the military offensive stated that if the air campaign had continued for another two or three weeks, the Iraqi army would have been forced to withdraw as a result of logistical strangulation.[65]

Denying transportation had a secondary effect: it became very hard for the Iraqis to deliver orders. Lieutenant General Sultan Hasim, the Iraqi deputy army chief of staff, noted that while he was preparing the withdrawal of forces from Kuwait, communication between Baghdad and Kuwait City was difficult "because of the bombardment of roads and the destruction of their vehicles."[66] Iraqi staff officers later reported that even if they managed to reach the tactical headquarters, they often found no commanding officer present. As one Iraqi officer complained, "When there is no company commander or a regimental commander or a brigade commander, then how can you carry out a withdrawal?"[67]

The ability of military operations to affect enemy morale has always been a controversial topic, and although the Iraqi soldiers doubtless experienced a gradual collapse of morale, it is difficult to assess whether a particular aspect of psychological stress had the greatest impact. The Coalition attacks certainly ensured that Iraqi soldiers were disoriented and experienced the paralysis of fear and shock, emotional effects such as loss of confidence and feelings of isolation, physiological effects resulting from sleep deprivation and the lack of adequate food and water, and intellectual effects that caused the Iraqi soldiers to question whether continued fighting served any purpose. Yet *morale* encompasses many abstract factors, and it is hard to establish a correlation between a certain type of attack and specific effects. However, common sense would indicate that lowered morale contributed to the Iraqi forces' physical inability to fight efficiently. For example, air strikes directly and significantly reduced the size of the Iraqi truck fleet, but the secondary effect was that fewer drivers were *willing* to make the trips from Baghdad and Basra to Kuwait.

DIRECT FORCE ATTACK: PREPARING THE BATTLEFIELD

The Coalition directed some two-thirds of the air-to-ground strikes in Operation Desert Storm against the Iraqi forces in the KTO. Strikes against Iraqi armor and artillery were the most distinctive feature of this effort, but trucks and troops were also prominent targets. The campaign targeted the Iraqi navy and Iraqi forces on the move, but the majority of the strikes were directed against the in-place Iraqi army and the Republican Guard. While much of the effort to gain control of the air and the strategic attacks on downtown Baghdad employed precision weapons and produced a sudden degradation of Iraqi capabilities, this portion of the air war can better be described as a gradual attrition of Iraqi forces. The Coalition's plan was to use the strikes to reduce Iraq's fighting capability by 50 percent—an unprecedented goal for air power—to ensure that Coalition ground forces would engage a weakened enemy.

Iraq had deployed forces in three echelons to meet the anticipated ground attack. The frontline forces, primarily Shiite conscript formations placed along the border between Kuwait and Saudi Arabia, were to meet the initial Coalition attack. Their role was to slow the enemy advance and cause attrition, while allowing the Iraqi military leadership to determine the Coalition's main axis of attack. The Iraqi III Corps divisions, which were part of the frontline and positioned along the coast, were the best trained and equipped of those deployed in the first line; the VII Corps divisions, positioned west of the Wadi al-Batin, were the worst. The second line consisted of tactical and operational reserves of armored and mechanized divisions deployed throughout central Kuwait and extending into Iraq. These forces would engage the Coalition forces that succeeded in breaching the front line. Eight Republican Guard divisions in the northwestern corner of Kuwait formed the third echelon. These forces represented the strategic reserves poised to counterattack the main Coalition formations. They were in essence an extension of the regime, as the Republican Guard was filled with very loyal officers, mostly Sunni Arabs and many of them from the area of Tikrit—Saddam Hussein's hometown. The commander of the Republican Guard saw his mission as a threefold defense: "Carry out operations to abort the enemy's attacks in depth of the region. Carry out counterattack operations in the locations where the enemy was able to achieve a foothold. . . . establish a confrontation line for the defense of al-Basra, if the situation required it."[68]

There was nothing sophisticated about the plan to destroy the Iraqi army, or the Republican Guard for that matter. The air planners divided Kuwait and southern Iraq into so-called kill boxes (225 square miles each) and assigned aircraft to eliminate as much of Iraq's weaponry and equipment as possible within each box. The Coalition basically pursued a strategy of attrition: of throwing air power up against an enemy in dug-in positions. Some aircraft dropped precision-guided munitions; others spread their loads of bombs and cluster bomb units over the desert landscape, hoping that even if they did not hit anything, they would at least undermine Iraqi morale.[69]

The first week of the air campaign saw 938 sorties in the KTO, the second week another 2,796, the third week 3,512, the fourth week 3,972, the fifth week an all-time high of 4,048, and in the sixth and final week, 3,807 sorties were recorded.[70] The planners based their choice of armament on the nature of the target and aircraft available for employment. Thus, the campaign was an odd mixture of new and old weapons systems, from F–117s and F–111Fs "plinking" tanks with five-hundred-pound laser-guided bombs to B–52s spreading fear and demoralization from high altitudes.[71] The B–52s conducted strikes throughout the theater and were the primary resource against area targets such as breaching sites, ammunition stockpiles, troop concentrations, or military field headquarters.[72] F–16s, F/A–18s, and F–15s (F–111s and A–6s at night) flew against the more distant and better equipped Republican Guard, while close to the front, other Coalition aircraft—F–5s, Jaguars, and A–4s—tackled the entrenched infantry. Army and Marine attack helicopters were available but mostly were used during the ground campaign.

In total, Coalition aircraft dropped 23,430 bombs on Iraqi formations.[73] The frontline infantry formations bore the brunt of the attacks and incurred the most physical and psychological damage, while the better trained and better equipped Republican Guard divisions farther from the front proved considerably more difficult to destroy.

In after-action reports, Iraqi prisoners spoke of dumb bombs randomly falling on and around them, inducing both a sense of helplessness and a willingness to surrender. According to some prisoner of war reports, the least accurate platform in the Coalition inventory, the B–52, had the greatest impact on their morale.[74] Iraqi officers also stated that the U.S. attack helicopters, and especially the Apache, had a profound effect on the psyche of many senior Iraqi ground commanders. They referred to the helicopters as "sneaking up" on armored formations from any direction with concentrated firepower and mentioned the frustration that resulted from the sense that while fixed-wing aircraft were out of reach, the Iraqi forces at least had a fighting chance against helicopters and failed to capitalize on it.[75]

While precision-guided munitions were effective in reducing the Iraqi war-fighting *capacity*—by destroying leadership and communication facilities, power plants, supply lines, shelters, and military hardware—the overall carpet-bombing in the KTO contributed to further shredding Iraqi morale. The combination of "smart" and "dumb" bombs left Iraqi units and formations on the brink of defeat and disintegration even before the Coalition ground offensive began. In total, the air offensive drew down Iraqi forces to a point where once the ground campaign began, it could advance in the certain knowledge that it would be engaging a largely incapacitated opponent.

CLOSE AIR SUPPORT AND THE GROUND OFFENSIVE: COMPLETING THE VICTORY

The Coalition designed its ground offensive to follow three major axes. Far to the west, XVIII Airborne Corps and the French Sixth Light Armored Division were to drive toward Tallil Air Base, just short of the Euphrates Valley, in a move that the Iraqis might well interpret as the first stage of an assault on Baghdad. In fact, the primary purpose was to establish a blocking position and to protect the main drive by the U.S. VII Corps. The corps, consisting of four heavy divisions and an armored cavalry regiment, together with one British division, was to sweep north and then east to attack the Republican Guard and the rear of the Iraqi army.[76] Finally, the U.S. Marine Corps would push "straight up the middle" into southeastern Kuwait toward Kuwait City, supported by Arab forces organized into Joint Force Command East on its right flank and Joint Force Command North on its left.[77]

The ground campaign depended on three preconditions, all of which rested on the effective use of air power. The first was that air power would allow the massive redeployment of Coalition forces to the far west, first by a substantial airlift of troops and supplies, and second by shielding the movement from Iraqi attacks. In fact, by mid-February, the Coalition's XVIII Airborne Corps had repositioned more than 115,000 soldiers and 21,000 wheeled and 4,300 tracked vehicles over a distance of 500 kilometers west of their initial deployment. At the same time, the Coalition's heavy VII Corps shifted 140,000 soldiers and 32,000 wheeled and 6,600 tracked vehicles more than 200 kilometers to the west.[78] Air supremacy enabled the troops to move undetected and thus permitted operational surprise. Saddam Hussein remained convinced that the main attack would come straight into Kuwait and would be accompanied by a supporting amphibious attack. The Iraqi leadership never realized that the preparations for an amphibious landing were merely a deception by the Coalition.

The second precondition was that the air campaign would reduce Iraqi fighting power by 50 percent, ensuring that the Coalition could start the ground war at its own choosing. When Washington decided in October that Schwarzkopf would be given the Army VII Corps, which was stationed in Germany at the time, Coalition planners accepted that if air operations were to start in mid-January, the ground campaign could not commence until mid- or late February. By the time the Coalition ground forces were ready to cross into Iraq on February 24, air attacks had in fact reduced combat effectiveness in many enemy units below that 50 percent level.[79]

The third precondition was that air assets would support the ground offensive proper, primarily with interdiction and deep strikes to prevent the Iraqis from concentrating their forces for counterattacks, and secondarily with CAS that would further smooth the Coalition advance. While interdiction and deep strikes occurred beyond the fire support coordination line, Horner had introduced the concept of "push CAS" inside that line—that is, air attacks constantly on call at the ground commander's demand. AV–8Bs and F/A–18s provided much of the ground support, but of all the aircraft, the A–10 "Warthog," flying at low altitude with its thirty-millimeter Gatling guns, had the greatest impact.[80]

As it turned out, Coalition ground forces had very little need for classic CAS: air power had pounded and degraded Iraqi ground troops for weeks, and in the four days of battle on the ground, CAS was not essential to accomplishing the mission.[81] The very lack of determined Iraqi resistance made CAS a rather peripheral aspect of Desert Storm. Thus, Desert Storm included few "troops in contact" situations that could serve as examples of how well CAS by fixed-wing aircraft and attack helicopters could be synchronized with the ground fire support system.[82]

By the end of February 27, Coalition forces controlled four-fifths of Kuwait's territory and had cut off virtually all routes of escape to Basra.[83] With the Iraqi forces withdrawn, destroyed, or surrendered, President Bush decided on the following morning to suspend operations. In military terms, Desert Storm constituted one of the most lopsided victories in modern military history.

THE UTILITY OF AIR POWER

The success of the Desert Storm military campaign derived from clear political and military objectives that were declared in advance, command and control arrangements that left no doubt as to who was responsible for what, a sound operational concept, and an "air power–friendly" environment. The utility of offensive air power is always highly situational and depends on the intensity of the campaign and the existence of identifiable targets. In this case, most targets were easy to "find, fix, and strike"— whether leadership facilities, electricity plants, infrastructure in the form of roads, bridges, and rail tracks, or tanks in the field. The Iraqi troops had few places to hide in the relatively flat and featureless desert of Kuwait.[84]

One of the most important factors in the Coalition's success—so obvious that it tends to be obscured by details—was the unambiguous chain of command. General Schwarzkopf, the theater commander, gave Lieutenant General Horner full responsibility for planning and executing the air campaign. Horner was the single point of contact for all aspects of air operations, and the understanding and trust between Schwarzkopf and Horner ensured that both worked toward the same objectives. Operation Desert Storm vindicated the "single manager" concept for the command and control of joint air operations, something airmen had dreamed of since the days of William "Billy" Mitchell.[85]

Most military analysts agree that the 1991 air campaign was a success, at least in operational and military terms, and that the foundation for that success lay in the Coalition's having gained air superiority from the outset. During the first few days of the war, allied attacks degraded the capabilities of the Iraqi air defenses to the point where the campaign could continue at acceptable levels of attrition for as long as Coalition leaders wanted.[86] Each Iraqi air base, including its fighter aircraft and SAMs, was isolated, with early warning radars blinded and the centralized command partly muted. Thus, the Iraqis had no *effective* defense against attacks on their civil and military infrastructure. In total, the Coalition lost 38 fixed-wing aircraft in combat,[87] a rather impressive record given that more than 110,000 flights took place. The Iraqis were able to mount 610 sorties, including combat support and fighters escaping to Iran, and lost 33 aircraft and 5 helicopters in air-to-air combat.

Four schools of thought have emerged regarding which aspect of the U.S.-led air campaign played the most important role in achieving the stated military objectives.[88] The first considers the strategic air attacks the decisive factor, as these strikes paralyzed the Iraqi leadership and thus prevented it from exercising effective command and control. According to these strategic air power advocates, the combination of stealth, precision, and standoff weapons inflicted a level of disruption unprecedented in terms of scale, immediacy, and effect. Denied any offensive option save a brave but brief and hopeless incursion into Saudi Arabia at al-Khafji, the Iraqi leadership could only act as a victim.[89]

The second school claims that the crucial element was that air power denied supplies to the troops. Precision-guided bombs stopped the flow of vehicles that brought water, food, and ammunition to Iraqi soldiers in the desert. The destruction of road and railway bridges, the ceaseless strafing of road traffic from Baghdad to Basra, and the prompt attacks on makeshift pontoon bridges forced the Iraqis to use the few roads that remained open; the resulting congestion in turn made their vehicles easier targets. Travel became slow, perilous, and sometimes impossible.[90] The flow of supplies was never completely halted, but it became erratic, irregular, and considerably below the level required to conduct operations effectively. The interrogation reports of prisoners who deserted or were captured give a strong impression that soldiers had a sense of futility: the Iraqis ran short of water, food, fuel, and spare parts.[91] Incessant, even if not necessarily accurate, bombing may or may not have demoralized them; the precision strikes on supply trucks certainly starved them.

The third school of thought holds that direct strikes on the Iraqi ground forces constituted the most useful application of air power.[92] These strikes left Iraqi troops with an unenviable choice: to stay in dug-in positions known to the enemy and be subjected to very deliberate attack, or to flee from these positions and run an even higher risk of being hit as the enemy attacked "targets of opportunity." In the end, eighty-six thousand Iraqis were taken prisoner. Most of them surrendered rather than being captured in action, and most of those who surrendered did so mainly because of the effect of air attacks. In short, however unsophisticated the attacks themselves, Desert Storm offered the first case in military history in which commanders and planners used air power directly as an operational tool to achieve immediate effects.[93] It seems fairly clear that thirty-eight days of intense and focused air operations against the Iraqi armed forces created the preconditions for one of the more rapid and crushing combined arms ground campaigns in modern military history.[94]

The fourth school of thought, espoused primarily by army traditionalists, represents the inverse of the various air power claims, basically asserting that the ground offensive was the decisive element. This school considers the air campaign merely a prelude to the real battle: however useful air power might have been in softening the resistance of Iraqi forces, it was boots on the ground that ensured the liberation of Kuwait.

Which viewpoint one favors is a matter of personal perspective and the criteria chosen for measuring effectiveness. In fact, probably no single cause accounted for Saddam Hussein's decision to withdraw his troops from Kuwait. The combination of actions—political, diplomatic, and military—added up to a situation in which all prospects of keeping Kuwait were blocked. However unsatisfactory this may be to proponents of a particular theory, it was the totality of the air campaign that ensured the allied victory: the combination of strategic attacks, interdiction, and direct attacks overlaid by air superiority and concluded by a ground offensive.[95] According to Kevin M. Woods, the author of *The Mother of All Battles*:

> It is difficult to determine which events contributed most to the simultaneous chaos in Iraq's government, military, and large parts of the population. Causes

close to the top of any list would certainly be the chaos created during the withdrawal, the vacuum created by fleeing and repositioning security forces inside Iraq, the lack of interior mobility due to destroyed bridges, and the unrelenting Coalition attacks on the Iraqi command and control system. The perception of omnipotent regime control and swift retribution for any infraction had, in the eyes of many inside Iraq and Washington D.C., evaporated.[96]

PERSPECTIVES: UNFINISHED BUSINESS

The applications of air power in Desert Storm, and their strengths and limitations, can be judged only in the framework of the adversaries' overall strategies. Air power certainly helped the Coalition to achieve its stated objectives of freeing Kuwait and securing continued access to Middle East oil. However, neither air power alone nor air power combined with the ground attack produced the result that the Bush administration had hoped for: the overthrow of Saddam Hussein by either humiliated Iraqi generals or a vengeful population.

In the short term, the strategic air offensive did cause the Iraqi leadership to lose firm control over the population. The systematic and precise bombing of Ba'ath Party institutions and government buildings apparently changed the Iraqi people's perception of the party as omnipotent. The offensive damaged a considerable amount of the command and control apparatus and disrupted the regime's ability to communicate effectively with the Iraqi people as well as with soldiers in the field. The cumulative functional disruption, confusion, and disorientation at the strategic and operational levels of command, coupled with the loosened grip of the Ba'ath Party at the local level, considerably reduced Saddam Hussein's ability both to direct military operations and to anticipate and prevent uprisings.[97] The Iraqi people's frustration and anger over intensifying deprivation in daily life, in additional to traditional grievances, helped to spark the Shiite and Kurdish rebellions that took place shortly after the war, and although they did not succeed, their scale was extraordinary for such a police state.[98]

Saddam Hussein believed that the uprisings came closer to overthrowing the regime than either the war with Iran or the recently ended "Mother of all Battles": "the traitorous rebellion was more difficult than the phase which had been before it."[99] Saddam himself suggested that this was in no small part owing to the strategic air campaign: when Ba'ath Party officials, government ministers, and officers were forced to "change locations," the opposition took advantage of the public belief that the state had lost control. He stated after the war that growing insurgent attacks

[s]pread out to the point that the governors would [have to] change the location of his ministry and the [local] security director would change his location, and the police director would change his location and so on. . . . What happened was the government was nonexistent. Well, the government was nonexistent. In such a way that whoever says he was a Sultan, it was possible for him to become a Sultan. So, traitors showed up . . . supported by elements trained and specially prepared to play such a role by Iran. And they erupted in al-Basra and they erupted in other places . . . even in the north.[100]

However, Desert Storm had left large portions of the Republican Guard intact, and they, together with some regular units and Iraq's vast security and intelligence network, succeeded in quelling both the Shiite rebellion in the south and the Kurdish resistance in the north. While the U.S.-led Coalition celebrated its victory, Saddam Hussein secured his regime's survival and, by extension, his personal power base.

This muddled aftermath of an apparently decisive military campaign demonstrates the importance of thinking beyond purely military operations to envision ways of achieving a sustainable peace. The Coalition's lack of any coherent concept or plan for war termination to a large extent negated the achievements of Operation Desert Storm; neither political nor military commanders had considered the endgame.

Saddam Hussein used the postwar period to rewrite history in his own terms. He boasted that he stood tall after an unprecedented air campaign and that the Coalition had declared a cease-fire because it did not have the stomach to fight the Iraqi armed forces any longer. He referred to himself as the first Arab leader who had been able and willing to attack deep into Israel and "dared stand against America."[101]

Undoubtedly, the invasion of Kuwait launched a series of events that eventually led to Saddam Hussein's downfall, but it took another U.S.-led military operation to succeed in toppling the Iraqi regime. The political objectives and overall strategy for Operation Iraqi Freedom (March 19–May 1, 2003) differed from those of Operation Desert Storm in many ways, but particularly in that the military campaign did not rely on effecting a palace coup d'état from a distance. This time, the operation to overthrow Saddam Hussein's regime and replace it with a "broad-based government" was designed to reach and to occupy Baghdad. The military campaign was once again well executed, but the insurgency and the death tolls in the years since 2003 raise questions as to the limitations of force, and the difference between winning battles and campaigns and the much more complex objective of winning the peace for which the war is waged.

OPERATION DELIBERATE FORCE, 1995

Robert C. Owen

— Often, they spent their entire lives without finding an opportunity to
express that hatred . . . but whenever the established order of things is
shaken by some important event, and reason and law are suspended . . . this
mob or rather a section of it . . . overflows into the town . . . and, like a flame
which has sought and has at last found fuel, these long-kept hatreds and
hidden desires for destruction and violence take over the town . . . until
some force larger than themselves suppresses them, or until they burn
themselves out and tire of their own rage.[1] —

AS IS THE CASE FOR MOST IF NOT ALL conflicts, the Bosnian civil war (1992–1995) was
as much about culture, politics, and economics as it was about the clash of arms.
Any assessment of North Atlantic Treaty Organization (NATO) air operations in
support of the United Nations (UN)–sanctioned intervention into that conflict must
account for its human and economic dimensions. This, of course, inserts a high
degree of messiness into what one could hope would otherwise be a simple account
of targeting strategies, weapons effects, and overall results achieved, for the UN and
NATO had plunged themselves into a region of ethnic and geographic complexity,
disproportionate external connections and importance, and political risk. Bosnia was,
in other words, not much different conceptually from other regions and conflicts
that the members of the intervention—the various UN and NATO member states
involving themselves directly in the conflict—might yet face again in other parts
of the world. The details would be different, of course, but the general lesson of
Bosnia—the criticality of understanding the true nature of a conflict before starting
to shoot—holds enduring value.

NATO air operations over Bosnia fell into two phases, the second of which had
two major subdivisions in both chronology and character. In the first phase, beginning

on October 16, 1992, several NATO states contributed aircraft to Operation Sky Watch to enforce a UN no-fly ban on all belligerents in the civil war. Sky Watch is not the subject of this study, since it involved no combat operations. But it was the failure of Sky Watch to dissuade the warring factions from using aircraft that led to the activation of Operation Deny Flight on March 31, 1993. For most of Deny Flight's duration, NATO patrolled the skies over Bosnia observing and reporting on violations of the no-fly ban and, after August 1993, was poised to strike military forces besieging Bosnian cities declared as "safe areas" by the UN or attacking UN troops and relief convoys. In the face of the continued aggression and savagery of the Bosnian Serb faction, NATO began planning for expanded operations not long afterward. This planning culminated in a short but intense air campaign against the military capabilities of the so-called Bosnian Serb Republic between August 30 and September 14, 1995. Though technically just a phase of Deny Flight, this campaign was distinct enough in its intensity, persistence, and somewhat relaxed rules of engagement (ROEs) that it received a separate designation as Operation Deliberate Force. In response to successful peace negotiations, the UN and NATO deactivated Deny Flight on December 20, 1995.

Military and civilian observers at the time recognized that precision weapons took on unprecedented strategic and tactical importance during both Deny Flight and Deliberate Force. Given political divisions within the intervention and strategic uncertainties over the causes of the conflict and the willpower of its factional leaders, the importance of conducting offensive operations quickly and with minimal risk of collateral noncombatant and even combatant casualties was a necessity. Thus, NATO pilots employed guided missiles, laser-guided bombs, and precision-aimed aircraft cannon to conduct most of the few offensive operations authorized during Deny Flight and most of those flown during Deliberate Force. In the case of Deliberate Force, NATO attacked Bosnian Serb targets with 708 precision-guided and only 318 nonprecision missiles and bombs: a 69:31 percent ratio, versus the 8:92 ratio of the Gulf War fought only a few years before. In a very real sense, Deliberate Force was the first "precision war," and few doubted that it pointed the way ahead for modern air forces.

If few observers questioned the value of precision weapons in the conduct of Deny Flight and Deliberate Force, there remains disagreement over the absolute and relative strategic effectiveness of the bombing itself. The complex background of the conflict makes such disagreement unavoidable. As described in the initial assessment of Deliberate Force by the U.S. Air Force (USAF), other forces influenced the end phase of the Bosnian civil war. These included:

- the general exhaustion of all sides after three years of vicious war;
- the desperation of Slobodan Milosevic, the president of Yugoslavia and presumed puppeteer of the indicted war criminals running the Bosnian Serb Republic, to escape the UN economic embargo;
- recent reversals of Bosnian Serb military fortunes at the hands of the armies of Croatia and of the UN-recognized Bosnian government;
- reaffirmed guarantees of Bosnian Serb postconflict territorial integrity and diplomatic autonomy by the UN and the so-called 5-Nation Contact Group (the United States, Britain, Germany, France, and Russia) working separately to broker a peace.

Given the complex interactions among these issues, the Air Force study asserted only that the air campaign was "*a* decisive factor in ending the . . . Bosnian conflict [emphasis added]," one that "at the instant of its application . . . stopped the attacks on the safe areas" and tipped Serb willingness to negotiate.[2] Others at the time emphasized the importance of the Croatian and Bosnian ground offensives as primary factors that forced the Serbian hand.[3]

Now is a good time to review the Bosnian air campaign and the more than a decade of further scholarship on its conduct and effects. Importantly, the linkage of precision weapons effects to the changing characteristics of the conflict and the intervention bears reexamination in light of hindsight. The *restrained* and sporadic use of precision weapons during Deny Flight generally only reinforced perceptions among warring factional leaders that NATO and the UN lacked the stomach for a real fight and, consequently, did much to encourage them to continue their aggressions. In contrast, while intervention politics and uncertainties still imposed significant restraints on targeting and tactics during Deliberate Force, the campaign nevertheless contributed to a rapid breakdown in Serb resistance. Was that because of the will and the weapons of the intervention, or because other factors simply made it a good time for the Serbs to quit? Or, viewed another way, were the other factors bearing on Serb decision making shaped at least in part by NATO's possession and ultimate use of superior air power?

This present reappraisal will begin by laying out the relevant background elements of the Bosnian civil war in enough detail to emphasize its complexity and to describe the constraints and restraints impinging on NATO air leaders, planners, and pilots. Then it will focus on the planning, execution, and outcomes of Deny Flight in general and Deliberate Force more specifically. In the end, these elements of context and operations cast a unique light on the general question of precision air power's effectiveness *relative* to land power, nonprecision air power, and even to some extent its independent decisiveness. The political and moral restraints operating on the intervention rendered precision air attacks and their land power equivalent—indirect artillery fires—its offensive options of first and probably only choice. But given the actual course of events, there is good reason to wonder whether concentrated offensive air strikes (OASs) could have been a viable option for the intervention prior to the summer of 1995. Timing, place, and human will influence the effectiveness of precision air power as much as they do any other element of military and political power.

STRATEGIC CONTEXT

No outsider in the mid-1980s, other than perhaps a few scholars of the region, would have expected the Yugoslavian province of Bosnia and Herzegovina to become a charnel house of ethnic violence in just a few years. After all, Sarajevo, the provincial capital, was the venue for the 1984 Winter Olympics. In that happy time, the city's "face" was all smiles and amity. Its beautiful young people danced in the streets and gave the opening ceremonies light and energy. The region was multiethnic, of course; it was the nexus of three major peoples in the polyglot Yugoslavian nation-state. The so-called Bosniak Serbs of Muslim descent, if not zeal, made up 44 percent of Bosnia's population. Serbs of Orthodox Christian descent composed 31 percent, and the mostly Catholic Croats, 18 percent. But ethnic identity did not seem to be something that could trigger widespread political violence. The general evenhandedness of President Josip Broz Tito and his communist Yugoslav government had rendered tensions over economic and political opportunity more an issue of ideology than of identity. All Bosnians spoke the same language, looked and dressed similarly, went to the same universities, served in the same army, sometimes married across ethnic lines, and otherwise existed in close proximity to one another as a matter of routine. Certainly, they could tell each other apart but generally not with enough enmity to go for each other's throats.

But there *were* signs of danger. President Tito's death in 1980 removed him and, eventually, the Yugoslav communist party as the arbiters of Yugoslavia as an equitable, multiethnic state. Also, the 1980s were a difficult time economically for Yugoslavia. The economy dropped by 40 percent, though non-Serbian regions, such as Croatia and Slovenia, did better than others. Most important, as the leaders of the various Yugoslavian states failed to settle on a postcommunist political dispensation, ethnic nationalists such as Slobodan Milosevic moved to exacerbate and exploit the internal divisions in the country to their own political and economic advantage.

Milosevic became the president of Yugoslavia in 1987 and quickly placed like-minded ethnic nationalists in control of the states of Serbia, Bosnia, Vojvodina, Kosovo, and Montenegro. Faced with the growing strength and militancy of the pan-Serb movement, other states dominated by non-Serb population groups became restive.

Yugoslavia melted down in 1991, when Slovenia and Croatia pulled out of the federation. The Yugoslavian National Army (*Jugoslovenska Narodna Armija*, or JNA) put up just a token fight to regain Slovenia, which contained only a small minority of Serbians. But the JNA and Croatia fought for several months over control of the Krajina region bordering Bosnia, which was populated mainly by Serbians and made up almost a third of Croatia's territory. Serbia ceased operations only in the face of harsh international criticism and after it had taken control of Krajina, which organized itself into the *Republika Srpska Krajina* (RSK). Taken together, these developments left Bosnia in the middle of unfriendly states—Serbia, Croatia, and the RSK—and with unhappy Christian Serb and Croat minorities in its own borders. Bosnia began to disintegrate when the Christian Serb minority created an independent Serbian republic, *Republika Srpska* (RS), in January 1992 under its own president, Radovan Karadzic, and with the avowed purpose of remaining linked to Serbia.

Bosnia exploded into vicious civil war in March, when most Bosnians voted for independence from Yugoslavia and inclusion of the Serbian Republic in the new state. The JNA promptly opened its arsenals to a hodge-podge of paramilitary groups, thugs, and military units of the forming Serb Republic Army. Quickly advancing around the northwestern and eastern regions of Bosnia, RS forces introduced the world to "ethnic cleansing," the premeditated process of depopulating whole areas of non-Serbs through forced displacement, mass murder, systematic rape, and robbery. Prisoners were beheaded, shot, or starved to death. Babies were killed in front of their mothers. Old men and women were murdered in their beds or thrown over cliffs. Villagers lost their houses to arson or occupation by Serb families. Ethnic cleansing was medieval savagery on a scale that stunned outside observers and against which the Bosnian government could put up only an incompetent defense.[4] In retaliation, Croat and Muslim soldiers also committed atrocities, though never on the scale or with the premeditation of the Serbs. Within a year, Bosnia controlled barely a third of its initial territory, and the Serbs were still advancing.

Almost dazed by the violence and fearful of being drawn into a conflict that could spread to other provinces of what was now being called the Former Republic of Yugoslavia (FRY), interested states responded to the Bosnian crisis hesitantly and indecisively. Anticipating the instability, if not the outbreak of civil war, the United Nations established a peacekeeping headquarters, the UN Protection Force

(UNPROFOR), in Bosnia in February 1992, but "blue-helmet" troops did not begin to arrive until June. In that same month, NATO's political leaders in the North Atlantic Council (NAC) authorized support for UN sanctioned arms boycotts and UNPROFOR units, should they come under attack. When the Serbs began to use transport and light-strike aircraft in support of their advance, NATO and the UN activated Operation Sky Watch in October 1992 to detect and report on such activities, but definitely not to shoot down violators.

The one UN Security Council Resolution (UNSCR) that had meat on its bones was UNSCR 757, issued on May 30, 1992, which called for a complete embargo on the export and transportation of "all commodities and products originating in the Federal Republic of Yugoslavia" (Serbia and Montenegro). Besides tacitly recognizing that the Bosnian Serbs were little more than stooges of Slobodan Milosevic, this resolution provided a clear and enforceable way to bring tremendous pressure on the Yugoslavian economy and military. Although the resulting embargo was never airtight, by late 1994 it undermined Milosevic's willingness to politically and economically underwrite the activities of the Bosnian Serbs. Without Milosevic's cover and funding, the Serbian advantage over the Bosnian Federation government and other factions would erode.

As one would expect, these halfhearted actions had minimal direct effect on the RS's objectives or day-to-day barbarism. The only checks on Serbian advances, apart from some improvements in the central government's military capabilities, were their own military limitations and Slobodan Milosevic's unwillingness to support actions that might prompt the UN and NATO to intervene more forcefully militarily and/or economically. This confrontation of interventionist timidity and Serbian calculation meant that the war ground on slowly, but it never ceased to grind.

DENY FLIGHT

When Serbian air attacks continued, the UN and NATO replaced Sky Watch with Deny Flight in March 1993. On paper, Deny Flight was a step-up in its enforcement provisions, but the intervention was slow to make them felt. The resolutions establishing Deny Flight allowed NATO planes to shoot down offending aircraft and to provide close air support to UNPROFOR units under attack. Subsequent resolutions also declared certain Bosnian cities as "safe areas" and permitted NATO offensive air strikes against Serbian military forces attacking them or, later, even just deployed in exclusion zones established by the UN around them. But all forms of offensive air operations always required simultaneous and specific UN and NATO political and military release. In the terminology of the time, NATO and UN leaders needed to "turn their keys" simultaneously. No "dual-key" approvals were given to NATO airmen during 1993. The allied intervention did not take a firmer stance until early 1994, largely in response to prodding by increasingly frustrated U.S. and British political leaders.[5] Even then, the interventionists had to work through fundamental disagreements over the nature of the conflict and, therefore, the correct course of action, before the important intervening nations could agree on unified and sustained action against the Serbs.

General agreement on the appropriate course of action was critical to the political unity of the interventionists, and political unity was indispensable to the success of any action taken. Both the UN and NATO are voluntary international organizations and generally require a plurality of support for any substantive military actions they take. As an organization of only sixteen member states at the time, NATO's political apex, the NAC, needed unanimous support, or at least acquiescence from all, before it would commit to large, sustained air operations. Sensitive to the views and political influence of over ten times that many states, the UN secretary general and the Security Council members were bound even more by the need to preserve unified political support for their actions in Bosnia. Many UN member states, of course, had little interest and no involvement in the intervention. But neither the secretary general nor the council could commit to an action that did not have the specific support of all permanent members of the council, of all states committing forces to the region, and at least the acquiescence of the General Assembly. Losing the support of any major contributing state or the General Assembly would have brought the intervention to a halt.[6]

Several factors made achieving unity for robust military actions difficult. First, none of the intervening powers wanted to be drawn into the Bosnian civil war more deeply than necessary. Second, the intervention was divided over the root causes of the conflict and, therefore, the appropriate intervention strategy. At the beginning of Deny Flight, most intervening government leaders subscribed to the theory that Bosnians were fighting over ancient and irreconcilable religious, ethnic, and historical enmities—the so-called ancient hatreds concept.[7] One well-established scholar of the region, Lenard Cohen, argued in 1993 that ethnic tensions were a constant of Balkan life and erupted into the current violence when Yugoslavian political leaders failed to develop a new, ethnically neutral, national political consensus after the fall of communism and instead turned to ethnic nationalism to build their personal political power.[8] Intervening in such circumstances, many believed, would only put off the inevitable struggle for dominance in the region and might in fact cause one or more of the Bosnian factions to turn on the peacekeepers. Thus, some proponents of the "ancient hatreds" explanation argued that the only sensible role for peacekeepers was to maintain absolute neutrality and to mitigate the suffering of noncombatants until the factions had fought the current spasm of violence to its conclusion.

While no one could disagree that the Bosnian conflict had aligned itself along ethnic lines, a growing number of intervening politicians argued that the sustaining cause of the conflict had become Bosnian Serb military ascendancy, not ancient hatreds. Unless Serbian military power was broken, this group argued, they would continue their offensives until they conquered the entire country and "cleansed" it of non-Serb populations. Breaking Serb military power, the argument went, would "level the playing field" between all factions and be the necessary first step toward effective peace negotiations. The proponents of focusing on the Serbs drew intellectual support from a growing number of scholars who argued that Bosnia's "long multicultural tradition where religious and ethnic differences were not generally reasons for hostility" had collapsed only in the face of misgovernment after World War I, and more recently in the face of Serb nationalism.[9] Serbian leaders, in other words, were the bad guys, and bad guys and their interests could be targeted.

Despite growing awareness that some kind of forceful military action might be needed to bring a halt to the war, the basic procedural arrangements played into the hands of those who remained reluctant to take action. While the encompassing Deny Flight resolution authorized member states to take "all necessary measures . . . to ensure compliance with the ban on flights," they could do so only "under the authority of the Security Council and subject to close coordination with the Secretary-General and UNPROFOR."[10] These requirements for "close coordination" remained in place when the Security Council further authorized "necessary measures, including the use of force, in reply to bombardments against the safe areas [or] obstruction . . . to the freedom of movement of UNPROFOR or of protected humanitarian convoys."[11] In the case of air strikes, these provisions required both NATO and the UN to approve an offensive strike, even in the heat of battle, when minutes could mean life and death. Worse, since the secretary general himself was the UN's approval authority for bombing, this so-called dual-key approval process actually could, and on occasion did, take hours. Even on the very eve of Deliberate Force, when the secretaries general of the NAC and the UN granted their military commanders greater authority to initiate strikes, the dual-key arrangement remained in place.[12]

Not surprisingly, operations involving actual weapons releases were infrequent events throughout most of Deny Flight. In February 1994, NATO jets shot down four Bosnian Serb light attack jets caught in the act of bombing Bosnian government–controlled targets. Next, in a demonstration of the clumsiness of the approval process, NATO aircraft were unable to attack a Serb artillery piece shelling Sarajevo because, by the time the UN secretary general's approval came, the gun had slipped under cover. NATO experienced more success in April, when air strikes in support of UN peacekeepers in the city of Gorazde forced attacking Serb forces to back off; and in August, when strafing attacks forced the Bosnian Serb army to return armored vehicles and heavy weapons it had taken from UN-guarded depots. But each of these actions was small scale, approved by the secretary general only reluctantly, and had no visible effects on the general determination of the Serbs to continue the war. The check placed on expeditious operations by the dual-key procedure rendered that arrangement an "unmitigated disaster" in the eyes of Richard Holbrooke, the principal American negotiator in the region.[13]

The largest single air operation of 1994, NATO's attack on the Bosnian Serb airfield of Udbina on November 21, gave the clearest indication of the limited potential of air strikes conducted halfheartedly and employing precision weapons to minimize rather than maximize effects. Located in Krajina, Udbina had been used for weeks by the Serbs to launch strikes against Bosnian forces attempting to open communications to the isolated city of Bihac. Admiral Leighton Smith, USN, commander in chief of NATO's Allied Forces Southern Europe (AFSOUTH) Command, headquartered in Naples, Italy, called for the complete destruction of the airfield; he wanted to make it into a "parking lot."[14] Concerned that a general attack would cause casualties and provoke Serb reprisals against peacekeepers, UN Secretary General Boutros Boutros-Ghali and his political representative in the region, Ambassador Yusushi Akashi, initially restricted Smith's air commander, Lieutenant General Michael Ryan, USAF, to attacking Udbina's runway with precision bombs. Ryan's bombers could not hit Serb antiaircraft systems or the offending Serbian aircraft parked openly on the airfield's ramp. Eventually, UN commanders did accede to Ryan's concerns for the safety of his aircrews and authorize them to hit air defense systems of "immediate" threat to the striking aircraft.[15]

These restrictions and the intervention's continued and obvious reluctance to take decisive action vitiated the strike of any real military or diplomatic value. Primarily utilizing laser-guided bombs, thirty-nine aircraft from the U.S., French, British, and Dutch air forces destroyed their targets easily and with great precision. But NATO's almost antiseptic application of these weapons really only created some large, easily filled holes in the ground, and they otherwise inflicted inconsequential military and no diplomatic pain on the enemy.[16] Worse, even as the dust was settling, Ambassador Akashi reassured the local Serb leader that the strike was a "necessary and proportionate response" to the deteriorating situation, and that the UN still was not taking sides in the conflict. Fearful that further attacks might prompt the Serbs to take UNPROFOR hostages, Britain and France blocked further strikes. Hostage-taking did not occur, possibly because NATO air attacks against Serb missile sites just before the ban went into effect convinced Serb forces that it was a good time to back off for a while. In the end, the diplomatic squirming of NATO and the UN probably did little more than convince the Serbs that they were not serious threats.[17]

By early 1995, the political balance within the UN and the NAC was in an accelerating swing in favor of robust air action against the Serbs.[18] One of the more influential proponents of pummeling the Serbs was U.S. ambassador Richard Holbrooke. He was the leader of the so-called Contact Group, which the United States, Britain, France, Germany, and Russia had formed in early 1994 to provide a negotiating team more agile and influential than the UN and NATO were proving to be. From the start, Holbrooke functioned as the de facto leader of the group's efforts to create a diplomatic structure for peace. Fully convinced that Serb leaders would respond only to force, he also worked tirelessly to coalesce American political leaders behind a more aggressive use of air power and, thereby, push their more reluctant European counterparts into line as well.[19] Others were beginning to think like Holbrooke as well, including British Lieutenant General Rupert Smith, the deputy commander of UNPROFOR.[20]

The expanding course of the war underwrote Holbrooke's zeal and effectiveness. The Serbs continued their offensives and accompanying ethnic cleansing operations, of course. But now the Bosnians and Croatians were demonstrating increased military effectiveness and, in April, the Croat army launched an offensive to begin clearing Krajina of Serb forces. Although Croat and Bosnian advances were accompanied by forced displacements, numerous but random murders, and looting, they produced nothing like the systematic mayhem practiced by Serb forces. Moreover, Serb military units had begun to make a habit of taking UN peacekeeping troops captive or hostage, whenever they felt in need of a negotiating or even just a tactical military advantage. As the violence increased and UNPROFOR's miserable helplessness became a daily humiliation, more and more political and military leaders recognized that the intervening alliance had to either toughen its military involvement or lose all credibility and influence over events.[21]

In late May 1995, the UN asked NATO to strike a Serbian ammunition depot in the town of Pale, near Sarajevo, and then gave another demonstration of the folly of conducting air attacks in an atmosphere of nearly complete political and military dishevelment. Having requested the strikes, UN commanders left their peacekeeping and observation units scattered in the midst of Serbian and Muslim forces, both of which had been taking UN hostages and stealing UN equipment over recent weeks. The bombing itself was anticlimatic. The jets released their laser-guided bombs, the ammunition bunkers vaporized in huge explosions, and the planes returned to their bases for lunch and to prepare for a second strike. But before they could return, the Serbs began taking what eventually would be nearly four hundred hostages and chained some of them to undamaged bunkers and to other potential targets in the area, including a communications tower and a bridge. In keeping with UN regulations, the tiny observer teams were completely unarmed and in some cases were taken by individual Serb soldiers sent out to round them up.[22] Predictably, the UN called off subsequent strikes. Even as these events unfolded, journalists, diplomats, and generals recognized that the intervention's failure in Bosnia undermined the very credibility of the UN and NATO, and perhaps even threatened the moral confidence and political survival of Europe and the West in general.[23]

Thereafter, UN and NATO leaders moved with unusual speed to set the stage for a sustained air campaign against the Serbs. Significantly, during June and July, NATO deployed a ten-thousand-strong Rapid Reaction Force (RRF) into Croatia and Bosnia. Equipped with infantry, helicopters, medium armor, and heavy artillery battalions, the RRF was clear evidence of the alliance's growing resolve and ability to protect its peacekeepers, even if commanders and diplomats remained uncertain of how it would be used, if at all.[24] The fall of the Bosnian city of Srebrenica on July 6 strengthened resolve for the intervention, or at least its desperation. The city fell to a well-planned Serb surprise attack, after the outnumbered Dutch peacekeeping battalion was forced into virtual hostage status and Serbian threats to kill hostages forced NATO to halt close air support strikes after only a few sorties.[25] The scale and shame of the debacle mounted as reports came out of the area that the Bosnian Serb forces had murdered thousands of Muslim men in cold blood after capturing the city. Faced with the potentially imminent collapse of other safe areas, NATO leaders met in London on July 21 and agreed somewhat reservedly to authorize strikes if the Serbian advances or attacks against the safe areas continued.[26] On August 10, UN Secretary General Boutros Boutros-Ghali and NATO Secretary General Willy Claes signaled their growing resolve by delegating authority to initiate air strikes to their military commanders, French General Bernard Janvier, the UNPROFOR commander, and Admiral Smith, AFSOUTH.[27]

Although not clearly understood by outside observers at the time, a series of defeats at the hands of the Croats and Bosnians in August began to undermine Serb long-term confidence in the course of the war. The Croats launched Operations Storm I, II, and III during that period and succeeded in clearing the Krajina of Serb forces and severely disrupting their defense structure in western Bosnia. In a series of smaller advances, the Bosnian army also disrupted Serb forces and recaptured small pieces of territory. To be sure, the Serbs were still advancing around eastern Bosnia, but, for the first time, they had reason to wonder if they would be able to complete their conquest of the country. In the evaluation of several knowledgeable observers, these Serb reversals on the ground deeply influenced their subsequent response to the bombing campaign and their willingness to make concessions at the peace talks in Dayton, Ohio.[28]

By August, NATO airmen had laid the foundations for a robust air campaign, though work remained to complete the structure.[29] The core document was Operational Plan (OPLAN) 40101. Coordinated by the NATO, AIRSOUTH, and UNPROFOR staffs through numerous iterations since April 1993, OPLAN 40101 was the core Deny Flight plan for enforcement of the UN's no-fly ban and operations in defense of UN personnel and the safe areas. Almost from the inception of Deny Flight, AIRSOUTH planners began building target information folders for possible offensive air strikes in protection of peacekeepers and the safe areas. After UNSCR 836 authorized "the use of air power, in and around the safe areas . . . to support UNPROFOR in performance of its mandate [to protect the safe areas]," planners divided these targets into three basic options. Option 1 targets generally were objects of military value involved directly in attacks against the safe area, such as artillery, combat vehicles, and munitions dumps. Option 2 targets typically fell in the safe areas and entailed objects involved directly in maintaining a siege, such as communications facilities and long-range artillery. Option 3 targets consisted of Option 2–type targets, plus military supply facilities and air assets that underpinned the actual capabilities and will of a faction's ability to continue fighting. Since Option 3 targets went beyond defensive measures and involved strikes outside of the twelve-mile-diameter exclusion zones around the safe areas, hitting them would be a sensitive political issue within both NATO and the UN.[30] After late 1994, and separate from the OAS provisions of UNSCR 836, NATO planners also put Deadeye, a plan for the suppression of Serbian air defenses threatening NATO aircraft, in place. Recognizing the engagement ranges and interlinkages of air defense and long-range communications systems, Deadeye divided Bosnia into two regions and presumed that NATO would be free to strike throughout a region, even if its jets were coming under attack only in a localized area within that region.[31]

As the likelihood of large-scale combat grew in the spring of 1995, the AIRSOUTH commander, now Lieutenant General Michael Ryan, directed his staff to use Deadeye as the basis for an offensive air campaign. His planners responded by dividing Bosnia into two offensive zones of action (ZOAs) roughly corresponding to the Deadeye boundaries and making provisions for air strikes throughout an entire ZOA should any city within it be attacked.[32] AIRSOUTH continued to refine this plan through the spring, and in the course of many briefings in May and June, the plan took on the name Deliberate Force.[33] On August 1, 1995, Ryan received permission from the NAC to conduct attacks throughout whichever ZOA contained a threatened city. By the end of that month, the Deliberate Force plan was advanced enough to provide a basis for a campaign, though it still needed refinement and exercising. Otherwise, all that remained to spark an air war was for the Bosnian Serbs to commit some act—a "trigger event"—that would galvanize the intervention into action under the provisions of the London agreement of the previous month.

DELIBERATE FORCE

A mortar attack on the crowded Mrkale marketplace in Sarajevo, which killed around thirty-eight civilians and wounded hundreds on August 28, 1995, was the trigger. Even though there was no real doubt among the intervening governments that the Serbian forces surrounding the city had fired the mortar bombs specifically at the civilian shoppers at the market, the tenuous commitment of many NATO and UN member states to taking strong action obliged both organizations to investigate the attack. The short delay was necessary in any case, since it allowed UN military forces to make final preparations. For UNPROFOR, these involved drawing its outlying observer and smaller peacekeeping units into main bases to minimize the threat of Serb military reprisals and hostage taking. Also, the RRF accelerated deployment of its combat units to key points, most importantly preparing its heavy artillery batteries for attacks against Serb forces in the vicinity of Sarajevo. At AFSOUTH, Admiral Smith used the time to call for additional aircraft from the U.S. and other NATO air forces. Meanwhile, NAC and UN leaders worked to firm up the tenuous political consensus for initiating sustained strikes. They had enough success to authorize NATO commanders on August 29 to attack if circumstances required, though a number of states clearly remained on the edge of withdrawing their support.[34] Thus, when NATO and UN investigators confirmed on August 30 that the Serbs were the culprits for Mrkale, Admiral Smith and General Janvier were ready to go and turned their keys.

General Ryan launched Deliberate Force with an air force that was substantial, though not huge, at least not in comparison to the one employed against Iraq only a few years before. At the start of operations, eight NATO states provided 269 combat and support aircraft to his air order of battle, a number that grew to 305 by the campaign's end.[35] Additionally, Ryan had access to several unmanned reconnaissance and surveillance systems, including General Atomics Gnats and Predators, and "national" assets, such as signals intelligence aircraft from several countries, U–2 high-altitude reconnaissance aircraft from the USAF, and satellite imagery from at least the United States, Britain, and France.

For the most part, the strike aircraft in Ryan's air force were equipped to deliver precision weapons.[36] Most of them would depend on laser-guided and optically guided, free-fall bombs, mainly American-made GBU–12s (five hundred pounds), GBU–16s (one thousand pounds), and GBU–10s, –15s, and –24s (two thousand pounds). Only the United States employed powered, standoff strike weapons, mainly the new standoff land attack missile for well-defended and hardened targets, the AGM–65 Maverick for smaller point targets, and the BMG–109 Tomahawk land attack cruise missile for long-range attacks against a variety of targets. All of these weapons were capable of striking reliably within a few feet of their intended aim points, which NATO planners referred to as desired mean points of impact (DMPIs).

All NATO air forces involved also utilized nonprecision weapons, except for Spain, which employed GBU–16s only, and Germany and Turkey, which conducted no offensive strikes. Mostly, they delivered Mk 82, 83, and 84 bombs weighing five hundred, one thousand, and two thousand pounds, respectively. When released by a "smart" aircraft equipped with advanced weapons delivery systems and flown by skilled pilots, these aircraft could and did routinely deliver their bombs to within a few tens of yards of their DMPIs. But the greater potential inaccuracy of these bombs, compared to precision-guided weapons, limited their use to targets well away from populated places. On several occasions, USAF A–10s and AC–130s employed their 30-millimeter (mm), 40mm, and 105mm cannons with extreme accuracy, and A–10s also fired a number of unguided 2.75-inch rockets, either to destroy targets themselves or to mark them for attack by other aircraft.[37]

Some of the most restrictive general ROEs in the history of air warfare would constrain General Ryan's employment of his forces and weapons. As a normal guideline, ROEs should be as general and unrestrictive as possible, consistent with the political objectives and military circumstances of a conflict, to give airmen in the heat of battle maximum latitude to protect themselves and accomplish their missions. In contrast, OPLAN 40101's ROEs annex, Security Council resolutions, and the general feeling that even small levels of collateral damage would undermine political support tightly restricted what NATO airmen actually could do. In addition to the dual-key arrangement for authorizing strikes, Deliberate Force's ROEs carefully spelled out the types of targets that could be struck, proportionality of usable force, high sensitivity to collateral damage, and a phasing of the air campaign to allow it to be controlled and cut off by civil authorities at any time.[38] Deny Flight's close air support operations and the attack on Udbina airfield revealed the almost obsessive requirement among UN and NATO civil leaders to have an on-off switch for the air attacks and their intolerance for collateral casualties of any kind, far exceeding the actual mandates of international law and of operational necessities.

Recognizing the political sensitivity of the situation and certain that a single incident of civilian casualties could bring the bombing to a halt, General Ryan also imposed tight special instructions (SPINs) on tactical operations. Only he could authorize strike aircraft to go "feet dry" from the Adriatic to the Balkan Peninsula. He and a small inner circle of planning officers made all poststrike battle damage assessments and approved all choices of DMPIs and weapons used in each day's strikes, and only he or Brigadier General Hal Hornburg, the director of the Combined Air Operations Center, could give final approval for weapons releases. Additionally, to preclude targeting errors by maneuvering pilots, General Ryan ordered that they release their weapons on assigned DMPIs only when they could identify them visually. For most of Deliberate Force, General Ryan, who was code-named "Chariot" over the radio nets, demanded that bombers go in only when supported by aircraft equipped for the suppression of enemy air defenses (SEAD) mission.[39] Since SEAD aircraft were in limited supply, this meant that some strikes would be canceled when their SEAD packages ran out of gas or had fired their weapons, usually high-speed antiradiation missiles (HARMs), in support of earlier strikes.

Beyond these general constraints, Ryan's planning team often issued additional SPINs to reduce the possibility that specific missions would create collateral casualties. Bridges, for example, generally were attacked at night, when people were not likely to be on them. Ryan also required his pilots to make their bomb runs along stream beds to ensure that malfunctioning weapons most likely would impact in the water, rather than in the towns at the ends of bridges under attack. When attacking munitions complexes, Ryan directed his pilots to strike the bunkers farthest away from their front gates and administrative buildings first, to give guards and other personnel warning and a chance to flee.[40] Usually, Chariot also directed his pilots to release only one weapon per pass. Everyone knew that this restriction would obligate strike aircraft to make multiple passes over the same targets, with a potential increase in risk to aircrews. But the need to reduce collateral casualties trumped concerns over increased risk and the strong preference of the airmen to "service" their targets as quickly as possible. Moreover, several analysts of the campaign have agreed that Ryan's restraints were a vital underpinning of the intervention's ability to lay the foundations of long-term peace in the region—that is, to achieve its strategic objectives, albeit at some increased cost in fuel, weapons, and flight time.[41]

Strategy differences probably constituted the Achilles' heel of the air campaign. Still hoping to be taken as a neutral broker in the conflict, the UN continued to justify its military actions as the minimum essential to getting the Serbs to cease their attacks on the safe areas and, perhaps, to talk more about peace. AIRSOUTH planners understood that the UN sought to limit its military operations or those conducted on its behalf. But they also believed that the Serbs would not talk until the bombing could "adversely alter the [Bosnian Serb Army's] advantage to conduct military operations against the BiH [Bosnian Army]."[42] Getting to that goal likely would require greater force than required to wring more, probably empty, promises from the Serbs to be good.

UNPROFOR, particularly the newly arrived RRF, was at odds over strategy. Most of UNPROFOR's units and national political authorities were incapable of operations other than peacekeeping. Overall, the UN's military arm seemed better at providing hostages for the Serbs than at conducting effective operations. But senior UNPROFOR commanders, particularly General Janvier's deputy, British Lieutenant General Rupert Smith, were more willing, even committed, to punishing the Serbs, and the RRF was clearly a combat force that could contribute to that. Also, since RRF artillery would be positioned in the Sarajevo safe area and would engage offending Serb forces directly, it had greater freedom to hit them with less concern about inflicting casualties. Finally, Ambassador Holbrooke and the Contact Group nations generally, but not completely, were pursuing an immediate end to the conflict, a goal that they believed the bombing could and should facilitate. In such a chaotic strategic environment, the bombing campaign would take on different meanings to different groups and individual countries, meanings that could change day to day as the campaign progressed. So much for the dictums of Carl von Clausewitz to link operations and political objectives rationally.

Trying to develop an operational concept that would survive among so many conflicting strategic visions and knowing that killing large numbers of Serbian soldiers was out of the question, General Ryan directed his planners to target a key Serb military advantage over Croatia and the Bosnian government rather than field forces. That advantage was the Serb ability to move, control, and supply its best fighting units. Against a Bosnian army of about twenty thousand troops of mixed capabilities, the Serbs fielded some sixty-five thousand soldiers, including about twenty thousand professionals, many drawn from the JNA, in seven mobile reserve brigades. These brigades were equipped with tanks, heavy artillery, and transport vehicles. While Serb generals employed most of their units in static defense, they used the mobile brigades to reinforce offensives and shore up faltering defenses wherever they might be needed. Since their effectiveness in these roles rested on the availability of clear roads, pre-positioned supplies, and a fairly robust communications system based on telephone landlines and microwave radio relay (RADREL) towers, Ryan directed his planners to target the Serb integrated air defense system (IADS) and matériel targets, such as road defiles, bridges, munitions dumps, and RADREL towers. He hoped that thus interdicting the Serbs' mobility would have the strategic effect of breaking their will and ability to carry on the war.

Returning to the operational narrative, once the necessary preparations were made and NATO peacekeepers were bunkered in their main camps, the Secretary General and the NAC cleared General Ryan to attack.[43] With General Ryan's approval, the first package of about sixty USAF and Marine aircraft, and F–18s and EA–6Bs from the USS *Theodore Roosevelt*, went "feet dry" from the Adriatic at 1:40 a.m. on August 30, 1995, to strike at Bosnian Serb air defenses around Sarajevo. This first package attacked missile sites, radar control vans, and RADREL towers. During the course of the day, five other strike packages of twelve to thirty bombers each went in primarily to hit Serbian ammunition dumps. All of these attacks were supported by numerous NATO airborne warning and control system (AWACS), airborne command and control center (ABCCC), aerial tanker, SEAD, and reconnaissance sorties. In all, NATO jets flew 122 sorties on day one and 242 sorties on day two, which included most of the first wave of strike packages. In those first two campaign days, about twenty-six hours in total length, NATO struck forty-eight DMPIs to disable or destroy several RADREL towers, munitions bunkers, radar antennas, and some tactical weapons. Meanwhile, RRF cannoneers coordinated their engagement windows to avoid endangering NATO jets and fired over six hundred 105mm and 155mm artillery rounds from British and French guns, and 120mm mortar rounds from the French and Dutch contingents, to hit Serb trenches, command bunkers, and weapons within the Sarajevo exclusion zone, wounding and killing a number of Serb soldiers.[44] On the next day, August 31, morning fog and overcast weather limited the bombing to three packages going after RADREL towers and munitions bunkers, while RRF guns attacked Serb mortar positions and armored vehicles.

There were immediate signs that the bombing instilled a sense of caution in Serb leaders, if it did not actually push them to surrender in so short a time. While Serb antiaircraft gunners and missileers worked hard to shoot down NATO aircraft, Serb ground forces limited themselves to only a few sniper and mortar attacks against NATO peacekeepers and RRF units. The sense that the Serbs were being more cautious than stunned was reinforced by their handling of the crew of a French Mirage 2000 shot down over Pale on the afternoon of August 30. In times past, they could have been expected to parade the pilots before the press and threaten to kill them in retaliation for continued bombing. But with waves of NATO jets roaring in and the RRF poised to attack, the Serbs merely sequestered the pilots and waited to see how they might use them.[45] Perhaps most significantly, Slobodan Milosevic in Belgrade handed Richard Holbrooke the so-called Patriarch Paper, in which the Bosnian Serb parliament authorized him to negotiate a peace settlement on its behalf, without directly involving Bosnian Serb president Radovan Karadzic and his strutting military commander Ratko Mladic, both of whom were indicted war criminals.[46] On August 31, Milosevic reported that the Bosnian Serbs were ready to talk on the basis of the UN demands, subject only to a halt to the bombing. After sometimes acrimonious discussions and to the disgust of some NATO civil and military leaders, Admiral Smith, General Janvier, and Boutros Boutros-Ghali agreed to halt the bombing and preemptive artillery strikes in the hope that the Serbs were finally serious about moving toward peace. Given the timid commitment of many NAC and UN members to the bombing, it would have not taken much sincerity from the Serbs to encourage the UN to continue the bombing halt.

As the world soon realized, Bosnian Serb leaders were not sincere about complying with UN resolutions. Moreover, the tirades and self-justifying public pronouncements of Karadzic and Mladic provided embarrassing evidence to UN and NATO leaders that they had been played for fools once again. Nevertheless, it still took the diplomatic proponents of the air campaign four days of frantic and heated shuttle diplomacy between the capitals of Europe, Washington, and at the Security Council and the NAC to cobble together enough of a consensus to restart the bombing.[47] Finally, after determining from Predator and ground observer reports that the Serbs had no intention of complying, Janvier and Admiral Smith recommended bombing on September 5.

Still not certain that the new political consensus would survive more than a few additional days of bombing, General Ryan, in close coordination with General Janvier and General Rupert Smith, resumed Deliberate Force with a vengeance.[48] Determined to increase the "pain" and psychological shock of the bombing, General Ryan and General Smith focused their attacks on the munitions, communications facilities, and road nets that General Mladic needed to control his forces and to move reserves to support his units being pressed in the west by Croat and Bosnian forces.

Ryan was pleased when the UN military commanders cleared him to strike twelve of the most important bridges in Mladic's transportation net. To hit those targets, Ryan sent in five strike packages on September 5. Poor weather limited NATO strikes the next day, but the alliance then flew about 270 sorties every day from September 7 to 10, 100 or so of which carried bombs on each day. Knowing that the Serbs had used the bombing pause to hone their air defense skills and concentrate their long-range air defense missile systems near their principal city of Banja Luka, Ryan also began preparations for strikes there. Most important, he sent requests through channels for the deployment of F–117 Nighthawk stealth fighters to the main American air base at Aviano, Italy, and for permission to use ship-launched Tomahawk land attack missiles (TLAMs) to soften up Serb air defense sites. His and General Smith's intent was to render the Serb Republic powerless to defend itself from continued air attacks and then finish off Mladic's ability to control and move his forces. Achieving those effects, Ryan hoped, would break down Mladic's will to continue the fight.

The launch of a new Croatian offensive, Operation Mistral 2, on September 8 only added to Serbian misery and uncertainty. Although the operation had been under preparation for weeks, the Croats probably timed the kickoff of Mistral 2 to take advantage of the rapid erosion of Serbian capabilities under the bombing. Most of the Serbian units they went up against had been mauled during Operation Storm and were full of untrained and demoralized recruits. Not surprisingly, the Croats rolled up the Serb units and took strategic highlands on the first day, rendering much of the Serbian defensive line in western Bosnia untenable. Over the next several days, the Croats broke up several Serbian defensive lines and kept them on the run. With his long-range communications system a shambles, General Mladic was helpless to coordinate a defense. The swelling retreat of Serb forces led some analysts to say that Mistral 2 was "an event of perhaps greater military significance" than the ongoing bombing.[49] In reality, then and now, distinguishing between the effects of the bombing and the ground war is difficult to do with any credibility, particularly since it was NATO's takedown of Serbian mobility and communications that set the stage for at least the rapidity of the Croatian advance.

Exploiting its arsenal of precision weapons and its near-complete dominance of the sky and resulting freedom of maneuver, AIRSOUTH prosecuted the campaign to maximize its military and psychological impact on the Bosnian Serbs while reducing operational risk nearly to zero. Each day, the command sent in a number of strike packages, usually consisting of eight to twenty planes and several dozen supporting aircraft conducting SEAD, reconnaissance, combat air patrol, airborne command and control, standby search-and-rescue, and air refueling missions. General Ryan usually focused each package on the DMPIs within either a single target or several located in proximity to one another. There were none of the search-and-destroy missions conducted by free-ranging fighters in other wars in search of targets of opportunity. Ryan's approach ensured that each bomb was dropped in a planned and controlled manner and that individual targets and DMPI sets were subjected to concentrated destruction and psychological shock in a matter of minutes. Also, NATO strike aircraft generally stayed above fifteen thousand feet to release their weapons, an altitude that rendered most Serb antiaircraft cannons and man-portable air defense systems (MANPADs) useless. F–16 crews operating out of Aviano Air Base quickly learned that their newly installed low-altitude navigation and targeting infrared for night systems allowed them to navigate and deliver their weapons accurately from medium altitudes.[50] NATO SEAD aircraft also stood ready to counterattack any Serb radar or missile launcher daring to threaten the strikers. As a result, when NATO deemed it time to destroy a particular set of DMPIs, it merely sent in a package of strikers, and they did the job, unstoppably destroying their targets and overwhelming Serb defenses. If a strike package missed some DMPIs or a re-strike was needed for other reasons, NATO went back in with the same implacable display of dominance.

Thus, Deliberate Force was the real debut of precision warfare by dominant air forces. In this kind of combat, there were few incidents of screeching fighter-bombers diving through curtains of fire and steel to rake their targets with cannon fire and salvos of bombs and rockets. Nor did it include pattern bombing of large tracts of real estate in the hope of hitting something valuable at high risk to civilians and their property. A few A–10s did go in with guns blazing during close air support missions and, in one case, cut down a RADREL tower, but the normal picture was of fighter-bombers and gunships in level flight releasing their weapons with exacting care. Unless they were leaving contrails, these aircraft were scarcely visible to the naked eye. With their safety largely secured by their altitude, speed, and SEAD support, the pilots of these aircraft had the luxury of maneuvering into the proper release "basket" of each of their weapons with little fear of or distraction from Serb defenses, and letting each go only when they were as sure as possible that it would hit its designated DMPI. A small percentage of smart weapons did go "stupid" or otherwise malfunctioned, but the great majority guided true. Even in the cases where Dutch and Italian aircraft released unguided bombs, they did so with the benefit of modern navigation and aiming systems that put them on their targets with accuracies that came remarkably close to those provided by guided weapons.[51] Thus, for most Bosnian Serbs—armed combatants and civilians alike—NATO's air war manifested itself in long periods of quiet in most locales, punctuated maybe once or twice by a few minutes of explosions against predictable military targets. Even in the midst of an attack, they were exceptionally safe, as long as they kept their heads down and did not happen to be located directly in a DMPI.

Meanwhile, Deliberate Force's diplomatic impact was reaching an apex. The mere continuation of the bombing in the background of preliminary truce talks conducted at Geneva on September 8 sent an unexpected and powerful message to the Bosnian Serbs and Milosevic in Belgrade of NATO and the UN's political will to stay the course. The TLAM attacks launched by the USS *Normandy* on the evening of September 10 unexpectedly reinforced the message that NATO was prepared to escalate its attacks as necessary to beat down the Serbs. Militarily, the *Normandy's* thirteen TLAMs struck their air defense and communications targets with near-perfect accuracy, eleven of them hitting within thirty feet of their DMPIs.[52] Most important, the destruction of a RADREL tower near General Mladic's headquarters cut off his communications with his western forces, just as they were crumbling before Operation Mistral 2. The use of the expensive and technologically advanced TLAMs stunned the Serbs and even many NATO diplomats not familiar with them or forewarned of their impending use. American planners viewed TLAMs merely as useful weapons for striking well-defended, high-value targets, particularly in poor weather. But to others they reflected a significant expansion of the bombing campaign—proof that NATO (or at least the United States) was willing to go to any length to force the Serbs to accept the UN's terms for peace. Ambassador Holbrooke, preparing at the time for the next round of meetings with Milosevic, reported that the missiles had "enormous" psychological impact on the Serbs. Probably echoing Holbrooke's assessment, Admiral Leighton Smith later reported that a diplomat involved in the negotiations told him that the TLAMs had "scared the shit out of the Serbs."

Ironically, just as the bombing was putting the Serbs under intense pressure, the intervention was heading into a possible diplomatic crisis of its own making; it was running out of Option 1 and 2 targets. By September 12, only eight southeastern ZOA and three Deadeye targets remained untouched. Given the pace at which Ryan's jets were taking them out, the campaign could come to an end in a few days for lack of new things to blow up. Ambassador Holbrooke was particularly concerned, since he believed that it was the bombing, not the Croatian and Bosnian land offensives, that was keeping the Serbs talking at the moment.[53] Realizing that AIRSOUTH might stop its attacks at any time, the ambassador moved his next face-to-face meeting with Milosevic up to September 13 and sent a message through channels asking that the bombing be stretched out as long as possible. While not directly aware of Holbrooke's concerns, but fully aware of the importance of his operations to negotiations, General Ryan had directed his staff already, on September 11, to scrub the target list to look for DMPIs worthy of attack or re-attack.[54] Perhaps fortuitously, bad weather slowed the pace of operations on September 13 and 14, allowing Holbrooke to continue negotiations before NATO had to make a hard and very public decision to stop the bombing or go after the more politically sensitive targets on the Option 3 list. Indeed, on September 14, *Time* magazine summarized the situation for the world, stating that moving to the power plants, bridges, and other economic facilities on the Option 3 list would be a "quantum leap" in the scale and intensity of the war. Key American leaders, the article went on, were willing to escalate and stay the course, but it was not clear if NATO and the UN were.[55]

As it turned out, the Serbs gave in on the day the *Time* article appeared. On arriving at Belgrade, Holbrooke found that Milosevic had lost heart and bullied Karadzic and Mladic into accepting the UN peace terms. The two war criminals were not happy, but they had little choice but to follow Milosevic's lead. As numerous analysts pointed out later, the sky was coming down on their heads. In addition to the improving military fortunes of their regional enemies, the Bosnian Serb army was beginning to suffer significantly from desertions, and Milosevic was distancing himself from it and restricting its supplies. Moreover, the outcomes of the September 8 Geneva Conference indicated that their opponents were prepared to allow the Bosnian Serbs to maintain substantial political and diplomatic autonomy within the Bosnian Federation and even to retain most of the land that they currently controlled. All that, and the unpredictable direction of the bombing campaign, indicated to anyone but a complete fool that the time had come to cut their losses. Therefore, in return for an immediate cease-fire, the Serb leaders signed an agreement to respect the safe areas and attend peace talks. By October 16, they were moving their forces out of the exclusion zones. On October 20, the UN and NATO announced that there was no reason to resume the air campaign and declared that Deliberate Force was over.

IMPLICATIONS: THE EFFICACY OF PRECISION AIR POWER

Deliberate Force was one of the most important factors in Serbian calculations to accept peace. To Richard Holbrooke, Deliberate Force "was the decisive factor in bringing the Serbs to the peace table," and precision bombing was a key capability enabling the intervention to undertake offensive operations.[56] As have most studies since the conflict, Ambassador Holbrooke ascribed NATO's success to a mix of the

Croat and Bosnian ground offensives, other diplomatic maneuvers (some of which he engineered), and Milosevic's exhaustion and domestic political vulnerability under the UN's economic embargo. But Holbrooke, the Air Force's after-actions study team, and others credited the bombing with causing a precipitous collapse in Serb military capabilities and political will. Ironically, the bombing probably also gave Slobodan Milosevic the leverage he needed to force his more fanatical and at-risk cronies, Karadzic and Mladic, to accept his own demands that they stop shooting and start talking.[57] In other words, Deliberate Force's unique contribution to the end of the Bosnian civil war was to move it up from some vague date in the future to something that happened after barely two weeks of serious bombing.

Despite first impressions, however, precision weapons were not critical to the successful outcome of Deliberate Force. Indeed, under the specific circumstances of the conflict, the *fact* of the bombing was more important to Serb calculations than its *means*. Serb resistance collapsed in the face of NATO's clear determination and ability to destroy key targets of military value. As nonprecision bombing accuracy during the campaign indicated, NATO could have destroyed any target on its Option 1, 2, and 3 lists with "smart" planes and "dumb" bombs. Such a nonprecision campaign would have required the commitment of more aircraft and/or time to service the target list, of course. It also would have produced more civilian and military casualties. But so long as the alliance had the will to persevere, it theoretically could have forced the Serbs to the conference table with dumb bombs just as certainly as it could with smart weapons.

This is not to say that precision weapons were not highly valuable to the intervention. In the first place, the confidence that NATO airmen and many political leaders had in the capabilities of such weapons lowered their decision threshold for action. They knew that precision weapons, when properly targeted and employed, could destroy the chosen targets rapidly, perhaps before political support waned, and with minimal collateral damage. NATO might have been able to "win" Deliberate Force without smart weapons, but it would be hard to assert that the alliance would have gone into the conflict without them. In the event, the U.S. ambassador overseeing the Balkan region, Christopher Hill, believed that the use of smart weapons "spooked" the Serbs, since they did not produce collateral civilian casualties with which to sway the Western press.[58] Last, the very existence of precision weapons obliged NATO to employ them. To use dumb weapons instead, with their higher likelihood of killing noncombatants, would have placed NATO in danger of violating the laws of war regarding the proportionate and discriminate use of force.

In the case of forcing an end to the Bosnian civil war in 1995, then, it would be fair to say that precision weapons made action more palatable to the intervention and allowed NATO to achieve its objectives with fewer engaged forces and with a vastly reduced butcher's bill in combatants and noncombatants alike. Their effect, in short, was incremental rather than revolutionary. But while this view is consistent with the general assertions of several prominent students of air power, Deliberate Force does not in itself prove the case.[59] In that instance, the limited leverage of precision clearly reflected the unique circumstances of political will and the list of easily located and vulnerable targets to be struck. In other conflicts where political will might be firmer and targets more fleeting, buried under ground, or surrounded by noncombatants, the leverage of precision would be profound, perhaps to the point of altering the interrelationships of surface and aerospace forces significantly. In high-intensity conflicts with peer or near-peer states, the pace of operations and shortage of time would place an absolute premium on precision weapons. In cases like those, joint commanders would be remiss in their responsibilities if they did not understand and exploit the capabilities of precision weapons fully.

10

OPERATION ALLIED FORCE, 1999

Tony Mason

THE CRISIS

IN 1989, SERBIA REVOKED the autonomy of Kosovo, then a part of Serbia within the Federal Republic of Yugoslavia (FRY); closed Albanian-language newspapers, radio, and television, and the Albanian Institute; changed street names from Albanian to Serbian; introduced a new Serbian curriculum for universities and schools; dismissed thousands of Albanians from public employment; and later resettled Serbs in Kosovo with loans and free plots of land. These measures were accompanied by widespread human rights abuses.[1] The Kosovar Albanians responded by establishing a parallel political structure, the League for a Democratic Kosovo (LDK), led by Dr. Ibrahim Rugova, which sought to achieve its objective of political independence by a combination of nonviolent resistance and international support.

In August 1993, U.S. ambassador Madeleine Albright warned President Slobodan Milosevic in the United Nations (UN) Security Council that "in the event of conflict in Kosovo caused by Serbian action, the U.S. will be prepared to employ military force against Serbians in Kosovo and Serbia proper."[2] Kosovo, however, was not included on the Dayton agenda in 1995.

In 1996, an organization calling itself the Kosovo Liberation Army (KLA) claimed responsibility for attacks on Serbian police and on alleged Albanian collaborators. In 1997, the KLA acquired large amounts of arms, supply routes, and training areas when the Albanian state apparatus across the border collapsed. The Serbian government proscribed the KLA as a terrorist organization, thereby justifying indiscriminate action against suspected KLA members, political activists, and other civilians.[3] The Yugoslav army entered Kosovo, operating alongside police and paramilitary units. Reports of Serbian brutality increased. A massacre of villagers in the Drenica area in March 1998, subsequently verified by a Human Rights Watch investigation, was classified by the Serbian authorities as an "operation to liquidate the heart of Kosovo terrorism."[4]

On March 31, 1997, the UN Security Council imposed an arms embargo on Yugoslavia, calling for autonomy and "meaningful self-administration" for Kosovo and warning that "additional measures" were possible if no progress was made toward a peaceful solution.[5] The Yugoslavs denied any armed conflict in Kosovo, asserting the absence of any threat to peace and security.

NATO'S RESPONSE

For the next twelve months, the North Atlantic Treaty Organization (NATO) debated how to support the UN resolution. The successful use of air power in Bosnia three years earlier was recalled. In April 1998, British foreign secretary Robin Cook asked General Wesley Clark, USA, supreme allied commander in Europe, if Milosevic's policy of increasing repression could be halted by the threat of air power. "Yes, probably," responded the general.[6] One month later, however, German General Klaus Naumann, chairman of the NATO Military Standing Committee, clearly identified the difference between Bosnia in 1995 and Kosovo. This time, there were no ground forces to threaten Milosevic with defeat. NATO air power alone offered no guarantee of success and might need to be accompanied by the threat of further escalation.[7]

U.S. Air Force (USAF) General Joseph Ralston, vice chairman of the Joint Chiefs of Staff, asked General Clark what would happen if Milosevic was not deterred: "You know that there are real limitations on what the Air Force can do. What if the bombing doesn't work?" The general responded, "I think that's unlikely but in that event I guess we'd have to do something on the ground, directed at Kosovo."[8] Nonetheless, in June, General Clark briefed General Henry Shelton, USA, chairman of the Joint Chiefs of Staff, saying that "Milosevic will pretend to negotiate but won't until he's under pressure. The air threat will provide the crucial leverage for the diplomats to be able to achieve a meaningful agreement."[9]

Milosevic's commitment to "Serbian" Kosovo and hostility to its Albanian inhabitants were very different from his interest in Bosnia. General Naumann, in meetings with Milosevic in early 1999, found that "as soon as you mentioned Kosovo in a way which may have triggered the thought in his mind that he may lose Kosovo one day, he got very emotional. He told us, I don't know how often, that Kosovo is really the cradle of Serb culture and religion."[10]

General Clark had already directed General John Jumper, the commander of U.S. Air Forces in Europe (USAFE), to draw up a plan for an air campaign against Yugoslavia that would "halt or degrade a systematic Serb campaign of ethnic cleansing in Kosovo [with the] intent that the air strike would be coercive in nature, on the Bosnia model, providing a strong incentive for Milosevic to halt operations."[11] Known as Nimble Lion, the plan envisaged attacks by a large number of U.S. and other aircraft against 250 targets.[12]

Allied aircraft and cruise missiles would fly phased operations. A demonstration element could be included, but if Belgrade failed to comply, the air operation would be extended to strikes on military targets throughout Yugoslavia: its integrated air defense (AD) system, command and control assets, airfields and/or aircraft, logistic sites, operational bases, and deployed heavy weapons within Kosovo.[13] Ground forces would include contingents from Germany, Italy, France, and the United States, possibly providing a NATO force of 36,000 troops, but only "to implement the military aspects of a peace agreement."[14]

On June 10, British prime minister Tony Blair asserted the need for military action if diplomacy were unable to end the crisis.[15] On June 16, NATO carried out an exercise involving eighty aircraft over Albanian and Macedonian territory within fifty miles of the FRY border, intended to demonstrate the alliance's ability to project air power into the region. Milosevic was not impressed. General Naumann later suggested that "Milosevic rightly concluded that the NATO threat was a bluff . . . and finished his summer offensive."[16] Serb forces inflicted several defeats on the KLA, ending its territorial control in several areas, shelling cities and villages, and driving civilians from their homes. Milosevic disregarded international condemnation and reports of NATO war plans. By August 1998, 260,000 Kosovars had been displaced within the province and another 200,000 had fled across the borders.[17] International television images of tens of thousands of refugees stimulated support of NATO's decision to resort to armed force.

On September 23, 1998, increasing Serbian violence against ethnic Kosovar Albanians prompted the UN Security Council to adopt Resolution 1199, which cited Chapter VII of the UN Charter. It called for a cease-fire and demanded the withdrawal of Yugoslav forces "used for civilian repression" and the return home of refugees and the internally displaced.[18] The following day, NATO issued "activation warnings" for Operations Flexible Anvil "Limited Air Response" and Allied Force "Phased Air Campaign."

On October 5, the Bill Clinton administration sent Special Envoy Richard Holbrooke, accompanied by USAF Lieutenant General Michael Short, to Belgrade to secure the presence of international observers from the Organization for Security and Cooperation in Europe (OSCE) in Kosovo, aerial verification by NATO aircraft, and withdrawal of additional Serbian forces from the province. After three days, Milosevic remained defiant, denouncing threats of NATO air strikes that "jeopardise the continuation of the political process."[19]

Consequently, on October 10, after an extensive debate in which each of the nineteen members expressed a different point of view on the bombing, the North Atlantic Council (NAC) approved "activation orders" that allowed General Clark to begin air strikes within ninety-six hours if Milosevic did not comply with the Holbrooke demands. On October 13, Holbrooke announced from Belgrade that the Yugoslav president had changed his mind and accepted the terms. He agreed to cease hostilities, withdraw mobilized forces from Kosovo, and allow international verification of compliance with Resolution 1199 by all parties. But by October 19, he had not fully complied, and the ninety-six-hour deadline was extended to October 27. Meanwhile, NATO readiness states were maintained, and deployment of aircraft to the theater continued. Despite Milosevic's further failure to apply restraint in, and withdraw from, Kosovo, the second deadline came and went with nothing more than a statement that "NATO remains ready to act. . . . The North Atlantic Council (NAC) will keep the situation in Kosovo under constant review and if they see evidence of substantial non-compliance in the future, NATO is ready to use force." NATO's focus, meanwhile, remained "ensuring the effectiveness of the verification regime."[20]

However, by the end of October 1998, large numbers of Yugoslav forces had withdrawn from Kosovo while OSCE Kosovo Verification Monitors (KVMs) had deployed. General Clark claimed a victory for coercion by air power: "This was diplomacy backed by threat. The air threat helped to halt the Serb campaign in Kosovo, just as I had expected. Milosevic was intimidated by NATO air power, even in the absence of a significant ground threat. We wouldn't have been able to stop the Serb campaign without the air threat."[21]

Milosevic saw things differently. Serbian government member Milorad Vucelic described him as "elated and euphoric" over the agreement with Holbrooke and asserted that Milosevic had regarded the deal as "the biggest victory ever for the Serbian people."[22]

Meanwhile, hostilities between the sides accelerated. In December, the UN secretary general reported that "Kosovo Albanian paramilitary units [had] taken advantage of the lull in the fighting" and ominously observed that "these actions . . . have only served to provoke the Serbian authorities, leading to statements that if the KLA cannot control their units the Government would. . . . Reports suggest that the number of [Serbian] forces deployed in Kosovo may exceed agreed figures."[23] The threat of air power had been able to induce temporary constraints on Milosevic but could not defuse the conflict, which by the beginning of 1999 assumed the character of a civil war.

On January 16, 1999, verification monitors confirmed the execution of forty-five ethnic Albanians in the village of Racak. Direct negotiations between Generals Clark and Naumann with President Milosevic broke down. The UN secretary general called for an immediate cessation of hostilities in the province and for dialogue to begin. As a result, the Contact Group (United States, United Kingdom, France, Italy, Germany, and Russia) invited representatives from Serbia and Kosovo to peace negotiations in Rambouillet, outside Paris. On March 19, the Kosovar Albanian delegation agreed to a plan that envisaged the disarming of the KLA, the withdrawal of Serb forces supervised by an "enabling" NATO force of thirty thousand, and the restoration of Kosovo's autonomy and independent institutions with the proviso that future political status be determined after three years.[24] But the FRY/Serbian delegation rejected the terms. On March 20, the OSCE–KVM observers were withdrawn, although heavy fighting had compelled another eighty thousand ethnic Albanians to flee their homes. President Milosevic refused to comply with a final request from Ambassador Holbrooke to stop attacks on the Kosovar Albanians or face air attacks.

On March 22, the NAC authorized the secretary general to decide, subject to further consultations, on a "broader range of air operations, if necessary."[25] The next day, the order to begin air strikes was given, and on March 24, 1999, Operation Allied Force began.

A STRATEGY OF COERCION

By December 1998, two very different NATO air plans existed: "There was a limited air option which was a short, sharp, punitive shock, rather like the attack on Iraq during 1998. Then there was the phased air option which went through a series of escalatory steps."[26] However, one feature, expressed in General Clark's initial directive to General Jumper, remained constant: the air operation was designed to coerce Milosevic, not to destroy either his forces or his government. Key requirements also remained fixed: minimize collateral damage, avoid any friendly losses, and preserve the Yugoslav civil infrastructure.[27]

The second option was chosen. President Clinton affirmed that the air operation had three goals: "To demonstrate the seriousness of NATO's opposition to aggression, to deter Milosevic from continuing and escalating his attacks on helpless civilians," and, if need be, "to damage Serbia's capacity to wage war against Kosovo by seriously diminishing its military capabilities." The president also said, "I don't intend to put our troops in Kosovo to fight a war."[28] Air power was confirmed as the sole coercive military instrument.

NATO objectives were expressed in similar terms: for the refugees to return safely home, for all Serb forces to withdraw from Kosovo, for an international force to oversee the peace, for Kosovo to be granted a wide measure of autonomy, and for a multicultural democracy to be established in the province. Serbia was identified as the aggressor. Prime Minister Blair outlined the moral tone and justification for NATO action: "We are taking this action to prevent Milosevic from continuing to perpetuate his vile oppression against innocent Kosovar civilians."[29]

UN Secretary General Javier Solana said, "Military action would be directed towards disrupting the violent attacks being committed by the Serb army and special police forces and weakening their ability to cause further humanitarian catastrophe."[30] General Clark stated, "We are going to systematically and progressively attack, disrupt, degrade, devastate and ultimately destroy those forces and their support unless Milosevic complies with the demands of the international community. The operation will be just as long and as difficult as Milosevic wants it to be." But he was confident: "Mr. Milosevic is wily, shrewd and calculating, but we are in a good position today because he respects NATO air power and is very much aware of what it can do."[31]

NATO air forces were tasked to coerce Milosevic into stopping Serbian oppression of Kosovar Albanian civilians and accepting the Rambouillet proposals. In Washington, a White House spokesman "made it clear they felt the bombing would last only three or four days."[32] Secretary of State Albright commented on television on March 24, "I don't see this as a long term operation. I think this is something . . . that is achievable with a relatively short period of time."[33] Lieutenant General Short, the USAF operational commander in theater, subsequently observed, "I can't tell you how many times the instruction I got was, 'Mike, you're only going to be allowed to bomb two, maybe three nights. That's all Washington can stand. That's all some members of the alliance can stand. That's why you've only got ninety targets. This will be over in three nights.'"[34]

General Charles Guthrie, chief of the UK Defence Staff, summed up the alliance position on March 25 in a Defense Ministry briefing after the first night of bombing: "This is a limited humanitarian action with a strictly humanitarian objective which we believe we can achieve through air strikes. We do not think it would be right to escalate this into a major ground invasion, in which many lives would be lost and the humanitarian crisis made worse." British defence secretary George Robertson confirmed that NATO had no intention of committing ground troops in Kosovo.[35] NATO military staff had concluded that even a relatively small Serbian force could disrupt or block the movement of NATO forces seeking to cross from Macedonia along the narrow Lepenac Valley. Other routes through Albania and Macedonia were poorly maintained and difficult for armored vehicles and other heavy traffic to traverse, and bridges would be rigged with antitank and antipersonnel mines. Operations to move NATO troops by helicopters behind Serbian lines would be constrained by mountains, restricting their range and endurance. Air power was the only military instrument NATO could use.

Operation Allied Force thus began with NATO expecting a speedy outcome, despite having rendered the precedent of Bosnia irrelevant by forswearing the use of ground forces. The susceptibility of Milosevic to any kind of coercion over Kosovo, in view of the visceral Serbian commitment to the province, was badly misjudged.

On March 24, eighty aircraft were involved in the first air attacks against forty widespread targets, including AD, other military installations, and arms factories near Belgrade, Pristina, Nis, Mitrovica, Podgorica, and Kraljevo. Cruise missiles were launched by the British and U.S. navies against AD south of Pristina to create a gap for manned aircraft to exploit against Serbian forces deployed in Kosovo.

USAFE had initially envisaged a replay of the Desert Storm air campaign with the first few days allocated to knocking out Serbian AD. General Jumper estimated that this defense suppression phase could last from four to six days, depending on the weather and the effectiveness of the Serb response. Presciently, the USAF planners noted that if the Serb AD simply "hunkered down," or declined to engage, the task would be much more difficult.[36]

Priority was, in accordance with doctrine, given to achieving control of the air. In the first seven days of the war, NATO air forces flew 1,700 sorties, of which 425 were attack missions, and over 100 cruise missiles were fired against more than 70 targets that included 4 secret police bases, 3 ammunition dumps, and a helicopter field in Kosovo, plus 42 assorted attacks on AD facilities across the FRY.[37]

These figures were frequently but unrealistically contrasted with the two thousand sorties flown on the first night of Desert Storm. General Guthrie admitted on March 30 that bad weather had forced the cancellation of planned NATO air attacks on three of the six nights since the air campaign began. Laser and optical weapons guidance systems could not work through clouds. There were insufficient aircraft to launch parallel attacks powerful enough to induce shock or paralysis on AD and deployed forces.

The fundamental contrast, however, stemmed from the difference between the previous strategy in Desert Storm of compulsion, anchored in a solid coalition, with clear objectives and strong determination, and this one of coercion, with uneasy partners, uncertain objectives, and political hesitation. NATO members would not agree to use their air power in a simultaneous strike on Belgrade and on Serbian deployed forces. The alliance was therefore committed to a "gradualist" use of air power, which would become highly contentious.

THE SERBIAN RESPONSE

The FRY air force had taken NATO threats seriously. Hardened Cold War shelters and underground hangars existed on many military and civilian airfields. In an exercise in October 1998, aircraft were dispersed from main bases and surface-to-air missiles (SAMs) relocated from static positions. Preparations for war included full-scale model decoys with frequent and different dispersals to airfields and major roads. Dispersals were well supported by ground crews, while communications were maintained by mobile phone and landline.[38] By March 1999, new sites for radars and AD missile batteries were identified. By March 24, 90 percent of material reserves and 70 percent of the FRY air force and AD (*Ratno Vazduhoplovstvo i Protiv Vazdusna Odbrana*, or RV i PVO) equipment had been moved from their peacetime locations, when the outbreak of war interrupted the deployment.[39]

NATO met little resistance from Serbian fighters. From a nominal strength of 154 aircraft, the RV i PVO had only 40 serviceable fighters and 40 fighter-bombers. Of these, only the MiG–29s of No. 127 Fighter Regiment engaged in combat.[40] Only nine of its sixteen aircraft were decreed serviceable on March 24. Five were scrambled on the first night. Three were shot down by NATO aircraft, one was probably destroyed by a Serbian SAM, and one returned to base with multiple systems failure. All suffered a failed radar, radio, or radar warning receiver. A further pair were scrambled from Batajnice the following day and were duly shot down.[41] Two MiGs were scrambled independently on April 5 and 6 but returned to base without engaging NATO aircraft. Five more MiG–29s were destroyed on the ground when even the most heavily constructed hardened aircraft shelter provided no protection.

The air intercept radars on the MiG–29s were constantly jammed, but communications with ground control were not. Pilots had been flying less than thirty hours a year, and aircraft serviceability was very poor. Little money had been allocated to the purchase of spares, while a UN embargo on weapons import had existed since 1992. Very often, an aircraft declared "operational" was simply "flyable." The handful of Serbian MiG–29 pilots were professional and brave. They were outnumbered, outranged, electronically blinded, and flying inferior and barely serviceable aircraft, but they still tried to engage their NATO opponents. But while No. 127 Regiment's aircraft were decimated, only two pilots were killed.

A small number of close air support sorties were flown at low level over Kosovo by Orao and Super Galeb G–4 fighter-bombers against KLA-fielded forces, with one aircraft lost to an undetermined cause. These activities by the Serbs were curtailed by systematic NATO attacks on air bases. No MiG–21 sorties were flown, for reconnaissance, AD, or ground attack.[42]

Subsequent reports that one-third of NATO fighters were flying combat air patrols over Macedonia, Albania, Bosnia, Hungary, and the Adriatic reflected alliance caution about an air-to-air threat. Yet no more than five Serbian fighters were in the sky at any one time, and that occurred only once. When a MiG–29 was shot down on May 4 by a USAF F–16, the caution appeared to be justified. The pilot was killed, and fragments of both an advanced medium-range air-to-air missile and Strela SA–7 hand-held SAMs were discovered in the wreckage. It was not known at the time that the frustrated MiG pilot was apparently seeking to take on the NATO air forces singlehandedly and without authorization.

Serbian ground AD, meanwhile, presented a substantial threat. AD structure and strategy were designed during the Cold War for survival, not the destruction of an enemy at any cost. Overwhelming NATO superiority simply reinforced the principle.[43] Between 1996 and 1999, the Serbs had studied the lessons of AD in the Gulf War of 1991 and the Bosnia conflict. Cold War AD procedures and rules were revised, emphasizing increased responsiveness and mobility. SA–3 and SA–6 missile batteries were moved frequently, usually before daybreak. Greater use was made of decoy transmitters, and older radars were reinstated. Radars purchased from the United States in 1982 were supplemented by Soviet equipment with additional surveillance radars borrowed from the army and navy. To the extent possible, radar crews were dispersed in hardened bunkers away from the radar heads.

Early warning ground radars, as well as SA–3 and SA–6 battery radars, provided early warning. Notice of NATO takeoffs was frequently provided by Serbian nationals or sympathizers by mobile phone from the neighborhoods of the NATO bases. No senior Serbian AD officer was prepared to admit to such information, but the statement "there are many Serbs overseas," accompanied by a cheerful grin, was confirmation enough.[44] Civilians in Novi Sad frequently received two hours' warning of a NATO attack, sufficient to influence decision making about attendance at football matches, barbecues, and other social activities.[45]

Several hundred SA–7 Strela were deployed across Serbia and Montenegro, usually some three kilometers away from expected targets in groups of four batteries per unit.[46] Operators were well-educated conscripts or reservists who deserved the respect shown to them by NATO aircrews. They had regular training to operate either as part of a division or independently. They expected their missiles to be effective up to seventy-five hundred feet but with effectiveness restricted by aiming at receding aircraft to maximize heat source engagement. One battery was at constant readiness, one on standby, and the other two at five minutes' readiness with operators concealed in nearby trenches. Each operator had two missiles. SA–7 operators defending Novi Sad oil installations received early warning from their unit commander by shortwave radio or voice. They had, however, no warning of cruise missile attacks on the Novi Sad bridges. Even had they received such warning, the operators were pessimistic about their prospects to intercept because of the small infrared signature and unpredictable approach path of their target. Their planning assumptions of four SA–7s to bring down a cruise missile were a little optimistic.

Benjamin Lambeth's assessment of the AD threat below fifteen thousand feet from the SA–7, its derivatives, and the SA–6 is well founded,[47] although an SA–3 accounted for an F–117 shot down forty miles northwest of Belgrade on March 26; its wreckage was gleefully displayed on Serbian television, testimony to counter the aura of invincibility that had hitherto surrounded the F–117. Serbian authorities subsequently revealed that the F–117 was destroyed by an SA–3 Neva missile of the Third Battalion of No. 250 Brigade.[48] It was detected at a distance of twelve kilometers and shot down at a height of approximately twenty-three thousand feet. No exact details of the shootdown were recorded at the time, as the SA–3 crew was not aware that it had engaged a stealth aircraft. It was not "ambushed" as a result of any previous aircraft flying a similar profile, nor was any information received about its impending presence. Ironically, the missile was fired by a Muslim serviceman, and the battery was commanded by a Hungarian.

The same battalion claimed to have damaged a second F–117 on May 1 and shot down an F–16 on May 2. SA–3 battery commanders of No. 250 Brigade believed they had shot down or damaged more than one F–117 when "blips" acquired by the battery radars disappeared after engagement. Other blips appeared and disappeared irregularly.[49] Such observations suggest that the F–117s were fleetingly visible to Serbian radars.

Two-thirds of the radars were hit by NATO air strikes, but SAMs remained a threat. All three AD sectors could be controlled from any one because of the relatively small area involved. Serbian AD officers confirmed NATO assessments that the AD command, control, and communications network was harassed and frequently jammed, but remained unbroken at the end of Allied Force.

AN EXPANDING CAMPAIGN

As the air campaign began, Serbian oppression in Kosovo intensified. Ground forces also had learned from Desert Storm and the Bosnian civil war.[50] Tactics of dispersal, deception, concealment, camouflage, mobility in small numbers, and placing military targets among civilians became standard practice. Headquarters, barracks, and other military installations, except for underground bunkers, were evacuated, while FRY troops deployed with their vehicles, armor, artillery, and antiaircraft weapons among the Albanian population: in factories, warehouses, barns, houses, and even wine cellars. In Novi Sad, at least one antiaircraft artillery battery was placed on the roof of a block of flats until angry civilian protests forced its removal, but only after a rare precision-guided munition (PGM) inaccuracy cratered the ground between the block and its neighbor. Denial and deception practices were employed:

> After the first week of KEZ [Kosovo Engagement Zone] strikes, the Serbs rarely drove military vehicles in the open during the day. They became masters of hiding during the day and making full use of night or bad weather. They also built and deployed ingeniously simple decoys to impersonate mortars, artillery, trucks, APCs [armored personnel carriers], and tanks. . . . They also parked vehicles in agricultural fields and painted them the same color as the growing crops. They built tunnels, some real, others not.[51]

One brigade could be spread over as many as fifteen villages. Vehicles were usually concealed by day in civilian surroundings or below dense foliage, with particular care being taken to mask heat emissions. One armored brigade entered Kosovo without detection by moving at night between tunnels. The tactics, however, incurred a penalty. While easily able to repress civilians, the dispersed, small units were vulnerable to KLA ambush and interception. The continuous threat from NATO air power therefore reduced the scale of oppression and induced heavier Serbian casualties at the hands of the KLA.

Lack of immediate success prompted Secretary General Solana on March 27 to initiate phase two of Operation Allied Force, saying, "I have taken the decision with the support of all allied governments, which are determined to bring a halt to violence in Kosovo and to prevent further humanitarian catastrophe. With this in mind, the broader range of operations will allow NATO commanders to intensify their action against Yugoslav forces."[52]

Amid increasing press criticism of the failure of air attacks to halt, or even slow down Serbian oppression and the flow of refugees,[53] George Robertson on March 29 repeated the arguments against using NATO ground troops offensively in Kosovo. European members did not have the forces that would be required. Even if they did, it would take two months or more to assemble and train them, with the risk of heavy combat losses. He emphasized the chances of success of the air campaign, with the possibility of Serbian armed forces overthrowing Milosevic as a result of the destruction of the FRY military infrastructure by NATO and from fear of being indicted as war criminals, but said, "It's not going to be quick and it's not going to be easy."[54]

This was the first suggestion from a NATO leader that Milosevic might not be coerced quite so easily as had been expected. Allegedly there was gloom in the White House because of fears that "the confident hope of Secretary of State Madeleine Albright, Defense Secretary William Cohen and National Security Adviser Sandy Berger, that a brief spell of bombing would bring Belgrade to heel, is proving unrealistic."[55]

NATO ambassadors met to consider extending targets to include ministries in Belgrade and other key components of Milosevic's regime. Previous references to a "Phase Three" in the bombing campaign were replaced by intentions to extend "the range and tempo of operations to maximize the effectiveness of the operation."[56] Rumors continued to spread regarding disagreements among NATO members about authorizing air attacks on the targets in Belgrade, and responding to a request by General Clark to "intensify and broaden" the assault on Yugoslavia.

On April 1, Secretary General Solana asserted, "We are degrading its [Serbia's] ability to carry out the current acts of violence in Kosovo. . . . The ring is closing around the Yugoslav armed forces. The impact of our air campaign will be increasingly cumulative." At the same NATO briefing, however, General Clark contradicted his previous assessments of the effectiveness of air power in the current crisis:

> We have always said from the outset that air power cannot stop paramilitary power on the ground. We know that. It has been widely recognised. As for what else might be done, I am going to defer that to the political leaders of NATO and NATO's governments, because these are questions governments have to resolve. They are not questions the military can resolve.[57]

The "what else" was diplomatic speak for "ground forces." At that time, the general had begun an attempt to introduce U.S. Army Apache helicopters into the theater.

After seven days, with expectations still not being met, five B–1 bombers, five EA–6Bs, six Canadian F–18s, and four Tornado GR–1 bombers were added to the allied force. The bombing campaign was extended on April 1, when the first bridge over the Danube was destroyed at Novi Sad, seventy-five miles north of Belgrade. Two days later, eight cruise missiles struck the interior ministry and police headquarters in Belgrade in the early hours. No collateral damage or casualties were reported.

Early reports of the impact of the limited attacks on Belgrade were contradictory, recording defiance, panic, and paranoia. Subsequent interviews with influential civilians in Belgrade reflected this ambiguity. Some believed that earlier heavy air attack would have induced extensive hostility to Milosevic and put pressure on him to accept the Rambouillet terms. Others recalled nonchalance in Belgrade and the angry response of the citizens of Novi Sad, directed against NATO, to the destruction of three of the city's Danube bridges. The civilian population seemed to quickly recognize the selectivity and precision of the air attacks and initially went about their business nonchalantly while avoiding military, security, and political buildings. Fewer than thirty civilians were killed in Belgrade, and one hundred civilians were injured.[58]

By April 3, widespread publicity about the plight of Albanian refugees led NATO spokesmen to acknowledge that Serbian oppression had not diminished. The British Foreign and Commonwealth Office lamented, "We did not expect Slobodan Milosevic to move the levels of population that he is moving. Perhaps, that was a failure of imagination."[59]

Fuel installations became primary but controversial targets. NATO estimated that 40,000 Serb troops in Kosovo would depend for mobility on some 7,000 vehicles, requiring some 150,000 gallons of fuel daily. But Serbian troop movements were relatively small, fuel supplies were readily available in Kosovo, and at least one U.S. oil company as well as Russian and Libyan tankers were delivering oil via the Montenegrin port of Bar.[60] Cutting such supply lines without UN authority could be provocative, as Russia naturally would oppose such a move. Nor could such operations be a substitute for direct attacks on deployed Serbian forces.

Hopes of increasing attacks on the fuel supply were raised when the Pentagon announced on April 4 that twenty-four AH–64A Apache helicopters, equipped with Hellfire antiarmor missiles, unguided rockets, and a 30mm machine gun, would deploy to the Balkans from their base in Germany. They began to arrive in Albania on April 20 but were not employed. They had trained for operations in which AD had been suppressed by multiple launch rocket systems and/or jammed by supporting fixed-wing aircraft. As long as Serbian AD had not been destroyed, Apache operations would have been severely inhibited.

Meanwhile, the air campaign continued to be constrained by tight rules of engagement that demanded positive identification of targets, validation from two sources, and, wherever there was a risk of civilian casualties or damage, the use of PGMs. Clouds frequently precluded or impeded target identification from medium level, inducing aborted missions. A–10 units were given a daily list compiled during the previous twelve hours of possible targets in Kosovo. But between the time targets were identified and aircraft were positioned to attack, Serbian forces usually moved, rendering the target information "hopelessly outdated and generally useless."[61]

Nevertheless, Prime Minister Blair on April 5 maintained that sending in ground troops "is not an alternative."[62] Greek foreign minister George Papandreou said, "Macedonia has already said it will not be the launching pad for any military operation. Therefore, any troops coming through Salonika will be sent purely for humanitarian reasons."[63]

On April 7, General Clark said he needed more strike and reconnaissance aircraft, illustrating once more that the scale of the task had been underestimated. He subsequently affirmed that he had asked for three hundred more U.S. aircraft and more than one hundred from other NATO allies.

On April 11, a ground offensive appeared to be no longer totally excluded in Washington. John Podesta, White House chief of staff, observed, "Last autumn, NATO did do an assessment of putting ground troops in and those plans and assessments could be updated quickly if we decided to do that, needed to do that." General Shelton added, "The build up of force of this size would depend on how many entry points you used, and we haven't excluded using more than one point of entry."[64] The suggestion that plans that had been discarded for both political and military reasons could now be easily resurrected and implemented was not convincing.

Every accidental attack that claimed civilian lives was prominently reported. On April 14, a refugee convoy in western Kosovo was mistakenly struck by a USAF F–16. In his subsequent debriefing to his squadron commander, the pilot described how he had circled the convoy for several minutes seeking to identify what he came to believe was a column of military tracked vehicles.[65] Eyewitness reports were conflicting, but several referred to the presence of Serbian troops and vehicles in the vicinity of the refugee convoy. Serbian television reported the attack on the convoy before the pilot or NATO headquarters was aware that any mistake had been made. NATO spokesmen could not accept responsibility solely on the evidence of anonymous destruction presented by a hostile news source. The full NATO explanation, accompanied by cockpit imagery, was only given on April 19. It revealed eight attacks before an OA–10 pilot, with binoculars, identified possible civilian vehicles among the convoy. The briefing also revealed the limited imagery available to the F–16 pilots on the monochrome four-and-a-half-inch screens in their cockpits.

The incident was a tragic example of human error even with the greatest care and the most rigid rules of engagement. A single low-level pass over the convoy might

Battle of Fleurus. French use of a balloon for observation at the battle of Fleurus contributing to their victory cited as the first use of aerial reconnaissance in warfare 26th July, 1794. *Heartstone*

Wright Flyer. *Heartstone*

Tornado GR4, 12 Squadron, RAF Lossiemouth, Moray, Scotland. *Nick Sidle/Heartstone*

Tristar KC1 Tanker, 216 Squadron, RAF, Refueling Tornado F3, 111 Squadron.
Nick Sidle/Heartstone

RAF E3-D Sentry AEW1 and Tornado F3, 111 Squadron with Tristar KC1
tanker of 216 Squadron. *Nick Sidle/Heartstone*

Hercules C-130K, 47/70 Squadron, KTTF–K Tactical Training Flight, RAF Lyneham, Southern England. *Nick Sidle/Heartstone*

Tornado GR4 / GR4A 11/1X/X111/31 Squadrons, RAF Marham, Cornwall, England.
Nick Sidle/Heartstone

Tornado F3, 43 Squadron, RAF Leuchers, Fife, Scotland. *Nick Sidle/Heartstone*

Jaguar GR3, 6 Squadron, RAF Coltishall. *Nick Sidle/Heartstone*

F15C Eagle, 493rd Fighter Squadron, USAF, based at RAF Lakenheath. *Nick Sidle/Heartstone*

KC–135RT Stratotanker, 351st Air Refueling Squadron, USAF from RAF Mildenhall,
F-15C Eagles, 493rd Fighter Squadron USAF. *Nick Sidle/Heartstone*

F-15E Strike Eagle, 49th Fighter Squadron from RAF Lakenheath over Highland Scotland.
Nick Sidle/Heartstone

Tornado F3, 43 Squadron, RAF, Loch Rannoch, Scotland. *Nick Sidle/Heartstone*

Red Arrows, Royal Air Force, Lincolnshire, England. *Nick Sidle/Heartstone*

Hercules C-130K, 47/70 Squadron, KTTF–K Tactical Training Flight, RAF Lyneham, Southern England. *Nick Sidle/Heartstone*

Harrier GR7, 20(R) Squadron, RAF England. *Nick Sidle/Heartstone*

Harrier GR7, 20(R) Squadron, RAF England. *Nick Sidle/Heartstone*

Jaguar GR3, 41 Squadron, RAF England. *Nick Sidle/Heartstone*

Harrier GR7, 20(R) Squadron, RAF England. *Nick Sidle/Heartstone*

F-16C, F-16D Falcon, 510th Fighter Squadron, United States Air Force, Dolomites, Italy.
Flown from Aviano Air Base. *Nick Sidle/Heartstone*

Hawk T1, 208 Squadron, RAF North Wales from RAF Valley, BAe Hawk India Program.
Nick Sidle/Heartstone

Nimrod MR2, North Sea, 42 Squadron from RAF Kinloss, Moray, Scotland.
Nick Sidle/Heartstone

F-15C Eagle, 493rd Fighter Squadron, USAF from RAF Lakenheath over Northern England.
Nick Sidle/Heartstone

F-15E Strike Eagle, 494th Fighter Squadron, USAF from RAF Lakenheath over
Northern Scotland. *Nick Sidle/Heartstone*

F-16A MLU, 331 Squadron, Royal Norwegian Air Force, Nordland, Norway. Flown from Bodo Main Air Station. *Nick Sidle/Heartstone*

F-16A MLU, 331 Squadron, Royal Norwegian Air Force, Lofoten Islands, Nordland, Norway. Flown from Bodo Main Air Station. *Nick Sidle/Heartstone*

P51 Mustangs, 332nd Fighter Group returning from bomber escort mission to their base in Italy.
Photo courtesy of Col. Roosevelt J. Lewis, Tuskegee Airmen

have left no doubt about its refugee character, but had it indeed been a military convoy, protected by mobile low-level AD, such a pass would have been most hazardous for the pilot and noncompliant with command guidance on aircrew risk.

Such guidelines were stimulated partly by legitimate concerns for force protection and partly by worries, especially in the United States, about an adverse public response to casualties. NATO commander General Wesley Clark was reported as issuing a "no loss of aircraft" restriction in November 1998.[66] Lieutenant General Short subsequently denied receiving such an order but acknowledged that "zero losses were a major goal."[67] In fact, General Clark had included a specific reference to aircraft losses in a videoconference on March 14, when he made the formal announcement to his commanders and staff of the order to execute phase one of the air campaign. He subsequently wrote,

> But we had to move the campaign along some general paths, in addition to minding the legal constraints in the order. I termed these "measures of merit.". . . the first measure of merit is not to lose aircraft, "minimize the loss of aircraft." This addressed Mike Short's biggest concern—to prevent the loss of aircrews. It drove our decisions on tactics, targets, and which airplanes could participate. But I was motivated by a larger political-military rationale. If we wanted to keep this campaign going indefinitely, we had to protect our air fleet. Nothing would hurt us more with public opinion than headlines that screamed, "NATO LOSES TEN AIRPLANES IN TWO DAYS." Take losses like that, divide it into the total number of aircraft committed, and the time limits on the campaign would be clear. Milosevic could wait us out.[68]

The media war continued to overlay the air campaign, whose effectiveness could be illustrated only by images of its impact, not by pictures of conscientious aircrews departing or returning from "successful" missions. The risk of civilian casualties increased proportionately. The problem for NATO was that Milosevic controlled instant access to the impact points, whereas NATO's own bomb damage imagery was sparse and tardy. Civilian casualties, albeit in small numbers, increased as NATO aircraft hit bridges, barracks, power supplies, and oil refineries and intensified attacks on ground forces in Kosovo.

Naturally, as air power was the only military instrument used by the allies, it dominated media reporting. Media anticipation of an easy allied victory, conditioned by the success of Desert Storm and encouraged by political forecasts at the outset of Allied Force, was frustrated by the apparent lack of progress.

By April 20, the number of aircraft committed to the campaign had risen to one thousand. Eight hundred were from the United States, which flew four-fifths of all sorties. Of 268 combat aircraft, 142 were U.S., 30 French, 27 British, 16 Dutch, 14 German, 12 Belgian, and the remainder from Canada, Denmark, Norway, Spain, and Portugal. Meanwhile, Serbian AD still posed a threat to NATO aircraft.

These increased numbers, together with better weather, enabled NATO target lists to be expanded still further to include President Milosevic's political party headquarters in Belgrade, which was struck by eight U.S. Navy (USN) Tomahawk cruise missiles at 3:30 a.m. on April 21. Two pro-Milosevic radio and television stations housed in the party headquarters building were also destroyed in the attack. NATO spokesman Jamie Shea observed, "From now on, any aspect of [Milosevic's] power structure is deemed a legitimate target."[69] The next day, Milosevic's official residence was destroyed, apparently to put psychological pressure upon him.

Meanwhile, the British position on the employment of ground forces was changing from using them as a peace implementation force to moving into Kosovo once there was no longer coordinated armed resistance, after the Serbian ground forces had been disrupted and weakened by air attack. On April 22, immediately before the fiftieth anniversary NATO summit conference in Washington, Prime Minister Blair sought to persuade President Clinton of the value of a "lightweight" invasion after Serbian troops had been weakened. The president rejected the suggestion in what General Clark referred to, albeit at second hand, as "a stormy session."[70]

At the summit meeting, the alliance rejected an invasion by ground troops but agreed to extend the target list by adding military-industrial infrastructure, media, and other strategic targets. They also conceded that, while any peacekeeping force would be NATO-led, it could include non-NATO troops, including a substantial Russian contribution.

On April 24, the air campaign and media war converged. The Yugoslav state television station was regarded by NATO as a legitimate target because of its "biased and distorted" coverage of the conflict. The TV center was destroyed at 2:00 a.m. by a B–2. Seventeen people were killed, and images of dead workers were flashed around the world. The deliberate attack on the studios and associated facilities, inflicting civilian casualties, was questionable in international law. In a campaign in which favorable TV coverage was eagerly sought by both sides, the attack was politically and psychologically misjudged. Militarily, it failed because the station quickly got back on the air, as its transmitters in the hills outside Belgrade had to be attacked. Yet when the media are manifestly being used by the enemy as an instrument of war, it is difficult to see how it can avoid becoming as much a legitimate target as a munitions factory.

Serbian civilian reaction in Belgrade to the destruction of the TV station was muted. Throughout the FRY, the population had access to international TV. The Belgrade station was generally vilified as the purveyor of Milosevic's lies, so first reports of its destruction were greeted with enthusiasm.

A NATO press release on April 27 affirmed that only 33 percent of Serbian oil stocks had been destroyed, that the AD system was still operating, and that 20 percent of ammunition storage depots had been significantly damaged. Five major bridges across the Danube had been destroyed and one damaged. Thirty-five days of air attacks had severely damaged the country's military infrastructure but left President Milosevic's ability to continue his repression in Kosovo largely untouched.

On May 2, however, came signs that the bombing was beginning to affect Serbian civilian morale. BBC world affairs editor John Simpson, reporting from Belgrade, noted a change in attitude among the civilian population. They were no longer instinctively supporting their president and were becoming fearful of the bombing campaign. Extensive opposition to Milosevic had existed in Belgrade before the bombing started, and attacks on empty government buildings had been regarded with equanimity by most civilians. On May 3, F–117s dropped nonlethal carbon graphite filament bombs on five main electricity power grids and transformer yards, with the primary objective of disrupting Serbian military headquarters' communications and computer services across the country. The power supply to Belgrade was cut off for several hours. The graphite particles were still causing short circuits in a generating plant three days later, intermittently cutting power to water supplies, domestic appliances, transport systems, and telephone switchboards. Meanwhile, gasoline was severely restricted in Belgrade, and the impact of sleepless nights as a result of the air raid sirens was being felt.

In an example of imaginative targeting of morale and the president's coterie, a cigarette factory at Nis was destroyed, creating a shortage in Belgrade and removing a primary source of income for Milosevic's family and friends. But after fifty days, the air campaign was widely criticized. NATO briefings were usually upbeat and consistently emphasized the number of sorties flown, targets attacked, and bombs dropped. Such "input" could readily be counted. It was, however, difficult at the time to assess how far the bombing of Belgrade was influencing Serb public opinion or to determine the coercive effect on Milosevic of attacks on Serbian forces in Kosovo.

During the night of May 6–7, the campaign was set back when the Chinese embassy in Belgrade was hit by three PGMs dropped from a B–2 bomber in the belief that it was a Yugoslav army headquarters. Apparently, targeting information provided by the Central Intelligence Agency was out of date.

This mistake undercut international efforts to persuade China to agree to the G–8 peace plan. The Russian government issued strongly worded criticisms and postponed visits to the West. It provided unexpected relief and a major propaganda coup for President Milosevic. The cumulative impact was to delay the end of the conflict and thereby unnecessarily prolong the suffering of the ethnic Albanians in Kosovo.

NATO spokesman Jamie Shea sought to put the Chinese embassy error into a military perspective by noting that allied planes had hit "1,900 aim points" and, out of a total of 9,000 missiles and bombs, only 12 had gone astray. But any military perspective had been overwhelmed by the international political reaction: a hostile mix of righteous indignation, suspicion, anger, incredulity, and ridicule.[71]

When on May 10, Milosevic offered to withdraw some of his troops from Kosovo, NATO spokesmen saw it as a "propaganda" ploy as oppression in Kosovo had, if anything, increased. There was widespread agreement that FRY forces had been engaged in a well-planned campaign of terrorism and expulsion of the Kosovar Albanians well before March 20.[72] While the perpetual threat of NATO air attack restricted the activities of Serbian forces, it was subsequently estimated that during the course of the air campaign, approximately 863,000 civilians sought or were forced into refuge beyond Kosovo's borders. An estimated additional 590,000 were internally displaced.[73]

On May 12, Shea's words reflected NATO's awareness of, and sensitivity to, criticisms of the air campaign: "We don't know when we are going to turn the corner. But we know we will, sooner or later. . . . We are satisfied that we are now having the type of military impact that will impress President Milosevic and will start making him think how he is going to get himself out of this crisis."[74] The statement coincided with the arrival in theater of the three hundred combat aircraft requested by General Clark, including additional A–10s and F–15Es, and the prospect of using airfields in Hungary and Turkey. NATO now deployed three times as many aircraft as it had at the start of the campaign, and their increased impact was soon obvious.

Unfortunately, public alliance disagreements on the use of ground troops continued. On May 17, British foreign secretary Cook called in Brussels for preparation of a ground force to be deployed before the Yugoslav government agreed to terms. Downing Street spokesmen suggested that it was now a question of "when" troops invaded, rather than "if."[75] Opposition came swiftly from French government officials and, by inference, from Jamie Shea, who reiterated the alliance agreement on an international security force only "once the violence has stopped." The following day, German chancellor Gerhard Schroeder and Italian prime minister Massimo D'Alema declared their opposition to such a move. The alliance was widely seen to be in disarray, encouraging, rather than coercing, Milosevic.

Nevertheless, the ground force issue receded as allied air attacks intensified. On May 20, there were antiwar demonstrations in Krusevac and reports of desertions among Serbian reservists deployed in Kosovo. On May 25, a Yugoslav army statement outlawed "illegal public gatherings" as antiwar protests and army desertions were reported. Meanwhile, NATO increased the pressure by agreeing to expand its "peace implementation force" from twenty-eight thousand to fifty thousand troops and authorized the improvement of the main road from the Albanian port of Durres to the Kosovo border. On the same day, Montenegrin president Milo Djukanovic, on an official visit to London, asserted that dissent was growing in Serbia and President Milosevic was preparing to sue for peace.

On May 27, U.S. deputy secretary of state Strobe Talbot, Russian special envoy Victor Chernomyrdin, and Finnish president Martti Ahtisaari began talks in Moscow, which led to Russia's support for NATO's settlement proposals. On the same day, the 308 air strikes conducted included more than 50 on Belgrade. The attacks followed close upon the International War Crimes Tribunal's indictment of President Milosevic for crimes against humanity.

By the end of May, B–52s and B–1s were dropping unguided ordnance on Kosovo daily, in an attempt to drive Serbian forces into the open, where they could be struck by PGMs.[76] As fighting between Serbian forces and the KLA intensified near the Albanian border, Serbian vulnerability to a NATO air attack increased, as the Serbs had to forsake their small unit mobility and begin to take up defensive positions. On June 1, 197 strike sorties were flown against Serbian forces opposing 4,000 KLA irregular troops near Mount Pastrik. By that date, total sorties had risen from fewer than one hundred a day in March to over seven hundred. Serbian defense authorities subsequently asserted, not entirely convincingly, that the Serbian forces engaging these KLA units comprised only small numbers of lightly armed "border guards" and, as elsewhere in Kosovo, suffered very few casualties to air attack.[77]

President Milosevic personally recognized more than five hundred Serbian troops killed in Kosovo, but the great majority were casualties to the KLA, not NATO air power. Individual military deaths were recorded in a book titled *Heroes of the Fatherland*, which Milosevic presented, with medals, to next of kin. The book, which was not available to the general public, recorded 1,004 killed or missing in action in all areas between February 1998 and June 1999. Many of those who died in Serbia and Montenegro served in AD radar and SAM units.[78] Those figures call to mind

Benjamin Lambeth's observation that "after the war ended, it was never established that any of the bombs dropped by the B–52s and B–1s had achieved any militarily significant effects, or that NATO's cooperation with the KLA had yielded any results of real operational value."[79]

THE END GAME

Reports of deserters from the Serbian army and the impact of NATO bombing on their morale continued to appear in the Western media, but there were no signs of any large-scale loss of control from Belgrade. Nonetheless, moves toward a diplomatic resolution to the conflict continued. President Milosevic was reported to have accepted the G–8 proposals after diplomatic pressure from Russia, but the position of Serbian forces in Kosovo after a peace agreement remained in doubt.

On June 3, the Yugoslav parliament accepted the peace proposals, but uncertainties remained over the nature of the Russian participation in the peacekeeping force. NATO, however, maintained its position that a "verifiable, substantial, Serbian withdrawal" had to begin before the bombing would cease.

On June 5, Lieutenant General Sir Mike Jackson, commanding NATO forces in Macedonia, met Serbian commanders on the Kosovo frontier to begin preparations for their withdrawal. An agreement on Serbian withdrawal was reached on June 9, and the bombing campaign ceased a few hours later. The refugees began to return home. All the objectives of Operation Allied Force had been achieved.

It seems that a combination of factors brought about Serbian capitulation. Milosevic had been depending on Russian support, which was withdrawn. He may have feared for his forces if NATO proceeded with tardy plans to deploy ground troops. He may have become concerned by his international isolation and rapidly dwindling support from both his inner circle and the general public. He may have reacted to his indictment as a war criminal. The absence of any one of those factors could have delayed the outcome, but the air campaign was the indispensable catalyst for its success. The sole military coercive instrument was air power.

USAF Chief of Staff General Michael Ryan had no doubts: "The lights went down, the power went off, petroleum production ceased, the bridges were down, communications were down, the economics of the country were slowly falling apart and I think he came to the realization, in a strategic sense, he wasn't prepared to continue this."[80]

"ALLIED" AIR POWER?

Yet despite its success, the conduct of the air campaign stimulated fierce debate. In the eight years since Desert Storm, the "air power differential"[81] (the capability gap existing between U.S. air power and everyone else's) had grown ever wider. It created problems of interoperability, generated a controversial dual command structure, and aggravated deep disagreements about bombing strategy, which in a less one-sided contest could have jeopardized the outcome.

The USAF had given priority to new families of PGMs, to development of unmanned aerial vehicles (UAVs), to speeding up the information-attack loop, and to all aspects of information warfare. Meanwhile, the European alliance partners, with one or two exceptions, had failed to reinvest in similar weapons and technology. Consequently, while the commander of Allied Air Forces Central Europe was able to take great pride in the achievements of NATO air forces in Allied Force, he also noted a significant number of operational deficiencies revealed in the air campaign.[82]

NATO aircraft had to be able to attack targets on the ground with an accuracy demanded by the rules of engagement in the glare of international exposure, but most could not deliver PGMs. There was a severe shortage of aircraft capable of designating targets for laser-guided bomb attack. Only the United States and, to a much lesser extent, France and the United Kingdom were able to drop precision-guided bombs. Even the United States began to run short of some kinds of PGMs, including cruise missiles, by the beginning of May. Many allied aircraft still required external laser or electro-optical guidance. Dependence on another aircraft for laser designation increased the overall aircraft requirement, complicated mission planning, and could increase the vulnerability of any target-marking aircraft that had to loiter in hostile airspace.

Only the United States possessed all-weather PGMs. The performance of those guided electro-optically or by laser was degraded by cloud, smoke, or bad weather. Over Kosovo, "there was 50–100% cloud cover 72% of the time, and only 21 of 78 days had good overall weather. In all, 3,766 planned sorties, including 1,029 sorties characterized as 'close air support' were aborted due to weather. Not until May did the weather become consistently favorable."[83]

Some air forces did not have secure air-to-air communications. Target and aircraft position information was frequently vulnerable to Serbian interception. Fortunately, no Serbian aircraft were available to take advantage, and even had they been alerted, autonomous Serbian AD units were unwilling to disclose their locations.

There was no standard "identification friend or foe" equipment. Nor were all NATO aircraft adequately equipped with radar warning receivers (RWR). Some were uncertain which SAM system was illuminating them or even whether the system was hostile. There was no alliance-wide reliable SAM threat warning system. Consequently, operational planners sought to mix different levels of RWR efficiency to provide adequate cover for a multinational package, clearly inhibiting the most effective aircraft involved. General Jumper sought "a reliable and flexible threat warning system, matched to the threats of our adversary."[84]

Potential vulnerability was increased by inadequate provision for defense suppression, which the USAF made a prerequisite for all missions. A RAND report in 1998 highlighted the atrophy of electronic warfare (EW) assets since Operation Desert Storm and prompted the creation of a new EW office in the Pentagon, with input to training, manning, and equipment. By March 1999, however, there had been little impact on operational capability.

EA–6B crews flew daily, six days a week, logging ninety hours a month, but the U.S. Navy had to reinforce the squadrons with instructors from training posts. The need to provide jamming support for the F–117 and B–2 stealth aircraft was, apparently, unexpected.[85] Shortfalls were compounded when the Serbian target signals sought by EC–135 Rivet Joint, the USN EP–3, and Army RE–12 Guardrail were simultaneously being jammed by EC–130 Compass Call and EA–6B Prowlers.

Differences in alliance capabilities affected not only operations, but also the way in which they were controlled. The forty-five sorties completed by the B–2 made up the first long-range precision strike offensive from bases in the United States to Europe, enabled by refueling twice in each direction. "Global reach, global power" became an air power reality, reducing the historical requirement for air bases in theater. The aircraft dropped 650 joint direct attack munitions (JDAMs),[86] 11 percent of the bombs dropped on fixed targets in Serbia and Kosovo, in less than half a percent of the total 9,500 strike sorties flown and with more than 80 percent of targets being hit in a single pass.[87] Serbian AD systems were never aware of the B–2's presence, and no B–2 crew was ever threatened by them. With onboard synthetic aperture radar and the Global Positioning System (GPS), the JDAM-equipped B–2 was impervious to weather that grounded or constrained all other combat aircraft. JDAMs could strike any static target by day or night, in all weathers, from heights of up to forty thousand feet, with a "near precision" accuracy of a few feet.

The B–2 was a NATO contributor in name only. "For the B–2 (and certain other systems) there was a structure in place that separated the most sensitive mission planning from the bulk of the planning for NATO sorties, segregating the pilots on what was called the 'U.S.-only' side of the operations."[88] Parallel U.S. and NATO command structures complicated operational planning and unity of command. B–2s, F–117s, and cruise missiles were allocated by U.S. European Command (USEUCOM) rather than by NATO. Within the Combined Air Operations Center (CAOC), there were separate USEUCOM and NATO targeting teams. Sometimes, AWACS crews were not notified of the presence in their areas of "sensitive" U.S. aircraft.

Some NATO partners were unhappy about independent operations being flown in an "allied" war zone. Had there been any hostile air activity in the region, the potential for confusion or worse would have been serious. The USAF, however, could not be expected to compromise the security and effectiveness of very high-value aircraft simply to alleviate alliance sensitivities. Tanking, intelligence, air cover, and SEAD support to B–2 missions were provided exclusively by U.S. resources. Conflict between U.S. security interests and allied operational interoperability would continue to present a practical obstacle to alliance cohesion.

In January 2001, the extent of allied tensions in executing Operation Allied Force was diplomatically confirmed by implication at a London conference by a senior British naval officer: [89]

> The dual key approach may dramatically reduce military effectiveness. . . . To maintain unity of effort, commanders, including our political masters need to effect liaison and coordination at each echelon of the command chain. . . . The promulgation of separate "need to know" Air Tasking Orders (ATOs) for "National Eyes Only" systems facilitates the full use of weapon capability . . . but careful coordination between the ATOs is required at the CAOC [as] the situation may partially undermine the "fully joint" principle of a coalition CAOC.[90]

Differences over command and control were accompanied by deep disagreements within the alliance over strategy. USAF commanders, in accordance with service doctrine, believed that "aerospace power is usually employed to greatest effect in parallel, asymmetric operations. This includes precision strikes against surface forces, information attack against command and control systems, or precision strikes against infrastructure and centers of gravity."[91] They preferred to hit targets associated with Milosevic and his inner circle: homes, businesses, command facilities, and others such as bridges, electrical grids, and other targets used by civilians, to bring pressure on the population. This was classical air power strategy of direct attack on, in Colonel John Warden's language, the "inner circle," plus pressure on civilian morale.[92] During the war, Lieutenant General Michael C. Short, alliance joint forces air component commander, said in an interview,

> Airmen would like to have gone after that target set [Serbian leadership] on the first night and sent a clear signal that we were taking the gloves off from the very beginning, that we were not going to try a little bit of this and see how you like it and try a little bit of that and see how you like it.[93]

Shortly after the end of the campaign, General Michael Ryan observed,

> The campaign did not begin the way that America would normally apply air power—massively striking at strategic centers of gravity that support Milosevic and his oppressive regime. A month into the campaign, it became apparent that a constrained, phased approach was not effective. NATO broadened the campaign to achieve strategic effects.[94]

In October 1999, General Short expressed himself more forcibly in testimony to the U.S. Senate Armed Services Committee:

> I believe the way to stop ethnic cleansing was to go at the heart of the leadership, and put a dagger in that heart as rapidly and directly as possible. . . . I'd have gone for the head of the snake on the first night. I'd have dropped the bridges across the Danube. . . . A nation that's providing less than eight percent of the sortie contribution to an effort [France] should not be in a position of restricting American aviators who are bearing seventy percent of the load.[95]

Beneath the arguments about strategy lay a fundamental problem of coalition warfare.[96] At the outset of the campaign, some NATO members did not wish to strike targets near Belgrade. Even the United Kingdom asked for "something more measured."[97] In his final press conference on May 4, 1999, General Naumann commented, "We need to find a way to reconcile the conditions of a coalition war with the principle of military operations such as surprise and overwhelming force. We did not apply either in Operation Allied Force and this cost time, effort and potentially additional casualties."[98]

In joint testimony to the Senate Armed Services Committee, Chairman of the Joint Chiefs of Staff General Henry Shelton observed,

> The fact that NATO needed to obtain and hold a consensus on its strategy required that a more gradualist approach be taken to the operation. Some NATO allies were reluctant to attack anything other than the troops and vehicles actually carrying out the ethnic cleansing of Kosovo, while others insisted that the fastest way to obtain Milosevic's compliance was with a strategic bombing effort on Serb centers of gravity.

Secretary of Defense Cohen was more emphatic:

The campaign would never have been launched at all—and Milosevic would have gotten away with ethnic cleansing—if demands had been made by some NATO members to pursue anything other than a gradually increasing air campaign. . . . Gaining consensus among 19 democratic nations is not easy.[99]

The debate over strategy went to the heart of air power doctrine. If air power can be effective only when applied with overwhelming force, claims of its inherent flexibility are groundless. USAF opposition to the "gradualism" of Allied Force had its roots in seared memories of Vietnam, while after Desert Storm thinking was heavily influenced by concepts of overwhelming parallel strikes. By 1999, USAF doctrine was dangerously close to congealing into dogma. For the first time in its history, air power had the capacity to be applied like a rapier, but there was a reluctance to abandon the bludgeon.

A NEW AIR POWER CENTURY

Allied Force rather than Desert Storm marked the beginning of a new era of air power: in its technology, in the evolution of asymmetric countermeasures, in the impact of humanitarian issues, in its exposure to the international media, and in its application within an uneasy alliance. Subsequent overwhelming successes and equally resounding problems in Iraq and Afghanistan had their roots in the war against Serbia in 1999 rather than in the larger and more spectacular success of 1991.

Satellites, in addition to facilitating communications, intelligence, surveillance, and reconnaissance, enabled air power finally to overcome a massive obstacle by providing all-weather platform navigation and precision weapon guidance, through GPS and JDAMs. The advent of an all-weather precision capability was perhaps the most important development in the evolution of air attack.

Shortfalls in timely reconnaissance and battle damage assessment remained, but for the first time, unmanned systems made a significant contribution. USAF RQ–1 Predators, USN RQ–2 Pioneers, and U.S. Army RQ–5 Hunters, together with a number of French, German, and British UAVs, provided target information and verification, battle damage assessment, and refugee monitoring. Attrition rates were comparatively high, perhaps close to 50 percent,[100] but their advantages and potential were now irrefutable. UAV losses involved no aircrew casualties, prompting neither public concern nor political embarrassment. Their cost was relatively small: $3.2 million for a Predator. They could fly below the weather within range of Serbian SAMs without putting the aircrew at risk. Their ability to loiter for many hours in an area of hostile activity was itself a deterrent to enemy movement on the ground.

At the end of the campaign, the USAF deployed into theater the first Predators to carry laser target designators. In Allied Force, unmanned systems stepped into the twenty-first century as their potential for even greater endurance, swifter communication, and weapons delivery became obvious.

In Desert Storm, the use of PGMs had been a desirable, operationally cost-effective reinforcement of air power, offering the prospect of fewer weapons, fewer aircraft, fewer air and ground crew, and smaller supporting infrastructure to achieve a desired effect. Of the total munitions expended, 9 percent were PGMs. In Operation Allied Force, when concerns about collateral damage and casualties had come to dominate strategy formulation, they became a political necessity. The proportion grew to 35 percent.[101] More than any other capability, possession or lack of PGMs determined the value of a contributor. General Jumper emphasized, "In the future we need to ensure that we each have the ability to *independently* participate in such precision warfare, where precision guided munitions, whatever their characteristics, are the weapons of choice."[102]

The combination in Allied Force of PGMs, an all-weather offensive capability, extended endurance and reach, and increasingly rapid relay of information would lay the technological basis for twenty-first-century air operations. Unfortunately, military technology, like strategy, does not advance in a political or even a technological vacuum.

In 1990 and 1991, Saddam Hussein had quickly realized the potential of manipulating the international media but lacked the skill or organization to do so consistently and successfully. Few reporters had instant satellite relays either in Baghdad or on the battlefield. By 1999, satellite technology had expanded television coverage of events worldwide, often in real time as events unfolded. Both sides were acutely conscious of the potential influence of the media. Civilian deaths and destruction were regularly reported with pictures facilitated by Serbian authorities, while justification or apologies came later by word from NATO briefings. Conversely, images of tragic refugees were issued daily by NATO, while defensive verbal explanations came later from Belgrade.

Heavier bombing inevitably increased the incidence of weapons malfunction or human error. Yet despite media coverage, such mistakes—Chinese embassy apart—had no effect on NATO's strategy and targeting, no influence on the outcome of the campaign, and little or no cumulative impact on public support. In the media war, NATO suffered a handful of tactical defeats, but the impact on public opinion of the plight of the Kosovar refugees was much greater and more sustained than the occasional images of NATO bombing errors. Moreover, the casualties incurred were infinitesimal compared with those that would have occurred had ground forces had to fight among the civilian population. By the end of April, British polls indicated support for the bombing campaign rising to more than three to one. Evidence from Kosovo suggests that public support for a cause is more tolerant of occasional bombing errors than some Western politicians and generals may have feared.

The humanitarian objectives aggravated differences in NATO over strategy, sensitivities to casualties, and "collateral" damage. The imposition of strict alliance rules of engagement demanding target validation, which was not always available, prompted operational frustration. After Allied Force, a combination of high public expectations, international media access, real-time image transmission, and unscrupulous political manipulation would continue to ensure that air power would pay some political penalty for even the rarest mistake, no matter how extensive the contrition.

The USAF and, to varying degrees, the other NATO air forces would seek to learn and apply the lessons from Allied Force. They would procure all-weather precision munitions, unmanned systems, and real-time secure networks of command, control, communications, intelligence, and response. One uncomfortable question lurked. Had the air power differential between the USAF and its allies widened so much that the military value of NATO to the United States was now outweighed by entangling political constraints? "The unavoidable impression was that the friction created in order to satisfy the political requirement for multi-nationality probably exceeded the tangible military benefit offered by that multi-nationality—a lesson that was not lost on the air power thinkers in Maxwell and Washington."[103]

Potential adversaries, however, would look for lessons in a different direction. They would recognize the impossibility of opposing the USAF, with or without allies, in the air. They would seek asymmetric countermeasures. They would copy Serbian tactics of dispersal, concealment, mobility, decoys, and deployment among civilian communities. They would deploy mobile SAMs, not depend on static installations and traditional AD command and control, seeking preservation rather than conventional engagements. Observing the vulnerability of democratic public opinion to casualties and apparent lack of success when a nation's vital interests were not at stake, they would elevate manipulation of the media to a primary strategic instrument. They would note the fragility of a NATO consensus when operations fell outside the original NATO mutual defense security area. In Allied Force, all that was missing from the asymmetric twenty-first-century counters to air power was an ability to strike at the U.S. heartland and an ideology that would confer perverted legitimacy on terrorism.

Air power had independently secured the objectives of Allied Force. At the threshold of the twenty-first century, U.S. air power was poised to become even more powerful. Both its potential and its asymmetric opposition had their roots in the Kosovo conflict.

PART IV: 2000–2006

INTRODUCTION

PART 4 OF THIS BOOK FOLLOWS air power into its second century. In chapter 11, Benjamin Lambeth characterizes Operation Enduring Freedom, the U.S.-led military campaign against al Qaeda and the Taliban in Afghanistan, as primarily an air campaign conducted in conjunction with special operations forces and friendly indigenous fighters. This represented a new way of war for the United States. Waged for more than five months during late 2001 and early 2002, Operation Enduring Freedom showed the ability of the United States to conduct successful force projection from land bases located thousands of miles away from the target area, as well as from carrier-based stations positioned farther away from a landlocked combat zone than ever before. Lambeth reviews the various phases of the war, devoting special attention to Operation Anaconda—the only part of Operation Enduring Freedom that involved conventional U.S. ground troops and that saw the greatest number of precision munitions dropped on the smallest geographic space in the history of warfare. Lambeth asserts that real-time imagery and improved communications connectivity tightened the sensor-to-shooter link and made it more efficient than ever, with impressive target-attack accuracy. While examining new elements in both warfighting concepts and technology, the author also emphasizes several problems that the Coalition encountered in Operation Enduring Freedom and warns nations against engaging in conflicts and relying on centralized, long-distance execution simply because they have the necessary technology to do so.

In chapter 12, Williamson Murray examines the U.S.-led campaign to topple Saddam Hussein and his Ba'athist regime in Operation Iraqi Freedom (March–April 2003). The author argues that air power played a critical role in meeting the political and military objectives of the campaign: not in the form of strategic attacks but in the form of air superiority, interdiction, and close air support. According to

Murray, strategic bombing to create "shock and awe" had little effect on the regime's willingness to continue the conflict but caused considerable damage to Iraq's civilian and bureaucratic infrastructure. This lack of effectiveness, according to Murray, stands in strong contrast to the other applications of air power. Undisputed Coalition air supremacy from the very beginning provided the basis for a campaign that was asymmetrical in almost every conceivable way, and air power in the form of direct attacks, combined with close air support to both the U.S. Army (Third Infantry Division) and the U.S. Marine Corps (First Marine Division), proved sufficient to facilitate the ground advance. Murray also suggests that the psychological effects of precision strikes against the Iraqi formations were just as important as the actual physical destruction. Drawing on Iraqi as well as Coalition reports, Murray concludes that, in terms of lessons learned, one should not read too much into this specific campaign at the tactical and operational levels, although many observations fit wider patterns of the utility and futility of air power.

The second Lebanon war, fought in 2006, stands out in military history as a war in which one party relied almost exclusively on air power, or, more specifically, as a war in which modern air power was used extensively against a terrorist and guerrilla organization that possessed significant military capability. Itai Brun argues in chapter 13 that this unique engagement led to controversial results: Hezbollah succeeded in withstanding attacks by the Israeli Air Force (IAF), and the Israel Defense Force (IDF) largely failed to defend the population of northern Israel. However, Israel achieved its goal of weakening Hezbollah, not only by reducing its military power, but also by revealing tensions among the organization's different identities. Contrary to conventional wisdom, the author claims that the IDF waged the second Lebanon war without a coherent doctrine: the priority it placed on air power resulted more from social and political constraints than from a concept of operations that relied on victory through air power. According to Brun, the lack of an appropriate doctrine led to a large gap between the IAF's impressive capabilities and its ability to apply air power properly during the conflict. In this regard, the need to develop a thoughtful, comprehensive doctrine before engaging in a military operation is the primary lesson of the second Lebanon war.

11

OPERATION ENDURING FREEDOM, 2001

Benjamin S. Lambeth

ON THE MORNING OF SEPTEMBER 11, 2001, a clear day that will be forever remembered in American history, four jetliners—two Boeing 757s and two Boeing 767s, all on scheduled transcontinental flights from the East Coast and each fully laden with fuel—were commandeered by Islamist terrorists almost simultaneously after their near-concurrent departures from Boston, Newark, and Washington, D.C. Upon being hijacked, the four aircraft were promptly turned into what would become de facto weapons of mass destruction against the United States and its citizens.[1]

The first two aircraft were flown within eighteen minutes of each other into the twin towers of the World Trade Center in New York City, ultimately reducing those familiar landmarks of the Manhattan skyline to 450,000 tons of rubble. The third aircraft was flown forty minutes later into the southwestern side of the Pentagon in Arlington, Virginia. The fourth aircraft, its intended target still unknown but thought to have been the White House or the U.S. Capitol building in Washington, D.C., fortunately had its mission thwarted by some brave passengers who turned on their captors once they learned, from frantic cell phone conversations with friends and relatives on the ground, what the other three airliners had just done. After a failed struggle between the terrorists and their resisters, that aircraft was brought to earth in a ball of fire in an empty field in western Pennsylvania.

The attacks caught the United States completely off guard. They also instantly defined the face of early twenty-first-century conflict. What for nearly a decade had come to be loosely called the "post–Cold War era," for lack of a better phrase to describe the still-unshaped period that followed the collapse of Soviet communism, was transformed in the short span of one morning into the era of fanatical Islamist extremism. The attacks, planned and executed by a determined band of murderous Islamist zealots, made for the boldest hostile act to have been committed on U.S. soil since Pearl Harbor. They also represented the single most destructive instance of terrorist aggression to have taken place anywhere in the world. The loss of life caused by the attacks exceeded that from Japan's attack on Pearl Harbor in 1941. In the final tally, nearly three thousand innocent civilians died as a result of the attacks.

Immediately after the attacks, the Federal Aviation Administration ordered all airborne domestic flights to land at the nearest suitable airport. It also banned any further nonmilitary takeoffs nationwide and, for the first time ever, halted all civil air traffic in the United States. As a result, some thirty-three thousand airborne passengers were taken in by Canada as U.S. airspace was closed and incoming international flights were rerouted. At the same time, at the direction of President George W. Bush, a continuity-of-government plan that was rooted in the early days of the Cold War was set into motion. As a part of that plan, the president was kept airborne and moving aboard Air Force One until the apparent terrorist threat had subsided.[2] Only at 7:00 p.m. did the president finally return to Washington to address the nation. In that address, he affirmed that in responding to the attacks, the United States would "make no distinction between the terrorists who committed these acts and those who harbor them."[3]

Earlier that day, even as the attacks were still under way, the alert status of U.S. forces around the world was raised to Defense Condition 3, the highest level since the Yom Kippur War of 1973. Air National Guard F–16 fighters were launched from Andrews Air Force Base, Maryland, to provide a continuous combat air patrol over the nation's capital. At the same time, Air Guard F–16s in Richmond, Virginia, were put on highest alert. E–3 airborne warning and control aircraft were also placed on airborne orbits to monitor the airspace over New York City and Washington as tight restrictions were imposed on access to U.S. military installations worldwide.[4] Many of those installations went to Force Protection Condition Delta, their most secure lockdown status.

Although no one immediately claimed responsibility for the attacks, it did not take long for the U.S. government to find strong evidence that Osama bin Laden and his Islamist al Qaeda terrorist network had been behind them. The attacks represented something fundamentally new with respect to international terrorism, elevating it from essentially an occasionally lethal nuisance to a core threat to U.S. security. Indeed, the conventional image of "terrorism" as it was most commonly understood before September 11 failed utterly to capture the full magnitude of what occurred that grim morning. At bottom, the attacks constituted the first truly unrestrained manifestation of an orchestrated and open-ended campaign of stateless asymmetrical warfare against the United States. What eventually became Operation Enduring Freedom, the initial military component of the ensuing U.S. global war on terrorism, did not begin until nearly a month later on October 7. Yet it was apparent from the earliest days after the attacks that the Bush administration would take forceful action in response to the outrage of September 11. There also was little doubt that the leading edge of that response would be an air-dominated campaign to extirpate bin Laden's al Qaeda network in Afghanistan and that country's ruling Taliban theocracy, which had provided the terrorists safe haven and a base of operations.

SHAPING A PLAN

As the initial shock and anger triggered by the attacks gave way to a more focused determination on the part of the nation's leaders, the first inklings of the administration's intended counteroffensive strategy began to emerge. Within minutes of having learned of the attacks, U.S. military commands throughout Europe, Asia, and the Middle East set up crisis action teams to implement heightened force-protection measures and to assess the status of the forces in their respective areas of responsibility (AORs) that might be committed to action in any short-notice military response. As Force Protection Condition Delta remained in effect for a second day at many U.S. installations worldwide, the nation began preparing for what President Bush described as "the first war of the 21st century."[5]

As the administration's response plan unfolded, its first challenge was to build a worldwide coalition so as to lend needed legitimacy and material support to the impending war on terrorism. A second entailed developing a concrete plan that specified the campaign's priorities and goals. A third was to craft a detailed concept of operations for meeting those priorities and achieving the administration's declared goals. Finally, there was the associated need to begin fielding and prepositioning the required assets of all services for any such action. All of that occurred within the scant twenty-six days that separated the attacks of September 11 and the onset of Operation Enduring Freedom on October 7.

As early as September 12, officials at the Pentagon and at U.S. Central Command (USCENTCOM) began closely reviewing the existing response options. It turned out that USCENTCOM had no planned contingency option in hand for dealing specifically with the Taliban and al Qaeda's terrorist organization in Afghanistan. Before long, however, the main goal of the emerging campaign came to be a complete takedown of the Taliban regime in addition to the destruction of al Qaeda's terrorist infrastructure in Afghanistan. The underlying strategy sought to rely on precision standoff weapons to the fullest extent possible, with any commitment of conventional ground forces in significant numbers to be undertaken only if deemed absolutely essential. In the space of just over three weeks, the U.S. government pulled together an effective international coalition, crafted the first outlines of a serviceable war strategy, moved needed forces and matériel to the region, developed alliances with indigenous anti-Taliban elements in Afghanistan, arranged for regional basing and overflight permission, laid the groundwork for an acceptable target approval process, and prepared to conduct concurrent humanitarian relief operations.

As for the instruments for implementing the strategy, USCENTCOM would rely heavily on Navy and Marine Corps carrier-based strike fighters, supported by U.S. Air Force and British Royal Air Force (RAF) tankers for providing inflight refueling owing to the limited number of accessible bases in the region within easy reach of Afghanistan by land-based fighters. The command also would draw on a highly redundant network of space-based and air-breathing intelligence, surveillance, and reconnaissance (ISR) platforms to provide it and those conducting the war at the tactical level with situational awareness of the highest possible fidelity. Initial troop and equipment deployments to USCENTCOM's AOR in Southwest Asia started even as the Bush administration was only beginning to crystallize its strategy and develop a plan for carrying it out. U.S. and British combat aircraft were already fielded in substantial numbers in Saudi Arabia and Kuwait and at Incirlik Air Base, Turkey, in support of Operations Northern and Southern Watch over Iraq. On September 19, President Bush ordered two dozen B–52 and B–1B heavy bombers and tankers moved forward to the Indian Ocean island of Diego Garcia, which had been made available by Great Britain, to put the aircraft within easier reach of Afghanistan.[6] On September 21, Secretary of Defense Donald Rumsfeld signed a second order dispatching 100 U.S. aircraft to the region to augment the 175 that were already in place there.

As for naval assets, two aircraft carriers, USS *Carl Vinson* and USS *Enterprise*, were already operating on station in the AOR with their embarked air wings ready for action, with a third carrier battle group led by USS *Theodore Roosevelt* ordered to deploy from its home port of Norfolk, Virginia, to the AOR on September 18. At the same time, the carrier USS *Kitty Hawk* departed for the AOR from her home port of Yokosuka, Japan, without her full air-wing complement to provide what came to be referred to as a sea-based "lily pad" from which U.S. special operations forces (SOF) teams would be staged into Afghanistan. To free up her flight and hangar decks to make room for a variety of SOF helicopters, *Kitty Hawk* carried only eight strike fighters from her air wing of more than fifty.[7]

Less than a week before Operation Enduring Freedom commenced, the number of U.S. aircraft in the region had grown to between four hundred and five hundred, including seventy-five on each of the Navy's three aircraft carriers on station.

That number included such support aircraft as tankers and electronic warfare and ISR platforms. Many dozens of Air Force combat aircraft were deployed to the Persian Gulf states of Kuwait, Saudi Arabia, and Oman; to Diego Garcia; and—in an unprecedented post–Cold War move—to the two former Soviet republics of Uzbekistan and Tajikistan, where Russia still maintained thousands of troops. These aircraft included B–52s, B–1Bs, F–15Es, and F–16s, as well as E–3s and tanker and other support aircraft.[8]

COMBAT HIGHLIGHTS

Operation Enduring Freedom began under clear skies on the night of October 7, 2001, against planned targets in and around Herat, Shindand, Mazar-i-Sharif, and the southern Taliban stronghold area of Kandahar. The attacks were carried out by five Air Force B–1B and ten B–52 heavy bombers operating out of Diego Garcia and by twenty-five Navy F–14 and F/A–18 fighters launched from the aircraft carriers *Enterprise* and *Carl Vinson* in the North Arabian Sea. Two Air Force B–2 stealth bombers flying nonstop from their home base at Whiteman Air Force Base, Missouri, also participated in the opening night attacks, each carrying sixteen two-thousand-pound satellite-aided GBU–31 joint direct attack munitions (JDAMs) directed against Taliban early warning radars and military headquarters buildings. The attack aircraft were supported by accompanying F–14 and F/A–18 fighter sweeps and by electronic jamming of enemy radar and communications transmissions by Navy EA–6B Prowlers.[9] H-hour for those attacks was 9:00 p.m. local time.

The heaviest bombing that night was conducted by Air Force B–52s, which rained both JDAMs and hundreds of five-hundred-pound Mk 82 unguided bombs on al Qaeda terrorist training camps in the valleys of eastern Afghanistan. For their part, strikes from the Navy's carriers involved distances to target of more than six hundred nautical miles, with an average sortie length of more than four and a half hours and a minimum of two inflight refuelings per fighter each way to complete the mission. Britain's RAF provided Tristar and VC–10 tankers to help supplement Air Force KC–135s and KC–10s in providing inflight refueling for the Navy fighters.[10] As part of a calculated effort to help mitigate the anticipated Taliban and al Qaeda propaganda offensive that the campaign would surely unleash, two C–17s flying from Ramstein Air Base, Germany, dropped 34,400 packets of food and medical supplies within 45 minutes after the first bombs hit their targets to provide interim sustenance for the thousands of refugees who were expected to flee Afghan cities during the bombing.

One goal of the initial attacks was to establish uncontested control of the air by neutralizing the Taliban's limited but nontrivial fighter force and its surface-to-air missile (SAM) and antiaircraft artillery (AAA) defenses. The former consisted of fewer than fifty MiG–21 and Su–22 fighter aircraft, many out of service, that had been captured from defeated post-Soviet Afghan factions in 1996. As for the latter, reports indicated that Taliban ground-based air defenses included three SA–3 SAM sites, but that their crews lacked the needed competence to keep the radars and missiles in usable condition.[11] It also was known to include man-portable SA–7 infrared SAMs, 300 to 550 AAA guns, and an undetermined number of U.S.-made Stinger shoulder-fired infrared SAMs left over from the original stock of around 1,000 that had been provided to the mujahedin by the United States during the last years of the Soviet occupation. Although rudimentary in the extreme, this air defense threat was not inconsequential from a U.S. mission planner's perspective. As many as forty Taliban pilots were believed capable of getting MiG–21s and Su–22s into the air.[12] USCENTCOM's main concern over those aircraft was not the traditional air combat challenge they represented, which was minuscule, but rather the finite chance that they might be loaded with explosives and flown on suicide missions into eventual U.S. ground encampments.

The second day of air operations saw only about half the number of aircraft that had been committed the first night. Attacks again began at night but this time continued on into daylight hours, indicating increased confidence at USCENTCOM that the Taliban's minimal air defenses had been largely neutralized. By the time the fifth consecutive day of strike operations arrived, mountain cave complexes harboring al Qaeda combatants and equipment were attacked for the first time using GBU–28 five-thousand-pound laser-guided hard-structure munitions.[13] Enemy AAA fire continued to be sporadic at best, with no confirmed reports of any Stinger infrared SAMs having been fired.

As the second week of Enduring Freedom got under way, two AC–130 gunships were committed for the first time as a part of a strike package that flew on October 15. Airborne forward air controllers (FAC–As) in F–14s also loitered overhead and identified Taliban targets for the gunships to attack, with the AC–130 aircrews functioning as their own onboard forward air controllers. The introduction of the AC–130, equipped with computer-aimed 105mm and 40mm cannons and a 25mm Gatling gun, reflected growing confidence at USCENTCOM that the surface-to-air threat had been largely eliminated—at least at night, when the AC–130 was normally employed in combat. The same day, large secondary explosions were set off by strike fighter and heavy bomber attacks against the enemy's cave hideouts, one of which started a raging underground fire that lasted for nearly four hours.[14]

Earlier, USCENTCOM's commander, U.S. Army General Tommy Franks, had requested that a dozen Air Force F–15E Strike Eagles be deployed to the AOR to take part in the campaign.[15] Accordingly, on October 17, F–15Es began operating out of al Jaber Air Base in Kuwait against Taliban troop positions, in the first use of land-based fighters in Enduring Freedom.[16] Because of the great distances involved, the two aircraft carriers deployed in the North Arabian Sea to conduct day and night strike missions into Afghanistan could each cover only around ten hours in country using a fourteen-hour first-launch-to-last-recovery window, making for only twenty hours of carrier coverage a day altogether. F–15Es out of al Jaber, along with F–16s equipped with Litening II infrared targeting pods, were accordingly used to fill the gaps in carrier coverage.[17]

After the campaign's tenth day, the Department of Defense announced that the effort had shifted from mainly attacking fixed targets to seeking out targets of opportunity, notably enemy troop concentrations and vehicles. Attention was turned to what were called "emerging targets," including Taliban vehicles that had been moved after the initial attacks, as well as other enemy troops and weapons as they were detected and identified. As a key part of this shift in emphasis, the successful insertion of a small number of SOF combatants into southern Afghanistan after more than a week of nonstop bombing signaled the beginning of a new use of air power in modern war. In this new phase of operations, FAC–As flying in carrier-based strike fighters would visually confirm and validate targets that had been designated by allied SOF teams and then clear other aircraft to attack them.

On November 9, friendly Afghan forces finally took Mazar-i-Sharif. They attacked with T–55 tanks, armored vehicles, infantry, and even by charging on horseback, advancing northward into a city that had already been stunned by precision aerial bombardment. The ensuing success made for the first tangible breakthrough in Operation Enduring Freedom, as well as a notable morale booster at a time when concerns about the campaign's initial halting progress had begun to mount.

The subsequent capture of Kabul by friendly Afghan forces, aided decisively by American air power working in close harmony with allied SOF teams, was another major breakthrough.[18] At the same time, the first phase of Enduring Freedom was by no means yet over. Taliban forces continued to fight hard to retain control of Kunduz and Kandahar, the latter of which was the movement's primary and last remaining stronghold. Accordingly, USCENTCOM's center of focus shifted to those two areas, where the majority of U.S. air strikes were now directed to be concentrated. Allied SOF teams now engaged systematically in enabling the aerial plinking of enemy targets by sealing off roads, selectively blowing up bridges, and calling in attacks on moving vehicles. All of this was aided by a multispectral ISR umbrella that stared relentlessly down from a multiplicity of air and space assets operating constantly overhead.

As the siege of Kunduz got under way in earnest, allied air strikes increased in number and intensity. In yet another sign of progress, the first reports, based on intercepted enemy radio traffic, that the bombing in the Kandahar area had finally succeeded in killing some senior al Qaeda leaders were confirmed.[19] Principal among the leaders was bin Laden's military chief, Mohammed Atef, who had intimate ties to the terrorist leader through his daughter's marriage to bin Laden's son.[20] He was killed while inside a targeted house by a laser-guided bomb dropped by an Air Force F–15E, which, by happenstance, was in the midst of conducting what turned out to have been the longest-duration combat sortie by a fighter ever recorded in history (15.8 hours).[21]

With the Taliban's remaining days in power now clearly numbered, the Pentagon indicated that the campaign had entered a new phase, with less well-defined front lines and with the emphasis now placed on "Taliban-plinking" and on rooting out al Qaeda combatants wherever they might be found. As for the campaign's level of effort to date, the Joint Staff's spokesman, Rear Admiral John Stufflebeam, reported that around ten thousand munitions had been expended during the first forty-five days of combat. That expenditure rate was roughly comparable to the weapons delivery rate of the North Atlantic Treaty Organization's air war for Kosovo in 1999, which saw 23,614 munitions employed over its 78-day course. A major difference between the two campaigns was the overall proportion of precision weapons employed (in percentage, twice as large in Operation Enduring Freedom as in Allied Force).[22]

On December 1, air attacks on Kandahar intensified as opposition forces moved to within ten miles of that last remaining Taliban holdout, and a loose encirclement of the city progressively became a siege. The first case of a fratricidal bombing error occurred on December 5 when a JDAM was inadvertently called in on a combat controller's own position. The mistaken aim point resulted in three U.S. and five Afghan soldiers killed and twenty American and eighteen Afghan soldiers wounded. Hamid Karzai, who eventually would become post-Taliban Afghanistan's leader, was nearby being protected by the SOF unit. He barely escaped being killed by a single two-thousand-pound bomb that had been dropped by a B–52.[23] It was at first thought that the wrong coordinates had been provided to the bomber's crew. It was later determined that the Global Positioning System receiver used by the controller to establish target coordinates had just been given a new battery pack and that the controller did not remember that the device was programmed to revert to its preset coordinates whenever the battery was changed. Remarkably, the controller survived the errant attack.[24]

The continuing battle for Kandahar was fought mainly from the air and entailed more than two months of strikes against the city's outskirts. An example that illustrates the discriminate force employment made possible by the precision weapons available to the United States was an attack by F–15Es that flattened three known al Qaeda houses that were lined up in a row. Yet two burlap tents directly adjacent to them that belonged to the United Nations Food and Agricultural Organization were left unharmed.[25]

With the fall of Kandahar sixty-three days after the start of the campaign, Secretary Rumsfeld declared that the war effort had now entered a new phase, with the main focus on finding bin Laden and his top lieutenants and on stabilizing post-Taliban Afghanistan. Hard-core al Qaeda combatants continued to hold out in the Tora Bora mountains, having found shelter there in as many as two hundred separate caves.[26] That made imminent what Chairman of the Joint Chiefs of Staff General Richard Myers called "a very tough battle" to root them out.[27] In connection with that effort, a B–52 delivered one AGM–142 Have Nap missile equipped with a rock-penetrating warhead against a target of special interest in Tora Bora: a cave entrance that presented a demanding access challenge requiring that a precision munition actually be flown into it.[28] Also, a fifteen-thousand-pound BLU–82/B bomb was dropped on a part of the Tora Bora cave complex believed to be housing al Qaeda leaders, such that no one could either enter or leave the complex.

The bombing of Tora Bora, which had continued nonstop for three weeks, was suspended briefly to allow friendly Afghan forces to advance on the caves in search of al Qaeda fugitives. Before the start of that interlude, U.S. and British SOF teams had begun checking some caves themselves after receiving a confirmed report that bin Laden had recently been spotted in the White Mountains.[29] In light of the unusual fierceness of the al Qaeda resistance, allied intelligence initially presumed that bin Laden had been surrounded and cornered in Tora Bora. Once that effort to track him down and capture or kill him was abandoned as a lost cause, however, administration spokesmen conceded that there was only a fifty-fifty chance that he was still there.

With the Tora Bora cave complex now all but obliterated, some of the al Qaeda survivors sought to regroup in caves in eastern Afghanistan at Zhawar Kili and nearby in the vicinity of Khost. That development prompted 118 consecutive attack sorties in the area over a four-day period, beginning on January 3, 2002, by B–52s, B–1Bs, F/A–18s, and an AC–130. The cave complex at Zhawar Kili covered nine square miles and featured seventy interconnected caves and tunnels offering literally miles of sheltered space.[30] Some 250 bombs were dropped on caves at Zhawar Kili alone.[31] It took nearly two weeks of bombing to complete the destruction of the al Qaeda complex there, with Air Force combat controllers attached to U.S. SOF teams identifying and designating most of the aim points.[32]

As in Operation Desert Storm, many weapons effects achieved in Enduring Freedom were primarily psychological in nature. Bombs dropped by aircraft that were too high to be seen or heard by the enemy exploded as though they had come out of nowhere. Friendly Afghan fighters often overheard Taliban soldiers on the radio speaking frantically of running for cover any time jet noise was heard. In one instance at night early in the campaign, Taliban forces were preparing to cross a bridge in foggy weather. The bridge was taken out by three concurrent JDAM hits right before their eyes.[33] Although intangible, unquantifiable, and unpredictable, such second-order effects most surely played a signal role in the unexpectedly early defeat of the Taliban.

On December 18, after more than nine weeks of nonstop combat operations, the aerial bombardment was finally brought to a halt. As the dust gradually settled, the Pentagon came under sharp criticism from many quarters for not having inserted U.S. ground forces in strength in a more timely way into the Tora Bora fighting to help prevent bin Laden and his closest associates from escaping. After the abortive effort in Tora Bora was called off, a British SOF officer who had participated in allied ground operations said of that failure: "We raided caves where al Qaeda fighters put up desperate holding actions in some places. But orders never came to move into the valleys where bin Laden and other leaders were escaping, despite suggestions from our part. The idea was for native troops to provide a blocking force who were simply not up to the task."[34]

By mid-January 2002, U.S. strike operations over Afghanistan had dwindled to a trickle. Said an F–14 pilot assigned to the air wing embarked on USS *Theodore Roosevelt* in late January,

> Here is a standard OEF flight: Launch, transit to the tanker, hold, hold, hold, hold, hold, top off at a tanker, hold, hold, hold, hold some more, hit a tanker again, come home for a night trap. Our mission now is equivalent to that of a relief pitcher hanging out in the bullpen, warming up, ready to go on a moment's notice. If he gets the call, his mission is singular—deliver the beanball. . . . [Our sorties now] are a far cry from all the action pre-Christmas.[35]

A month later, Operation Enduring Freedom had largely evolved from its initial character as a high-technology air war into a domestic policing action, in effect, as the United States found itself striving to manage and pacify feuding warlords, protect the embryonic interim Afghan government, and ensure adequate force protection from sniper fire and other hostile action for the four thousand U.S. ground troops who were in the country.

From the campaign's opening moments, the U.S. goal had not been to "defeat" Afghanistan, but rather to bring an end to Taliban rule and to destroy al Qaeda's network and support structure in that country. True to that goal, the Taliban regime was brought down only 102 days after the terrorist attacks of September 11. General Franks later remarked that his strategy had not envisaged a linear progression starting with air operations and then followed in sequence by the introduction of SOF and then conventional ground troops, but rather a concurrent use of all available tools as needed. Although indigenous Afghan forces and allied SOF teams were essential to the success of this strategy, American air and space power were the principal enabling elements.

OPERATION ANACONDA

After two months of relative quiescence following the fall of the Taliban and the installation of the interim Karzai government, U.S. ground forces met their fiercest test of the war in a bold attempt to encircle and capture or kill those al Qaeda fugitives who remained in Afghanistan through an offensive that came to be called Operation Anaconda. This planned push into the high mountains of eastern Afghanistan was to be the first and only substantial combat involvement by conventional U.S. ground troops in Enduring Freedom. The Shah-i-Kot valley area had been under close surveillance by USCENTCOM ever since early January 2002 because intelligence reports showed that hard-core Taliban and foreign al Qaeda holdouts were regrouping there.

Two considerations underlay the steps that ultimately led to Anaconda: a desire on USCENTCOM's part to preempt the growing concentration of al Qaeda fighters who were reequipping themselves in the Afghan hinterland and threatening the fragile Karzai government, and mounting intelligence indicating a conviction by al Qaeda leaders that U.S. forces would not pursue them into the mountains and take them on in winter weather.[36] After weeks of experimentation with alternative command and control (C²) arrangements, the lead role for the planning and execution of Anaconda fell to Army Major General Franklin Hagenbeck, the commander of the Tenth Mountain Division, who, for the upcoming operation, was formally designated commander of Combined Joint Task Force (CJTF) Mountain, an amalgam of forces from the Tenth Mountain and 101st Airborne Divisions, along with a small overt SOF contingent and a larger number of indigenous Afghan fighters.[37] All of these forces would execute Anaconda at the appointed time.

Despite its nominal designation as a "joint" entity, CJTF Mountain had no service representation other than from the Army in its organizational makeup. Moreover, beyond General Hagenbeck himself, only two other personnel in CJTF Mountain had any previous experience operating in a joint environment. Even more important, at no time in the elaborate planning for Anaconda almost up to the day of its scheduled execution had Hagenbeck made any attempt to enlist the air component's involvement, notwithstanding the fact that the mission had grown under his direction into the largest pending commitment of U.S. ground troops (more than one thousand) to combat since Operation Desert Storm more than a decade before. By his own later admission, Hagenbeck assumed—incorrectly, as it turned out—that his attached Air Force air liaison officer had been routinely communicating CJTF Mountain's intentions and needs to the air component from the start of Anaconda's planning and that his own action officers and the air component's staff were busy at work seeing to the necessary air support integration.[38] That unfounded assumption would prove to have near-disastrous consequences once it came time to implement Operation Anaconda.

The declared mission of the operation was to capture or kill any al Qaeda and Taliban fighters who might be encountered by allied forces in the Shah-i-Kot area of Afghanistan's eastern hinterland. Toward that end, more than fourteen hundred conventional U.S. Army infantrymen and an additional two hundred overt SOF troops were assigned to participate, along with around one thousand friendly Afghan fighters who were also involved in the planned blocking and trackdown effort. CJTF Mountain's plan was to surround the Shah-i-Kot valley with overlapping rings of forces aimed at bottling up and then capturing or killing the several hundred al Qaeda fighters who were thought to be hiding in the area. In the end, however, Anaconda would instead prove to be a series of intense individual firefights starting on March 2, after repeated delays caused by high winds and other weather complications, in which al Qaeda holdouts, rather than retreating as before at Tora Bora, would stay on and fight to the death. It also would prove to be an experience in which fixed-wing air power, largely left out of the initial planning and summoned in full force only at the eleventh hour when events seemed headed for a major calamity, would be pivotal in producing what ultimately was a successful, if costly, outcome.

In one of the first harbingers of further trouble yet to come, a flight of U.S. Army AH–64 Apache attack helicopters preceded CJTF Mountain's move into the valley by reconnoitering the air assault's planned landing zones (LZs). Because no al Qaeda presence in the area was detected from the air, the Apache flight leader erroneously reported the LZs as cold. Almost immediately after being inserted, however, CJTF Mountain's troops found themselves beset by withering enemy mortar and machine gun fire from both the valley floor and the adjacent high ground. Equipped only with their personal weapons and with light machine guns and mortars, they lacked sufficient firepower of their own to negate the al Qaeda pressure. Accordingly, they called the Apaches back to perform a suppressive sweep of the suspected areas from which the hostile fire was emanating. Upon returning to the now-embattled valley, the Apache aircrews found themselves unable to provide the needed support because of the high density of enemy fire coming at them from multiple directions.[39]

In the end, all seven of the Apaches that had initially been committed to the fight were hit by al Qaeda fire. They eventually succeeded in flying the one-hundred-mile distance back to their main operating facility at Bagram but were inoperable on arrival and accordingly were out of the fight until they underwent extensive field repairs and were recertified as being airworthy. After the seven battle-damaged Apaches were withdrawn from the fight, and with only half of CJTF Mountain's initially planned forces having been inserted owing to weather complications, the complexion of Anaconda changed significantly, in the words of one informed account, "from an operation focused primarily on land power to an operation increasingly dependent on Air Force, Navy, and later Marine air assets."[40]

However, because CJTF Mountain had not enlisted the involvement of the air component or laid the groundwork for an optimally effective joint air-ground operation until the last minute, this sudden dependence on fixed-wing air naturally encountered trouble when a need for emergency close air support (CAS) arose. No CAS cell was manned in the air component's Combined Air Operations Center (CAOC) at the time Anaconda commenced. The two air liaison officers attached to CJTF Mountain quickly learned that their undermanned and poorly equipped air support cell, which had been jury-rigged only the previous February 20, when the Anaconda operations order was first issued, was on the brink of being swamped by the need to prioritize multiple CAS requests and to deconflict the limited airspace over the valley. A profusion of calls for immediate fire support came pouring simultaneously into CJTF Mountain's command post from the thirty-seven Air Force enlisted tactical air controllers (ETACs) who were deployed throughout the area.[41]

Once the air contribution to Anaconda improved in effectiveness, Air Force combat controllers and ETACs controlled hundreds of munitions deliveries from every type of attack platform in every U.S. and allied service involved in Enduring Freedom, with no fratricide and no friendly losses to enemy fire. On occasion, Army mortar fire would keep al Qaeda troops pinned down at their mountain positions to prevent them from fleeing as air assets entered the fight to attack them with laser-guided bombs or JDAMs, in what General Hagenbeck later agreed was a role reversal from the traditional air-ground relationship, with air power in this case being the supported force element.[42]

Phase Two of Operation Anaconda, from March 5 to March 12, saw a heightened intensity of CAS operations that ultimately rendered the surviving al Qaeda forces unable to sustain their resistance. Phase Three finally laid waste to al Qaeda's positions in the valley as dozens of aircraft operated continuously without incident in the cramped airspace above it. In a situation in which five times the expected enemy strength was taken on by CJTF Mountain, air support to Anaconda saw the greatest number of precision munitions dropped into the smallest geographic space in the history of air warfare.[43]

From an air perspective, the biggest problem presented by the initial planning for Anaconda entailed coordinating the many concurrent strike operations with too little advance preparations. The sudden and unexpected demand for air support led to an airspace congestion problem of formidable proportions, with allied aircraft frequently stacked eight miles high over the combat zone. B–52s at the highest altitude of thirty-nine thousand feet dropped JDAMs through the flight paths of B–1 bombers and formations of fighters orbiting at twenty-two thousand to twenty-five thousand feet, EP–3s at lower altitudes, and AC–130s lower still at night, all followed by RQ–1 and MQ–1 Predator unmanned aerial vehicles (UAVs), A–10s, and attack helicopters at the lowest altitudes.[44] In addition, three civil air routes ran through the airspace over the Shah-i-Kot valley beneath the operating altitudes of the B–52s, which created yet another deconfliction challenge for the CAOC. The overriding concern was not running out of aircraft but rather running out of usable airspace. Often lower priority requests would be denied because of a lack of sufficient airspace. With multiple JDAMs falling through this densely occupied airspace, only the most exacting air discipline, combined with a significant measure of good luck, prevented a major inflight disaster.

Viewed in hindsight, during its initial workups for Anaconda, CJTF Mountain failed repeatedly to make the most of the potential synergy of land and air power that was available to them in principle. Because of the initial absence of a full-up Air Support Operations Center (ASOC) equipped to translate Hagenbeck's intent into a systematic CAS prioritization scheme, at his headquarters, friction and confusion ensued at first as terminal attack controllers on the ground competed for limited CAS assets on an ad hoc basis over a single tactical air direction frequency.[45] As a result, near-pandemonium ensued in the congested airspace over the Shah-i-Kot area as numerous aircraft of all types literally were forced to dodge one another (as well as one another's falling bombs) as they simultaneously serviced multiple urgent requests for CAS. Eventually, an eleventh-hour effort was made to cobble together a usable set of assigned run-in start points for individual aircraft target attacks to help smooth out this result of the land component's failure to have engaged the CAOC at the outset of its planning for Anaconda. That did not occur, however, until well into the operation.[46] Because the CAOC was not engaged in Anaconda's planning from the very start, it was not integrated into the plan, even though it proved in the end to have provided the overwhelming preponderance of force for CJTF Mountain.

More to the point, had General Hagenbeck been willing to slip the scheduled start of Anaconda by merely the week or so that would have been needed for the CAOC to prepare itself fully for any contingency needs, the air component commander, Lieutenant General Michael Moseley, and his staff could have developed any number of measures to ensure that the operation would have the fullest support from USCENTCOM's air assets in all services. Such measures would have involved a pre-positioning of all needed aircraft and matériel before the start of the operation, including a forward deployment of A–10s in time for them to be ready from the outset. It also would have included preparation of the air component's infrastructure and the determination of sustainment requirements, such as the number of AC–130s needed and proper crew-to-aircraft ratios for all platforms; the use of all available ISR assets to map out known enemy cave locations; the establishment of tanker requirements and planning of airborne tanker tracks; the development of aircraft stacking arrangements and deconfliction schemes above the various assigned heli-copter LZs; a land component fully fleshed out in its representation in the CAOC; and the development of a proper command and control arrangement, including the timely provision of a full-up ASOC assigned to CJTF Mountain's field headquarters at Bagram. Once those arrangements had been duly attended to, General Moseley and the CAOC staff could then have "chair-flown" the entire operation beforehand with all involved air component principals—not only the mission commanders and flight leaders but also every other key participant, right down to the combat controllers and ETACs.[47]

Nevertheless, fixed-wing air power in the end did most of the work originally envisaged for organic Army fires. Although there is no evidence to suggest that the CAOC was deliberately cut out of the planning for Anaconda by the land component, numerous faulty assumptions nonetheless resulted in CJTF Mountain having been only barely covered by needed air support once its insertion on day one encountered resistance and the going got unexpectedly rough. Upon reflection, the former CAOC director during the first phase of Enduring Freedom aptly concluded, "The message that needs to come out of this issue is that to optimize air-ground synergy, the air component must be included in all phases of planning surface operations and vice versa. That is what went awry in Anaconda, not CAS."[48]

DISTINCTIVE ASPECTS

Operation Enduring Freedom was an SOF-centric application of joint and combined air power that, in the end, added up to a new way of war for the United States. Among other things, even more than in the case of Operation Desert Storm more than a decade before, the campaign's results showed the U.S. ability to conduct successful force projection from land bases located thousands of miles away from the target area, as well as from carrier operating stations positioned farther away from a land-locked combat zone than ever before in the history of naval air warfare.[49] As attested by statistics compiled by the CAOC during the seventy-six days of bombing between October 7, when Enduring Freedom began, and December 23, when the first phase of the war ended after the collapse of the Taliban, some 6,500 strike sorties were flown altogether, during which approximately 17,500 munitions were dropped on more than 120 fixed targets, 400 vehicles and artillery pieces, and a profusion of concentrations of Taliban and al Qaeda combatants. Of the total number of allied munitions expended, 57 percent were precision guided. U.S. carrier-based strike fighters accounted for 4,900 of the strike sorties flown during that period, making up 75 percent of the total. More than half of those sorties were flown by Navy and Marine Corps F/A–18s.

The three pivotal ingredients that made this achievement possible were long-range precision air power managed by a uniquely sophisticated and capable CAOC; consistently good real-time tactical intelligence; and mobile SOF teams on the ground working in close concert with indigenous Afghan resistance forces and equipped with enough organic firepower and electronic support to maintain adequate situation awareness, operate independently, and avoid ambushes. As for air warfare "firsts" registered during Operation Enduring Freedom, the war saw the first combat employment of the wind-corrected munitions dispenser and the RQ–4 Global Hawk high-altitude UAV, as well as the first operational use of MQ–1 Predators armed with Hellfire missiles and the first combat employment of JDAM by the B–1 and B–52. (During Operation Allied Force over Serbia and Kosovo in 1999, only the B–2 had been configured to deliver that satellite-aided weapon.) The integration of combat controllers on the ground with heavy bombers for enabling precision attacks on emerging targets was also novel, as was the use, for the first time, of the vastly improved CAOC at Prince Sultan Air Base in Saudi Arabia and the provision of live Predator UAV video feed directly to airborne AC–130 gunship crews.[50]

Finally, Operation Enduring Freedom saw a continuation of some important trends that were set in motion during the first Persian Gulf War of 1991. Precision weapons accounted for only 9 percent of the munitions expended during Operation

Desert Storm, yet they totaled 29 percent in Operation Allied Force and nearly 60 percent in Enduring Freedom. That overall percentage can be expected to continue to grow in future contingencies as precision-guided munitions (PGMs) become ever more plentiful and, as a result, as even small groups of combatants, such as a handful of enemy troops manning a mortar position, may eventually be deemed worthy of a PGM in some circumstances. That dramatic improvement in overall force leverage reaffirmed that one now can speak routinely not of the number of sorties required to engage a given target, but rather of how many desired weapon aim points can be successfully attacked by a single sortie.[51]

Yet another operational trend that continued in Enduring Freedom had to do with extended-range operations. In Desert Storm, the proportion of tanker sorties among the total number of air sorties flown was 12 percent. In Allied Force, it was 20 percent. In Enduring Freedom, it was 27 percent. By the same token, long-range bombers have delivered a steadily increasing percentage of the overall numbers of weapons expended throughout the succession of U.S. combat engagements since 1991. In Desert Storm, it was 32 percent. In Allied Force, it was roughly 50 percent. In Enduring Freedom, it was about 70 percent.[52]

For the first time in the history of modern warfare, an operation was conducted under an overarching ISR umbrella that stared down relentlessly in search of enemy activity. That umbrella was formed by a constellation of overlapping sensor platforms, starting with various satellites on both low and higher orbits in space. It also included a multiplicity of manned and unmanned aircraft sporting a broad spectrum of electro-optical, radar, and other sensor suites and packages. These interlinked and mutually supporting platforms enabled a greatly increased refinement of ISR input over that which had been available during earlier conflicts. It also permitted a degree of ISR fusion that distinguished Enduring Freedom from all previous air campaigns.

Still another notable innovation pioneered during Operation Enduring Freedom was the uniquely close synchronization of air and land power that dominated the war effort. Allied SOF teams performed three major missions throughout the campaign. First, they marshaled and directed the unorganized forces of the indigenous Northern Alliance of friendly Afghan fighters. Second, they built small armies out of anti-Taliban Pashtun tribesmen in the south. Third, they provided accurate and validated target information to U.S. aircrews for conducting precision air attacks.

The integration of Air Force terminal attack controllers with U.S. and allied SOF teams on the ground was arguably the single greatest tactical innovation of the war. These controllers would rack and stack a dozen or more fighters and bombers like layers of a wedding cake over a segment of the battlefield and then talk pilots' eyes onto specific targets to be attacked. In that manner, aircraft could service six or more separate target aim points with as many JDAMs in a single drop. As the campaign shifted from attacking fixed targets to engaging emerging time-sensitive targets, aircrews would routinely get airborne without any preassigned targets. By the time the air war was over, some 80 percent of all targets attacked by allied aircrews had not been planned but rather were assigned while their aircraft were en route to their designated holding points over Afghanistan.

By every measure that matters, the major combat portion of Operation Enduring Freedom from October 7, 2001, through March 2002 was a resounding success as far as it went. Never before in modern times had the United States fought an expeditionary war so far removed from its base structure. The tyranny of distance that dominated the campaign redefined the meaning of endurance in air warfare and made for an unprecedented test of American combat flexibility. One B–2 sortie lasted 44.3 hours from takeoff to landing, becoming the longest-duration air combat mission flown in history. With the aid of multiple inflight refuelings, it was not uncommon for fighter sorties to last ten hours or more. Indeed, the war saw the longest range carrier-based strike operations conducted in the history of naval air warfare. People rather than equipment constituted the main limiting factor in USCENTCOM's ability to maintain a persistent combat presence over Afghanistan.

PROBLEMS IN EXECUTION

At the same time, Operation Enduring Freedom was not without inefficiencies and friction points. To begin with, much as in the previous case of Operation Allied Force against Serbia in 1999, some severe shortcomings in target approval under tight time constraints were revealed.[53] Thanks to the recent revolution in global communications and ISR fusion, sensor-to-shooter data cycle time (known more colloquially as the "kill chain") was reduced from hours—or even days—often to single-digit minutes. Yet an overly cumbersome target approval process with multiple layers of involved participants often nullified the potential effects of that breakthrough by extending decision timelines, making the human factor rather than the C^2 and ISR system the principal rate limiter.

Many of the problems in execution that were encountered during Enduring Freedom had to do with unusually restrictive rules of engagement that flowed from the highest levels, as well as a tendency toward both centralized adaptive planning and centralized execution of operations by USCENTCOM. This trend was made possible by the unprecedented worldwide sensor and communications connectivity, both horizontal and vertical, that dominated the role played by C^2 and ISR in the war.

Once allied SOF teams were finally on the ground in Afghanistan and the campaign shifted from attacking fixed targets to engaging emerging time-sensitive targets, the rules of engagement required that at least one SOF team member have eyes on the target before the target could be struck. Any target that could create even one noncombatant casualty if attacked with less than perfect precision and discrimination had to be briefed first to USCENTCOM by the CAOC and then reviewed by General Franks, if not by even higher level civilian leaders in Washington. That requirement entailed a time-consuming process of briefing preparation that often undermined the effectiveness of the CAOC's air effort.

Some complaints about the rules of engagement and about target-approval restrictions were entirely appropriate. Yet at the same time, it is important to understand where the rules of engagement came from and what considerations underlay them. The fact is that they emanated from the highest echelon of the U.S. government and were anything but arbitrary. On the contrary, President Bush was personally determined to avoid any untoward occurrence that might even remotely suggest that the campaign was an indiscriminate war against the Afghan people or against Islam. That determination led to a requirement for a minimally destructive air campaign using tactics that would not risk alienating the Afghan rank and file, further damaging an already weak Afghan economy and infrastructure, and inflaming popular passions elsewhere in the Arab world. For that reason, infrastructure targets were expressly excluded from attack. Moreover, a relentless effort was made in target assessment to ensure that the amount and type of force employed were proportionate to the target's value. These and related constraints were characterized by USCENTCOM's director of operations as having been as exacting as any in the history of warfare.[54]

As it turned out, however, in what amounted to preemptive surrender to the strictest interpretation of the rules of engagement, the approach followed by USCENTCOM sometimes occasioned a tendency on the part of CAOC staffers to be gun-shy in proposing targets out of anticipatory fear of USCENTCOM's disapproval on the grounds of collateral damage sensitivities. At times, matters got to a point where mission accomplishment took a backseat to collateral damage avoidance. Clearly, it is the rightful prerogative of national leaders to impose collateral damage constraints in the interest of achieving desired objectives and avoiding undesirable turns of events. Yet there was a tendency at all levels to forget that information on time-sensitive targets is highly perishable and often must be acted on within minutes to produce intended results. More than any previous campaign, Operation Enduring Freedom saw not only centralized planning, but also a pronounced expansion of centralized execution that reached from the highest echelons of government all the way down to engaged combatants at the tactical level. The result was a complex target approval process involving many tiers of the chain of command that had the effect of lengthening rather than shortening the kill chain.

How did such a situation develop? A pronounced downside consequence of the expanded bandwidth and situation awareness at all levels that have evolved since Desert Storm is that at the same time that they have made possible more efficient operations than ever before, they also have increasingly come to enable direct senior leadership involvement in the finest details of force employment. Even before the terrorist attacks of September 11, the traditional and long-familiar U.S. command and control arrangement had already been transformed into what some observers have called a "meshwork" of communications linkages yielding "metastasized command and control," wherein virtually any element can talk to any other element irrespective of its placement in the chain of command. This was a fundamentally new reality, and senior leaders exploited it to the hilt in Enduring Freedom because they both felt a need to and, more to the point, were *able* to. Ultimately, they often intervened in execution at the tactical level not because political or operational circumstances required it, but simply because they *could*. All of this raised a valid question in the minds of many about the appropriateness of having live Predator video feed (or, for that matter, *any* real-time sensor feed) at the combatant command headquarters, at the Pentagon, and in the White House.[55]

A related unwelcome aspect of the heightened communications connectivity and battlespace awareness that predominated throughout Enduring Freedom was the growing frustration created by the emergence of powerful distributed organizations, all of whose principals wanted to be hands-on players. The systems and capabilities that have evolved since Desert Storm to give every interested principal a shared operating picture demand an unprecedented degree of discipline by commanders and senior leaders to ensure that innovations intended to speed up operations do not end up instead being brakes on those operations. This calls for command and support relationships aimed at enabling and ensuring flexibility and rapidity of action instead of the opposite if component commanders are to be properly empowered to be commanders in fact as well as in name.

Some argue that centralized execution of the sort that predominated in Enduring Freedom may by now have become an irreversible fact of twenty-first-century military life. Insofar as that may be the case, it bodes ill for the long-term interests of U.S. security if operators accept it uncritically and simply surrender to it without challenging it. True enough, some kinds of operations in which the political content and consequences of failure are exceptionally high will continue to require both stringent rules of engagement and centralized execution. However, national leaders need to remain mindful of the potential impact of such constraints. Centralized execution worked in spite of itself in a small war such as Operation Enduring Freedom but would be impossible in a larger war requiring a thousand or more combat sorties and weapon aim points a day. Time-sensitive targeting will, no doubt, continue to be the wave of the future in many circumstances. Yet the United States needs a faster way of getting timely approval for such targeting on a large scale. As they well discovered during the three-week period of major combat in Operation Iraqi Freedom a year later, senior leaders and commanders cannot expect to have the luxury of approving the placement of every weapon aim point when thousands of targets are being struck every day.

To sum up, there is an inherent tension between the imperatives of political control and those of efficient execution in the new C² and ISR environment that senior operators and national leaders need to understand and deal with. If centralized execution is increasingly going to be the norm, at least for certain kinds of conflicts, the system needs a way to process and integrate incoming battlespace information more quickly and efficiently. Beyond that, senior leaders need to remain focused on their proper level of war and to know when their hands-on involvement is appropriate and when it is not. Even though the American command and control meshwork has now evolved to a point where centralized execution has become routinely possible in principle, decentralized execution remains both the preeminent virtue of American military culture and the one feature that distinguishes it from its polar opposite, namely the inflexible and discredited top-down approach of the former Soviet High Command.[56] As the former air commander during the 1991 Persian Gulf War, retired U.S. Air Force General Charles Horner, bluntly observed, "The most dangerous thing we face [as a result of increased ISR and communications connectivity worldwide] is the 8,000-mile screwdriver simply because it is possible."[57] Doctrine and practice must accordingly recognize this new reality and find a way to address it preemptively lest that reality be allowed, by operator default, to undermine and ultimately destroy one of America's most precious military advantages.

CONCLUSIONS

Beyond its overarching role as the first major military move in the global war on terrorism, Operation Enduring Freedom was a battle laboratory for testing, in a live combat setting, some of the most significant air power developments to have appeared in more than two decades. Among other things, the war saw the first use of an unmanned ISR platform, the MQ–1 Predator UAV, as a precision-attack weapon. The campaign's dominant features were persistence of pressure on the enemy and rapidity of execution, thanks to the improved data fusion enabled by new technologies, a better managed CAOC, more help from space, and smarter concepts of operations. Much of the persistent pressure stemmed from the widespread availability of precision weapons. During Allied Force, only the B–2 stealth bomber was configured to drop JDAMs. In Enduring Freedom, nearly every strike platform was equipped with that capability.

Furthermore, a new concept of offensive air employment against enemy ground forces was successfully tested in Enduring Freedom. Although often mistakenly equated with CAS, it was, in fact, something fundamentally new by way of air power application that entailed air attacks against fielded enemy forces that were *not* in direct contact with friendly troops.[58] As for collateral damage avoidance, it is now an entrenched fact of life that as air power has become ever more accurate, lethal, and effective, it also has come under ever more intense public attention, scrutiny, and questioning. At the same time, these air power capabilities have heightened not only the nation's political imperatives but also the legal need to be more discriminate in the use of force. Moreover, as concern for avoiding enemy noncombatant casualties has steadily risen in recent years, it has spawned an increasingly stringent rules-of-engagement regime aimed at minimizing the incidence of collateral damage.

Without question, the heightened aversion to the potential costs of unintended consequences that pervaded the chain of command from the White House on down allowed more than a few lucrative but fleeting opportunities to kill enemy leaders to slip away. There was abundant good reason for that aversion to collateral damage in principle, however, and such cases of missed chances were fortunately exceptions to the rule. On this important point, the air commander during Operation Desert Storm, General Horner, rightly noted that in Enduring Freedom, "collateral damage concerns [indeed] became more important than mission success. But then, in part, mission success depended on avoiding collateral damage."[59]

Timely and accurate intelligence has become increasingly paramount for providing top leaders with the needed confidence to approve attacks against time-sensitive targets. Such high-quality intelligence will come only from multiple sources and consistently good analysis. It is now a given that clever adversaries will use the international laws of armed conflict as a weapon, in what the Air Force's current deputy judge advocate general has aptly referred to as "lawfare."[60] Denying opponents the opportunity to reap propaganda advantages from that stratagem will be increasingly essential if the war on terrorism is to succeed in winning the support of those throughout the Muslim world among whom the terrorists would seek to embed themselves and draw strength.

That said, Operation Enduring Freedom represented a unique blend of air power, allied SOF, and indigenous Afghan opposition group combatants on the ground. It was further marked by a complete absence of heavy-maneuver U.S. ground forces. Notwithstanding the later involvement of a large number of conventional ground troops in Operation Anaconda, the campaign was not a land war but an SOF-centric air war that largely accounted for the ultimate successes of the Afghan resistance forces. SOF teams and air power produced a unique synergy in which each enabled the other. The SOF units rendered air power more effective than it would have been otherwise, and air power enabled the SOF teams to succeed with opposition groups in land operations against Taliban and al Qaeda forces in a fashion that otherwise would not have been possible. SOF units on the ground further enabled a patient waiting process of monitoring potential targets, acquiring precise geolocation and target characterization information, holding out for the best possible time to attack, and then calling in strikes when the enemy was most exposed. In this, the SOF presence was critical to Enduring Freedom's outcome. Neither air power alone nor air power in support of conventional ground troops could have produced the same results. Yet the integration of SOF operations with strike aviation turned the enemy's cave redoubts from safe hideaways into death traps. SOF combatants are now most decidedly a part of the overall air power equation. Thanks to their close and imaginative involvement, Operation Enduring Freedom saw more target kills per combat sortie than ever before.

If there was anything "transformational" about the way Operation Enduring Freedom was conducted, it was the dominance of fused information over platforms and munitions as the principal enabler of the campaign's success in the end. That new dynamic made all other major aspects of the war possible, including the integration of SOF teams as human ISR sensors with precision-strike air power, the minimization of target-location error, and collateral damage avoidance. Thanks to real-time imagery and increased communications connectivity, the kill chain was shorter than ever, and target-attack accuracy was truly phenomenal. Such network-enabled operations are now the cutting edge of an ongoing paradigm shift in combat style that may be of greater potential influence on future warfighting by the world's most advanced air arms than was the introduction of the tank at the beginning of the twentieth century.

12

OPERATION IRAQI FREEDOM, 2003

Williamson Murray

THE AIR WAR AGAINST SADDAM HUSSEIN'S Ba'athist regime represented a throwback to the earliest days of air power, when the most significant contribution that aircraft made was to the ground campaign. In the First World War, the airplane proved to be a crucial component in the combined arms approach to war that in 1918 finally broke the deadlock on the Western front. It had provided air superiority, so that reconnaissance aircraft could supply the targets for artillery; it had given close air support to the advancing infantry; and it had interdicted the enemy's supply lines and reinforcements, while attacking his formations before they could reach the battlefront. The few strategic bombing attacks that occurred caused considerable furor while killing substantial numbers of civilians, yet they achieved virtually nothing of military or strategic value.

Ironically, then, most airmen in the interwar period, particularly in the United States and Britain, rejected the lessons of the last war and marched into the future sure that the proper role for air power was to bomb the heart of the enemy's nation, namely to destroy his cities and industries.[1] Not until well into World War II did the British and Americans utilize air power's potential to its fullest. Unfortunately, conceptions that air power can do it all alone have remained popular among airmen to the present day, despite the fact that history has consistently shown that air power has rendered its greatest contributions when combined with efforts on the ground and at sea.[2]

Nevertheless, that has not been how most air power advocates and theorists have seen the future. A memorandum the British air staff provided the chiefs of staff in March 1924 summed up their attitude toward the usefulness of history. It argued that the air forces attacking an enemy nation

> can either bomb military objectives in populated areas from the beginning of
> the war, with the objective of obtaining a decision by moral[e] effect which such

attacks will produce, and by the serious dislocation of the normal life of the country, or, alternatively, they can be used in the first instance to attack enemy aerodromes with a view to gaining some measure of air superiority and, when this has been gained, can be changed over to the direct attack on the nation. The latter alternative is the method which the lessons of military history seem to recommend, but the Air Staff are convinced that the former is the correct one.[3]

In effect, then, the conduct of the air campaign against Iraq in 2003 was considerably ironic. The reversion to what had been historically effective was obvious from the beginning to the end of the campaign. There was no prolonged air campaign; instead, most of the Coalition air power concentrated on supporting the drives of the Third Infantry Division and the First Marine Division. Yet as usual in the history of American military power, the focus on the land campaign by Coalition air power represented more of an accident than a deliberate effort to learn from history.

In the early 1980s, the U.S. Army and the U.S. Air Force had led a campaign to integrate America's military forces into a joint force, but each did so for quite different reasons. The Army believed that a true joint force incorporating the capabilities of all the services would represent a more effective fighting force. The Air Force, on the other hand, seems to have been more narrowly focused on obtaining control of air campaigns and ensuring that the air assets of the Marine Corps and Navy were fully integrated into its plans for any given effort.[4]

The result of these efforts, and the profound dissatisfaction throughout the civilian defense community at failures in joint operations such as Desert One and Grenada, led to the Goldwater–Nichols Department of Defense Reorganization Act of 1986, which forced the services to cooperate in a more coherent and effective fashion. Ironically, some American air power advocates now express dissatisfaction with the results of jointness because, while on one hand, the air component commander has control of air assets, on the other, he is under the control of the combatant command's commander, who in most cases is a ground commander.

A second and entirely new problem has arisen with the use of air power, particularly in strategic campaigns such as the one waged against Serbia in the late 1990s, when collateral damage is more apparent. Paradoxically, the problem has resulted from the advent of precision weapons. During World War II, the nature of air power was such that even with the precision capabilities available, air campaigns, such as the extremely effective offensive against the German transportation network in France prior to the Normandy invasion, still resulted in the "acceptable" collateral killing of approximately ten thousand French civilians.[5] But the introduction of precision weapons in the 1990s and their success during the Gulf War's air campaign created expectations of accuracy that have considerably hobbled air power employment. The problem now is that precision weapons, no matter how impressive their accuracy might be, are only as good as the intelligence about the target. The ill-fated attack on the Chinese embassy in Belgrade during the air campaign against Serbia is a case in point. A senior British army general has cogently expressed the difficulties involved with the expectations concerning the use of precision weapons that commanders now face:

> The target effect of a 1,000 bomber raid can now be delivered through a single aircraft; a similar tale can be told on artillery and rocket GPS [Global Positioning System] technology, so our ability to strike is getting better. But Newton's second law informs us "there is no force without an equal and opposite"; precision for all its advantages brings with it an increasing liability to ensure safer and accountable target selection. We see no strike lists, collateral damage profiles, legal obligations, moral obligations, approval procedures, the sum of which moves us further away from mass and rapidly towards "insistence precision," from indirect to very direct with the constraint that if you cannot find the target, verify it, confirm that it remains within the agreed attack profiles you probably cannot strike it; find is the 21st century turn-key. And the targets, whether you are seeking to merely understand them or kill them, just keep getting smaller: individuals, extremists, terrorists, the architects of chaos who disappear in the urban vomit that is the modern city . . . and even with precision, all our options start to look like needles in haystacks.[6]

Our task in this chapter, then, is to examine some of these larger aspects of the contributions as well as the difficulties that the Coalition's air campaign faced in its efforts to destroy Saddam's Ba'athist regime in March and April 2003. We will begin with the planning and development of the joint campaign, as well as Iraqi planning and expectations, that would contribute to the Coalition's success and then turn to the actual conduct of air operations, in terms of both striking at the heart of the regime and supporting the drives of the Third Infantry Division and the First Marine Division to Iraq's center and the capture of Baghdad.

PLANNING THE AIR CAMPAIGN

The crucial planning for the overall campaign and the air effort took place in the last half of 2002. U.S. and Coalition air forces' air commanders—particularly those of the British—possessed a thorough understanding of Iraqi air defense capabilities, which they brought to that planning. The efforts of the Operations Northern Watch and Southern Watch air campaigns had lasted for most of the period from the Gulf War to the Iraq War. Thus, Coalition commanders had few illusions about the nature of Iraqi military effectiveness, in stark contrast to their overestimations in 1990.[7] In fact, the Iraqi performance was to prove even more incompetent than they expected for reasons examined below.

The initial planning focused on how long the air campaign should last before the ground campaign would begin. Senior Air Force officers argued for a prolonged air campaign, and ground commanders for a relatively short one; finally, both compromised on a synchronous start to the offensive.[8] The compromise also reflected the meddling of civilian leaders in the planning from the beginning. Secretary of Defense Donald Rumsfeld demanded a running start that would see operations launched as the buildup of ground forces was still under way, as opposed to the massive buildup that occurred during the Gulf War.[9] Thus, ground operations would begin with only a part of the force available, while the remainder, if needed, transited from the United States. In the short run, that approach worked to the U.S. advantage because it misled the Iraqis as to when operations might begin, but in the long run it proved disastrous, since U.S. Central Command had insufficient ground forces to bring order and stability to Iraq in the aftermath of the collapse of Saddam's regime.[10]

Meetings between the air and ground commanders in May 2002 brought out the differences. Lieutenant General T. Michael "Buzz" Moseley argued that air power needed approximately ten days to two weeks to wreck Iraq's air defense system and attack leadership targets throughout Baghdad and the center of Iraq. Moseley's approach reflected the experiences of the past decade. It may also have reflected the sloppy thinking that abounded in the defense intellectual communities around Washington. One of the most prominent manifestations of this sloppiness was the infamous *Shock and Awe* study by Harlan K. Ullman and James P. Wade. The authors argued that air power, with its precision weapons, would allow for the achievement of "rapid dominance" over the battlefield, leading to the collapse of the enemy politically and militarily. Rumsfeld certainly found the concept intriguing.

To a certain extent, the decision in the summer of 2002 to carry out an aggressive, stepped-up version of Southern Watch finessed Moseley's arguments for the need for a sustained air campaign before the onset of the ground war.[11] As the war approached, the consensus moved to favor a simultaneous beginning for the ground and air campaigns. Since the ground offensive would start with a number of divisions not yet in the theater, the air campaign would have to focus heavily on the ground effort and support the Third Infantry Division and the First Marine Division in the rush into Iraq. Here, precision as well as intelligence, surveillance, and reconnaissance (ISR) capabilities would allow for greater integration of fires between air and ground than had been the case in the Gulf War. Moreover, precision capabilities would increase the deadliness of interdiction missions aimed at disrupting the concentration of the Republican Guard as the advance closed in on Baghdad.

Still, throughout the last months of 2002, there was no clear decision as to the number of days, if any, by which the air campaign would precede the ground offensive. In October, the Marines received the warning order to deploy to Kuwait in preparation of Operation Iraqi Freedom (OIF). Major General James Amos had just taken over the Third Marine Air Wing in July; in November, he found himself in Kuwait with his 150-man advance team, all deeply involved in planning for the upcoming air and ground operations. Plans were still nebulous, with discussions of the air campaign ranging from a thirty-day head start to the concept of a simultaneous launch of ground and air forces. Moreover, a number of crucial issues involved in OIF besides the length of the air campaign would not be resolved almost until the campaign began.[12]

The Iraqi perspective is particularly interesting because of the regime's obvious misreadings as to Coalition intentions, as well as the complete lack of understanding of America's resolve by Saddam and his henchmen. Captured Iraqi documents underline that throughout the buildup to the war, Saddam refused to recognize the Bush administration's intention to wage a ground war that would drive the Coalition into the heart of Iraq with the explicit aim of overthrowing the Ba'athist regime.[13] Given his experience with Western air power, Saddam did expect the Americans might launch an extensive air campaign similar to Operation Desert Fox, which had shaken his regime in the late 1990s. As one of his ministers commented at the time: "I believe if any incident occurs, the Americans will utilize their air strike method, which they prefer and used recently, instead of sending ground troops, based on their horrific experience in Somalia."[14]

Immediately before the invasion, Saddam commented to the director general of the Republican Guard that there was no way the United States was going to engage in a ground war and that "there was no way the air force was going to win a battle or a war as long as there is a single Iraqi soldier left."[15] On several occasions, Saddam did opine that the Coalition might use ground forces to seize the oil-rich regions to the north and west of Basra, but even then he quickly persuaded himself that a ground war was simply not a possibility. Not surprisingly, Saddam's view found enthusiastic agreement among Iraq's senior officers. The commander of the Iraqi air force stated after the conflict, "We thought that this war would be like the last one in 1991. We figured that the United States would conduct some operations in the south and then go home."[16]

In terms of meeting the threat of an air offensive, the Iraqis had had extensive experience with American and Coalition air power over the course of the previous twelve years. Thus, they buried as much as they could, dug extensive hiding positions for their ground forces, and decided that they would make no direct response to the expected Coalition air offensive beyond firing unguided antiaircraft guns and missiles wildly into the sky in the hope they might hit something or at least reassure Iraqi civilians the regime was striking back at the enemy.[17] Simply put, the Iraqi strategy was to hunker down and wait for the international community to force the Coalition to end the air campaign.

Saddam's own attitude toward a potential air campaign is best encapsulated in a remark he made immediately after the Gulf War in early March 1991:

> How many were scared? I mean what kind of proportionality do we have for this attack? . . . Where is it written in the [history] books to have a preparatory [air] bombardment for one month and a half. . . . Which book is it? Was it ever recorded in a war? . . . we should say in a decisive manner that [Iraq] is the master of the world, when it comes to faith . . . mental and nervous capabilities . . . and human tenacity because there has never been anything like this attack in history.[18]

Because Saddam discounted the possibility of a Coalition ground offensive, the Iraqis made no preparations to launch an insurgency, as defenders of the Bush regime have claimed in the disastrous aftermath of OIF.[19] Saddam's focus was on other issues. His greatest fear was that the air campaign might unleash another uprising along the lines of the March 1991 rebellion that came perilously close to toppling his regime. That fear explains why the Iraqis made few efforts to blow up Iraq's bridges, which remained intact for the Third Infantry Division and the First Marine Division to capture and which then sped them on their way into the heartland of the Mesopotamian Valley. In 1991, Coalition air attacks had destroyed most of the bridges, which seriously complicated Saddam's efforts to put down the rebellion that had followed immediately after the Gulf War.[20] Thus, the Iraqis left the bridges untouched because Saddam believed they would prove critical to redeploying forces to nip any signs of rebellion in the bud.

Given his experiences with American air power to this point, Saddam had no confidence his air force could achieve anything against enemy air attacks. As a result, he ordered that his aircraft make no response against the Coalition. Instead, the order went out to disperse the few remaining aircraft away from airfields; in one case, local commanders went so far as to bury fighter aircraft in the sand. From the beginning of the war, the Coalition enjoyed complete and total air superiority. Its losses over the course of the three-week campaign speak volumes as to the completeness of its control of Iraqi air space: four Army Longbow Apache helicopters, two Marine Cobra helicopters, and one A–10 close air support aircraft.[21]

FORCE STRUCTURE AND LOGISTICAL PREPARATIONS

The United States deployed four sets of air power capabilities to the Middle East in support of OIF: Air Force, Marine, Navy, and Army air all contributed to an innovative, flexible, and impressive campaign, directly linked to efforts on the ground. The British also contributed substantial forces. The air component commander, General Moseley, was no doctrinaire. Rather, he made every effort to use the forces at his disposal to the greatest extent possible in support of OIF's larger objectives. Each of the American air forces brought different strengths, force structures, and subcultures to the fight.

The largest and best prepared force in terms of a strategic air campaign was the U.S. Air Force. It would deploy 293 fighters (F–15Cs and Es, F–16s, A–10s, and F–117s), 51 bombers (B–1s, B–2s, and B–52s), and a whole host of support aircraft. The Marines brought 130 fighters (F–18s and AV–8s), EA–6Bs, large numbers of helicopters, and specially modified C–130s for ground logistical support; the Navy brought 232 fighters (F–18s and F–14s) and EA–6Bs. The Army in turn brought a host of attack and support helicopters. In addition to the American effort, Coalition partners, particularly the United Kingdom and Australia, contributed a number of fighter aircraft. Unmanned aerial vehicles (UAVs) also made their first appearance in support of major ground combat operations; four Predators and Global Hawks opened a new chapter in ISR missions—a chapter with considerable possibilities for the future.

The buildup of Coalition air power throughout the Gulf in 2002 pointed at the possibility of a major air campaign. Planning for the air war picked up over the last half of 2002, particularly as Southern Watch increased the number of targets its aircraft were attacking. Because the period of hot weather would start in April–May, there was only a limited time frame for Coalition ground operations to begin. The one weakness in Coalition air power concerned close air support. Since World War II, it has been the stepchild of the Air Force, and as a result that service has been unwilling to provide sufficient forward air controller teams to the Army.[22] As one officer put it to this author, the Air Force is stuck in "old-think." The Marines were far better prepared to deliver close air support because that mission, as opposed to interdiction and strategic attack missions, is fundamental to their conception of the Marine Air-Ground Task Force.[23]

In this regard, Moseley proved an adaptive and imaginative air commander rather than an ideologue. He went out of his way to ensure close cooperation with his Marine subordinate, Major General James Amos. Moseley made it clear that he was the boss of the air campaign but that he also understood the particular needs of Marine ground forces for support from their air assets.[24] Mosley proved to be a man of his word. Throughout the campaign, there would be minimal friction between Marine air commanders and the Air Force.

The buildup of Marine air in Kuwait had to overcome a number of difficulties that did not confront either the deployment of Air Force units or the concentration of naval air power. The Navy, of course, simply had to move its carriers into the Red Sea to be ready for operations. The Air Force had access to a large number of bases throughout the Gulf region—bases from which its aircraft had been operating for over a decade, and which therefore were well equipped with maintenance facilities, fuel, ammunition, spare parts, and excellent quarters for those who flew or maintained aircraft. For the Marine Harriers, initially operating off ships, support did not represent a problem, although plans to deploy the planes forward as Marine ground units pushed into Iraq would require the forward movement of supplies, ammunition, and fuel after they left their shipboard homes.

The Marines, however, were arriving in theater with none of that support structure and had to create one. It required close cooperation between operators, supply, and the Seabees (the Navy's shore construction arm). With five squadrons of F–18s scheduled to bed down at the Kuwaiti air base of al Jaber in early January, the Marines faced a major set of problems. Luckily, there was already a considerable Air Force presence: two squadrons of A–10s and one squadron of F–16s with a support structure of twenty-five hundred airmen, all with first-class accommodations and messing facilities. The Marines now descended on their comfortable life and created a tent city for forty-five hundred Marine airmen to support both the Hornets and the air wing.

Even with the facilities of al Jaber, the Marines faced major problems in building sufficient infrastructure to support the Third Marine Aircraft Wing (MAW) as well as the ground troops that poured into Kuwait with their vehicles. This effort included building tent cities for the three regimental combat teams arriving in early January; laying an additional pipeline from Kuwait City's port to al Jaber for fuel; pouring concrete for an eight-hundred-by-thirteen-hundred-foot ramp and matting thirteen hundred square feet. Moreover, the Marines used the hard-packed desert sands to build a runway in the desert near the regimental encampments for the use of the C–130s, whose crews all had to become night-landing qualified. The logistical issues confronting the Marines are important to keep in mind because they reflect the potential difficulties involved in the future projection of American air power, when the kind of base structure and facilities to which the Air Force has become accustomed in the Gulf may not be available.[25]

THE OPENING MOVES: "SHOCK AND AWE"

Shortly after 2200 hours local time on March 20, Moseley's chief of strategy received word from Washington that the Central Intelligence Agency was nearly 100 percent sure it had located Saddam. He and his two sons were supposedly meeting at Dora Farms, a location that Saddam's family had used occasionally in the past. In fact, there is no evidence the dictator had used the site in the years immediately preceding the war. Since the American ultimatum to Iraq was due to expire at 0400, it seemed possible to put together a hurried F–117 mission to attack Dora Farms and decapitate the regime.

Despite the fact the war was not scheduled to begin for another forty-eight hours, President George Bush gave the go-ahead. There then followed a desperate period of briefing the pilots, getting the aircraft armed and ready, and alerting the Navy to launch its Tomahawk land attack missiles (TLAMs) for strikes at other key command and control sites. From beginning to end, friction plagued the mission— the sort of friction the advocates of the frictionless environment that technology was going to provide had totally ignored in their efforts to dismiss reality.[26]

A little over five hours later, two F–117s were airborne, each equipped with two EGBU–27 bunker-busting bombs. Friction continued to dog the mission. As the aircraft approached Baghdad, the GPS unit on one of the bombs went dead. Lieutenant Colonel David Toomey, flying the aircraft, desperately worked to get the unit back on line; he restored it just in time for the aircraft to drop their four bombs directly on Dora Farms. The target was obliterated, but Saddam was not there. As was to occur on a number of occasions throughout the three-week campaign, intelligence identified Saddam's location, aircraft responded and destroyed the target, but neither Saddam nor anyone else of importance was at the site. In fact, the evidence available today indicates that none of the attacks managed even to get close to Saddam's actual location. Precision weaponry is wonderful, but it attacks with precision only what it is told to attack. Without precise, accurate intelligence, precision weapons are no more effective than the "dumb" munitions of the past.[27]

A salvo of forty-five TLAMs from Navy vessels in the Gulf was supposed to accompany the attack on Dora Farms. However, someone in the Navy's bureaucracy had decided to take the extremely high-frequency system down for routine maintenance, and so the required targeting data had to be loaded by means of a slower system. As a result, only thirty-nine of the missiles were ready for firing—another of the types of friction inevitable in human endeavors.[28] While these missiles targeted command and control centers, there is no evidence that any of the regime's senior leaders were significantly harmed, merely inconvenienced by having to trundle around Baghdad to meet Saddam at one of his many hiding places scattered throughout the capital.[29] As one of the leading works on the war notes,

> As the war was waged, allied planes would carry out strikes against other time sensitive targets, including Chemical Ali. But not one of the top 20 figures in the regime was killed by an air strike. The United States' reconnaissance, communications, and precision weapons gave it the capability to strike enemy leaders, and to strike quickly. But such attacks would be only as good as the intelligence they were based on, and as the opening night of the war demonstrated, that intelligence was often not reliable.[30]

The attempt to decapitate the regime by blowing up Saddam threw the strategic air campaign off kilter. The full-scale effort to attack the regime at its heart started on the next evening, but by then the ground campaign had already begun. By that time, ministers, bureaucrats, and generals were ensconced in safe locations. The display of ordnance hitting targets throughout the Baghdad area did indeed provide spectacular pictures on media outlets worldwide. Adding to the fireworks display were the unaimed, uncoordinated efforts of the Iraqi air defense system, blasting away into the skies over Baghdad. In one case, on the third night of the war, a stripped-down Predator UAV circled the Iraqi capital drawing a blistering barrage of missiles and antiaircraft fire, all of which missed the drone, which was moving at a speed of approximately eighty miles per hour.[31] That one incident alone underlined the futility of the Iraqi air defense system, which fired no less than 1,660 surface-to-air missiles (SAMs), none of which managed to achieve any hits, as well as innumerable antiaircraft shells, all to little effect.[32]

The attacks on the government structures in Baghdad raise a number of important questions about the effectiveness of strategic air power. First, there is no evidence they had the slightest impact on Saddam and his colleagues in terms of their willingness to continue the war. Second, given Iraqi experiences with Coalition bombing efforts, these strikes at the center did only minimal damage to the regime's ability to use its communications systems to direct its military units. As an Iraqi commander noted after the conclusion of hostilities: "The early air attacks hit only empty headquarters and barracks buildings. It did not affect our communication switches which were still based in those buildings. We primarily used schools and hidden command centres in orchards for our headquarters—which were not hit."[33]

The third point is that the "Shock and Awe" campaign, while doing little substantive damage to the regime's willingness to continue the conflict,[34] did inflict considerable damage on the civilian and bureaucratic infrastructure that would be necessary in putting Iraq back together.[35]

INTERDICTION AND CLOSE AIR SUPPORT: THE GROUND CAMPAIGN

While the strategic attacks on Iraq's center continued, Coalition ground forces began their rapid advance into Iraq from their launching points in Kuwait. On the right, emerging from deployment areas in Kuwait, British forces with support from U.S. Marines drove north to Basra and the Rumaila oil fields. The main Army and Marine drives toward Baghdad moved west and north toward the Euphrates River. The Marines then crossed that river at Nasiriya, where they ran into a hornet's nest of opposition. An incompetently led Army supply column had wandered into the city and fully alerted the Iraqi defenders. To that point, the Marines had run into relatively light opposition. Cobra helicopters from the Third MAW had suppressed most of the dispirited Iraqi units south of the Euphrates. But Nasiriya was a nasty fight at close quarters, mostly with Iraqi fedayeen, but with some units from the Iraqi Eleventh Infantry Division.

After crossing the canal on the far side of the Euphrates against heavy opposition, the lead Marine unit, already under heavy attack by fedayeen, was hit by an A–10 Warthog, which misidentified the Marine amphibious assault vehicles and blasted them. Six Marines died as a result.[36] This was not the only time that Air Force A–10s misidentified Coalition combat vehicles; the other casualty was a British Warrior light armored vehicle. The A–10s hit no U.S. Army vehicles, but the two friendly fire incidents suggest a lack of training in identifying vehicles other than those possessed by the Army, with whom the A–10s worked closely.

Despite the friendly fire incident, the Marines continued to receive heavy fire support from air assets. Amos's Cobras played a particularly important role in suppressing the Iraqi defenders. In a Marine pilot's words,

> That night, we returned to where the Grunts were located where we had left
> them to go get gas. It's dark now. The marine vehicles were parked in a coiled

formation . . . so that each individual can fire in a specific direction to protect the rest of the vehicles in the coil. Each tank and LAV [light armored vehicle] is assigned a particular sector of fire. As we approached, we could see they were in a pretty decent dog fight. As we moved to get over their position, fire is going out in every direction from their coil. TOW [tube-launched, optically tracked, wire-guided] missiles, 25mm chain gun, M–1 tank main gun, and heavy machine gun fire. We were so low over them the firing from the machine guns made your teeth rattle. Every couple of minutes a FAC [forward air controller] would give me a roll out heading and I'd either ripple a pod of rockets, or blast away with cannon. Everything was danger close.[37]

The battle through Nasiriya broke the First Marine Regimental Combat Team loose to advance on Al Kut on the Euphrates, while the Fifth and Seventh Regimental Combat Teams moved to the northwest along the western bank of the river toward Ad Diwaniyah. Meanwhile, Major General Buford Blount's Third Infantry Division moved up the right bank of the Euphrates and masked the major cities along the river until the division approached the Karbala Gap, through which they planned to advance on Baghdad from the west. As they moved north the division's helicopter assets, the Apaches, moved with them, providing support and cover for the long columns snaking north, which confronted ill-led and ill-trained but nevertheless ferocious fedayeen attacks emanating from the cities.

On the evening of March 22, the Eleventh Attack Helicopter Regiment launched a deep attack aimed at chewing up elements of the Republican Guard Medina Division. Pushed by senior officers worried about the Medina's armored strength as well as the fact that a major storm was coming in from the west, the Eleventh mounted its attack with little intelligence on the mission area and only the most cursory planning. The fuel required for the mission arrived just before nightfall, requiring a complicated refueling process in unfamiliar terrain and darkness. So difficult was the process that the mission commander reduced the number of attack helicopters by a third, which reduced the number of targets by a third. So late did the mission get off the ground that by the time it launched, suppressive fires from artillery and the Air Force had already occurred.

To add to the mission's difficulties, V Corps refused the Eleventh's request to fly into the target area from the north—relatively uninhabited territory—which left only a southern route. The mission profile took the helicopters over heavily defended territory where an operating power grid would silhouette them against the night sky.[38] And finally, to add to the extent of the attackers' troubles, the Iraqis were ready and waiting.[39] Despite extraordinary heroism on the part of the aircrew, the mission was a complete failure. The attackers lost one Apache, and all the rest were damaged. The bottom line, at least to this author, is that helicopters, enormously useful aerial vehicles for any number of missions, should be considered a deep-attack asset only as a last resort, especially when there are fixed-wing aircraft available.

Throughout the movement north by Marines and soldiers, interdiction strikes, informed by ISR assets, had continuously pounded the Iraqis with precision munitions. In most cases, these weapons proved as effective from the psychological point of view as they did in terms of the actual damage inflicted.[40] In a postwar interview, Lieutenant General Majid Husayn Ali Ibrahim Al-Dulaymi, commander of the Republican Guard's I Corps, commented, "Our units were unable to execute anything due to worries induced by psychological warfare. They were fearful of modern war, pinpoint bombing war in all climates and in all weather."

After visiting the Adnan Republican Guard Division shortly after the precision attack had wrecked one of its battalions, the general added that "the level of precision of these attacks put real fear into the soldiers of the rest of the division. The Americans were able to induce fear throughout the army by using precision air power."[41]

The destruction of the Republican Guard Al-Nida Division, which was one of Saddam's best-equipped forces, further underlines the connection between psychological and actual destruction. At the beginning of the war, the division had thirteen thousand soldiers. After the first two weeks of ground operations, when ordered to pull back on Baghdad, it was down to only two thousand men. The division had yet to fight a ground battle with the advancing Americans. By the time it reached the capital, it had barely one thousand. As the dispirited commander noted after the war,

> Every day the desertions increased. We had no engagements with American forces. When my division pulled back across the Diyala Bridge, of the more than 500 armored vehicles assigned to me before the war, I was able to get barely fifty or so across the bridge. Most were destroyed or abandoned on the east side of the Diyala River.[42]

A study of the 2003 Iraq War, based on Iraqi military documents and postwar interviews with senior Iraqi officers, notes,

> Considering that the Al-Nida Division was never really engaged in ground fighting during the course of the war, what happened to it suggests that

psychological operations, integrated with precision fire, created a generalized dread of seemingly inevitable destruction; this combination quite literally broke the will of many Iraqi units subjected to it. In the eyes of the average Iraqi soldier, Iraq's inability to stop the United States from "flying 8,000 miles to drop its trash [pamphlets]" on them proved the regime's impotence. The fact that the Coalition seemed to know exactly where to drop the "trash" made every soldier in the Republican Guard feel as if they were in a "sniper's sight." Witnessing the effects of precision weapons that devastated exposed positions did not help already poor morale.[43]

During the early days of the air war, the Al-Nida Division had largely escaped heavy attacks. But in one case, its 153d Artillery Battalion, which had dispersed into three hide sites, received devastating attention from Coalition aircraft, which destroyed the entire battalion in a matter of minutes. During the second week, as Coalition ground forces broke into the center of the Mesopotamian Valley, two of the division's brigades received heavy attacks. According to the division commander,

> In the 42nd Brigade sector, the troops were in their prepared positions and were hit very effectively for five days. The continuous nature of the attacks did not allow us to track the number of losses. After the attacks many of the soldiers "escaped" [deserted]. By the end of the war more than 70 percent of the Al-Nida Republican Guard Division "escaped," between the air strikes and desertions only 1,000–1,500 soldiers remained out of more than 13,000.[44]

What is perhaps astonishing from a Western perspective is that the failure to destroy Iraqi communications actually contributed to Saddam's and his regime's inability to understand what was actually happening, as American ground forces chewed through what was left of Iraqi ground forces after the devastating air attacks had wrecked most of Iraq's fighting strength. The tyrannical system that the dictator had established created a culture in which only good news passed up the chain of command, while bad news remained buried for as long as one could escape the consequences. Certainly, everyone within Saddam's reach understood that passing along bad news to the dictator was a sure way to end one's career—and that was the best of all possible outcomes.

The result was that the information Saddam received from the battlefront was almost entirely good news. The Ba'athist officials at As Samawah, An Najaf, Al Hillah, and Ad Diwaniyal all reported the Iraqi forces had dramatically defeated

American attempts to break into their cities, when, in fact, the Americans had merely masked those towns, so that the fedayeen could not break out to interfere with the logistical flow north. One of the more sophisticated—and competent—Iraqi generals commented after the war,

> Part of the problem with reporting on the ground was the political leadership. The Ba'ath officials in command of the local units in the mid-Euphrates Region did not understand what was happening. [Nevertheless] Saddam gave great credit to an idealized vision of tribal war. In Saddam's eyes this kind of close combat was what the Ba'ath Party could deliver. Saddam thought that the Ba'ath commanders knew more than the professional military. The Ba'ath destroyed the army.[45]

The damage done to units by Coalition air attacks remained buried in a military reporting system in which news steadily improved as it moved up the bureaucratic ladder. Part of the reason was that most Iraqi Ba'ath officials—the ones to whom Saddam listened—did not understand what they were seeing, while those who did knew enough to stay silent. Thus, the Iraqi information minister known as "Baghdad Bob," who passed along what appeared to Western eyes to be sheer and utter nonsense, was, in fact, reporting what the regime believed was actually happening.[46]

DENOUEMENT: TACTICAL AIR POWER AND THE REGIME'S COLLAPSE

Between March 28 and 30, Lieutenant General David McKiernan, the land component commander, ordered the ground forces to halt for refit, resupply, and preparation for the final push to Baghdad. The Marines needed the pause less than their Army counterparts did. Admittedly, they had to move less distance and therefore used up less fuel than the Army units; and with the exception of the furious battle at Nasiriya, they had not faced heavy fighting. But there was an additional reason that underlines the difference between the Air Force's integration with the ground campaign and the Marine Corps' integration of its air assets with its ground forces. Since the Vietnam War, the Air Force has largely regarded its C–130 fleet as a force to transport paratroopers and carry supplies from one base to another.[47] By contrast, the Marines have regarded their C–130s as combat aircraft: flexible, useful assets that can be used to directly support the lead units of Marine forces, if necessary. The Marines had fitted four of the C–130s in their inventory with a forty-thousand-pound fuel tank in the cargo bay, which added to the forty thousand pounds of fuel that the

C–130T could dispense and provided the Marine Corps with an enormous ability to supply their spearheads with fuel.

The question was solved by selecting several straight sections of four-lane highway—after removing the guardrail. The Fifth Regimental Combat Team carried fuel bladders with it, and as it approached An Numaniyah, its supply organization and ground personnel from the Third MAW laid out the improvised airfield and the fuel stations to unload the fuel for the M–1s. Meanwhile, conventional C–130s flew in ammunition and the needed spare parts. Thus, the First Marine Division was able to cross the Tigris and swing up its eastern bank to come in from the east. As General Amos remarked to the author, "There is nothing I would not have done for Jim Mattis [commander of the First Marine Division]."[48]

The result was that the two American drives struck Saddam's crumbling empire at its heart, Baghdad, at approximately the same time. By now, the American air offensive against the Iraqi Republican Guard and regular army was hitting full stride. The level of cooperation between Moseley and Amos had reached the point where without the slightest haggling Amos provided the air component commander with some of his F–18C high-speed antiradiation missile shooters in return for what he termed almost "unlimited support from air force A–10s." Virtually everyone this author talked to after the war praised the Marine system of close air support as far more responsive and capable than its Air Force counterpart because it put more forward air controllers where they could provide the guidance for even "danger close" missions.

For the Iraqis, this last week of the war represented a catastrophe during which massive attacks from the air savaged those units that still maintained some combat capabilities. On April 2, General Raad Hamdani, II Republican Guard Corps commander, asked for the third or fourth time for permission to blow the Al-Qa'id Bridge (Objective Peach) over the Euphrates, which gave direct access to the Karbala Gap. He finally received permission, but at almost that exact moment, he received word that the Americans had taken the bridge. He then received the order to retake the bridge. That night he struggled to cobble together a unit from what was left of the Medina Division and various Iraqi special forces units. He describes the dismal results in his memoirs written after the war:

> The attack moved forward slowly because we did not have night vision. . . . The Medina Division's commander and I followed the 10th Armored Brigade with our communications groups. At 0200 American jets attacked our force as we moved down the road. We were hit by many missiles. Most of the Medina Division's staff were killed. My corps communications staff was also killed.

When we reached the area near the bridge where the special forces battalion had set up a headquarters, we immediately came under heavy fire. Based on the volume of fire, I estimated at least 60 armored vehicles.[49]

For all intents and purposes, the war was over. The Americans had a straight run in on Baghdad. A few more days of slaughter followed, but the regime, totally unprepared for what was now happening, collapsed with a whimper and not a bang.

THE WAR IN THE NORTH

While the decisive ground war was occurring in the south, a combination of air and air-supported ground forces kept the Iraqis occupied in the north. Since the efforts of the American diplomats and senior military leaders to open Turkey for the deployment of the Fourth Infantry Division failed, the decision was made to drop paratroopers from the 173d Airborne Brigade onto an airstrip at Bashur, already under the control of U.S. special forces and Kurdish guerrillas.

Within four days, 2,160 soldiers and a substantial number of pieces of combat equipment, including tanks, had arrived.[50] The U.S. force lacked any real mobility, but with the available air support, it was hardly in any danger from the Iraqis. Moreover, the Iraqi documents make clear that Saddam and his military were desperately worried about American airborne capabilities. In addition, the operation seems to have reinforced the dictator's belief that the real American drive was coming not from the south, but rather from the north or the west. American commanders did nothing to play down the impression that substantial Coalition military power was building up in the north.

CONCLUSION

The air war against Iraq represented a battle of Goliath against David in which David had no chance at all. Is there much to be learned from this conflict? The answer is clearly yes, but only in the broadest sense. Airmen in their dogmatic approach to air power have all too often confused their narrow desire for unity of command over all air assets with the larger issue of why and for what purpose nations wage war. It is the larger strategic and political context as well as the nature of the enemy that must determine how air power should be used. In the campaign against Serbia, too many senior air commanders missed the political constraints under which the North Atlantic Treaty Organization was fighting the war. Admittedly, the political and strategic context resulted in a less than effective air war, but also allowed the war to continue through to its successful conclusion.

In the Iraq War of 2003, the strategic air campaign was largely ineffective. It certainly did not lead to the fall of Saddam's regime and was unlikely to have achieved that result even if it had continued. Only a ground invasion that moved into the center of the Mesopotamian Valley and occupied Baghdad could succeed in overthrowing Saddam. Air forces and navies cannot occupy territory. Even considering their extraordinarily important role in the history of the twentieth century, they have been, for the most part, major enablers that have paved the way for successful ground campaigns. Only soldiers and marines can occupy ground, and it is control of the ground that results in political and strategic victory. In the end, air power allowed Coalition ground forces to win their overwhelming conventional victory. In actuality, the driving effect of the ground forces helped pull the enemy out into the open, where close air support and interdiction strikes destroyed much of his force. Moreover, logistical support from Marine C–130s, particularly fuel, helped keep the Marine prong of the American drive on Baghdad moving forward.

Does the Iraq War provide a picture of war in the future? From this writer's perspective, it offers little more than some hints. The future is never foreseeable, no matter how aggressively one ransacks the past. But the war does at least suggest that air power has returned to its roots as part of a joint team, supporting ground forces in controlling the land and its terrain.[51]

13

THE SECOND LEBANON WAR, 2006

Itai Brun

THE "SECOND LEBANON WAR" is the official name the Israeli government gave, post facto, to the armed conflict between the State of Israel and the Lebanese Hezbollah between July 12 and August 14, 2006.[1] This war represented a new phase in the ongoing conflict, which began with the creation of Hezbollah in 1982. The war started after Hezbollah attacked an Israel Defense Forces (IDF) patrol along the Israeli-Lebanese border, killed three IDF soldiers, and kidnapped another two. It ended when both sides accepted United Nations (UN) Security Council Resolution 1701, which called for a cease-fire and reinforcement of the UN force in Lebanon. Simultaneously with the war on the northern front, Israel conducted a major military operation against Hamas and other terrorist groups in the Gaza Strip, following another kidnapping in that area.

As a direct result of the second Lebanon war, Israel enjoyed more than two years of exceptional peace along its northern border—one of the positive strategic outcomes of the conflict. However, public opinion in Israel views the war as a missed opportunity: not because of the number of Israeli losses (120 soldiers and 42 civilians killed), but rather because of the wide gap between expectations at the beginning of the war and its final outcomes. The IDF, with its advanced capabilities, could not prevent the continuous firing of rockets into Israel's northern region and had failed to defeat Hezbollah by the time the war ended after thirty-four days. To many Israelis, the four thousand rockets that landed in Israel demonstrated the limitations of military might and particularly of air power.

This chapter deals with the employment of the Israeli Air Force (IAF) during the second Lebanon war. The war offers an interesting case study in the history of air warfare, mainly because Israel chose to use primarily firepower from its air force and artillery and was very reluctant to employ troops on the ground. No major ground operation, as opposed to minor raids, was initiated until the late stages of the war, and when Israel finally decided to conduct such an operation, it was terminated before achieving its objectives. The second Lebanon war, therefore, enriches historical experience and provides an opportunity to examine fundamental questions related to current challenges to air power and its role in military might in general. In this sense, the war reflects changes in the nature of warfare and the new challenges that result from it.

During the war, the IAF's fighters and helicopters carried out about nineteen thousand sorties, of which some twelve thousand were fighter sorties in attack and support missions (an average of about three hundred sorties a day). Attack and transport helicopters carried out some forty-two hundred additional sorties. Most of the air activity was directly aimed at Hezbollah. During the war, the IAF attacked about seven thousand targets, using about nineteen thousand bombs and about two thousand missiles; approximately 35 percent of the ammunition used during the war was precision-guided munitions (PGMs). In parallel to the kinetic operations, the IAF also operated in the information realm and dropped about 17.3 million flyers.

From an operational perspective, the uniqueness of this war lies in the encounter between modern air power, such as Israel's, and a terrorist and guerrilla organization with significant military capabilities and a semi-military structure, such as Hezbollah. The analysis in this chapter emphasizes the strategic and the operational aspects of the employment of air power during the war.

This chapter was written about three years after the war. Therefore, the author had to confront several inherent difficulties that should be acknowledged from the beginning. First and foremost, they concern information itself. Although Israel revealed an unprecedented amount of sensitive information about the conduct of the war and about decision-making processes both before and during the war, some facts remain obscure.[2] On other issues, some of them very important, the information available makes it impossible to choose among different approaches and interpretations. Hezbollah, by contrast, provided very little reliable information about the war and has used the incomplete information that it spreads for propaganda purposes.[3] This chapter does draw on this information, among other sources, to assess the outcomes achieved by the IAF, but years must certainly elapse before a full, reliable picture can emerge on this subject.

A second major difficulty concerns the perspective from which to analyze the war. Three years is certainly too short a time frame to confer a sufficiently broad perspective. The main problem relates to assessing the strategic results. While there is a relatively broad consensus on the tactical outcomes of the war, its strategic outcomes are the subject of major dispute in both Israel and the Arab world. Perhaps the war, in this respect, also reflects the need to update the generally accepted interpretation of the terms *decision* and *victory*. This need stems from the way that changes in the nature of adversaries and in the characteristics of military conflicts challenge the conceptual framework and the familiar imagery developed during the era of modern war.

THE STRATEGIC CONTEXT

HEZBOLLAH

Hezbollah has multiple identities: a terrorist and guerrilla organization, a political party, an ideological movement, and a social network.[4] The organization was founded by Iran in 1982 following the IDF invasion of Lebanon, which destroyed the military and political infrastructure of the Palestinian terrorist organizations operating against Israel from that country. That war (known as the Peace for Galilee war or the first Lebanon war) temporarily weakened Syria's hegemony in Lebanon but failed to restore the authority of the central government in Beirut, which collapsed during the civil war of 1975–1976. Iran identified an opportunity to exploit this strategic change by exporting its revolution to the Lebanese arena—to the very heart of the Arab world—and from there to act against Israel and the United States without being directly involved. Iran decided to operate mainly among the Shiite community, which traditionally suffered from political, economic, and social discrimination despite being the largest community in Lebanon.

However, despite its strong ties to Iran, Hezbollah is an authentic Lebanese organization, and its creation primarily reflected the forces that had propelled the Lebanese Shiite community into political activism during the second half of the twentieth century. Indeed, within a few years, Hezbollah also became a political party participating in the Lebanese political scene. Since 1992, it has represented a large part of the Shiite community in the parliament, and since 2005, the Lebanese government has included ministers who belong to the Hezbollah party. Hezbollah's character as a hybrid organization has proved a crucial factor in the difficulties that Israel has faced in trying to cope with the organization.[5]

THE "LEBANESE MUD"

During the 1980s, Hezbollah battled another Lebanese Shiite organization, Amal, for supremacy. However, since the beginning of the 1990s, a combination of Iranian and Syrian interests turned Hezbollah into the dominant Lebanese force carrying out attacks against Israel. Hezbollah directed its primary efforts against the IDF forces in the security zone that Israel has maintained under its control since it made the unilateral decision to withdraw from the territories conquered in 1982. Hezbollah carried out a wide variety of terrorist attacks, relying mainly on improvised explosive devices and the firing of rockets, mortars, and antitank guided missiles (ATGMs), as well as attacks and suicide bombings against IDF positions. In February 1992, after Israel took out the general secretary of the organization, Hezbollah for the first time launched rockets into Israeli territory to retaliate and to deter Israel from similar operations. This course of action escalated over time and effectively prevented Israel from resorting to what Hezbollah termed "exceptional activities."

The sustained presence of the IDF in the security zone in southern Lebanon generated popular opposition in Israel. It first surfaced in the bitter public debate concerning the Peace for Galilee war and went on to create the public impression that the price of staying in Lebanon was too high in terms of human lives. The sense that Israel had "sunk into the Lebanese mud" increased during the 1990s and reached its climax near the end of that decade, after a series of bloody events that culminated in a helicopter accident in which seventy-three IDF soldiers were killed. The resulting wave of public protest had an especially significant impact on the decision to withdraw from Lebanon in May 2000.

THE ISRAELI WITHDRAWAL (2000)

Israel's withdrawal was designed to end eighteen years of frustrating military presence in Lebanon.[6] After the withdrawal, Prime Minister Ehud Barak publicly declared that Israel held Syria responsible for ensuring peace in Lebanon because of its hegemonic position and military presence in the country. In fact, however, Syria's relationship with Hezbollah was undergoing a major change. In June 2000, Syrian president Hafez al-Assad died and was succeeded by his son, Bashar. During Bashar's first years in power, the balance in Syria's relationship with Hezbollah shifted as Syria grew weaker while the Israeli withdrawal dramatically empowered Hezbollah. Syria's perception of its Lebanese partner also changed; it no longer saw Hezbollah as a mere tool in the conflict with Israel but as a genuine strategic partner. Because of this, a unique and close relationship developed between the inexperienced Bashar Assad and Hezbollah's leader Hassan Nasrallah.

The first challenge to Israel's post-withdrawal strategy came a few months later, in October 2000, when Hezbollah kidnapped three IDF soldiers and a reserve IDF colonel. Israel did not retaliate against either Hezbollah or Syria, primarily because the kidnapping occurred in parallel with the beginning of the violent confrontation with the Palestinians known as the Second Intifada, and Israel did not want to cope with two fronts simultaneously. But the absence of retaliation also demonstrated a greater unwillingness among both the political and senior military leadership to return to the Lebanese mud so soon. After the 9/11 attacks in the United States, the international community became more aware of what Hezbollah had been doing and what it was capable of. That recognition was reflected in UN Security Council Resolution 1559, calling for the withdrawal of Syrian forces from Lebanon and for the disbanding of armed militias. In Israel, many hoped that the international community would solve the Hezbollah problem.

THE "CEDAR REVOLUTION"

The situation in Lebanon changed radically on February 14, 2005, when former Lebanese prime minister Rafik Hariri was killed in Beirut. The assassination shook public opinion; hundreds of thousands of Lebanese took to the streets calling for the withdrawal of Syrian forces. Those rallies, known as the Cedar Revolution, achieved their desired goals: the last Syrian soldier left Lebanon on April 26, 2005. One month later, an anti-Syrian coalition, led by Rafik Hariri's son Saad, won the election with an absolute majority (72 out of 128 members). The former Lebanese minister of the treasury, Fouad Siniora, who held anti-Syrian views, was elected prime minister.

The withdrawal of the Syrian forces from Lebanon was perceived in Israel as a positive strategic change, but in fact it undermined the basis of Israel's strategy toward Hezbollah and called for a new, more direct approach. This understanding was the basis for a new operational plan prepared by the IDF, centered on a massive ground campaign. Simultaneously, the IDF developed a competing plan that avoided such a ground campaign and instead sought to alter the situation in the Lebanese arena by using only firepower. Because there was no sense of urgency, neither plan was completed until the second Lebanon war began in July 2006. However, these plans to a large extent shaped the conceptual framework in which the IDF operated during the war.

HEZBOLLAH'S ORDER OF BATTLE

One of Hezbollah's unique characteristics is its combination of political and social activities and advanced military capabilities.[7] In 2006, Hezbollah was active throughout Lebanon but was concentrated in southern Lebanon, near Beirut and Baalbek. The nerve center was the Dahia neighborhood in the Shiite quarter of Beirut. It was the main symbol of Hezbollah's sovereignty in Lebanon, and the location of the organization's headquarters as well as Nasrallah's offices. Dahia was a tightly controlled neighborhood, where guards checked everyone entering and leaving.

When the war began, Hezbollah had an impressive arsenal of rockets. It included 13,000 107mm and 122mm short-range rockets (maximum range of 20 kilometers [km]), as well as about 1,000 Iranian and Syrian medium-range rockets. The Iranian rockets were Fajr-3 (45 km) and Fajr-5 (70 km) mounted on mobile launchers (civilian cars) and on fixed launchers hidden in civilian houses. Hezbollah also had vehicle-mounted Syrian 220mm and 302mm rockets with ranges of 70 km and 115 km, respectively, and Iranian rockets (Zelzal) for longer ranges (250 km). In addition, Hezbollah possessed an air unit operating unmanned aerial vehicles (UAVs) for attack missions; a marine unit operating antiship missiles; a large ground force (about ten thousand fighters), armed with advanced ATGMs and antiaircraft artillery, and a well-developed underground infrastructure.

Most of Hezbollah's operational personnel were located in the Nabatieh region and south of the Litani River, where all the short-range and some of the medium-range rockets were deployed. In this sector, Hezbollah built complex arrays with ATGMs, underground facilities, and logistics to support prolonged fighting. This sector was directed to launch rockets into Israeli territory and delay IDF forces in case of an Israeli ground offensive.

Hezbollah's operational depth, including medium-range rockets, was located north of the Litani River. The role of this zone was as a staging area to launch some of the medium-range rockets (mainly the 302mm deployed between the Litani and the Awali rivers) and to engage Israeli ground forces in the case of an attempted flanking maneuver into the heart of the Lebanese territory. The launchers for the long-range Zelzal were positioned north of the Awali River.

Hezbollah's training and logistic infrastructures were located in the Lebanese Bekaa, far from the Israeli border. Syrian and Iranian supplies were received there and distributed to the various units.

Israel's Strategic Objectives

It is generally accepted that the war revealed severe shortcomings in the Israeli decision-making process at the strategic level.[8] Clearly, although the threat of kidnapping (which Hezbollah had already attempted to implement, unsuccessfully, in November 2005) was always present, Israel's higher level political and military leadership had no coherent and comprehensive concept for coping with such a challenge and its wider implications.

This state of affairs stemmed from various causes, some of them related to the fact that the war took place during a period of dramatic change in the political and military leadership in Israel. In January 2006, Prime Minister Ehud Olmert succeeded Ariel Sharon, who was ill and had slipped into a coma. In May 2006, about one month prior to the war, Olmert appointed Amir Peretz as minister of defense. Previously, Peretz had dealt mainly with social and economic issues. Both Olmert and Peretz lacked significant previous national security or military experience—an extraordinarily rare situation in Israel.

The military high command had also changed almost completely during the year before the war. The Israeli chief of the general staff was Lieutenant General Dan Halutz, the first airman named to that position. The main challenge that he had faced during the first year of his tenure (2005) was the Israeli disengagement from the Gaza Strip, which the IDF carried out with great success. Halutz's general staff did not differ in its composition from that of his predecessor's and consisted primarily of army representatives. Two IAF major generals served on the general staff: Amos Yadlin, whom Halutz appointed in January 2006 to the sensitive position of head of the Directorate of Military Intelligence, and Eliezer Shkedi, who replaced Halutz as IAF commander in April 2004.

Determining Israel's goals in the second Lebanon war is difficult. From the published record, it emerges quite clearly that the higher political leadership had made no clear basic assessment of political objectives before going to war. During the initial cabinet discussion most ministers did not realize that Israel had entered a genuine war, and many of them considered the current military engagement a retaliation operation of limited time and scope. They were convinced of the need for a strong response to the kidnapping of the two IDF soldiers, but no serious debate was held concerning the wider meaning of an Israeli retaliation operation and its political objectives. At the end of the discussion, the government issued a press release that characterized the kidnapping as a serious event and held the Lebanese government responsible, but also singled out Hezbollah as its perpetrator and announced the organization would pay a high price. The press release also warned of the possibility of significant attacks against the homeland.

The government appointed a smaller ministerial committee to oversee individual military operations.[9] As it turned out, this committee mainly approved targets, rather than formulating more general objectives for the military operation or determining how the targets were related to such objectives.

The clearest expression of the political objectives of the second Lebanon war can be found in a speech made by Prime Minister Olmert at the Knesset on July 17, 2006, some five days after the war had begun.[10] In this speech, Olmert presented very ambitious political objectives, which included securing the return of the kidnapped soldiers, driving Hezbollah out of southern Lebanon, and ensuring deployment of the Lebanese army in that area in accordance with UN Security Council Resolution 1559. However, in his testimony before the Winograd Commission after the war, the prime minister downplayed the importance of the speech and claimed that he had other reasons for making these statements, such as the need for deterrence and for bolstering the morale of the Israeli population and troops.[11]

In many respects, the military provided the clearest articulation of more tangible war aims. On the first day of the fighting, military representatives gave a presentation to the government that described how the military conceived the war's political objectives.[12] The military appeared to understand that the primary strategic objective was to restore—and increase—Israel's deterrence of Hezbollah. This would be achieved by demonstrating Israel's readiness to exact a disproportionately high price for any hostile operation, despite the threat against its own territory. The military presentation also revealed the emphasis given to the Lebanese government's responsibility for the security situation in southern Lebanon.

The general impression that emerges from the material published about the discussions at the beginning of the war is that Israel was primarily concerned with restoring its deterrent capability, which it believed had been damaged by the kidnappings in areas from which Israel had withdrawn unilaterally (on June 25, Palestinians in the Gaza Strip had kidnapped an IDF soldier). Under these circumstances, Israeli decision makers believed that they had to react harshly. Indeed, an analysis of the discussions that took place on July 12, the first day of the war, shows that the government concerned itself more with the extent and magnitude of the Israeli military response than with any political gains that might result. In essence, Israel's government decided to conduct a military operation in order to convey a clear message that would prevent future kidnappings, rather than to wage war.

IDF MISSIONS
The debate within the government during the first day of fighting reveals three different opinions regarding the primary target of Israeli forces. Some called for the use of force against the Lebanese state; others claimed that force should be directed against Syria; and yet others stated that force must be used against Hezbollah itself.

The chief of the general staff, Lieutenant General Halutz, believed that Israel's reaction to the kidnapping would mark a turning point in the way Israel dealt with Hezbollah and the Lebanese government's responsibility for it. He presented to the political leadership the strategic concept developed by the general staff on that day, which emphasized exerting strong pressure on the Lebanese government and forcing it to fulfill its responsibility to deal with Hezbollah. This would be accomplished by inflicting severe damage on the Lebanese national infrastructure, mainly to the electrical and transportation systems. Specifically, the military proposed to strike two power plants, thus decreasing the total capacity of the Lebanese power grid by 20 to 30 percent, and to attack Hezbollah's assets, including its broadcasting station. General Halutz was certainly aware of the Lebanese government's weakness; therefore, this proposal was apparently based on the assumption that such attacks would encourage the international community to intervene and to assist the Lebanese government in controlling Hezbollah. An additional aspect was that the damage caused would lead the Lebanese population to recognize that the actions of Hezbollah, which presented itself as "the Shield of Lebanon," had in fact led to severe destruction.

The political leadership rejected both this concept of operations and an alternative concept that advocated an attack on Syria. Instead, they favored a strategic concept based on attacking Hezbollah directly. One of the reasons was a message from the U.S. government that emphasized the need to maintain Fouad Siniora's regime, which U.S. officials considered a genuine expression of the change in Lebanon and one of the greatest successes of the campaign to move the Middle East toward democratization and reforms. The political leadership feared that an attack on the Lebanese national infrastructure would lead to the collapse of the current government.

In the end, Israel's leaders directed the IDF to execute an operational plan that the IAF had prepared years before, whose centerpiece was a preemptive attack on Hezbollah's deployed rockets. In fact, the military opposed attacking these targets in the current situation, fearing massive civilian casualties. Attacking rocket launchers had far-reaching consequences and was even more dangerous than a strike on the Lebanese national infrastructure, since most rocket launchers were hidden in private homes, generally on the outskirts of villages. Ultimately, civilian casualties were far lower than the military had feared, but the political leadership's permission to attack reflects its view of the magnitude of the response required.

The operational order issued on July 12 reflects the military's understanding of the specific list of missions assigned to it. This order instructed the IDF to destroy Hezbollah's long-range rocket launchers and to damage the organization's launch capability, attack its soldiers, commands, and infrastructure, strike its symbols and assets, and destroy Hezbollah infrastructures next to the Israeli border in order to establish a special security zone. At the same time, the IDF was instructed to set up an aerial and naval blockade to prevent Syria and Iran from supplying arms to Hezbollah.

A ground offensive was not discussed seriously on the first day. When the topic was raised in the following days, the majority of decision makers, both political and military, opposed it.

Interestingly, the instructions given to the IDF did not specifically call for eliminating the short-range rocket launchers. It can generally be assumed that both the political leadership and the military high command underestimated the importance of short-range rockets and largely overlooked their central place in Hezbollah's strategic and operational concepts. Yet they undoubtedly realized that the Israeli home front would be attacked by missiles—a possibility underlined in private debates and public declarations. In addition, the decision makers seem to have believed that Israel lacked a proper mechanism for responding to the rocket problem; they considered a ground offensive incapable of stopping the missile attacks.

Doctrine: Priority to Air Power

The emphasis Israel placed on its firepower, primarily by its air force and artillery, was heavily criticized after the war.[13] In the three years since the second Lebanon war, many, both in Israel and worldwide, have claimed that during the years immediately preceding the war, the IDF abandoned its traditional ground-campaign-centered doctrine in favor of a new doctrine focused on achieving victory by air power alone. Some theorists identified the new doctrine with the old concept of strategic bombing, while others identified it with the new effects-based operations (EBO) approach. These theorists usually attributed the change in doctrine to the IDF officers' having been dazzled by advanced technology and by the U.S. success in applying this technology in the military conflicts of the previous decade, particularly against Serbia in 1999. They claim that the new doctrine was developed by the first Israeli chief of the general staff, who came from the IAF, and that it failed dramatically. From this analysis, they draw various conclusions, all of which demand a return to traditional concepts.

These conclusions provide a superficial answer to a question that merits much serious analysis. A deeper examination shows that Israel's application of military power was not based on an established perception that wars can be decided from the air. The priority accorded to air power did not reflect adoption of either EBO or strategic bombing as a foundation. Instead it was, first and foremost, the outcome of a long process of increasing social and political restraints on military operations.

The IDF's original doctrine had been shaped during the 1950s and 1960s. At its heart lay the concept of bringing the war to the enemy's territory. This stemmed from Israel's lack of strategic depth and the need to end every war with a rapid and unequivocal victory. Central to the concept was a ground maneuver, and the IDF was structured primarily to allow the execution of this concept. The IAF was always a central element of Israel's overall military power. Its achievements, which reached their high point in Operation *Moked* during the first day of the Six Days War (see chapter 6 in this book), greatly reinforced its status but did not undermine the principles that continued to identify military success with the concept of a ground maneuver.

The IDF's original doctrine took Israeli social perspectives into account, but until the Yom Kippur War (1973) these considerations had only a limited effect on the way military power functioned. War was accepted as a situation imposed upon Israel, and nobody doubted that the very existence of the state was threatened. Only a few resisted the general consensus that Israelis had to fight for their homeland. The entire nation was enlisted to fight against the existential threat, and neither the public nor the media questioned the ability of the political and military leadership to make hard decisions on military and security matters. The IDF's successes in the War of Independence (1948), the Sinai campaign (1956), and the Six Days War (1967) reinforced the Israeli public's confidence in its military, its commanders, and its doctrine.

The original IDF doctrine began to change after the Yom Kippur War. It is generally assumed that this conflict marked a turning point in Israeli public attitudes in many domains. The war triggered an unprecedented wave of protest, directed primarily against the leadership, and undoubtedly greatly contributed to the political upheaval in 1977, when, for the first time, the Labor Party lost power. The combination of loss of trust in the political and military leadership and the awareness of the heavy price of war led to a basic shift in public attitudes toward war. This shift, which intensified during the two following decades, is the development that most significantly influenced the IDF's ability to apply its original doctrine.

The implications of this change had already become apparent in the 1990s, during two major operations conducted in Lebanon against Hezbollah (Operation Accountability in 1992 and Operation Grapes of Wrath in 1996). In these two operations, Israel used only its air power and artillery and avoided large-scale operations on the ground. This was the first obvious digression from its original doctrine and a clear contradiction to the way it had dealt with the threat from Lebanon in Operation Litani (1978) and in the Peace for Galilee war (1982).

One school of thought sees a direct link between these two operations and the lessons that Israel learned from the Gulf War of 1991. However, the attempt to link these operations with only the lessons learned from this war misses the effect of the social and political process in Israeli society. By that time, the fundamental change in civil-military relations was very clear, demonstrated by a dramatic decrease in support for the collectivist, national model of the "nation in uniform" that appeared in the 1950s and persisted in Israel until the beginning of the 1980s.

In fact, during the decade that preceded the war, the IDF high command engaged in many debates about doctrine. These debates were prompted in part by the reduced security budget, but they also reflected a certain readiness for a fundamental, critical debate about the original doctrine. In mid-2003, the IDF initiated a formal process to shape and codify an updated doctrine. The discussions were summarized in a document outlining the new IDF doctrine, published in April 2006 and signed by General Halutz.

As the Winograd Commission later stressed, the document itself had little impact on decision makers or on how forces operated in the second Lebanon war and how those operations were flawed. The document was published in April, and it is unlikely that readers had time to give it serious consideration before the war began. In fact, it did not even represent a complete doctrine. Its importance stems from the fact that it reflected the way the senior military leadership interpreted the series of changes in both the Israeli strategic environment and Israeli society itself.

One of the document's key conclusions was that the changes forced a review of the importance and significance of territorial issues, severely limiting the legitimacy of territorial conquest and occupation as a bargaining chip. The document also stated that an occupation by large forces aids the enemy, risks promoting guerrilla warfare, and forces Israel to control a hostile population. These statements express a basic divergence from the original doctrine, which centered on moving the war into the enemy's territory, which implies occupying territory.

The new doctrine emphasized the shift in the role of air power from a supporting element to a main factor in bringing about a military decision. The document did not state that it is possible to win wars from the air alone, and it did not disregard ground operations, but it did indicate the need for a different form of operation than the classical maneuver that had been executed in the Yom Kippur War. The new doctrine was influenced by the campaign in which the U.S. military was involved, but the Gulf War of 2003, which reflected a doctrine combining firepower and ground maneuver, affected it far more than the way the United States had used air power in Kosovo.

CHRONOLOGY: THE PHASES OF THE WAR
PHASE I: JULY 12–19
The war began on July 12, 2006, after the attack on the patrol and the kidnapping of the two IDF soldiers.[14] A few hours after the kidnapping, Nasrallah declared

in a speech that the objective of the kidnapping was the return of Lebanese and Palestinian prisoners detained by Israel. While the Israeli government held the crucial meetings that shaped how the military would operate during that war, the IAF was already dispatched on attack missions that included thirty-five targets, mainly bridges over the Litani and Zahrani rivers, Hezbollah outposts, and command posts. That same day, twenty-two rockets landed on Israeli territory, some of them during the kidnapping itself, apparently in an attempt to distract Israel's attention. Some rockets even hit the IAF northern air control unit.

During the night of July 12–13, Israel made its decision to respond harshly to the kidnapping and begin the first phase of the war, in which the IDF acted primarily to neutralize Hezbollah's strategic capability and to signal the radical change in Israeli containment policy. During this phase, which lasted for a week, the IAF carried out about 2,300 fighter sorties—some 20 percent of all the sorties made during the war (an average of about 330 sorties a day). In the same period, 625 rockets hit Israel (an average of 90 rockets a day), and 13 civilians and 14 soldiers were killed, including the soldiers who had been killed on the first day.

During the first phase, Israel relied primarily on air power and used it mainly against Hezbollah's medium- and long-range rocket launchers. The IAF also attacked symbols of Hezbollah's sovereignty in Lebanon (the Dahia neighborhood in Beirut and the organization's facilities in Baalbek), bridges, traffic intersections, and command posts. Simultaneously, the aerial and naval blockade of Lebanon came into force. In addition, the IAF conducted raids against convoys transporting weapons from Syria to Lebanon. Ground forces were used only to begin destroying Hezbollah outposts adjacent to the Israeli border. Israel received wide support from domestic and international public opinion during this phase of the war.

In the early hours of July 13, Israel carried out a preemptive attack against the medium-range rocket deployment, mainly the Iranian-made Fajr-3 and -5 rockets. This operation represented the culmination of years of intelligence and operational effort. In less than one hour, the IAF destroyed dozens of mobile rocket launchers concealed in the houses of Hezbollah activists and Shiite families in southern Lebanon. During the day, the IAF carried out another raid against dozens of additional targets, including the Beirut airport and the Hezbollah broadcasting station. Nasrallah warned that if Israel attacked Beirut, Hezbollah would attack Haifa; in fact, one of the 125 rockets that landed in Israeli territory the first day did hit that city.

On July 14, the IAF continued its raids on targets in Lebanon. Despite Nasrallah's warnings, the IAF for the first time attacked the Dahia neighborhood, which thereafter became its primary target in the Beirut area. During that evening,

Hezbollah launched two Chinese C–802 antiship missiles, one of which hit an Israeli navy ship enforcing the naval blockade around Lebanon. The Israeli navy was unaware that Hezbollah had such a missile in its arsenal, and the standing instructions given to ships did not provide for appropriate defensive measures. This incident, in which four sailors were killed, was widely publicized by Nasrallah, who reported it in a real-time telephone interview that was also broadcast live on Israeli TV. As a result, Nasrallah gained credibility among the Lebanese and Israeli public.

The next day, Hezbollah rockets for the first time hit the city of Tiberias by Lake Kinneret, about thirty-five kilometers from the Lebanese border. The IAF attacked primarily in three sectors: the Dahia neighborhood of Beirut, targets related to the logistical rear of Hezbollah in the Baalbek region, and Hezbollah's infrastructures and rocket launchers in southern Lebanon.

This day also marked the beginning of widespread international activity related to the war. The Arab League held a meeting at which some of the more moderate Arab countries openly opposed Hezbollah. Lebanese prime minister Siniora criticized Hezbollah and called on the international community to craft a cease-fire declaration. The next day, a meeting of the Group of 8 (G-8) heads of government in St. Petersburg, Russia, resulted in a declaration that condemned Hezbollah and included a four-point program for resolving the crisis. Israel welcomed the final declaration, which incorporated almost all its demands.

On July 16, Hezbollah launched about fifty rockets at Israeli territory. One of them, a Syrian medium-range missile, struck a train hangar in Haifa, killing eight civilians—the largest number of civilian casualties on the Israeli home front in a single attack during the war. This tragic event clearly demonstrated to the Israelis the different nature of the conflict that they were facing: although Haifa had been hit by Iraq during the Gulf War of 1991 and had suffered major terrorist attacks during the years of confrontation with the Palestinians, it had not undergone a heavy attack since the War of Independence.

On July 17, Hezbollah launched about ninety rockets that hit mainly Haifa, Safed, Migdal Haemek, and Afula. That day, Prime Minister Olmert declared Israel's ambitious war objectives in his speech to the Knesset.

The following day, the IAF carried out another significant attack against the Hezbollah rocket deployment. This time, the attack targeted the long-range Zelzal rockets that threatened Tel Aviv and its surroundings.

Phase II: July 20–31

In hindsight, the Israeli operation clearly reached its culmination point after the first week of the war. Israel relied mainly on its prior intelligence about Hezbollah to guide the operations against rockets and other facilities. The IDF's operational plans, prepared before the war, had identified the one-week point as the appropriate time to stop the attacks, analyze their impact, and, if needed, begin a significant ground maneuver. However, while plans acknowledged this option, the decision makers never considered it seriously.

Nevertheless, the sense that the air effort had failed to cause significant damage to Hezbollah and the ongoing rocket attacks produced some changes in Israel's pattern of operations. The second phase of the war, July 19–31, included continuous aerial hunting for rocket launchers and a limited ground operation that was not intended to conquer territory or even to hinder deployment of short-range rockets. The primary emphasis in this phase was on more general strikes at Hezbollah activists, carried out in the form of limited raids on sectors under Hezbollah's control. These raids focused on the villages of Bint Jbeil and Maroun A-Ras, and later on additional sectors. During this phase, IAF fighters carried out about 4,000 sorties (an average of about 360 sorties a day), representing some 35 percent of all the sorties made during the war. In the same period, about 1,250 rockets hit Israeli territory (an average of about 115 rockets a day), and 7 civilians and 21 soldiers were killed.

On July 26, an international conference assembled in Rome to discuss the conflict in Lebanon reached no significant decision except to call to send a UN multinational force into Lebanon. The meeting is remembered mainly because Lebanese prime minister Siniora burst into tears and accused Israel of destroying his country.

The same day, eight IDF soldiers were killed during fighting in Bint Jbeil. These casualties, and the limited success achieved by the ground operations, caused Israeli decision makers to question the use of ground forces—a feeling partly related to the difficulty of accepting that Israel had been dragged into a "real war."

On July 27, the Israeli cabinet ordered the IDF to carry out an extended reserve mobilization of several divisions but did not yet authorize a major incursion into Lebanon. However, the mobilization marked both the acknowledgment that air power had failed to bring about a significant reduction in rocket attacks, and the growing recognition of the rockets' central role in Hezbollah's general concept of operations. On the following day, July 28, Hezbollah for the first time fired rockets at the city of Afula, about fifty-five kilometers from the Lebanese border.

The IDF completed the reserve mobilization on July 29. That day, the prime minister instructed the IDF to present options for an extended operation in southern Lebanon. Most decision makers still believed that the damage caused by implementing such an option would outweigh the benefits.

One of the main features of this phase of the war was the significant decline in international support for Israel's actions, which fell to its lowest point at the end of July. On July 30, the collapse of a building in Kafr Qana following an IAF attack killed twenty-eight civilians. This tragedy awakened bad memories on both sides: it occurred in the same village that Israel had hit by mistake during Operation Grapes of Wrath in 1996. That earlier incident, in which about one hundred Lebanese civilians were killed, had led Israel to terminate the operation before it could achieve its objectives.

The IAF had carried out the strike against the Kafr Qana building in the framework of its operations against short-range rockets. During the days preceding the attack, Hezbollah had fired about 150 rockets from this village and its surroundings; several times, immediately after the launches, surveillance spotted groups of armed men running for cover into the built-up area in the village. The building hit was very close to a launch site used prior to the attack.

The attack in Kafr Qana marked a turning point in public opinion. In an attempt to explain the attack, Israel launched a media campaign and broadcast video clips showing the firing from civilian buildings, but the images showing the Lebanese casualties had greater impact. From then on, a consensus in Lebanon opposed Israeli actions. Partly because of this incident, Europe also withdrew public support from the IDF offensive. Many countries were shocked by the daily images of Beirut under attack, and Europeans saw the magnitude of Israel's attacks and the high number of victims on the Lebanese side as a disproportionate response to the relatively small numbers of Israeli casualties from Hezbollah rockets. By the end of July, the United States was the only country supporting the Israeli operation.

Initial information about the incident led U.S. secretary of state Condoleezza Rice, who was then in Israel, to cancel a scheduled visit to Beirut that was intended to bring about a cease-fire and a political settlement to the conflict. On July 31, Israel (under U.S. pressure) halted its attacks on populated areas for forty-eight hours. During those two days, neither side carried out significant operations; only ten rockets landed on Israeli territory. However, Hezbollah used the two-day temporary cease-fire to reorganize its rocket deployment.

Phase III: August 1–14

A cabinet discussion held on July 31 resulted in the IDF receiving authorization to expand the ground campaign in Lebanon and to create a special six-kilometer-wide security zone. This discussion marked the beginning of the third phase of the war and a significant change in the nature of the ground operations: near the end of the war, Israel planned to conduct a large-scale ground offensive south of the Litani River.

During this phase, about 2,080 rockets hit Israeli land (an average of about 150 rockets a day). Twenty-three civilians and eighty-four soldiers were killed, thirty-three of them during the last two days of the war, until the end of the large-scale ground offensive. The IAF carried out 5,300 fighter sorties (an average of about 380 sorties a day), accounting for some 45 percent of the total number of sorties during the war.

On the night of August 1, Israeli special forces, transported by helicopters, raided Hezbollah targets in Baalbek. Unusually, the command of the operation was given to the air force commander, who was responsible for the battlefield north of the Litani River. Part of the operation took place in an urban environment, supported by air intelligence, surveillance, reconnaissance, and ground power.

On August 2, the Israeli air attacks resumed. In parallel, Hezbollah resumed its rocket attacks on Israeli territory, and on that day 230 rockets hit Israel—the highest number of launches on a single day. On August 4, about two hundred rockets fell on Israeli territory, and for the first time rockets struck the city of Hadera, by the Mediterranean Sea, about fifty kilometers north of Tel Aviv. Two days later, a rocket killed twelve reservist soldiers deployed in Kfar Giladi. The rocket strike, which caused the highest number of military casualties in a single incident, reinforced awareness of the threat not only on the civilian home front, but also in the military rear. After this event, Israeli public support for the war declined significantly.

Participants in a security meeting held in the prime minister's office on August 7 emphasized the importance of stopping the rocket attacks, and later that day, the minister of defense approved a major ground offensive in Lebanon. The next day, the chief of the general staff nominated his deputy, General Moshe Kaplinski, to take over the northern command—a public expression of the tensions that emerged during the war between the general headquarters and the northern command. Many believe that Kaplinski's assignment reflected the reversal of Israeli public opinion regarding the war.

On August 9, the security cabinet authorized the major ground offensive in Lebanon. Meanwhile, diplomatic negotiations sought a political solution to the conflict, and the next day Israel and the United States agreed on a draft cease-fire resolution. On August 11, while the debates in the UN Security Council continued, the prime minister authorized a widespread ground offensive in southern Lebanon, and the operation began at the same time that the Security Council's member states agreed on the proposed cease-fire resolution.

The ground offensive in southern Lebanon continued on August 12. That day, Hezbollah shot down a CH–53 helicopter as it took off after dropping troops into Lebanon. The same day, the UN Security Council unanimously adopted Resolution

1701, which called for an end to the hostilities and for the dispatch of fifteen thousand armed UN troops into southern Lebanon. In fact, the resolution meant the termination of the ground offensive before it attained all of its objectives. On August 13, Israel accepted the resolution, and the United Nations announced that the cease-fire would go into effect at 0800 on August 14. Fighting in southern Lebanon continued until that time; the IAF shot down two Hezbollah UAVs in an attack mission, and the IAF attacked the Dahia neighborhood for the last time.

During the following weeks, both the cease-fire and the aerial and naval blockades of Lebanon were maintained. The territories conquered by the IDF were gradually handed over to the UN Interim Force in Lebanon, and an intensive search located much of Hezbollah's fighting equipment. On September 7–8, Israel lifted the blockades, and the IDF withdrew from Lebanon on October 1.

HEZBOLLAH AT WAR

Although Hezbollah was surprised that the kidnappings led to war, it had prepared in advance for an armed conflict very similar to the one that actually occurred.[15] The concept that guided Hezbollah's force buildup and deployment later became known as "victory through non-defeat." It represents a variation of the concept of attrition, based on a deep understanding of basic Israeli military and security perceptions. Hezbollah correctly identified Israel's need for a clear and unambiguous victory in a short war. Thus, Hezbollah had only to survive and, more important, to demonstrate its survivability. Hezbollah chose to do so by means of continuous rocket attacks on Israel.

During the war, Hezbollah launched about thirty-five hundred short-range rockets from villages, open areas, and special underground facilities it had built. In the first phase, firing was intermittent throughout the day, but later Hezbollah began launching salvos at more or less fixed times, mainly in the daytime.

Hezbollah also launched about 200 medium-range rockets in 40 launching salvos (most from mobile multiple rockets) and about 400 extended-range 122mm rockets in 150 launch sessions. During the first few days, these attacks targeted mainly small settlements close to the Lebanese border. From the middle of the first week of the war until the end of the second week, rockets also hit large towns in northern Israel, including Haifa. Near the end of the second week, rocket attacks decreased, apparently because Israel succeeded in destroying the launchers. Near the end of July, Hezbollah introduced 302mm rocket launchers into the battle, allowing it to shoot at more distant locations.

The strip of Israeli settlements close to the border suffered the bulk of the rocket attacks. The city of Kiryat Shmonah, in the Finger of Galilee, endured the largest number of rockets (about 520). The town of Neharyah, by the Mediterranean Sea, was hit by about three hundred rockets. The cities of Akko and Carmiel, about twenty kilometers from the border, were each hit by between eighty and a hundred rockets. Haifa, about forty kilometers from the border, was hit by about fifty rockets. A few rockets also fell farther away from the border—for instance, on the towns of Afula (about fifty-five kilometers from the border), Beth Shean (about sixty-five kilometers from the border), and Hedera (about seventy-five kilometers from the border and about fifty kilometers from Tel Aviv).

Hezbollah's objective in fighting the IDF ground forces was to cause as many casualties as possible and to slow the IDF advance so that Hezbollah could continue the rocket attacks. Most of Hezbollah's tactics involved firing antitank missiles and mortars and concealing explosive charges along the roads; Hezbollah forces rarely engaged in direct confrontation with IDF soldiers.

OUTCOMES OF THE WAR

After the war, the Israeli public experienced a strong sense of disappointment and frustration, mainly owing to the wide gap between the prewar expectations of a decisive victory and the actual outcomes.[16] The expectations had stemmed in part from the leaders' declarations of ambitious objectives at the beginning of the war, and in part from the precedents of successful wars that Israel had initiated. Israel had plenty of time to plan its attack, and in the beginning the military operation enjoyed almost unanimous support. Nevertheless, contrary to expectation, when the war ended, Hezbollah was still standing and had not been disarmed.

Public pressure led the Israeli government to establish a commission of inquiry, headed by retired judge Eliyahu Winograd, which singled out Prime Minister Olmert, Minister of Defense Peretz, and Chief of the General Staff Halutz as bearing primary responsibility for the failures that came to light. Yet mainly for legal reasons, the commission refrained from recommending disciplinary action. Nevertheless, even in the absence of clear conclusions by the commission, the public feeling of disappointment and frustration led to the resignation of almost all the leaders involved in the war. The first to resign were the commanders of the ground forces, Major General Udi Adam, commander of the northern command, and Brigadier General Gal Hirsch, commander of the northern division. Next, Chief of General Staff Dan Halutz and the Israeli navy commander (who was sharply criticized after an antiship missile hit a missile boat) also resigned. The deputy chief of the general staff, Major General Kaplinski, was not appointed chief of staff and finished his military service after about two and a half years as deputy. Changes also occurred at the political level. Defense Minister Amir Peretz resigned from the government. Prime Minister Ehud Olmert also resigned, though for reasons not directly related to the war itself.

Beyond the widespread disappointment, the strategic results of the war are at the center of a huge Israeli debate, which also has political aspects. The discussions concern primarily the effect of the war on Israel's deterrence posture, both in general and toward Hezbollah in particular. One side maintains that Israel failed in the war and that its deterrence capability has been greatly damaged. This viewpoint dominated immediately after the war and served as the basis for the public discussions at the time. The interim report of the Winograd Commission, published in April 2007, reflects this perspective.

However, about two years after the war, a different, far more balanced view emerged, asserting that the war actually reinforced Israeli deterrence. Proponents also claimed that Israel achieved its more realistic objectives, even though the results did not meet the Israeli public's unreasonable expectations. The Winograd Commission's final report, published at the end of 2007, contains a preliminary, highly limited expression of this viewpoint. The commission chose not to include a chapter assessing the outcomes of the war in the report, stating that it was too early to determine them.

The more balanced perspective stresses both the tactical achievements of the war and its strategic outcomes. In the tactical context, Israel undoubtedly succeeded in surprising Hezbollah and in causing significant damage to its rocket deployments. The number of Hezbollah fighters killed was estimated at over six hundred—a very high price for an organization that previously had not lost many fighters. Hezbollah also suffered severe economic damage, losing expensive armaments and vital infrastructure. In addition, the war damaged the symbol of Hezbollah's sovereignty in Beirut and the main organization nerve center. The IDF destroyed the array of positions that Hezbollah had built along Lebanon's border with Israel, uncovered the system of underground facilities the organization had established, and seriously damaged its rocket deployment. The Shiite villages that were Nasrallah's main stronghold endured severe damage, and Nasrallah himself went into hiding for the two years following the war, fearing an Israeli attempt on his life.

In the strategic context, this assessment points to the calm that prevailed along Israel's northern border for two years after the war and relates it to the outcomes of the war, in particular to the damage inflicted on Lebanon. This view, furthermore, holds that the outbreak of the war itself significantly reduced the effect of Hezbollah's strategic weaponry and the deterrence that Hezbollah had achieved during the years that preceded the war. In addition, the very acceptance of Resolution 1701 (which has been only partially implemented) changed the state of affairs because of the banning of Hezbollah's armed presence in southern Lebanon, the widespread deployment of UN forces, and the unprecedented deployment of the Lebanese army in southern Lebanon. This viewpoint also highlights the strategic aspect of the loss of assets that Iran had built up after much hard work and years of effort.

A similar discussion is taking place in the Arab world, where the prevailing view is that Hezbollah achieved significant success. However, another school of thought holds that Hezbollah's actions caused severe destruction in Lebanon and in fact failed to achieve much of importance.

LESSONS LEARNED
ROCKETS

Because of the special character of the war, most of the lessons learned concern how the IAF dealt with Hezbollah's rocket deployment.[17] Overall, the execution of the preemptive attacks against the medium- and long-range rockets was very impressive. The Iranian Fajr-3 and -5 launchers were severely attacked on July 13, and the missiles were never actually used during the war. The operations on July 18 caused severe damage to the Zelzal long-range rockets, and despite Nasrallah's explicit promises these weapons were never used against Tel Aviv.

The hunt for mobile medium-range rocket launchers also proved successful. The IAF destroyed almost every rocket launcher (thirty of the approximately forty launchers after they had already fired a missile). These achievements seriously damaged the 220mm and 302mm rocket deployments. These results show that the IAF succeeded in implementing a sophisticated system of detection and destruction that functioned throughout the war and enabled the search operations.

By contrast, the 122mm rockets proved a real problem, since their radar signature remained below the level the IAF needed to conduct an air strike. Hezbollah used the 122mm launches primarily for sustained pressure on northern Israeli cities, although these rockets caused far less damage than the 220mm and 302mm rockets.

The effort against short-range rocket launchers bore no fruit whatsoever. Although the IAF managed to hit a few dozen launchers, they represented only a small part of the total. The IAF attacked hundreds of targets in attempts to degrade the launchers' operative capability and identified hundreds more locations as weapons storage or command and control sites, but Hezbollah continued firing short-range rockets at Israel.

From Hezbollah's perspective, the rocket deployment achieved mixed results. In many respects, the use of rockets achieved its objectives and represented a central element in the implementation of the concept of "victory through non-defeat." This achievement must be attributed mainly to the short-range rockets, which maintained continuous pressure on Israeli cities, with Hezbollah succeeding in firing a relatively fixed number of 100 to 160 rockets per day. The medium-range rockets, which Hezbollah viewed as its strategic weapon, neither prevented Israel from starting the war nor curbed Israel's activities during it. This arsenal suffered severe damage at the beginning of the war and during the war itself. The long-range rocket deployment had no effect at all and was also severely damaged during the extensive attack on July 18.

The physical damage that the rocket attacks caused to the Israeli home front was comparatively low and corresponded to IDF expectations. The rockets killed a total of fifty-four people (forty-two civilians and twelve soldiers), an average of one casualty for every seventy-five rockets. Few buildings were destroyed. The main damage was to morale, since about one million civilians, not believing the IDF could protect their homes, were forced to stay in shelters or leave their homes for over a month.

The IAF failure against the short-range rockets triggered an argument among the experts. One school of thought maintained that the IAF could achieve better results but had not properly prepared for this mission, while the other claims that air power is ineffective against this type of weapon.

However, the lessons at the strategic level regarding the rocket deployment deviate considerably from those at the tactical level. The conflict revealed that the Israeli concept of war still demanded a quick and unambiguous victory. Hezbollah fully understood this attitude and focused on depriving Israel of such a victory. Hezbollah's main mechanism for achieving its goals was continuously firing rockets at Israel. By contrast, the decision makers in Israel, at the top political and military levels, did not consider the short-range rockets a serious threat and therefore did not direct significant activity against them. Yet these rockets undoubtedly contributed most strongly to Hezbollah's survival and Israel's inability to achieve a decisive victory.

Given the current state of technology, the large number of rockets (thousands of short-range rockets) and their characteristics (particularly their small radar signature) made it impossible to target them from air attacks. Therefore, in the 2006 war, only a ground operation could have stopped the launching of these rockets. In the longer term, the IAF must develop a capability to deal with such weapons systems.

Ground Operations

More generally, the war demonstrated the need for significant ground maneuvers to defeat an enemy such as Hezbollah. Because of Israel's geostrategic situation, the lesson is apparently even more universal and concerns the necessity for ground operations in most conflict scenarios that Israel may confront.

The war showed the need to develop an operation tailored to the mission of dealing with rocket and surface-to-surface missile launchers. Such an operation should not seek merely to reach certain geographic positions or even to control territory; rather, it should involve significant elements of searching and clearing the conquered area of rockets and missiles. The main goal should be to draw the adversary's forces out into the open so that they reveal their position for an effective air strike. In this sense, ground forces would assist air forces as much as the air forces assist them.

CLOSE AIR SUPPORT

The need for ground operations naturally leads to a debate on close air support (CAS). In the IDF structure, ground forces do not have their own army aviation; thus, the IAF is also responsible for providing CAS to the ground forces using its airplanes and helicopters. The IAF carried out several thousand fighter and combat helicopter sorties to support the northern command, which was also assigned to the fight against short-range rockets south of the Litani River. These sorties, executed in CAS missions, searched for rocket launchers, disrupted launch operations, attacked infrastructures, and provided air cover to forces under attack.

The IAF established its headquarters within the northern command to supervise all IAF operations there. Northern command selected and prioritized the targets. However, years of not practicing CAS caused many difficulties and problems in executing this mission. The Winograd Commission noted many shortcomings in the IAF participation in the ground campaign that resulted from serious weaknesses in planning, preparation, and preliminary exercises. Differences in interpreting doctrine caused additional problems.

These problems also became apparent in the ground forces' logistics, and this had a major influence on how air power was used. During the war, about 350 wounded and about 20 dead soldiers were evacuated by air, the majority by helicopter. The evacuation operations were conducted in response to an urgent need by the ground forces, while a method was being adapted to evacuate troops under fire from the battle zone.

Another result of the logistics problems was seen in supply missions assigned to the IAF. In this framework, the IAF parachuted several hundred tons of equipment from C–130s. Because the IAF was determined to respond rapidly to the ground forces' needs, the high-risk supply drops took place very close to the contact line.

A few helicopter sorties were carried out to transport several hundred troops to the ground operation near the end of the war. One of the helicopters was shot down by a shoulder-launched missile. By contrast, combat helicopters carried out about 16 percent of all the sorties during the war. They operated at relatively high altitudes to avoid being hit.

Strategic Bombing

The second Lebanon war provided no lessons relevant to the debate about strategic bombing, since Israel did not use this concept of operations during the war. Although Israel attacked targets related to the Lebanese national infrastructure, this type of operation was very limited and was linked to other missions given to the IAF. Nevertheless, Israel paid a heavy price for these attacks in terms of its tarnished image in the international community. The widespread impression was that Israel was deliberately attacking Lebanon's infrastructure and even its population.

This confusion came about because a small portion of this infrastructure was damaged during other missions. The IAF carried out limited attacks on the Lebanese transportation infrastructure, mostly during the first three days of the fighting; planes also targeted one fuel reservoir and destroyed runways at the Beirut, Rayak, and Kleyate airports. In addition, the IAF attacked many buildings, including civilian dwellings used for weapons storage and other Hezbollah activities.

The air strikes did cause severe damage in Lebanon, estimated by Lebanese sources at several billion dollars. Most of the damage resulted from attacks on the transportation infrastructure (over one hundred bridges or road bypasses), the Dahia neighborhood in Beirut, buildings used for weapons storage, and rocket-launching bases.

According to a UN report, 1,191 Lebanese civilians were killed and 4,405 were wounded in this war. About nine hundred thousand Lebanese fled their homes, and about thirty thousand residential units were destroyed or extensively damaged.[18] The restraint that has characterized Hezbollah in the years since the war is very likely linked to the destruction in Lebanon, since Hezbollah recognizes that it depends on popular support for its military actions and must therefore reconcile those actions with its image as a community benefactor.

UAVs

The war illustrated the challenge of intercepting UAVs on attack missions, given their low radar signatures. During the war, the IAF carried out about one thousand sorties on air defense missions. Israel had information that Hezbollah possessed the Iranian Ababil UAV model, since Hezbollah had carried out sorties into Israeli territory with this type of aircraft at the end of 2004 and the beginning of 2005. The IAF hindered such attempts, using Python 4 air-to-air missiles, capable of total defense interception, to shoot down two Ababil UAVs, one on July 7 and one on July 13. Another UAV crashed in Israel while being followed by IAF fighters. The main lesson here is the need for advance information on both the characteristics of the aircraft and their operating concept. Prior information concerning the location of the launch site almost guarantees successful interception.

RESILIENCE

The second Lebanon war was another in the series of military confrontations in the last decades that caused very little damage to air power. Israel did not lose a single fighter in combat action during the war, although the crew of an F–16I had to abandon the plane during takeoff. A CH–53 helicopter participating in the transport operations during the last days of fighting was shot down and destroyed immediately after taking off; five air team members—two pilots and three mechanics, one of them female—were killed. The helicopter units also experienced some accidents: two Apache choppers collided (one air team member was killed and three wounded), and an Apache Longbow crashed because of a mechanical problem, killing two team members.

Another significant lesson relates to the operational capability of air power when its bases are under attack. The development of rockets and surface-to-surface missiles (SSMs) makes air force bases more vulnerable. During the second Lebanon war, one IAF base and several other important sites (including the IAF central command post in the northern region) came under rocket attack. This necessitates appropriate protection of the air teams and other entities and the development of an operational capability under continuous rocket and SSM attacks.

INTELLIGENCE AND BATTLE DAMAGE ASSESSMENT

The war again proved the importance of intelligence as the basis for air operations against the full range of targets. The nature of the confrontation and the characteristics of the enemy increased the need for real-time information about most types of targets: not only real-time target positions, but also the whereabouts of civilians.

At the tactical level, it was very difficult to assess the battle damage from this war, largely because of the fleeting nature of the targets. The outcomes were more noticeable at the strategic and operational levels of war. As the definition of the linkage between the operation of forces and its strategic outcomes becomes more complex, assessment also becomes more problematic.

PREEMPTIVE ATTACK

Strategically, the war revealed the increasing importance of a preemptive attack on an enemy whose assets are concentrated and vulnerable. Of course, such an attack has political drawbacks, but the expected benefit may be so high that it outweighs the potential damage. In this context, the early attack on the medium-range rocket arsenal highlighted the importance of a well-prepared, powerful opening move. Such a move can demonstrate air power's capability at its best by using an orderly preparation process, high-quality intelligence, and surprise.

Israel's success in dealing with the medium-range rocket launchers reflects the importance of complete and organized preparedness for war. The IAF's years of preparation included developing a relevant concept, equipping the force with appropriate weapons, and training continuously. The IAF had put these capabilities in place on the basis of a huge intelligence effort, which enabled the detection of Hezbollah's deployments and allowed both the preemptive attack and the launchers hunting campaign during the war.

CONCLUSIONS

One of the most prominent features of wars in the modern era has been a clear and unambiguous military decision. Such decisions have been followed by famous surrender ceremonies, such as those at the end of World Wars I and II and some of the Israeli-Arab wars. No such decision marked the end of the second Lebanon war: both sides had successes and failures. Hezbollah had managed to withstand Israel's military power, and the IDF largely failed to defend the population of northern Israel. However, Israel did succeed, thanks mainly to its employment of air power, in increasing the tensions between Hezbollah's different identities and enhancing the system of restraints that limit Hezbollah's freedom of action.

The absence of a clear and unambiguous decision characterizes the changed nature of warfare in the so-called postmodern era. Indeed, the second Lebanon war directed the attention of more informed observers to the new types of conflicts typical of the current era: low-intensity conflicts, usually protracted and conducted in an urban environment against asymmetric threats and nonstate adversaries—unlike the nation-states involved (on both sides) in major military conflicts of the nineteenth and twentieth centuries. They differ fundamentally from the conflicts that air forces were designed to deal with during the first hundred years of military aviation. These new types of conflicts create an increasing gap between impressive advanced capabilities and the ability to apply them to a significant extent in military conflicts.

Indeed, the capabilities of air power have undoubtedly undergone a fundamental change over the last decades. The survivability of air power and its capability to penetrate deep into the adversary's territory have improved significantly owing to developments in electronic warfare, stealth technology, and UAVs, and the ability to launch at a distance, that is, outside the threat range. Precision-guided munitions and the adoption of new information collection tools and control systems have greatly increased the effectiveness of air power. Thanks to these developments, from which the IAF has benefited, it is now possible to conduct a massive attack on a large number of targets, stationary and mobile, at short and long ranges, under bad weather conditions, with uncertain light, and in complex threat areas.

Hezbollah was aware of these capabilities and of the technological superiority they conferred on Israeli forces. Therefore, like other adversaries in recent years, Hezbollah adopted the logic of a weaker side that must deal with a far stronger, technologically superior adversary. This logic rests on the assumption that the stronger side has weaknesses and vulnerabilities that can be exploited to offset technological advantages. Hezbollah succeeded in translating this idea into the concept of asymmetric warfare, which generally has three main elements. The first is enhancing resilience and survivability. This primarily allows the weaker side to withstand the stronger side's lethal capabilities and to preserve its own power. The second is deterrence, which is essential to moving the war into areas more favorable to the weak side. Deterrence can also offset some of the stronger side's technological advantages without direct military confrontation. The third is a combination of attrition and the negation of legitimacy, which represent keys to victory in asymmetric wars because of the stronger side's inability to tolerate long wars with many losses.

As noted earlier, the result of the encounter between this concept and the IAF's technological capabilities was ambiguous. This outcome stems in part from the IDF's inexperience with various technologies to deal with Hezbollah's unique characteristics, but primarily from Israel's lack of a comprehensive strategic concept for defeating Hezbollah. Contrary to accepted opinion, the IDF waged the second Lebanon war without a coherent doctrine. The original doctrine, which had been formulated in the first years of the IDF's existence and had been successful until the 1970s, was considered irrelevant. The collection of understandings developed in the decade preceding the war did not represent an alternative doctrine that could have served as a solid basis for responding to the challenge presented by Hezbollah.

The lack of a relevant doctrine and concept directly damaged Israel's ability to use its air power efficiently. Because of this lack, the IAF operated in separate missions that did not form a comprehensive conceptual framework. The need to develop such a doctrine is thus the main lesson learned from the second Lebanon war.

This issue is connected to the shortcomings of the decision-making process in Israel at both the political and senior military levels and to a more fundamental problem related to the mind-sets of air forces. The second Lebanon war therefore also demonstrated the need for strategic and operational thinking among air forces themselves and for an appropriate planning process that would best translate that thinking into action. The IAF executed its assigned missions very efficiently, but the logic behind these missions has drawn the majority of criticism in regard to the way Israel employed military force during the war. The IAF has always concentrated on maintaining its tactical excellence. The second Lebanon war and the importance of employing air power in this and other conflicts compel the IAF and other air forces to develop operational and strategic excellence as well.

PART V: PERSPECTIVES

AFTER TRACING THE ROLE OF AIR POWER in military campaigns from World War I to the second Lebanon war—a span of almost one hundred years—the book concludes with three chapters that assess the overall utility of air power throughout its history. James Corum focuses in chapter 14 on the use of air power in "small wars"—counterinsurgencies and irregular warfare—from 1913 to the present day. He takes a critical look at air policing operations in French and British colonies prior to World War II, when the European powers attempted to use air power as an inexpensive substitute for ground operations—an approach quickly proven ineffective in controlling restive populations in remote areas. He next examines how air power was applied throughout the Cold War in Greece, Malaya, and the Philippines, how the French dealt with counterinsurgency in Algeria and Vietnam, and how the United States misapplied air power in Vietnam. Corum also provides an overview of how air power has performed in counterinsurgency campaigns in Latin America since the 1980s, how the Soviet Union struggled against Afghan forces, and how the Russians used and misused air power against Chechnya, and he outlines key features of recent air operations in Afghanistan, Iraq, and Lebanon. He concludes that the primary role of air power in counterinsurgency operations is to support police and military forces on the ground, and that success in small wars depends on a comprehensive strategy combining judicious applications of force with civil-economic actions that address the underlying causes of the uprising.

In chapter 15, Martin van Creveld analyzes the development of air warfare from the Italian-Turkish war in 1911 to the latest war between Israel and Hezbollah in 2006 by examining various air power theories and the impact of technological improvements. Van Creveld asserts that air power, growing rapidly from very modest beginnings, proved itself as a strong and influential instrument of force in wars between nation-states; it had a devastating effect in World War II and has since demonstrated its worth in many conventional wars from the Middle East to the Falklands, and from the Persian Gulf to Kosovo. However, he suggests that manned air power has not followed a trajectory of ever-increasing influence: beginning as early as 1945, some of its most important missions, such as "strategic" bombardment, deterrence, and reconnaissance, were taken over by ballistic missiles and later by various unmanned air- and spaceborne vehicles. At the same time, as unconventional warfare has spread around the world, Van Crevald argues that it has become increasingly clear that in such conflicts the usefulness of air power is limited at best. As a result, over the last decade alone, the number of combat aircraft in the world's most important air forces has declined by an average of one-third; if this trend continues, and the author argues that it almost certainly will, then in another generation or so manned aircraft will all but disappear. Van Creveld concludes that some of the remaining elements of air power—missiles, various unmanned devices, and helicopters—will probably be reabsorbed into ground and naval forces, whereas others will be reorganized in the framework of a space command.

In chapter 16, Richard P. Hallion surveys the history of air and space power through the lens of evolving technology, doctrine, expectations, and combat experience, assessing the continuing debate over their nature and value. He notes that while little consensus exists, the contradictory nature of many differing interpretations has fueled a "virtually continuous re-examination" of the subject. As is evident from the title of his chapter, "Air and Space Power: Climbing and Accelerating," Hallion offers a counterpoint to the views of Martin van Creveld, noting that skepticism about air and space power (and aerospace development overall) has generally proved unwarranted and concluding, "It is premature to bury the manned military airplane, air forces, or air power." Among other points, Hallion argues that vantage is the "single most significant capability" furnished by air and space power; that air dominance is the "most important enduring requirement"; that the demarcation between "air" and "space" power and the debate over "weaponizing" space have become increasingly irrelevant; that air and space power work best when applied according to the principles of effects-based operations; that unmanned aircraft can be expected to transform air forces but not to the exclusion of manned aircraft; and that while all services have their own reasons for projecting and exploiting air power, only manned air forces are "full service" air power providers.

14

AIR POWER IN SMALL WARS: 1913 TO THE PRESENT

James S. Corum

ALMOST AS SOON AS THE AIRPLANE was developed, it assumed an important role in warfare against irregular forces. In 1913–1914, the French army deployed a detachment of airplanes to assist the French forces in their ongoing pacification campaign in Morocco. From the start, the airplane proved extremely useful in the reconnaissance role. One airplane could put a large area under observation far more efficiently than a cavalry company. The French experimented with dropping bombs on hostile tribesmen, and their initial impression was that the airplane had a significant psychological effect on the enemy—far greater than the physical damage caused. The first experiments in employing air power against irregular enemies were promising, but they ended with the start of the First World War in August 1914 and the recall of air detachments to France.

During the war, all the major powers created large air forces, and the technology of air power evolved rapidly. Long-range strategic bombing became a feature of war, and heavy bombers could carry a bomb load of one ton over one hundred miles. Airplanes also became the primary means of gathering tactical intelligence. By 1917, airplanes were regularly used in the ground attack role, and joint air-ground operations were a normal feature of war by 1918.

The use of air power against colonial insurgents was resumed after World War I, when Britain and France faced several colonial conflicts. Order had to be restored in colonies that had been ignored during the war. Trouble flared up along India's Northwest Frontier, and the French campaign in Morocco was renewed. The most difficult problems were the new colonial mandates that Britain and France had gained from the collapse of the Ottoman Empire. Britain had acquired Iraq, Jordan, and Palestine as new mandates, and France had acquired Syria and Lebanon. Opposing the British and French mandates were Arab and nationalist factions vying for power amid the ruins of the Ottoman Empire.

In the Caribbean region, the United States was involved in conducting military interventions and establishing pro-American governments in the Dominican Republic and Haiti. Other colonial powers, namely Italy and Spain, also faced conflicts in their expanding empires. These powers would deploy air units to their colonies and dependencies to support the pacification effort.[1]

THE CONCEPT OF AIR CONTROL

Air power played a dramatic role in one of Britain's first postwar colonial operations. In 1919, the British dispatched a squadron of two-seat light bombers to help local troops deal with the bandit forces of the "Mad Mullah" of Somaliland, who had bedeviled British colonial efforts for years in one of the most remote colonies of the empire. In a short campaign that featured the aerial bombardment of the Mad Mullah's forces, which had never encountered aircraft before, the rebels panicked and were defeated with relative ease. The Royal Air Force (RAF), which was frantically looking for a specialized mission as a means of maintaining its newly won independence as a separate service, argued that it could police the colonies cheaply with a system of "air control." Air control would use aerial bombardment, or the threat of it, to keep hostile tribes and factions in line.[2]

Under the doctrine of air control, the airplane would replace the punitive expedition, which had long been the standard military operation against rebellious tribesmen on the frontiers of the empire. Instead of spending weeks traveling to reach a hostile village in an isolated country, an airplane could fly to the spot in hours, drop some bombs, inflict the necessary punishment, and fly home in time for dinner. Airplanes could produce the desired effects—namely, punishment for the rebels and bandits—and do it quickly and at minimal cost. For financially strapped postwar Britain and France, now responsible for garrisoning large new colonies, air power seemed an ideal solution.

The idea that air power by itself could serve as a colonial garrison force was soon put to the test and found wanting. In 1920, Iraq, which had recently become a British mandate, erupted in a massive rebellion that started with the Kurds and spread to other groups. The Kurdish and Arab rebels were relatively well armed, largely with stocks of modern weapons seized when the Turkish Empire had collapsed.[3] Many of the leaders of the revolt had served in the Ottoman and Arab armies during the war and had an understanding of modern warfare.[4] At first, the sixty thousand British troops in Iraq were hard pressed to respond, and the British had to dispatch thirty thousand additional soldiers and two more RAF squadrons as reinforcements.[5]

The RAF performed well in its role as a support arm of the ground forces, providing reconnaissance and close support as it had done in the First World War.

One of the notable innovations of the Iraq conflict was the use of RAF aircraft for transportation. Army garrisons surrounded by the rebels were saved by aircraft that dropped food and ammunition to the troops. Despite the advantages of air power and modern weapons, it still took a year of hard fighting and heavy casualties for the British to suppress the Iraq rebellion.[6]

The financial cost of the war, over forty million pounds, came as a great shock to the government. After the rebellion was crushed, the British government accepted the offer by RAF chief Hugh Trenchard to use the force to police Iraq "on the cheap" by means of air control. The British army units were withdrawn from Iraq, the RAF force was strengthened to eight squadrons, and military forces in Iraq were placed under an RAF commander. Contemporary articles give the impression that the RAF was the predominant military force in some colonies and that air operations had been substituted for ground operations. The reality was different. Only in relatively minor cases of banditry was an aerial attack on the offending tribe employed as the primary military response. In any serious case of tribal rebellion, the military employed significant ground forces with the air units in support. In Iraq, the British administration ensured that large ground forces garrisoned the country. British army units withdrawn from Iraq in 1922 were replaced with Indian army brigades, paid for by the Indian state.[7] The British also created an Iraqi army, officered and trained by the British.[8] Iraqi and Indian army forces fought against several major rebellions in Kurdistan that occurred between 1922 and Iraqi independence in 1932.

Thus, while much was made of "air policing" in the popular press, most RAF operations in the colonies in the interwar years were actually joint operations. Although the RAF often bombed rebel towns, its primary missions in the campaigns against Kurdish rebels and hostile tribes on India's Northwest Frontier were reconnaissance and close air support. In the reconnaissance role, a couple of aircraft could perform the mission faster and better than a cavalry regiment. RAF light bombers were substituted for heavy artillery and provided effective close air support. In short, air power served as an effective force multiplier. Aircraft also proved to be flexible. Light bombers could carry supplies and fly wounded men back for medical care as well as bomb the enemy.

The employment of air power by other colonial powers in the interwar period paralleled the British experience. General Maxime Weygand, the French commander in Syria after World War I, was enthusiastic about using air power to police the colonies.[9] The directives he issued to his air units in 1924 very much resembled the British air control doctrine. Aircraft were used to bomb tribal groups to intimidate them into compliance with the French regime.[10]

France fought a major campaign against rebels in Morocco (the Rif war) from 1923 to 1925 and in Syria (the Druze revolt) from 1925 to 1927. Both campaigns were conventional wars that required large ground forces and were fought as joint operations.[11] In Morocco, at the height of the Rif campaign in 1925, the French army deployed thirty-six battalions supported by ten air squadrons that flew almost two thousand sorties per month.[12] As with the RAF in Iraq, the primary uses of air power were in reconnaissance, artillery spotting, and close support. The French proved innovative in their use of air power. In Morocco, they relied heavily upon aerial resupply to maintain isolated garrisons. By keeping forces deep in the Rif, the French were able to inhibit rebel operations.[13] The use of aerial photography for mapping was also an important contribution of air power.[14] In Morocco, the French established the first large-scale aerial medical evacuation system system. The French air service modified light bombers to carry wounded personnel and formed air detachments with the sole mission of evacuating the sick and wounded.[15] During the fighting in 1925, the French evacuated 987 wounded and sick soldiers to rear hospitals by air.[16] The system did not just save many soldiers' lives; simply knowing that good medical care was quickly available provided a tremendous morale boost for the colonial soldier.

In the early 1920s, there was considerable enthusiasm within the military and political leadership about the potential of air forces to suppress colonial banditry and insurgency quickly and cheaply by bombing the rebels' home villages. In Iraq, the RAF even bombed tribes for nonpayment of taxes, even though the Colonial Office in London considered this policy to be a bit heavy-handed.[17] Officially, the RAF announced that it would bomb rebellious areas only after warnings were issued so that civilian casualties would be minimized.[18] However, officers in the field often preferred that bombing take place without warning so as to get the maximum psychological effect from an air attack. This was a variation of the standard argument justifying the bombing of civilians used by the major air power theorists of the interwar period: in the long run, casualties and costs were lower in war if the maximum shock effect by aerial bombardment was inflicted at the onset of hostilities. The expectation was that the shock effect of bombing would quickly break rebel morale.

At first, the British were able to carry out bombing operations with little public outcry because Kurdistan, Aden, and the Northwest Frontier were all isolated regions. On the frontiers of the empire, one could punish whole tribes or villages without many questions asked by the press or Parliament. But by the 1930s, the traditional heavy-handed methods of keeping native peoples in line were no longer acceptable to the public and home government. Senior British officials in India, including the viceroy, disliked the air control doctrine and argued that bombing villages and attacking civilians in order to punish a tribe for the actions of some of its bandits were not only morally doubtful, but also politically risky. Such actions were likely to increase the hatred that the border tribes felt for the British.[19] By the mid-1930s, the policy of air policing in the colonies was quietly ended.

One reason for ending the air policing doctrine was that its effectiveness was clearly diminishing. Although bombing tended to have a significant psychological effect the first time it was used, it had less effect once it became a common tactic. During the Kurdish revolts in Iraq in the 1920s and 1930s, the British found that rebels subjected to months of aerial bombing effectively learned how to adapt to British air power. The rebels camouflaged their bases and hid by day and moved at night, so they could not be observed by aerial reconnaissance. They dug bomb shelters that were impervious to anything but a direct hit, and they organized a ground observer corps to spot incoming aircraft and provide warning.[20]

Colonial air power operations ought to have provided some valuable military lessons for the major powers. But the actual effect on air power thinking for conventional warfare was minimal. In the colonies, the British and French air forces had conducted joint air-ground operations very competently. Yet at the outbreak of World War II, the RAF and the French air force were incapable of conducting joint operations against the Germans. Moreover, even though the importance of air transport had been demonstrated time and again in colonial warfare, neither the French nor the British possessed a specialized air transport force. Finally, the colonial campaigns ought to have taught the European air forces that civilian populations were less vulnerable to aerial bombardment than the theorists had predicted.

THE EARLY COLD WAR ERA

During World War II, air power had evolved dramatically in its capabilities. At the same time, the theory and practice of insurgency and revolutionary war also changed. In the immediate postwar era, the Western powers would face a series of threats that were far more serious than the prewar colonial insurgencies. In the 1920s and 1930s, Mao Zedong developed the doctrine of "people's war" in which Marxist insurgent leaders first organized the population and developed a strong shadow government. The next step in this process was to initiate a guerrilla war and refrain from risking their fighting forces against the government's regular forces as the insurgents built up their strength. After creating a strong political and military base and wearing down the government forces by guerrilla action, the insurgents would move to the final phase of conventional war. For the next several decades, the Western powers and their allies would face several variations of people's war.

In the post–World War II era, the wrecked countries of Europe and the Western colonies in Asia that had suffered through Japanese occupation provided fertile ground for powerful communist insurgencies ready to employ their own versions of people's war. Britain and France also faced a much stronger form of nationalism in their colonies. In several colonies, notably Indochina and Malaya, nationalists guided by a version of communist ideology were able to exploit the long-repressed sentiments of the population and found strong support to overthrow the colonial regimes.

During the Second World War, the Western powers had covertly sent arms and military trainers to help partisan groups in occupied territory. The fact that those groups were often organized by the communists was irrelevant to military leaders focused on defeating the Axis powers. Thanks to these covert Allied operations, by the end of the war there were large, well-trained, and well-equipped communist partisan forces in Greece, Malaya, the Philippines, and elsewhere. These groups were now ready to use the postwar disorder as an opportunity to seize power.

Greece

The first major postwar confrontation between communism and the Western powers took place in Greece. During the war, the communists had created substantial partisan forces and controlled a large part of the country. In the fall of 1944, the Germans withdrew, and British and Greek exile forces landed in Athens. In short order, a full-scale civil war broke out between the communists and the pro-Western Greek royal government supported by the British. At first, the British and Greek forces concentrated around Athens were hard pressed simply to hold out, but over time British air power in the form of RAF Spitfire and Beaufighter fighter-bombers played a big role in defeating the insurgent attacks.[21]

Once the rebels were defeated in Athens, the Greek government reestablished its control in the country with British support, and a truce was established. But in 1946, war broke out again between the Greek government and the communists. In many respects, it was a war by proxy between the West and the Soviet Union, as the communists received military aid from the Soviet Union sent through its Yugoslavian and Albanian allies, and the Greek government was supported by Britain and America. Although the British helped the Greeks reestablish their army and air force, the Greek military of 1946 was in poor shape to fight insurgents. It was badly trained and organized, suffered from mediocre leadership, and performed poorly against the insurgents in the early fighting. The communists soon controlled large parts of central and northern Greece.[22]

The Royal Hellenic Air Force (RHAF) had been organized during the Second World War from Greek air units that had escaped the invasion of their homeland.[23] In 1947, the British delivered two hundred surplus aircraft to the RHAF, including Spitfires, C–47 transports, Anson transports, and light liaison aircraft.[24] By the middle of 1947, the force had grown to five thousand officers and men. The Greeks' problem at this point lay not in resources but in the ability of their commanders to coordinate joint operations effectively.

The British government, bankrupted by the Second World War, found itself unable to maintain its support for the Greeks as their situation deteriorated. In early 1947, the British asked the United States to take over strategic responsibility for Greece. The American response was outlined in a speech to Congress by President Harry S. Truman in March 1947. The Truman Doctrine was a commitment to provide aid, training, equipment, and military advisers to support friendly nations threatened by communist subversion. For the next decades, the Truman Doctrine would be a core part of American counterinsurgency policy.[25]

Although the American public opposed the idea of sending U.S. combat troops to fight in Greece, it strongly supported providing aid to help the Greeks fight their own war. U.S. aid included large amounts of equipment and supplies for the Greek military, along with six hundred military trainers and advisers. Although the British could no longer assist Greece, the RAF left behind 150 personnel to help train and advise their Greek counterparts. Between those personnel and the U.S. advisers who arrived in 1947, the RHAF had over 250 British and American personnel to support its efforts.

A turning point in the conflict came in late 1947 when Truman appointed U.S. Army General James Van Fleet as the head of the U.S. military mission to Greece. Van Fleet, who had been a dynamic corps commander in World War II, concentrated his efforts on pushing the Greek leaders to reorganize and reform the armed forces. Following Van Fleet's advice, the Greeks established a force of elite infantry battalions to conduct offensive operations against the communists, while a large home guard force secured the rear areas against guerrillas. On Van Fleet's advice, better military commanders were appointed. American advisers helped the Greek staffs plan and coordinate joint operations.

In 1949, the Greek communists made the strategic mistake of fighting conventional battles rather than a guerrilla war. Hoping to break the Greek army's morale by inflicting massive casualties, the communists established strong defensive positions in the rugged Vitsi and Grammos Mountains. But this gave the Greek government the opportunity to use its heavy firepower in the form of artillery and aircraft to methodically destroy the rebel strongpoints. Supported by the RHAF's flying T–6 trainers, which spotted targets for the artillery and air strikes, the Greek army reduced the communist defenses. Heavy-fire support was provided by forty surplus Curtis Helldiver dive-bombers supplied by the United States. During the final campaign in the Grammos Mountains from August 24 to 29, the RHAF flew 826 attack sorties.[26] The communist forces collapsed, and the survivors retreated to exile in Bulgaria and Albania.

THE PHILIPPINES

On the other side of the world, the newly independent Philippines also faced a communist insurgency in the form of the Huk movement. The Huks, who had fought the Japanese as guerrillas during the Second World War, exploited the long-term grievances of the Philippine peasantry to organize a large-scale insurgency against a weak government. As in Greece, the American response was to provide aid, military equipment, and advisers to the Philippine government. In 1947, a Joint Military Advisory Group was established, and two officers who served with the advisory group, U.S. Air Force (USAF) Lieutenant Colonel Edward Lansdale and U.S. Army Major Charles "Bo" Bohannan, were instrumental in defeating the Huks.[27] Both had a sound understanding of counterinsurgency warfare: Lansdale knew the Philippines well and specialized in psychological warfare, and Bohannan was an authority on unconventional warfare.

The Philippine military responded in a heavy-handed manner. Heavily armed Army units swept into rebel areas, and the Philippine air force, equipped with surplus American F–51 fighters, bombed rebel villages. These early attempts to crush the insurgency by force actually contributed to the dissatisfaction of the peasants with their government.[28]

As the insurgency grew, the U.S. and Philippine governments changed their strategy to emphasize reform of the Philippine economy and military and to deal with the just grievances of the peasants.[29] A turning point was reached when the highly capable Ramon Magsaysay was appointed defense secretary in 1950. Magsaysay, supported by American advisers Lansdale and Bohannan, reorganized the army to concentrate on civic action projects. Generous amnesty conditions were provided to rebels who surrendered. Those who resisted were relentlessly hunted by elite light infantry units supported by the Philippine air force.

The Philippine air force deployed its squadrons as task forces to support regional military districts, and each district had a small air force of liaison, transport, and fighter planes to support the ground forces. Light aircraft kept rebel areas under constant observation. Aircraft also flew psychological warfare missions, dropping leaflets and broadcasting messages over rebel areas. The surveillance and psychological operations, when combined with pressure from ground forces, were highly effective in demoralizing the Huk rebels.

Since the Huk campaign was essentially a low-level guerrilla war, there were few cases of dramatic employment of air power such as had occurred in Greece. The Philippine air force supported the army in the campaign. Reconnaissance planes provided intelligence and kept pressure on the rebels. Transport aircraft quickly flew army units into isolated areas to reinforce any major efforts. When firefights occurred between Huk forces and army units, aircraft were on call to provide effective close air support.[30] The Philippine government regained control of the countryside and pushed the Huk rebels deep into the jungle and away from the population. By 1954, the insurgency was defeated.

MALAYA AND BRITISH COLONIAL OPERATIONS

From 1948 to 1960, British, Commonwealth, and Malayan government forces fought and defeated a Maoist-style insurgency in Malaya. As with Greece and the Philippines, many insurgents were former wartime guerrilla fighters. The insurgency, supported mostly by the large Chinese population of Malaya, was led by the communists and rooted in legitimate economic and political grievances.

For the first three years, the British countered the insurgency with a massive increase in military and police forces and large-scale military sweep operations. Despite such an application of force, attacks on the British and casualties to British and Malay forces increased, and the rebel numbers continued to grow. The first years of the insurgency included the application of heavy aerial firepower in the form of Lincoln heavy bombers that blasted large sections of jungle where rebels were believed to be hiding. Even though the British dropped one thousand tons of ordnance, there is no evidence that the jungle bombing actually inflicted any casualties on the rebels.

By early 1952, Malaya had become a quagmire for the British. However, that year marked the start of a dramatic turnaround when the British government sent a new leadership team to Malaya headed by General Gerald Templer, who served as both military commander and governor-general. Templer instituted a series of major political and military reforms. To deal with the legitimate grievances of the Chinese community and its unfair exclusion from the government of the Malay states, Templer instituted a strategy to bring more Chinese into the government and armed forces. He resettled civilians away from areas of strong insurgent activity, gave them land, and provided government services. The intelligence system was overhauled and the Malay police and army reformed. Templer's political reforms effectively reduced insurgent support among the population.[31] With better trained and led military and police forces, supported by better intelligence, Templer put the insurgents on the defensive.

Because the Malayan insurgency featured mostly small unit actions, there was little scope for major strike operations. Air power proved most useful in the support role. Air transport enabled the British and Malay forces to maintain garrisons deep in the jungle, and for the first time in a counterinsurgency campaign, helicopters saw extensive use. RAF and Royal Navy helicopters were used to lift light infantry units deep into previously inaccessible jungle areas where they could engage the guerrillas in their strongholds. These tactics denied guerrillas a place of sanctuary where they could train and regroup.

Another major feature of the campaign was the use of aircraft in psychological operations. The RAF mounted loudspeakers on transports and flew them over known rebel areas, broadcasting prerecorded messages that encouraged rebel units to accept the amnesty conditions offered by the government. Many rebels who surrendered said that these broadcast messages had convinced them to accept the amnesty. Such operations were key in defeating the insurgency by 1954.[32] When Malaya became independent in 1957, the once-powerful insurgency had been reduced to a handful of guerrillas hiding deep in the jungle.

FRENCH COUNTERINSURGENCY CAMPAIGNS

INDOCHINA

From 1946 to 1954, the French fought to retain their colonies in Indochina against an exceptionally well-organized nationalist movement led by Ho Chi Minh. Having been driven out of their colonies by the Japanese during the Second World War, the French were at a huge disadvantage in trying to reestablish their power after the war. To put it simply, the French never had the troops, aircraft, or funds to try to maintain a colonial empire on the other side of the world against a very capable and determined opposition. The fundamental strategic problem was that no European power could realistically maintain a colonial empire in the face of the nationalist movements that spread across the third world after World War II.

The Vietnamese insurgents, under the military command of General Vo Nguyen Giap, fought the better war. Sometimes the Viet Minh fought a guerrilla war of ambush and raid and avoided open battles. At other times, they concentrated their forces and fought conventional battles. Although the French deployed large forces to Indochina and had a conventional firepower advantage, it was always a case of too few soldiers and aircraft for too much territory.[33]

The final act for France in Indochina came about as a result of overestimating the capabilities of air power and underestimating the enemy's resourcefulness. In 1954, the French decided to establish a large force deep in Viet Minh territory at Dien Bien Phu and to maintain the force by air supply. The Viet Minh responded by concentrating their forces and secretly transporting large numbers of antiaircraft guns through the jungle and mountains and emplacing them in the hills overlooking the French garrison. It was an action that the French had discounted as impossible. When the Viet Minh began their offensive, their antiaircraft guns and artillery fire on the French airfield made it impossible for the French to fly in supplies and reinforcements. After a siege of several weeks, the garrison of over ten thousand troops surrendered. French recognition of Vietnamese independence came soon afterward.[34]

ALGERIA

Conditions were very different for France as it battled a nationalist insurgency in Algeria from 1954 to 1962. Although Algeria and its vast majority of Muslim inhabitants were treated by the French as a colony, legally Algeria was part of metro-politan France. Because Algeria had more than a million ethnically French settlers and had long been France's premier possession, the French government committed the best part of the armed forces to fight the *Front de Libération Nationale* (FLN) rebels. At the height of the French counterinsurgency campaign, from 1957 to 1959, more than 450,000 French soldiers, sailors, and airmen were serving in Algeria. In addition to these forces, tens of thousands of Algerian Muslims served in government-organized home guard units. A large part of the French air force was deployed to support operations in Algeria. The Algerian War also saw the large-scale use of helicopters: the conflict is notable for being the first to employ helicopters modified as gunships.

In most respects, Algeria is a good model for the effective use of air power at the tactical and operational levels. With overwhelming forces and plenty of air power, the French had a huge military advantage in Algeria. Key to the French strategy was to aggressively seek out the FLN rebel forces operating mostly in the countryside. The rugged mountainous areas of Algeria provided good shelter and plenty of hiding places for the rebels. Because of the nature of the terrain, air power was an essential element of French operations. The French divided Algeria into districts and ensured that each district commander would have his own force of reconnaissance and strike aircraft as well as helicopter units available.

The French approach to counterinsurgency relied on an extensive communications network. Joint air-ground operations were key, and several joint operations centers were set up to coordinate operations. Each district commander had an air control center and an aerial support brigade to provide for logistics, aircraft maintenance, and base support.[35]

The French strategy was to saturate a district with troops and systematically clear it. T–6 reconnaissance planes kept areas of rebel activity under constant surveillance. When rebel forces were spotted, helicopter units quickly brought light infantry units into the remote areas to set up blocking positions and cut off the rebel detachments. When the French brought the FLN to battle, their forward controllers could quickly bring strike aircraft and heavy firepower to the scene. Faced with this degree of mobility and firepower, FLN units caught by the French had little chance of survival.

In December 1958, President Charles de Gaulle appointed air force general Maurice Challe as commander in chief in Algeria. Challe, an exceptionally capable commander, refined the air command and control system and created a force of three divisions that carried out systematic operations to clear whole regions of the FLN. Using his air power advantage was a key element to Challe's strategy, and more than four hundred helicopters made Challe's offensive force highly mobile. Helicopter groups were organized into detachments ("combat cells") of seven heavy H–21s and one light Alouette helicopter for command and reconnaissance. These units could rapidly move companies in two shifts.[36] Using light infantry and helicopters for mobility, Challe's offensive force sought out and destroyed the FLN forces in several districts. French civic action detachments moved in behind the mobile forces to ensure the countryside would stay pacified.[37] By the end of 1959, thousands of rebels had been killed, large swathes of the countryside had been cleared of insurgents, and FLN morale had collapsed. By early 1960, Challe's innovative and aggressive strategy had broken the FLN as a military force.[38]

But in counterinsurgency, military victory does not necessarily mean strategic victory. Although the French clearly won the Algerian war militarily, by 1960, the French nation was tired of paying a heavy price to keep Algeria. Peace negotiations with the FLN rebels soon led to a French decision favoring Algerian independence. Having won all the battles, the French nonetheless withdrew and gave the Algerians their independence in July 1962.

THE SOUTHEAST ASIAN WARS

Vietnam

America's longest counterinsurgency experience was in Vietnam. From the birth of the South Vietnamese state in 1955 to its collapse in 1975, the United States played a central role in South Vietnam's conflict with the Viet Cong guerrillas and the North Vietnamese army.

The American involvement in the Indochina war began in 1955 when a small U.S. advisory and training mission was deployed to South Vietnam to help the new government of Ngo Dinh Diem. The initial American commitment to South Vietnam was made in the context of the Truman Doctrine, later adopted by the Eisenhower administration, which emphasized military aid to threatened nations while avoiding the commitment of American combat forces.

While popular at first, President Diem managed to alienate many of South Vietnam's political and religious factions by the late 1950s, and he faced a major insurgency. As the situation deteriorated, the Americans poured in increasing amounts of military aid. By the time the John F. Kennedy administration came into office in 1961, the plight of South Vietnam was seen as a major challenge. The Kennedy administration dramatically increased the levels of military support to South Vietnam. In answer to President Kennedy's call for a more dynamic response to the threat of communist subversion, the USAF stood up a special warfare unit tasked with the mission of training and advising foreign air forces. The USAF group, soon renamed "Air Commandos," was deployed to South Vietnam in late 1961. For the next three years, the United States would build up the South Vietnamese Air Force (VNAF) and train it in army support operations. The South Vietnamese were equipped with an array of surplus American airplanes, including heavy helicopters and the A–1 Skyraider fighter-bomber—a rugged and dependable propeller plane that proved extremely effective in the counterinsurgency role.[39] By 1964, the VNAF had grown into a capable strike force of ninety-two A–1 Skyraiders with a cadre of well-trained pilots, and it began to conduct strike missions in support of the South Vietnamese army.[40]

Despite the increased American aid, South Vietnam's strategic position deteriorated after Diem was deposed in November 1963. In early 1965, President Lyndon Johnson decided to deploy large American combat forces to South Vietnam and to "Americanize" the war. Although the U.S. military had the recent successful experiences of Greece and the Philippines as models for counterinsurgency operations, most U.S. military and political leaders discounted the traditional counterinsurgency approach and preferred to treat the Vietnam conflict as a conventional war. The American leadership believed that the center of gravity in Vietnam was not the indigenous insurgency, but the communist state of North Vietnam, which supported the insurgents. The Joint Chiefs of Staff and key presidential advisers such as Walt Rostow advocated an air campaign to destroy strategic targets in the North. They promised a quick end to the insurgency by swiftly destroying the North's warmaking potential. Thus began a bombing campaign that lasted for three years. In addition to the bombing of North Vietnam, the USAF and Navy carried out a massive interdiction campaign to cut the flow of supplies moving from North Vietnam through Laos to the South.

Treating Vietnam as a conventional war was a strategic mistake of the first order. The bombing campaign failed badly in its goal to cripple the North's ability to wage war. North Vietnamese morale remained high despite the heavy air attacks, and plenty of troops and supplies from the North were flown into South Vietnam. In the South, American troops supported by U.S. air power inflicted massive casualties upon the North Vietnamese army and Viet Cong. However, the downside of American tactical success was the indiscriminate use of firepower throughout much of South Vietnam. This resulted in many casualties among the same South Vietnamese population that the United States had pledged to protect.

At a relatively late point in the conflict, 1969, U.S. leaders changed their strategy, and the U.S. military turned its attention to building up the South Vietnamese forces. Previously, this had been considered a low-priority mission, and more than a decade into the U.S. training and advisory effort, most of the South Vietnamese army was still poorly trained and equipped. As U.S. forces began withdrawing from Vietnam in 1969, they turned the war over to the Vietnamese, who were largely unprepared. After years of U.S. involvement, some South Vietnamese units were effective, but most were consistently poor performers. The U.S. advisory efforts, which never received the full support of the U.S. military establishment, were not able to overcome the serious internal flaws of the South Vietnamese army.[41]

In contrast to the South Vietnamese army, the VNAF's combat performance throughout the war was very good. By 1968, the VNAF had expanded into a force of 362 aircraft and 16,000 personnel. The Tet offensive of 1968 was a major test for the VNAF that it passed with high marks when it flew more than four thousand close support sorties in January and February 1968.[42]

As the United States turned more of the war over to the South Vietnamese, the VNAF quickly expanded into a force of several thousand aircraft. When the North Vietnamese mounted a major offensive in early 1972, the VNAF flew thousands of sorties in support of the South Vietnamese army.[43] It was an outstanding effort, and the North Vietnamese army was so badly battered that it was unable to carry out any major offensive operations for the next two years. Shortly afterward, the last of the U.S. forces were withdrawn from South Vietnam. Yet despite its capable air force, South Vietnam remained a country with enormous internal weaknesses. South Vietnam collapsed in 1975 not to insurgents but to an armored blitzkrieg executed by North Vietnamese regular forces.

THAILAND

At the same time as the United States suffered a strategic defeat in Vietnam, the Thais, supported by the Americans, waged a highly successful counterinsurgency campaign against communist rebels in Thailand's northern provinces. Unlike the case in Vietnam, a commonsense approach prevailed in Thailand. There was no attempt to Americanize the war there, and the American involvement was limited to training, advice, and providing equipment. From the start, the counterinsurgency effort was much better organized than that in Vietnam, and in 1966, a single U.S. official was placed in charge of all programs to support the Thais. In short, there was better unity of effort and interservice coordination than ever existed in Vietnam.

In Thailand, a small number of military advisers, along with U.S. Agency for International Development civilians, supported the Thai government's efforts to combat a growing insurgency.[44] In contrast to the conventional war approach in Vietnam, the Thais developed a strategy based on civic action programs and on building local defense forces. The key to the Thai effort was a long-term strategy to develop the northern provinces and provide security for the local population. The USAF advisers encouraged the Thai efforts to employ classic counterinsurgency techniques rather than the highly kinetic warfare preferred by most senior American officers in Vietnam. After the U.S. forces left Vietnam, American military advisers remained in Thailand. Their low-key approach was highly successful, and although the communists won in South Vietnam, they were in decline in Thailand.

COUNTERINSURGENCY IN LATIN AMERICA

EL SALVADOR

Failure in Vietnam made Congress and military leaders highly reluctant to commit U.S. forces to a counterinsurgency campaign. When a major Marxist insurgency, supported by Cuba and Nicaragua, broke out in El Salvador in 1980, the U.S. response was limited to providing aid, training, and advisers. Congress limited the number of U.S. troops in the country so severely that most of the U.S. effort consisted of training the Salvadorans outside the country.

In El Salvador, the U.S. military got it right. There was no belief that the conflict could be won quickly or by conventional means. The U.S. military applied classic doctrine and worked with the Salvadoran government to develop a strategy for remedying the severe economic and social problems that generated the insurgency. The Salvadoran military's serious problems of leadership, corruption, and lack of training and equipment were addressed by a long-term U.S. plan to rebuild and retrain the Salvadoran forces.

The Americans began their involvement by developing a comprehensive strategy to fight the insurgents. In 1981 and 1982, the Pentagon and State Department put together a strategy that emphasized economic aid (of $5 billion in U.S. aid to El Salvador from 1981 to 1992, $4 billion was economic aid and $1 billion was military aid) and fundamental reforms of the Salvadoran government and military. Over a twelve-year period, the U.S. military advisers worked patiently to transform a poorly trained and led military into a very capable organization.[45]

The effort to build a capable Salvadoran air force took up a large part of the U.S. military aid. The force in 1981 was a motley collection of old planes, many of them barely flyable. The U.S. Army and Air Force set out to help the Salvadorans to expand their air force from less than two thousand personnel to over five thousand. Salvadoran pilots and personnel were trained in the United States and at U.S. bases in Panama. By 1984, the Salvadoran air force had more than one hundred aircraft, mostly U.S.-supplied UH–1 helicopters and some modified A–37 trainers that served as strike aircraft.

The improvement in the Salvadoran air force had a major impact on the military side of the war. By 1984, the U.S. training efforts began to pay off when the Salvadoran military proved that it could conduct joint operations and coordinate effective air support for the ground troops. Supported by the air force's helicopter squadrons, the army could respond quickly to rebel attacks and reinforce threatened sectors. The helicopter force also enabled the Salvadoran army to take the offensive against the rebel strongholds in previously inaccessible mountain areas. Constant surveillance by light reconnaissance planes inhibited rebel movement and had a strong effect on lowering insurgent morale. Old transports, such as the C–47, were converted into gunships and proved to be highly accurate and effective close air support systems.

After 1985, government forces were in the ascendancy. The training and leadership reforms and the receipt of new American equipment made a notable improvement in the combat effectiveness of the Salvadoran forces. Although the insurgency dragged on, the *Frente Farabundo Martí para la Liberación Nacional* rebels understood that the opportunity for a military victory had long passed. After years of negotiations, a peace settlement was reached in 1992, which resulted in rebel disarmament and the incorporation of the former rebels into a democratic party system.

Colombia

Since the 1960s, Colombia has faced two major insurgencies. Fueled by revenue from the illegal drug trade, the two main insurgent groups, *Fuerzas Armadas Revolu-*

cionarias de Colombia (FARC) and *Ejército de Liberación Nacional*, became quite powerful by the 1990s. As in El Salvador, the United States has supported Colombia as a long-term ally and has provided the Colombian military and national police forces with equipment, training, and logistics support. The U.S. military commitment to Colombia remains limited, and the four hundred U.S. military trainers and advisers in the country are not permitted to take part in combat operations.

The insurgencies in Colombia, which are of the classic Maoist type, were ascendant until 2000 when the Colombians and Americans agreed upon a long-term counterinsurgency strategy: "Plan Colombia." Under the plan, the United States gave Colombia $1.3 billion in aid,[46] part of which went to helping the Colombians stand up elite counterdrug battalions. Another major portion of Plan Colombia was aviation support; the United States provided Colombia with several dozen helicopters to support the elite light battalions.[47] All aircraft provided by the U.S. aid program came with training and logistics support, and the Colombian flying personnel were trained by the USAF at the Inter-American Air Force Academy in Texas.[48]

The Plan Colombia strategy of 2000, followed by the "Plan Patriota" strategy of the Colombian government, were important steps in providing the government with the right kind of forces to aggressively pursue the rebel groups. After 2002, the enlarged Colombian forces, equipped with arms and aircraft from the United States, went on the offensive against the rebel forces.[49] The Colombian air force and the aviation arms of the national police and the army have carried out well-coordinated joint operations against the rebels that included paratroop drops, helicopter-borne infantry operations, and air support with precision munitions. Thanks to successful operations that have cleared large areas of rebels, the Colombian death rate dropped dramatically between 2000 and 2005. Colombian police and military operations increased and rebel attacks declined. By 2008, the once-powerful rebel FARC group had been reduced to 60 percent of its 2000 strength.[50]

In the first decade of the twenty-first century, Colombia's air force has emerged as a model of effective counterinsurgency operations by a small nation. Although Colombia's decades-long war with the Marxist insurgents has not yet been won, the Colombian government continues to make progress.

SOVIET-RUSSIAN COUNTERINSURGENCY OPERATIONS

The fairly sophisticated counterinsurgency strategies and employment of air power in El Salvador, Colombia, and Thailand stand in contrast to the Soviet-Russian approach to counterinsurgency. From 1979 to 1989, the Soviet Union found itself embroiled in a bloody counterinsurgency campaign against tribesmen in Afghan-istan. From 1995 to the present, the Russian Federation has waged a ruthless war against separatist insurgents in Chechnya. In both campaigns, the Russians have em-phasized the use of air power and technology against insurgents, and both campaigns illustrate the limitations of technology in counterinsurgency.

AFGHANISTAN

When the Soviet Union invaded Afghanistan in 1979, Moscow expected the oper-ation to replace the Afghan government with one more amenable to its interests to be short.[51] To the surprise of the Soviets, the overwhelming majority of Afghans rejected the puppet government installed in Kabul and took up armed resistance. Soon, the 110,000 Soviet troops in the country found themselves confined to heavily fortified enclaves in the midst of a hostile land.

The Afghan tribes, which had the advantage of living in one of the most rugged and isolated pieces of terrain in the world, carried on a guerrilla war of ambush, raid, and harassment of Soviet bases. The armor-heavy Soviet army of 1979 was confined to operating in the few areas in Afghanistan that had roads. However, the Soviets quickly adapted and transformed their force in Afghanistan into a helicopter-mobile army. They expanded their heliborne forces and deployed their elite special warfare units. New tactics were developed around helicopters, and the Mi–8 and Mi–6 transport helicopters and Mi–24 helicopter gunships performed very well. With greater mobility, the Red Army took the fight to the rebel mountain strongholds.[52] Yet despite heavy losses, the Afghans continued the struggle against the Soviets.

Frustrated at fighting a no-mercy guerrilla war, the Soviets retaliated with a ruthless policy of bombing Afghan villages. The suffering of the Afghan population was immense. Most estimates put the number of Afghans dead in the hundreds of thousands, and more than two million Afghans made the dangerous trek across the mountains to live as refugees in Pakistan. For their part, the Soviets may have lost as many as twenty thousand.

Despite all the advantages of modern weaponry and the massive application of air power, the Soviets were unable to pacify the Afghans. The Afghans developed good tactics of their own and received weapons and aid from the West, including Stinger antiaircraft missiles, through neighboring Pakistan. The Stingers forced the Soviets to use their air power more cautiously. By 1985, the war had become a quagmire for the Soviets, and they began withdrawing their troops. By 1989, the Soviet troops had departed, and Afghanistan was left in the hands of warring factions.

CHECHNYA

In 1991, as the Soviet Union collapsed, the small region of Chechnya in the Caucasus declared independence. The new Russian state refused to accept Chechen independence, but for four years the Chechens and Russians maintained a truce. In 1995, war broke out when the Russians sent in armored forces, supported by fighter-bombers, to take the Chechen capital of Grozny. Although outgunned, the Chechens managed a brilliant defense of Grozny and dealt some heavy defeats to the Russians. The poor performance of the Russian troops demonstrated the steep decline in military capabilities since the Soviet era. Attacks were poorly coordinated; tactics themselves were poor. The Russians needed a long period to reorganize their forces after the initial battles. The Russians then put Grozny under siege and eventually occupied the city, but not before many of the Chechen insurgents had retreated to the mountainous areas to carry on a guerrilla campaign.[53] As in Afghanistan, the Russians in Chechnya relied heavily on firepower and brute force. There was little care taken to minimize civilian casualties, and Grozny was a complete ruin by the time the Russians occupied it. Still, Chechen morale remained high, and resistance continues to this day in the mountainous regions of southern Chechnya.

POST-COLD WAR INSURGENCIES

In many respects, the insurgencies since the 1980s have been different from those from the 1940s to the 1980s. Most insurgencies of the earlier era were of the Maoist type and were motivated primarily by nationalism and the desire for political reform. The Maoist insurgencies tended to have strong central organizations. Some post–Cold War insurgencies, such as Colombia's, still follow the Maoist model. But with the end of the Cold War, the primary motivators for insurgents and terrorists became long-standing ethnic and religious tensions, such as the ones motivating the current insurgencies involving Lebanese Shiites, Afghan tribesmen, and al Qaeda supporters in Iraq. Unfortunately, such conflicts tend to be waged with a higher intensity of passion. Another characteristic of contemporary insurgency is that the insurgent organization tends to be built around local groups and leaders, which work together in a loose network with other local groups.[54]

Israel's campaign against Hezbollah in Lebanon from 1982 to 2007 provides a good example of the new conditions faced by a counterinsurgent and some of the problems of employing air power. In the aftermath of the Israeli invasion of Lebanon in 1982, which culminated in the siege of Beirut and the destruction of the Palestine Liberation Organization (PLO) as a military force, the Israelis occupied part of southern Lebanon as a security zone. The Israelis found themselves the targets of a guerrilla war waged by Hezbollah, the organization of the Lebanese Shiite population that lived mostly in southern Lebanon. The Israelis used their large and modern air force to carry out precision strikes against Hezbollah training camps, command centers, and infrastructure inside Lebanon. Although such strikes had worked against the highly centralized PLO, the same strategy was ineffective against the more decentralized Hezbollah.

A strategy of precision air strikes requires modern technology, careful planning, skilled employment of joint forces, and excellent intelligence—all strengths of the Israeli forces. The Israeli Air Force campaign against Hezbollah inflicted heavy casualties, but for every lost member, there were many more recruits ready to join. The air campaign failed to produce a deterrent effect or any crippling damage to Hezbollah.[55] On two occasions, the Israelis used their air power to take out top Hezbollah leaders, but even these strikes failed to produce strategic effects. The organization was less vulnerable to such attacks because it was directed by a council and could replace lost leaders quickly. Its units were not dependent upon a central organization and had considerable leeway to conduct their own small raids.

Hezbollah never expected to defeat the Israelis in a pitched battle. Its strategy was to inflict a steady rate of casualties upon the Israelis and break the Israeli will to stay in Lebanon. In order to kill a small number of Israelis, Hezbollah was willing to accept heavy casualties. By 2000, the Israeli government had failed to make progress against Hezbollah, and under strong public pressure Israeli forces were withdrawn from southern Lebanon, which was ceded to Hezbollah control.[56]

In the summer of 2006, after a series of rocket attacks and cross-border raids by Hezbollah, Israel launched a six-week campaign to break its forces in southern Lebanon. A series of precision air strikes against Hezbollah targets was followed by a ground invasion by the Israeli army. The Israeli Air Force was to be the main player in the campaign, but Israel had greatly underestimated the size and sophistication of Hezbollah's huge rocket arsenal and put too much faith in the ability of its air force to cripple Hezbollah. Therefore, too few ground troops were readied for the invasion of southern Lebanon.

There were also major failures on the part of Israeli intelligence, and these failures are still being analyzed by the Israeli forces. Hezbollah forces were larger and better prepared than the Israelis had expected.[57] Although the Israeli Air Force hit many known Hezbollah targets, Hezbollah remained an effective fighting force. The army's progress into the Hezbollah strongholds was slow, even with strong air support. Over six weeks, Hezbollah was able to fire thousands of rockets at Israeli civilian targets, and the Israeli Air Force could do little to stop the bombardment.[58] Although

Hezbollah suffered heavy casualties and eventually accepted a truce, it could credibly claim a moral victory for standing up to overwhelming Israeli air power and surviving.

AIR POWER IN AFGHANISTAN AND IRAQ

In late 2001, American air power played the leading role in defeating the Taliban regime in Afghanistan. A handful of U.S. special forces personnel coordinated precision air strikes for America's outnumbered Afghan allies fighting the Taliban and al Qaeda. These indigenous forces, supported by American air power, quickly occupied most of Afghanistan without the commitment of significant U.S. ground forces. Popular defense analysts and many USAF leaders argued that the brilliant performance of American air power and high-tech weaponry in Afghanistan in October to December 2001 signified a "New American Way of War"—a revolution in warfighting in which America could leverage its air power and technological superiority to defeat enemies swiftly while using minimal ground forces.[59]

But a few weeks later, in the mountains of eastern Afghanistan, Taliban and al Qaeda forces demonstrated that they could adapt to American air power tactics. Al Qaeda fighters effectively hid their fighting positions from the Coalition's huge aerial surveillance effort. The USAF identified less than half of the numerous al Qaeda fighting positions before the Tora Bora offensive was launched.[60] When the fight began, some Coalition forces walked into al Qaeda traps. Although Coalition ground and air forces inflicted heavy casualties on al Qaeda forces, many escaped to fight again.

In Afghanistan in 2001 and in Iraq in 2003, American and Coalition air power proved decisive in initial conventional war operations. However, after the opposition factions turned to insurgency, traditional counterinsurgency tactics proved necessary. Allied air power, to include sophisticated unmanned aerial vehicle surveillance systems and pinpoint strike capability with precision munitions, has been an important weapon in Afghanistan and Iraq. But counterinsurgency remains a manpower-intensive form of war, and the primary role of air power in both Afghanistan and Iraq has been to support the ground forces.

One area where the Western air forces have performed poorly has been in the effort to help the Afghan and Iraqi governments to build their own air forces. In both countries, the effort to train and equip indigenous air forces started late and has remained very small.

The effort to create an Afghan air corps began in the spring of 2006. More than four years after the Hamid Karzai regime was established, a handful of U.S. advisers began training an Afghan air corps as an adjunct to the Afghan army.[61] While there has been generous support to help build an Afghan army, minimal support has been available for Afghan aviation.[62] For the foreseeable future, Afghanistan will be almost completely dependent upon the United States and Western nations for air support.

A serious effort to develop a new Iraqi air force began only in 2006 when the USAF set up an advisory squadron to train Iraqi air force personnel.[63] As of mid-2008, the Iraqi air force had only eighty aircraft, including helicopters and training planes.[64] An American report of late 2007 assessed the Iraqi air force as an organization that had low morale and was plagued by a high desertion rate.[65] Currently, the Iraqi air force has not even a fraction of the transport and strike capabilities it will need to support its forces in the ongoing campaign against insurgents. These minimal results in Afghanistan and Iraq stand in very dramatic contrast to the USAF assistance programs of the past.[66]

In promoting the idea that air power has revolutionized warfare, the USAF leadership has generally ignored the mission of training and equipping allied nations. In August 2007, the USAF published a counterinsurgency doctrine that extolled its high-tech capabilities and ignored the training and advisory mission.[67] In contrast to the Air Force position, the U.S. Army and Marine Corps in December 2006 published a counterinsurgency doctrine that stressed traditional counterinsurgency concepts and argued that "developing effective host nation security forces is one of the highest priority counterinsurgency tasks."[68] The Army-Marine doctrine included an annex on the use of air power in counterinsurgency that outlined the principles of training an allied air force.[69] The differences between the more traditional approaches to counterinsurgency favored by the Army and Marines and the high-tech approach favored by airmen will likely remain an issue of contention in the next decade.

AIR WAR, COUNTERINSURGENCY, AND THE MODERN MEDIA

Since the Algerian war, insurgent groups have shown themselves very adept at manipulating the media of the third world and the West in order to present the insurgent cause in a favorable light and the counterinsurgent forces as cruel aggressors. The use of air power by the counterinsurgent force is consistently held up as excessive and aimed primarily at civilians. Even precision air strikes carefully planned to minimize collateral damage are commonly characterized in the media as indiscriminate warfare. Insurgents have often managed to portray air power in a negative light and gain propaganda victories out of military defeats. For example, the 1982 Israeli bombing of PLO targets in Beirut, which was carefully restricted to clearly military targets, was referred to as "terror bombing" and "indiscriminate bombing of

Muslim civilians" in much of the world's press.[70] Israel's 2006 campaign in Lebanon was countered by a sophisticated propaganda campaign waged by Hezbollah and its supporters in the world's media. Outrageous claims of indiscriminate Israeli bombing were accompanied by doctored photos and inflated claims that fifteen thousand houses in Lebanon had been destroyed by bombing. Indeed, a common Hezbollah tactic has been to deliberately place insurgent forces in the midst of civilians to ensure high civilian casualties and to follow such campaigns with media reports sympathetic to insurgent and terrorist forces.

Similar charges are routinely made that accuse North Atlantic Treaty Organization forces in Afghanistan and Coalition forces in Iraq of indiscriminately targeting civilians. Improbable and unsubstantiated casualty figures presented to the Western and third-world press are often accepted at face value.[71] For example, during the heavy fighting in Fallujah, Iraq, in 2004, insurgents stored munitions in twenty mosques, which were used as fighting positions. Although Coalition air forces in Iraq employed only precision weapons and attempted to keep the damage to mosques to a minimum during the heavy fighting, there was enough destruction to allow the insurgents to paint the Americans as aggressors conducting attacks upon Islam itself.

This type of propaganda, often directed specifically at air power, puts Western airmen in the dilemma of having to choose between gaining the military advantage and losing the propaganda war. Moreover, with air power constantly presented in a negative light, some Western human rights groups and even some Western governments are now pushing for an international ban on various air weapons such as cluster bombs.[72]

CONCLUSION

The lessons of air power in counterinsurgency have been remarkably consistent since 1913. For example, the basic missions of air power in conflict with nonstate forces have changed little since air power was first employed in such operations. Despite the hopes of airmen, the primary role of air power in counterinsurgency is supporting the army and police. Although aviation technology has become highly sophisticated, there is little evidence that air power has changed the fundamental dynamics of counterinsurgency operations. Indeed, insurgents and irregular forces have shown an ability to adapt to the advances in air power technology and find means to limit the effects of air power.

Wars against nonstate forces are very different from conventional wars against states. In fighting insurgencies and irregular forces, military success does not necessarily determine the outcome. While air power technology provides great advantages to the counterinsurgent, success still depends upon having a sound strategy, good leadership, good training, and the ability to coordinate joint operations. All the successful counterinsurgency campaigns contained those elements. On the other hand, the cases of Vietnam and Algeria show that tremendous air power capability cannot overcome a bad strategy.

THE RISE AND FALL OF AIR POWER
Martin van Creveld

WHERE HAS AIR POWER COME FROM, where is it now, and where might it be going? Does independent air power have a future, or is it past its peak? Given the enormous cost that building and maintaining a modern air force entails, as well as the central role air power allegedly plays in national defense, these questions are extraordinarily important. Here, an attempt will be made to answer them by means of a short survey of air power's history, its present situation, and its possible future.

THE BEGINNINGS

Thanks to the vast literature that exists on the subject, the history of air power is easily told. Visions concerning the use of air power in war, some of them extremely sadistic, are probably as old as humanity itself. An early form of air power was used by the Lord when he rained down stones from Heaven on Joshua's Canaanite enemies. During the Napoleonic Wars, English caricaturists toyed with the possibility that the troops of the Grande Armée, complete with horses and guns, would climb into newly invented Montgolfier-type balloons. Waiting for a favorable wind, they would ignore the navy, fly across the English Channel, land at Dover, and proceed to conquer England. Observation balloons were used during the American Civil War, and the French used balloons to fly mail and passengers out of their besieged capital during their war against the Prussians. By the first years of the twentieth century, the majority of the world's most important armed forces incorporated observation balloons into their order of battle almost as a matter of course.

During World War I, observation balloons, usually organized as part of the signal corps, were extensively used both over land and at sea. The idea was to use them to provide surveillance, advance warning, target spotting, and damage assessment. However, in the absence of good portable wireless communications, there were often limits on what they, and the observers they carried, could do. By this time, several countries, with Germany at the head, had also started building rigid, lighter-than-air devices and putting them into service. Such devices differed from balloons in that they had engines and a steering mechanism and thus did not depend entirely on the wind but could be flown in any direction. On many occasions, German dirigibles crossed the North Sea and dropped bombs on English towns, causing some damage and fatalities. However, such were the technological limitations of the time that the raids in question constituted no more than pinpricks and probably cost the Germans more than they were worth.

Invented in 1903, heavier-than-air devices were first used in war shortly thereafter. Some of the very first missions were flown during the Italian-Turkish war when Italian aircraft in Libya conducted reconnaissance and dropped small bombs on their opponents. When World War I broke out, aircraft on both sides quickly took to the air to serve as the "eyes" of their respective armies. A French reconnaissance aircraft was even able to play a critical part in the Battle of the Marne when the pilot observed and reported that the Germans who were approaching Paris had changed direction. Instead of marching southwest, they had turned to the southeast, thus presenting their right flank to the city and enabling the French to counterattack.

From reconnaissance and primitive attempts at bombing—at first, it was necessary to throw the bombs by hand—it was but a small step to air-to-air combat. Right from the beginning, pilots carried handguns for self-defense in case enemy action or a mechanical defect forced them to land in enemy territory. Soon enough, they started using those guns against one another too. Somewhat later, handguns were replaced by machine guns—some aircraft carried two men, the pilot and the gunner—and by 1916, a way had been found to synchronize those guns with the propeller so that they could fire straight ahead. This in turn led to formation flying, intended to provide mutual protection, as well as the development of various air combat tactics. One result of the progressive improvement of aircraft was that lighter-than-air devices proved to be too vulnerable and were driven from the sky.

By 1916–1917, aircraft were being categorized into different types, such as reconnaissance, fighters, close support aircraft (with armor under the front of the body), light bombers, and even heavy bombers capable of carrying a large load deep into enemy territory. Reconnaissance, which increasingly relied on photography instead of the pilots' eyes, was developing at a furious pace. Soon, corps of specialists charged with interpreting the resulting images were formed; down below, the first improvised antiaircraft guns and batteries were being fielded. By the last years of the war, each of the principal belligerents had several thousand aircraft in its order of battle. Since losses, whether to enemy action or accidents, were enormous, sustaining these numbers meant production figures reaching into the tens of thousands. Developing, deploying, supplying, maintaining, and operating those aircraft, as well as training the necessary personnel and directing operations, presented a formidable task. During most of the war, this task was entrusted to a specialized organization within the ground and, in some countries, naval forces. However, on April 1, 1918, Britain took the lead in establishing the world's first independent air force in the form of the Royal Air Force (RAF).

By that time, too, air power had already developed most of the different sorts of missions that were to characterize it to the present day. They included reconnaissance, air-to-air combat, artillery spotting, close air support (both bombing and strafing), interdiction, strategic bombing (in the sense that the targets were civilian and located deep in the rear), and liaison. Looking back, the only important omissions were air transport and airborne operations; both would be developed during the interwar period and play a major role in World War II. Air power was critical in many campaigns from the Battle of St. Mihiel in the west to those of General Edmund Allenby in Palestine. Especially around the British Isles, it helped fend off the German submarine threat. Nevertheless, it would be difficult to point to even one major campaign or battle in which its role was decisive. When all is said and done, air power assisted the ground and naval forces but could not decide the battle in their stead.

Not long after the war ended, the first classic treatise on air power—by Italian general Giulio Douhet (1869–1930)—was published. Originally an engineering officer, Douhet was an early air power enthusiast. In 1912, he was tasked with writing air power lessons learned from the Italian-Turkish war, and a year later he was put in command of his country's first air battalion at Turin. After Italy entered World War I in 1915, he wrote about the incompetence of the high command—which, in view of the terrible attrition suffered on the Isonzo front in the northeast, was not difficult to do. For this, he was sentenced to a year in jail.

In November 1917, soon after the defeat at Caporetto had validated his critique of the Italian army, Douhet was released and placed at the head of the air commissariat. Later he resigned from the army and continued to advocate building a powerful air force. Eventually, in 1921, as part of his advocacy efforts, he published the book *Il dominio dell'aria* (*Command of the Air*). In many ways, the book is a period piece, yet it remains worth reading decades after it was published, and indeed it would be hard to think of any single volume that had a greater impact on air power.

In essence, Douhet's message was simple. The invention of the internal combustion engine had enabled man to fly for the first time. He could do so in all directions regardless of the presence of highways, railways, and other transport arteries. At the same time, he could ignore all kinds of obstacles such as rivers, lakes, mountains, forests, and the like. Compared with the capabilities of the traditional services (the army and the navy), air power had the great advantages of speed, range, and flexibility. Aircraft could concentrate and strike rapidly over long distances, thus making it possible to achieve surprise. Furthermore, these qualities made air power into an offensive instrument par excellence. The enemy would never be able to defend every point; the larger the territory he ruled, the more difficult trying to do so became.

All these were important considerations that have retained their validity to the present day. Douhet, however, went much further. The way he saw it, in the future air power would be able not merely to complement ground and sea forces but also to take their place. Air power provided the means with which the great problem that bedeviled all armies in World War I—namely, how to break through a fortified front—could be solved. Instead it would enable the side best prepared to do so to strike directly at the enemy's vulnerable (read: civilian) rear. Fleets of aircraft, carrying high explosives as well as gas, would take off on the first day and head straight for the enemy's principal demographic and industrial centers. Dropping their bombs, they would inflict so much damage and cause so much panic that the enemy government would be forced to surrender—if, indeed, that government was not first overthrown by a maddened, despairing mob.

Like all great prophets, Douhet pretended that his theories derived from the very nature of his subject matter and thus possessed a universal validity. In fact, they were particularly suitable for a country such as Italy, which, owing to its peninsular shape and the mountains that line its northern borders, experienced difficulty in launching a large-scale attack on its neighbors. The same consideration explains why, consciously or unconsciously, island nations such as Britain and the United States also adopted those theories to a large extent. To the senior military personnel of such nations, Douhet suggested a method by which they could cross the water and get at their continental enemies without need for building an invasion fleet and without having to mount that most difficult of all operations, an amphibious landing. The parallel even extended to personalities. In the United States, the leading contemporary advocate of air power was General William "Billy" Mitchell (1879–1936). Much like Douhet, his reward was to be tried and imprisoned for insubordination in 1925.

Countries that had traditionally relied on their ground forces tended to see things in a different light. In particular, the Germans, though they were familiar with Douhet—his book was translated in 1935, the year in which Hitler unveiled his new

Luftwaffe, and some people read him long before that—did not accept his work in its entirety. Like Douhet, the Wehrmacht high command considered air power primarily an offensive instrument whose effectiveness depended on its speed, flexibility, and, perhaps most important of all, ability to concentrate. Like him, initially they tended to overestimate the effect that bombing civilian targets could and would have. On the eve of World War II, plans were even in place to deal with the tens of thousands of bomb-crazed lunatics that would result from "strategic" bombing; in the event, hardly any materialized.

Unlike Douhet, however, the Germans never considered that air power on its own was capable of winning a war; that could be achieved only by an effective combination of all arms. Following the Clausewitzian idea that the strength of any country lay primarily in its armed forces and that victory should therefore be won by attacking and annihilating those forces first of all, they also rejected the idea that the primary target should consist of enemy civilians. In a sense, what the Germans were saying was that mere civilians were not worthy of being attacked. Instead, the Germans intended to coordinate the Luftwaffe's operations with those of the ground forces. The target should be the enemy's front—this was known as close air support, or CAS—and his zone of communications, including headquarters, bases, transportation arteries, convoys, and the like.

To a large extent, systems of organization reflected each country's geographical position as well as its military doctrine. As already noted, the first country to establish an independent air force was Britain. Counting "great powers" only, it was followed by Italy, France, and, when it started to rearm, Germany as well. In addition to the RAF, Britain also developed a naval air arm—a logical thing to do for a global empire whose very life depended on its maritime communications. By contrast, neither the United States nor Japan established an independent air force. Instead, they divided their aviation between their respective armies and navies. The Soviet Union, with its age-old tradition of overwhelming land power, adopted a somewhat similar system. Here, the air force was an integral part of the Red Army, whereas the navy had its own air arm. In both Germany and the Soviet Union, gliders and parachutists were added to the order of battle, and late in World War II the Luftwaffe even had its own ground divisions. Germany was unique in that the Luftwaffe was also in charge of antiaircraft defense, a fact that probably reflected Hermann Göring's political position as second only to Hitler himself.

Throughout the interwar period, technical innovation proceeded at a furious pace. Lighter-than-air devices all but disappeared. Balloons remained in use only for antiaircraft work (as part of Britain's air defenses against the Blitz and later the V–1) and observation (over the Atlantic, where the Allies did not have to worry about

German aircraft and could therefore use balloons to detect submarines). Monoplanes took the place of biplanes; all-metal craft replaced planes made of wood, wire, and fabric. Engines became steadily more reliable and developed more horsepower per unit of weight. The most important performance characteristics, such as speed, range, ceiling, and climbing rate, steadily improved. So did armament, which gradually came to consist of 20- and even 37-millimeter (mm) cannons rather than simple machine guns. For some types of air-to-ground work, rockets were introduced. Bombs grew larger and heavier, although, since bombing would be carried out from greater altitude and while flying at greater speed, accuracy did not always improve. In the 1930s, Germany and the Soviet Union experimented with airborne forces in the form of gliders and parachutists. Other countries followed suit during World War II.

Finally, in all countries, air transport came of age, as was perhaps most dramatically illustrated in 1936 when Italian aircraft carried Francisco Franco's troops across the Strait of Gibraltar and thus enabled him to start the Spanish civil war. In terms of volume and cost, air transport could not—still cannot—compete with land and sea transport. Other complicating factors were the extreme vulnerability of transport aircraft and their need for fairly extensive ground facilities; hence, rarely could they come very close to the front. As against these disadvantages, air transport did provide exceptional speed and flexibility. In every armed force worth its salt, its place, like that of air power as a whole, was secure.

FROM WARSAW TO BAGHDAD

Though the Italian-Ethiopian war, the Spanish civil war, the Japanese-Chinese war, and the Russo-Finnish war all saw the use of air power, in all of them it was still employed on a relatively small scale, and much of it remained experimental. Not so during World War II, when the scale on which operations was conducted was gigantic and air power really came of age. The very first campaign—the German attack on Poland—showed how far things had come. It demonstrated the ability of the Luftwaffe to gain air superiority, effectively assist the advance of the ground forces, and finally bring a city—Warsaw—to its knees by means of what would later become known as strategic bombing.

The campaigns Germany fought in the West in the spring of 1940 were even more spectacular. First, it was necessary to achieve air superiority, which, given that the French and the British—each in their own way—held their air forces back, did not prove too difficult. Next the Luftwaffe, using interdiction, CAS, and airborne operations in the form of both parachutists and gliders, opened the way into the Netherlands, Belgium, and France. Had it not done so, the German campaigns against those countries might very well have stalled, as had happened in the autumn of 1914. Given the immense superiority that the British navy enjoyed at sea, the April 1940 German campaign against Norway was even more dependent on air power in the form of interdiction, CAS, and airborne operations. Had it not been for the Luftwaffe, that campaign could not have been carried out at all.

From this point on, the role of air power could only grow. First came the Battle of Britain, during which the Germans, having lost much of their navy in Norway, tried to use their air force to bring that country to its knees. Fortunately for Britain, the Luftwaffe had never been built with strategic operations in mind. The bomb loads its aircraft could carry were too small for the task, and those aircraft capable of hitting pinpoint targets (the famous Stukas) were too slow, ill protected, and vulnerable. This, as well as the facts that the Luftwaffe was operating at the far end of its aircrafts' range and the British had radar, enabled the RAF to put up an effective resistance. Though the battle was close run, in the end the RAF inflicted such losses as to break the power of the offensive and force the Germans to desist. Later, having switched from attacks on the RAF to civilian targets, the Germans continued to suffer unsustainable losses. In all, contrary to Douhet's theory, the campaign was a triumph for defensive air power. As Winston Churchill put it, seldom in history did so many owe so much to so few.

Next, confirming and extending lessons that had been learned in Norway and the Low Countries, the Germans carried out an airborne landing in Crete. Receiving very little support from the sea, the campaign in question was probably the most spectacular one of all time; when it was over, Hitler told the Reichstag, "The German soldier can do anything!" In fact, so heavy were the invaders' casualties that even Hitler did not care to repeat the experiment against Malta. Barely a month later, operations in Crete were dwarfed by the German invasion of the Soviet Union. Taking the enemy by surprise, during the first four days alone the Luftwaffe destroyed some eight thousand enemy planes, most of them on the ground. It thus opened the way to an impetuous ground advance that, six months after it had started, brought the Wehrmacht to the gates of Moscow.

After Pearl Harbor led to the U.S. entry into the war, the conflict assumed global dimensions. But for air power, to which the Germans, lacking any form of naval aviation, did not really have an answer, the submarine war in the Atlantic might very well have ended differently, with Britain forced to surrender owing to lack of food, raw materials, and oil. But for the very effective forms of air power, especially torpedo aircraft, that Japan had developed during the interwar years and tested in China, its expansion into the Pacific and Southeast Asia would have been utterly impossible. Later, American air power, both land- and sea-based but always closely coordinated with naval forces in particular, played a critical role in the advance that pushed the Japanese back onto their home islands. Air power, mainly in the form of CAS and interdiction, also played an important role in the titanic struggle between the Wehrmacht and the Red Army. First the Luftwaffe enjoyed air superiority, and then, toward the end of the war, the Red Army gained the advantage. The role of air superiority in the war between Germany and the Western Allies was, if anything, even greater, albeit that it was considerably more effective over flat, open terrain of the kind found in North Africa and Western Europe than it was over the mountains of Italy.

Depending on geography, strategy, technology, and industrial capability, some belligerents developed air power to a greater extent than others did. Between them, however, they used it in all possible forms and in all possible combinations. Though the war against Japan differed from that against Germany and Italy, in both cases land- and sea-based air power was used on an enormous scale. Operations ranged from land-based to carrier-based; from attack to defense; from reconnaissance to surveillance; from liaison to the use of light aircraft as flying command posts; from CAS to interdiction; and from transport to airborne assault. On at least one occasion (the Red Army's encirclement of German troops on the Eastern front in 1941–1942, known as the Demyansk pocket), a considerable ground force was kept alive for several months from the air alone. By contrast, the attempt to do the same at Stalingrad failed. For a time, transport aircraft flying over the "Hump" provided the only link between the Allies and China. Had it not been for the superior air power at their disposal, the Allied landings in Sicily, Salerno, Anzio, and Normandy would have been impossible. On the other hand, air power also had its failures, as happened at Arnhem in September 1944.

Though the Battle of Britain ended with a defeat for the Luftwaffe, Douhet's theories concerning the utility of strategic bombing were confirmed to a considerable extent on other occasions and in other theaters. Whereas, in 1941, British air attacks on the German homeland resulted in more casualties among the air crew than among the civilians below, May 1942 saw the RAF mounting its first "thousand aircraft" raid, which left much of the city of Cologne in ruins. In 1943–1945, thousands upon thousands of British and American bombers systematically set out to smash Germany to pieces. They attacked first cities, then industrial installations, then oil refineries, and finally transportation centers. Starting with the U.S. Strategic Bombing Survey of 1945–1946, the precise role air power in general, and strategic bombing in particular, had played in bringing the Third Reich to its knees has been hotly debated by historians. Yet to anyone who has seen images of Berlin in the immediate aftermath of the war, when for miles around the city center not one building was left with an intact roof, there can be no doubt that the role in question was very great indeed.

Distances in the Pacific were greater than in Europe, which meant that Allied air power took a longer time before it could make its impact felt. However, during the last months of the war, Japan also was subjected to a vast strategic bombing offensive that systematically reduced its cities to ashes. The coup de grace of that offensive came in August 1945. First Hiroshima and then Nagasaki were incinerated from the air, with casualties numbering in the hundreds of thousands. Thereupon, all Japan could do was surrender. Robert Oppenheimer, the man who built the bomb, described his handiwork with a quotation from the Bhagavad-Gita: "Now I am become Death, the destroyer of worlds." Air power, it seemed, had attained a position where it was literally capable of ruling the world. Put just a few bombs on any target, and any kind of opposition would be evaporated.

Instead, rather than finally vindicating Douhet's belief in the ability of air power to decide wars with little or no assistance from other forces, August 1945 proved to be the point from which that power (and, to a large extent, conventional war as understood from the Stone Age on) went into decline. Certainly this was not for lack of effort, investment, or ingenuity. Already during the last months of the conflict itself, the Germans put the first jet aircraft into service. Within a few years, those aircraft had relegated almost all propeller-driven planes to the scrap heap. Leading the development, combat aircraft kept growing larger, faster, and better armed. But so did transport aircraft, reconnaissance aircraft, and every other kind of aircraft that air forces need in order to operate and fight. Starting in the late 1950s, antiaircraft guns were to a large extent replaced by surface-to-air missiles so that the former remained in use only for defending pinpoint targets against low-altitude attacks. Fighter aircraft, too, began to be armed with air-to-air and air-to-surface missiles. The introduction of helicopters after 1945 provided air forces with an ability to take off and land without the need to prepare extensive ground facilities first. However, in terms of speed, carrying capacity, and cost, helicopters never approached the capabilities of fixed-wing aircraft.

Above all, this was the missile age. The Germans in World War II had built and used both missiles and cruise missiles on a very large scale, even though, given how inaccurate these devices were, they probably cost more than they were worth. Once the war had ended, development of these weapons, often supported by German scientists, engineers, and technicians, continued. During the 1950s, all the most important countries started incorporating ballistic missiles into their arsenals. By the end of the decade, missiles had acquired sufficient range to enable air power to expand from the atmosphere into outer space. As more and more Earth-circling satellites were put into orbit, they assumed increasing importance for weather prediction, reconnaissance, surveillance, damage assessment, navigation, communication, and a variety of similar missions.

Most important of all was the development of surface-to-surface missiles, some of them with intercontinental range capable of reaching almost any point on Earth from any other. Unlike manned aircraft, which could be intercepted in the air or shot down from the ground, these missiles could not be stopped while making their way to their targets. Provided their bases were mobile, or else properly concealed or hardened, they were also extremely difficult to destroy before they were launched. The very power of air power, its ability to "put an end to civilization as we know it," as the phrase went, was now beginning to work against it. As Bernard Brodie, probably the most prescient post-1945 strategist, was one of the first to point out, a weapon so powerful that it cannot be countered cannot be used either. Rather, using it is tantamount to suicide.

As one might expect, air force commanders everywhere did not simply acquiesce in this situation. For several decades, they spent fortunes as well as immense intellectual capital trying to find ways to make the most powerful weapons at their disposal usable without necessarily turning the world into a radioactive desert; in the end, however, they did not succeed. While more and more states acquired nuclear weapons and their delivery vehicles, not one of them ever made use of those weapons. Instead, most found themselves increasingly constrained in their relations with other states.

Still worse from the point of view of those responsible for running their respective countries' air power, as missiles became the principal instruments for putting nuclear weapons on target, there really was no compelling reason why those missiles should be part of the air force, or, indeed, why the air force should be independent of the other services. For example, already in World War II, it was the German army, not the Luftwaffe, that developed, built, and operated the V–2 ballistic missile. By the time the war ended, production of the missile had come under the SS (which, given its commander's vast ambition, might in time have come to supervise its deployment and use as well). In 1948, the U.S. Navy, afraid of being outclassed by the newly formed Air Force, demanded and obtained its own nuclear-capable aircraft. Later, the same navy pioneered a submarine-launched missile force almost as capable of putting warheads on targets as the Air Force was. Insofar as submarines were easier to defend than land-based missile bases, it was a superior force. One superpower, the

Soviet Union, split its air force into two: a tactical one and a strategic one. The latter
was put in charge of both long-range bombers, of which the Soviets had but a few,
and intercontinental ballistic missiles, of which they had a great many. Whatever the
merits of this particular arrangement, it certainly showed that there was more than
one way to do things and that putting "everything that flies" under the command of
a single service, as Hermann Göring once formulated it, was not necessarily the only
possibility or even the best one.

Unable to use the most powerful weapons by far at their disposal against the
most powerful enemies by far, air forces turned their attention to lesser operations.
As they did so, one generation of aircraft, missiles, and (perhaps most important)
electronic equipment succeeded another. The speed of aircraft, their range, their
service ceiling, their ability to climb, and, from about 1975 on, their maneuverability
(which earlier generations of jets tended to sacrifice in favor of speed) all increased
by leaps and bounds. Nevertheless, though things became much more complicated
and sophisticated, in many ways there was no fundamental change. Following the
system that had emerged from World War II, air power was still usually divided into
strategic, operational (meaning interdiction), and CAS, although in truth only one
country now retained a sufficient number of heavy bombers to mount any kind of
strategic air offensive at all.

As the Korean War, the October 1973 war (when cloud cover was one of the
reasons that prevented the Israelis from launching a preemptive strike against Syria in
particular), and Kosovo proved, the effectiveness of air power continued to depend
to some extent on the terrain and the weather. A conventional force that did not have
air power; that lost it at the beginning of hostilities (as happened to the Egyptians in
1967 and the Iraqis in 1991) or that did not know how to operate it properly found
itself in great difficulty. On the other hand, seldom if ever did air power on its own
bring about victory. The Middle East wars, the Indo-Pakistani wars, the Falklands
war, and the wars in the Persian Gulf came and went. Until at least and including
1991, on the whole, they brought little that commanders such as Albert Kesselring,
Adolph Galand, Hugh Dowding, Charles Portal, Ira Eaker, "Hap" Arnold, and the
rest would not have recognized and, after some study, mastered.

While the quality of aircraft and their ancillary systems was improving all the
time, quantitatively the situation went downhill after 1945. To cite just one example
of the way things were moving, at the height of World War II, the U.S. Army Air
Force numbered four million men and women. Half a century later, the U.S. Air
Force (USAF) has barely one-eighth that number. In 1944, one military aircraft was
coming off America's assembly lines every five minutes on average. By contrast, in the

whole of 1995, the United States, as the sole "hyperpower" left on Earth, produced only 127 of them, transports and helicopters included. Some of the aircraft the USAF did operate were decades older than the pilots who flew them. Conversely, as Air Force Chief of Staff General Merrill McPeak told this author in 1993, so slowly did the acquisition of new aircraft proceed that those who would one day fly them were still in kindergarten at the time the procurement was authorized.

In part, the decline was owing to the fact that some missions previously carried out by manned aircraft were being overtaken by missiles and, later, unmanned systems such as remotely piloted vehicles (RPVs) and the like. In large part, however, it was because proliferating nuclear weapons prevented major war from breaking out among the major powers—a major power being defined as one that either already possessed nuclear weapons or was capable of fielding them so quickly that it hardly mattered. Coming on top of these considerations was the question of cost. As the fate of, first, the Soviet Union and, currently, the United States shows, so expensive were many of the new weapon systems, not just airborne ones but ground- and sea-based ones as well, that no country could really afford any number of them without bankrupting itself in the process.

With the use of air power (and of conventional war as a whole) now confined almost entirely to wars between, or against, third- and fourth-rate states, perhaps it is no wonder that theory stalled. To focus on the USAF as the most important air force of all, as late as the 1980s it was still framing the debate—close support and interdiction on the one hand versus "deep" strategic bombing on the other—in terms that came straight out of World War II, if not before. There was, indeed, precious little in the vaunted AirLand Battle that the Luftwaffe had not practiced in 1939–1941. Every so often, some self-styled genius would cause a stir with some new theory as to how new aircraft and missiles were revolutionizing warfare and how air power could and should be used. One day it was missiles that were supposed to bring about the change, the next, helicopters. However, in most cases, it turned out that there was less to their theories than met the eye.

During the entire period, perhaps the thinker who came closest to devising a new "paradigm," as theorists like to say, was USAF Colonel John Warden (1943–). The way Warden saw it, the factor most responsible for the change was precision-guided munitions (PGMs). Given proper intelligence and command and control (with many of those functions supplied by, or assisted from, outer space), those munitions should be capable of being used with such precision, and to such effect, as to obliterate the distinction between "strategic" on the one hand and "operational and tactical" on the other. The way to proceed was to divide targets into "rings," of which the innermost one was formed by the enemy's command and control facilities and the outermost one by his armed forces. With stealth aircraft and PGMs leading the way, those rings should be attacked from the inside out, spreading first paralysis, and then, if that did not work, destruction. In this way, Warden argued, Clausewitz could and should be stood on his head. The old airman's dream, which goes back all the way to Douhet himself, of smashing the enemy and winning the war from the air alone would finally be realized.

In 1991 in Iraq, and again in 1999 in Kosovo, Warden's theory was put to the test. Arguably, in both cases, it worked—but only against opponents who turned out to be so weak that they were hardly able to put up any kind of opposition, and then only after weeks of attacks by fleets of aircraft mightier than any that had been assembled since World War II or are likely to be assembled in the future. Furthermore, in neither campaign was the victory complete. In the case of Iraq, it turned out that air power was unable to complete the job so that the actual liberation of Kuwait had to be carried out by land forces maneuvering on the ground more or less as they had always done. In the case of Kosovo, it later turned out that the Serb army, taking cover, had remained largely untouched. Though President Slobodan Milosevic did surrender, this was not so much because of the effectiveness of the North Atlantic Treaty Organization's air campaign but because Russia, which was then at the nadir of its political-economic standing, withdrew its support.

As for Warden himself, his reward for his innovative theories was the one so often reserved for prophets of his kind. He was denied promotion and finally sent into retirement. To that extent, his fate merely reflected that of his predecessors Mitchell and Douhet.

AIR POWER VERSUS GUERRILLAS

While Cold War–era air warriors, as well as their fellows in the ground and naval forces, continued building forces for fighting each other but were increasingly prevented from putting those forces to use by their own enormously powerful weapons, an altogether different form of war was spreading and making its impact felt. Over the decades, the names that were applied to this form of war varied: banditry, irregular war, partisan war, people's war, revolutionary war, brushfire war, low-intensity war, guerrilla war, asymmetric war, terrorism, and insurgency, to mention but a few.

As these and other names show, the wars in question were extremely varied— more so, perhaps, than the regular interstate wars whose place they have increasingly usurped. Still, it is precisely by contrasting them with interstate war that one may get at least a superficial impression of what they are all about. Their first and most important characteristic is that they are *nontrinitarian*. By this I mean that the classical division into a government that runs the war, armed forces that fight and die, and a civilian population that pays and suffers does not exist in the same form. Instead, all three elements of the trinity are mixed with one another; indeed, the fact that they are mixed, and thus to some extent are beyond the enemy's reach, constitutes one very important factor in their long run of successes.

Second, these forms of war constitute the weapon of the weak against the strong. From this proposition, as well as the previous one, everything else follows. Being weak, insurgents, terrorists, guerrillas, freedom fighters, and the rest cannot afford to set up regular armed forces (which, in turn, is one very important reason why they ignore the trinity). Lacking this capacity, they cannot engage in a strategy of annihilation but are obliged to rely on attrition and protracted warfare (*On Protracted Warfare*, not *On Guerrilla Warfare*, is the original title of Mao Zedong's treatise on the subject). The same reason explains why, other than at the lowest tactical level, they must disperse their forces and hide among the civilian population and rely on it for their supplies; why most of their operations are conducted by stealth; why it is hard, if not impossible, for them to obey the international law of war; and so many other things that have been discussed so often by so many people that it is unnecessary to repeat them.

Such, then, are the most important characteristics of the wars in question. But how has air power fared *against* them? On the whole, the answer is: very badly indeed. If counterinsurgent, counterguerrilla, and counterterrorism operations, and the like have anything in common, it is this: in over one hundred such struggles since 1945, with hardly any exception, the regulars, or occupants, or counterinsurgents, or "forces of order," or whatever names they chose to call themselves, had absolute or near absolute command of the air.

Take, for example, RAF efforts in the Palestinian Arab revolt of 1936–1939. Whether the RAF, in its conduct of "air police" operations in Iraq immediately after the First World War, was really as effective as its heads (who were fighting to establish their service on an equal footing with the two older ones) claimed will not be discussed here. Suffice it to say that, when the Palestinian Arabs rose in revolt, the RAF, which was in charge of security in the country, was unable to cope with the uprising as, quoting its alleged success in Iraq, it had promised to do.[1] RAF aircraft certainly provided intelligence concerning insurgents. However, they often could not do so early enough and in sufficient detail to enable those insurgents to be brought to battle and destroyed; on other occasions, they were hampered by the weather. RAF aircraft escorted military convoys making their way by road but were unable to provide cover at all times owing to their limited endurance. RAF aircraft engaged guerrillas, dropping bombs and firing their machine guns, but too often, instead of destroying them, they merely caused them to hide and disperse. RAF aircraft also performed a variety of other tasks such as liaison, casualty evacuation, and the like. Except for villagers armed with World War I–vintage rifles who sometimes took potshots at them, the aircraft in question were totally unopposed. Still, they did not succeed in overcoming the insurgency.

In 1937, the British themselves drew conclusions from these facts. Ever since the Mandate was created in 1922, overall responsibility for the defense of Palestine had been in the hands of the RAF. Now it was taken away and transferred to the army and, behind it, the War Office. Two army divisions, complete with some artillery and armored cars, were sent to put down the insurgency. In charge were some of Britain's most promising commanders, such as Generals John Dill and Bernard Montgomery, both destined to rise to the position of chief of the Imperial General Staff. To be sure, the RAF continued its operations—but this time as an auxiliary and not as the main operator.

In the end, the results were mixed. Having killed over five thousand Palestinian Arab insurgents (and losing no more than two hundred of their own troops) and inflicted vast destruction, the British did succeed in crushing the revolt, militarily speaking. Yet insofar as victory had to be bought by political concessions, the job was clearly incomplete. When the government of Neville Chamberlain published its White Book in 1939, it granted almost all Palestinian demands, even including "evolution towards independence" within ten years.

The most important aircraft used by the RAF in these operations was the Gloster Gladiator. It was a 3,000-pound biplane with an 850-horsepower engine and a top speed of 250 miles per hour, and it was armed with machine guns mounted under the lower wings. Other aircraft carried bombs and dropped them. To be sure, this was a far cry not only from later supersonic jets, but also from the most advanced fighters of the time, such as the British Hurricane. Still, given that they faced no enemy in the air and that opposition from the ground was negligible, the Gladiators were not without advantages. They could take off and land from short, simple airstrips without any need for elaborate ground facilities. They were easy to maintain and operate, which translated into the ability to fly numerous sorties within short periods of time. They were slow enough to be capable of escorting ground forces on the move (just try to imagine an F–16 doing that) and extremely maneuverable. This gave them an advantage when it came to shooting guerrillas in the kind of closed terrain the latter preferred. Last but not least, each sortie flown did not cost a fortune. For all their comparative disabilities, the aircraft of the time were in many ways well suited for the purpose they served.

To a large extent, the story written by the British forces in Palestine in 1936–1939 was repeated by the German occupiers in the Balkans and the Soviet Union in 1941–1944. Perhaps because combined arms had always been their motto, the Germans, unlike the British, never had any illusions that air power on its own was capable of holding down "bandits." Far more than the British, who always maintained some scruples and feared indiscriminate slaughter would only make the population more determined to resist, the Germans were prepared to do whatever they thought it would take. That the Luftwaffe did not use its first-line aircraft in combating "bandits" is self-evident—those aircraft were put to better use when it was supporting the great offensives of 1939–1942, and later, when it was desperately trying to resist the Allied air attack on Germany proper. Yet given that, especially in the Balkans, the Luftwaffe enjoyed absolute command of the air, the aircraft it did use were powerful enough. For example, though the Stukas were too vulnerable to operate against Britain's Spitfires, they could and did deliver accurate firepower against Josip Broz Tito's partisans. As in the case of the Gladiators, compared with what was to come later, they even enjoyed considerable advantages.

Shall we continue to spin this sad story? For any reader who is even slightly familiar with the history of warfare from 1945 on, surely doing so is unnecessary. All the most important air forces of the world were busily preparing to drop nuclear bombs on each other's countries. All the most important air forces also prepared to wage conventional war against each other. However, afraid as they were of nuclear escalation, in reality they were only able to fight against third- and fourth-rate opponents.

Even as they did all this, the British in Palestine, Malaysia, Kenya, Cyprus, and Aden enjoyed absolute command of the air. The same applies to the French in Indochina (except for Dien Bien Phu, where the Viet Minh used antiaircraft artillery provided to them by the Chinese) and Algeria, the Americans in Vietnam (except when flying over North Vietnam), the Soviets in Afghanistan, the Israelis in Lebanon, and so many other cases that it is easy to lose count. Almost every time some new technical device appeared and was incorporated into air forces— be it jet engines, swept-wing fighters, air-to-ground missiles, helicopters, electronic gear, heads-up display, forward-looking infrared radar, whatever—it was quickly put to use in counterinsurgency too. Yet neither technical innovation nor command of the air brought victory to the air forces in question. And neither, of course, did the tremendous expenditure and effort that backed those air forces and made them possible.

Each time a "counterinsurgent" was defeated and sent packing, there were many explanations as to why he had failed to achieve his goals. Now, the air force was not given enough independence, meaning that ignorant ground commanders misused its capabilities. Now, it was given too much, meaning that it did not coordinate with the ground forces as it should. Now, it was decided that the aircraft the counterinsurgent used, having been designed to fight others of their kind, were not suitable for counterinsurgency operations. On other occasions, they *were* deemed suitable, only to be "micromanaged" from the top and "set up" for defeat. Some claimed that, to speed up the observe, orient, decide, and act (OODA) loop and succeed in catching the "nimble" guerrillas, a dedicated air force with its own fighters, transport aircraft, helicopters, intelligence, signals, and airborne units needed to be formed. Others responded that in World War II, the Luftwaffe *did* operate units made up of all kinds of different aircraft and *did* have airborne troops under its own command. To cite but one example, Operation Rösselsprung, in January 1944, made use of such troops. Yet it still did not succeed in defeating the Yugoslav partisans against which it was directed.

These and similar questions might be subject to debate. Still, almost everybody agreed that the most powerful instruments at the disposal of modern air forces— their high-performance combat aircraft—were hardly ideal for counterinsurgency missions. See Indochina and Algeria, where the French operated both fixed-wing aircraft and helicopters, whereas their enemies did not have a single such machine in their order of battle. See Vietnam, where the most powerful fleet, made up of the most powerful aircraft ever fielded to that time, dropped six million tons of bombs, twice as many as were dropped on Germany and Japan together during World War II, without being able to avert defeat. See also Iraq, where U.S. air power has played only a very limited role since President George W. Bush proclaimed the end of "major combat operations" in May 2003, to say nothing of current operations in Afghanistan.

Perhaps the most interesting case in point is Israel's 2006 war against Hezbollah in Lebanon. During the first few days, its F–15s and F–16s, flown by personnel widely believed to be the best of their kind in the world, operated very effectively indeed.

They succeeded where Norman Schwarzkopf and Charles Horner in 1991 utterly failed, destroying almost all the enemy's long-range (sixty-mile) missile launchers within minutes after they were discovered. However, during the remaining forty days of the war, those same machines, flying thousands of sorties, achieved little. Pitted against thousands upon thousands of relatively small, mobile, well-concealed, short-range Katyusha rockets, they were virtually helpless. Whereas each rocket cost only a few hundred dollars at most, the price tag of each F–15 or F–16 stood at perhaps $40 million to $100 million, with operating costs in proportion. Merely training a pilot to be capable of operating these machines takes years and costs millions. Under such circumstances, all an air force can do is to increase the national debt of the country in whose name it operates.

What applies to air power applies a fortiori to outer space. Half a century after the launch of Sputnik, space has become vital for the conduct of both nuclear and conventional air warfare. This fact is reflected in the growing number of countries that launch Earth-circling satellites as well as the increasing amount of space junk flying about. Nevertheless, half a century after the launch of Sputnik, satellites still do not shoot. Whether, some day, they will be provided with weapons that enable them to do so is moot. Given the expense of operating in space, putting weapons in it makes little sense unless those weapons can deliver a big bang indeed. On top of this, space-based weaponry may in some ways be more vulnerable to enemy action than its ground- or sea-based equivalents. On the other hand, we have long possessed what it takes to destroy any point on Earth from practically any other. If so, why bother with space? Even if weapons are based in space, though, firing them in the direction of Earth, whatever else it may achieve, is extremely unlikely to be helpful in combating terrorists.

As counterinsurgents went from one defeat to the next, attempts were made to solve, or at least alleviate, these problems by the use of new technologies such as helicopters, RPVs, and, most recently, unmanned aerial vehicles (UAVs). On the face of it, these vehicles are much better suited to counterinsurgency operations than are high-performance fighters. This is because they are smaller, slower, more maneuverable, capable of getting closer to their targets (which often translates into greater accuracy), and, in the case of RPVs and UAVs at any rate, cheaper and more dispensable, so that their loss is more easily tolerated. Precisely because they are all those things, though, they raise the question whether they should really be part of the air force. Suppose, as is often the case, that the main threat is insurgency and its various cousins. Suppose, too, as some analysts claim, that the most important problem in combating insurgency is how to shorten the counterinsurgent's OODA loop. If these propositions are true, one may well wonder whether an independent air force is still needed at all.

As if to clinch the argument so far, amid the wasteland of failed counterinsurgency campaigns here and there, it *is* possible to find insurgencies that were successfully combated and, ultimately, defeated. Two very good, if radically different, examples are the "Troubles" in Northern Ireland (1969–2003) and the Syrian suppression of the Islamic revolt in the city of Hamma in January 1982.[2] Except for the British use of helicopters and RPVs, air power played no role at all in these struggles. Indeed, as of the writing of this chapter in April 2008, in the United States, there were claims that the USAF was not doing enough to assist the Army and Marines in Iraq and Afghanistan.[3] Caught between the various forms of asymmetric warfare, in which it is of very limited use (and in which, if it is to be of greater use, it might very well be reabsorbed into the ground forces) on the one hand, and nuclear warfare (which it can wage only at the cost of committing suicide, and which in any case is much more likely to make use of surface-to-surface missiles) on the other, air power clearly is in real trouble. Whoever tries to deny this is merely putting his head in the sand.

TOWARD THE END OF AIR POWER?

The time: summer 1996; the place: a congress hall in Canberra, Australian Capital District; the occasion: a conference to honor the seventy-fifth anniversary of the Royal Australian Air Force (RAAF); the subject: air power 2020. In front of some three thousand servicemen and women, this author, making use of some of the above arguments, said that, in 2020, there probably would not be any air power. To the audience's great credit, they received the message not merely with good humor but with considerable applause. Perhaps this was because they knew that, by that time, almost all of them would be retired.

We are already halfway through the period in question. To what extent is the prophecy on its way to being realized? A look at the RAAF provides part of the answer. In all those years, it has neither shot down a single enemy aircraft nor purchased a single new combat aircraft. Accordingly, the number of such aircraft in its order of battle has gone down from 106 to 72. For the United States, the corresponding figures are 3,002 and 2,159. For China, they are 4,600 and 2,785; for Germany, 360 and 269; for Japan, 360 and 263; for Singapore, 137 and 101; for India, 778 and 738 (excluding naval aviation); and for Israel, 449 and 335. It would thus seem that, in most of these forces, wear and tear is causing the order of battle to go down by about 3 percent per year. In the case of Russia, according to an interview with Foreign

Minister Igor Ivanov published in the Israeli paper *Yediot* on April 11, 2008, the number of new military aircraft purchased went down from 100 in 1992–1997 to just 2 in 2000–2007. It is true that advances in air-to-air and air-to-ground missiles as well as electronics have made many of the aircraft available in 2006 much more capable than their predecessors. This presumably means that, if they are ever going to clash, attrition will bring operations to an end within just a few days—after which the only "airborne vehicles" that people will have left to fight each other with will be kites.

While the number of combat aircraft has been going down, that of space vehicles, surface-to-surface missiles, helicopters, RPVs, and UAVs has been rising sharply. Without a doubt, all these have increased the ability of air power to reach its targets and destroy them many times over. With the exception of space vehicles, though, there really is no convincing reason why they should be part of an independent service. Except perhaps for those with the longest range (which can also serve as space launch vehicles), surface-to-surface missiles can be (and are being) deployed equally well by armies and navies. The same applies to helicopters, RPVs, and UAVs. Supposing that twenty-first-century wars will be mainly of the low-intensity kind, as postulated above, there probably is no compelling case for independent air power at all.

To be sure, depending on size, geography, strategic interests, and so on, different countries will handle these questions in different ways. No single formula, no single system of organization will satisfy them all. In a way, it does not matter. With every passing day, the steadily declining number of combat aircraft means that the "core" mission of air forces everywhere is being eroded. Those ignoring this process do so at their own peril.

AIR AND SPACE POWER: CLIMBING AND ACCELERATING

Richard P. Hallion

A CENTURY HAS PASSED SINCE the advent of the military airplane, and almost a century since the establishment of the world's first air force. Invented in 1903, adopted by the military in 1908, flown in combat in 1911, the airplane proliferated and matured at a rate remarkable even by the standards of the electronic revolution of the same century. And in much the same fashion that the computer's potential impact was largely missed—in 1945, a prominent member of a National Research Council study committee stated baldly that the United States would never need more than five or six electronic computers, missing the American computer market of a half-century later by a factor of tens of millions—the airplane's impact upon military affairs was, likewise, something few foresaw or appreciated.[1]

A TROUBLED BIRTH

Developers and demonstrators of new technology typically encounter skepticism or derision, and in aeronautics it was ever thus. In August 1783, when Benjamin Franklin watched the ascent of a small unmanned hydrogen balloon over Paris as a "technology demonstrator" by scientist J. A. C. Charles and the brothers Jean and Noël Robert, an onlooker remarked, "Of what possible use is it?" Franklin shot back, "What is the use of a newborn babe?"[2] The babe grew quickly: the balloon gave humanity its first "off-the-planet" observational vantage point, and not surprisingly, the balloon was soon adopted for military purposes. In April 1794, France's Committee of Public Safety organized the world's first aerial combat unit, and the following month it went to war for *"l'observation des marches et mouvements des enemis."*[3] At the Battle of Fleurus on June 26, 1794, aeronaut Jean Coutelle and General Antoine Morelot remained aloft in the balloon *l'Entreprenant* for nine hours, observing enemy forces and dropping messages to be carried to French headquarters. Aided by this primitive intelligence, surveillance, and reconnaissance (ISR) system, French forces were overwhelmingly victorious over their Austro-Dutch foes in the most crucial battle of the revolutionary period.[4]

More than a century later, with the balloon now an accepted commonplace, attention turned to its successor, the airplane. In the 1890s, both the French and American governments recognized its potential value, particularly since, unlike the balloon, it was not at the mercy of the winds. Two remarkable political figures, France's Charles-Louis de Freycinet and America's Theodore Roosevelt, launched the first attempts to develop military airplanes. From this sprang the *Avion III* of Clément Ader and the "Great Aerodrome" of Samuel Langley. Each failed to fly, though both are, fortunately, preserved in museums for study and examination.[5] Their failures, and those of other pre–Wright Brothers pioneers, hardened skeptics; when invited to join the Aeronautical Society of Great Britain, British scientist Lord Kelvin crushingly replied, "I have not the smallest molecule of faith in aerial navigation other than ballooning, or of expectation of good results from any of the trials we hear of."[6]

But he was, of course, wrong. A revolution in propulsion, structural concepts, and aerodynamic theory was under way, and within just a few years, the Wrights flew at Kitty Hawk. To indicate how surprising its development was, just two years previously, futurist H. G. Wells, an aviation enthusiast, had written, "Long before the year 2000 A.D., and very probably before 1950, a successful aeroplane will have soared and come home safe and sound."[7] Less than five years after their first flight, the Wright brothers designed, built, and flew the world's first military airplane, demonstrated by Orville Wright at Fort Myer, Virginia, in 1908, coincident with Wilbur Wright's demonstrating their designs in Europe. Even so, skepticism persisted. In 1910, attending an air show in France, Ferdinand Foch, arguably the most distinguished military theorist of his time, dismissed the airplane as having "zero" value for the French army.[8] The next year, Italian forces used the airplane in war against Libya. By August 1914, several hundred were in service with the armies of the Great Powers. German, British, and French reconnaissance aircraft critically influenced the outcome of the two "shaping" battles at the opening of the Great War, Tannenberg and the Marne; their influence was altogether disproportionate to their small numbers. Converted by this and other wartime experience, Foch, just six years after dismissing the airplane, would issue (to his credit) an operational order stating "only superiority in aviation permits the superiority in artillery that is indispensable for having superiority in the actual battle," adding "victory in the air is the preliminary to victory on land."[9] After the war, he remained a noted air enthusiast.

MATURING AIR POWER

During the interwar years, the capabilities of aircraft increased dramatically, and fear of international air attack came to dominate popular literature, encouraging alarmist predictions of impending national disaster and the rise of aerial nationalism. However exaggerated such predictions were, by the end of the interwar period national survival unquestionably depended on retaining control of the air. In 1945, the conjoining of the atomic bomb and the long-range airplane ushered in the atomic era. That fateful year, the great military theorist Major General J. F. C. Fuller published a seminal text on armament and its influence upon history, in which he characterized the "powers and limitations" of weapons according to their range of action, striking power, accuracy of aim, volume of fire, and portability. Of all of these, it was range that he selected as "the dominant characteristic—that is, the characteristic which dominates the fight." He noted,

> Therefore the parts played by all other weapons should be related to the dominant one. Otherwise put, the weapon of superior reach or range should be looked upon as the fulcrum of combined tactics. Thus, should a group of fighters be armed with bows, spears and swords, it is around the arrow that tactics should be shaped; if with cannon, muskets and pikes, then around the cannon; *and if with aircraft, artillery and rifles, then around the airplane* [emphasis added].[10]

Fuller's credentials as both a military analyst and historian were impeccable, and his conclusions all the more worthy of reflection and consideration given that he was neither an airman nor, certainly, an air power zealot. Height, reach, and speed have always been important verities in military affairs, and in the air power era, it was their combination that, when coupled with mobility and payload, synergistically worked to make such a difference in military affairs. Free to move within three dimensions, unconstrained by the convolutions of terrain and rolling dynamic of the ocean's surface, the airplane could achieve effects in time unachievable by other military forces. By the time Fuller penned his words, the propeller-driven airplane, even given its pre–jet age immaturity, had already overturned centuries of naval and land warfare. In the Pacific theater, Allied aircraft were directly responsible for 45 percent of Japan's maritime losses (submarines, the twentieth century's other "three-dimensional system," were responsible for 48 percent). In the European theater, Royal Air Force (RAF) aircraft sank 51 percent of Axis ships destroyed by air or sea action. Moreover, Allied aircraft sank 47 percent of the 785 U-boats lost at sea.[11] On land, the director of Nazi Germany's military medical services judged that Allied air attack was, by 1945, "far ahead of either artillery or infantry weapons as a cause of casualties in the

German armed forces." Furthermore, it was more lethal: German casualties shifted from a ratio of one killed to eight wounded at the beginning of the war to a deadlier one to three ratio at war's end, thanks to the "devastating effect of aerial warfare," something echoed by numerous high-ranking German combat commanders.[12] No wonder that Joseph Goebbels, in recording one of his last conversations with Adolf Hitler, noted, "Again and again we return to the starting point of our conversation. Our whole military predicament is due to enemy air superiority."[13]

The high-speed revolution—a product of the development of the turbojet and the refinement of transonic aerodynamics that reshaped the airplane (most notably encapsulated by the swept wing, the iconic symbol of the "jet age")—when conjoined with air refueling produced the ability to reach across the globe within hours, redefining crisis intervention (whether for humanitarian or combat purposes) and theater-level warfare.[14] Its joining to the burgeoning electronic revolution created both the "systems" airplane and, via the advent of computerized flight controls and advanced sensors, the "smart" airplane and "smart" weapon as well, and, in the modern era, their extension to the autonomous unmanned aerial vehicle (UAV) of contemporary interest. With the precision revolution, air power achieved maturity, rendered unique among all forms of combat power for its combination of "speed, range, flexibility, precision, and lethality." It was a potent combination of characteristics first enunciated in Secretary of the Air Force Donald B. Rice's *Global Reach—Global Power*, a strategic planning framework for the U.S. Air Force issued, significantly, in June 1990, as Saddam Hussein put the finishing touches on his plan to seize Kuwait.[15] Highly controversial, it proved prescient within months and formed the intellectual underpinning for both the subsequent restructuring and reorganization of the Air Force in the post–Gulf War era undertaken by Rice and Chief of Staff General Merrill A. McPeak, and for the service's adaptation of an effects-based model of warfare, one adopted largely by airmen worldwide in the years since.

Like the airplane, the rocket, too, went from strength to strength in the face of skepticism and ridicule. Its first recorded military use dates to AD 1232, when Chinese defenders fired black powder rockets against Mongol invaders during the siege of K'ai-feng. The rocket gave the soldier a reach beyond the range of the arrow or lance, an advantage, in the pre-cannon era, not lost on those who witnessed it. Simple in design and concept, it had lasting power. More than five centuries later, Tipu Sultan, the self-styled "Tiger of Mysore," made extensive use of similar rockets, inspiring artillerist Sir William Congreve to develop a British equivalent that was little advanced save for industrial standardization. Royal Navy rocketeers fired twenty-five thousand against Copenhagen in a single night during the Napoleonic wars, when Admiral Nelson destroyed the Danish fleet, and its appearance in the British attack upon Fort McHenry during the War of 1812 is immortalized in "the rockets' red glare" of the American national anthem.[16] Then came the rapid proliferation of long-range rifled artillery, and the black powder rocket became a military anachronism, used thereafter largely as a means of firing lifesaving lines from shore to foundering ships and launching harpoons, and for public spectacle.

By the early twentieth century, derided as little more than a celebratory firework and the stuff of science fiction, the rocket had such a poor reputation that when Clark University physics professor Robert H. Goddard suggested that a rocket could reach the moon, and thereafter fired off small experimental ones, he encountered widespread derision.[17] Vannevar Bush, wartime chief of the Office of Scientific Research and Development (OSRD), remarked to California Institute of Technology's Robert Millikan and Theodore von Kármán, "I don't understand how a serious scientist or engineer can play around with rockets."[18] Nor was he alone in such sentiments. When given the choice of federal funding for research on rockets or windshield deicing, Jerome Hunsaker, chief of the Massachusetts Institute of Technology's aeronautical engineering program and chairman of the National Advisory Committee for Aeronautics, flippantly chose deicing, stating, "Kármán can have the Buck Rogers job" (von Kármán, undoubtedly delighted, subsequently launched what eventually evolved into the prestigious National Aeronautics and Space Administration Jet Propulsion Laboratory).[19]

Then came the Second World War, with battlefield rockets such as the *Nebelwerfer* and Katyusha, rocket-boosted antiship missiles, the bazooka and *Panzerfaust*, the over-two-hundred-mile-range V–2, and a host of concepts for rocket-accelerated supersonic airplanes and missiles. Rocketry quickly leapt to the forefront of weapons research; in April 1945, Hugh Dryden, member of an Army Air Forces (AAF)–sponsored, von Kármán–led study team assessing the state of aeronautics technology, rightly judged long-range ballistic missile research "vital to the future defense of our nation."[20] Within months, the AAF Air Materiel Command issued a study contract to the Douglas Aircraft Company for a report on the feasibility of Earth-orbiting satellites; in May 1946, the Douglas team—which would become the RAND Corporation—submitted an impressively detailed analysis enumerating the challenges, prospects, operational environment, and design requirements of a "world-circling spaceship." They reviewed two different designs (one conservative, another more challenging), forecast the value of the satellite for reconnaissance and communications, ruminated on the prospects of manned spaceflight, and concluded that despite all the difficulties, "technology and experience have now reached the point where it is possible to design and construct craft which can penetrate the atmosphere and achieve sufficient velocity to become satellites of the earth."[21]

Even so, a surprising number of ostensibly knowledgeable authorities continued to downplay or miss altogether the implications of such weapons. Just months after Dryden penned his recommendation, in June 1945, a distinguished scientific panel chaired by Sir Henry Tizard for the UK Chiefs of Staff concluded, "The military advantages of very long-range bombardment by rocket are liable, in our view, to be grossly exaggerated."[22] Four years later, Vannevar Bush argued that, even if it could be built, the intercontinental ballistic missile would "never stand the test of cost analysis."[23] He sarcastically chided those "eminent military men, exhilarated perhaps by a short immersion in matters scientific," who thought otherwise, and ridiculed satellites as well, adding in a tone of evident disbelief, "We even have the exposition of missiles fired so fast that they leave the Earth and proceed about it indefinitely as satellites, like the moon, for some vaguely specified military purposes."[24]

Less than a decade later, the shock of *Sputnik* demonstrated to even the most obstinate that a new era had indeed dawned; within another decade, global-ranging nuclear-tipped intercontinental missiles stood alert in silos and submarine launch tubes of various nations, defining the "balance of terror" that characterized the Cold War, even as the Soviet Union and the United States engaged in a rocket-boosted "space race" to land on the moon, and each side orbited intelligence-collecting satellites to learn as much as they could about the other. The spaceflight revolution transformed reconnaissance, warning, communication, weather prediction, and (perhaps most notably) navigation.[25] Out of all this came a transformation in military power projection and application, glimmerings of which were evident as early as the Vietnam War. It was revealed to the world in a more complete form with the Desert Storm campaign of 1991, which affirmed in dramatic fashion what on-call satellites could mean to the prospects of a military campaign.[26]

THE IMPACT OF DESERT STORM

The Gulf War generated an intense debate on air (and space) power's merits even before the last bombs of the campaign had landed. Already, after decades of neglect, a new generation of practitioner-thinkers—particularly Britain's Air Vice Marshal R. A. "Tony" Mason and U.S. Air Force Colonel John A. Warden III—had infused air power doctrine and education with a new vibrancy, their work extrapolating and then expanding well beyond an older conceptual framework dating to Douhet, Trenchard, Mitchell, Slessor, and Tedder. Their influence upon more junior officers who subsequently rose to positions of great responsibility (for example, Timothy Garden of the RAF and David Deptula and Philip Meilinger of the USAF) was profound.[27] Consequently, the years since Desert Storm have witnessed a proliferation of studies (most consistently by America's RAND Corporation and Australia's Air Power Development Centre) and a virtually continuous global debate on the strengths, limitations, attributes, and nature of air and space power that dwarfs the debates and exchanges of the interwar years, or those after the Second World War.[28] For airmen, the new "normative" attitude on power projection was succinctly captured by Group Captain Andrew P. N. Lambert, RAF, who boldly wrote in 1996,

> Power for Caesar, Mohammed, and Charlemagne resided in the strength and potency of their respective armies. By the Second Millennium AD power also embraced another medium, and for Philip II of Spain, for Elizabeth I and Victoria, power stemmed from naval fleets which circumnavigated the globe. Now, as we approach the Third Millennium, and with powered flight still less than 100 years old, it is clear that power delivered via the medium of the air can be equally decisive. *As technology accelerates, and as night and poor weather are mastered, Air Power will progressively evolve to dominate older forms of warfare* [emphasis added].[29]

Although far from universally accepted, particularly by traditionalists in sister services, there was, nevertheless, a post–Gulf War resonance to such sentiment. The next year, the air-minded U.S. Senator Saxby Chambliss (R–GA), introducing a provocative and wide-ranging study of air and space power by the prestigious Center for Strategic and International Studies (CSIS), stated that "the two-dimensional—horizontal—battlefield has its place in history; the focus has now shifted into a third dimension—the vertical. This is the realm of air and space forces."[30] Subsequent conflicts and crises—particularly Operation Allied Force, followed by the near-decade-old struggle against terrorism in the wake of the 9/11 attacks upon the United States—have added their own impulse to this dialogue, with "lessons" eagerly sought and promulgated by various champions as they come to grips with the challenges of the twenty-first century.[31]

The international discussion over air and space power has taken place against a historiographical backdrop in which an increasing number of notable surveys and compilations have appeared, supplementing and expanding upon older established works, and complementing the proliferation of narrower specialist studies and doctrinal works.[32] It is refreshing to note the seemingly inexhaustible production of new studies in air and space history—biographies included—many characterized by thoughtful, analytical, and incisive examination of issues long thought settled and resolved. Since little consensus still exists within both the military history and history of technology communities on the broad perspective and narrative of aerospace history, many are frankly contradictory, a circumstance helping fuel an almost continuous reexamination of the field and its players.[33]

What now might be said of the state and prospects of air and space power, in an era where the Second World War is a fading memory, Korea almost so, Vietnam well on the way, and even the Cold War a period of crisis that many of today's military members have not themselves experienced? The following are some personal considerations derived from reviewing both the chapters in this volume and the larger history of aviation and military affairs.

THE ADVANTAGE OF VANTAGE

The single most significant capability furnished by air and space power is timely vantage, the ability to furnish a "position giving a strategic advantage, commanding perspective, or comprehensive view."[34] Successful warfare is all about—and has always been all about—acquiring and exploiting information: as one U.S. Air Force study of the mid-1990s concluded, "Both micro wars and major regional contingencies have become information intensive conflicts."[35] A decade later, in the emergent era of cyberspace warfare, securing and retaining information dominance are of even greater importance. Significantly, the very first uses of the balloon, the airplane, and the orbital spacecraft were for the purpose of reconnaissance. Indeed, the most advanced operational aircraft of their day were often first put to use as reconnaissance platforms: The first German fighter, the Fokker *Eindecker* of 1915, was a modified reconnaissance airplane. The de Havilland Mosquito, Britain's jack-of-all-trades, first flew as a reconnaissance aircraft before achieving equal distinction as a bomber and night fighter. The only operational Mach 3 airplane ever introduced into American service, the Lockheed Blackbird, was designed for gathering strategic intelligence. History has now repeated itself yet again, with the first combat use of UAVs being for reconnaissance.

Today, air or space observation, whether by aircraft, spacecraft, UAVs, and specialized platforms such as the Joint Surveillance Target Attack Radar System, EP–3, Rivet Joint, Nimrod R1, and so forth, is encompassed in the acronym *ISR*, though it is more properly prefixed by the C^4 for command, control, communications, and computers. C^4ISR is the central nervous system sine qua non of combined force joint-service combat operations.[36] The critical challenge—one encountered notably in the Gulf War and in conflicts since—is less the *acquisition* of ISR and more its timely *processing and distribution*—the turning of raw ISR feed into actionable intelligence that is then returned to deployed forces in time for incorporation into operational plans and combat execution. It is entirely fitting for all services to incorporate ISR acquisition, processing, and distribution systems and architectures, just as it is equally so for them to possess air and space forces. But as with the latter, it is to be expected that the most robust, capable, and sophisticated of those systems will be those possessed by independent air forces and/or national intelligence organizations.

THE ESSENTIALITY OF AIR DOMINANCE . . .

The single most important enduring requirement of air power forces is ensuring air dominance. As a rule, as Philip Meilinger noted more than a decade ago, "whoever controls the air generally controls the surface."[37] And generally speaking, loss of control of the air usually equates to the inability to control or to hold the surface and, more importantly, to exert national sovereignty. But more than this, loss of air dominance compromises all other military operations, for air dominance is, per se, the effective guarantor of all other operations. At Normandy in 1944, General Dwight Eisenhower memorably said, in a comment to his son, "If I didn't have air supremacy, I wouldn't be here."[38] Having it, he enjoyed massing and maneuver advantages unknown to his opponents. Overwhelming Allied air power denied German ground forces any ability to intervene decisively. "The enemy's air superiority has a very grave effect on our movements," German Field Marshal Erwin Rommel confided to his wife, noting, "There's simply no answer to it."[39] With it, as Rommel's naval aide Vice Admiral Friedrich Ruge ruefully wrote, "Our movements are extremely slow, supplies hardly get through; any deployment of tactical units is becoming impossible; the artillery cannot move to its firing positions anymore. *Precisely the same thing is happening on land here as happened at sea in the Tunisian campaign*" (emphasis added). Altogether, he concluded, "utilization of the Anglo-American air force is the modern type of warfare, turning the flank not from the side but from above."[40]

Air dominance, air supremacy, and air superiority are not the same thing. *Air dominance* is the overarching control of the air over one's forces and territory, and/or over those of the foe as well. *Air supremacy* is the greatest expression of air dominance, the ability to conduct one's operations with at most only passing concern for the enemy's ability to intervene. *Air superiority* is the lesser form of air dominance, where one is able to prosecute air operations successfully in spite of enemy efforts to intervene. Of the two, air supremacy is always preferred, for air superiority implies a rate of loss that, in the modern era of decreasing numbers of platforms, may well be unacceptable. Technically, in both the Arab-Israel war of 1973 and the Falklands war, the victorious powers—Israel and Great Britain—never "lost" air superiority. In reality, because neither possessed air dominance over their opponents, they experienced losses threatening the outcome of the conflict. Israel lost 35 percent of its prewar combat air strength in just nineteen days; Great Britain endured a war of attrition at sea that nearly saw its relatively modern fleet forced to retire in the face of 1950s aircraft dropping "dumb" bombs.

Air dominance is of particular significance to great powers, which may have to intervene in crisis regions with deployed forces possessing numerical disadvantages with respect to foes that have to be concerned only about their own "backyard." To paraphrase Isaiah Berlin's reference to Archilochus's memorable distinction between the hedgehog and the fox, the great power is the fox that knows and does many things; the regional actor is the hedgehog that needs to know only the "one big thing," namely, keeping charge of his territory. That means denying his airspace to intruders, and so, for the intervening power, there is, likewise, only "one big thing," namely, securing and retaining control of the air—possessing air dominance.

. . . AND HOW IT MAY BE LOST

Even if long established, air dominance can be lost, and lost quickly. Because air dominance necessarily depends upon a mix of technological investment, timely acquisition, proper choice, adequate force structure, and suitable training, a nation's air dominance advantage can wither should any one of these internal factors prove insufficient or inadequate. The external environment—political and economic structure and decision making, changes in the nature of threats and technological progression, for example—renders it vulnerable as well. For example, France ended the First World War as the strongest European aeronautical nation. It had the largest and most powerful air arm, and a robust and inventive industry. Nevertheless, through a series of poor decisions over the next twenty years, France lost its aeronautical dominance, collapsing in 1940 before a nation that had been literally prostrate just two decades previously. In the postwar era, questionable political and industrial decision making robbed Britain of any opportunity it had to lead the postwar military aircraft revolution. Instead, the leadership in military aircraft technology passed to the United States—a nation that had had to rely upon British initiative for both its best conventional fighter (the Merlin-powered North American P–51 Mustang), and its first jet-engine experience (the license-built GE I–A, a modified Power Jets—Frank Whittle—design). Enthralled with supersonic flight and nuclear war scenarios, the U.S. Air Force, having handily won the Korean air war with a superb fighter aircraft (the North American F–86 Sabre), proceeded to make development and training choices that gave it the wrong aircraft and the wrong training and doctrine by the time it went to war in Vietnam in the 1960s. The air war over North Vietnam, certainly during the Rolling Thunder phase, constituted an air dominance crisis for the United States (and particularly the Air Force), just over a decade after the overwhelming success of the air war in Korea. The result was hundreds of aircraft lost and airmen captured and killed, and a bitter series of hard-learned lessons before the service embarked upon the development of new and far more appropriate designs in the post-Vietnam era. Just six years after enjoying a stunning aerial victory, Israel, overconfident that it could readily replicate the success of its 1967 campaign, missed the significance of the internetting of fixed and mobile surface-to-air missiles and light, rapid-firing, radar-cued mobile gun systems, perilously skirting disaster in its 1973 war.[41]

A particular problem is the increasing time taken by systems acquisition in the face of rapidly changing technology and a quickly transforming external world. Since 1945, for example, there has been an approximate tenfold increase in fighter aircraft development times, from 2.5 to roughly 25 years between conception and introduction into operational service. This increase reflects the evolution of the highly complex systems of airplanes armed with weapons that are themselves highly sophisticated (if small) aerial vehicles. In an era of technological change encapsulated in the well-known Moore's Law of computational power (essentially doubling every eighteen to twenty-four months), this poses great challenges to ensure that a design remains relevant over the length of its development and deployment cycle. Acquisition reform—and not only for air forces, but also for all combatant forces—remains one of the greatest unresolved challenges of the early twenty-first century.

CONFRONTING THE CULTURE OF COMPLACENCY

The greatest danger to ensuring air dominance is complacency, particularly the belief—expressed through the years—that the era of air combat is, somehow, past. This claim, which can be documented with examples drawn from every war, from the Western front to the Persian Gulf, typically holds that the nature of air defenses and the capabilities of new weapons render the air dominance fighter either obsolete or irrelevant. Before the Second World War, belief that the era of air combat had passed caused the RAF to develop rigid, stylized "Vic" formation section attacks that resulted in unnecessary losses of RAF fighter aircrew during the Battle of Britain, precisely at a time when their loss could be least tolerated. In 1949, a year before the onset of the bitter Korean air war with its swirling battles over "MiG Alley," Vannevar Bush predicted that aerial combat between opposing aircraft was "probably now a thing of the past."[42] In 1957, the infamous Sandys White Paper gutted RAF fighter development on the premise that the future belonged to the missile. In the 1960s, Robert McNamara decreed as much for the Department of Defense, consuming approximately eight years of development time before being set straight.

More recently, in the two decades since the end of the Cold War, commentators and even senior political and defense officials in various Western nations have repeatedly (and surprisingly) minimized the risk of losing air dominance, even in the face of evidence of rapid proliferation of new and derivative combat designs, many with systems, sensors, countermeasures, and weapons that negate the technical edge long enjoyed by Western forces. The United States, for example, whose Air Force has maintained a continuous wartime tempo since August 1990 and the Iraqi occupation of Kuwait (and whose fighter, attack, bomber, ISR, mobility, and tanker forces have been hard flown since that time) possesses, as of 2009, an aging fleet badly in need of recapitalization. Perhaps dazzled by the apparent (and somewhat illusory) disparities of performance evident from the combat experience of Desert Storm, senior civilian defense and political leaders over the past fifteen years have repeatedly ignored the strenuous warnings of successive service (civil and military) leaders and have opted not to invest in large numbers of new replacement airplanes. As a consequence, the U.S. fighter force averages twenty-five years in age, its F–15Cs so old that, were they automobiles, they would wear classic car plates. The KC–135 tanker fleet and the B–52 bomber fleet are both well over forty years old. Worse, with such age come structural and performance penalties that reflect themselves in reduced permissible performance and reduced flight safety—two F–15s have already disintegrated in flight from structural failure, one killing its pilot, the other nearly so—further adding to the possible disparity in power projection capabilities among deployed American forces and the hostile forces they may encounter in some far-flung contingency.[43]

In a larger international sense, will the fighter aircraft as it is currently known remain a constant? Of course not—no more than the fighter of today resembles the fighter of the 1960s, or the 1940s, or the "Great War." Whether piloted aircraft or UAV, capabilities, sensors, weapons, and performance are all in play. The essential point, the historical verity, is not: air dominance has been, is, and will continue to be the essential requirement for guaranteeing the success of joint and combined force warfare.

OF AIRMEN, SPACEMEN, AND THE "WEAPONIZATION" OF SPACE

The demarcation between "air" and "space" power is increasingly irrelevant, as is the debate over "weaponizing" space. Since the earliest days after the shock of *Sputnik*'s launch, space has been increasingly important to international security. For the United States, successive administrations from Eisenhower onward framed national space policy via a series of presidential directives, public law, policy pronouncements, and international agreements.[44] By the mid-1980s, American space operators had established a discrete set of abilities, most highly classified, to furnish support to combatant forces. Their success in the first Gulf War highlighted the maturation of space as a coequal player with traditional air power. An influential study of the future of Air Force space requested by General Merrill McPeak concluded, rightly, that "robust space operations are critical to the security of our nation," that "national accomplishments in space are and will remain a barometer of international status and prestige, technological prowess, and military capability," and that "the single most important reason to be in space is to acquire Global View. . . . Global View is the enabler for Global Reach, Global Power."[45] General Charles Horner, air chief of the Gulf War, became chief of American space forces, overseeing the creation of a Space Warfare Center and the Fourteenth Air Force, wartime space component of the Air Force. These organizational and structural changes transformed the Air Force space community from one focused primarily on research and development ("launch when ready"), to one focused on timely "launch-on-warfighter-demand" to support deployed forces.[46]

In the immediate aftermath of Desert Storm, an uncomfortable undercurrent ran through Air Force long-range strategic planning meetings: what was the future of space? Would the space community become a "corps" affiliated with the Air Force in much the same fashion that the U.S. Marine Corps is partnered in a special relationship with the U.S. Navy? Would the space community "do a Mitchell" and "split" with the Air Force in much the same fashion that the Air Force had sprung from the Army? And if it did, what would be the organizational model? Would the model be an Air Force one or a *Star Trek*–like "Star Fleet?" Would there be space generals or space admirals? Colonels or captains? Space planes or space cruisers? The answers to these questions remain unknown; perhaps, in time, space will form a corps or even a distinct military service of its own, and if so, at that point it might likely continue to evolve as the predominant partner in an air-space relationship where both serve to observe, inform, intervene, and control what happens in the Earth's atmosphere and upon the Earth's surface below.

As contributors to force projection, space power and air power are so inextricably linked and interrelated that the issue of space weaponization is largely moot. The strike aircraft of the present era takes off, flies to a target area identified on the basis of space-derived intelligence, navigates to the point of weapon release using space-based navigation and space-based communication, follows a route taking into account space-derived weather information, and then likely drops a weapon such as a joint direct attack munition (JDAM) guided to its target by satellite. It makes no difference to the fate of the targeted facility whether it is destroyed by a bomb dropped from an airplane using a self-contained laser designation system or one such as a JDAM that is guided by satellite input. The result is the same. This is not to say that there are not many other issues involving military weapons in space, or that nations should be necessarily free to employ whatever sort of weapon they choose within the space environment. Certainly, since the advent of the Global Positioning System and JDAMs, it is past time to drop the fiction that space, somehow, is a pristine environment untrammeled by the military art. When military forces—land, sea, and air—are as dependent upon space-based communication, weather, intelligence, warning, cueing, and navigation as they now are (and that dependency is near-total, certainly for mechanized mobile forces), and when individuals and facilities come under attack based upon space-derived information and using space-cued weapons, it is fair to state that space is already weaponized. The only question remaining is the *degree* to which it is weaponized, not whether it *is*, in fact, weaponized.

AIR AND SPACE POWER AND EFFECTS-BASED OPERATIONS

Air and space power work best when applied as part of an overarching effects-based strategy, one that emphasizes simultaneous, parallel, time-compressing, and nodal power projection. For much of military history, commanders projected power in linear and sequential fashion: along a single line of approach, against a succession of fortresses or along a succession of battlefields, one following the other, until the enemy surrendered or outlasted the attacker. For much of its history, air warfare proceeded in similar fashion, until the advent of the precision weapon (which reversed the measure of aerial merit from "sorties per target destroyed" to "targets destroyed per sortie"). Thus, the Combined Bomber Offensive of the Second World War was essentially a "classic" linear-sequential form of attack, despite the aerial medium. So, too, were the bomber offensive against Japan, Rolling Thunder in Vietnam, and even Linebacker as well. Air power was seen in "support" terms, as a necessary element "supporting" the theater commander's overall campaign objectives but lacking any distinctive contribution of its own.

The Gulf War changed all that. Given the tremendous number of possible aim points, target sets were evaluated on the basis of nodal, cascading effects, rather than a "fair-sharing" notion that all targets in any particular category (say power, or transportation, or air defense, or fielded forces) were essentially coequal. Planners recognized as well the powerful psychological stress that air attack induces in those who are attacked, a stress, ironically, that seems greater for the individual enemy soldier than for the individual enemy civilian. The result was an air campaign plan that was simultaneous, not sequential, and parallel, not linear. Multiple target sets were attacked simultaneously from opening night onward in a campaign that one planner termed "death by a thousand cuts."[47] Simply put, planners first targeted Iraq's ability to defend itself: its integrated air defense system. Once that was shattered—once the effect had been achieved—then other cascading effects followed: attacks against power generation, against the machinery of the Saddam Hussein regime, against its transportation and fielded forces. As postwar interrogation reports revealed, Iraqi commanders and fielded force personnel found themselves effectively operating out of the time dimension of their attackers, who—thanks to information and decision-making advantages furnished by their air and space C[4]ISR systems, and the air dominance that secured the Coalition unrestricted maneuver while pinning Iraqi forces in place—were able to act and react ever more quickly and decisively than Saddam's hard-pressed forces. Air power essentially imprisoned the Iraqi army in Kuwait itself until, in desperation, it fled in disorder. By war's end, senior Iraqi commanders had no idea what precise area of Iraq they still occupied, or where the forward line of Coalition forces actually was, and, in their first meeting with Coalition leaders, literally had to be shown their own positions on a map.

The success of the Desert Storm air campaign encouraged the widespread adaptation of effects-based operations (EBO), despite an undercurrent of persistent reluctance and even outright opposition from traditionalists who rejected EBO's implications that combat operations could be executed rationally by treating an opponent as a system of networks and nodes that could be precisely targeted. Opponents stressed the continuing "chaotic" and "unpredictable" nature of war (recalling Clausewitz's "fog and friction"), implying that the future of warfare would (indeed, must) remain at its essence a series of punishing force-on-force close-fight encounters. More recently, in the post-9/11 period, critics have called for the reversal, even the banning, of the notion and terminology of effects-based warfare.[48] Such efforts, in the long term, are unlikely to change the actual application of EBO principles by the global military community (except, ironically, perhaps in the land of their "birth"). It is a curious campaign, given that even a cursory examination of military history shows that victory most often goes to the commander who best seeks to understand his opponent and the opponent's intent, identifies what the opponent holds most dear and needs to achieve, and then seeks to rationalize and order the battlefield ("prepare the battlespace" in today's jargon), using carefully apportioned force to achieve his own defined, desired effects. In short, EBO is more than an air war conceit: it is intrinsically "common sense," essential to the efficient employment of all forms of combat power and particularly suited to the capabilities of joint and combined force air (and space) power.

SCIENCE, TECHNOLOGY, AND AIR AND SPACE POWER

Air and space power is inherently dependent upon the power of science and technology. Moreover, it must inherently reflect progressive technological change if it is to remain relevant, particularly given the nature of evolving threats. Flight through the atmosphere or into space requires absolute mastery of some of the most complex scientific and technological disciplines, so much so that air and space power forces, more than other military services, require the fullest possible investment in advanced science and technology. The challenge for planners is to determine the requisite level of appropriate technology needed to fulfill a particular requirement, while being flexible enough to address "pop-up" challenges (such as the surface-to-air missile [SAM] crisis of the 1960s and 1970s) or opportunities (such as the turbojet engine or low observables) when they arise. Overly fanciful thinking generates as many problems as too conservative, as does a misreading of "lessons learned."[49]

Because of the inherently complex nature of aerospace science and technology, air and space power requires the maintenance of a robust aerospace industrial base (national in the case of the United States, international in the case of the European alliance), one that supports both civil and military aircraft development, for civil and military aeronautics are inextricably intertwined. That aerospace industrial base is little recognized but profoundly significant. It is vulnerable to program reduction, fluctuating job markets, changes in educational policy, student choice, and political whim. In an era where defense policy is too often caught up in a "boots-on-the-ground" mind-set, and where "crisis du jour" prioritization and planning substitute for a rational examination of future requirements and capabilities, air power—which is inherently expensive, time consuming to produce, and focused on the long-term future—can easily be neglected. And here is the rub: once neglected, it is very difficult to reconstitute. The over-two-decade replacement cycle for new aircraft; the challenge of interesting, training, hiring, and retaining adequate numbers of science, technology, engineering, and mathematics–qualified personnel; the shifting priorities in program management and acquisition objectives—all work to seriously constrain and compromise the smooth and orderly progression of air (and space) power capabilities and force structure over successive political administrations, as does the demanding and rapidly changing external "real world."

AIR AND SPACE POWER: MISSIONS, PEOPLE, AND COMBAT ENVIRONMENTS

Air (and space) power should be held to the same standards as other forms of military power, and not simplistically typecast. This may seem a small or even unnecessary point to make, but it is not. All too often, air power is criticized because it is not 100 percent effective, 100 percent of the time: true, but then, neither is any other form of military power projection. Certainly, air power is not a "perfect" form of power projection: none is. Certainly, it can be misused, and cases exist where the expectations of its success were unwarranted and proven so by actual combat application. It requires an expensive investment in large fixed or mobile bases (airfields or aircraft carriers), and large numbers of trained personnel; it lacks persistence in loiter (aside from some specialized vehicles and systems); and it requires high levels of maintenance to ensure basic flight safety, not simply combat effectiveness. It is not a panacea; it is at best rarely capable of winning conflicts on its own. Nevertheless, on balance, if not as omniscient and omnipotent as its most zealous adherents would wish it, nevertheless, has proved more efficient and effective than its critics have generally alleged. Combat experience—from Kasserine to Operation Anaconda—indicates that when ground commanders do not adequately address the potentialities of air power they suffer unnecessary casualties to their own forces as a result. Indeed, one of the most interesting aspects of air operations since 9/11 is how effective air attack by manned and unmanned systems has been in targeting enemy forces—and how dependent friendly surface forces have been on air power to save and extract them when their various schemes of ground maneuver and insertion have gone awry.

Air power is about more than opting for either "strategic bombardment" or "close air support." Popular discussion of air power, even in a war college environment, often degenerates into advocacy for just this sort of mutually exclusive "choice." In truth, of course, air power is multifaceted, across the spectrum of conflict, and at varying levels of investment and application. These are two kinds of mission areas that air power can fulfill, but it can fulfill (and has fulfilled) many others as well: air interdiction, leadership attacks, air mobility, maritime surveillance and strike, reconnaissance. Likewise, Air Force leadership is more complex and nuanced than the "struggle" often depicted between "fighter generals" and "bomber generals" over who gets a new set of shiny airplanes. Certainly, anyone exposed to the decision-making environment within the higher councils of an air force—for example, the U.S. Air Force's periodic *Corona* meetings—realizes quite quickly how cartoonish such depictions are.

Air power enables striking at a foe from a distance, quickly, and usually out of effective range for response, reducing the risk to one's own forces. As such, this works to obviate or minimize the necessity of engaging in the close fight, where the greatest losses of combatants and innocents and the greatest collateral damage traditionally occur. The close fight is a muddle to be avoided at almost any cost. It is a means of losing one's own advantage, of effectively stripping one's own forces of their technological, equipment, and training strengths and placing them on a level playing field with opponents who may, in the present world, simply be seeking an opportunity for "martyrdom." Strange indeed, however, is the frequently heard criticism that air power is too "clean," too "risk-free," that it does not place sufficient personnel "at risk" to demonstrate national or coalition moral resolve. This latter argument, echoing the churchmen and knights in the Middle Ages who railed against the "immorality" of the firearm and cannon (which, able to strike at a distance, kept their gunners beyond the reach of the foe), is itself at heart devoid of both logic and ethics. Ignoring or minimizing the value of one's own air (and space) power forces while putting one's troops in close proximity to enemy forces to send a misguided ethical "signal" solves the enemy's engagement problems, not one's own. It reflects a disturbing mind-set that seeks to make not only a necessity, but also a virtue, of the punishing and bloody close fight.

THE DISTINCTION OF AIR FORCES

All services have a legitimate need to project and/or exploit air and space power, but only air forces are "full service" air and space power providers. It is entirely to be expected that military services will find their own way to exploit the air and space medium for their own advantage. But that is not to say that all military services furnish the same level of air and space awareness, mobility, and force application, nor the same rate of response. Air forces deploy and respond to the onset of a crisis at transonic speeds, what one British official termed the "six-hundred-knot gunboat." Naval air forces respond at the speed of a carrier strike group, and land warfare aviation forces (as shown by Task Force Hawk in Kosovo) at the speed of a mechanized vehicle. Thus, while air forces deploy within hours to a crisis region, naval forces take significantly longer, and land warfare forces longer still. The capabilities and combat effectiveness vary greatly as well. Air forces possess a wide range of assets to prosecute air war across the spectrum of conflict and across an entire theater of operations; naval aviation forces possess systems to support and protect fleet operations and prosecute littoral warfare, typically within the naval battlespace, but not across an entire theater; land warfare forces possess systems to furnish on-call fire support to engaged combat forces, typically across a divisional area or, at most, the front of a corps.

These differences are significant, but, likewise, mutually supportive. The challenge is achieving the fullest integration and coordination of air effort (again, something echoing EBO concepts) so that the joint force air campaign can meet the needs and achieve the objectives of the theater commander. For this reason, it is essential that, first, the differences between the kind and quality of air power that the various services project be clearly understood and appreciated; second, that combatant commanders understand the necessity of submitting their needs for air support and intervention through the joint force air component commander (JFACC); and third, that the JFACC be an airman. The JFACC need not be an "Air Force" airman—but he or she must be an individual who is cognizant of the nuances of air warfare and committed to seeking the best and most effective packaging and utilization of available air and space power resources to best fulfill the campaign plan of the theater commander.

REPORTS ARE GREATLY EXAGGERATED

It is premature to bury the manned military airplane, air forces, or air power. This is more than a kneejerk reaction to those who predict the imminent (or even longer term) demise of the manned airplane, the air force, and air power itself. Without question, all change—all *have* changed—and will continue to change over time. Certainly, the force mix of military manned and unmanned aircraft, the roles and missions of air power, and the nature of air forces will continue to evolve.

First, the airplane: over time, UAVs will supplant manned combat aircraft in many high-risk roles. As information distribution networks proliferate, as sensor and onboard flight control programs become more "intelligent" and nearly or totally autonomous, the need for the inhabited fighter or strike aircraft transiting into a high-threat area will decrease. In this role, unmanned combat aerial vehicles (UCAVs) will swiftly emerge. Systems such as Predator and Global Hawk have already pointed to this, as has the heavy and consistent investment made by Israel in UAV systems, technology, and combat operations over many years. The hard-maneuvering 9G manned fighter and the overflying manned bomber are likely to be replaced by autonomous or near-autonomous UAVs monitored or controlled by airborne or ground controller-pilots.

Consider the jet fighter today: it is far different from the cannon- or machine gun–armed fighter of the Korean War, or even the missile-armed fighter of the Vietnam era. It is really a very complex information-sharing system employing robotic aerial weapons, such as the advanced medium-range air-to-air missile, as substitutes for fighter aircraft: in short, it is a fighter launching an interceptor. The future fighter may be a manned platform aircraft launching several small UCAV fighters engaging the enemy and launching advanced air-to-air missiles. (Indeed, a case already exists where a missile-toting UAV took an opportunistic shot at an Iraqi MiG, nearly shooting it down).

The future bomber may be a platform aircraft (manned or unmanned) loitering outside the effective range of an enemy integrated air defense system and then using advanced air-breathing hypersonic missiles to engage the foe. The technology for such missiles is well in hand, achievable today by many nations, and their advantage, aside from enabling great standoff outside the enemy's threat range, is that their speed renders them particularly well suited to address "pop-up" targets and threats at distances of six hundred to one thousand nautical miles, turning fleeting intelligence into actionable intelligence. Today's cruise-missile-firing bomber, ship, or submarine, or even an airborne strike fighter, is ill suited to address such targets itself, and not simply from the dangerous nature of the defensive system. Indeed, it makes little sense to speak of closing the "sensor-to-shooter" loop when the "shooter-to-target" loop is so slow—exemplified by the firmly subsonic cruise missile, or the need to transit large swaths of contested airspace at transonic speeds—that one enters a veritable "zone of 'are we there yet?'" until finally reaching the target area. The netting of long-range loitering systems, manned or unmanned, with space-based ISR and hypersonic weapons promises to dramatically transform combat force application.

The nature of ground operations since 9/11 has compelled some to call for a return to the "counterinsurgency aircraft" mind-set of the McNamara era. Nothing could be more foolish, given the state of current air defense capabilities of even lightly armed insurgent forces. One need only consider the loss rates experienced by loitering and low-altitude attackers in Southeast Asia and the Middle East almost four decades ago, in an era when air defense technology was far less advanced (and thus far less lethal) than it is today. Introduction of the SA–7 during the 1972 North Vietnamese spring offensive drove propeller-driven "strike" and Forward Air Control (FAC) airplanes—even the robust and heavily armed Douglas A–1— from the sky. During the 1973 Middle East war, nearly 60 percent of the estimated 109 aircraft Israel lost fell during close air support missions (and roughly the same percentage of Arab aircraft fell to Israeli SAM and gun defenses as well). The Soviet air experience in Afghanistan after the introduction of the Stinger missile is, of course, now well appreciated.[50] The modern man-portable missile system, ever increasing in its own capabilities, is so lethal as to prohibit the routine operation of latter-day O–1, O–2, and OV–10 aircraft. Rather than invest in such platforms, crewed by one or two individuals, planners should devote greater attention to UAVs, and, particularly, so-called micro-UAV systems, using distributed information-sharing to more sophisticated "on call" strike aircraft or artillery-equipped ground forces.

With regard to UAVs, it is again oversimplification to allege that airmen of various services, particularly air forces, have been slow to adapt to the unmanned aerial vehicle. While such is often stated, in fact, the record of UAV development indicates that such development took place consistent with the requisite technical requirements and capabilities needed to make it so. The reliable, reusable combat UAV—for example, Predator or Global Hawk—simply could not have been built in the precomputer, preelectronic, fly-by-wire, advanced-sensor era. When the age of computerized flight arrived, military services were quick to seize on the potential of the UAV, again first looking to its capabilities as an ISR system. By the late 1980s, major UAV development activities were under way, certainly in the United States. As with early American transonic and supersonic aircraft programs, early UAV efforts were characterized by an often costly and expensive series of disappointments and failures (such as the Army's Aquila program, the Air Force's Tacit Rainbow, and the Defense Advanced Research Projects Agency's Dark Star). When successful systems did appear, such as Predator and Global Hawk, they were enthusiastically supported within the higher councils of the military, particularly the Air Force, and quickly exploited for combat purposes.[51]

UAVs represent another powerful tool within the air and space power tool box, and their proliferation will drive a restructuring of air power forces, particularly air forces, away from a primarily manned focus. For the U.S. Air Force, this means that over time, the greater number of its combat assets will likely be UAVs, and such is likely to be true for other nations' air forces as well. There is an important precedent: already, a significant portion of Air Force personnel operate unmanned systems—the space operators who control the satellites so crucial to American and coalition forces. Sociologically, over time it is likely that fewer operators of UAVs will be rated pilot officers, and more will be skilled enlisted operators or perhaps a new cadre akin to the Army's warrant officer airmen.

Of air forces, it is unlikely in the short term, or even in the long term, that they will disappear. The range of capabilities that air forces possess, the responsibilities that they fulfill, their nature as "full service" air power providers ensure that they occupy now, and will likely continue to occupy, a special place beyond the service-focused air arm of an army or navy. Armies and navies are so necessarily focused on their own sphere of operations that they cannot reasonably be expected to assume the full range of air and space power functions that air forces now fulfill. Having said this, armies and navies quite rightly must continue to refine and hone their own aviation capabilities, particularly (for armies) in the development of UAVs and micro-UAVs to furnish the soldier with the "over-the-hill-and-behind-the-next-building" ISR information needed to prosecute modern, multidimensional war. Airborne counters to even seemingly intractable problems such as the improvised explosive device have proved surprisingly effective and point toward even more efficient service aviation capabilities in the future.[52] For navies, UAVs offer a means of ensuring the continued relevance and survivability of the carrier strike group by complementing, and perhaps eventually dominating, the composition of the carrier air wing. For both, as for air forces, hypersonic missiles will become a necessity—for armies, for corps defense against the theater's weapons of mass destruction threat; for navies, for fleet defense and fleet power projection against shore targets. Air forces will remain, as they have been, the primary means of furnishing space launch, global and theater ISR, theater and homeland air dominance, long-range, high-capacity strike, air mobility (both long range and in theater), and theater-wide special operations.

As for air power, it can never be returned to the simple context of two-dimensional surface warfare, any more than flight itself can be uninvented. Air power, it must be recognized, is like other forms of military power: always in an evolving and transitional form. The creation of the RAF in 1918 marked not only the establishment of the world's first independent air force, but also the recognition that air power—the air medium, in a larger sense the *three-dimensional medium*—had achieved such an importance and significance in military affairs as to warrant its own special service.[53] That recognition was a signal that air power is reflective of an arena of conflict—the "third dimension"—that has its own special attributes and characteristics. That dimension extends to the fringes of the atmosphere, where the laws of aerodynamics are succeeded by the laws of ballistics and Keplerian orbital mechanics. Everything from there on is the province of space. In time, the air-space relationship might well change. Air forces have become air and space forces and are arguably on their way to becoming space and air forces. Air power, as defined as an "atmospheric" form of power projection, may well be subsumed into a larger category of three-dimensional power in which space predominates. In that case, however, it is important to reflect that while space might well offer a global perspective enabling its vantage and control over the air, air power will continue to maintain its vantage and control over the surface.

In the century since the advent of the military airplane, the world has experienced profound transformation. Conceived in an era of global empires, the airplane played a role in destroying that world, in defeating the totalitarian forces that sprang from its rubble, and, assisted by burgeoning space power, in maintaining an uneasy forty-year Cold War that preserved freedom in the face of a persistent global threat. In the years since 1989, air and space power have had to adjust to new global environments, confronting enemies rarely thought of since the earliest days of British air control in the Middle East and Southwest Asia. The airplane has become the greatest and most reliable means of civil and military mass mobility. The satellite has become the great enabler of modern society: deliverer of information, source of guidance, furnisher of warnings of weather and security risk, and provider of means of communication. None of this has taken place without the careful, conscientious, and courageous work of men and women who have made the aerospace revolution—particularly the military aerospace revolution—the force of profoundly significant global transformation that it is. Works such as this book are to be welcomed, not merely for stimulating the on-going debate and discussion that are necessary to refresh thinking and perspective, but for recalling the service and sacrifice of those upon whose shoulders we stand.

NOTES

INTRODUCTION

1. Sir Michael Howard, *The Causes of Wars* (London: Unwin Paperbacks, 1983), 215–217. See also John Keegan, *The Face of Battle* (London: Penguin Books, 1978), 20–35.
2. Howard, *The Causes of Wars*, 215–217.
3. Pieter Geyl, *Use and Abuse of History* (New Haven, CT: Yale University Press, 1955), 70. The statement comes from his wartime study of French historiography on Napoleon Bonaparte.
4. Ibid., 62.
5. H. L. Mencken, "The Divine Afflatus," in *A Mencken Chrestomathy* (New York: Random House, 1949), 443. This essay was originally published in the *New York Evening Mail*, November 16, 1917, and reprinted in *Prejudices: Second Series* (New York: Alfred A. Knopf, 1920).
6. Geyl, *Use and Abuse of History*, 61.
7. I would like to acknowledge H. P. Willmott for this observation.
8. Carl H. Builder, *The Icarus Syndrome: The Role of Air Power Theory in the Evolution and Fate of the U.S. Air Force* (New Brunswick, NJ, and London: Transaction Publishers, 1994), 36.
9. Colonel Peter Faber, "The Evolution of Air Power Theory in the United States: From World War I to Colonel John Warden's *The Air Campaign*," in *Asymmetric Warfare*, ed. John Andreas Olsen (Trondheim: Royal Norwegian Air Force Academy, 2002), 45–116.

CHAPTER 1

1. Albert Robida, *La Guerre au Vingtième Siècle* (Paris: G. Decaux, 1887).
2. Ivan S. Bloch, *The Future of War in Its Technical, Economic and Political Relations: Is War Now Impossible?* trans. R. C. Long (New York: Doubleday & McClure, 1899).
3. Alfred Gollin, *No Longer an Island: Britain and the Wright Brothers, 1902–1909* (Stanford: Stanford University Press, 1984), 19.
4. H. G. Wells, *The War in the Air* (London: George Bell & Sons, 1908).
5. Philippe Bernard, "A propos de la stratégie aérienne pendant la Première Guerre Mondiale: Mythes et réalités," *Revue d'histoire moderne et contemporaine* 16 (1969): 354–355.
6. Felix P. Ingold, *Literatur und Aviatik: Europäische Flugdichtung* (Basel: Birkhäuser Verlag, 1978), 96, 104, 116–117.

7. Kriegswissenschaftliche Abteilung der Luftwaffe (KAdL), *Die Militärluftfahrt bis zum Beginn des Weltkrieges 1914*, ed. Militärgeschichtliches Forschungsamt, 3 vols., 2d rev. ed. (Frankfurt: Mittler und Sohn, 1965–1966), 2: 86.

8. Jürgen Eichler, "Die Militärluftschiffahrt in Deutschland 1911–1914 und ihre Rolle in den Kriegsplänen des deutschen Imperialismus," *Zeitschrift für Militärgeschichte* 24, no. 4 (1985): 407–410.

9. *Flight* 5, no. 10 (March 7, 1914): 248–249.

10. John R. Cuneo, *Winged Mars*, 2 vols. (Harrisburg: Military Service Publishing Co., 1942, 1947), 2: 92–94.

11. Charles Christienne et al., *Histoire de l'aviation militaire française* (Paris: Charles Lavauzelle, 1980), 88.

12. John H. Morrow Jr., *German Air Power in World War I* (Lincoln: University of Nebraska Press, 1982), 16–17.

13. Peter Mead, *The Eye in the Air: History of Air Observation and Reconnaissance for the Army 1785–1945* (London: Her Majesty's Stationery Office, 1983), 51–58.

14. *Flight* 3, no. 41 (October 9, 1914): 1026.

15. Bernard, "Stratégie aérienne," 359–360; correspondence, Flandin to D'Aubigny, September 21, 1915, File A81, Service Historique de L'Armée de l'Air (SHAA).

16. File AIR1/2319/223/29/1–18, Public Record Office (PRO).

17. *Flight* 7, no. 26 (June 25, 1915): 446–448, 455; *Flight* 7, no. 30 (July 23, 1915): 525–526, 539–542; *Flight* 7, no. 43 (December 22, 1915): 798, 802.

18. Frank J. Cappelluti, "The Life and Thought of Giulio Douhet" (Ph.D. diss., Rutgers University, 1967), 67–110 passim.

19. Louis Thébault, *L'Escadrille 210* (Paris: Jouve, 1925), 29, 49, 53, 59.

20. Johannes Werner, *Boelcke. Der Mensch, der Flieger, der Führer der deutsche Jagdfliegerei* (Leipzig: K. F. Köhler, 1932), 158–168.

21. Douglas H. Robinson, *Giants in the Sky: A History of the Rigid Airship* (Seattle: University of Washington Press, 1973), 122.

22. Hugh Trenchard, "Short Notes on the Battle of the Somme 1 July–11 November 1916," File MFC 76/1/4, Trenchard Papers (TP), Royal Air Force Museum (RAFM), Hendon.

23. "L'Aéronautique militaire française pendant la Guerre de 1914–1918," vol. 2, "1917–1918," *Icare, revue de l'aviation française*, no. 88 (Printemps 1979), 17.

24. Guy Pedroncini, *Pétain: Général en chef 1917–1918* (Paris: Presses Universitaires de France, 1974), 41, 57.

25. Ibid., 41–42.

26. Lieutenant Marc [Jean Béraud Villars], *Notes d'un pilote disparu (1916–1917)* (Paris: Hachette, 1918). Translated by Stanley J. Pincetl and Ernst Marchand as *Notes of a Lost Pilot* (Hamden: Archon, 1975), 211–221.

27. Bernard, "Stratégie aérienne," 363.

28. American Expeditionary Force account of the aviation plan of bombardment, November 18, 1917, AIR 1/1976/204/273/40, PRO; Pedroncini, *Pétain*, 58.

29. Georg P. Neumann, ed., *In der Luft unbesiegt* (Munich: Lehmanns, 1923), 79–91, 166–175.

30. Correspondence, Haig GHQ no. O.B./1826 to Secretary, War Office, May 18, 1917, AIR 1/2267/209/70/34, PRO.

31. George Kent Williams, "Statistics and Strategic Bombardment: Operations and Records of the British Long-Range Bombing Force during World War I and Their Implications

for the Development of the Post-War Royal Air Force, 1917–1923" (Ph.D. diss., Oxford University, 1987), 45–64, 186.

32. MFC 76/1/1, TP, RAFM.

33. Cappelluti, "Douhet," 138–145.

34. Weir to Trenchard, September 10, 1918, MFC 76/1/94, TP, RAFM.

35. Williams, "Statistics," 233–251, 257, 260–262.

CHAPTER 2

1. See, for example, Karl-Heinz Völker, *Dokumente und Dokumentarfotos zur Geschichte der deutschen Luftwaffe* (Stuttgart: VDA, 1968), 469, document 200, "Luftkriegführung."

2. See James Corum, "From Biplanes to Blitzkrieg: The Development of German Air Doctrine between the Wars," *War in History* 3 (1996): 85–101.

3. Robert J. Young, "The Strategic Dream: French Air Doctrine in the Inter-War Period, 1919–1939," *Journal of Contemporary History* 9 (1974): 59–61.

4. Philip Meilinger, "Trenchard and 'Morale Bombing': The Evolution of Royal Air Force Doctrine before World War II," *The Journal of Military History* 60 (1996): 243–270. On Sykes, see Eric Ash, *Sir Frederick Sykes and the Air Revolution 1912–1918* (London: Taylor and Francis, 1999).

5. National Archives II, College Park, MD, RG18/223 Box 1, RAF War Manual Part I, Operations (May 1935), 1, 57.

6. German figures from Klaus Maier et al., *Das Deutsche Reich und der Zweite Weltkrieg: Band II, Die Errichtung der Hegemonie auf dem europäischen Kontinent* (Stuttgart: DVA, 1979), 339–340. Allied figures in Ernest May, *Strange Victory: Hitler's Conquest of France* (New York: Hill & Wang, 2000), 477, 479; F. R. Kirkland, "The French Air Force in 1940," *Air University Review* 36 (1985): 101–102.

7. Kirkland, "French Air Force," 103, 110; J. Truelle, "La production aéronautique militaire française jusqu'en juin 1940," *Revue d'histoire de la Deuxième Guerre Mondiale* 19 (1969): 98–102.

8. See Richard Overy, "Air Power, Armies and the War in the West, 1940," 32d Harmon Memorial Lecture, United States Air Force Academy, Colorado Springs, 1989, 8–17.

9. See Maier, *Das Deutsche Reich und der Zweite Weltkrieg: Band II*, 369–371, 375–382, for details of German planning.

10. Details in Richard Overy, *The Battle of Britain* (London: Penguin, 2000), 34–35, 40–41, 124.

11. British figures from the National Archives, Kew, London, AIR 22/293, "Statistics: Aircraft Production, Imports and Exports," June 1–September 30 [1940].

12. Maier, *Das Deutsche Reich und der Zweite Weltkrieg: Band II*, 391; National Archives, Kew, AIR 16/365, "Fighter Command Operational Strength," September 19, 1940.

13. Maier, *Das Deutsche Reich und der Zweite Weltkrieg: Band II*, 388–390.

14. Hans-Adolf Jacobsen, ed., *Generaloberst Halder: Kriegstagebuch: Band II* (Stuttgart: Kohlhammer, 1963), 98–100, entry for September 14, 1940; Maier, *Das Deutsche Reich und der Zweite Weltkrieg: Band II*, 390–392.

15. On Douhet, see Philip Meilinger, "Giulio Douhet and the Origins of Airpower Theory," in *Paths of Heaven: The Evolution of Airpower Theory* (Maxwell Air Force Base, AL: Air University Press, 1997), 1–40.

16. Cited in Charles Webster and Noble Frankland, *The Strategic Air Offensive against*

Germany: Volume IV (London: Her Majesty's Stationery Office, 1961), 36–37. On Hitler's attitude toward air power, see Richard Overy, "Hitler and Air Strategy," *Journal of Contemporary History* 15 (1980): 405–421.

17. *Fuehrer Conferences on Naval Affairs 1939–1945* (London: Greenhill Books, 1990), 172, Report on Conferences with the Fuehrer on January 8 and 9, 1941.

18. Williamson Murray, *Luftwaffe* (London: George Allen and Unwin, 1985), 59–60; Maier, *Das Deutsche Reich und der Zweite Weltkrieg: Band II*, 397, gives two hundred bombers destroyed or damaged in October 1940 alone, of which 67 percent were the victims of noncombat loss.

19. Murray, *Luftwaffe*, 77. The figures were 1,711 in 1940, 1,511 in 1941.

20. See Reginald V. Jones, *Most Secret War: British Scientific Intelligence 1939–1945* (London: Hamish Hamilton, 1978), chaps. 16–18; Alfred Price, *Instruments of Darkness: The History of Electronic Warfare, 1939–1945* (London: Greenhill Books, 2005), 25–50.

21. Calculated from statistics in Maier, *Das Deutsche Reich und der Zweite Weltkrieg: Band II*, 407.

22. John Ray, *The Night Blitz, 1940–1941* (London: Arms and Armour, 1996), 260.

23. On the social history of the Blitz, see Angus Calder, *The Myth of the Blitz* (London: Jonathan Cape, 1991); Amy H. Bell, *London Was Ours: Diaries and Memoirs of the London Blitz* (London: I. B. Tauris, 2008); Brad Beaven and John Griffiths, "The Blitz, Civilian Morale and the City," *Urban History* 26 (1999): 71–88; Helen Jones, *British Civilians in the Front Line: Air Raids, Productivity and Wartime Culture, 1939–1941* (Manchester: Manchester University Press, 2006).

24. Marco Bragadin, *The Italian Navy in World War II* (Annapolis: U.S. Naval Institute Press, 1957), 365–366.

25. Vera Zamagni, "Italy: How to Lose the War and Win the Peace," in *The Economics of World War II: Six Great Powers in International Comparison*, ed. Mark Harrison (Cambridge: Cambridge University Press, 1998), 192–193.

26. Edward von der Porten, *The German Navy in World War II* (London: Macmillan, 1969), 174–178. Also see Kenneth Poolman, *Focke–Wulf Condor: Scourge of the Atlantic* (London: Macdonald and Janes, 1978).

27. Wesley F. Craven and James L. Cate, *The Army Air Forces in World War II*, 7 vols. (Chicago: University of Chicago Press, 1948), 1: 538–553; Samuel E. Morison, *The Two-Ocean War: A Short History of the United States Navy in the Second World War* (Boston: Little, Brown, 1963), 122–129.

28. Craven and Cate, *The Army Air Forces in World War II*, 2: 387–388; J. R. Butler, *Grand Strategy III, Part II: June 1941–August 1942* (London: Her Majesty's Stationery Office, 1964), 302–308.

29. See the excellent discussion in John Buckley, "Atlantic Airpower Co-operation, 1941–1943," in *Airpower: Theory and Practice*, ed. John Gooch (London: Frank Cass, 1995), 175–197.

30. Horst Boog et al., *Das Deutsche Reich und der Zweite Weltkrieg: Band IV: Der Angriff auf die Sowjetunion* (Stuttgart: DVA, 1983), 313.

31. Evan Mawdsley, *Thunder in the East: The Nazi-Soviet War, 1941–1945* (London: Hodder Arnold, 2005), 86–87.

32. Mawdsley, *Thunder in the East*, 58–59; Boog et al., *Das Deutsche Reich und der Zweite Weltkrieg: Band IV*, 689, 699–700.

33. Boog et al., *Das Deutsche Reich und der Zweite Weltkrieg: Band IV*, 701–703.

34. Ibid., 312–316.

35. Comparative figures in Richard Overy, *The Air War 1939–1945*, 2d ed. (Washington, DC: Potomac Books, 2005), 150. On German aircraft production, the best history is Lothar Budrass, *Flugzeugindustrie und Luftrüstung in Deutschland 1918–1945* (Düsseldorf: Droste Verlag, 1998), parts V and VI.

36. John Erickson, "Alexander Novikov," in *Stalin's Generals*, ed. Harold Shukman (London: Weidenfeld and Nicholson, 1993), 163–172.

37. Robert Kilmarx, *A History of Soviet Air Power* (London: Faber and Faber, 1962), 176–179; Alexander Boyd, *The Soviet Air Force since 1918* (London: Macdonald and Janes, 1977), 142–146; Erickson, "Novikov," 163–164.

38. Joel Hayward, *Stopped at Stalingrad: The Luftwaffe and Hitler's Defeat in the East, 1942–43* (Lawrence: University Press of Kansas, 1998), 309–310, 322–323.

39. Andrew Brookes, *Air War over Russia* (London: Ian Allen, 2003), 125–130.

40. Mawdsley, *Thunder in the East*, 201–202, 266–267.

41. Overy, *Air War*, 57. For a general history of Soviet battlefield aviation, see Kenneth Whiting, "Soviet Air-Ground Coordination," in *Case Studies in the Development of Close Air Support*, ed. Benjamin F. Cooling (Washington, DC: Office of Air Force History, 1990), 115–152.

42. Overy, *Air War*, 67–68.

43. Craven and Cate, *The Army Air Forces in World War II*, 2: 137, 205–206; 3: 806–807.

44. See Ian Gooderson, *Air Power at the Battlefront* (London: Frank Cass, 1998). For a general history of ground-attack aircraft, see Richard Hallion, *Strike from the Sky: The History of Battlefield Air Attack, 1911–1945* (Washington, DC: Smithsonian Institution Press, 1998), chaps. 13–14; Will A. Jacobs, "The Battle for France, 1944," in *Case Studies in the Development of Close Air Support*, 237–294.

45. Jodl quotation in National Archives II, College Park, United States Strategic Bombing Survey, Interview no. 62, Colonel General Alfred Jodl, June 29, 1945.

46. Cited in Arthur Tedder, *Air Power in War* (London: Hodder and Stoughton, 1948), 52.

47. See, for example, Tami D. Biddle, "British and American Approaches to Strategic Bombing: Their Origins and Implementation in the World War II Combined Bomber Offensive," in Gooch, *Airpower Theory and Practice*, 97–114; Richard Overy, "Allied Bombing and the Destruction of German Cities," in *A World at Total War: Global Conflict and the Politics of Destruction, 1937–1945*, eds. Roger Chickering, Stig Förster, and Bernd Greiner (Cambridge: Cambridge University Press, 2005), 279–287.

48. See, for example, Malcolm Smith, "The RAF and Counter-Force Strategy before World War II," *Journal of the Royal United Services Institute* 121 (1976): 69–72.

49. National Archives, Kew AIR 14/225, Air Staff "Western Air Plans," December 9, 1937.

50. Hayward S. Hansell, *The Air Plan that Defeated Hitler* (Atlanta: Higgins-McArthur, 1972), 81–83, 92–93, 298–307.

51. On France see Danièle Voldman, "Les civils, enjeux du bombardement des villes," in *La violence de guerre 1914–1945*, eds. Stéphane Audoin-Rouzeau, Annette Becker, Christian Ingrao, and Henry Rousso (Brussels: Editions complexes, 2002), 161–162; on Italy, Marco Patricelli, *L'Italia sotto le bombe* (Rome-Bari: Laterza, 2007). See too Gabriella Gribaudi, *Guerra Totale: Tra bombe alleate e violenze naziste, Napoli e il fronte meridionale 1940–44* (Turin: Bollati Boringhieri, 2005), chaps. 5–7.

52. On the recent debate, see Jörg Friedrich, *Der Brand: Deutschland im Bombenkrieg 1940–1945* (Munich: Propyläen Verlag, 2002); Hermann Knell, *To Destroy a City: Strategic Bombing and Its Human Consequences in World War II* (Cambridge, MA: Da Capo Press, 2003); Anthony Grayling, *Among the Dead Cities: Was the Allied Bombing of Civilians in World War II a Necessity or a Crime?* (London: Bloomsbury, 2006).

53. Martin Gilbert, *Finest Hour: Winston S. Churchill, 1939–1941* (London: William Heinemann, 1983), 329–330.

54. Winston Churchill, *The Second World War: Volume II* (London: Cassell, 1949), 567.

55. Gilbert, *Finest Hour*, 1136.

56. On the role of propaganda see Nicholas Cull, *Selling War: The British Propaganda Campaign against American "Neutrality" in World War II* (Oxford: Oxford University Press, 1995), chap. 5; Mark Connelly, "The British People, the Press, and the Strategic Air Campaign against Germany, 1939–1945," *Contemporary British History* 16 (2002): 39–58.

57. On Roosevelt, see Jeffrey S. Underwood, *The Wings of Democracy: The Influence of Air Power on the Roosevelt Administration* (College Station: Texas A&M University Press, 1992); on Spaatz, see Richard G. Davis, *Carl A. Spaatz and the Air War in Europe* (Washington, DC: Smithsonian Institution Press, 1992), 106–116.

58. See, for example, Lamberto Mercuri, *Guerra psicologica. La propaganda anglo-americana in Italia 1942–46* (Rome: Archivio Trimestrale, 1983).

59. On German deception, see Edward Westermann, "Hitting the Mark but Missing the Target: Luftwaffe Deception Operations, 1939–1945," *War in History* 10 (2003): 206–221.

60. Webster and Frankland, *Strategic Air Offensive: Volume IV*, 205–213, appendix 13, "Report by Mr. Butt to Bomber Command, 18 August 1941."

61. Ibid., 143–148, appendix 8 (xxii), Air Ministry Directive, February 14, 1942.

62. RAFM, Hendon, London, Harris Papers, Misc. Box A, Folder 4, Ministry of Economic Warfare, "100 German Cities" [n.d.].

63. Webster and Frankland, *Strategic Air Offensive: Volume IV*, 153–154, appendix 8 (xxviii), "Combined Chiefs of Staff Directive, January 21, 1943."

64. On the history of prewar air raid precautions, see Bernd Lemke, *Luftschutz in Grossbritannien und Deutschland 1923 bis 1939* (Munich: Oldenbourg, 2005), part IV.

65. Keith Lowe, *Inferno: The Devastation of Hamburg 1943* (London: Viking, 2007), 322–323.

66. F. Golucke, *Schweinfurt und der strategische Luftkrieg, 1943* (Paderborn: Schöningh Verlag, 1980).

67. Murray, *Luftwaffe*, 214–218.

68. W. Hays Park, "'Precision' and 'Area' Bombing: Who Did Which, and When?" in *Airpower: Theory and Practice*, 162; J. Kreis, *Piercing the Fog: Intelligence and Army Air Forces Operations in World War II* (Washington, DC: Office of Air Force History, 1996), 237–246.

69. On the issue of diminishing returns, see Jurgen Brauer and Hubert van Tuyll, *Castles, Battles and Bombs: How Economics Explains Military History* (Chicago: University of Chicago Press, 2008), 197–243. On Dresden, see the discussion in Donald Bloxham, "Dresden as a War Crime," in *Firestorm: The Bombing of Dresden, 1945*, eds. Paul Addison and Jeremy Crang (London: Pimlico, 2006), 180–208; Stefan Goebel, "Coventry und Dresden: Transnationale Netzwerke der Erinnerung in den 1950er und 1960er Jahren," in *Deutschland im Luftkrieg: Geschichte und Erinnerung*, ed. Dietmar Süss (Munich: Oldenbourg, 2007), 111–120.

70. See Richard Overy, "World War II: The Bombing of Germany," in *The War in the Air 1914–1994*, ed. Alan Stephens (Fairbairn, Australia: Air Power Studies Centre, 1994), 117–132; Adam Tooze, *The Wages of Destruction: The Making and Breaking of the Nazi Economy* (London: Allen Lane, 2006), chap. 19.

71. See, for example, the discussion of bombing and morale in Richard J. Evans, *The Third Reich at War* (London: Allen Lane, 2008), 441–466.

CHAPTER 3

1. A most useful overall survey of the course of the U.S.-Japanese war in the Pacific is Ronald Spector, *Eagle against the Sun: The American War with Japan* (New York: Free Press, 1985). Alan Levine provides a nuanced and compact treatment of events in the theater, to include diplomacy and grand strategy, in *The Pacific War: Japan versus the Allies* (Westport, CT: Praeger, 1995). Excellent short treatments of air power in the Pacific may be found in Richard J. Overy, *The Air War, 1939–1945* (New York: Stein and Day, 1981), 85–101; and John Buckley, *Air Power in the Age of Total War* (Bloomington: Indiana University Press, 1999), 170–197. This chapter also relies heavily on Samuel Eliot Morison, *History of United States Naval Operations in World War II*, 15 vols. (Boston: Little, Brown, 1947–1962); the same author's condensation *The Two-Ocean War* (Boston: Atlantic, 1963); and Wesley F. Craven and James L. Cate, *The Army Air Forces in World War II*, 7 vols. (Washington, DC: Office of Air Force History, 1983).

2. A marvelous discussion of the operating environment can be found in Eric Bergerud, *Fire in the Sky: The Air War in the South Pacific* (Boulder, CO: Westview, 2000).

3. Overy, *Air War*, 85–101.

4. William Mitchell, *Winged Defense: The Development and Possibilities of Modern Air Power, Economic and Military* (New York: Putnam's, 1925), 71.

5. On ACTS, see Peter R. Faber, "Interwar U.S. Army Aviation and the Air Corps Tactical School: Incubators of American Air Power," in *The Paths of Heaven: The Evolution of Airpower Theory*, ed. Philip Meilinger (Maxwell Air Force Base, AL: Air University Press, 1997), 183–238.

6. Haywood S. Hansell, *The Air Plan that Defeated Hitler* (Atlanta: Higgins-MacArthur, 1972), 298.

7. Craven and Cate, *Army Air Forces*, 6: 202–203.

8. Spector, *Eagle against the Sun*, 43.

9. Edward S. Miller, *War Plan Orange: The U.S. Strategy to Defeat Japan, 1897–1945* (Annapolis: U.S. Naval Institute Press, 1991).

10. William Trimble, *Admiral William Moffett: Architect of Naval Aviation* (Washington, DC: Smithsonian Institution Press, 1994).

11. Craig C. Felker, *Testing American Sea Power: U.S. Navy Strategic Exercises, 1923–1940* (College Station: Texas A&M University Press, 2007), 2.

12. Ibid., 58–59.

13. All data on ship types is from *Conway's All the World's Fighting Ships, 1922–1946* (Annapolis: U.S. Naval Institute Press, 1997).

14. Lisle Rose, *The Ship that Held the Line* (Annapolis: U.S. Naval Institute Press, 1995).

15. Data on aircraft types in this chapter is drawn from René J. Francillon, *Japanese Aircraft of the Pacific War* (Annapolis: U.S. Naval Institute Press, 2000); and Gordon Swanborough and Peter M. Bowers, *United States Navy Aircraft since 1911* (Annapolis: U.S. Naval Institute Press, 1990).

16. Steve Ewing, *Reaper Leader: The Life of Jimmy Flatley* (Annapolis: U.S. Naval Institute Press, 2002), 104–105.
17. Clark Reynolds, *The Fast Carriers: The Forging of an Air Navy* (Annapolis: U.S. Naval Institute Press, 1968), 15.
18. U.S. Marine Corps, *Small Wars Manual* (Washington, DC: U.S. Government Printing Office, 1940), chap. IX.
19. Edward C. Johnson, *Marine Corps Aviation: The Early Years, 1912–1940* (Washington, DC: USMC History and Museums Division, 1977), 35.
20. The best treatment of the subject in English is Mark R. Peattie, *Sunburst: The Rise of Japanese Naval Air Power, 1909–1941* (Annapolis: U.S. Naval Institute Press, 2001). Also David C. Evans and Mark R. Peattie, *Kaigun* (Annapolis: U.S. Naval Institute Press, 1997), chap. 9.
21. Peattie, *Sunburst*, 77ff.
22. Evans and Peattie, *Kaigun*, 312.
23. John Dower, *War without Mercy: Race and Power in the Pacific War* (New York: Pantheon, 1986), 99ff.
24. Peattie, *Sunburst*, 155–159; Buckley, *Air Power in the Age of Total War*, 178.
25. Saburo Sakai, *Samurai!* (Annapolis: U.S. Naval Institute Press, 1991), 26–27.
26. Horst Boog, "Higher Command and Leadership in the Luftwaffe, 1935–1945," in *Air Power: Promise and Reality*, ed. Mark K. Wells (Chicago: Imprint, 2000), 135.
27. Osamu Tagaya, "The Imperial Japanese Air Forces," in *Why Air Forces Fail: The Anatomy of Defeat*, eds. Robin Higham and Stephen J. Harris (Lexington: University Press of Kentucky, 2006), 179.
28. Gordon Prange, *At Dawn We Slept: The Untold Story of Pearl Harbor* (New York: McGraw-Hill, 1981).
29. Roberta Wohlstetter, *Pearl Harbor: Warning and Decision* (Stanford: Stanford University Press, 1962). Also Irving Janis, *Groupthink: Psychological Studies of Policy Decisions and Fiascoes*, 2d ed. (Boston: Little, Brown, 1982), chap. 4.
30. William H. Bartsch, *December 8, 1941: MacArthur's Pearl Harbor* (College Station: Texas A&M Press, 2003), 413ff; Levine, *Pacific War*, 37–39.
31. Peattie, *Sunburst*, 171–172.
32. Spector, *Eagle against the Sun*, 154; Craven and Cate, *Army Air Forces*, 1: 438–444; John B. Lundstrom, *The First Team* (Annapolis: U.S. Naval Institute Press, 1984), 136ff.
33. Morison, *Naval Operations*, 4: 60.
34. Standard sources on Midway include Gordon Prange, *Miracle at Midway* (New York: Penguin, 1982); Walter Lord, *Incredible Victory* (New York: Harper and Row, 1967); and Mitsuo Fuchida and Masatake Okumiya, *Midway: The Battle that Doomed Japan* (Annapolis: U.S. Naval Institute Press, 1992). A more recent treatment, Jonathan Parshall and Anthony Tully, *Shattered Sword: The Untold Story of the Battle of Midway* (Washington, DC: Potomac Books, 2005), substantially adds to our understanding of the battle.
35. Morison, *Naval Operations*, 4: 84.
36. John S. Thach, "A Beautiful Silver Waterfall," in *Carrier Warfare in the Pacific: An Oral History Collection*, ed. E. T. Wooldridge (Washington, DC: Smithsonian Institution Press, 1993), 58.
37. Captain Bruce R. Linder, USN (Ret.), "Lost Letter of Midway," *Proceedings* (August 1999): 32.

38. Craven and Cate, *Army Air Forces*, 1: 459.
39. Peattie, *Sunburst*, 174–175.
40. Parshall and Tully, *Shattered Sword*, 387–388.
41. For Guadalcanal, see Richard B. Frank, *Guadalcanal: The Definitive Account of the Landmark Battle* (New York: Random House, 1990); John Lundstrom, *The First Team and the Guadalcanal Campaign* (Annapolis: U.S. Naval Institute Press, 1994); and Morison, *Naval Operations*, vol. 5.
42. Robert Sherrod, *History of Marine Corps Aviation in World War II* (San Rafael, CA: Presidio, 1980), 85–86.
43. James B. Wellons, "General Roy S. Geiger, USMC: Marine Aviator, Joint Force Commander" (master's thesis, USAF School of Advanced Air and Space Studies, June 2007), 81–82.
44. Morison, *Naval Operations*, 5: 371.
45. Sakai, *Samurai!* 31.
46. Morison, *Naval Operations*, 5: 107.
47. George C. Kenney, *General Kenney Reports: A Personal History of the Pacific War* (New York: Duell, Sloan and Pearce, 1949), 28–29.
48. Thomas E. Griffith Jr., *MacArthur's Airman: General George C. Kenney and the War in the Southwest Pacific* (Lawrence: University Press of Kansas, 1998), 27.
49. Kenney, *General Kenney Reports*, 52–53.
50. Griffith, *MacArthur's Airman*, 69.
51. Ibid., 96.
52. Kenney, *General Kenney Reports*, 185.
53. Morison, *Naval Operations*, 6: 63.
54. Spector, *Eagle against the Sun*, 229.
55. Morison, *Naval Operations*, 6: 290.
56. *U.S. Navy War Photographs* (New York: U.S. Camera, 1945), 15.
57. Spector, *Eagle against the Sun*, 271–272.
58. Ibid., 422–423; Levine, *Pacific War*, 115.
59. Hansell, *Air Plan that Defeated Hitler*, 108.
60. William H. Tunner, *Over the Hump* (Washington, DC: Office of Air Force History, 1985), chap. III.
61. Henry Probert, *The Forgotten Air Force: The Royal Air Force in the War against Japan, 1941–1945* (London: Brassey's Ltd., 1995), 192.
62. Max Hastings, *Retribution: The Battle for Japan, 1944–45* (New York: Knopf, 2008), 133.
63. H. P. Willmott, *The Battle of Leyte Gulf: The Last Fleet Action* (Bloomington: Indiana University Press, 2005).
64. M. G. Sheftall, *Blossoms in the Wind: Human Legacies of the Kamikaze* (New York: NAL Caliber, 2005), 33–48.
65. James J. Fahey, *Pacific War Diary* (Boston: Houghton Mifflin, 1963), 228–232.
66. On the B–29 program, see Jacob Vander Meulen, *Building the B–29* (Washington, DC: Smithsonian Institution Press, 1995).
67. Kenneth P. Werrell, *Blankets of Fire: U.S. Bombers over Japan during World War II* (Washington, DC: Smithsonian Institution Press, 1996), 71.
68. Ibid., 90–91.
69. Thomas R. Searle, "'It Made a Lot of Sense to Kill Skilled Workers': The Firebombing of Tokyo in March 1945," *The Journal of Military History* 66 (January 2002), 103–134.

70. Robert S. Burrell, *The Ghosts of Iwo Jima* (College Station: Texas A&M University Press, 2006), 30–31.

71. Ibid., 106. Spector is also skeptical but concedes that "it is probably true that the airmen saved exceeded the number of marines killed in taking the island." Spector, *Eagle against the Sun*, 502.

72. Werrell, *Blankets of Fire*, 159–163.

73. Vander Meulen, *Building the B–29*, 8.

74. Conrad Crane, *Bombs, Cities and Civilians: American Airpower Strategy in World War II* (Lawrence: University Press of Kansas, 1993), 133.

75. Alvin D. Coox, "Strategic Bombing in the Pacific, 1942–1945," in *Case Studies in Strategic Bombardment*, ed. R. Cargill Hall (Washington, DC: Office of Air Force History, 1998), 321.

76. Overy, *Air War*, 99.

77. Morison, *Naval Operations*, 14: 234–237.

78. Sherrod, *History of Marine Corps Aviation*, 390.

79. John Hersey, *Hiroshima* (New York: Vintage, 1989): 49.

80. An excellent discussion of sources and interpretations is Barton Bernstein, "Truman and the A-Bomb: Targeting Noncombatants, Using the Bomb, and Defending His 'Decision,'" *The Journal of Military History* 62, no. 3 (1998): 547–570.

81. Craven and Cate, *Army Air Forces*, 5: 734.

82. Morison, *Two-Ocean War*, 282.

83. Levine, *Pacific War*, 83.

84. Evans and Peattie, *Kaigun*, 312.

85. Craven and Cate, *Army Air Forces*, 1: 17.

86. *The United States Strategic Bombing Survey (European War) (Pacific War)* (Maxwell Air Force Base, AL: Air University Press, 1987), 107.

CHAPTER 4

1. The precise contributions by sorties were U.S. Air Force, 69.3 percent; U.S. Navy, 16.1 percent; U.S. Marine Corps, 10.3 percent; and land-based friendly foreign troops, 4.3 percent. Robert Frank Futrell, *The United States Air Force in Korea 1950–1953* (Washington, DC: Office of Air Force History, 1983), 689–691.

2. Xiaoming Zhang, *Red Wings over the Yalu* (College Station: Texas A&M University Press, 2002), 201.

3. Bernard Brodie, ed., *The Absolute Weapon: Atomic Power and World Order* (New York: Harcourt Brace, 1946), 76.

4. Prior to the establishment of the U.S. Air Force in September 1947, American air power had been operated primarily by the U.S. Navy and the U.S. Army Air Forces.

5. The term most widely used to describe offensive air operations for ground forces in contact with the enemy is *close air support*. The word *support* can, however, be misleading, so this chapter will use the description *close air attack*.

6. M. J. Armitage and R. A. Mason, *Air Power in the Nuclear Age* (Urbana: University of Illinois Press, 1985), 22.

7. Other nations to contribute air forces included Australia, South Africa, Greece, the United Kingdom, South Korea, Thailand, Canada, and Turkey.

8. The first carrier sorties were flown by strike fighters from the U.S. Navy's Task Force 77

on July 3, 1950. Over the course of the war, twenty-three carriers saw action: seventeen from the United States, five from the United Kingdom, and one from Australia.

9. MacArthur also held the positions of commander in chief, Far East, and supreme commander Allied powers, the former being a U.S. appointment, the latter an Allied appointment responsible for the postwar occupation of Japan.

10. Futrell, *The United States Air Force in Korea 1950–1953*, 50–51, 693.

11. Quoted in David Halberstam, *The Fifties* (New York: Random House, 1993), 67.

12. Futrell, *The United States Air Force in Korea 1950–1953*, 46.

13. Ibid., 692. Of the remaining 225, 147 were shot down in air-to-air combat, and 78 were lost to other enemy actions.

14. Matthew B. Ridgway, *The Korean War* (New York: Doubleday, 1967), 244. Ridgway replaced MacArthur as commander of the UNC in April 1951.

15. See, for example, Jeffrey Grey, "Definite Limitations: The Air War in Korea 1950–1953," in *The War in the Air 1914–1994*, ed. Alan Stephens (Maxwell Air Force Base, AL: Air University Press, 2001): 158–160, 162.

16. William T. Y'Blood, "The U.S. Air Force in Korea—1950–1953," *Air Power History* 47, no. 2 (Summer 2000): 24–25.

17. Halberstam, *The Fifties*, 82.

18. Armitage and Mason, *Air Power in the Nuclear Age*, 29–30.

19. Zhang, *Red Wings over the Yalu*, 208–209.

20. "The basic mission of the [air force] . . . is tactical support of the ground forces." Raymond L. Garthoff, *Soviet Military Doctrine* (Glencoe, NY: Free Press, 1953), 325–326.

21. Walter J. Boyne, *Beyond the Wild Blue* (New York: St. Martin's Press, 1997), 64. Vladimir Lenin once remarked, "The capitalists will sell us the rope with which we will hang them." The sale of the Nene engines early in the Cold War lends substance to Lenin's sardonic observation.

22. Zhang, *Red Wings over the Yalu*, 252, n. 37.

23. The legendary USAF strategist and fighter pilot John Boyd developed his "OODA [observe, orient, decide, and act] Loop" concept after pondering why F–86 pilots were so successful against the MiG–15 in Korea. Boyd concluded that the response speed of the F–86's hydraulic controls conferred a critical advantage on its pilots for the "act" phase of the OODA cycle.

24. Zhang, *Red Wings over the Yalu*, 122–123.

25. For an examination of kill ratio claims, see ibid., 202–203.

26. Boyne, *Beyond the Wild Blue*, 70.

27. Armitage and Mason, *Air Power in the Nuclear Age*, 39.

28. Halberstam, *The Fifties*, 407.

29. "Reconnaissance" was the name used at the time; the more descriptive title "intelligence, surveillance, reconnaissance" is a relatively recent elaboration.

30. Futrell, *The United States Air Force in Korea 1950–1953*, 548–549.

31. Ibid., 572.

32. Ibid., 569.

CHAPTER 5

1. This chapter relies mostly on the author's *To Hanoi and Back: The U.S. Air Force and North Vietnam, 1966–1973* (Washington, DC: Smithsonian Institution Press, 2000),

and Jacob Van Staaveren, *Gradual Failure: The Air War over North Vietnam, 1965–1966* (Washington, DC: Air Force History and Museums Program, 2002). There, readers can find extensive documentation. Books that give an overview of naval air operations include Edward J. Marolda, *By Sea, Air, and Land: An Illustrated History of the U.S. Navy and the War in Southeast Asia* (Washington, DC: Naval Historical Center, 1994); Peter B. Mersky and Norman Polmar, *The Naval Air War in Vietnam* (Baltimore: Nautical and Aviation Publishing Company of America, 1986); and John B. Nichols and Barrett Tillman, *On Yankee Station: The Naval Air War over Vietnam* (Annapolis: U.S. Naval Institute Press, 1987). The notes below suggest more good books on some of the topics discussed.

2. Edwin E. Moise, *Tonkin Gulf and the Escalation of the Vietnam War* (Chapel Hill: University of North Carolina Press, 1996), argues the predominant view that while the torpedo boat attack of August 2 occurred, that of August 4 did not.

3. William J. Duiker, *Ho Chi Minh* (New York: Hyperion, 2000); Military Institute of Vietnam, *Victory in Vietnam: The Official History of the People's Army of Vietnam, 1954–1975*, trans. Merle L. Pribbenow (Lawrence: University Press of Kansas, 2002); Ilya V. Gaiduk, *The Soviet Union and the Vietnam War* (Chicago: Ivan R. Dee, 1996); Qiang Zhai, *China and the Vietnam Wars, 1950–1975* (Chapel Hill: University of North Carolina Press, 2000).

4. Jack Broughton, *Thud Ridge* (Philadelphia: J. B. Lippincott, 1969). See also his *Going Downtown: The War against Hanoi and Washington* (New York: Orion Books, 1988) and *Rupert Red Two: A Fighter Pilot's Life from Thunderbolts to Thunderchiefs* (St. Paul, MN: Zenith Press, 2007).

5. Timothy N. Castle, *One Day Too Long: Top Secret Site 85 and the Bombing of North Vietnam* (New York: Columbia University Press, 1999).

6. Stephen P. Randolph, *Powerful and Brutal Weapons: Nixon, Kissinger, and the Easter Offensive* (Cambridge, MA: Harvard University Press, 2007).

7. Nixon's White House discussion with Bunker on February 3, 1972, was tape-recorded. See Aloysius Casey and Patrick Casey, "Lavelle, Nixon, and the White House Tapes," *Air Force Magazine* (February 2007): 86–90.

8. John Darrell Sherwood, *Afterburner: Naval Aviators and the Vietnam War* (New York: New York University Press, 2004); Carol Reardon, *Launch the Intruders: A Naval Attack Squadron in the Vietnam War, 1972* (Lawrence: University Press of Kansas, 2005).

9. Jeffrey Ethell and Alfred Price, *One Day in a Long War: May 10, 1972, Air War, North Vietnam* (New York: Random House, 1989).

10. Todd P. Harmer and C. R. Anderegg, *The Shootdown of Trigger 4* (Washington, DC: Headquarters U.S. Air Force, 2001).

11. Marshall L. Michel III, *Clashes: Air Combat over North Vietnam, 1965–1972* (Annapolis: U.S. Naval Institute Press, 1997).

12. Benjamin F. Schemmer, *The Raid* (New York: Harper and Row, 1976).

13. Stuart I. Rochester and Frederick Kiley, *Honor Bound: The History of American Prisoners of War in Southeast Asia, 1961–1973* (Washington, DC: Office of the Secretary of Defense, 1998); Vernon E. Davis, *The Long Road Home: U.S. Prisoner of War Policy and Planning in Southeast Asia* (Washington, DC: Office of the Secretary of Defense, 2000).

14. Marshall L. Michel III, *The Eleven Days of Christmas: America's Last Vietnam Battle* (San Francisco: Encounter Books, 2002).

15. General John Vogt, interview with Lieutenant Colonel Arthur W. McCants Jr. and James

C. Hasdorff (Air Force History Program), August 8–9, 1978. See also "Linebacker II USAF Bombing Survey," in Herman L. Gilster, *The Air War in Southeast Asia: Case Studies of Selected Campaigns* (Maxwell Air Force Base, AL: Air University Press, 1993), 75–115.

16. U. S. Grant Sharp, *Strategy for Defeat: Vietnam in Retrospect* (San Rafael, CA: Presidio Press, 1978); William W. Momyer, *Air Power in Three Wars* (Washington, DC: U.S. Government Printing Office, 1978).

17. Mark Clodfelter, *The Limits of Air Power: The American Bombing of North Vietnam* (New York: Free Press, 1989). See also Earl H. Tilford Jr., *Crosswinds: The Air Force's Setup in Vietnam* (College Station: Texas A&M University Press, 1993).

CHAPTER 6

1. Shmuel L. Gordon, *30 Hours in October* (Tel Aviv: Maarhot, 2008).

2. The author served in the Israeli Air Force (IAF) throughout this period and participated as a fighter pilot and commander in these wars. The author hopes that his active service has not affected his judgment or tempered his criticism.

3. Max Weber, "Doctrine of the German Air Force," in *The Impact of Air Power*, ed. Eugene Emme (Princeton: D. Van Nostrand Co., 1959); originally printed in German in 1935.

4. Yigal Allon, *The Making of Israel's Army* (London: Sphere Books Ltd., 1971); Moshe Dayan, *Story of My Life* (New York: Morrow, 1976); Dan Horowitz, "The Israeli Concept of National Security," in *National Security and Democracy in Israel*, ed. Avner Yaniv (Boulder, CO: Westview Press, 1993).

5. Yizhak Shteigman, *From the War of Independence to Operation* Kadesh *1949–1956* (Tel Aviv: Israeli Air Force History Branch, 1990), 16.

6. David Ben-Gurion, government meeting (December 21, 1958), government archive, quoted by Avi Cohen, *The Defense of the Water Sources* (Tel Aviv: Ministry of Defense, IAF, 1992), 26–27.

7. David Ben-Gurion, *Diary of the War*, vol. 3, ed. Gershon Rivlin and Elhanan Oren (Tel Aviv: Ministry of Defense, 1982), 622.

8. Ezer Weizman, *On Eagle's Wings: The Personal Story of the Leading Commander of the Israeli Air Force* (Tel Aviv: Stimatzky's Agency Ltd., 1976).

9. IAF Document, Operation Branch (November 2, 1955).

10. Yoash Zidon-Chatto, *By Day, By Night, Through Haze and Fog* (Tel Aviv: Maariv Library, 1995), 223–227.

11. Yizhak Shteigman, *Operation Kadesh: The IAF in 1950–1956: Strengthening and Activities* (Tel Aviv: Ministry of Defense, IAF, 2006), 301–305; interview with General Dan Tolkowsky (May 1982).

12. Moti Havakuk, "The Development of the IAF in Light of the Conclusions of the 1956 War," in *Roar of Engines: 50 Years to Sinai War 1956*, ed. Hagai Golan and Shaul Shai (Tel Aviv: Ministry of Defense, 2006), 301–305.

13. Shmuel L. Gordon, *Air Leadership, Modern Operational Culture* (Tel Aviv: Ministry of Defense, Maarhot, 2003).

14. Moti Hod, lecture to the Command and Staff School, January 23, 1976.

15. Ze'ev Zahor, "Everything Is Dependent on the IAF, ROTEM Case 1960," in *Restless Decade: Chapters in the IAF History 1956–1967*, ed. Ze'ev Lahish and Meir Amitai (Tel Aviv: Ministry of Defense, IAF, 1995), 225–248.

16. Yigal Sheffy, *The "Rotem" Affair and the Israeli Security Perception 1957–1960* (Tel Aviv: Maarhot, 2008).

17. The story of the campaign on air superiority in the Six Days War is mainly based on the official IAF study. Yossi Abudi, ed., *The IAF in the Six Days War: Achievement of Air Superiority* (Tel Aviv: IAF, 1972).

18. Numerous books, studies, and articles deal with the Six Days War. An interesting book that represents the Arab outlook is Ibrahim Abu-Laghod, ed., *The Arab-Israeli Confrontation of June 1967: An Arab Perspective* (Evanston, IL: Northwestern University Press, 1970). A Western perspective is presented by Nadav Safran, *From War to War: The Arab-Israeli Confrontation 1948–1967* (New York: Pegasus, 1969).

19. Moti Havakuk, *Air-to-Air Warfare: November 1956–June 1967* (Tel Aviv: IAF, 1993), 62–68; Cohen, *The Defense of the Water Sources*, 176.

20. Zahor, "Everything Is Dependent on the IAF, ROTEM Case 1960," 225–248.

21. Weizman, *On Eagle's Wings*, 259 (Hebrew version).

22. Shlomo Aloni, *IAF Air Campaign: The Six Days War* (Tel Aviv: Decal Publishers, 2008), 181. This book is the most detailed description of Operation *Moked* in terms of missions, targets, casualties, and success.

23. Rafi Harlev, "40 Years to the Six Days War," in *40 Years for the Six Days War and 25 Years for the Lebanon War: Essays Collection 36*, ed. Oded Marom (Tel Aviv: Fisher Institute for Air and Space Strategic Studies, August 2007), 11; Abudi, *The IAF in the Six Days War*, appendix 1, 502.

24. *Operation Order MOKED* (March 23, 1967), updated version (private collection).

25. Ehud Yonay, *No Margin for Error* (New York: Pantheon House, 1993), 208–213.

26. Weizman, *On Eagle's Wings*, 189–246.

27. *Operation Order MOKED.*

28. Ibid., 2; Abudi, *The IAF in the Six Days War*, 33–43.

29. Dani Shapira, *Alone in the Sky* (Tel Aviv: Sifriat Maariv, 1994), 244–257.

30. Harlev, "40 Years to the Six Days War," 9.

31. Abudi, *The IAF in the Six Days War*, 454.

32. Harlev, "40 Years to the Six Days War," 11.

33. Aloni, *IAF Air Campaign: The Six Days War*, 183.

34. Abudi, *The IAF in the Six Days War*, appendix G, 502.

35. A detailed analysis based on the data in ibid., 351–358.

36. Ibid., 458.

37. Yitzhak Rabin, *The Rabin Memoirs* (Berkeley, CA: University of California Press, 1996), 18 (Hebrew version).

38. Gordon, *Air Leadership, Modern Operational Culture.*

39. Hod lecture.

40. Gordon, *Air Leadership, Modern Operational Culture.*

41. Fouad Ajami, *The Arab Predicament* (Cambridge: Cambridge University Press, 1981), 12–13.

42. Henry Kissinger, *My Years in the White House* (Boston: Little, Brown, 1979), 605–606.

43. A relevant essay that presents the Egyptian perspective is Ahmed S. Khalidi, "The War of Attrition," *Journal of Palestine Studies* (Autumn 1973): 60–87. A different perspective is presented by Yaacov Bar Siman-Tov, *The Israeli-Egyptian War of Attrition 1969–1970* (New York: Columbia University Press, 1980).

44. Yzhak Grinberg, *Planning the IDF Order of Battle between the Six Days War and Yom Kippur War* (Tel Aviv: Ministry of Defense, 2005), 34, table 3.

45. Dan Schiftan, *Attrition: The Political Strategy of Nasser's Egypt after the 1967 War* (Tel Aviv: Maarhot, 1989), 97–110.

46. Abdel Magid Farid, *Nasser: The Final Years* (Reading: Ithaca Press, 1994), 135–136.

47. Golda Meir, *My Life* (New York: Dell, 1975), 279 (Hebrew version).

48. General Eli Zeira, head of military intelligence in the Yom Kippur War, discussion with the author, May 10, 2007.

49. Daniel Dishon, ed., *Middle East Record 1969–1970* (Jerusalem: Israel University Press, 1977), 159.

50. Amos Amir, *Fire in the Sky* (Barnsley, UK: Pen and Sword Books, 2005), 218–224.

51. Elliezer "Cheetah" Cohen, *Israel's Best Defense* (New York: Orion Books, 1993), 310 (Hebrew version).

52. Moti Havakuk and Niv Faran, *Israeli Air Force Losses in Air Combats* (Tel Aviv: IAF Headquarters, 2001), 31–36.

53. Schiftan, *Attrition*, 239 (calculations by the author).

54. Ibid.

55. Ibid.

56. Mohamed Abdel Ghani el Gamasy, *The October War: Memoirs of Field Marshal El-Gamasy of Egypt* (Cairo: American University in Cairo Press, 1993), chapter 2.

57. This section is based on long, thorough, and detailed research on IAF formal debriefings, Arab writings, and interviews with most of the key people in the IAF headquarters at that time.

58. Lon Nordeen, *Fighters over Israel* (New York: Orion Books, 1990); Martin van Creveld, *Military Lessons of the Yom Kippur War: Historical Perspectives* (Beverly Hills, CA: Sage, 1975).

59. Anwar Sadat, *In Search of Identity: An Autobiography* (New York: Harper and Row, 1978); Hasan Al-Badri et al., *The Ramadan War 1973* (Dunn Loring, VA: T. N. Dupuy Associates, 1978), chapter 3.

60. Among the many other interesting books that present the Egyptian perspective are Muhamed Heikal, *The Road to Ramadan* (London: Collins, 1975), and Al-Badri et al., *The Ramadan War 1973*. An interesting study is Insight Team of the Sunday Times, *Insight on the Middle East War* (London: Andre Deutsch Ltd., 1974).

61. Uri Bar-Josef, *The Watchman Fell Asleep: The Surprise of Yom Kippur and Its Sources* (Albany: State University of New York Press, 2005).

62. Amir, *Fire in the Sky*, 239–240.

63. Recording of Operational Forum of the IAF Headquarters, October 6, 1973 (personal collection).

64. Cohen, *Israel's Best Defense*, 324–325.

65. Saad el Shazly, *The Crossing of the Suez* (San Francisco: American Mideast Research, 1980), 180–182 (Hebrew version). Another source mentions 250 aircraft. See Suhir al-Husaini, "Amazing Cooperation," *Maarhot*, no. 332 (October–November 1993): 75.

66. Dayan, *Story of My Life*, 581.

67. Recording of General David Elazar in the IAF Command Cell, October 7, 1973 (personal collection).

68. Shazly, *The Crossing of the Suez*, 168–169, 173–174.

69. Updating General Elazar, Operation Center, October 7, 1973 (personal collection); Avraham "Bren" Adan, *On the Banks of the Suez* (London: Arms and Armour, 1980), 39 (Hebrew version). General Elazar updated by the commander of the Southern Command, October 7, 1973. Recording of a discussion in Elazar's personal room (personal collection).

70. IAF Operational Department, *The IAF Annual Assessment* (August 29, 1973), table: Operational Plans (personal collection).

71. Colonel Avihu Ben Nun, head of the Offensive Branch in the IAF headquarters in the 1973 war and later commander of the IAF, interview by the author, July 24, 2006.

72. General David Ivri, General Peled's deputy and IAF commander in the 1982 war, interview by the author, February 5, 2007.

73. Michael R. Rip and Joseph F. Fontanellam, "A Window on the Arab-Israeli 'Yom Kippur' War of October 1973: Military Photo-Reconnaissance from High Altitude and Space," *Intelligence and National Security* 6 (January 1991), 15–89.

74. Ze'ev Lahish, "Intelligence Assessments for Operation Dugman 5, October 7, 1973," *Special Intelligence Review* (Tel Aviv: IAF, 1983), 18.

75. "The Israeli Air Force in the Yom Kippur War," report prepared for General Beni Peled, the IAF commander's debriefings in the United States (Tel Aviv: IAF Headquarters, 1974), 25.

76. Gordon, *30 Hours in October*, part 6; Amir, *Fire in the Sky*, 243–248.

77. Weizman, *On Eagle's Wings*, 329.

78. Shazly, *The Crossing of the Suez*.

79. Havakuk and Faran, *Israeli Air Force Losses in Air Combats*, 38.

80. For an outstanding Syrian perspective of the 1982 war, see Mustafa Tlas, ed., *The Israeli Invasion of Lebanon* (Damascus: Tashrin, 1983). For a broad observation, see Itamar Rabinovich, *The War for Lebanon 1970–1985* (Ithaca, NY: Cornell University Press, 1985).

81. Some of the systems developed and produced in Israel that played significant roles in the 1982 war are documented in Ze'ev Bonen and Dan Arkin, *RAFAEL: From Laboratory to Campaign* (Tel Aviv: N. D. D. Media, 2003).

82. The ambassador was shot and remained severely crippled for the rest of his life.

83. Yossi Abudi, ed., *The Operations of the IAF in the "Peace of Galilee" War* (Tel Aviv: IAF Headquarters, 1984), 25.

84. Tlas, *The Israeli Invasion of Lebanon*, 189–190.

85. David Ivri, "How We Destroyed the SAM Array in SHELEG War," in *40 Years for the Six Days War and 25 Years for the Lebanon War*, 23–29.

86. Abudi, *The Operations of the IAF in the "Peace of Galilee" War*, 354.

87. Ivri, "How We Destroyed the SAM Array in SHELEG War."

88. Tlas, *The Israeli Invasion of Lebanon*, 191.

89. Ivri, "How We Destroyed the SAM Array in SHELEG War," 28.

90. David Ivri, "Operational Command System," in *Essays Collection 10*, ed. Oded Marom (February 2003), 2–3.

91. Shmuel L. Gordon, *Conflict in the Air: Issues in Air Strategy of Germany and Britain 1914–1945* (Tel Aviv: Maarhot, 1985), 109–144.

CHAPTER 7

1. This chapter is largely based on Lawrence Freedman, *Official History of the Falklands Campaign*, vol. II, *War and Diplomacy*, rev. ed. (London: Routledge, 2007). For other

sources, see Despatch by Admiral Sir John Fieldhouse, GCB, GBE, commander of the Task Force Operations in the South Atlantic: April to June 1982, December 14, 1982; supplement to the *London Gazette,* December 13, 1982: David Brown, *The Royal Navy and the Falklands War* (London: Leo Cooper, 1987); Rodney Burden, Michael Draper, Douglas Rough, Colin Smith, and David Wilton, *Falklands: The Air War* (London: Arms and Armour Press, 1986); Michael Clapp and Ewan Southby-Tailyour, *Amphibious Assault: Falklands: The Battle of San Carlos Waters* (London: Leo Cooper, 1996); James Corum, "Argentine Airpower in the Falklands War," *Air and Space Power Journal* (Fall 2002); Jeffrey Ethell and Alfred Price, *Air War South Atlantic* (London: Sidgwick and Jackson, 1983); Major General Sir Jeremy Moore and Rear Admiral Sir John Woodward, "The Falklands Experience," *Journal of the Royal United Services Institute* (March 1983); and Admiral Sandy Woodward with Patrick Robinson, *One Hundred Days: The Memoirs of the Falklands Battle Group Commander* (London: HarperCollins, 1992).

2. Freedman, *Official History of the Falklands Campaign,* 79.
3. Ibid., 442.
4. Ibid., 431.

CHAPTER 8

1. Edward N. Luttwak, *Strategy: The Logic of War and Peace,* rev. ed. (Cambridge, MA: Belknap Press of Harvard University Press, 2001), 271–273.
2. See, for example, Richard P. Hallion, *Storm over Iraq: Air Power and the Gulf War* (Washington, DC: Smithsonian Institution Press, 1992); Richard G. Davis, *On Target: Organizing and Executing the Strategic Air Campaign against Iraq* (Washington, DC: Air Force History and Museums Program, 2002); and Luttwak, *Strategy,* 185–205.
3. Rather than dealing with the full spectrum of air operations—which includes important elements such as air-to-air tanking, airlift, reconnaissance, electronic warfare, command and control, and a range of other supporting activities—this chapter focuses on Coalition aircraft that dropped bombs and delivered missiles against Iraq's political, economic, and military infrastructure, as well as against the Iraqi armed forces.
4. Kevin M. Woods, *The Mother of All Battles: Saddam Hussein's Strategic Plan for the Persian Gulf War* (Annapolis: U.S. Naval Institute Press, 2008), provides excellent insight into Iraqi perspectives. This is an official U.S. Joint Forces Command report and part of the larger *Iraqi Perspective Project.* See also Ofra Bengio, *Saddam Speaks on the Gulf Crisis: A Collection of Documents* (Syracuse, NY: Syracuse University Press, 1992).
5. Woods, *The Mother of All Battles,* 65.
6. Ibid., 60–92; Kenneth M. Pollack, *Arabs at War: Arab Military Effectiveness, 1948–1991* (Lincoln: University of Nebraska Press, 2002), 235–237.
7. For a very good discussion on the background of the invasion, see Amatzia Baram, "The Iraqi Invasion of Kuwait: Decision-making in Baghdad," in *Iraq's Road to War,* ed. Amatzia Baram and Barry Rubin (London: Macmillan, 1993), 5–36. See also Anthony H. Cordesman and Abraham R. Wagner, *The Gulf War: The Lessons of Modern War* (Boulder, CO: Westview Press, 1996), 4: 33–61; Lawrence Freedman and Efraim Karsh, *The Gulf Conflict 1990–1991* (London: Faber and Faber, 1993), 19–63; Ghazi A. Algosaibi, *The Gulf Crisis: An Attempt to Understand* (London: Kegan Paul International, 1993), 1–19; Saad al-Bazzaz, "An Insider's View of Iraq," *Middle East Quarterly* 2, no. 4 (1995).
8. "Address to the Nation Announcing the Deployment of United States Armed Forces

to Saudi Arabia," August 8, 1990, in *Public Papers of the Presidents of the United States: George Bush, 1990* (Washington, DC: U.S. Government Printing Office, 1991), 1,108.

9. John Lewis, *Days of Fear: The Inside Story of the Iraqi Invasion of Kuwait* (Dubai: Motivate Publishing, 1997); Kanan Makiya, *Cruelty and Silence: War, Tyranny, Uprising, and the Arab World* (New York: St. Martin's Press, 2006).

10. For details, see Amatzia Baram, "Calculation and Miscalculation in Baghdad," in *International Perspectives on the Gulf Conflict 1990–1991,* ed. Alex Danchev and Dan Keohane (London: Macmillan, 1994), 23–58.

11. Department of Defense, *Conduct of the Persian Gulf War: Final Report to Congress* (Washington, DC: U.S. Government Printing Office, 1992), 33.

12. On the air power debate, see, for example, John Andreas Olsen, *John Warden and the Renaissance of American Air Power* (Washington, DC: Potomac Books, 2007); Richard T. Reynolds, *Heart of the Storm: The Genesis of the Air Campaign against Iraq* (Maxwell Air Force Base, AL: Air University Press, 1995); James C. Slife, *Creech Blue: Gen Bill Creech and the Reformation of the Tactical Air Forces, 1978–1984* (Maxwell Air Force Base, AL: Air University Press, 2004); and Barry D. Watts, "Doctrine, Technology and Air Warfare," in *Air Power Confronts an Unstable World,* ed. Richard P. Hallion (London: Brassey's Ltd., 1997), 13–50.

13. Department of Defense, *Conduct of the Persian Gulf War,* 84.

14. Eliot A. Cohen et al., *The Gulf War Air Power Survey,* vol. 2, part 2: *Effects and Effectiveness* (Washington, DC: U.S. Government Printing Office), 79.

15. Woods, *The Mother of All Battles,* 130.

16. Ibid., 133.

17. For personal accounts on airmen's view, see Tom Clancy, *Every Man a Tiger,* with Chuck Horner (New York: G. P. Putnam's Sons, 1999), and Buster C. Glosson, *War with Iraq: Critical Lessons* (Charlotte, NC: Glosson Family Foundation, 2003).

18. In alphabetical order, the countries that contributed combat aircraft were: Bahrain, Canada, Egypt, France, Italy, Kuwait, Oman, Qatar, Saudi Arabia, United Arab Emirates, United Kingdom, and the United States.

19. For insight into the Iran-Iraq War and the performance of the Iraqi air force, see Pollack, *Arabs at War,* 182–235.

20. Woods, *The Mother of All Battles,* 71. On the Iraqi air defense system, see Michael R. Gordon and Bernard E. Trainor, *The Generals' War: The Inside Story of the Conflict in the Gulf* (Boston: Little, Brown, 1995), 102–122, and Cohen et al., *Gulf War Air Power Survey: Operations,* vol. 2, part 1, 77–82.

21. Benjamin S. Lambeth, *The Transformation of American Air Power* (Ithaca, NY: Cornell University Press, 2000), 112.

22. Richard G. Davis, *Decisive Force: Strategic Bombing in the Gulf War* (Washington, DC: Air Force History and Museums Program, 1996), 36.

23. Woods, *The Mother of All Battles,* 182–185.

24. Cohen et al., *Gulf War Air Power Survey: Operations,* vol. 2, part 1, 145.

25. Woods, *The Mother of All Battles,* 189–190; Cohen et al., *Gulf War Air Power Survey,* vol. 2, part 2, 109. See also Clancy, *Every Man a Tiger,* 536–544.

26. Lambeth, *The Transformation of Air Power,* 114.

27. Woods, *The Mother of All Battles,* 190.

28. Ibid., 281. In the end, the air attacks destroyed 375 of 594 hardened shelters on 44 airfields. Cohen et al., *Gulf War Air Power Survey,* vol. 2, part 2, 146.

29. Woods, *The Mother of All Battles*, 204.

30. Cohen et al., *Gulf War Air Power Survey*, vol. 2, part 2, 109–111.

31. Woods, *The Mother of All Battles*, 177.

32. Ibid., 193.

33. Ibid.

34. Cohen et al., *Gulf War Air Power Survey*, vol. 2, part 1, 95, 155.

35. Department of Defense, *Conduct of the Persian Gulf War*, 124–129. See also Davis, *Decisive Force*, 47.

36. Woods, *The Mother of All Battles*, 182. For details, see Hazim Abd al-Razzaq al-Ayyubi, "Forty-Three Missiles on the Zionist Entity," first published in *Amman al-Arab al-Yawm*, translated by Foreign Broadcast Information Service (FBIS), October 25–November 12, 1998.

37. Woods, *The Mother of All Battles*, 184–192; Cohen et al., *Gulf War Air Power Survey*, vol. 2, part 1, 189.

38. Woods, *The Mother of All Battles*, 265.

39. Cohen et al., *Gulf War Air Power Survey*, vol. 2, part 2, 148.

40. Quoted in Woods, *The Mother of All Battles*, 273.

41. Cohen et al., *Gulf War Air Power Survey*, vol. 2, part 1, 5.

42. Davis, *Decisive Force*, 4–5.

43. Cohen et al., *Gulf War Air Power Survey*, vol. 2, part 2, 148; author's discussions with General Wafiq Samarrai (Ret.), former chief of Iraqi intelligence.

44. Woods, *The Mother of All Battles*, 206.

45. Cohen et al., *Gulf War Air Power Survey*, vol. 2, part 2, 277.

46. Ibid., 285.

47. Woods, *The Mother of All Battles*, 187.

48. Ibid.

49. Cohen et al., *Gulf War Air Power Survey*, vol. 2, part 2, 349; Daniel T. Kuehl, "Airpower vs. Electricity: Electric Power as a Target for Strategic Air Operations," in *Airpower: Theory and Practice*, ed. John Gooch (London: Frank Cass, 1995), 237–266.

50. Gordon and Trainor, *The Generals' War*, 324–327.

51. Cohen et al., *Gulf War Air Power Survey*, vol. 2, part 2, 345; William M. Arkin, "Baghdad: The Urban Sanctuary in Desert Storm," *Airpower Journal* 11, no. 1 (Spring 1997): 4–21.

52. Cohen et al., *Gulf War Air Power Survey*, vol. 2, part 2, 167.

53. See Wayne W. Thompson, "Al Firdos: The Last Two Weeks of Strategic Bombing in DESERT STORM," *Air Power History* (Summer 1996): 63.

54. Davis, *Decisive Force*, 43.

55. Cohen et al., *Gulf War Air Power Survey*, vol. 2, part 2, 171.

56. Ibid., 159.

57. Ibid., 170.

58. Ibid., 161.

59. Ibid., 170–202.

60. Fred Frostic, *Air Campaign against the Iraqi Army in the Kuwaiti Theater of Operations*, Project Air Force (Santa Monica, CA: RAND, 1994), 6.

61. Davis, *Decisive Force*, 66.

62. Ibid., 68.

63. Woods, *The Mother of All Battles*, 186; Stephen T. Hosmer, *Psychological Effects of U.S. Air*

Operations in Four Wars 1941–1991: Lessons for U.S. Commanders (Santa Monica, CA: RAND, 1996), xxvii.

64. Cohen et al., *Gulf War Air Power Survey*, vol. 2, part 2, 197–199.

65. Pollack, *Arabs at War*, 246.

66. Woods, *The Mother of All Battles*, 228.

67. Ibid., 232, 234.

68. Ibid., 142.

69. Cohen et al., *Gulf War Air Power Survey*, vol. 2, part 1, 342.

70. Ibid., 269–286.

71. Ibid., 320; Cohen et al., *Gulf War Air Power Survey*, vol. 2, part 2, 97, note 38.

72. Cohen et al., *Gulf War Air Power Survey*, vol. 2, part 2, 98–99.

73. Lambeth, *The Transformation of American Air Power*, 130.

74. Cohen et al., *Gulf War Air Power Survey*, vol. 2, part 1, 250.

75. Woods, *The Mother of All Battles*, 287.

76. Cohen et al., *Gulf War Air Power Survey*, vol. 2, part 1, 295.

77. For details on the ground war, see, for example, Robert H. Scales, *Certain Victory: The U.S. Army in the Gulf War* (London: Brassey's Ltd., 1997); Richard M. Swain, *"Lucky War": Third Army in Desert Storm* (Fort Leavenworth, KS: U.S. Army Command and General Staff College Press, 1994); Pollack, *Arabs at War*, 246–256; and Department of Defense, *Conduct of the Persian Gulf War*, 226–296.

78. Scales, *Certain Victory*, 146.

79. Cohen et al., *Gulf War Air Power Survey*, vol. 2, part 1, 294.

80. Ibid., 306.

81. Ibid., 311, 313–315 (for controversy on the fire support coordination line).

82. Cohen et al., *Gulf War Air Power Survey*, vol. 2, part 2, 245.

83. Pollack, *Arabs at War*, 256.

84. Lambeth, *The Transformation of American Air Power*, 103.

85. For the controversy on the JFACC role, see, for example, James A. Winnefeld and Dana J. Johnson, *Joint Air Operations: Pursuit of Unity of Command and Control, 1942–1991* (Annapolis: U.S. Naval Institute Press, 1993).

86. Cohen et al., *Gulf War Air Power Survey*, vol. 2, part 1, 156.

87. Cohen et al., *Gulf War Air Power Survey*, vol. 2, part 2, 114.

88. For a debate on air power effectiveness, see *Security Studies* 7, no. 2 (Winter 1997–1998): 93–171; and *Security Studies* 7, no. 3 (Spring 1998): 182–238.

89. For an Iraqi view on al-Khafji, see Woods, *The Mother of All Battles*, 14–30.

90. Luttwak, *Strategy*, 194–199.

91. Cohen et al., *Gulf War Air Power Survey*, vol. 2, part 1, 322–325.

92. A strong advocate of this school is Robert A. Pape, *Bombing to Win: Air Power and Coercion in War* (Ithaca, NY: Cornell University Press, 1996).

93. Cohen et al., *Gulf War Air Power Survey*, vol. 2, part 1, 332.

94. Cohen et al., *Gulf War Air Power Survey*, vol. 2, part 2, 12; Frostic, *Air Campaign against the Iraqi Army in the Kuwaiti Theater of Operations*, 5.

95. John G. Heidenrich, "The Gulf War: How Many Iraqis Died?" *Foreign Policy* 90 (Spring 1993); and John Muller, "The Perfect Enemy: Assessing the Gulf War," *Security Studies* 5, no. 1 (Autumn 1995): 77–117. The Americans suffered 148 combat fatalities and 458 wounded out of a total of more than 500,000 military personnel deployed to the theater.

It is difficult to assess how many Iraqis died, but several studies indicate that the number of soldiers and civilians killed by Coalition action during Desert Storm combined was considerably less than ten thousand.

96. Woods, *The Mother of All Battles*, 243.
97. For more on how the strategic bombing affected the regime and the construct of the security apparatus, see John Andreas Olsen, *Strategic Air Power in Desert Storm* (London: Frank Cass, 2003). For further insight on sectarian-religious and tribal elements, see Amatzia Baram, *Building toward Crisis: Saddam Husayn's Strategy for Survival* (Washington, DC: Washington Institute for Near East Policy, 1998).
98. Davis, *Decisive Force*, 54–55.
99. Woods, *The Mother of All Battles*, 249.
100. Ibid.
101. Ibid., 299.

CHAPTER 9

1. Ivo Andric, *Gospodjica* (Zagreb: Mladost, 1961), 77, drawn from Lenard J. Cohen, *Broken Bonds: The Disintegration of Yugoslavia* (Boulder, CO: Westview Press, 1993), 268.
2. Robert C. Owen, "Summary," in *Deliberate Force: A Case Study in Effective Air Campaigning*, ed. Robert C. Owen (Maxwell Air Force Base, AL: Air University Press, 2000), 513–514.
3. Norman Cigar, "How Wars End: War Termination and Serbian Decisionmaking in the Case of Bosnia," *South East European Monitor* (January 1996).
4. Even today, it is difficult to believe the systematic savagery of ethnic cleansing, but it is well documented in many reports and encapsulated in several books, including Roy Gutman, *A Witness to Genocide* (New York: Macmillan, 1993), and David Rieff, *Slaughterhouse: Bosnia and the Failure of the West* (New York: Simon & Schuster, 1995).
5. Karl A. Mueller, "The Demise of Yugoslavia and the Destruction of Bosnia: Strategic Causes, Effects, and Responses," in Owen, *Deliberate Force*, 21.
6. Robert A. Hunter, interview by author, July 23, 1996, tape 1, side a, index 50, held in the USAF Historical Research Center's Balkans Air Campaign Study (BACS) files.
7. Though the origins of the term are vague, two books on the region clearly underpin the "ancient hatreds" notion: Rebecca West, *Black Lamb and Grey Falcon* (London: Penguin Books, 1941), and Robert Kaplan, *Balkan Ghosts: A Journey through History* (New York: St. Martin's Press, 1993).
8. Cohen, *Broken Bonds*, throughout and chapter 9 in particular.
9. Carole Rogel, *The Breakup of Yugoslavia and the War in Bosnia* (Westport, CT: Greenwood Press, 1998), 47.
10. United Nations Security Council Resolution (UNSCR) 816, March 31, 1993, 2.
11. UNSCR 836, June 4, 1993, 3.
12. Bradley S. Davis, "The Planning Background," in Owen, *Deliberate Force*, 57. Smith was commander in chief, Allied Forces Southern Europe (AFSOUTH).
13. Richard Holbrooke, interview by Mark McLaughlin and Karl Mueller, May 24, 1996, n.p., BACS.
14. Leighton Smith, "NATO Operations in Bosnia-Herzegovina: Deliberate Force, 29 August–14 September 1995," presentation to the Air War College, Maxwell Air Force Base, AL, November 9, 1995, videotape, index 1280, BACS.

15. Smith, "NATO Operations," 1270–1330.

16. Scott G. Walker, interview by author, February 28, 1997, BACS. Walker was the deputy mission commander of the strike.

17. "NATO Jets Knock Out Base for Serb Planes," *Stars and Stripes*, November 22, 1994, 1–2; Roger Cohen, "NATO, Expanding Bosnia Role, Strikes a Serbian Base in Croatia," *New York Times*, November 22, 1995, 1.

18. Holbrooke interview, May 24, 1996, side A, index 567, BACS.

19. In his memoir of the conflict, Holbrooke declared, "The Western mistake . . . had been to treat the Serbs as rational people. . . . In fact, they respect only force or an unambiguous and credible threat to use it." Richard Holbrooke, *To End a War* (New York: Random House, 1998), 152.

20. Tim Ripley, *Operation Deliberate Force: The UN and NATO Campaign in Bosnia 1995* (London: Centre for Defence and International Security Studies, 1995), 47.

21. Ibid., 96–112.

22. Adrian Humphreys, "Canadian's Saga Puts NATO Strike on Trial," *Canadian National Post*, June 14, 2008.

23. For a most bitter and pessimistic assessment of the Bosnian debacle, see Rieff, *Slaughterhouse*, 224–225, and throughout. Also see Roger Cohen, "Conflict in the Balkans: The Overview; After 2d Strike from NATO, Serbs Detain U.N. Troops," *New York Times,* May 27, 1995.

24. Christopher Bellamy, "BOSNIA CRISIS: Rapid Reaction Unit Starts to Take Shape," *Independent* (London), July 13, 1995; Mike O'Connor, "Bosnian Government Said to Hamper New, Stronger U.N. Force," *New York Times,* August 17, 1995.

25. Ripley, *Deliberate Force*, 140–142.

26. Michael Evans, "Muted Threat Falls Short of Summit Hopes," and "American Deal Sours Over Dinner," *Times* (London), July 22, 1995.

27. Bradley S. Davis, "The Planning Background," in Owen, *Deliberate Force*, 57.

28. Ripley, *Operation Deliberate Force*, 195.

29. The most thorough and professionally competent discussion of NATO air planning during the Bosnian intervention remains Christopher M. Campbell, "The Deliberate Force Air Campaign Plan," BACS, 87–126. At the time that Colonel Campbell wrote his study, he was serving as an instructor in the USAF's Joint Doctrine Air Campaign Planning Course and had served previously in several NATO air planning positions and on the staff of the United Nations Protection Force.

30. UNSCR 836, 3, and North Atlantic Council, Memorandum to the Secretary General, NATO, subject: NAC Decision Statement MCM–KAD–084–93, "Operational Options for Air Strikes in Bosnia-Herzegovina," August 8, 1993.

31. Campbell, "Campaign Plan," 101.

32. NATO Military Committee, memorandum to the Secretary General, NAC MCM–KAD–57–95, BACS; also see Richard L. Sargent, "Deliberate Force Targeting," 282–283.

33. Mark A. Bucknam, *Responsibility of Command: How UN and NATO Commanders Influenced Airpower over Bosnia* (Maxwell Air Force Base, AL: Air University Press, 2003), 204–206; AIRSOUTH, briefing, subject: NATO Air Operations in Bosnia-Herzegovina—Deliberate Force, about August 1, 1995, BACS.

34. Holbrooke, *To End a War*, 99.

35. Number of aircraft, August 30, 1995, and September 15, 1995, respectively: France, 44/47; Germany, 0/14; Italy, 20/20; the Netherlands, 18/18; NATO, 8/8; Spain, 11/11; Turkey, 18/18; United Kingdom, 28/28; and United States, 122/141. Total: 269/305. Information taken from charts in Richard L. Sargent, "Aircraft Used in Deliberate Force," in Owen, *Deliberate Force*, 203–205. Sargent's chapters, which also include "Weapons Used in Deliberate Force," "Deliberate Force Targeting," and "Deliberate Force Tactics," remain the best unclassified sources for information on those topics.

36. Germany did not conduct air-ground strikes during Deliberate Force. Italian strike aircraft were capable of precision strikes but did not utilize precision weapons during the campaign. Dutch fighters could drop laser-guided bombs but only if another aircraft designated the target with a laser beam.

37. Sargent, "Weapons," 259–268.

38. See Ronald M. Reed, "Chariots of Fire: Rules of Engagement in Operation Deliberate Force," in Owen, *Deliberate Force*, 381–421, for a detailed discussion of the evolution of Deliberate Force's rules of engagement.

39. Mark J. Conversino, "Executing Deliberate Force, 30 August–14 September 1995," in Owen, *Deliberate Force*, 150–163.

40. John A. Tirpak, "Deliberate Force," *Air Force Magazine* (October 1998).

41. Reed, "Chariots of Fire," 406; Robert C. Owen, "Operation Deliberate Force: A Case Study on Humanitarian Constraints in Aerospace Warfare," *Proceedings of Humanitarian Challenges in Military Intervention Workshop*, Carr Center for Human Rights Policy, John F. Kennedy School of Government, Harvard University, November 29–30, 1999, 69–71.

42. AIRSOUTH, "Air Campaign Targeting," briefing, June 2, 1995, BACS; and Sargent, "Targeting," 285.

43. This abbreviated narrative of the air campaign is drawn mainly from Owen, *Deliberate Force*, throughout, and Ripley, *Deliberate Force*, particularly his excellent narrative, 245–291. Other sources are indicated below as appropriate.

44. Daniel Williams, "NATO Continues Extensive Bombing across Bosnia," *Washington Post*, August 31, 1995, A1; Ripley, *Deliberate Force*, 217.

45. Williams, "NATO Continues," A1.

46. Holbrooke, *To End a War*, 106. Milosevic's role was essential, since both the president of the Serb Republic, Radovan Karadzic, and his military commander, Ratko Mladic, were indicted war criminals and faced immediate arrest should they leave the area under their control to participate in international negotiations.

47. For detailed discussions of the diplomacy behind restarting the bombing, see Holbrooke, *To End a War*, 18–98, and Ripley, *Deliberate Force*, 261–267.

48. Daniel R. Zoerb, interview by Wayne Thompson and Tim Reagan, October 20, 1995, BACS. Then-Colonel Zoerb was General Ryan's chief planner for Deliberate Force.

49. Ripley, *Deliberate Force*, 276.

50. Tim Ripley, "F–16 Precision Strikers, Operation Deliberate Force over Bosnia," *Code One* (January 1996). The Low-Altitude Navigation and Targeting Infrared for Night system coupled a high-resolution infrared sensor with the aircraft's terrain radar to provide pilots with a detailed display of a target area and a laser designator to provide terminal weapon guidance.

51. Evaluation of 5 ATAF Deputy Commander, USAF Brigadier General David Sawyer, in Ripley, "F–16 Precision Strikers."

52. Tirpak, "Deliberate Force."

53. Holbrooke, *To End a War*, 144–148.

54. Conversino, "Executing Deliberate Force," 156–157.

55. Bruce W. Nelan, "More Talking, More Bombing," *Time*, September 18, 1995.

56. Tirpak, "Deliberate Force."

57. Ripley, *Deliberate Force*, 314–315.

58. Ibid., 296.

59. For a recent exploration of the operational meaning of precision air power, see Robert A. Pape, "The True Worth of Air Power," *Foreign Affairs* (March–April 2004). Addressing the effect of precision weapons on the independent decisiveness of air power, Pape argues that "precision air weapons have fundamentally changed military power, but they have not brought about the revolution often proclaimed by many air power advocates. . . . rather, precision weaponry has revolutionized contemporary warfare by multiplying the effectiveness of using air and ground power together. The United States, in other words, still wins its wars the old-fashioned way. But with new precision air weapons, it now does so better than ever."

CHAPTER 10

1. *Kosovo Report: Independent International Commission on Kosovo*, annex 2 (Oxford: Oxford University Press, 2000), 42.

2. Ibid., 56.

3. Ibid., 53.

4. Ibid., 69.

5. United Nations Security Council Resolution (UNSCR) 1160, 1998.

6. Wesley K. Clark, *Waging Modern War* (New York: Public Affairs, 2001), 112.

7. Ibid., 117.

8. Ibid., 119.

9. Ibid., 117.

10. PBS *Frontline* interview with General Naumann. Cited in Louis Sell, *Slobodan Milosevic and the Destruction of Yugoslavia* (Durham, NC: Duke University Press, 2002), 267.

11. Clark, *Waging Modern War*, 122.

12. Benjamin S. Lambeth, *NATO's Air War for Kosovo: A Strategic and Operational Assessment*, DRR–2449–AF (Santa Monica, CA: RAND, December 2000), 11.

13. United Kingdom Ministry of Defence (UK MOD), Press Release 148/98, June 12, 1998.

14. Ibid.

15. Report in the *Boston Globe*, June 11, 1998, A2, cited in *Kosovo Report*, 73.

16. Sell, *Slobodan Milosevic*, 287.

17. UN High Commission for Refugees, cited in *Kosovo Report*, 74.

18. UNSCR 1199, 1998.

19. Sell, *Slobodan Milosevic*, 289.

20. Headquarters Allied Forces Southern Europe, website briefing notes, March 27, 1999.

21. Clark, *Waging Modern War*, 153.

22. Sell, *Slobodan Milosevic*, 291.

23. Report of the Secretary-General Prepared Pursuant to Resolution 1160, 1199, and 1203 of the United Nations Security Council, UN Doc/Si998/1221, December 24, 1998, 3.

24. *Kosovo Report*, 82.

25. Headquarters Allied Forces Central Europe, website release, March 27, 1999.
26. General Sir Rupert Smith, DSACEUR, in evidence to the House of Commons Defence Committee, May 17, 2000, *Lessons of Kosovo,* vol. II, para. 934.
27. Wesley K. Clark, testimony before U.S. Senate Armed Services Committee, October 21, 1999.
28. *New York Times,* March 25, 2004.
29. *Guardian* (London), March 25, 1999.
30. Press Conference, HQ NATO, March 23, 1999.
31. *Guardian* (London), March 29, 1999.
32. David Halberstam, *War in a Time of Peace* (New York: Touchstone, 2002), 425.
33. Ibid.
34. Ibid.
35. *Aviation Week and Space Technology,* March 29, 1999, 30.
36. Clark, *Waging Modern War,* 123.
37. UK MOD and Pentagon Briefings, March 31, 1999.
38. Interview with Colonel Nebojsa Djukanovic, HQ Serbian Air Force and Air Defense Command, Belgrade, June 12, 2005.
39. Alexandar Radic and Vladimir Jovanovic, *Air Forces Monthly,* April 2002, 30.
40. For a comprehensive analysis of the air war from Western sources, see Lambeth, *NATO's Air War for Kosovo.*
41. For a detailed and authentic description of the Serbian MiG–29 opposition, see Mark Nixon, "The Knights," *Air Forces Monthly* (January 2002).
42. Interview with Lieutenant Colonel Nebojsa Nikolic, HQ Serbian Air Force and Air Defense Command, Belgrade, June 12, 2005.
43. Interview with Colonel Jovica Draganic, former OC, No. 250 Missile Brigade, Belgrade, June 13, 2005.
44. Conversations with senior serving and retired air defense officers, Belgrade, June 9–13, 2005.
45. Interview with staff of Novi Sad University, June 11, 2005.
46. Interview with SA–7 operator, Novi Sad, June 11, 2005.
47. Lambeth, *NATO's Air War for Kosovo,* 102–120.
48. Interview with Colonel Jovica Draganic, Belgrade, June 13, 2005.
49. Ibid.
50. Interview with Serbian Defence Staff, Belgrade, June 9, 2005.
51. Christopher Haave and Phil Haun, *A–10s over Kosovo* (Maxwell Air Force Base, AL: Air University Press, 2003), 106.
52. *Daily Telegraph* (London), March 28, 1999.
53. See, for example, John Keegan, "Why Air Strikes Are Not Working," *Daily Telegraph,* March 30, 1999.
54. *Guardian* (London), March 30, 1999.
55. *Daily Telegraph* (London), April 2, 1999.
56. James Shea, NATO HQ Briefing, March 31, 1999.
57. *Daily Telegraph* (London), April 2, 1999.
58. Belgrade interviews, June 9–13, 2005.
59. *Sunday Telegraph* (London), April 4, 1999.
60. *Daily Telegraph* (London), April 26, 1999.

61. Haave and Haun, *A–10s over Kosovo*, 138.

62. *Sunday Telegraph* (London), April 4, 1999.

63. *Guardian* (London), April 6, 1999.

64. *Daily Telegraph* (London), April 12, 1999.

65. Author's interview with F–16 pilot's squadron commander, Washington, DC, August 16, 1999.

66. *Washington Post,* May 30, 1999.

67. *Washington Watch,* U.S. Air Force Association, June 10, 1999, 5.

68. Clark, *Waging Modern War,* 182–183.

69. HQ NATO Media Briefing, April 21, 1999.

70. Clark, *Waging Modern War,* 268.

71. NATO Briefing, May 8, 1999.

72. Organization for Security and Cooperation in Europe Report on Kosovo, viii, cited in *Kosovo Report,* 88.

73. United Nations High Commissioner for Refugees Estimate, May 1999, cited in *Kosovo Report,* Annex 1, 304.

74. *Guardian* (London), May 13, 1999.

75. *Daily Telegraph* (London), May 18, 1999.

76. *Washington Post,* May 30, 1999.

77. Interviews with defense officials in Belgrade, June 2005.

78. Interviews in Belgrade, June 2005.

79. Lambeth, *NATO's Air War for Kosovo,* 56.

80. General Michael E. Ryan, Chief of Staff, USAF, in Air Force Policy letter, August 1999.

81. See the author's *Air Power: A Centennial Appraisal* (London: Brassey's Ltd., 1994), 235–278, for the origin and explanation of this expression.

82. General John Jumper, Commander U.S. Air Force in Europe and Commander Allied Air Forces Central Europe, "Kosovo Victory: A Commander's Perspective," *Air Power Review* 2, no. 4 (Winter 1999): 7–9.

83. Bruce R. Nardulli et al., *Disjointed War: Military Operations in Kosovo 1999* (Santa Monica, CA: RAND Arroyo Center, 2002), 48.

84. Jumper, "Kosovo Victory," 8.

85. *Aviation Week and Space Technology,* November 15, 1999.

86. Brigadier General Leroy Barnidge, Commander, 509th Bomber Wing, Aerospace Education Foundation Colloquium on NATO Air Operations in Kosovo, Washington, DC, September 17, 1999.

87. Lambeth, *NATO's Air War for Kosovo,* 91.

88. Rebecca Grant, *The B–2 Goes to War* (Arlington, VA: Iris Press, 2001), 30.

89. Rear Admiral I. R. Henderson, Royal Navy, "Coalition Operations—Learning the Lessons," Shephard Airpower Conference and Exhibition, London, January 29, 2001.

90. Ibid.

91. Air Force Doctrine Document 2, *Organization and Employment of Aerospace Power,* USAF, September 28, 1998, 6–7.

92. John Warden, *The Air Campaign: Planning for Combat* (Washington, DC: National Defense University Press, 1988).

93. *New York Times,* May 13, 1999.

94. *Washington Post,* June 4, 1999.

95. Lieutenant General Michael C. Short, testimony to the U.S. Senate Armed Services Committee, October 21, 1999; *Washington Post*, October 22, 1999, 14.

96. *Daily Telegraph* (London), April 28, 1999.

97. Clark, *Waging Modern War*, 124.

98. *Daily Telegraph* (London), May 5, 1999.

99. William S. Cohen and General Henry H. Shelton, USA, in a joint statement before the Senate Armed Services Committee, October 1999, as reported in *Air Force Magazine*, December 1999.

100. Tim Ripley, *Defence Systems Daily*, December 1, 1999.

101. Lieutenant General J. W. Handy, USAF, in testimony to the U.S. Military Readiness Committee, October 26, 1999.

102. Jumper, "Kosovo Victory," 9.

103. Air Commodore Stuart Peach, RAF, "Air Warfare: A Contemporary Perspective," in *Effects Based Warfare*, ed. Christopher Finn (London: London Stationery Office, 2002), 92.

CHAPTER 11

1. This chapter is an excerpt from the author's book *Air Power against Terror: America's Conduct of Operation Enduring Freedom* (Santa Monica, CA: RAND Corporation, 2005).

2. James R. Asker, "Washington Outlook," *Aviation Week and Space Technology*, September 7, 2001, 33.

3. Michael Grunwald, "Terrorists Hijack Four Airliners, Destroy World Trade Center, Hit Pentagon; Hundreds Dead," *Washington Post*, September 12, 2001.

4. The fullest available details on these and other immediate U.S. military responses may be found in *The 9/11 Commission Report: Final Report of the National Commission on Terrorist Attacks upon the United States* (New York: W. W. Norton and Company, 2004), 20–46.

5. David von Drehle, "Bush Pledges Victory," *Washington Post*, September 14, 2001.

6. Eric Schmitt and Michael R. Gordon, "U.S. Dispatches Ground Troops and Top Officer," *New York Times*, September 21, 2001.

7. Rebecca Grant, "An Air War Like No Other," *Air Force Magazine*, November 2002, 33.

8. Thomas E. Ricks, "Warplanes Begin Deploying to Gulf, Central Asia," *Washington Post*, September 20, 2001.

9. Thomas E. Ricks and Vernon Loeb, "Initial Aim Is Hitting Taliban Defenses," *Washington Post*, October 8, 2001.

10. Michael Evans, "U.S. Troops and Helicopters Set for Ground War," *Times* (London), October 11, 2001.

11. David A. Fulghum, "Afghanistan Crash Reveals U.S. Intel Operation," *Aviation Week and Space Technology*, October 1, 2001, 28.

12. Conversation with then–Lieutenant General Charles F. Wald, USAF, Headquarters U.S. Air Force, Washington, DC, May 15, 2002.

13. Bradley Graham and Vernon Loeb, "Cave Complexes Smashed by Bombs," *Washington Post*, October 12, 2001.

14. Thom Shanker and Steven Lee Myers, "U.S. Sends in Special Plane with Heavy Guns," *New York Times*, October 16, 2001.

15. Steven Lee Myers and Thom Shanker, "Pilots Told to Fire at Will in Some Zones," *New York Times*, October 17, 2001.

16. Karen DeYoung and Vernon Loeb, "Land-Based Fighters Join Airstrikes in Afghanistan," *Washington Post*, October 18, 2001.

17. "Afghan War Continues for Second Month," *Air International,* December 2001, 323.

18. Coalition countries that provided special operations forces for Enduring Freedom included Australia, Canada, Denmark, France, Germany, Norway, Poland, Turkey, and the United Kingdom. See Nora Bensahel, *The Counterterror Coalitions: Cooperation with Europe, NATO, and the European Union* (Santa Monica, CA: RAND, 2003), 55–63.

19. James Dao, "More U.S. Troops in bin Laden Hunt; Hideouts Bombed," *New York Times,* November 19, 2001.

20. Only three of al Qaeda's top twenty leaders believed to have been in Afghanistan at the start of the war were thought to have been killed by U.S. military action. In addition to Atef, Fahmi Nasr and Tariq Anwar, both senior leaders of the Egyptian Islamic Jihad movement, were later designated as killed in action.

21. Comments on an earlier draft by then–Lieutenant General T. Michael Moseley, USAF, who at the time was the air component commander for Operation Enduring Freedom.

22. Tony Capaccio, "Sixty Percent of Bombs Dropped on Afghanistan Precision-Guided," Bloomberg.com, November 20, 2001.

23. James Dao and Eric Schmitt, "Bin Laden Hunted in Caves; Errant U.S. Bomb Kills Three GIs," *New York Times,* December 6, 2001.

24. Vernon Loeb, "'Friendly Fire' Deaths Traced to Dead Battery," *Washington Post,* March 24, 2002; John Hendren and Maura Reynolds, "The U.S. Bomb That Nearly Killed Karzai," *Los Angeles Times,* March 27, 2002.

25. John Pomfret, "Kandahar Bombs Hit Their Marks," *Washington Post,* December 12, 2001.

26. Anthony Cordesman, *The Lessons of Afghanistan: Warfighting, Intelligence, Force Transformation, Counter-Proliferation, and Arms Control* (Washington, DC: Center for Strategic and International Studies, June 28, 2002), 20.

27. Susan B. Glasser, "U.S. Attacks on al Qaeda Intensify," *Washington Post,* December 10, 2001.

28. Thom Shanker and Eric Schmitt, "Marines Advance Toward Kandahar to Prepare Siege," *New York Times,* December 5, 2001.

29. Stephen Farrell and Michael Evans, "SAS Searches bin Laden Cave System," *Times* (London), December 4, 2001.

30. Steve Vogel, "Al Qaeda Tunnels, Arms Cache Totaled; Complex Believed Largest Found in War," *Washington Post,* February 16, 2002.

31. Esther Schrader, "U.S. Keeps Pressure on al Qaeda," *Los Angeles Times,* January 8, 2002.

32. Steve Vogel and Walter Pincus, "Al Qaeda Complex Destroyed; Search Widens," *Washington Post,* January 15, 2002.

33. Keith Richburg and William Branigan, "Attacks Out of the Blue: U.S. Air Strikes on Taliban Hit Military Targets and Morale," *Washington Post,* November 18, 2001.

34. Martin Arostegui, "The Search for bin Laden," *Insight Magazine,* September 2, 2002.

35. E-mail to the author, dated January 30, 2002, partly quoted in Sandra I. Erwin, "Naval Aviation: Lessons from the War," *National Defense,* June 2002, 16.

36. David A. Fulghum, "U.S. Troops Confront al Qaeda in Vicious Mountain Battle," *Aviation Week and Space Technology,* March 11, 2002, 24–25.

37. The addition of the word *combined* to a multiservice Joint Task Force designator indicates the inclusion of allied representation (in this case, coalition special operations forces personnel) in the organization.

38. Conversation with Lieutenant General Franklin L. Hagenbeck, USA, Headquarters U.S. Army, Washington, DC, July 1, 2004.

39. For an informed and vivid account of Army Apache operations on day one of Anaconda, see Dodge Billingsley, "Choppers in the Coils: Operation Anaconda Was a 'Back to Basics' Campaign for U.S. Combat Helicopters," *Journal of Electronic Defense*, September 2002.

40. Major Mark G. Davis, USA, "Operation Anaconda: Command and Confusion in Joint Warfare" (master's thesis, School of Advanced Air and Space Studies, Maxwell Air Force Base, AL, June 2004), 113.

41. Conversation with Lieutenant General John D. W. Corley, USAF, Headquarters U.S. Air Force, Washington, DC, May 13, 2003. The year before, General Corley was the air component's Combined Air Operations Center director throughout the course of Operation Anaconda.

42. Conversation with Lieutenant General Hagenbeck.

43. Conversation with General Corley.

44. Comments during a panel presentation by Enduring Freedom carrier air wing commanders at the Tailhook Association's 2002 annual reunion and symposium, Reno, NV, September 6, 2002.

45. Elaine M. Grossman, "Operation Anaconda: Object Lesson in Poor Planning or Triumph of Improvisation?" InsideDefense.com, accessed August 12, 2004.

46. Lieutenant Colonel John M. Jansen, USA, et al., "Lines One Through Three . . . N/A," *Marine Corps Gazette*, April 2003, 34.

47. Conversation with General Moseley.

48. Comments on an earlier draft by Major General David A. Deptula, USAF, Director of Operations, Pacific Air Forces, Hickam Air Force Base, Hawaii, October 4, 2002.

49. For a fuller treatment of the U.S. Navy's important contributions to Operation Enduring Freedom, see Benjamin S. Lambeth, *American Carrier Air Power at the Dawn of a New Century* (Santa Monica, CA: RAND, 2005), 9–38.

50. David A. Fulghum, "Afghanistan Crash Reveals U.S. Intel Operation," *Aviation Week and Space Technology*, October 1, 2001, 28; and "U.S. Girds for Demands of Long Winter War," *Aviation Week and Space Technology*, November 12, 2002, 34.

51. Christopher J. Bowie, Robert P. Haffa Jr., and Robert E. Mullins, *Future War: What Trends in America's Post–Cold War Military Conflicts Tell Us about Early 21st Century Warfare* (Arlington, VA: Northrop Grumman Analysis Center, January 2003), 60.

52. Ibid., 4.

53. For more on the many execution problems associated with Operation Allied Force, see Benjamin S. Lambeth, *NATO's Air War for Kosovo: A Strategic and Operational Assessment* (Santa Monica, CA: RAND, 2001), especially 101–218.

54. Conversation with Major General Victor E. Renuart, USAF, USCENTCOM J–3, Washington, DC, September 5, 2003.

55. One report noted that President Bush himself had constant access to live Predator feed in the White House. Peter Pae, "Future Is Now for Creator of Predator," *Los Angeles Times*, January 3, 2002.

56. For further discussion of how the Soviet approach to command and control stifled initiative and hampered the flexibility of Soviet forces at the operational and tactical levels, see Benjamin S. Lambeth, *Russia's Air Power in Crisis* (Washington, DC: Smithsonian Institution Press, 1999), 71–109.

57. Comments by General Charles A. Horner on an earlier version of this chapter.

58. For more on this new approach to the use of air power in land warfare, see Major General David A. Deptula, USAF, Colonel Gary Crowder, USAF, and Major George L. Stamper, USAF, "Direct Attack: Enhancing Counterland Doctrine and Joint Air-Ground Operations," *Air and Space Power Journal*, Winter 2003, 5–12.
59. Comments by General Horner on an earlier version of this chapter.
60. Brigadier General Charles J. Dunlap Jr., USAF, "Air and Information Operations: A Perspective on the Use of 'Lawfare' in Modern Conflicts," presentation at a conference on Current Issues in the Law of Armed Conflict, Naval War College, Newport, RI, June 2003.

CHAPTER 12

1. For a brief discussion of these theories of air power and their weaknesses, see Williamson Murray, *Luftwaffe* (Baltimore, MD: Nautical and Aviation Publishing Company of America, 1985), appendix 1.
2. See, in this regard, John A. Warden III, *The Air Campaign: Planning for Combat*, rev. ed. (Washington, DC: National Defense University Press, 1998).
3. Public Record Office, Air 20/40, Air Staff Memorandum No. 11 A, March 1924.
4. This was not necessarily a parochial or narrow-minded effort. The air campaigns against North Vietnam, particularly the Rolling Thunder effort (1965–1968), had been marked by an almost complete lack of cooperation between the Navy's efforts and those of the Air Force. For the best discussion of these issues, see Mark Clodfelter, *The Limits of Air Power: The American Bombing of North Vietnam* (Lincoln: University of Nebraska Press, 2006).
5. Sir Charles Webster and Noble Frankland, *The Strategic Air Offensive against Germany*, vol. 3, *Victory* (London: Her Majesty's Stationery Office, 1962), 32–41.
6. Lieutenant General G. C. M. Lamb, Commander Field Army, United Kingdom, "Keeping the High Intensity Warfare Flame Alive" (paper delivered at the Royal United Services Institute's Land Warfare Conference, 2008). This paper is in the possession of the author.
7. In 1990, as the military confrontation with Iraq loomed over its occupation of Kuwait, not only pundits but also the intelligence agencies clothed the Iraqis with military capabilities that equated their ground forces to the combat-hardened veterans of the Waffen SS. The estimates of their air capabilities were more restrained. See Williamson Murray, *Operations*, vol. 2, rep. 1, *Gulf War Air Power Survey*, ed. Eliot Cohen (Washington, DC: Air Force Historical Studies Office, 1993).
8. Interview with Lieutenant General James Amos, commander, Marine Corps Development Command, May 23, 2008.
9. Michael R. Gordon and Bernard Trainor, *Cobra II: The Inside Story of the Invasion and Occupation of Iraq* (New York: Pantheon, 2006), 50.
10. In effect, the running start concept represented a symptom rather than the cause of subsequent U.S. difficulties. It reflected Rumsfeld's bizarre belief that few U.S. troops would be needed for operations, and particularly for the postconflict period.
11. Gordon and Trainor, *Cobra II*, 67–68.
12. The British would decide as late as December 2002 to deploy their forces not in the north, but rather in the south, while the American Fourth Division was denied entry into Turkey in February–March 2003 and thus had to deploy through Kuwait, arriving after the war was over.
13. The following discussion is based on an extensive reading of translated Iraqi documents and transcripts as well as the published discussion of those documents. See Kevin M.

Woods, *Iraqi Perspectives Project: A View of Operation Iraqi Freedom from Saddam's Senior Leadership*, with Michael R. Pease, Mark E. Stout, Williamson Murray, and James G. Lacey (Washington, DC: U.S. Government Printing Office, 2006).

14. Captured media tape circa 1995, "Saddam and Senior Advisors Discuss International Reaction to UN Inspection Report."

15. Iraqi Perspectives Project interview with Major General Hamid Isma'aeli Dawish al R'baei, director general of Republican Guard General Staff, November 18, 2003.

16. Iraqi Perspectives Project interview with Lieutenant General Hamid Raja Shala al Hadithi al Tikriti, commander, Iraqi Air Force, November 12, 2003.

17. A response that was quite similar to the German response during the Second World War, when the Luftwaffe's antiaircraft artillery was largely ineffective against high-flying British and American bombers, but was made to keep firing by the regime's political leadership largely for the effect it had on the German population's morale.

18. Kevin M. Woods, *The Mother of All Battles: Saddam Hussein's Strategic Plan for the Persian Gulf War* (Annapolis: U.S. Naval Institute Press, 2008), 270.

19. Woods, *Iraqi Perspectives Project*, 149.

20. In fact, the Iraqi documents make it clear that Saddam and his henchmen believed that the rebellion had come far closer to overthrowing his regime than the war waged by American and allied air and ground forces in January and February 1991.

21. U.S. Air Forces Central (USCENTAF), "Operation Iraqi Freedom—By the Numbers," Assessment and Analysis Division, April 30, 2003, 3. One British Tornado was shot down by a Patriot missile battery that failed to recognize the Tornado's identification friend or foe.

22. For perfectly understandable reasons, given the enormous numbers the USAF faced on the Central front against the Red Air Force, commanders had prioritized the gaining of air superiority as their first task and close air support as their bottom priority.

23. From the Marine point of view, close air support must always be available because Marines have shorted artillery in their table of organization and replaced that firepower with that available from aircraft.

24. Interview with Lieutenant General James Amos, Quantico, VA, June 2008.

25. Ibid.

26. In this regard, see particularly Bill Owens and Ed Offley, *Lifting the Fog of War* (Baltimore, MD: Johns Hopkins University Press, 2001). For a more detailed discussion of the frictions that arose in the planning and execution of the mission, see Gordon and Trainor, *Cobra II*, 169–176. For the inevitability of friction not only in war but also in human affairs, see Barry D. Watts, *Clausewitzian Friction and Future War* (Washington, DC: National Defense University Press, 1996).

27. In fact, during the Gulf War, the B–52 with its massive use of dumb bombs—which even then were dropped on inaccurate computer coordinates—was by far the most feared aircraft in the American arsenal.

28. Gordon and Trainor, *Cobra II*, 175.

29. For a discussion of the measures taken to protect Saddam's location, see Woods, *Iraqi Perspectives Project*, 127.

30. Gordon and Trainor, *Cobra II*, 177.

31. Eric Schmitt, "In the Skies over Iraq, Silent Observers Become Futuristic Weapons," *New York Times*, April 18, 2003.

32. USCENTAF, "Operation Iraqi Freedom," 2.

33. Woods, *Iraqi Perspectives Project*, 128.

34. Given the regime's savagery in putting down the March 1991 uprising (suppression tactics included the use of mustard and probably sarin gas against crowds in rebel cities), popular morale mattered not a whit because no Iraqis were going to risk rebelling against the regime until it was clear that Saddam had been overthrown.

35. This was one more indication of the general sloppiness of the Bush administration's approach to preparing for the postwar period. There are innumerable outstanding books on this subject, but perhaps the most telling item is the documentary film *No End in Sight*, which is available on DVD.

36. Williamson Murray and Robert H. Scales Jr., *The Iraq War: A Military History* (Cambridge, MA: Harvard University Press, 2003), 121–122.

37. Jamie Cox, "Callsign 'Deadly'—Snakes in the Attack: A Personal Account of an AH–1W Pilot during the War with Iraq," unpublished manuscript.

38. Murray and Scales, *The Iraq War*, 105–108.

39. Woods, *Iraqi Perspectives Project*.

40. This was, of course, the claim that RAF commanders were making at the end of the First World War, but more on the impact of bombing on civilians rather than on military formations. For an examination of these issues, see Murray, *Luftwaffe*, appendix 1.

41. Woods, *Iraqi Perspectives Project*, 125.

42. Ibid., 126.

43. Ibid., 125.

44. Ibid., 128–129.

45. Ibid., 139.

46. And he understood, as American units drove into the center of Baghdad even as he reported more glorious Iraqi victories, that he might die accidentally from a coalition bullet, but that if he reported what Saddam thought was not the proper Ba'athist line, he would die immediately—at least as long as the regime managed to survive.

47. There are, of course, the special mission C–130s in the Air Force's special operations units, which can execute any number of highly classified missions, in addition to the AC–130 gunships that provide devastating fire from the air in support of ground forces.

48. Interview with Lieutenant General Amos.

49. Woods, *Iraqi Perspectives Project*, 147.

50. Gordon and Trainor, *Cobra II*, 340.

51. USCENTAF, "Operation Iraqi Freedom." *Number of Enemy Responses*: AAA events, 1,224; SAM/rockets launched, 1,660; SAM emitters active, 436; SSM launches, 19. *Number of Aircraft*: USAF (Fighters: 293, Bombers: 51, Tankers: 182, ISR: 60, Sp Ops/ Rescue: 58, Airlift: 111, SOF: 73); USMC (Fighters: 130, Tankers: 22); USN (Fighters: 232, Tankers: 52, ISR: 18); Royal Australian AF (Fighters: 14, Airlift: 3); RAF (Fighters: 66, ISR: 9, Tankers: 12, Sp Ops/Rescue: 14, Airlift: 4). *Number of Sorties Flown*: USAF (Fighters: 8,828, Bombers: 505, Airlift: 7,413, Tankers: 6,193, ISR: 452, Rescue: 191); USMC (Fighters: 3,794, Tankers: 454, ISR: 305); USN (Fighters: 5,568, Tankers: 2,058, ISR: 357), RAF (Fighters: 1,736, Tankers: 359, ISR: 273); Australian (Fighters: 302). *Amounts of Munitions Expended*: Guided munitions: 19,948; Unguided munitions: 9,251; 20mm: 16,901; 30mm: 311,597.

CHAPTER 13

1. The author would like to express his deep gratitude to Chaim Meyer and Elena Ratz for their contribution to this article, written in 2008.

2. The most detailed information concerning the Israeli side can be found in the two Winograd reports: Winograd Commission of Inquiry, *Interim Report*, 2007, and Winograd Commission of Inquiry, *Final Report*, 2008. Against the opinion of the committee members, the Israeli Supreme Court ruled in favor of publishing some testimonies given before the commission (cf., the testimonies given to the Agranat Commission of Inquiry [after the Yom Kippur War] were published only in 2008, thirty-five years after the war). However, both the reports and the testimonies were heavily censored. Reliable information can also be found in a subdivision of Israeli literature that was published after the war: Amos Harel and Avi Issacharof, *34 Days: Israel, Hezbollah and the War in Lebanon* (New York: Palgrave MacMillan, 2008); Amir Rapaport, *Friendly Fire: How We Defeated Ourselves in the Second Lebanon War* (in Hebrew) (Tel Aviv: Ma'ariv, 2007); Ofer Shelah and Yoav Limor, *Captives of Lebanon: The Truth on the Second Lebanon War* (in Hebrew) (Tel Aviv: Yedioth Ahronoth and Hemed, 2007). The data used in this chapter concerning the decision-making process in Israel is mainly based on these sources.

3. Reuven Erlich and Yoram Kahati, "Hezbollah as a Case Study of the Battle for Hearts and Minds," Intelligence and Terrorism Information Center, May 2007.

4. On Hezbollah's history and background, see Augustus Richard Norton, *Hezbollah: A Short History* (Princeton: Princeton University Press, 2007); Judith Palmer Harik, *Hezbollah: The Changing Face of Terrorism* (London: I. B. Tauris, 2005).

5. Frank Hoffman, *Conflicts in the 21st Century: The Rise of Hybrid Wars* (Arlington, VA: Potomac Institute for Policy Studies, 2007).

6. On Israel's post-withdrawal strategy and on the IDF's operational plans, see the sources cited in note 2. For a good description of the processes in Lebanon and Hezbollah, see Reuven Erlich, "The Road to the Second Lebanon War: The Lebanese Scene in the Years 2000–2006," Intelligence and Terrorism Center, http://www.intelligence.org.il/, accessed November 18, 2008.

7. Erlich and Kahati, "Hezbollah as a Case Study."

8. For more, see Efraim Inbar, "Strategic Follies: Israel's Mistakes in the Second Lebanese War," Begin-Sadat Center for Strategic Studies, perspective paper no. 21, September 10, 2006, http://www.biu.ac.il/SOC/besa/perspectives21.html; Giora Eiland, "The Decision Making Process in Israel," in *The Second Lebanon War: Strategic Perspectives*, ed. Shlomo Brom and Meir Elran (Tel Aviv: Institute for National Security Studies, 2007).

9. Cabinet secretary Israel Maimon's announcement on the official website of the prime minister's office, http://www.pmo.gov.il/PMO/Archive/Spokesman/2006/07/ spoke gov120706.htm.

10. Address by Prime Minister Ehud Olmert in the Knesset on the official website of the prime minister's office, http://www.pmo.gov.il/PMO/Archive/Speeches/2006/07/ speechkneset170706.htm.

11. The testimony of Ehud Olmert on the website of the Winograd Commission of Inquiry, http://www.vaadatwino.org.il/statements.html, 47–48. See also Winograd Commission of Inquiry, *Interim Report*, 101.

12. Winograd Commission of Inquiry, *Interim Report*, 70.

13. For a description on the traditional Israeli doctrine, see Israel Tal, *National Security: The Israeli Experience* (Westport, CT: Praeger, 2000). For an American perspective on the traditional Israeli doctrine, see Eliot Cohen, Michael Eisenstadt, and Andrew Bacevich, *Knives, Tanks and Missiles: Israel's Security Revolution* (Washington, DC: Washington Institute for Near East Policy, 1998). For the voices about the change of the IDF doctrine in the years preceding the second Lebanon war, see Sarah Kreps, "The 2006 Lebanon War: Lessons Learned," *Parameters* (Spring 2007): 72–84; Ron Tira, *The Limitations of Standoff Firepower-Based Operations: On Standoff Warfare, Maneuver, and Decision* (Tel Aviv: Institute for National Security Studies Memorandum 89, March 2007); Avi Kober, "The Second Lebanon War," Begin-Sadat Center for Strategic Studies, perspective paper no. 22, September 28, 2006; Efraim Inbar, "How Israel Bungled the Second Lebanon War," *Middle East Quarterly Magazine* (June 22, 2007); Amir Kulick, "The IDF's Combat Approach vs. Hizbollah," *Strategic Assessment* 9, no. 3 (November 2006).

14. All data in this chapter is taken from the interim and final reports of the Winograd Commission of Inquiry, as well as from announcements of the IDF spokesman and the Israeli Air Force's reports during the war, which can be found on the Israeli Air Force's official website, http://www.iaf.org.il. See also Amos and Issacharof, *34 Days*.

15. On Hezbollah's operational activities during the war, see Steven Erlanger and Richard Oppel, "A Disciplined Hezbollah Surprises Israel with Its Training, Tactics and Weapons," *New York Times*, August 7, 2006; Andrew Exum, *"Hezbollah at War: A Military Assessment*, policy focus no. 63 (Washington, DC: Washington Institute for Near East Policy, December 2006); Kulick, "The IDF's Combat Approach vs. Hizbollah"; Ralph Peters, "Lessons from Lebanon: The New Model Terrorist Army," *Armed Forces Journal*, no. 144 (October 2006).

16. For the different opinions about the outcomes of the war and the reasons for them, see Shai Feldman, "The Hezbollah-Israel War: A Preliminary Assessment," *Middle East Brief* (Waltham, MA: Crown Center for Middle East Studies, September 2006); Avi Kober, "The Israel Defense Forces in the Second Lebanon War: Why the Poor Performance?" *Journal of Strategic Studies* 31, no. 1 (February 2008): 3–40; Edward Luttwak, "Misreading the Lebanon War," *Jerusalem Post*, August 20, 2006; David Makovsky and Jeffery White, *Lessons and Implications of the Israel-Hizballah War: A Preliminary Assessment*, policy focus no. 60 (Washington, DC: Washington Institute for Near East Policy, October 2006); Shlomo Brom, "Political and Military Objectives in a Limited War against a Guerrilla Organization," in *The Second Lebanon War: Strategic Perspectives*; Eyal Zisser, "The Battle for Lebanon: Lebanon and Syria in the Wake of the War," in *The Second Lebanon War: Strategic Perspectives*.

17. For a detailed description of the rocket campaign and the way Israel dealt with it, see Uzi Rubin, *The Rocket Campaign against Israel during the 2006 Lebanon War*, Begin-Sadat Center for Strategic Studies, June 2007, 23 and below.

18. Information concerning the damage caused to Lebanon is taken from the United Nations Environment Program Lebanon Post-Conflict Environmental Assessment, http://post conflict.unep.ch/publications.php?prog=lebanon, accessed January 2, 2009.

CHAPTER 14

1. James Corum and Wray Johnson, *Airpower and Small Wars* (Lawrence: University Press of Kansas, 2003). On the use of air power by U.S. forces in military interventions in the

Caribbean and Latin America, see 11–50; on Spanish and Italian use of air power in the interwar era, see 66–73, 80–81.

2. For an overview of the RAF and air control doctrine, see Peter Gray, "The Myths of Air Control and the Realities of Imperial Policing," *RAF Air Power Review* 4, no. 2 (Summer 2001): 37–52, and James Corum, "Air Control: Reassessing the History," *RAF Air Power Review* 4, no. 2 (Summer 2001): 15–36.

3. David Omissi, *Air Power and Colonial Control: The Royal Air Force 1919–1939* (Manchester: Manchester University Press, 1990), 25–27.

4. Howard Sachar, *The Emergence of the Middle East 1914–1924* (New York: Alfred Knopf, 1969), 369–372.

5. Mark Jacobsen, "Only by the Sword: British Counter-Insurgency in Iraq, 1920," *Small Wars and Insurgencies* 2, no. 2 (August 1991): 351–352, 358. Considering the size of the Iraqi population in 1920 (about four million), the British soldier-to-population ratio employed to fight that insurgency was more than two and a half times the soldier-to-population ratio of the U.S. forces fighting Iraqi insurgents in 2006–2007.

6. Ibid., 357. The Iraq revolt was suppressed at the cost of 1,040 British soldiers killed and missing.

7. In the summer of 1923, there were six Indian army infantry battalions in Iraq.

8. By 1926, the British had created an Iraqi army, which had training centers and six infantry battalions, four cavalry regiments, four artillery batteries, and supporting units. See Lieutenant Colonel R. H. Beadon, "The Iraqi Army," *RUSI Journal* (May 1926): 343–354.

9. Arnaud Teyssier, "L'Aviation Contre les Insurrections: L'Expérience Français au Levant au Lendemain de la Première Guerre Mondiale," *Revue Historique des Armées* no. 169 (December 1987): 48–54, esp. 52.

10. Ibid., 54.

11. Ibid., 55.

12. Jérome Millet, "L'Aviation Militaire Français dans la Guerre du Rif," *Revue Historique des Armées*, no. 166 (March 1987): 46–58.

13. S. Lainé, "L'Aéronautique Militaire Français au Maroc 1911–1939," *Revue Historique des Armées*, no. 4 (1978): 107–120, esp. 112–118.

14. Charles Christienne and Pierre Lissarague, *A History of French Military Aviation* (Washington, DC: Smithsonian Institution Press, 1986), 231.

15. Capitaine W. Breyton, "L'Aviation Sanitaire au Maroc en 1933," *Revue de L'Armée de L'Air*, no. 56 (March 1934): 243–264.

16. Lainé, "L'Aéronautique Militaire Français au Maroc 1911–1939," 118.

17. Omissi, *Air Power and Colonial Control*, 174.

18. Ibid., 20–21.

19. Philip Towle, *Pilots and Rebels: The Use of Aircraft in Unconventional Warfare, 1918–1988* (London: Brassey's Ltd., 1989), 40–43.

20. Omissi, *Air Power and Colonial Control*, 119–121.

21. For a good overview of the air actions in the Greek civil war, see Victor Flintham, *Air Wars and Aircraft* (New York: Facts on File, 1990), 9–13. See also Corum and Johnson, *Airpower and Small Wars*, 93–110.

22. For an overview of the Greek civil war, see Edgar O'Ballance, *The Greek Civil War, 1944–1949* (New York: Frederick A. Praeger, 1966). On the U.S. involvement in Greece, see

Lawrence Wittner, *American Intervention in Greece, 1943–1949* (New York: Columbia University Press, 1982).

23. The prewar Greek air force was destroyed during the German invasion of 1941. Some Greek personnel escaped the debacle and were formed into three squadrons by the RAF: a light bomber squadron (No. 13 Squadron) and two Spitfire fighter squadrons (Nos. 335 and 336 Squadrons). These units served under RAF command until 1946, when they were transferred to the Greek government to form the nucleus of a new Greek air force (which, at the time, possessed only fifty-eight obsolete aircraft and fewer than three hundred experienced pilots).

24. M. Campbell, E. W. Downs, and L. V. Schuetta, *The Employment of Airpower in the Greek Guerrilla War, 1947–1949*, Project No. AU–411–62–ASI (Maxwell Air Force Base, AL: Concepts Division, Aerospace Studies Institute, Air University, December 1964), 8.

25. On the U.S. decision to aid Greece, see Harry S. Truman, *Memoirs* (Garden City: Doubleday, 1956), 2: 100–109. For an overview of U.S. military aid programs, see Duncan Clarke and Daniel O'Connor, *Send Guns and Money: Security Assistance and U.S. Foreign Policy* (Westport, CT: Praeger, 1997).

26. J. C. Murray, "The Anti-Bandit War, Conclusion," *Marine Corps Gazette* (May 1954): 52.

27. Parker Borg, *The United States, the Huk Movement, and Ramon Magsaysay*, Government 644 (April 26, 1965), 6–8. Edward Lansdale wrote an autobiographical account of his experience in the Philippines in his book *In the Midst of Wars: An American's Mission to Southeast Asia* (New York: Harper and Row, 1972). Charles Bohannan coauthored a book with Napoleon Valeriano, a senior Philippine army officer, titled *Counter-Guerrilla Operations: The Philippine Experience* (1962; repr., New York: Praeger, 2006).

28. Valeriano and Bohannan wrote that "clobbering an area" by air often led to civilian casualties and was counterproductive. See Bohannan and Valeriano, *Counter-Guerrilla Operations*, 105–106.

29. In 1950, President Truman signed National Security memo NSC 84/C, which underscored that the U.S. aid should emphasize economic and political solutions rather than the mostly military approach used in Greece.

30. On the use of air power in the Philippines, see H. Peterson, George C. Reinhardt, and E. E. Conger, eds., *Symposium on the Role of Airpower in Counterinsurgency and Unconventional Warfare: The Philippine Huk Campaign*, RM–3652–PR (Santa Monica: RAND, July 1963).

31. For an analysis of the Malaya counterinsurgency program, see James Corum, *Training Indigenous Forces in Counterinsurgency: A Tale of Two Insurgencies* (Carlisle, PA: U.S. Army War College, Strategic Studies Institute, March 2006).

32. On RAF operations in Malaya, see Royal Air Force, *The Malayan Emergency 1948–1960* (London: Ministry of Defence, June 1970).

33. For an overview of the French air force operations in Indochina, see Patrick Facon, "L'Armée de l'Air et la Guerre d'Indochine (1945–1954)," *Revue Historique des Armeés*, no. 177 (December 1989): 95–107.

34. On the Dien Bien Phu battle, see Bernard Fall, *Hell in a Very Small Place* (Philadelphia: Lippincott, 1966). On the French air force at Dien Bien Phu, see Patrick Facon, "L'armée de l'Air et Dien Bien Phu," *Revue Historique des Armeés*, no. 158 (March 1985): 79–87.

35. Christienne and Lissarague, *A History of French Military Aviation*, 464–465.

36. John Talbot, "The War Without a Name—France in Algeria 1954–1962," in *The Chopper Boys: Helicopter Warfare in Africa*, ed. J. Ventner (London: Greenhill Books, 1994), 37–44.

37. See Lieutenant Colonel Claude Carré, "Aspects Opérationnels du Conflit Algérien 1954–1960," *Revue Historique des Armeés*, no. 166 (March 1987): 82–111.

38. Alistair Horne, *A Savage War for Peace: Algeria 1954–1962* (London: Penguin Books, 1977), 335–338.

39. On the early years of the U.S. mission to the VNAF, see Robert Futrell, *The United States Air Force in Southeast Asia: The Advisory Years to 1965* (Washington, DC: Office of Air Force History, 1981).

40. Ibid., 149, 239, 263.

41. On the U.S. advisory efforts in Vietnam, see James Willbanks, *Abandoning Vietnam* (Lawrence: University Press of Kansas, 2004).

42. Major A. J. C. Lavalle, USAF, *The Vietnamese Air Force, 1951–1975: An Analysis of Its Role in Combat and Fourteen Hours at Koh Tang* (Washington, DC: Office of Air Force History, 1985), 33.

43. In April 1972, the VNAF flew almost 30 percent of the total allied air sorties—4,904 out of a total of 17,000 air sorties. The next month the VNAF flew over 5,500 sorties out of a total of 18,444. A. J. C. Lavalle, *Airpower and the 1972 Spring Invasion*, USAF Southeast Asia Monograph Series, vol. II (Washington, DC: U.S. Government Printing Office, 1976).

44. Thomas Marks, "Thailand: Anatomy of a Counterinsurgency Victory," *Military Review* (January–February 2007): 35–51, and Warren Trest, *Air Commando One: Heinie Aderholt and America's Secret Air Wars* (Washington, DC: Smithsonian Institution Press, 2000).

45. For an overview of this campaign, see James Corum, "The Air War in El Salvador," *Airpower Journal* (Summer 1998).

46. On the strategic situation in Colombia in 2001, see Max Manwaring, "United States Security Policy in the Western Hemisphere: Why Colombia, Why Now, and What Is to Be Done?" *Small Wars and Insurgencies* (Autumn 2001): 67–96.

47. In 2001, eighteen UH–60 Black Hawk helicopters were provided to the Colombian forces along with forty-two older UH–1 helicopters. Karen DeYoung, "Colombia to Get Fewer, Stronger, Helicopters," *Washington Post*, October 13, 2000, 18.

48. The Colombian air force has a mix of fixed-wing and rotary-wing aircraft. It is well configured to carry out liaison, strike, surveillance, and troop transport missions. For strike aircraft, it has A–37 modified trainers and Embraer Super Tucanos. Israeli-made Kfir fighter-bombers are able to employ precision-guided munitions. The Colombians have Cessna Skymasters for liaison, OV–10 Broncos for reconnaissance, and CE 208 and CASA 212 light transports. C–130s serve as heavy transports. The Colombian air force and aviation forces are primarily helicopter forces with UH–60s, refurbished UH–1s, and surplus Mi–17s. Colombia has organized its air force into six regional commands, each with a strong air detachment to support operations in the command's area. Each command has a mix of liaison, strike, and reconnaissance and transport aircraft.

49. A key element of the U.S. aid program was training for the Colombian armed forces. In 2002, 6,230 Colombian military and police personnel went through U.S. training courses. Courses for Colombian personnel in the United States included helicopter pilot training, aviation maintenance, radar operation, ground defense skills, communications, and search and rescue. Figures from the U.S. State Department.

50. Rich Lowry, "Colombia Comeback," *National Review*, November 23, 2007.

51. For a good overview of the Afghanistan war, see Lester W. Grau, ed., *The Bear Went over the Mountain: Soviet Combat Tactics in Afghanistan* (Washington, DC: National Defense University Press, 1996).

52. An excellent book presenting the Soviet view of the war is Lester W. Grau and Michael Gress, eds. and trans., *The Soviet Afghan War: How a Superpower Fought and Lost: The Russian General Staff* (Lawrence: University Press of Kansas, 2002), 314–318.

53. On the fighting in the 1990s in Chechnya, see Anatol Lieven, *Chechnya: Tombstone of Russian Power* (New Haven, CT: Yale University Press, 1998). On the Russian use of air power during the 1999–2000 fighting, see Marcel de Haas, "The Use of Russian Air Power in the Second Chechen War," *RAF Air Power Review* 6, no. 1 (Spring 2003): 35–60.

54. For a discussion of leadership and organization in contemporary insurgency, see T. X. Hammes, *The Sling and the Stone* (St. Paul: Zenith Press, 2004).

55. An excellent account of Israel's bombing campaign against Hezbollah is found in Kenneth Schow, "Falcons against the Jihad" (master's thesis, Maxwell Air Force Base, AL: Air University Press, November 1995).

56. Accounts of the Israeli operations in South Lebanon are found in Clive Jones, "Israeli Counter Insurgency Strategy and the War in South Lebanon, 1985–97," *Small Wars and Insurgencies* (Winter 1997): 82–108; Shmuel Gordon, *The Vulture and the Snake: Counter-Guerrilla Air Warfare: The War for Southern Lebanon*, Study 39, Begin-Sadat Center for Strategic Studies, July 1998; Brigadier General Ephraim Segoli, IAF (Ret.), *The Israeli-Lebanese Dilemma* (Maxwell Air Force Base, AL: School of Advanced Airpower Studies, 1998).

57. Steven Erlanger and Richard Oppel Jr., "A Disciplined Hezbollah Surprises Israel with Its Training, Tactics and Weapons," *New York Times*, August 7, 2006.

58. Over one hundred Israeli civilians were killed by Hezbollah attacks, and millions of dollars of damage was inflicted upon Israeli homes and businesses. See Bill Gertz, "Mossad Missed Hezbollah Threat," *Washington Times*, August 16, 2006; and "Lebanon's New Crisis," *Washington Post*, November 15, 2006.

59. On the argument that air power had revolutionized warfare, see Max Boot, "The New American Way of War," *Foreign Affairs* 82, no. 4 (July–August 2003); Richard Andres and Colonel Thomas Griffith, USAF, "Winning with Allies: The Strategic Value of the Afghan Model," *International Security* 30, no. 3 (Winter 2005): 124–160; Major General Charles Dunlap, USAF, "Making Revolutionary Change: Airpower in COIN Today," *Parameters* (Summer 2005): 52–66.

60. For a good critique of the argument of the primacy of air power advocates, see Stephen Biddle, *Afghanistan and the Future of Warfare* (Carlisle, PA: U.S. Army War College, Strategic Studies Institute, November 2002). On the failure to identify al Qaeda positions at Tora Bora, see page 29. For a rejoinder to the Andres–Griffith arguments, see Stephen Biddle, "Allies, Airpower and Modern Warfare," *International Security* 30, no. 3 (Winter 2005), 161–176.

61. As of October 2007, the Afghan Air Corps consisted of five transport planes (only two serviceable), seven Mi–17 helicopters, and six Mi–35 helicopter gunships.

62. Jason Straziuso, "Afghan Air Force Struggles to Take Flight," *Air Force Times*, October 10, 2007.

63. See Staff Sergeant Jon Cupp, USAF, "Iraqi Air Force Makes Strides Toward Transition," USAF Office of Public Affairs, September 7, 2007; Technical Sergeant Kevin Williams, USAF, "Iraqi Air Force Takes Flight with Help from U.S. Airmen," USAF Office of Public Affairs, April 4, 2007.

64. The Iraqi air force was organized into four small squadrons: a reconnaissance squadron, a transport squadron, and two helicopter squadrons. In 2008, it had no strike capability.

65. See *The Report of the Independent Commission on the Security Forces of Iraq*, Gen. James Jones, USMC (Ret.), Chair, September 6, 2007. As of May 2008, a total of only fifteen hundred Iraqi air force personnel had completed training programs. See also Anthony Cordesman, *Iraqi Force Development* (Washington, DC: Center for Strategic and International Studies, May 2008).

66. In 2008, the USAF capability to support a training and advisory mission remained minimal: fewer than three hundred personnel were specifically assigned to the mission. A RAND study has criticized the USAF for its approach and has argued for a specialist advisory force of at least wing strength. See Alan J. Vick et al., *Air Power in the New Counterinsurgency Era* (Santa Monica, CA: RAND, 2006), 126–127, 129–132, 136–143.

67. Air Force Doctrine Document 2–3, *Irregular Warfare* (August 2007).

68. Field Manual 3–24, *Counterinsurgency* (December 2006), para. 6–22.

69. Ibid., annex E, paras. E–17–18, E–31.

70. Corum and Johnson, *Airpower in Small Wars*, 406–409.

71. An example of a false claim of civilian casualties was the one made by some Iraqis in November 2006 that more than thirty women and children had been killed by American bombing in the Iraqi city of Ramadi during heavy fighting there. In fact, there had been no air strikes. The initial report was published widely, but the correction to the story was printed only several weeks later. Solomon Moore, "Marines Deny Airstrikes Used against Insurgents in Ramadi," *Los Angeles Times*, December 29, 2006.

72. For examples of the broad agitation in the West to ban cluster bombs, see "No Place for Cluster Bombs," *New York Times*, August 26, 2006; "Norway Plans Talks on Cluster-Bomb Ban," *Washington Times*, November 18, 2006.

CHAPTER 15

1. The most recent work on this subject is R. Yermiash, "The Wings of Empire: The Royal Air Force in Palestine and Transjordan, 1919–1939" (Ph.D. dissertation, Hebrew University of Jerusalem, 2008, in Hebrew).

2. This author discussed both of these cases in Martin van Creveld, *The Changing Face of War: Lessons of Combat, from the Marne to Iraq* (New York: Presidio, 2007), 229–256.

3. "Air Force Not Doing Enough in Iraq and Afghanistan," http://www.ar15.com/forums/topic.html?b=1&f=5&t=701310&page=5.

CHAPTER 16

1. The National Research Council member was Howard Aiken, a Harvard mathematician. For the context of this astonishing estimate, see Paul E. Ceruzzi, *A History of Modern Computing*, 2d ed. (1998; repr., Cambridge, MA: MIT Press, 1999), 13.

2. Général Pierre Lissarrague, *Premiers envols* (Paris: Éditions Joël Cuénot, 1982), 17; and Tom D. Crouch, *The Eagle Aloft: Two Centuries of the Balloon in America* (Washington, DC: Smithsonian Institution Press, 1983), 14.

3. Quoted in Alain Dégardin and Francis Villadier, "Des ballons pour la République," in Antoine Dumas et al., eds., *Les temps des ballons* (Paris: Éditions de la Martinière and the Musée de l'Air et de l'Éspace, 1995), 76, and J. Jobé, *The Romance of Ballooning: The Story of the Early Aeronauts* (New York: Edita Lausanne and the Viking Press, 1971), 66–67.

4. Dumas et al., eds., *Les temps des ballons*, 76–83; Frederick S. Hayden, *Aeronautics in the Union and Confederate Armies, with a Survey of Military Aeronautics Prior to 1860,* (Baltimore, MD: Johns Hopkins University Press, 1941), 1: 7–11.

5. Ader plays to mixed reviews; see Pierre Lissarrague's *Clément Ader: Inventeur d'avions* (Toulouse: Bibliothèque Historique Privat, 1990), and Charles H. Gibbs-Smith's far more critical *Clément Ader: His Flight Claims and His Place in History* (London: Her Majesty's Stationery Office, 1968). For Langley, see Samuel P. Langley, with Charles M. Manly, *Langley Memoir on Mechanical Flight,* parts 1–2, a study in the *Smithsonian Contributions to Knowledge* series, vol. 27, no. 3 (1911).

6. Kelvin to Major B. F. S. Baden-Powell, December 8, 1896, letters files, folder 13, Library and Archives of the Royal Aeronautical Society, London. I thank Brian Riddle for making it available.

7. In Charles M. Westenhoff, ed., *Military Airpower: The CADRE Digest of Airpower Opinions and Thoughts* (Maxwell Air Force Base, AL: Air University Press, 1990), 51.

8. "L'aviation pour l'Armée, c'est zéro," quoted in Patrick Facon, "L'armée française et l'aviation (1891–1914)," *Revue historique des armées,* no. 164 (September 1986): 77.

9. Foch to commander, troisième bureau, no. 6145 (November 3, 1916), reprinted in Bernard Pujo, "L'evolution de la pensée du général Foch sur l'emploi de l'aviation en 1915–1916," Institute d'histoire des conflits contemporains, Service historique de l'armée de l'air, et Fondation pour les études de defense nationale, *Colloque air 1984* (Paris: École Militaire, September 1984), 221.

10. Major General J. F. C. Fuller, *Armament and History: A Study of the Influence of Armament on History from the Dawn of Classical Warfare to the Second World War* (New York: Charles Scribner's Sons, 1945), 7.

11. Pacific data computed from Joint Army-Navy Assessment Committee, *Japanese Naval and Merchant Shipping Losses during World War II by All Causes* (Washington, DC: U.S. Government Printing Office, February 1947), table II, vii. European data computed on the basis of statistics in Captain Stephen W. Roskill, *The War at Sea, 1939–45,* vol. 3 (London: Her Majesty's Stationery Office, 1961), appendices XX and Y, tables III and IV, 457–461, 471–472.

12. Lieutenant Colonel Richard L. Meiling, Medical Corps, "Interview with Professor Doctor Siegfried Handloser, Lt. Gen., Chief Medical Officer, OKW," interview no. 75 (July 27, 1945), appendix 2, U.S. Strategic Bombing Survey, *Consolidated Report of the Medical Sciences Branch* (Washington, DC: U.S. Strategic Bombing Survey Morale Division, 1945), archives of the Air Force Historical Research Agency, Maxwell Air Force Base, Alabama. I thank Air Commodore Andrew P. N. Lambert for making me aware of this document. For an example of the views of other commanders, see Seymour Freidin and William Richardson, eds., *The Fatal Decisions* (New York: William Sloane Associates, 1956), 215, 227, 286, and 290, a series of commentaries by six former Nazi generals: Werner Kreipe, Günther Blumentritt, Fritz Bayerlein, Kurt Zeitzler, Bodo Zimmerman, and Hasso von Manteuffel.

13. Goebbels diary, entry for March 21, 1945; Joseph Goebbels, *Final Entries, 1945: The Diaries of Joseph Goebbels*, ed. Hugh Trevor-Roper (New York: G. P. Putnam's Sons, 1978).

14. See, for example, James O. Young, "Riding England's Coattails: The Army Air Forces and the Turbojet Revolution," Richard P. Hallion, "The Air Force and the Supersonic Breakthrough," and Thomas A. Julian, "The Origins of Air Refueling in the United States Air Force," all in *Technology and the Air Force: A Retrospective Assessment*, ed. Jacob Neufeld, George M. Watson Jr., and David Chenoweth (Washington, DC: U.S. Government Printing Office, 1997), 3–39, 49–99; Richard K. Smith, *Seventy-Five Years of Inflight Refueling* (Washington, DC: Air Force History and Museums Program, 1998); Keith A. Hutchinson, *Air Mobility: The Evolution of Global Reach* (Vienna, VA: Point One VII, 1999); and A. Timothy Warnock, ed., *Short of War: Major USAF Contingency Operations 1947–1997* (Maxwell Air Force Base, AL: Air University Press in association with the Air Force History and Museums Program, 2000).

15. Secretary Donald B. Rice, *The Air Force and U.S. National Security: Global Reach—Global Power, A White Paper* (Washington, DC: Office of the Secretary of the Air Force, June 1990), 1. Principal author of this watershed document, a product of the Secretary of the Air Force's Staff Group (SAF/OSX), was then–Lieutenant Colonel David A. Deptula, USAF, assisted by Dr. Christopher Bowie of the RAND Corporation, with primary inputs from Colonel John A. Warden III, Colonel John Piazza, and Lieutenant General Charles Boyd. (Personal recollection of author, who served in SAF/OSX as a senior issues and policy analyst for Secretary Rice).

16. Joseph Needham, *Science in Traditional China: A Comparative Perspective* (Cambridge: Harvard University Press, 1981), 30–52; Denys Forrest, *Tiger of Mysore: The Life and Death of Tipu Sultan* (London: Chatto and Windus, 1970), 140; Frank H. Winter, *The First Golden Age of Rocketry: Congreve and Hale Rockets of the Nineteenth Century* (Washington, DC: Smithsonian Institution Press, 1990), 1–11.

17. Milton Lehman, *This High Man: The Life of Robert H. Goddard*, 2d ed. (1963; repr., New York: Pyramid Books, 1970), 102–103; David A. Clary, *Rocket Man: Robert H. Goddard and the Birth of the Space Age* (New York: Hyperion, 2003), 134–136.

18. Theodore von Kármán, *The Wind and Beyond: Theodore von Kármán—Pioneer in Aviation and Pathfinder in Space*, with Lee Edson (Boston: Little, Brown, 1967), 243.

19. Ibid.; see also Frank J. Malina, "The U.S. Army Air Corps Jet Propulsion Research Project, GALCIT Project No. 1, 1939–1946: A Memoir," in *Essays on the History of Rocketry and Astronautics: Proceedings of the Third through the Sixth History Symposia of the International Academy of Astronautics*, vol. 2, ed. R. Cargill Hall, National Aeronautics and Space Administration (NASA) Conference Publication 2014 (Washington, DC: NASA, 1977), 155. It is hard to fathom why Hunsaker is as revered among American aeronautical engineering pioneers as he is. He advised Donald Douglas not to enter the aviation field (a suggestion young Douglas wisely ignored); dissuaded Britain's Barnes Wallis from immigrating to America; overemphasized the value of the airship even after the R 101, *Akron, Macon*, and *Hindenburg* disasters; missed the significance of the rocket; and argued against wartime turbojet research on the grounds that the jet would not be ready in time to influence the outcome of the war. Afterward, as the National Advisory Committee for Aeronautics grappled with the postwar world, he persisted in his hostility toward rocketry and spaceflight before abandoning the agency on the eve of *Sputnik* and leaving the eminently more qualified James H. Doolittle and Dr. Hugh L. Dryden to

sort out its future. For three views of Hunsaker, see William F. Trimble's hagiographic *Jerome C. Hunsaker and the Rise of American Aeronautics* (Washington, DC: Smithsonian Institution Press, 2002); Jack C. Kerrebrock's slightly more balanced "Jerome Clarke Hunsaker, 1886–1984," in National Academy of Sciences, *Biographical Memoirs,* no. 78 (Washington, DC: National Academies Press, 2000), 94–107; and James H. Doolittle's straightforward *I Could Never Be So Lucky Again: An Autobiography,* with Carroll V. Glines (New York: Bantam, 1991), 516–517.

20. Hugh L. Dryden, "Present State of the Guided Missile Art," 1, a study paper in the Technical Intelligence Supplement to Theodore von Kármán et al., *Where We Stand: First Report to General of the Army H. H. Arnold on Long-Range Research Problems of the AIR FORCES with a Review of German Plans and Developments* (August 22, 1945), Papers of General Henry H. Arnold, Microfilm Reel 194, Manuscript Division, Library of Congress, Washington, DC.

21. Francis H. Clauser et al., *Preliminary Design of an Experimental World-Circling Spaceship,* Report No. SM–11827 (Santa Monica, CA: Douglas Aircraft Company, Inc., Santa Monica Plant Engineering Division, May 2, 1946), 1; see also 9–16, and the telling comments of Louis Ridenour. This report was prepared under Army Air Forces contract authorization W33–038–ac–14105, and marked one of the first research efforts of the newly created RAND, which began as a division of Douglas. The report is available from the RAND Corporation website at http://www.rand.org/pubs/special_memoranda/SM11827/. See also RAND, *The RAND Corporation: The First Fifteen Years* (Santa Monica, CA: RAND, 1963), 9.

22. Sir Henry Tizard et al., "Future Development in Weapons and Methods of War: Report by Sir Henry Tizard's 'Ad Hoc' Committee," Chiefs of Staff Committee Report C.O.S. (45) 402 (O), Copy No. 94, June 16, 1945, 17, in the Papers of General Muir Fairchild, Box 4, "Joint Strategic Survey" file, Manuscript Division, Library of Congress, Washington, DC. The Tizard Ad Hoc Committee consisted of Tizard, P. M. S. Blackett, C. D. Ellis, C. P. Thomson, and J. D. Bernal.

23. Vannevar Bush, *Modern Arms and Free Men: A Discussion of the Role of Science in Preserving Democracy,* 2d ed. (1968; repr., Cambridge, MA: MIT Press, 1949), 86.

24. Ibid., 85.

25. For *Sputnik*'s impact, see Walter A. McDougall, *The Heavens and the Earth: A Political History of the Space Age* (New York: Basic Books, Inc., 1985), 141–156; and Howard E. McCurdy, *Space and the American Imagination* (Washington, DC: Smithsonian Institution Press, 1997), 62–63; for the Soviet perspective, see Asif A. Siddiqi, *Challenge to Apollo: The Soviet Union and the Space Race, 1945–1974,* SP–2000–4408 (Washington, DC: NASA, 2000), 167–169.

26. David N. Spires, *Beyond Horizons: A Half Century of Air Force Space Leadership* (Peterson Air Force Base, CO: Air Force Space Command, 1997), 243–269.

27. See Air Vice Marshal R. A. Mason, *War in the Third Dimension: Essays in Contemporary Air Power* (London: Brassey's Defence Publishers, 1986); and Colonel John A. Warden III, *The Air Campaign: Planning for Combat* (1988; repr., New York: toExcel Press, 2000). For Warden and his influence, see John Andreas Olsen, *John Warden and the Renaissance of American Air Power* (Washington, DC: Potomac Books, 2007). Garden rose to senior RAF command and subsequently became a major figure in international strategic studies; Deptula rose to senior USAF command and was responsible for strategic targeting of Iraq

during the first Gulf War. He has since generated his own acolytic following. Meilinger became the first commander of the USAF's School of Advanced Airpower Studies (now the School of Advanced Air and Space Studies) and was an influential thinker in air doctrine.

28. For example, Alan Stephens, ed., *Smaller but Larger: Conventional Air Power into the 21st Century* (Canberra: RAAF Air Power Studies Centre, 1991); Norman Friedman, *Desert Victory: The War for Kuwait* (Annapolis: U.S. Naval Institute Press, 1991); Group Captain Gary Waters, RAAF, *Gulf Lesson One—The Value of Air Power: Doctrinal Lessons for Australia* (Canberra: RAAF Air Power Studies Centre, 1992); Richard P. Hallion, *Storm over Iraq: Air Power and the Gulf War* (Washington, DC: Smithsonian Institution Press, 1992); Thomas A. Keaney and Eliot A. Cohen, *Gulf War Air Power Survey Summary Report* (Washington, DC: U.S. Government Printing Office, 1993); James A. Winnefeld and Dana J. Johnson, *Joint Air Operations: Pursuit of Unity in Command and Control, 1942–1991* (Annapolis: U.S. Naval Institute Press and RAND, 1993); Christopher Bowie, Fred Frostic, Kevin Lewis, John Lund, David Ochmanek, and Philip Propper, *The New Calculus: Analyzing Airpower's Changing Role in Joint Theater Campaigns*, Report MR–149–AF (Santa Monica, CA: RAND, 1993); Major General Robert H. Scales Jr., USA, *Certain Victory: The U.S. Army in the Gulf War* (Washington, DC: Brassey's, Inc., 1994); Squadron Leader S. A. Mackenzie, RNZAF, *Strategic Air Power Doctrine for Small Air Forces* (Canberra: RAAF Air Power Studies Centre, 1994); Group Captain Andrew P. N. Lambert, RAF, *The Psychology of Air Power* (London: Royal United Services Institute for Defence Studies, 1995); and Colonel David A. Deptula, USAF, *Firing for Effect: Change in the Nature of Warfare* (Arlington, VA: Aerospace Education Foundation of the Air Force Association, 1995).

29. Group Captain Andrew P. N. Lambert, RAF, and Arthur C. Williamson, eds., *The Dynamics of Air Power* (Bracknell, UK: Royal Air Force Staff College, 1996), xi.

30. In the foreword to Daniel Gouré and Christopher M. Szara, eds., *Air and Space Power in the New Millennium* (Washington, DC: Center for Strategic and International Studies in cooperation with VII Inc., 1997), vii.

31. For example, Group Captain Andrew G. B. Vallance, RAF, *The Air Weapon: Doctrines of Air Power Strategy and Operational Art* (London: Macmillan Press Ltd., 1996); Lambert and Williamson, eds., *The Dynamics of Air Power*; G. A. S. C. Wilson, ed., *British Security 2010* (London: Ministry of Defence, 1996); Alan Vick, David T. Orletsky, John Bordeaux, and David A. Shlapak, *Enhancing Air Power's Contribution against Light Infantry Targets*, MR–697–AF (Santa Monica, CA: RAND, 1996); George and Meredith Friedman, *The Future of War: Power, Technology, and American World Dominance in the 21st Century* (New York: St. Martin's Griffin, 1996); Gouré and Szara, eds., *Air and Space Power in the New Millennium*, xvii–xxii, 48–87, 107; Richard P. Hallion, ed., *Air Power Confronts an Unstable World* (London: Brassey's Ltd., 1997); Allan D. English, ed., *The Changing Face of War: Learning from History* (Montreal: McGill–Queens University Press and the Royal Military College of Canada, 1998); Alan Vick et al., *Aerospace Operations in Urban Environments*, MR–1187–AF (Santa Monica, CA: RAND, 2000); Donald Kagan and Frederick W. Kagan, *While America Sleeps: Self-Delusion, Military Weakness, and the Threat to Peace Today* (New York: St. Martin's Griffin, 2000); Stephen T. Hosmer, *Why Milosevic Decided to Settle When He Did*, Report MR–1351–AF (Santa Monica, CA: RAND, 2001); Stephen T. Hosmer, *Operations against Enemy Leaders*, MR-1385-AF

(Santa Monica, CA: RAND, 2001); John Andreas Olsen, ed., *From Manoeuvre Warfare to Kosovo?* (Trondheim: Royal Norwegian Air Force Academy, 2001); John Andreas Olsen, ed., *A Second Aerospace Century* (Trondheim: NATO Combined Air Operations Centre 3 and Royal Norwegian Air Force Academy, 2001); Michael Evans, *Australia and the Revolution in Military Affairs* (Duntroon: Australian Army Land Warfare Studies Centre, 2001); Michael Evans and Alan Ryan, *From Breitenfeld to Baghdad: Perspectives on Combined Arms Warfare* (Duntroon: Australian Army Land Warfare Studies Centre, 2003); Wing Commander J. W. Waller, RAAF, *Effects-Based Operations and the Royal Australian Air Force* (Canberra: RAAF Aerospace Centre, 2003); Benjamin S. Lambeth, *Air Power against Terror: America's Conduct of Operation Enduring Freedom*, Report MG–166 (Santa Monica, CA: RAND, 2005); Frederick W. Kagan, *Finding the Target: The Transformation of American Military Policy* (New York: Encounter Books, 2006); Matthew Butler, *Effects-Based Targeting: The Future of Targeting for the Royal Australian Air Force* (Canberra: RAAF Air Power Development Centre, 2008); Sanu Kainikara, *A Fresh Look at Air Power Doctrine* (Canberra: RAAF Air Power Development Centre, 2008).

32. Notably, Air Vice Marshal Tony Mason, *Air Power: A Centennial Appraisal* (London: Brassey's Ltd., 1994); Alan Stephens, ed., *The War in the Air, 1914–1994* (Canberra: RAAF Air Power Studies Centre, 1994; Maxwell Air Force Base, AL: Air University Press, 2001); Colonel Philip S. Meilinger, USAF, ed., *The Paths of Heaven: The Evolution of Airpower Theory* (Maxwell Air Force Base, AL: Air University Press, 1997); Sebastian Cox and Peter Gray, eds., *Air Power History: Turning Points from Kitty Hawk to Kosovo* (London: Frank Cass Publishers, 2002); Stephen Budiansky, *Air Power: From Kitty Hawk to Gulf War II: A History of the People, Ideas and Machines That Transformed War in the Century of Flight* (New York: Viking, 2003); and Walter J. Boyne, *The Influence of Air Power upon History* (Gretna, LA: Pelican Publishing Co., 2003). For "classic" works still possessing much value, there is Robin Higham's *Air Power: A Concise History* (New York: St. Martin's Press, 1972); and Eugene M. Emme's *The Impact of Air Power* (Princeton: D. Van Nostrand Co., 1959).

33. For example, the Battle of Britain, the subject of continuing examination, such as Richard Overy's thoughtful *The Battle of Britain: The Myth and the Reality* (New York: W. W. Norton and Co., 2000); Paul Addison and Jeremy A. Crang, eds., *The Burning Blue: A New History of the Battle of Britain* (London: Pimlico, 2000); Christine Goulter, Andrew Gordon, and Gary Sheffield, "The Royal Navy Did Not Win the 'Battle of Britain;' but We Need a Holistic View of British Defences in 1940," *RUSI Journal* (October 2006): 66–67; and Anthony J. Cumming's revisionist "Did Radar Win the Battle of Britain?" *The Historian* 69, no. 4 (Winter 2007): 688–705. Another is RAF Bomber Command and the strategic air offensive against Nazi Germany, the subject of two meticulously researched, vigorously argued, and provocative works, differing greatly in conclusion and interpretation: Air Commodore Henry Probert, *Bomber Harris: His Life and Times: The Biography of Marshal of the Royal Air Force Sir Arthur Harris, the Wartime Chief of Bomber Command* (London: Greenhill Books, 2001); and Tami Davis Biddle, *Rhetoric and Reality in Air Warfare: The Evolution of British and American Ideas about Strategic Bombing, 1914–1945* (Princeton: Princeton University Press, 2002). A third is the ever-fascinating Brigadier General William "Billy" Mitchell, subject of two differing and strongly argued works: Rondall R. Rice, *The Politics of Air Power: From Confrontation to Cooperation in*

Army Aviation Civil-Military Relations (Lincoln: University of Nebraska Press, 2004); and Douglas Waller, *A Question of Loyalty: Gen. Billy Mitchell and the Court-Martial that Gripped a Nation* (New York: HarperCollins Publishers, 2004).

34. Philip B. Gove, ed., *Webster's Seventh New Collegiate Dictionary* (Springfield, MA: G. and C. Merriam Company, Publishers, 1971), 981.

35. Dr. Charles L. Morefield, "Air Force Information Applications in the 21st Century," in *Information Applications*, a volume in the *New World Vistas: Air and Space Power for the 21st Century* study series (Washington, DC: Air Force Scientific Advisory Board, 1996), vii. The *New World Vistas* study was an ambitious effort by Air Force Secretary Dr. Sheila Widnall, supported by Air Force Chief of Staff General Ronald Fogleman, to both revitalize the Air Force Scientific Advisory Board and to assess the likely scientific and technological future environment, and the opportunities and challenges that might present themselves. It was, overall, an excellent initiative, and one that established important baseline markers both for long-range planning and future Air Force investment and acquisition.

36. For example, see Committee on C⁴ISR for Future Naval Strike Groups, *C⁴ISR for Future Naval Strike Groups* (Washington, DC: National Research Council, 2006), xii.

37. Colonel Philip S. Meilinger, USAF, *Ten Propositions on Air Power* (Washington, DC: Air Force History and Museums Program, 1994), proposition 1.

38. John S. D. Eisenhower, *Strictly Personal* (Garden City, NY: Doubleday and Co., 1974), 72.

39. B. H. Liddell Hart, ed., *The Rommel Papers*, with Lucie-Maria Rommel, Manfred Rommel, and General Fritz Bayerlein (New York: Harcourt, Brace, and Co., 1953), 491.

40. Friedrich Ruge, *Rommel in Normandy: Reminiscences by Friedrich Ruge* (San Rafael, CA: Presidio Press, 1979), 181, 187.

41. For more detail, see Richard P. Hallion, "A Troubling Past: Air Force Fighter Acquisition since 1945," *Airpower Journal* 4, no. 4 (Winter 1990): 4–23.

42. Bush, *Modern Arms and Free Men*, 49.

43. For example, a case exists where a senior Air Force officer was assigned a particular F–15 when he first flew as a lieutenant. More than twenty years later, as a regional commander deployed to Europe, he found himself flying the same airplane. More than ten years after that, his son was assigned to that very airplane. This would be equivalent to the son of a Great War SPAD pilot being assigned to fly the same SPAD in the early 1950s.

44. For an excellent examination of the evolution of American national security space policy, see R. Cargill Hall, "The Evolution of U.S. National Security Space Policy and Its Legal Foundations in the 20th Century," *Journal of Space Law* 33, no. 1 (2007): 1–103, an essential work by a superb scholar who had privileged archival access.

45. Air University, *Spacecast 2020* (Maxwell Air Force Base, AL: Air University Press, 1994), 1: ix–x.

46. After General Charles Horner took over Space Command, he sat through successive meetings in which participants gave updates on a Titan IV missile experiencing continuous delays preventing its launch with a national security payload. Finally, experiencing one meeting too many, Horner barked, "If that missile isn't off the pad in two weeks, I'm gonna paint it brown and give it a building number." Space Command, to its credit, quickly launched the Titan and its payload, and moved on with a more operationally focused mind-set. For Horner's reaction to the space community and the challenges he faced, see Tom Clancy, *Every Man a Tiger*, with General Chuck Horner, USAF (Ret.)

(New York: G. P. Putnam's Sons, 1999), 518–524; conversation with General Horner, January 2009, Shalimar, Florida.

47. Colonel John A. Warden III to the author.

48. See, for example, Ann Roosevelt, "USJFCOM Drops Effects Based Operations Terms and Concepts," *Defense Daily* (August 19, 2008), relating the decision of General James Mattis, USMC, commander of U.S. Joint Forces Command, to drop the reference to EBO, and related terms such as "effects-based approach," "operational net assessment," and "system of system analysis" in Joint Professional Military Education.

49. After Korea, for example, the U.S. Navy rigorously restructured its aircraft and weapons acquisition programs to address shortfalls identified in the crucible of the Korean conflict. The Air Force, having had a "good" war, determined that Korea was an anomaly and turned back to what its planners perceived as the "normative" form of future war: high-Mach nuclear scenarios. The result after 1953 was a succession of aircraft and weapons programs unrelated to the service's real needs, so much so that, a decade later, the Air Force had to acquire fighter and attack aircraft originally designed for the U.S. Navy (the F–4 Phantom II, A–7 Corsair II, and A–1 Skyraider) in order to fulfill its national security responsibilities. That lesson stayed with the service, which next acquired families of aircraft much more closely related to its future needs.

50. David K. Mann, *The 1972 Invasion of Military Region I: Fall of Quang Tri and Defense of Hue* (Hickam Air Force Base, HI: Headquarters Pacific Air Forces, Directorate of Operations Analysis, contemporary historical examination of current operations/Corona Harvest Division, March 15, 1973); John F. Kreis, *Air Warfare and Air Base Air Defense, 1914–1973* (Washington, DC: Office of Air Force History, 1988), 325–338.

51. Personal recollections of the author from his service on the Air Force Air Staff between 1991 and 2006.

52. For example, the U.S. Air Force's *Horned Owl* C–12-based counter–improvised explosive device (IED) program, which used a combination of forward-looking infrared and ground-penetrating radar, coupled with a real-time ground station, to frustrate IED-planting terrorists and locate weapons and explosive caches (personal recollection of author).

53. Then why not a separate service for submarines, it might be asked? Because they could under only the most special circumstances influence what was happening on land, with their mobility constrained to less than the three-fifths of the world's surface covered by water, whereas the airplane is unconstrained across the entire globe.

SELECTED BIBLIOGRAPHY

Addison, Paul, and Jeremy Crang, eds. *The Burning Blue: A New History of the Battle of Britain.* London: Pimlico, 2000.

———. *Firestorm: The Bombing of Dresden 1945.* London: Pimlico, 2006.

Aloni, Shlomo. *IAF Air Campaign: The Six Days War.* Tel Aviv: Decal Publishing, 2008.

Amir, Amos. *Fire in the Sky.* Barnsley, UK: Pen and Sword Books, 2005.

Anderegg, C. R. *Sierra Hotel: Flying Air Force Fighters in the Decade after Vietnam.* Washington, DC: Air Force History and Museums Program, 2001.

Armitage, M. J., and R. A. Mason. *Air Power in the Nuclear Age,* 2d ed. Urbana: University of Illinois Press, 1985.

Ash, Eric. *Sir Frederick Sykes and the Air Revolution, 1912–1918.* London: Taylor and Francis, 1999.

Bar, Siman-Tov Yaacov. *The Israeli-Egyptian War of Attrition, 1969–1970.* New York: Columbia University Press, 1980.

Bartsch, William H. *December 8, 1941: MacArthur's Pearl Harbor.* College Station: Texas A&M University Press, 2003.

Beckett, Ian, ed. *The Roots of Counterinsurgency: Armies and Guerrilla Warfare, 1900–1945.* London: Blandford Press, 1988.

Bell, Amy H. *London Was Ours: Diaries and Memoirs of the London Blitz.* London: I. B. Tauris, 2008.

Bensahel, Nora. *The Counterterror Coalitions: Cooperation with Europe, NATO, and the European Union.* Santa Monica, CA: RAND, 2003.

Bergerud, Eric. *Fire in the Sky: The Air War in the South Pacific.* Boulder, CO: Westview Press, 2000.

Biddle, Tami Davis. *Rhetoric and Reality in Air Warfare: The Evolution of British and American Ideas about Strategic Bombing, 1914–1945.* Princeton: Princeton University Press, 2002.

Boyd, Alexander. *The Soviet Air Force since 1918.* London: Macdonald and Jane's, 1977.

Boyne, Walter J. *Beyond the Wild Blue: History of the United States Air Force, 1947–1997.* New York: St. Martin's Press, 1997.

Bragadin, Marco. *The Italian Navy in World War II.* Annapolis: U.S. Naval Institute Press, 1957.

Brauer, Jurgen, and Hubert van Tuyll. *Castles, Battles, and Bombs: How Economics Explains Military History.* Chicago: University of Chicago Press, 2008.

Brodie, Bernard, ed. *The Absolute Weapon: Atomic Power and World Order.* New York: Harcourt Brace, 1946.

Brom, Shlomo, and Meir Elran, eds. *The Second Lebanon War: Strategic Perspectives*. Tel Aviv: Institute for National Security Studies, 2007.

Brookes, Andrew. *Air War over Russia*. London: Ian Allen, 2003.

Broughton, Jack. *Thud Ridge*. Philadelphia: J.B. Lippincott, 1969.

———. *Going Downtown: The War against Hanoi and Washington*. New York: Orion Books, 1988.

———. *Rupert Red Two: A Fighter Pilot's Life from Thunderbolts to Thunderchiefs*. St. Paul, MN: Zenith Press, 2007.

Brown, David. *The Royal Navy and the Falklands War*. London: Leo Cooper, 1987.

Buckley, John. *Air Power in the Age of Total War*. Bloomington: Indiana University Press, 1999.

Bucknam, Mark A. *Responsibility of Command: How UN and NATO Commanders Influenced Airpower over Bosnia*. Maxwell Air Force Base, AL: Air University Press, 2003.

Budiansky, Stephen. *Air Power: The Men, Machines, and Ideas That Revolutionized War, from Kitty Hawk to Gulf War II*. New York: Viking, 2004.

Builder, Carl H. *The Icarus Syndrome: The Role of Air Power Theory in the Evolution and Fate of the U.S. Air Force*. New Brunswick: Transactions Publisher, 1994.

Burden, Rodney, Michael Draper, Douglas Rough, Colin Smith, and David Wilton. *Falklands: The Air War*. London: Arms and Armour Press, 1986.

Burrell, Robert S. *The Ghosts of Iwo Jima*. College Station: Texas A&M University Press, 2006.

Butler, J. R. *Grand Strategy III, Part II: June 1941–August 1942*. London: Her Majesty's Stationery Office, 1964.

Calder, Angus. *The Myth of the Blitz*. London: Jonathan Cape, 1991.

Castle, Timothy N. *One Day Too Long: Top Secret Site 85 and the Bombing of North Vietnam*. New York: Columbia University Press, 1999.

Chickering, Roger, Stig Förster, and Bernd Greiner, eds. *A World at Total War: Global Conflict and the Politics of Destruction, 1937–1945*. Cambridge: Cambridge University Press, 2005.

Christienne, Charles, and Pierre Lissarague. *A History of French Military Aviation*. Washington, DC: Smithsonian Institution Press, 1986.

Churchill, Winston. *The Second World War: Volume II*. London: Cassell, 1949.

Clapp, Michael, and Ewan Southby-Tailyour. *Amphibious Assault: Falklands: The Battle of San Carlos Waters*. London: Leo Cooper, 1996.

Clark, Wesley K. *Waging Modern War*. New York: Public Affairs, 2001.

Clarke, Shaun. *Strategy, Air Strike, and Small Nations*. RAAF Base Fairbairn, ACT, Australia: Airpower Studies Center, 1999.

Clary, David A. *Rocket Man: Robert H. Goddard and the Birth of the Space Age*. New York: Hyperion, 2003.

Clodfelter, Mark. *The Limits of Air Power: The American Bombing of North Vietnam*. New York: Free Press, 1989.

Cohen, Elliezer. *Israel's Best Defense*. New York: Orion Books, 1993.

Cohen, Eliot A. et al. *Gulf War Air Power Survey*. Vol. 1, *Part I: Planning*. Washington, DC: U.S. Government Printing Office, 1993.

———. *Gulf War Air Power Survey*. Vol. 1, *Part II: Command and Control*. Washington, DC: U.S. Government Printing Office, 1993.

———. *Gulf War Air Power Survey*. Vol. 2, *Part I: Operations*. Washington, DC: U.S. Government Printing Office, 1993.

———. *Gulf War Air Power Survey*. Vol. 2, *Part II: Effects and Effectiveness*. Washington, DC: U.S. Government Printing Office, 1993.

————. *Gulf War Air Power Survey*. Vol. 5, *Part A: A Statistical Compendium*. Washington, DC: U.S. Government Printing Office, 1993.

Cohen, Lenard J. *Broken Bonds: The Disintegration of Yugoslavia*. Boulder, CO: Westview Press, 1993.

Cooling, Benjamin F., ed. *Case Studies in the Development of Close Air Support*. Washington, DC: Office of Air Force History, 1990.

Cooper, Malcolm. *The Birth of Independent Air Power: British Air Policy in the First World War*. London: Allen and Unwin, 1986.

Cordesman, Anthony J. *The Lessons and Non-Lessons of the Air and Missile Campaign in Kosovo*. Westport, CT: Praeger, 2001.

————. *The Lessons of Afghanistan: Warfighting, Intelligence, Force Transformation, Counter-Proliferation, and Arms Control*. Washington, DC: Center for Strategic and International Studies, June 28, 2002.

Cordesman, Anthony J., and Abraham R. Wagner. *The Gulf War: The Lessons of Modern War*. Volume IV. Boulder, CO: Westview Press, 1996.

Corum, James, and Wray Johnson. *Airpower and Small Wars*. Lawrence: University Press of Kansas, 2003.

Cox, Sebastian, and Peter Gray, eds. *Air Power History: Turning Points from Kitty Hawk to Kosovo*. London: Frank Cass Publishers, 2002.

Crane, Conrad. *Bombs, Cities and Civilians: American Airpower Strategy in World War II*. Lawrence: University Press of Kansas, 1993.

Craven, Wesley F., and James L. Cate. *The Army Air Forces in World War II*. 7 vols. Chicago: University of Chicago Press, 1948.

Crouch, Tom D. *The Eagle Aloft: Two Centuries of the Balloon in America*. Washington, DC: Smithsonian Institution Press, 1983.

Cull, Nicholas. *Selling War: The British Propaganda Campaign against American "Neutrality" in World War II*. Oxford: Oxford University Press, 1995.

Daalder, Ivo, and Michael O'Hanlon. *Winning Ugly: NATO's War to Save Kosovo*. Washington, DC: Brookings Institution Press, 2000.

Davis, Richard G. *Carl A. Spaatz and the Air War in Europe*. Washington, DC: Smithsonian Institution Press, 1992.

————. *Decisive Force: Strategic Bombing in the Gulf War*. Washington, DC: Air Force History and Museums Program, 1996.

————. *On Target: Organizing and Executing the Strategic Air Campaign against Iraq*. Washington, DC: Air Force History and Museums Program, 2002.

Davis, Vernon E. *The Long Road Home: U.S. Prisoner of War Policy and Planning in Southeast Asia*. Washington, DC: Office of the Secretary of Defense, 2000.

Doolittle, James H. *I Could Never Be So Lucky Again: An Autobiography*. With Carroll V. Glines. New York: Bantam, 1991.

Douhet, Giulio. *The Command of the Air*. New York: Coward-McCann, Inc., 1942. Originally published as *Il Dominio dell'Aria: Saggio sull' Arte della Guerra Aerea, con una Appendice Contentente Nozioni Elementari di Aeronautica*. Rome: Stabilimento Poligraphico per l'Amministrazione della Guerra, 1921.

Dower, John. *War without Mercy: Race and Power in the Pacific War*. New York: Pantheon, 1986.

Duiker, William J. *Ho Chi Minh*. New York: Hyperion, 2000.

El-Gamasy, Mohamed Abdel Ghani. *The October War Memoirs of Field Marshal El-Gamasy of Egypt*. Cairo: American University in Cairo Press, 1993.

Ethell, Jeffrey, and Alfred Price. *Air War South Atlantic*. London: Sidgwick and Jackson, 1983.
———. *One Day in a Long War: May 10, 1972, Air War, North Vietnam*. New York: Random House, 1989.
Emme, Eugene M. *The Impact of Air Power*. Princeton: D. Van Nostrand Co., 1959.
Evans, David C., and Mark R. Peattie. *Kaigun*. Annapolis: U.S. Naval Institute Press, 1997.
Evans, Richard J. *The Third Reich at War*. London: Allen Lane, 2008.
Ewing, Steve. *Reaper Leader: The Life of Jimmy Flatley*. Annapolis: U.S. Naval Institute Press, 2002.
Fahey, James J. *Pacific War Diary*. Boston: Houghton Mifflin, 1963.
Felker, Craig C. *Testing American Sea Power: U.S. Navy Strategic Exercises, 1923–1940*. College Station: Texas A&M University Press, 2007.
Finn, Christopher, ed. *Effects Based Warfare*. London: London Stationery Office, 2002.
Flintham, Victor. *Air Wars and Aircraft*. New York: Facts on File, 1990.
Francillon, René J. *Japanese Aircraft of the Pacific War*. Annapolis: U.S. Naval Institute Press, 2000.
Frank, Richard B. *Guadalcanal: The Definitive Account of the Landmark Battle*. New York: Random House, 1990.
Freedman, Lawrence. *Official History of the Falklands Campaign*. Vol. II, *War and Diplomacy*. Rev. ed. London: Routledge, 2007.
Freedman, Lawrence, and Efraim Karsh. *The Gulf Conflict, 1990–1991: Diplomacy and War in the New World Order*. London: Faber and Faber, 1993.
Frostic, Fred. *Air Campaign against the Iraqi Army in the Kuwaiti Theater of Operations*. Santa Monica, CA: RAND, 1994.
Fuchida, Mitsuo, and Masatake Okumiya. *Midway: The Battle That Doomed Japan*. Annapolis: U.S. Naval Institute Press, 1992.
Fuller, J. F. C. *Armament and History: A Study of the Influence of Armament on History from the Dawn of Classical Warfare to the Second World War*. New York: Charles Scribner's Sons, 1945.
Futrell, Robert Frank. *The United States Air Force in Southeast Asia: The Advisory Years to 1965*. Washington, DC: Office of Air Force History, 1981.
———. *The United States Air Force in Korea, 1950–1953*. Washington, DC: Office of Air Force History, 1983.
Gaiduk, Ilya V. *The Soviet Union and the Vietnam War*. Chicago: Ivan R. Dee, 1996.
Gibbs-Smith, Charles H. *Clément Ader: His Flight Claims and His Place in History*. London: Her Majesty's Stationery Office, 1968.
Gilbert, Martin. *Finest Hour: Winston S. Churchill, 1939–1941*. London: William Heinemann, 1983.
Gilster, Herman L. *The Air War in Southeast Asia: Case Studies of Selected Campaigns*. Maxwell Air Force Base, AL: Air University Press, 1993.
Gollin, Alfred. *No Longer an Island: Britain and the Wright Brothers, 1902–1909*. Stanford: Stanford University Press, 1984.
Gooch, John, ed. *Airpower: Theory and Practice*. London: Frank Cass, 1995.
Gooderson, Ian. *Air Power at the Battlefront*. London: Frank Cass, 1998.
Gordon, Michael R., and Bernard E. Trainor. *The Generals' War: The Inside Story of the Conflict in the Gulf*. Boston: Little, Brown, 1995.
———. *Cobra II: The Inside Story of the Invasion and Occupation of Iraq*. London: Atlantic Books, 2006.

Goure, D., and C. M. Szara. *Air and Space Power in the New Millennium*. Washington, DC: Center for Strategic and International Studies, 2006.

Grant, Rebecca. *The B–2 Goes to War*. Arlington, VA: Iris Press, 2001.

Grau, Lester, ed. *The Bear Went over the Mountain: Soviet Combat Tactics in Afghanistan*. Washington, DC: National Defense University Press, 1996.

Gray, Peter W., ed. *British Air Power*. London: London Stationery Office, 2003.

Grayling, Anthony. *Among the Dead Cities: Was the Allied Bombing of Civilians in WWII a Necessity or a Crime?* London: Bloomsbury, 2006.

Griffith, Thomas E., Jr. *MacArthur's Airman: General George C. Kenney and the War in the Southwest Pacific*. Lawrence: University Press of Kansas, 1998.

Gutman, Roy. *A Witness to Genocide*. New York: Macmillan, 1993.

Haave, Christopher, and Phil Haun. *A–10s over Kosovo*. Maxwell Air Force Base, AL: Air University Press, 2003.

Halberstam, David. *War in a Time of Peace: Bush, Clinton and the Generals*. London: Bloomsbury, 2002.

Hall, R. Cargill, ed. *Case Studies in Strategic Bombardment*. Washington, DC: Air Force History and Museums Program, 1998.

Hallion, Richard P. *Rise of the Fighter Aircraft, 1914–1918*. Baltimore: Nautical and Aviation Publishing Company of America, 1984.

———. *Storm over Iraq: Air Power and the Gulf War*. Washington, DC: Smithsonian Institution Press, 1992.

———. *Strike from the Sky: The History of Battlefield Air Attack, 1911–1945*. Washington, DC: Smithsonian Institution Press, 1998.

Hallion, Richard P., ed. *Air Power Confronts an Unstable World*. London: Brassey's Ltd., 1997.

Hammes, T. X. *The Sling and the Stone*. St. Paul, MN: Zenith Press, 2004.

Hammond, Grant T. *The Mind of War: John Boyd and American Security*. Washington, DC: Smithsonian Institution Press, 2001.

Hansell, Haywood S., Jr. *The Air Plan that Defeated Hitler*. New York: Arno Press, 1972, 1980.

Harel, Amos, and Avi Issacharof. *34 Days: Israel, Hezbollah and the War in Lebanon*. New York: Palgrave Macmillan, 2008.

Harik, Judith Palmer. *Hezbollah: The Changing Face of Terrorism*. London: I. B. Tauris, 2006.

Harmer, Todd P., and C. R. Anderegg. *The Shootdown of Trigger 4*. Washington, DC: Headquarters U.S. Air Force, 2001.

Harrison, Mark, ed. *The Economics of World War II: Six Great Powers in International Comparison*. Cambridge: Cambridge University Press, 1998.

Hastings, Max. *Retribution: The Battle for Japan, 1944–45*. New York: Knopf, 2008.

Hayden, Frederick S. *Aeronautics in the Union and Confederate Armies, with a Survey of Military Aeronautics Prior to 1860*. Vol. 1. Baltimore: Johns Hopkins University Press, 1941.

Hayward, Joel. *Stopped at Stalingrad: The Luftwaffe and Hitler's Defeat in the East, 1942–43*. Lawrence: University Press of Kansas, 1998.

Heikal, Muhamed. *The Road to Ramadan*. London: Collins, 1975.

Hersey, John. *Hiroshima*. New York: Vintage, 1989.

Higham, Robin. *Air Power: A Concise History*. New York: St. Martin's Press, 1972.

Higham, Robin, and Stephen J. Harris, eds. *Why Air Forces Fail: The Anatomy of Defeat*. Lexington: University Press of Kentucky, 2006.

Holbrooke, Richard. *To End a War*. New York: Random House, 1998.

Hosmer, Stephen T. *Psychological Effects of U.S. Air Operations in Four Wars, 1941–1991: Lessons for U.S. Commanders.* Santa Monica, CA: RAND Corporation, 1996.

———. *The Conflict over Kosovo: Why Milosevic Decided to Settle When He Did.* Santa Monica, CA: RAND, 2000.

Hutchinson, Keith A. *Air Mobility: The Evolution of Global Reach.* Vienna, VA: Point One VII, 1999.

Jackson, Mike. *Soldier.* London: Bantam, 2007.

Jamison, Perry D. *Lucrative Targets: The U.S. Air Force in the Kuwaiti Theater of Operations.* Washington, DC: Air Force History and Museums Program, 2001.

Janis, Irving. *Groupthink: Psychological Studies of Policy Decisions and Fiascoes.* 2d ed. Boston: Little, Brown, 1982.

Jobé, J. *The Romance of Ballooning: The Story of the Early Aeronauts.* New York: Edita Lausanne and Viking Press, 1971.

Johnson, Edward C. *Marine Corps Aviation: The Early Years, 1912–1940.* Washington, DC: U.S. Marine Corps History and Museums Division, 1977.

Jones, Helen. *British Civilians in the Front Line: Air Raids, Productivity and Wartime Culture, 1939–1941.* Manchester: Manchester University Press, 2006.

Jones, Reginald V. *Most Secret War: British Scientific Intelligence, 1939–1945.* London: Hamish Hamilton, 1978.

Kaplan, Robert. *Balkan Ghosts: A Journey through History.* New York: St. Martin's Press, 1993.

Kármán, Theodore von. *The Wind and Beyond: Theodore von Kármán—Pioneer in Aviation and Pathfinder in Space.* With Lee Edson. Boston: Little, Brown, 1967.

Kennett, Lee. *The First Air War, 1914–1918.* New York: Free Press, 1991.

Kenney, George C. *General Kenney Reports: A Personal History of the Pacific War.* New York: Duell, Sloan and Pearce, 1949.

Kilmarx, Robert. *A History of Soviet Air Power.* London: Faber and Faber, 1962.

Kissinger, Henry. *My Years in the White House.* Boston: Little, Brown, 1979.

Knell, Hermann. *To Destroy a City: Strategic Bombing and Its Human Consequences in World War II.* Cambridge, MA: Da Capo Press, 2003.

Kreis, J. *Air Warfare and Air Base Air Defense, 1914–1973.* Washington, DC: Office of Air Force History, 1988.

———. *Piercing the Fog: Intelligence and Army Air Forces Operations in World War II.* Washington, DC: Air Force History Program, 1996.

Kumaraswamy, P. R., ed. *Revisiting the Yom Kippur War.* London: Frank Cass, 2000.

Laghod, Ibrahim Abu, ed. *The Arab-Israeli Confrontation of June 1967: An Arab Perspective.* Evanston, IL: Northwestern University Press, 1970.

Lambert, Andrew. *The Psychology of Air Power.* London: Royal United Services Institute for Defence Studies, 1995.

Lambert, Andrew, and Arthur C. Williamson, eds. *The Dynamics of Air Power.* Bracknell, UK: Royal Air Force Staff College, 1996.

Lambeth, Benjamin S. *Russia's Air Power in Crisis.* Washington, DC: Smithsonian Institution Press, 1999.

———. *The Transformation of American Air Power.* Ithaca, NY: Cornell University Press, 2000.

———. *NATO's Air War for Kosovo: A Strategic and Operational Assessment.* Santa Monica, CA: RAND, 2001.

———. *Air Power against Terror: America's Conduct of Operation Enduring Freedom.* Santa Monica, CA: RAND, 2005.

———. *American Carrier Air Power at the Dawn of a New Century*. Santa Monica, CA: RAND, 2005.

Lavalle, A. J. C. *Airpower and the 1972 Spring Invasion*. USAF Southeast Asia Monograph Series, Vol. II. Washington, DC: U.S. Government Printing Office, 1976.

———. *The Vietnamese Air Force, 1951–1975: An Analysis of Its Role in Combat and Fourteen Hours at Koh Tang*. Washington, DC: Office of Air Force History, 1985.

Lehman, Milton. *This High Man: The Life of Robert H. Goddard*. 2d ed. New York: Pyramid Books, 1970.

Levine, Alan. *The Pacific War: Japan versus the Allies*. Westport, CT: Praeger, 1995.

Liddle, Peter H. *The Airman's War, 1914–18*. Poole, Dorset: Blandford, 1987.

Lord, Walter. *Incredible Victory*. New York: Harper and Row, 1967.

Lowe, Keith. *Inferno: The Devastation of Hamburg 1943*. London: Viking, 2007.

Lundstrom, John B. *The First Team*. Annapolis: U.S. Naval Institute Press, 1984.

———. *The First Team and the Guadalcanal Campaign*. Annapolis: U.S. Naval Institute Press, 1994.

Luttwak, Edward N. *Strategy: The Logic of War and Peace*. Rev. ed. Cambridge, MA: Belknap Press of Harvard University Press, 2001.

Mackenzie, S. A. *Strategic Air Power Doctrine for Small Air Forces*. Canberra: RAAF Air Power Studies Centre, 1994.

Magid, Nasser Farid Abdel. *The Final Years*. Reading: Ithaca Press, 1994.

Marolda, Edward J. *By Sea, Air, and Land: An Illustrated History of the U.S. Navy and the War in Southeast Asia*. Washington, DC: U.S. Naval Historical Center, 1994.

Mason, R. A. *War in the Third Dimension: Essays in Contemporary Air Power*. London: Brassey's Defence Publishers, 1986.

———. *Air Power: A Centennial Appraisal*. London: Brassey's Ltd., 1994.

Mawdsley, Evan. *Thunder in the East: The Nazi-Soviet War, 1941–1945*. London: Hodder Arnold, 2005.

McCurdy, Howard E. *Space and the American Imagination*. Washington, DC: Smithsonian Institution Press, 1997.

McDougall, Walter A. *The Heavens and the Earth: A Political History of the Space Age*. New York: Basic Books, 1985.

Mead, Peter. *The Eye in the Air: History of Air Observation and Reconnaissance for the Army 1785–1945*. London: Her Majesty's Stationery Office, 1983.

Meilinger, Philip S. *Ten Propositions on Air Power*. Washington, DC: Air Force History and Museums Program, 1994.

Meilinger, Philip S., ed. *Paths of Heaven: The Evolution of Airpower Theory*. Maxwell Air Force Base, AL: Air University Press, 1997.

Mersky, Peter B., and Norman Polmar. *The Naval Air War in Vietnam*. Baltimore, MD: Nautical and Aviation Publishing Company of America, 1986.

Michel, Marshall L., III. *Clashes: Air Combat over North Vietnam, 1965–1972*. Annapolis: U.S. Naval Institute Press, 1997.

———. *The Eleven Days of Christmas: America's Last Vietnam Battle*. San Francisco: Encounter Books, 2002.

Military History Institute of Vietnam. *Victory in Vietnam: The Official History of the People's Army of Vietnam, 1954–1975*. Translated by Merle L. Pribbenow. Lawrence: University Press of Kansas, 2002.

Miller, Edward S. *War Plan Orange: The U.S. Strategy to Defeat Japan, 1897–1945*. Annapolis: U.S. Naval Institute Press, 1991.

Mitchell, William. *Winged Defense: The Development and Possibilities of Modern Air Power, Economic and Military*. New York: Putnam's, 1925.

Moise, Edwin E. *Tonkin Gulf and the Escalation of the Vietnam War*. Chapel Hill: University of North Carolina Press, 1996.

Momyer, William W. *Air Power in Three Wars*. Washington, DC: U.S. Government Printing Office, 1978.

Morison, Samuel Eliot. *History of United States Naval Operations in World War II*. 15 vols. Boston: Little, Brown, 1947–1962.

———. *The Two-Ocean War: A Short History of the United States Navy in the Second World War*. Boston: Little, Brown, 1963.

Morrow, John H., Jr. *Building German Air Power, 1909–1914*. Knoxville: University of Tennessee Press, 1976.

———. *German Air Power in World War I*. Lincoln: University of Nebraska Press, 1982.

———. *The Great War in the Air: Military Aviation from 1909 to 1921*. Washington, DC: Smithsonian Institution Press, 1993.

Murray, Williamson. *Luftwaffe*. Baltimore, MD: Nautical and Aviation Publishing Company of America, 1985.

———. *The Luftwaffe, 1933–1945: Strategy for Defeat*. Washington, DC: Brassey's, Inc., 1996.

Murray, Williamson, and Robert H. Scales Jr. *The Iraq War: A Military History*. Cambridge: Harvard University Press, 2003.

Nardulli, Bruce R., et al. *Disjointed War: Military Operations in Kosovo 1999*. Santa Monica, CA: RAND, 2002.

National Commission on Terrorist Attacks upon the United States. *The 9/11 Commission Report: Final Report of the National Commission on Terrorist Attacks upon the United States*. New York: W. W. Norton and Company, 2004.

Neufeld, Jacob, George M. Watson Jr., and David Chenoweth, eds. *Technology and the Air Force: A Retrospective Assessment*. Washington, DC: U.S. Government Printing Office, 1997.

Nichols, John B., and Barrett Tillman. *On Yankee Station: The Naval Air War over Vietnam*. Annapolis: U.S. Naval Institute Press, 1987.

Norton, Augustus Richard. *Hezbollah: A Short History*. Princeton: Princeton University Press, 2007.

O'Ballance, Edgar. *The Greek Civil War, 1944–1949*. New York: Frederick A. Praeger, 1966.

Olsen, John Andreas. *Strategic Air Power in Desert Storm*. London: Frank Cass, 2003.

———. *John Warden and the Renaissance of American Air Power*. Washington, DC: Potomac Books, 2007.

Olsen, John Andreas, ed. *Asymmetric Warfare*. Trondheim: Royal Norwegian Air Force Academy, 2002.

———. *A Second Aerospace Century*. Trondheim: Royal Norwegian Air Force Academy, 2001.

Omissi, David. *The Royal Air Force, Air Power and Colonial Control, 1919–1939*. Manchester: Manchester University Press, 1990.

Overy, Richard J. *The Air War, 1939–1945*. New York: Stein and Day, 1981.

———. *The Battle of Britain: The Myth and the Reality*. London: Penguin, 2000.

Owen, Robert C., ed. *Deliberate Force: A Case Study in Effective Air Campaigning*. Maxwell Air Force Base, AL: Air University Press, 2000.

Owens, Bill and Ed Offley. *Lifting the Fog of War*. Baltimore: Johns Hopkins University Press, 2001.

Pape, Robert A. *Bombing to Win: Air Power and Coercion in War*. Ithaca, NY: Cornell University Press, 1996.

Parshall, Jonathan, and Anthony Tully. *Shattered Sword: The Untold Story of the Battle of Midway*. Washington, DC: Potomac Books, 2005.

Peattie, Mark R. *Sunburst: The Rise of Japanese Naval Air Power, 1909–1941*. Annapolis: U.S. Naval Institute Press, 2001.

Peterson, H., G. C. Reinhardt, and E. E. Conger, eds. *Symposium on the Role of Airpower in Counterinsurgency and Unconventional Warfare: The Philippine Huk Campaign*, RM–3652–PR. Santa Monica, CA: RAND, July 1963.

Pisano, Dominick A., Thomas J. Dietz, Joanne M. Gernstein, and Karl S. Schneide. *Legend, Memory, and the Great War in the Air*. Seattle: University of Washington Press, 1992.

Pollack, Kenneth M. *Arabs at War: Arab Military Effectiveness, 1948–1991*. Lincoln: University of Nebraska Press, 2002.

Poolman, Kenneth. *Focke–Wulf Condor: Scourge of the Atlantic*. London: Macdonald and Janes, 1978.

Prange, Gordon. *At Dawn We Slept: The Untold Story of Pearl Harbor*. New York: McGraw Hill, 1981.

———. *Miracle at Midway*. New York: Penguin, 1982.

Price, Alfred. *Instruments of Darkness: The History of Electronic Warfare, 1939–1945*. London: Greenhill Books, 2005.

Probert, Henry. *The Forgotten Air Force: The Royal Air Force in the War against Japan, 1941–1945*. London: Brassey's Ltd., 1995.

———. *Bomber Harris: His Life and Times: The Biography of Marshal of the Royal Air Force Sir Arthur Harris, the Wartime Chief of Bomber Command*. London: Greenhill Books, 2001.

Putney, Diane T. *Airpower Advantage: Planning the Gulf War Air Campaign, 1989–1991*. Washington, DC: Air Force History and Museums Program, 2005.

Raleigh, Walter, and H. A. Jones. *The War in the Air*. 6 vols. Oxford: Clarendon Press, 1922–1937.

Randolph, Stephen P. *Powerful and Brutal Weapons: Nixon, Kissinger, and the Easter Offensive*. Cambridge: Harvard University Press, 2007.

Ray, John. *The Night Blitz, 1940–1941*. London: Arms and Armour, 1996.

Reardon, Carol. *Launch the Intruders: A Naval Attack Squadron in the Vietnam War, 1972*. Lawrence: University Press of Kansas, 2005.

Report of the Independent International Commission on Kosovo. Oxford: Oxford University Press, 2000.

Reynolds, Clark. *The Fast Carriers: The Forging of an Air Navy*. Annapolis: U.S. Naval Institute Press, 1968.

Reynolds, Richard T. *Heart of the Storm: The Genesis of the Air Campaign against Iraq*. Maxwell Air Force Base, AL: Air University Press, 1995.

Rice, Rondall R. *The Politics of Air Power: From Confrontation to Cooperation in Army Aviation Civil-Military Relations*. Lincoln: University of Nebraska Press, 2004.

Ridgway, Matthew B. *The Korean War*. New York: Doubleday, 1967.

Rieff, David. *Slaughterhouse: Bosnia and the Failure of the West*. New York: Simon & Schuster, 1995.

Ripley, Tim. *Operation Deliberate Force: The UN and NATO Campaign in Bosnia 1995*. London: Centre for Defence and International Security Studies, 1995.

Robinson, Douglas H. *The Zeppelin in Combat: A History of the German Naval Airship Division, 1912–1918*. London: Foulis, 1962.

————. *Giants in the Sky: A History of the Rigid Airship*. Seattle: University of Washington Press, 1973.

Rochester, Stuart I., and Frederick Kiley. *Honor Bound: The History of American Prisoners of War in Southeast Asia, 1961–1973*. Washington, DC: Office of the Secretary of Defense, 1998.

Rogel, Carole. *The Breakup of Yugoslavia and the War in Bosnia*. Westport, CT: Greenwood Press, 1998.

Rose, Lisle. *The Ship That Held the Line*. Annapolis: U.S. Naval Institute Press, 1995.

Sachar, Howard. *The Emergence of the Middle East 1914–1924*. New York: Alfred Knopf, 1969.

Sadat, Anwar. *In Search of Identity: An Autobiography*. New York: Harper and Row, 1978.

Safran, Nadav. *From War to War: The Arab Israeli Confrontation 1948–1967*. New York, Pegasus, 1969.

Sakai, Saburo. *Samurai!* Annapolis: U.S. Naval Institute Press, 1991.

Scales, Robert H. *Certain Victory: The U.S. Army in the Gulf War*. London: Brassey's Ltd., 1997.

Schemmer, Benjamin F. *The Raid*. New York: Harper and Row, 1976.

Sell, Louis. *Slobodan Milosevic and the Destruction of Yugoslavia*. Durham, NC: Duke University Press, 2002.

Sharp, U.S. Grant. *Strategy for Defeat: Vietnam in Retrospect*. San Rafael, CA: Presidio Press, 1978.

Shazly, Saad el. *The Crossing of the Suez*. San Francisco: American Mideast Research, 1980.

Sheftall, M. G. *Blossoms in the Wind: Human Legacies of the Kamikaze*. New York: NAL Caliber, 2005.

Sherrod, Robert. *History of Marine Corps Aviation in World War II*. San Rafael, CA: Presidio Press, 1980.

Sherwood, John Darrell. *Fast Movers: Jet Pilots and the Vietnam Experience*. New York: Free Press, 1999.

————. *Afterburner: Naval Aviators and the Vietnam War*. New York: New York University Press, 2004.

Shukman, Harold, ed. *Stalin's Generals*. London: Weidenfeld and Nicholson, 1993.

Siddiqi, Asif A. *Challenge to Apollo: The Soviet Union and the Space Race, 1945–1974*, SP–2000–4408. Washington, DC: National Aeronautics and Space Administration, 2000.

Slife, James C. *Creech Blue: Gen Bill Creech and the Reformation of the Tactical Air Forces, 1978–1984*. Maxwell Air Force Base, AL: Air University Press, 2004.

Smith, Herschel. *A History of Aircraft Piston Engines*. Manhattan, KS: Sunflower University Press, 1986.

Smith, Richard K. *Seventy-Five Years of Inflight Refueling*. Washington, DC: Air Force History and Museums Program, 1998.

Spector, Ronald. *Eagle against the Sun: The American War with Japan*. New York: Free Press, 1985.

Spires, David N. *Beyond Horizons: A Half Century of Air Force Space Leadership*. Peterson Air Force Base, CO: Air Force Space Command, 1997.

Stephens, Alan, ed. *Smaller but Larger: Conventional Air Power into the 21st Century*. Canberra: RAAF Air Power Studies Centre, 1991.

————. *The War in the Air, 1914–1994*. Fairbairn, Australia: Air Power Studies Centre, 1994.

Summers, Harry G., Jr. *On Strategy II: A Critical Analysis of the Gulf War*. New York: Dell Publishing, 1992.

Swain, Richard M. *"Lucky War": Third Army in Desert Storm*. Fort Leavenworth, KS: U.S. Army Command and General Staff College Press, 1994.

Swanborough, Gordon, and Peter M. Bowers. *United States Navy Aircraft since 1911*. Annapolis: U.S. Naval Institute Press, 1990.

Tal, Israel. *National Security: The Israeli Experience*. Westport, CT: Praeger, 2000.

Tedder, Arthur. *Air Power in War*. London: Hodder and Stoughton, 1948.

Thompson, Wayne. *To Hanoi and Back: The U.S. Air Force and North Vietnam, 1966–1973*. Washington, DC: Smithsonian Institution Press, 2000.

Tilford, Earl H., Jr. *Setup: What the Air Force Did in Vietnam and Why*. Maxwell Air Force Base, AL: Air University Press, 1991.

———. *Crosswinds: The U.S. Air Force's Setup in Vietnam*. College Station: Texas A&M University Press, 1993.

Tlas, Mustafa, ed. *The Israeli Invasion of Lebanon*. Damascus: Tashrin, 1983.

Tooze, Adam. *The Wages of Destruction: The Making and Breaking of the Nazi Economy*. London: Allen Lane, 2006.

Towle, Philip. *Pilots and Rebels: The Use of Aircraft in Unconventional Warfare, 1918–1988*. London: Brassey's Ltd., 1989.

Trest, Warren. *Air Commando One: Heinie Aderholt and America's Secret Air Wars*. Washington, DC: Smithsonian Institution Press, 2001.

Trimble, William. *Admiral William Moffett: Architect of Naval Aviation*. Washington, DC: Smithsonian Institution Press, 1994.

———. *Jerome C. Hunsaker and the Rise of American Aeronautics*. Washington, DC: Smithsonian Institution Press, 2002.

Tunner, William H. *Over the Hump*. Washington, DC: Office of Air Force History, 1985.

Underwood, Jeffery S. *The Wings of Democracy: The Influence of Air Power on the Roosevelt Administration*. College Station: Texas A&M University Press, 1992.

United States Strategic Bombing Survey (European War) (Pacific War). Maxwell Air Force Base, AL: Air University Press, 1987.

U.S. Department of Defense. *Conduct of the Persian Gulf War: Final Report to Congress*. Washington, DC: U.S. Government Printing Office, 1992.

U.S. Marine Corps. *Small Wars Manual*. Washington, DC: U.S. Government Printing Office, 1940.

Vallance, Andrew G. B. *The Air Weapon: Doctrines of Air Power Strategy and Operational Art*. London: Macmillan Press Ltd., 1996.

Vander Meulen, Jacob. *Building the B–29*. Washington, DC: Smithsonian Institution Press, 1995.

Ventner, J., ed. *The Chopper Boys: Helicopter Warfare in Africa*. London: Greenhill Books, 1994.

Vergnano, Piero. *Origins of Aviation in Italy, 1783–1918*. Genoa: Intyprint, 1964.

Van Creveld, Martin. *Military Lessons of the Yom Kippur War: Historical Perspectives*. Beverly Hills: Sage, 1975.

———. *The Changing Face of War: Lessons of Combat, from the Marne to Iraq*. New York: Presidio Press, 2007.

Van Creveld, Martin, S. L. Canby, and K. S. Brower. *Airpower and Maneuver Warfare*. Maxwell Air Force Base, AL: Air University Press, 1994.

Van Staaveren, Jacob. *Gradual Failure: The Air War over North Vietnam, 1965–1966*. Washington, DC: Air Force History and Museums Program, 2002.

Von der Porten, Edward. *The German Navy in World War II*. London: Macmillan, 1969.

Waller, Douglas. *A Question of Loyalty: Gen. Billy Mitchell and the Court-Martial That Gripped a Nation*. New York: HarperCollins Publishers, 2004.

Warden, John A. III. *The Air Campaign: Planning for Combat*. Washington, DC: U.S. Government Printing Office, 1988.

Warnock, A. Timothy, ed. *Short of War: Major USAF Contingency Operations 1947–1997*. Maxwell Air Force Base, AL: Air University Press in association with the Air Force History and Museums Program, 2000.

Waters, Gary. *Gulf Lesson One—The Value of Air Power: Doctrinal Lessons for Australia*. Canberra: RAAF Air Power Studies Centre, 1992.

Watts, Barry D. *Clausewitzian Friction and Future War*. Washington, DC: Institute for National Strategic Studies, National Defense University, 1996.

Webster, Charles, and Noble Frankland. *The Strategic Air Offensive against Germany: Volume IV*. London: Her Majesty's Stationery Office, 1961.

Weizman, Ezer. *On Eagle's Wings: The Personal Story of the Leading Commander of the Israeli Air Force*. Tel Aviv: Stimatzky's Agency Ltd, 1976.

Wells, H. G. *The War in the Air*. London: George Bell and Sons, 1908.

Wells, Mark K., ed. *Air Power: Promise and Reality*. Chicago: Imprint, 2000.

Werrell, Kenneth P. *Blankets of Fire: US Bombers over Japan during World War II*. Washington, DC: Smithsonian Institution Press, 1996.

West, Rebecca. *Black Lamb and Grey Falcon*. London: Penguin Books, 1941.

Willbanks, James. *Abandoning Vietnam*. Lawrence: University Press of Kansas, 2004.

Willmott, H. P. *The Battle of Leyte Gulf: The Last Fleet Action*. Bloomington: Indiana University Press, 2005.

Winnefeld, James A., and Dana J. Johnson. *Joint Air Operations: Pursuit of Unity of Command and Control, 1942–1991*. Annapolis: U.S. Naval Institute Press, 1993.

Winter, Denis. *The First of the Few: Fighter Pilots of the First World War*. London: Penguin, 1982.

Winter, Frank H. *The First Golden Age of Rocketry: Congreve and Hale Rockets of the Nineteenth Century*. Washington, DC: Smithsonian Institution Press, 1990.

Wittner, Lawrence. *American Intervention in Greece, 1943–1949*. New York: Columbia University Press, 1982.

Wohlstetter, Roberta. *Pearl Harbor: Warning and Decision*. Stanford: Stanford University Press, 1962.

Woods, Kevin M. *The Mother of All Battles: Saddam Hussein's Strategic Plan for the Persian Gulf War*. Annapolis: U.S. Naval Institute Press, 2008.

Woods, Kevin M. *Iraqi Perspectives Project: A View of Operation Iraqi Freedom from Saddam's Senior Leadership*. With Michael R. Pease, Mark E. Stout, Williamson Murray, and James G. Lacey. Annapolis: U.S. Naval Institute Press, 2006.

Woodward, Sandy. *One Hundred Days: The Memoirs of the Falklands Battle Group Commander*. With Patrick Robinson. London: HarperCollins, 1992.

Wooldridge, E. T., ed. *Carrier Warfare in the Pacific: An Oral History Collection*. Washington, DC: Smithsonian Institution Press, 1993.

Zhai, Qiang. *China and the Vietnam Wars, 1950–1975*. Chapel Hill: University of North Carolina Press, 2000.

Zhang, Xiaoming. *Red Wings over the Yalu*. College Station: Texas A&M University Press, 2002.

INDEX

A-1 Skyraiders, 339, 390
A-4 Skyhawks
  Desert Storm, 194
  Falklands War, 159, 160, 161, 163, 164–166, 169, 171
  Israel-Arab Wars, 137, 139, 150
  Vietnam War, 111, 114, 119
A4Bs, 170
A4Cs, 161, 169
A4Qs, 161, 169
A-6 Intruders, 115–116, 119–120, 125, 194
A6M Zeros, 58, 59, 61–62, 69
A-7 Corsair IIs, 119, 125
A-10 Warthogs
  Allied Force, 238, 242
  Bosnian civil war, 214, 220
  Desert Storm, 184, 196
  Enduring Freedom, 268, 269
  Iraqi Freedom, 285, 286, 289, 294
A-37 Dragonflies, 342
AAV (amphibious assault vehicle), 289
ABCCC (airborne command and control center), 217
Abrams, Creighton, 119
AC-130s, 116, 214, 260, 263, 268, 269, 270
acquisition reform, 381
ACTS (Air Corps Tactical School), 55–56, 67, 74
AD (air defense). *See* air defense systems
Adam, Udi, 315
Ader, Clément, 372
advanced medium-range air-to-air missile (AMRAAM), 233, 389
aerial medical evacuation, 329, 330
aerial photography, 7–8, 117, 330, 352
Aerial Warfare (Hearne), 6

aerodynamics, 372, 374, 392
AEW (airborne early warning), 172
Afghan forces, friendly, 261, 263–265, 270, 271
Afghanistan
  Operation Enduring Freedom (*See* Operation Enduring Freedom)
  Soviet occupation, 343–344
AFSOUTH (Allied Forces Southern Europe), 209, 211, 213
Afula, 310, 311, 315
AGM-65 Mavericks, 214
AH-64 Apaches, 184, 194, 236–237, 266–267, 285, 290–291, 321
Ahtisaari, Martti, 243
air campaign success debate, 244–249
Air Commandos, 72, 79, 339
air control concept, 328–331
Air Corps Tactical School (ACTS), 55–56, 67, 74
air defense systems, 100–101
  Allied Force, 176, 227, 231–234, 237, 240, 241
  Bosnian civil war, 217, 220
  Desert Storm, 178, 182, 183–186, 191
  Falklands War, 162, 173
  Iraqi, 282, 288, 385
  Israel-Arab Wars, 135, 138, 146, 148, 150, 152
  Korean War, 89, 100
air dominance, 326, 379–382
Air Force, South Vietnamese, 339, 340
Air Force, US. *See* US Air Force (USAF)
air forces, about, xvi, 127, 327. *See also specific air forces*
  establishment of, 20, 86, 355

future of, 391–392
speed of, 388
Air Forces in Europe, US (USAFE), 226–
        227, 231
air loss rates, 373–374, 390
    Desert Storm, 197, 202
    Israel-Arab Wars, 135, 140–141, 154
    Korean War, 89, 100, 101
    Vietnam War, 112, 123
    WWII, 31, 37, 40, 48, 51
air policing, 329–331, 364
Air Power Development Centre, Australia,
        377
air power differential, 244–245, 251
air power history and evolution, 279–280
    counterinsurgency, 328–331, 349,
        366–369
    early history, 1, 3–6, 327, 351–356,
        371–372
    future, 154–155, 389–393
    guerrilla warfare, 363–366
    military distinctions, 388–389
    missile age, 359–361, 374–376
    necessity of air power, 369–370
    post-Desert Storm, 376–378
    standards, 387–388
    technology and production, 249–250,
        323, 361–362, 371–374, 386,
        389–393
    theory, 353–354, 362–363
    WWII, 356–359, 360
air-refueling tankers, 112, 161, 164, 168,
        259, 374
Air Solomons, 68, 78
air superiority, concept of, 127–128, 152–
        153, 155, 186, 253–254, 379–380
Air Support Operations Center (ASOC),
        268–269
air supremacy, concept of, 186, 379
air tasking order (ATO), 247
air-to-air combat, 5, 352–353
    Falklands War, 159, 173
    Israel-Arab wars, 135, 138, 140–141,
        153–154
    Korean War, 85–86, 101
    Vietnam War, 123
air-to-air missiles, 359, 389–390. See also
        missiles; specific types
    Allied Force, 233
    Falklands War, 168

Israel-Arab Wars, 139, 149, 152, 321
    Vietnam War, 100, 111, 122
air-to-air tankers, 112, 161, 164, 168, 259,
        374
air-to-surface missiles, 150, 214, 359. See
        also missiles; specific types
air transport, 71, 161, 329, 331, 353, 356
Air Transport Command, 71
Air War Plans Division Plan 1 (AWPD-1),
        43–44, 56
Air War Plans Division Plan 42 (AWPD-
        42), 70
airborne command and control center
        (ABCCC), 217
airborne early warning (AEW), 172
airborne warning and control system
        (AWACS), 217, 246, 256, 259
aircraft, military, 369. See also specific aircraft
    Allied Force, 232–233, 236, 240, 242
    Bosnian civil war, 213–214
    Desert Storm, 183
    Enduring Freedom, 258–259, 260
    Falklands War, 160–162
    Iraqi Freedom, 285
    Israel-Arab Wars '67–'82, 130–131, 138,
        149–150
    Korean War, 85–86, 88, 90–92, 93,
        98–99, 103
    Second Lebanon War, 302
    Vietnam War, 111–113, 116, 118–119
    WWI, 8–10, 11–12, 14, 17, 19–20
    WWII, 29, 56, 58, 59–60, 69, 372–373
aircraft carriers, 29. See also specific carriers
    Japan, 2, 72
    US, 2, 58, 88
aircraft production, 14–17, 18–23, 31, 40,
        361–362, 381
airlift campaigns
    Desert Storm, 195
    Falklands War, 161
    Korean War, 104
    Kuwait, 178
    Pusan, 91–92, 94, 105
    WWII, 71–72, 74, 92
airships, 1, 3, 4–5, 57
AIRSOUTH (Allied Air Forces Southern
        Europe), 212–213, 216, 219,
        221–222
Akagi, 64
Akashi, Yusushi, 209–210

Akko, 315
Akron, 57
Al Jaber air base, 261, 286
al Qaeda, 256–257, 259–260, 262–267, 270,
    345, 347
al-Assad, Hafez, 300
Albania, 231, 233, 238, 334
Albanians, Kosovo, 225, 226, 227, 229, 235, 242. *See also* Kosovo
    Liberation Army (KLA); refugees
al-Basra, 193, 200
Albatros fighters, 12, 17, 18
Albright, Madeleine, 225, 230, 236
Al-Dulaymi, Mjid Jusayn Ali Ibrahim, 291
Algeria, 337–338, 350, 366, 367
Allied Air Forces Southern Europe
    (AIRSOUTH), 212–213, 216, 219, 221–222
Allied Force. *See* Operation Allied Force
Allied Forces Southern Europe
    (AFSOUTH), 209, 211, 213
all-weather capabilities, 245, 249–250, 251
Al-Nida Republican Guard Division, 291–292
Alouette helicopters, 338
Al-Qa'id Bridge, 294–295
Aluminum Trail, 71, 74, 358
Amal, 299
Amar, Abd El-Hakim, 129
American Volunteer Group (AVG), 54, 71
Amos, James, 283, 286, 289–290, 294
amphibious assault vehicle (AAV), 289
AMRAAM (advanced medium-range air-to-air missile), 233, 389
Anaconda, Operation. *See* Operation
    Anaconda
ancient hatreds concept, 207–208
Antelope, HMS, 169–170
antiaircraft artillery (AAA)
    Allied Force, 235
    Desert Storm, 184
    Enduring Freedom, 259–260
    Israel-Arab Wars, 139–140, 144, 302
    Korean War, 100
    Vietnam War, 114
antiradiation missiles (ARM), 113, 165, 184, 215, 294
antiship missiles, 159, 161, 168, 171–174, 302, 309–310, 375

antisubmarine warfare, 19, 23, 35, 36, 58, 60, 162
antitank guided missiles (ATGM), 300, 315
Anti-U-Boat Warfare Committee, 36
Antrim, HMS, 169
AOR (area of responsibility), 257, 258
Apache helicopters, 184, 194, 236–237, 266–267, 285, 290–291, 321
Arab air forces, 130, 141–147. *See also*
    specific air forces
Arab League, 181, 310
Ardent, HMS, 169
area of responsibility (AOR), 257, 258
Argentina, Falklands War, 82–83
    air power of, 160–162
    attrition attempts, 162–167
    background and overview, 157–160, 172–174
    Battle of San Carlos, 168–172
Argonaut, HMS, 169
Arizona, USS, 61
Ark Royal, HMS, 172
Armament Development Authority
    (RAFAEL), 149
armies, future of, 391–392
ARMs (antiradiation missile), 184, 215, 294
Army, US. *See* US Army
Army Air Corps, US. *See* US Army Air
    Corps
Army Air Forces, US (USAAF), 36, 42, 48, 55–56, 75, 78–79, 128
Arnold, Henry H. "Hap," 43–44, 62, 73–74, 75, 362
Arras, battle of, 17
Ascension Island, 160, 161, 163–164
ASOC (Air Support Operations Center), 268–269
Assad, Bashar, 300
Assad, Hafez, 132
asymmetric warfare, 256, 323
    Allied Force, 247, 249, 251–252, 254
    Desert Storm, 176
    Enduring Freedom, 256
    Israel-Arab Wars, 155
Atef, Mohammed, 262
ATGM (antitank guided missile), 300, 315
Atlantic Conveyor, HMS, 167, 170–171, 173
ATO (air tasking order), 247
atomic bombs, 2, 76–77, 78–79, 86–87, 359, 373

attrition, 370
　Allied Force, 249
　Desert Storm, 193–195, 197
　Falklands War, 162–167, 380
　guerrilla warfare, 364
　Israel-Arab Wars, 136–141, 146, 314,
　　　323
　Korean War, 98
　WWI, 15–21
　WWII, 38, 40, 42, 48–50, 51
Australia, 87, 369, 377
　Iraqi Freedom, 285
　Korean War, 90–91
　WWII, 53, 54–55, 67–68
AV-8B Harriers, 196, 285
AVG (American Volunteer Group), 54, 71
aviation history. *See* air power history and
　　evolution
Avion III, 372
Avro Lancaster bombers, 34
AWACS (airborne warning and control
　　system), 217, 246, 256, 259

B-1 Lancers, 236, 243–244, 258–259, 263,
　　268, 270, 285
B-1Bs, 258, 259, 263
B-2 Spirits, 246–247, 259, 270, 272, 276, 285
B-17 Flying Fortresses, 34, 46, 56, 61, 64, 65
B-24 Liberators, 36, 56
B-25 Mitchells, 62, 67
B-26s, 93
B-29 Superfortresses, 2, 70, 73–77, 78, 86,
　　88, 93
B-36 Peacemakers, 79, 88
B-47 Stratojets, 88
B-52s, 82, 382
　Allied Force, 243–244
　Desert Storm, 175, 184, 194
　Enduring Freedom, 258, 259, 262, 263,
　　　268, 270
　Iraqi Freedom, 285
　Vietnam War, 52, 107–108, 112–113,
　　　117–118, 124–125
B5N Kates, 59–60
B6N Jills, 69
Baalbek, 309, 310, 313
Ba'ath party, 189, 190, 199, 283, 292–293
backseaters, 122
Baghdad, 188–193, 288–289, 294–296
Baker, James, 187

Baldwin, Stanley, 154
Balfour, Herbert, 9
Balkans, German occupation of, 366
Ball, Albert, 15
ballistic missiles, 86, 155, 186–187, 191,
　　326, 359–361, 375–376
balloon flight, 3, 4, 351–352, 355–356,
　　371–372, 378
Banja Luka, 219
Barak, Ehud, 300
Barbarossa campaign, 32, 33
battle damage assessment (BDA), 215, 249,
　　267, 321
Battle of Arras, 17
Battle of Berlin, 48
Battle of the Bismarck Sea, 67–68
Battle of Britain, 30–35, 357, 358, 381
Battle of Bull's Run, 72–73
Battle of Chemin des Dames, 15–16, 17, 20
Battle at Chongchon River, 96
Battle of the Coral Sea, 63–64, 66
Battle of Fleurus, 371
Battle of Imphal, 72
Battle of Kohima, 72
Battle of Marne, 6, 352, 372
Battle of Midway, 2, 63–65, 66
Battle of the Philippine Sea, 70
Battle of San Carlos, 159, 167–172
Battle of the Santa Cruz Islands, 66
Battle of Somme, 11, 12, 14–15, 24
Battle of Tannenberg, 7, 372
Battle of Verdun, 11, 15, 24
BDA (battle damage assessment), 215, 249,
　　267, 321
Beaverbrook, Lord, 44–45
Béchereau, Louis, 12
BEF (British Expeditionary Force), 7, 9
Beirut, 299, 301, 309–310, 312, 316, 320,
　　345, 348–349
Belgium, 9, 29, 30, 240, 357
Belgrade, 176, 236–237, 240–242, 243–244
Ben-Gurion, David, 128
Berger, Sandy, 236
Berlin, 32, 43, 48, 72, 92, 359
Berlin, Isaiah, 380
Berlin Airlift, 72, 92
Bf 109s, 69
bin Laden, Osama, 256–257, 262–264
Bint Jbeil, 311
biplanes

evolution, 3–4, 58, 356, 365
  WWI, 6, 8, 12–14, 17, 19, 22, 24
Bismarck, 36
Bismarck Sea, Battle of the, 67–68
Blackbirds, 378
Blair, Tony, 227, 230, 238, 240
Blériot, Louis, 4
blind bombing, 49
Blitz, London, 2, 32–35, 37, 44, 47, 355
Bloch, Ivan S., 3
"Bloody April," 17, 18
Blount, Buford, 290
Blowpipe missiles, 168, 169
BMG-109s. *See* Tomahawk land attack
  missiles (TLAM)
Boelcke, Oswald, 10, 12, 15
Bohannan, Charles, 334
Bolo, 113
bombardment, strategic, 4, 387
  colonial insurgencies, 328, 330–331
    Vietnam War (*See* Linebacker I
        campaign; Linebacker II
        campaign; Rolling Thunder
        campaign)
  WWI, 1, 6, 8, 10–12, 25
  WWII, 33, 50, 55–56, 74
Bomber Command, RAF, 25, 32, 35–36,
    43, 45–46, 49
Bomber Command, US, 74
Bosnia, 205–206, 211. *See also* Bosnian civil
    war
Bosnia and Herzegovina province, 204. *See*
    also Bosnian civil war
Bosnian Army, 210, 211–212, 216, 218,
    222–223
Bosnian civil war, 175, 201–224
  background and overview, 201–208
  evaluation, 222–224
  Operation Deliberate Force (*See*
      Operation Deliberate Force
      (ODF))
  Operation Deny Flight, 175, 202–204,
      206–213, 215
Bosnian Serb Republic, 202, 204–206
  Bosnian Serb Army, 203, 206, 208–212,
      216–218, 222–224
Boutros-Ghali, Boutros, 209, 211, 218
BQM-74 drones, 184
Bradley, Omar, 89
Breguet, Louis, 12

Breguet bombers, 12, 17, 20, 22
bridge bombing, 121
  Allied Force, 236–237, 241
  Deliberate Force, 215, 218–219
  Desert Storm, 191–192, 197
  Iraqi Freedom, 284, 294–295
  Korean War, 93, 95–96, 97
  Second Lebanon War, 309, 320
  Vietnam War, 114–115, 118, 120–121
Brilliant, HMS, 166
Bristol F2 fighters, 14, 17
Britain, Allied Force, 229, 240, 245, 248
Britain, Bosnian civil war, 203, 209–210,
    214, 217
Britain, Cold War, 99, 166
Britain, colonial insurgencies
  post WWI, 327, 328–329, 330–331
  post WWII, 332–334, 335–336
Britain, Desert Storm, 195
Britain, Enduring Freedom, 258, 259, 263
Britain, Falklands War, 82–83, 157–174
  air power, 160–161
  attrition attempts, 162–167
  background and overview, 157–160,
      172–174
  Battle of San Carlos, 167–172
Britain, Iraqi Freedom, 285, 289
Britain, Israel and, 129
Britain, Korean War, 88
Britain, WWI, 5–7, 9–10, 15, 18–23
Britain, WWII, 372
  aircraft fleet, 30–32
  antisubmarine campaign, 30–35
  Battle of Britain, 30–35, 153
  pre-war strategy and planning, 28–30
  war in Pacific, 61, 71–72
  Western Europe, 40–49
British Expeditionary Force (BEF), 7, 9
British Western Air Plans, 43
Broadsword, HMS, 166, 169, 170
Brodie, Bernard, 86, 360
Broughton, Jack, 110
Builder, Carl, xv–xvi
Buna, 67
Bunker, Ellsworth, 119
Burckhardt, Jacob, xiv
Burdett, Edward, 116
Bureau of Aeronautics (BuAer), US, 57, 58
Burma, 53, 71–72, 79
Bush, George H.W., 177, 179–180, 196

Bush, George W., 256–257, 258, 273,
    287, 367
Bush, Vannevar, 375–376, 381–382
Butt, D. M., 46
Butt Report, 46

C² (Command and control), 265, 272,
    274–275
C³I (Command, control, communications,
    and intelligence), 129, 131, 138, 154
C⁴I (Command, control, communications,
    computers, and intelligence), 149,
    151–152, 153–154, 378–379
C⁴ISR, 378–379, 385
C-17s, 259
C-47s, 88, 92, 333, 342
C-54s, 88, 91–92
C-130 Hercules, 111, 114, 285, 287, 293–
    294, 296, 319
Cactus Air Force, 68
Cairo, 137–138
Cam Pha, 110
Cambodia, 107, 117, 118, 120, 126
Canada, 240, 256
Canberra B62s, 161, 163, 171
CAOC (combined air operations center),
    246–247, 267–269, 270, 273, 276
Caproni, Gianni, 6, 19–20
Caproni bombers, 10, 15, 19–20, 23–24
Carl Vinson, USS, 258, 259
Carmiel, 315
carrier operations, 387, 388, 392
    Desert Storm, 270
    Enduring Freedom, 258–259, 261,
        270, 272
    Falklands War, 160–161, 162–163,
        168, 174
    Korean War, 88, 96, 104
    Vietnam War, 110, 112, 118–119
    WWII, 2, 57–58, 61–63, 65–66, 69–70,
        72–73, 77–79
Carrier Pigeon Unit Ostende, 7
CAS (close air support). See close air support
    (CAS)
CBI theater (China-Burma-India), 55,
    71–72, 79
Cedar Revolution, 301
CENTCOM (US Central Command), 257–
    258, 260–261, 265, 269, 272–273
Center for Strategic and International
    Studies (CSIS), 377

Central Pacific (CENTPAC), 2, 54, 66,
    68–72
centralized execution, 274–275
CH-53s, 137, 313, 321
chain of command
    Allied Force, 246–247
    Desert Storm, 197
    Enduring Freedom, 274–275, 276
    Iraqi Freedom, 292
    Vietnam War, 111–112, 119
Challe, Maurice, 338
Chamberlain, Neville, 365
Chambliss, Saxby, 377
Charles, J.A.C., 371
Chechnya, 344, 345
Chemin des Dames, battle of, 15–16, 17, 20
Cheney, Richard, 181
Chennault, Claire, 56, 71
Chernomyrdin, Victor, 243
Cherwell, Lord, 45
China, 369, 374
    Korean War, 85–86, 93, 94–97, 98,
        99, 101
    Kosovo war, 241–242
    Vietnam War, 82, 108, 109, 110, 114, 120
    WWII, 53–54, 60, 63, 71–72, 74
China-Burma-India theater (CBI), 55,
    71–72, 79
Chinooks, 160, 165, 168, 171, 172
Chongchon River, 96, 98
Chosin Reservoir, 96
Christian Serbs, 204–205. See also Bosnian
    civil war
Churchill, Winston
    WWI, 5–6, 9
    WWII, 36, 44–46, 51–52, 357
civilian deaths
    Allied Force, 176, 237, 238, 239,
        240, 250
    Bosnian civil war, 213, 215, 223
    Chechnya, 345
    Enduring Freedom, 276, 349
    insurgencies, 330–331, 349
    invasion of Kuwait and Desert Storm,
        180, 190
    Iraqi Freedom, 349
    Second Lebanon War, 297, 305, 310,
        312, 313, 318, 320
    September 11th attacks, 256
    Soviet occupation of Afghanistan, 344

Vietnam War, 124, 126, 340
WWI, 25
WWII, 35, 44, 75–77, 280
CJTF (Combined Joint Task Force), 265–269
Claes, Willy, 211
Clark, Wesley, 226, 228–230, 236, 238–240, 242
Clausewitz, Carl von, 105, 216, 355, 363, 385
Clemenceau, Georges, 17, 22
Clinton, Bill, 229, 240
Clodfelter, Mark, 126
close air attacks, 88, 90, 92, 94, 96
close air support (CAS), 145, 327, 355, 387
　Allied Force, 232–233, 245
　Bosnian civil war, 206, 211, 215, 220
　colonial insurgencies, 329
　Desert Storm, 178, 195–196
　early Cold War counterinsurgency, 335
　El Salavador, 342
　Enduring Freedom, 267–269
　Iraqi Freedom, 253, 276, 285–286, 289–293, 294, 296
　Israel-Arab Wars, 143, 144, 145, 319–320, 390
　Korean War, 88, 90, 92, 94, 96
　Vietnam War, 117
　WWI, 20
　WWII, 67, 72, 75, 76, 357, 358, 361
Coastal Command, RAF, 35–36
Cobra helicopters, 285, 289
Cohen, Lenard, 207
Cohen, William, 236, 248–249
Cold War, 77, 86–87, 99, 166, 233, 376, 392
collateral damage, 280–281, 348, 387–388
　Allied Force, 176, 250–251
　Bosnian civil war, 214–215, 223, 229
　Desert Storm, 180, 190
　Enduring Freedom, 273, 276, 277
　Iraqi Freedom, 280–281
Colombia, 342–343
colonial air power operations, 328–331
combined air operations center (CAOC), 246–247, 267–269, 270, 273, 276
Combined Bomber Offensive, 46–47, 87–88, 384
Combined Joint Task Force (CJTF), 265–269
Command of the Air (Douhet), 25, 353–354

Command, control, communications, computers, and intelligence (C⁴I), 149, 151–152, 153–154, 378–379
Command, control, communications and intelligence (C³I), 129, 131, 138, 154
Command and control (C²), 265, 272, 274–275
Committee of Public Safety, France, 371
communist insurgencies, 334–336
complacency, 60–61, 381–382
Congreve, William, 374
Coningham, Arthur, 42
Contact Group, 5-Nation, 203, 210, 216, 229
continuity-of-government plan, 256
Cook, Donald, 123, 242
Cook, Robin, 226
Coral Sea, Battle of the, 63–64, 66
counterinsurgencies
　air power, 349–35, 366–369
　early Cold War, 331–338
　Latin America, 341–343
　media, 348–349
　post Cold War, 345–348
　post WWI, 327–331, 364–366
　Southeast Asian, 338–341 (*See also* Vietnam War)
　Soviet-Russian, 343–345
Coutelle, Jean, 371
Coventry, HMS, 170, 173
Crete, 357
Croatia, 203–205, 210–212, 216, 218, 221–223
cruise missiles
　Exocet, 159, 161, 168, 171, 172, 173, 174
　Tomahawks (*See* Tomahawk land attack missiles (TLAM))
CSIS (Center for Strategic and International Studies), 377
Cuba, 341
Cunningham, Randall, 122
Curtiss, Glenn, 19
Curtiss Helldivers, 69, 334
Czechoslovakia, 129

D3A Vals, 60
D4Y Judy's, 69
Daggers, 160–161, 163, 166, 169, 171
Dahia, 301, 309–310, 314, 320
Daily Express, 9–10

D'Alema, Massimo, 243
Day, George "Bud," 123
Dayan, Moshe, 129, 132, 139, 144, 145
Deadeye plan, 212–213, 221
DeBellvue, Charles, 122
decentralized execution, 275, 346
decision-making process, 7, 51, 145–147,
        302, 324, 380
de Gaulle, Charles, 130, 338
Dehavilland bombers, 14, 19, 102, 378
Deliberate Force, Operation. *See* Operation
        Deliberate Force (ODF)
demilitarized zone, 116–117, 124
Demyansk pocket, 38, 358
Denmark, 240, 375
Deny Flight, Operation. *See* Operation
        Deny Flight
Deptula, David, 377
Desert Storm, Operation. *See* Operation
        Desert Storm
desired mean point of impact (DMPI),
        214–215, 217, 219–221, 222
deterrence, 86–87, 105, 326
        Israel-Arab Wars '67–'82, 128, 129,
                147, 155
        Second Lebanon War, 304, 316, 323
Devastators, 58
Dicta Boelcke guidelines, 12
Diego Garcia, 258, 259
Dien Bien Phu, 337, 366
Dill, John, 365
dirigibles, 1, 3, 4–5, 57
Djukanovic, Milo, 243
DMPI (desired mean point of impact),
        214–215, 217, 219–221, 222
doctrine, war, 328
        Allied Force, 231, 247, 249
        Desert Storm, 181, 188, 376
        Enduring Freedom, 275
        Israel-Arab Wars, 128–129, 136, 144–
                146, 150, 153, 254, 306–308,
                323
        Korean War, 89, 104
        small war insurgencies, 330–331, 341, 348
        WWI, 6, 10
        WWII, 27, 28, 41–42, 58–59, 78
Dominican Republic, 328
Doolittle, James H., 62–63
Doolittle raid, 62–63, 64
Dora Farms, 287–288

Dornier bombers, 34
Douglas Aircraft Company, 375
Douhet, Guilio
        about, 23, 353–355
        theories and WWI, 6, 10, 15, 19–20
        theories and WWII, 25, 33, 358–359
Doumer Bridge, 114–115, 120
Dowding, Hugh, 153, 361
Drenica, 225
Driscoll, William, 122
drones, 184, 288
Druze revolt, 330
Dryden, Hugh, 375–376
dual key approval process, 207, 208–209,
        214–215, 245, 247
Dumesnil, J. L., 16–17
Dutch. *See* Netherlands

E-2C Hawkeyes, 150
E-3s, 217, 246, 256, 259
EA-6B Prowlers, 217, 246, 259, 285
EAF (Egyptian Air Force), 129, 132–135,
        139–143, 147–148
Eaker, Ira, 45
EB-66s, 113
EBO (effects-based operations), 306,
        384–386
EC-135 River Joints, 246
ECM (electronic countermeasure), 140,
        149–150, 172–173
effects-based operations (EBO), 306,
        384–386
Egypt, 128–130, 149
        Kuwait, 180
        Six Days War, 130–135
        War of Attrition, 136–141
        WWII, 40, 41–42
        Yom Kippur War, 141–148
Egyptian Air Force (EAF), 129, 132–135,
        139–143, 147–148
Eighteenth Airborne Corps, 195
Eighth Air Force, 45, 46, 48, 74, 124
Eighth Army, 96, 103
Eighth Tactical Fighter Wing, 113, 121
Eindeckers, 10, 378
Eisenhower, Dwight D., 107, 339, 379
Ejército de Liberación Nacional (ELN),
        342–343
El Salvador, 341–342, 343
Elazar, David, 144, 145, 146

electronic countermeasures (ECMs), 140,
        149–150, 172–173
electronic revolution, 371, 374
electronic warfare
    Allied Force, 246
    Enduring Freedom, 259
    Israel-Arab Wars, 129, 138, 140, 151,
        153, 323
    Vietnam War, 113
    WWII, 34
Eleventh Attack Helicopter Regiment, 290
Eleventh Infantry Division, Iraqi, 289
ELN (Ejército de Liberación Nacional),
        342–343
embargoes, 54, 203, 206, 223, 226, 232
Enduring Freedom, Operation. *See*
        Operation Enduring Freedom
enlisted tactical air controller (ETAC),
        267, 269
Enterprise, USS, 58, 62, 64, 66, 258–259
Entreprenant, l', 371–372
EP-3s, 246, 268, 378
escort carriers, 35, 36, 69, 72, 73
Essen, 6, 8, 9–10
Essex class carriers, 69
ETAC (enlisted tactical air controller),
        267, 269
ethnic cleansing, 205, 210, 211, 225,
        248–249
Exocet antiship missiles, 159, 161, 168,
        171–174
expenditure rates, munitions, 262
    Allied Force, 246, 250
    Enduring Freedom, 262, 268, 270–271
    Israel-Arab Wars '67–'82, 134–135, 138
    Second Lebanon War, 298, 309, 311,
        313–315, 317–318
    Vietnam War, 117
    WWII, 48–49
extended-range operations, 271

F-1s, 183, 185
F2A Buffalos, 58
F-4 Phantoms, 137, 138, 139, 141, 146, 150
    Desert Storm, 184
    Israel-Arab Wars, 150
    Vietnam War, 111, 113, 116, 119, 120,
        122, 125–126
F4F Wildcats, 58
F4U Corsairs, 69

F-5s, 194
F6F Hellcats, 69
F-8 Crusaders, 111, 112, 119
F-14s, 259, 260, 285
F-15s, 149, 152, 184, 194, 367–368, 382.
        See also F-15Cs; F15-Es
F-15Cs, 185, 285, 382
F-15Es, 242, 259, 260–263, 285
F-16s
    Allied Force, 233, 234, 238
    Desert Storm, 184, 188, 194
    Enduring Freedom, 256, 259, 261
    Iraqi Freedom, 285, 286
    Israel-Arab Wars, 149, 152, 321,
        367–368
F-18s, 217, 236, 285, 286, 294
F-18Cs, 294
F-51 Mustangs, 88, 90, 92, 334
F-80 Shooting Stars, 88, 90, 98
F-84s, 88, 98
F-86 Sabres, 88, 99, 103, 380–381
F-94s, 98
F-105 Thunderchiefs, 110–111, 113, 116,
        119, 125
F-111s, 116, 119, 125, 194, 184185–186
F-117 Nighthawks
    Allied Force, 234, 241, 246
    Deliberate Force, 219
    Desert Storm, 175, 184, 188, 190, 194
    Iraqi Freedom, 285, 287
F/A-18s, 184, 194, 196, 259, 263, 270
FAC–A (forward air controller–airborne),
        260, 261, 390
Fahey, James J., 73
Falcon missiles, 111
Falklands War, 82–83, 157–174, 380
    air power of, 160–162
    attrition attempts, 162–167
    background and overview, 157–160
    Battle of San Carlos, 167–172
    summary, 172–174
Far East Air Forces (FEAF), 88, 94, 101, 104
FARC (Fuerzas Armadas Revolucionarias de
        Colombia), 342–343
Farman, Henri, 3–4
Farman biplanes, 8–9, 11
Fauzi, Mahmud, 136–137
FEAF (Far East Air Forces), 88, 94, 101, 104
Fearless, HMS, 170
Feinstein, Jeffrey, 122

Fieldhouse, John, 167–168
Fifth Air Force, 67, 68, 78, 88, 103
Fifth Fleet, 70
Fifth Marine Regimental Combat Team,
    290, 294
fighter aces, 10, 12, 15, 24–25, 60, 122–
    123. *See also specific aces*
First Air Commandos, 72
First Bombardment Group (GB1), 6
First Lebanon War, 127, 148–152, 154,
    299, 345–346
First Marine Air Wing, 66, 88
First Marine Division, 254, 280, 281, 283,
    284, 294
First Marine Regimental Combat Team, 290
5-Nation Contact Group, 203, 210,
    216, 229
Flatley, Jimmy, 58
Fleet Problems, 57–58
Fletcher, Frank Jack, 63, 64, 65
Fleurus, battle of, 371
flight history. *see* air power history and
    evolution
FLN (Front de Libération Nationale),
    337–338
floatplanes, 13, 22
flying boats, 19, 58, 60
Flying Tigers, 54
Foch, Ferdinand, 372
Fokker fighters, 8, 10, 12, 17, 22, 378
Fonck, René, 16, 22
Force Protection Condition Delta, 256, 257
Ford, Gerald, 118
formation flying, 8, 115–116, 128, 139,
    352, 381
Former Republic of Yugoslavia. *See*
    Yugoslavia, Federal Republic of
    (FRY)
Forward Air Control (FAC), 260, 261, 390
432nd Tactical Reconnaissance Wing,
    121–122
Fourteenth Air Force, 71, 383
France
    air power history, 355, 367, 380
    Allied Force, 240, 242, 245
    balloons, 351, 371–372
    Bosnian civil war, 203, 209–210, 214, 217
    colonial insurgencies, 327, 328–330,
        332, 336–338
    Desert Storm, 195
    Falklands War, 161

Israel, 129, 130
    pre-WWI aviation, 3–5, 6, 327
    WWI, 6–7, 8, 11–12, 15–17, 20–22
    WWII, 29–30, 372
Franco, Francisco, 356
Franklin, Benjamin, 371
Franks, Tommy, 260–261, 265, 273
French, John, 7
Frente Farabundo Martí para la Liberación
    Nacional (FMLN), 341–342
Freycinet, Charles-Louis de, 372
Front de Libération Nationale (FLN),
    337–338
Fuerzas Armadas Revolucionarias de
    Colombia (FARC), 342–343
Fuga Magisters, 131
Fuller, J.F.C., 373

G4M Bettys, 60
Garden, Timothy, 376–377
Garros, Roland, 10
Gaza Strip, 297, 303, 304
GBUs (guided bomb unit), 185–186, 214,
    259, 260
Geiger, Roy S., 66
General Atomics Gnats and Predators, 214
General Belgrano, ARA, 83, 159, 163
George, Harold, 43
Germany, 369
    Allied Force, 229, 240
    Bosnian civil war, 203, 210, 214
    Israel, 128
    pre-WWI aviation, 3–5, 6
    WWI, 6–9, 12–15, 17–18, 20–23
Germany, WWII
    air power history and theory, 354–359,
        360, 366, 372
    aircraft fleet, 29, 30–33, 37–38
    antisubmarine campaign, 35–37
    Battle of Britain, 30–34
    Eastern front, 37–38, 39–40
    pre-war strategy and planning, 27–29
    Western Europe, 42–43, 47–50
Geyl, Pieter, xiv
Gilbert Islands, 62
Glasgow, HMS, 166
gliders, 72, 355, 356
Global Hawks, 270, 285, 389, 391
Global positioning system (GPS), 246, 249,
    262, 281, 384
Global Reach – Global Power (Rice), 374

Global View, 383
Gloster Gladiator, 365–366
Goddard, Robert H., 375
Goebbels, Joseph, 374
Golan Heights, 134, 142–145, 147
Goldwater, Barry, 108
Goldwater-Nichols Department of Defense
    Reorganization Act, 280
Gonen, Shmuel, 144
Goose Green, 159, 164, 172
Gordon, Shmuel, 82
Göring, Hermann, 30, 31–32, 33, 355, 361
GPS (global positioning system), 246, 249,
    262, 281, 384
GQG (High Command, France), 6, 8, 11,
    16, 21–22
GR-1 Tornados, 184, 236
GR-3 Harriers, 160, 167, 174
Grammos Mountains, 333–334
Great Aerodrome, 372
Greece, 332–334
ground operations, 327, 390
    colonial insurgencies, 329, 331, 337–338
    Enduring Freedom, 264, 267
    Iraqi Freedom, 282–283, 288, 291
    Israel-Arab Wars '67–'82, 143–145
    Korean War, 104, 110
    Second Lebanon War, 297–298, 306–
        309, 311–314, 318–319
    WWI, 21
    WWII, 27–30, 37–39, 40–42, 55
Groupe de Bombardment (GB1), 6
Groves, Leslie, 77
Grozny, 345
Guadalcanal, 2, 65–66, 79
Guam, 70, 74, 112
guerrilla warfare, 363–365
    early Cold War era, 331, 333, 334–335
    Korean War, 92
    post Cold War, 345–346
    Second Lebanon War, 254, 308
    Soviet-Russian counterinsurgencies,
        344, 345
Gulf War. See Operation Desert Storm
Guthrie, Charles, 230, 231
Guynemer, Georges, 10, 12, 15, 16

H-21s, 338
Hagenbeck, Franklin, 265–266, 267–269
Hague, The, 4

Haifa, 187, 309–310, 314–315
Haig, Alexander, 158–159
Haig, Douglas, 18, 19, 21
Haiphong, 108, 110, 111, 115, 120, 124, 126
Haiti, 328
Halsey, William F. "Bull," 58, 62, 68, 70, 72
Halutz, Dan, 303, 304–305, 308, 315
Hamas, 297
Hamdani, Raad, 294–295
Hanoi, 108, 110, 111, 114, 120, 121,
    124–126
Hansell, Haywood S., 74
Hariri, Rafik, 301
Hariri, Saad, 301
HARMs (high-speed antiradiation missiles),
    184, 215, 294
Harmsworth, Alfred, 3
Harris, Arthur, 46, 48
Hasim, Sultan, 192
Hawker, George Lanoe, 10
Hawker fighters, 30, 42
Hearne, R. P., 5
Heinkel, Ernst, 13–14, 22
Heinkel bombers, 34
helicopters, 359, 370. See also specific types
    Afghan Soviet occupation, 344
    Algeria, 337
    Allied Force, 236
    Desert Storm, 184
    Enduring Freedom, 266–267, 268
    Falklands War, 160
    Iraqi Freedom, 285, 290–291
    Israel-Arab Wars, 137, 150, 313, 321
    Korean War, 103–104, 105
Henderson Field, 65
Hercules, 111, 114, 160–161, 285, 287,
    293–294, 296, 314
Hermes, HMS, 160, 168, 172, 174
Heroes of the Fatherland, 243
Hezbollah and Second Lebanon War
    background, 254, 297–302, 304–
        305, 307
    Israeli combat against, 309–314
    operations, 314–315
    outcomes, 316–317, 345–347
    rocket deployment, 309, 311, 313–315,
        317–318
    strategy and planning, 301–302, 349
High Command, France, 11, 16, 21–22, 68
High Command, Germany (OHL), 6–7, 22

high-speed antiradiation missiles (HARMs), 184, 215, 294
Hill, Christopher, 223
Himalayas, 71
Hindenburg, Paul von, 13
Hindenburg Program, 13–14, 18
Hiroshima, 76–77, 359
Hirsch, Gal, 315
Hiryu, 64–65
Hispano-Suiza engines, 12, 17
history
    air power (*See* air power history and evolution)
    study of military, xiii–xvi
Hitler, Adolf, 30, 32, 51–52, 61, 354–355, 357
Ho Chi Minh, 107, 109, 336
Ho Chi Minh Trail, 107, 118, 120
Hod, Moti, 129, 135, 137, 139, 153
Hoeppner, Ernst von, 13
Hofi, Yzhak, 145
Holbrooke, Richard, 209, 210, 216, 218, 221–223, 227–229
Hornburg, Hal, 215
Horner, Charles A., 383
    Desert Storm, 183, 186, 190, 196, 197, 368
    Enduring Freedom, 275, 276
Hornet, USS, 58, 62, 65, 66
hostage taking, 210–211, 216. *See also* kidnappings, terrorist
Howard, Michael, xiii–xiv
Huk movement, 334–335
humanitarian relief, 208, 230, 238, 251, 258, 259
Hump, 71, 74, 358
Hungary, 233, 242
Hunsaker, Jerome, 375
Hussein, Saddam
    Desert Storm, 178, 182–183, 185–189, 191, 195, 199–200
    invasion of Kuwait, 178–179, 180–181
    Iraqi Freedom, 253, 283–285, 287–288, 292–293, 295
    media manipulation, 250

I Operation, 68
IADS (integrated air defense system), 217, 390. *See also* air defense systems
IAF (Israeli Air Force). *See* Israeli Air Force (IAF)

Icarus syndrome, xv–xvi
identification friend or foe (IFF), 245
IDF (Israel Defense Force). *See* Israel Defense Force (IDF)
IJN (Imperial Japanese Navy). *See* Imperial Japanese Navy (IJN)
Il Dominio dell'aria (Douhet), 25, 353–354
Ilyushin transporters, 186
Immelman, Max, 10, 12
Imperial Japanese Navy (IJN)
    Allied offensive-defensive phase, 65–66, 70, 72–73
    background and strategy, 58, 59–60
    fleet of, 69, 72
    Japanese offensive phase, 60–62, 63–65
Imphal, Battle of, 72
incendiary weapons, 13, 34, 62, 73–75
Inchon, 94
Independence class carriers, 69
India, 55, 71–72, 79, 327, 329, 330–331, 369
Indochina, 332, 336–337, 367
industry as targets
    Desert Storm, 188–190
    Vietnam War, 115–116
    WWI, 33
    WWII, 43–45, 46–47, 76
information dominance, 378–379
insurgencies
    air power, 349–35, 366–369
    early Cold War, 331–338
    Latin America, 341–343
    media, 348–349
    post Cold War, 345–348
    post WWI, 327–331, 364–366
    Southeast Asian, 338–341 (*See also* Vietnam War)
    Soviet-Russian, 343–345
integrated air defense system (IADS), 217, 390. *See also* air defense systems
intelligence, 378–379. *See also* intelligence, surveillance, and reconnaissance (ISR)
    Desert Storm, 190
    Israel-Arab Wars, 132, 142
    Korean War, 87, 102
    precision weapons and, 287–288, 321
    WWI, 327
    WWII, 31, 60–61
intelligence, surveillance, and reconnaissance (ISR)

early, 371–372
Enduring Freedom, 258, 261, 269, 271, 272, 275–276
evolution of, 378–379, 391
Iraqi Freedom, 203, 205, 291
Second Lebanon War, 313, 346
Inter-Allied Aviation Committee, 21, 36, 41
interdiction, 387
  Desert Storm, 191–193, 196, 197–198
  Iraqi Freedom, 253, 283, 291, 296
  Korean War, 92–97, 105
  Vietnam War, 108, 116, 117–118, 119, 340
  WWII, 38, 356–357, 358, 361
international law of war, 4, 6, 215, 240, 276, 364
interpretations of history, xiv
interservice rivalry, 19, 79, 88–89, 104–105, 122–123
Invincible, HMS, 160, 172
Iran
  Desert Storm, 186, 197
  Iran-Iraq war, 178, 183
  Lebanon, 299, 302, 305
Iraq, 258
  air force, 178, 183, 185–186, 348
  Desert Storm (*See* Operation Desert Storm)
  Iran-Iraq war, 178, 183
  Iraqi Corps divisions, 193
  Israel-Arab Wars, 130, 133, 142
  navy, 178
  post–WWI, 327, 328–329, 330–331
Iraqi Freedom, Operation. *See* Operation Iraqi Freedom (OIF)
Iron Hand, 113
irregular warfare and air power, 327. *See also* guerrilla warfare
ISR (intelligence, surveillance, and reconnaissance). *See* intelligence, surveillance, and reconnaissance (ISR)
Israel, 369, 381. *See also* Israel Defense Force (IDF); Israeli Air Force (IAF)
  Israel-Arab Wars (*See* Israel-Arab Wars)
  Kuwait and Desert Storm, 180, 181, 183, 186–187
  withdrawal from Lebanon, 300–301
Israel-Arab Wars, 127–155
  background and overview, 127–130

First Lebanon War, 127, 148–152, 154, 299, 345–346
Second Lebanon War (*See* Second Lebanon War)
Six Days War, 82, 127, 129–136, 154
summary, 152–155, 348–349
War of Attrition, 127, 136–141, 153–154
Yom Kippur War, 82, 127, 130, 141–148, 154, 380
Israel Defense Force (IDF)
  about, 128–130
  between First and Second Lebanese Wars, 299–301, 303–304
  Second Lebanon War, 254, 297, 304–305, 308–314, 319, 323
  war doctrine history, 306–308, 323
  War of Attrition, 137
  Yom Kippur War, 141–148
Israeli Air Force (IAF)
  about, 82, 128–132, 307
  First Lebanon War, 148–152
  Second Lebanon War, 254, 297–298, 305, 308–314, 317–321
  Six Days War, 130–135
  War of Attrition, 136–141
  Yom Kippur War, 141–147
Italy
  air power history and theory, 355
  Bosnian civil war, 220
  colonial insurgencies, 328
  Italian-Turkish War, 352, 353
  Kosovo war, 229
  pre-WWI aviation, 6
  WWI, 10, 14–15, 19–20, 23–24, 353
  WWII, 29, 35, 42, 45, 54, 358
Ivanov, Igor, 369–370
Ivri, David, 151–152
Iwo Jima, 74–75

Jackson, Mike, 244
Jaguars, 194
jamming, electronic, 47, 113, 150, 232, 234, 246, 259
Janvier, Bernard, 211, 213, 218
Japan, 369
Japan, Korean War, 87
Japan, WWII
  Allied offensive-defensive phase, 65–69, 70, 71–72

background and strategy, 53–54, 59–60
Japanese offensive phase, 60–65
summary, 77–79, 357–358, 359
US bombing offensive phase, 74–77
JDAM (joint direct attack munition).
      See joint direct attack munition
      (JDAM)
Jeschonnek, Hans, 33
Jet Propulsion Laboratory, 375
JFACC (joint force air component
      commander), 389
JNA (Yugoslavian National Army), 205,
      216–217. *See also* Bosnian civil war
Jodl, Alfred, 42–43
Johnson, Gerald W., 124
Johnson, Lyndon, 82, 108–109, 110, 113–
      115, 119, 339
joint direct attack munition (JDAM), 384
      Allied Force, 246, 249
      Enduring Freedom, 259, 262, 267–268,
            270, 272, 276
joint force air component commander
      (JFACC), 389
joint warfare
      early Cold War insurgencies, 333,
            337–338
      Falklands War, 174
      Iraqi Freedom, 280
      Korean War, 103–105
      Latin America, 342, 343
      post–WWI insurgencies, 329–331
      Vietnam War, 116–117
      WWI, 327
jointness, concept of, 79, 280
Jordan, 132, 133, 137, 327
Joynson-Hicks, William, 10
Jumper, John, 226–227, 229, 231, 246, 250
Junkers, 18, 34, 39

KA-3s, 112
Kafr Qana, 312
Kaga, 64
Kai-Shek, Chiang, 71, 95
kamikazes, 73, 76
Kammhuber, Josef, 47
Kammhuber Line, 47
Kandahar, 259, 261–263
Kaplinski, Moshe, 313, 315
Karadzic, Radovan, 205, 218, 222, 223
KARI (integrated air defense system), Iraq,
      178, 182, 183–186, 191

Kármán, Theodore von, 375
Karzai, Hamid, 262, 265
Katyusha rockets, 148, 368, 375
KC-10s, 259
KC-135s, 112, 259, 382
Kennedy, John F., 107–108, 339
Kenney, George, 56, 66–68, 74, 78, 79, 95
Kérillis, Henri de, 16
Kfar Giladi, 313
Khost, 263
kidnappings, terrorist, 297, 300–301, 302–
      304, 308–309
Kido Butai, 60, 64, 66
kill chain, 272, 274, 277
kill ratios. *See* air loss rates
King, Ernest J., 36, 57, 58–59, 61
Kiryat Shmonah, 314–315
Kissinger, Henry, 119, 123, 136
Kitty Hawk, USS, 258
KLA (Kosovo Liberation Army), 225, 227–
      229, 232–233, 235, 243–244
Kogenluft, 13, 18
Kohima, Battle of, 72
Korean War, 85–106
      air superiority, 97–101, 380–381
      background and overview, 81, 85–89
      interdiction campaign, 92–97, 105
      joint warfare, 103–105
      Pusan Perimeter, 90–92, 94, 106
      reconnaissance, 102–103
      strategic bombing campaign, 101–
            102, 106
      summary, 105–106
Kosovo, 176, 205, 225. *See also* Operation
      Allied Force
Kosovo Liberation Army (KLA), 225, 227–
      229, 232–233, 235, 243–244
Kosovo Verification Monitors (KVM),
      228–229
Krajina region, 205, 209, 210, 212
Krusevac, 243
KTO (Kuwaiti Theater of Operations), 191,
      194–195
Kunduz, 261–262
Kurdish rebellions, 199–200, 328–329, 331
Kurdistan, 329, 330
Kurita, Takeo, 72
Kursk, 40
Kuwait
      Enduring Freedom, 258, 259, 261

invasion of, 178–181 (*See also* Operation Desert Storm)

Iraqi Freedom, 286, 289

Kuwaiti Theater of Operations (KTO), 191, 194–195

KVM (Kosovo Verification Monitors), 228–229

Laffey, USS, 76

Laird, Melvin, 119, 121

Lambert, Andrew P.N., 377

Lambeth, Benjamin, 234, 244

landing zones, 266, 269

Lang Chi plant, 121

Langley, Samuel, 372

Langley, USS, 58

Lansdale, Edward, 334

Laos, 107, 108, 110–112, 115–118, 120, 126, 340

laser guidance systems, 114, 231, 245, 249–250, 384. *See also* laser-guided bombs (LGB)

laser-guided bombs (LGB)
    Allied Force, 245
    Bosnian civil war, 202, 209, 211, 214
    Desert Storm, 194
    Enduring Freedom, 260, 267
    Korean War, 82, 114, 120, 121, 126

Lavelle, John, 119–120

Le Châtelier, A., 8

Le Duan, 109–110

Le Duc Tho, 109

leadership targeting, 108, 188–191, 282

League for a Democratic Kosovo (LDK), 225

Lebanon
    First Lebanon War, 82, 148–152
    France, 327
    Second Lebanon War (*See* Second Lebanon War)
    Six Days War, 133

LeMay, Curtis E., 74–76, 107–108, 126

l'Entreprenant, 371–372

Lexington, USS, 58, 63

LGBs (laser-guided bomb). *See* laser-guided bombs (LGB)

Libya, 237, 352, 372

Lichtenstein radar, 47

Lieth-Thomsen, Hermann von der, 13

Limits of Air Power, The (Clodfelter), 126

Linebacker I campaign, 81–82, 117–123

Linebacker II campaign, 81–82, 118, 124–126

Litani River, 302, 307, 309, 312, 313, 319

Lloyd George, David, 9, 21

London bombings, 2, 9, 32–35, 37, 44, 47, 355

long-range bombers, 55, 59, 86, 88, 271, 361

Lord Kelvin, 372

loss rates, air. *See* air loss rates

Loucheur, Louis, 22

low-intensity conflicts, 322

Ludendorff, Erich, 13, 18

Luftwaffe, 33, 60, 128, 354–355, 356–357, 366. *See also* Germany, WWII

LZs (landing zone), 266, 269

MacArthur, Douglas
    Korean War, 89, 94–97
    WWII, 54–55, 61, 66–67, 68, 71, 77, 95

MacArthur-Pratt agreement, 55

Macedonia, 227, 230–231, 233, 238, 244

Macon, 57

Mad Mullah, 328

Magsaysay, Ramon, 334

MAGTAF (Marine air-ground task force), 286

Mahan, Alfred Thayer, 56–57

Malaya, 61, 332, 335–336

Manchuria, 53, 54, 97, 99

Manhattan Project, 77

man-portable air defense system (MANPAD), 220, 260, 390

Mao Zedong, 85, 95, 98, 331, 364

Mariana Islands, 2, 70, 74–75

Marine Air-Ground Task Force (MAGTAF), 286

Marine Corps, US. *See* US Marine Corps (USMC)

Marne, Battle of, 6, 352, 372

Maroun A-Ras, 311

Marshall, George C., 36, 56

Marshall Islands, 62, 70

Mason, R.A., 376

Mattis, Jim, 294

Mazar-i-Sharif, 259, 261

McCain, John S., III, 123

McCain, John S., Jr., 123

McKiernan, David, 293

McNamara, Robert, 119, 382

McPeak, Merrill, 362, 374, 383

Me-262s, 98
media
    Allied Force, 176, 190, 239, 240–241,
        244, 249–251
    counterinsurgencies, 348–349
    Second Lebanon War, 307, 312
Meilinger, Philip, 377, 379
Meir, Golda, 137
Mencken, H. L., xiv
Mentors, 165, 171
Meteor 13 NFs, 98, 129
Meyer, John C., 124
MH-53 Pave Lows, 184
Mi- helicopters, 344
Michelin brothers, 5, 6
Middleton, Linley, 174
Midway, Battle of, 2, 63–66
MiG fighters. *See also specific types*
    Allied Force, 232–233
    Desert Storm, 183, 185
    Israel-Arab Wars, 130, 133, 137–139,
        141, 149
    Korean War, 94, 98–99, 100–101, 103,
        381–382
    Vietnam War, 111, 113–114, 122, 125
    WWII, 37
MiG-3s, 37
MiG-15s, 94, 98–99, 100–101, 103
MiG-17s, 122
MiG-21s, 122, 130, 137–139, 141, 183,
    233, 260
MiG-23s, 149, 183
MiG-25s, 149, 183
MiG-29s, 183, 185, 232–233
military history, study of, xiii–xvi
Miller, Carl, 121
Millikan, Robert, 375
Milosevic, Slobadan
    Allied Force, 176, 225–231, 236, 237,
        241–244
    Bosnian civil war, 203, 204–206, 218,
        221–222, 223
Mirages, 132, 136, 139, 141, 186, 218
    F-1Es, 183
    IIIs, 161, 163, 165, 171
missiles. *See also specific types*
    Allied Force, 231, 232, 233–235, 242
    Bosnian civil war, 202, 214, 215, 219
    Desert Storm, 183, 184, 186–187
    Enduring Freedom, 259–260

evolution, 326, 359–362, 370, 375–376,
    382, 389–390
Falklands War, 159, 161, 164, 166–168,
    171–173
Iraqi Freedom, 287–288
Israel-Arab Wars '67-'82, 130, 134, 139,
    146–147, 150–151, 153–154
Second Lebanon War, 298, 300, 302,
    306, 310, 315, 317–319, 321
Vietnam War, 11, 109, 113, 122–123, 125
Missouri, USS, 77
Mitchell, William "Billy," 21, 55, 57, 197,
    354, 376
Mitscher, Marc, 58–59, 70
Mladic, Ratko, 218–219, 221–223
Moffett, William A., 57
Moltke, Helmuth von, 5
Momyer, William "Spike," 111–112, 126
monoplanes, switch to, 58, 356
Montenegro, 205, 206, 233, 243
Montgomery, Bernard, 365
Moore, Jeremy, 167
Moorer, Thomas, 119
morale as a target
    Allied Force, 241, 244, 247
    Desert Storm, 189, 192–193, 194–195
    Second Lebanon War, 318
    small war insurgencies, 330, 333, 338
    WWI, 4–5, 9, 16, 19, 20, 24–25
    WWII, 2, 27, 28, 33, 35, 43, 46, 50
Morelot, Antoine, 371
Morocco, 42, 327, 330
Moseley, Michael, 269, 282, 285, 286, 294
Mosquitos, 378
Mother of all Battles, The (Woods), 198–199
Mountbatten, Louis, 71
MQ-1 Predators, 268, 270, 275–276
Mrkale marketplace, 213
Mubarak, Hosni, 141
munitions expenditure rates. *See* expenditure
    rates, munitions
Murderer's Row, 693
Muslims, 180, 204, 205, 211, 337, 347–348
mutual assured destruction (MAD), 86
Myers, Richard, 263
Mystères, 131

N1K2J Georges, 69
Nabatieh, 302
NAC (North Atlantic Council). *See* North
    Atlantic Council (NAC)

Nagasaki, 77, 359
Nagumo, Chuichi, 60, 64
Napoleonic wars, 351, 374–375
Nasiriya, 289–290, 293
Nasrallah, Hassan, 300, 301, 308–310, 316, 317
Nasser, Abdul, 135, 136–138, 139
NATO (North Atlantic Treaty Organization), 140
NATO (North Atlantic Treaty Organization), Allied Force
  background, 226–229
  operations, 235–244
  Southern Europe (*See* Allied Forces Southern Europe (AFSOUTH))
  strategy, 229–231
  success debate, 245–249, 250–251
NATO (North Atlantic Treaty Organization), Bosnian civil war
  background and overview, 201–203
  Operation Deliberate Force, 213–215, 217–222, 223–224
  Operation Deny Flight, 206–207
  Rapid Reaction Force (RRF), 211, 213, 216–218
Naumann, Klaus, 226–227, 229, 248
navies, future of, 391–392
navigation technology, 33–34, 47, 88, 220, 249, 360, 376
Navy, US. *See* US Navy (USN)
NBC (nuclear, biological, and chemical weapons), 181, 189–190
Nebelwerfer, 375
Neharyah, 315
Neosho, USS, 63
Netherlands
  Allied Force, 240
  Bosnian civil war, 209, 211, 217, 220
  WWII, 29, 54, 356
New Britain, 62, 68
New Guinea, 54–55, 62, 63, 65, 67, 68
Ngo Dinh Diem, 107, 339
Nguyen Cao Ky, 107
Nguyen Chi Thanh, 109–110
Nguyen Van Thieu, 107
Nicaragua, 341
Nieuport biplanes, 12
Nimble Lion, 226–227
Nimitz, Chester A., 61, 64, 70, 71, 73, 75

Nimrods, 160, 163, 378
Nivelle, Henri, 15–16
Nixon, Richard, 82, 109, 118–121, 123–124, 126, 136, 139
Nixon Doctrine, 136
NKAF (North Korean Air Force), 89, 97–98
No. 77 Squadron, 90–91
No. 127 Fighter Regiment, 232
No. 250 Brigade, 234
no-fly ban, Bosnian, 202, 212
nontrinitarian, concept of, 364
Normandy, 42, 358, 379
Normandy, USS, 221
North Africa, 29, 35, 38, 41, 50
North Atlantic Council (NAC)
  Bosnian civil war, 206–208, 210, 213, 217, 218
  war in Kosovo, 228, 229
North Atlantic Treaty Organization (NATO). *See* NATO (North Atlantic Treaty Organization)
North Korea, 85, 101–102. *See also* Korean War
North Korean Air Force (NKAF), 89, 97–98
North Vietnam, 81–82, 107–108, 112–113, 117–118, 122, 126. *See also* Vietnam War
Northern Alliance, 271
Norway, 240, 357
Notes of a Lost Pilot (Villar), 16
Novi Sad, 233–237
Novikov, Alexander, 38–39
nuclear weapons, 86–87, 96, 181, 189–190, 360–361, 362, 366
Nungesser, Charles, 12, 16

Oberste Heeresleitung, 6–7, 22
observation balloons, 3, 351, 355–356, 371, 378
observe, orient, decide, and act (OODA), 367, 368–369
ODF (Operation Deliberate Force). *See* Operation Deliberate Force (ODF)
OHL (Oberste Heeresleitung), 6–7, 22
OIF (Operation Iraqi Freedom). *See* Operation Iraqi Freedom (OIF)
Okinawa, 76
Olds, Robin, 113, 121
Olmert, Ehud, 302–303, 310, 315–316
Oman, 259

On Guerrilla Warfare (Zedong), 364
101st Airborne Division, 265
Onishi, Takijiro, 73
OODA (observe, orient, decide, and act), 367, 368–369
Operation A, 70
Operation Accountability, 307
Operation Allied Force, 225–252
    background and overview, 176, 225–229
    evaluation, 249–252, 262, 270–272, 363
    ground force use debate, 225, 230–231, 235–236, 238, 240, 242–243
    Phase 1, 231–235
    Phase 2, 235–244
    strategy, 229–231, 247–249
Operation Anaconda, 253, 265–269, 277
Operation Argument, 48
Operation Arzav, 150–152
Operation Black Buck, 163–165
Operation Cartwheel, 68
Operation Deliberate Force (ODF), 213–222
    background and overview, 175–176, 202–204, 208
    precision bombing implications, 222–224
    resources and planning, 213–216
    strategy differences, 216–217
Operation Deny Flight, 175, 202–204, 206–213, 215
Operation Desert Shield, 179–180
Operation Desert Storm, 177–200, 384–385
    Allied Force contrasts, 231–232, 250, 270–271
    effects of, 199–200
    goals and strategies, 181–183
    ground offensive, 193–196
    incapacitating the Iraqi regime, 187–191
    invasion of Kuwait, 178–181
    overview and summary, 175, 177–178, 196–199, 308, 345
    supply interdiction, 191–193
    suppressing Iraq's air defense, 183–187
Operation Dugman, 145–146, 149, 151, 152
Operation Enduring Freedom, 255–277
    background and overview, 253, 255–257
    conclusions, 275–277
    early operations, 259–265
    execution problems, 272–275, 347–348, 363

Operation Anaconda, 265–269
    strategy and planning, 257–259
    successes and firsts, 270–272, 347
Operation Gomorrah, 47–48
Operation Grapes of Wrath, 307, 312
Operation Iraqi Freedom (OIF), 200, 279–296
    background and overview, 253–254, 279–281
    conclusion, 295–296, 347–348
    ground campaign, 289–296
    "shock and awe" phase, 287–289
    strategy and planning, 281–285
    structure and preparation, 285–287
Operation Litani, 307
Operation Matterhorn, 74
Operation Meetinghouse, 75
Operation Mistral 2, 219, 221
Operation MO, 63–64
Operation Moked, 129, 131–135, 147, 307
Operation Northern Watch, 258, 282
Operation Priha, 137–138
Operation Rösselsprung, 367
Operation Saturate, 97
Operation Sealion, 30, 32–33
Operation Sky Watch, 201–202, 206
Operation Southern Watch, 258, 282, 285
Operation Spring Thaw, 97
Operation Starvation, 76
Operation Storm I, II and III, 211–212, 219
Operation Strangle, 97
Operation Tagar, 144–146
Operation Tarawa, 70
Operation Thursday, 72
Operation Torch, 42
Operation Watchtower, 65–66, 79
Operation Zela, 129, 131
Oppenheimer, Robert, 359
Organization for Security and Cooperation in Europe (OSCE), 227–229
Ottoman Empire, 179, 327, 328
Ouragans, 131
Ozawa, Jisaburo, 70, 72

P-36 Mowhawks, 56
P-38 Lightnings, 42, 48, 56, 68
P-39 Airacobras, 56
P-40 Warhawks, 56
P-47 Thunderbolts, 42, 48
P-51 Mustangs, 48, 74–75, 380

Painlevé, Paul, 6, 15–16
Pakistan, 344
Pale, 210–211, 218
Palestine, 327, 364–366
Palestine Liberation Organization (PLO), 345–346, 348
Panzerfaust, 375
Papandreou, George, 238
paratroopers, 158, 159, 293, 295, 343, 355–356
Park, Keith, 153
Patriarch Paper, 218
Patriot anti-air missiles, 187
Paulus, Friedrich, 39
PBY Catalinas, 58
Peace for Galilee War, 127, 148–152, 154, 299, 345–346
peace talks
    Allied Force, 229, 242, 244
    Bosnian civil war, 212, 218, 221–222
    Vietnam War, 109, 117, 123–124
Pearl Harbor, 2, 41, 54, 60–61, 63, 255–256
Peled, Beni, 142–143, 145, 146
People's Liberation Army (PLA), 95–96
People's Liberation Army Air Force (PLAAF), 85–86, 94, 98–101
people's war doctrine, 331–332
Peretz, Amir, 303, 315–316
Pétain, Henri, 15–16, 20, 21–22
Peterson, Douglas "Pete," 123
PGM (precision-guided munition). See precision-guided munition (PGM)
Phantoms. See F-4 Phantoms
Philippine Sea, Battle of the, 70
Philippines, 61, 72–73, 332, 334–335
photography, aerial, 7–8, 117, 330, 352
Phuc Yen, 113–114, 116
pipelines, oil, 117, 121
PLA (People's Liberation Army), 95–96
PLAAF (People's Liberation Army Air Force), 85–86, 94, 98–101
Plan Colombia, 343
Plan Patriota, 343
PLO (Palestine Liberation Organization), 345–346, 348
Podesta, John, 238
Pointblank Directive, 46–47
Poland, 29, 62, 356
Portugal, 240
Powell, Colin, 181, 191

precision warfare
    Allied Force, 176, 237, 250
    Bosnian civil war, 176, 202–204, 214, 220–221, 222–224
    Enduring Freedom, 270–271, 276, 347
    Iraqi Freedom, 280–281, 291–292
    Second Lebanon War, 298, 346
precision-guided munition (PGM), 362–363
    Allied Force, 235, 237, 246, 250
    Bosnian civil war, 202, 214
    Desert Storm, 177, 188, 195
    Enduring Freedom, 270, 271
    Israel-Arab Wars, 149, 151–152, 298, 323
Predators, 218, 249–250, 268, 270, 275–276, 285, 389, 391
preemptive attacks, 128, 135, 305, 309, 317, 322
Prince of Wales, HMS, 61
propaganda, 276
    Allied Force, 242
    Enduring Freedom, 259
    Second Lebanon War, 298
    small war insurgencies, 348–349
    Vietnam War, 121, 126
    WWII, 63
psychological warfare, 42, 327, 331. *See also* morale as a target
    Bosnian civil war, 219–220, 221
    Desert Storm, 192
    Enduring Freedom, 264
    Iraqi Freedom, 254, 291–292
    Malaya, 336
    Philippines, 334–335
    WWI, 7
    WWII, 73
public opinion, 61, 239, 241, 250–251, 297, 309, 312–313
Pucarás, 160, 165, 169, 171
Pumas, 165, 166, 168
pursuit aviation, 8, 10–12, 15, 20, 24–25, 56
Pusan Perimeter, 81, 90–92, 94, 106
push CAS, 196
Python 4s, 321

RAAF (Royal Australian Air Force), 369
Rabaul, 62, 65, 68
Rabin, Yitzhak, 130, 135
Racak, 229
radar jamming. *See* jamming, electronic

radar technology
  Allied Force, 232–234, 245–246
  Desert Storm, 184
  Israel-Arab Wars, 153
  Korean War, 88, 99, 100–101
  Vietnam War, 113, 122
  WWII, 28, 30, 34, 36–37, 47
radar warning receivers (RWR), 245–246
Radio Hanoi, 125–126
radio relay (RADREL), 188, 217, 220, 221
Raeder, Erich, 32–33
RAF (Royal Air Force). *See* Royal Air Force
  (RAF)
RAFAEL (Armament Development
  Authority), 149
railroads in North Vietnam, 109, 114–115,
  117, 118, 120
Ralston, Joseph, 226
Rambouillet peace talks, 229, 230, 237
RAND Corporation, 246, 375, 377
Rapid Reaction Force (RRF), 211, 213,
  216–218
Rapier missiles, 167, 169, 173
Rathenau, Walther, 7
RB-17s, 103
RB-29s, 103
RE-12s, 246
reconnaissance
  Allied Force, 249
  Bosnian civil war, 214, 217, 219
  counterinsurgencies, 328–330, 335,
    338, 342
  early aviation and history, 4–8, 327,
    352–353, 372, 378
  Israel-Arab Wars, 132, 146
  Korean War, 102–103, 105
  satellites, 375–376
  Vietnam War, 110
  WWII, 57
Red Army, 37, 344, 355, 358
Red River, 114–115, 121
Red River Valley Fighter Pilots Association,
  123
refugees
  Afghan, 259, 344
  Kosovo, 176, 227, 229–230, 237–239,
    242, 244, 250
Reichenau, Franz von, 7
Reims, 3–4, 16
remotely piloted vehicles (RPV), 362,
  368–370

Republican Guard, 178, 181, 191–195,
  200, 290–292, 294–295
Republican Guard Medina Division, 290,
  294–295
Republika Srpska (RS), 205–206
Republika Srpska Krajina (RSK), 205
Repulse, HMS, 61
resilience, 321, 323
Revolt of the Admirals, 79
Revue générale de l'aéronautique militaire, 4
Reynolds, Clark, 59
RF-51s, 103
RF-80s, 103
RFC (Royal Flying Corps), 7, 9, 14, 18–19,
  20, 23
RHAF (Royal Hellenic Air Force), 333–334
Rice, Condoleezza, 312
Rice, Donald B., 374
Richthofen, Manfred Freiherr von, 12, 17, 22
Ridgway, Matthew, 90, 97, 102, 104
Rif war, 330
Rio Grande airfield, 165–166
Ritchie, Richard "Steve," 122
RNAS (Royal Naval Air Service), 7, 9, 14,
  19, 23
Robert, Jean and Nóel, 371
Robertson, George, 230, 235–236
Robida, Albert, 3
Rochefort, Joseph, 63, 64, 65
rockets, 374–376. *See also* missiles
ROE (rules of engagement). *See* rules of
  engagement (ROE)
Rolling Thunder campaign, 81–82, 108–
  117, 118–122, 381, 384
Rolls, Charles, 3
Rolls-Royce engines, 14, 19, 48, 99
Rommel, Erwin, 379
Roosevelt, Franklin D., 43, 44–45, 51–52,
  62, 63, 71
Roosevelt, Theodore, 372
Rostow, Walt, 339
Rotem, 129–130
route package system, 111–112, 116,
  120, 124
Royal Air Force (RAF)
  beginnings, 353
  counterinsurgencies, 328–329, 330,
    333, 336
  Enduring Freedom, 258, 259
  Falklands War, 160–161, 163–165

Israel, 128–129
Palestine, 364–366
WWI, 23
WWII, Europe, 28, 30–32, 34–36,
    40–43, 48–49, 128, 357
WWII, Pacific, 53, 72
Royal Australian Air Force (RAAF), 90–
    91, 369
Royal Australian Navy, 87
Royal Flying Corps (RFC), 7, 9, 14, 18–19,
    20, 23
Royal Hellenic Air Force (RHAF), 333–334
Royal Marines, 158
Royal Naval Air Service (RNAS), 7, 9, 14,
    19, 23
Royal Navy, 166, 374–375
    colonial operations, 336
    Falklands War, 83, 158–160, 169–171,
        172–174
    WWII, 35–36
RPVs (remotely piloted vehicle), 362,
    368–370
RQ-1 Predators, 218, 249–250, 268, 270,
    275–276, 285, 389, 391
RQ-2 Pioneers, 249
RQ-4 Global Hawks, 270, 285, 389, 391
RQ-5 Hunters, 249
RRF (Rapid Reaction Force), 211, 213,
    216–218
RS (Republika Srpska), 205–206
RSK (Republika Srpska Krajina), 205
Ruge, Friedrich, 379
Rugova, Ibrahim, 225
rules of engagement (ROE)
    Allied Force, 176, 237–239, 245, 251
    Bosnian civil war, 175–176, 202,
        214–215
    Enduring Freedom, 272, 273–275, 276
    Falklands War, 162–163
    Vietnam War, 110–111, 122–123
rules of study, history, xiii–xiv
Rumsfeld, Donald, 258, 263, 282
Rundstedt, Gerd von, 43
Russia, 369
    Bosnian civil war, 203, 210
    Chechnya, 344, 345
    Kosovo war, 229, 237, 240, 242, 363
RV i PVO (Yugoslav Air Force and Air
    Defense), 232–235, 242, 243, 244
RWR (radar warning receivers), 245–246

Ryan, John, 120
Ryan, Michael
    Allied Force, 244, 248
    Bosnian civil war, 209, 212–220, 222

SA-2s, 112, 124, 134, 138, 183
SA-2Es, 138
SA-3s, 138, 146, 153, 183, 233–234, 260
SA-6s, 146, 149–150, 183, 233–234
SA-7s, 233–234, 260, 390
SA-8s, 149, 151, 183
SA-9s, 149, 151
SAC (Strategic Air Command), 112,
    124–125
Sadat, Anwar, 141
SAF (Syrian Air Force), 132–133, 142–
    149, 152
Sakai, Saburo, 60, 66
SAMs (surface-to-air missile). *See* surface-to-
    air missiles (SAMs)
San Carlos, Battle of, 159, 167–172
Sandys White Paper, 382
Santa Cruz Islands, Battle of the, 66
Sarajevo, 204, 213, 216, 217
Saratoga, USS, 58
SAS (Special Air Service), 165–166, 169
satellites, 249, 250, 271, 360, 368, 375–
    376, 393
Saudi Arabia
    Enduring Freedom, 258, 259, 270
    invasion of Kuwait and Desert Storm,
        179–181, 185, 187
Savo Island, 66
SB2C Helldivers, 69, 334
SBD Dauntless, 58
Schmitt, Paul, 6
Schroeder, Gerhard, 242–243
Schutzstaffeln, 13, 17–18
Schwarzkopf, Norman, 181–182, 186, 190,
    191, 197, 368
Scud missiles, 186–187, 191
SE5s, 14, 17
Sea Darts, 162, 166, 168, 170, 173
Sea Harriers, 82
    Falklands War, 158, 160–162, 164–165,
        167–169, 171, 172–173
    Iraqi Freedom, 286
Sea Kings, 160, 172
Sea Wolfs, 166, 168, 170, 173
Seabees, 286

SEAD (suppression of enemy air defenses), 184, 215, 219–221, 247
Second Battle of Alamein, 42
Second Intifada, 300–301
Second Lebanon War, 297–324
    background and overview, 254, 297–301, 304–308
    combat phase I, 308–310
    combat phase II, 310–312
    combat phase III, 312–314
    conclusions, 322–324
    Hezbollah operations, 314–315, 323
    lessons, 317–322
    outcomes, 315–317, 345–347, 367–368
    strategy and planning, 301–304
security zone, 299–300, 305, 312, 345
Senate Armed Services Committee, 248
September 11th attacks, 255–257
Serb Republic Army, 205
Serbia, 205–206, 225. *See also* Bosnian civil war; Operation Allied Force
Serbian Republic, 205–206
Seventh Air Force, 119, 121, 125
Seventh Corps, US, 195–196
Seventh Marine Regimental Combat Team, 290
Shah-i-Kot valley, 265–269
Sharon, Ariel, 302–303
Sharp, Grant, 111–112, 126
Shazly, Saad el, 143, 144
Shea, Jamie, 240, 242
Sheffield, HMS, 159, 166
Shelton, Henry, 226, 238, 248
Shenandoah, USS, 57
Shiites
    Iraqi, 193, 199–200
    Lebanese, 299, 309, 316, 345–346
Shkedi, Eliezer, 303
Shock and Awe (Ullman and Wade), 282
Shoho, 63
Shokaku, 63–64
Short, Michael, 227, 230, 239, 247, 248
short-range rockets, 302, 306, 311, 312, 314, 317–318
Shrike missiles, 113, 165
Sidewinder missiles, 111, 122, 168
Siegert, Wilhelm, 13
Sijan, Lance, 123
Simpson, John, 241
Sims, USS, 63

Sinai Peninsula, 128, 130, 134, 135, 141, 147
Singapore, 54, 61, 369
Siniora, Fouad, 301, 305, 310, 311
Sir Bedivere, HMS, 170
Sir Galahad, HMS, 159–160, 170
Sir Lancelot, HMS, 170
Sir Tristram, HMS, 159–160
Site 85, 115–116
Six Days War, 82, 127, 129–136, 154
skip bombing, 67
Skyhawks. *See* A-4 Skyhawks
Skyraiders, 339, 390
Skyvans, 165
Slovenia, 204–205
Smith, Leighton, 209, 211, 213, 218, 221
Smith, Rupert, 210, 216, 218, 219
Smuts, J. C., 19
SN2 radar, 47
SOF (special operations force), 253, 258, 261–262, 270–271, 273, 277
Solana, Javier, 230, 235–236
Soloman Islands, 65, 66, 68
Somme, Battle of, 11, 12, 14–15, 24
Sopwith fighters, 14
sortie rates, 384
    Allied Force, 240, 243, 245, 246
    Bosnian civil war, 217, 219, 231–233
    Desert Storm, 185, 194, 197
    Enduring Freedom, 263, 270–272, 275, 277
    Falklands War, 168, 172
    Greece, 334
    Iraqi Freedom, 285
    Israel-Arab Wars '67–'82, 134–135, 139–143, 148, 151
    Korean War, 85–86
    Rif war, 330
    Second Lebanon War, 298, 309, 311, 313
    Vietnam War, 340
Soryu, 64
South African Air Force, 92
South Georgia, 158
South Korea, 85, 89, 98. *See also* Korean War
South Vietnam, 81–82, 107, 108–110, 117–118, 126. *See also* Vietnam War
South Vietnamese Air Force (VNAF), 339–340
South Vietnamese army, 339–340
Southern Resource Zone, 54, 62

Southwest Pacific theater (SWPAC), 2, 53, 54–55, 66–68, 79
Soviet Union, 355, 360–361
  Afghanistan, 343–344
  Cold War, 86–87, 99
  Greece, 332
  Israel-Arab wars, 82, 130, 136–141, 146
  Korean War, 85–87, 96, 100, 101, 105
  Kuwait, 181
  Vietnam War, 109, 110
  WWII, 28, 37–40, 53–54, 357, 366
Spaatz, Carl, 45
space power
  effects-based operations, 384–386
  evolution, 382–384, 386
  standards, 387–388
Space Warfare Center, 383
space-based technology, 258, 368, 370, 376–378, 383–384, 390
SPAD fighters, 12, 17, 20
Spain, 214, 240, 328, 377
Sparrow missiles, 111, 122
Special Air Service (SAS), 165–166, 169
Special Attack Corps, 73
special instructions (SPIN), 215
special operations forces (SOF), 253, 258, 261–266, 270–271, 273, 277
Spector, Ronald, 56
SPIN (special instructions), 215
Spitfires, 31, 102, 332, 333, 366
Sprague, Clifton, 72
Spruance, Raymond, 64, 65, 70
Sputnik, 368, 376, 382–383
Srebrenica, 211
SSMs (surface-to-surface missile), 150, 155, 319, 321, 360, 369, 370
St. Lo, USS, 73
Stalin, Josef, 38, 45, 85, 87
Stalingrad, 38, 39, 358
Stanley, 159–165, 172
Stealth bombers, 246–247, 259, 270, 272, 276, 285
Steichen, Edward, 69
Stennis, John, 115
Stillwell, "Vinegar Joe," 71
Stinger antiaircraft missiles, 169, 260, 344, 390
Stockdale, James, 123
stormfliers, 17–18
Strasser, Peter, 7, 13–14, 18

Strategic Air Command (SAC), 112, 124–125
strategic bombing, 1, 353, 355
  Allied Force, 248, 254
  Desert Storm, 175, 188–191, 197
  Iraqi Freedom, 253–254
  Korean War, 101–102, 106
  Second Lebanon War, 306, 320
  WWI, 8, 10, 14–15, 19–20, 22–24, 279, 327
  WWII, 1, 54, 78–79, 327, 355, 356, 358
Stratemeyer, George E., 88, 89, 92–96, 99, 101
Stufflebeam, John, 262
Stukas, 357, 366
Su-22s, 260
subjectivity of military history, xiv–xv
submarines
  Falklands War, 159, 162–163
  WWI, 19, 20, 23
  WWII, 34–37, 57, 60–61, 76, 77–79, 357, 360
Suez Canal, 130, 134, 135, 137–139, 141, 143–144
Sukhois, 186
Sullivan, Glenn, 124
Sultan, Tipu, 374
Super Étendards, 159, 161, 163–165, 171, 172
Super Galeb G-4s, 232–233
suppression of enemy air defenses (SEAD), 184, 215, 217, 219–221, 247
surface-to-air missiles (SAMs), 153, 359. See also specific types
  Allied Force, 232–234, 245, 251
  Desert Storm, 183–184, 187
  Enduring Freedom, 259–260
  Falklands War, 164, 167–169, 171, 173
  First Lebanon War, 148
  Iraqi Freedom, 288
  Six Days War, 130, 131, 134, 135
  Vietnam War, 109, 112–114, 116, 125
  War of Attrition, 138
  Yom Kippur War, 141–142, 144–148
surface-to-surface missiles (SSM), 150, 155, 319, 321, 360, 369, 370
surveillance, 360, 671, 678
  Allied Force, 233, 249
  Bosnian civil war, 214
  colonial wars, 335, 338

Enduring Freedom, 258, 265, 347
Falklands War, 160
Iraqi Freedom, 283
Israel-Arab Wars, 142, 150, 313
Korean War, 87
WWI, 351
Sutherland, Richard, 67
SWPAC theater (Southwest Pacific), 2, 53,
    54–55, 66–68, 79
Sykes, Frederick, 28
Syria, 369
    First Lebanon War, 148–152, 299
    France, 327
    Kuwait, 180
    post–WWI, 329–330
    Second Lebanon War, 301, 302, 304,
        305, 309
    Six Days War, 130, 132–134
    War of Attrition, 136
    Yom Kippur War, 142–148
Syrian Air Force (SAF), 132–133, 142–
    149, 152

T-6s, 334, 338
Tajikistan, 259
Talbot, Strobe, 243
Taliban, 257–262, 264, 265–266, 270, 347
Tannenberg, Battle of, 7, 372
Tarawa Operation, 70
target selection, 10, 93, 273, 281, 303, 362
TBF Avengers, 69
Tedder, Arthur, 41–42, 376
Templer, Gerald, 335–336
Tenth Mountain Division, 265
terrorism, 148, 149, 256–257, 276, 297,
    299. See also specific organizations
Tet offensive, 109, 115, 340
Thach, Jimmy, 58
Thailand, 110, 112, 113, 116, 119, 121–
    122, 341
Thanh Hoa Bridge, 114, 120
Theodore Roosevelt, USS, 217, 258, 264
theory, air power
    1990s, 175
    Desert Storm, 198
    early, xv–xvi, 372
    Korean War, 101
    post WWI, 25, 27–28, 279–280, 330, 354
    Second Lebanon War, 306
    war against third/fourth rate states,
        362–363

WWII, 55, 56–57, 60, 74, 331, 358, 373
Third Infantry Division, 254, 280–284, 290
Third Marine Aircraft Wing (MAW), 286,
    289, 294
thirty-eighth parallel, 85, 90, 94, 97, 104
Thompson, Julian, 167
Thorsness, Leo, 123
Thud Ridge (Broughton), 110
Tibbets, Paul, 76
Tiberias, 310
Time magazine, 222
Tito, Josip Broz, 204, 366
Tizard, Henry, 376
TLAM (Tomahawk land attack missile). See
    Tomahawk land attack missiles
    (TLAM)
Tlas, Mustafa, 150
Tojo, Hideki, 77–78
tokko forces, 73, 76
Tokyo bombings, 62–63, 75
Tokyo Express, 65, 66
Tolkowsky, Dan, 129
Tomahawk land attack missiles (TLAM)
    Allied Force, 240
    Deliberate Force, 214, 219, 221–222
    Desert Storm, 175, 184, 188
    Iraqi Freedom, 287, 288
Toomey, David, 287
Tora Bora, 263–264, 347
torpedo attacks, 58, 65, 159
torpedo planes, 58, 59–60, 64, 69, 357
training, pilot
    Afghanistan, 347–348
    El Salvador, 341–342
    Greece, 333–334
    Korean War, 88, 90, 99–100
    Kosovo, 233
    South Vietnam, 339, 340
    Vietnam War, 123, 340
    WWI, 14
    WWII, 31–32, 40, 46, 60–61, 73,
        78, 100
transonic aerodynamics and speed, 374,
    388, 390, 391
Trenchard, Hugh "Boom," 14, 18–19, 23,
    28, 329, 376
Tripartite Pact, 54
Truman, Harry S., 87, 95, 96–97, 333
Truman Doctrine, 333, 339
Tunner, William H., 71–72

Turkey, 214, 242, 258, 295, 352
Turk's Cross, 18
Twentieth Air Force, 74, 78
Twentieth and Twenty-first Bomber
    Commands, 74
25 de Mayo, ARA, 161, 162–163

U-2s, 214
UAVs (unmanned aerial vehicle). *See*
    unmanned aerial vehicles (UAVs)
UCAVs (unmanned combat aerial vehicle),
    389
Udbina, 209, 215
Ullman, Harlan K., 282
UN (United Nations). *See* United Nations
    (UN)
UNC (United Nations Command). *See*
    United Nations Command (UNC)
uncertainties of history, xiv–xv
unconventional warfare, 326, 334. *See also*
    guerrilla warfare
United Kingdom. *See* Britain
United Nations (UN)
    Bosnian civil war (*See* Bosnian civil war)
    Falklands War, 158, 159
    invasion of Kuwait and Desert Storm,
        179–180, 181
United Nations Command (UNC), 81, 85
    air forces, 98–101, 102, 106
    interdiction campaign, 92–97
    Korean War, 88–89
    Pusan Perimeter, 90, 91, 94, 106
    reconnaissance, 102–103
United Nations Protection Force
    (UNPROFOR)
    Deliberate Force, 213, 216
    Deny Flight, 206, 208, 210
    Sky Watch, 205–206
United Nations Security Council Resolution
    (UNSCR)
    Bosnian civil war, 206–207, 208, 212, 214
    invasion of Kuwait, 179–180
    Korean War, 85
    Second Lebanon War, 297, 301, 303–
        304, 313–314, 316–317
    war in Kosovo, 225–226, 227
United States, Allied Force, 229, 240, 245
United States, Bosnian civil war, 203,
    209–210, 214
United States, Cold War, 86–87

United States, counterinsurgencies, 328,
    333–334, 341–343
United States, Desert Storm. *See* Operation
    Desert Storm
United States, Enduring Freedom. *See*
    Operation Enduring Freedom
United States, Falkland Wars, 158–159
United States, Israeli-Arab wars, 82, 130,
    135–136, 138, 305, 312, 313
United States, Korean War. *See* Korean War
United States, Vietnam War. *See* Vietnam
    War
United States, WWII in Europe, 36, 41,
    42–49
United States, WWII in Pacific
    Allied offensive-defensive phase, 65–70,
        73–77
    background and strategy, 53–59
    Japanese offensive phase, 60–65
    summary, 77–79
    war in Asia, 71–72
United States Strategic Bombing Survey,
    78–79
unmanned aerial vehicles (UAVs), 368, 370
    Allied Force, 245, 249–250
    Enduring Freedom, 268, 270, 347
    evolution of, 374, 378, 389–392
    Iraqi Freedom, 285, 288, 347
    Israel-Arab Wars '67–'82, 149, 150, 155
    Second Lebanon War, 302, 314,
        320–321
unmanned combat aerial vehicles (UCAV),
    389
UNPROFOR (United Nations Protection
    Force). *See* United Nations
    Protection Force (UNPROFOR)
UNSCR (United Nations Security Council
    Resolution). *See* United Nations
    Security Council Resolution
    (UNSCR)
US Air Force (USAF), 72, 361–362, 369
    aircraft technology and production, 382
    Allied Force, 231, 245, 246, 247,
        249, 251
    assistance programs, 343, 348
    Bosnian civil war, 202–203, 214, 217,
        223
    Colombia training, 343
    Enduring Freedom, 258
    Iraqi Freedom, 280, 285–286, 293–294

Korean War, 85–86, 88, 90–92, 99–100, 380–381 (*See also* United Nations Command (UNC))
space, 383
Vietnam War, 110–116, 118–126, 339–340
US Air Forces in Europe, (USAFE), 226–227, 231
US Army
  counterinsurgency doctrine, 348
  Iraqi Freedom, 280, 285, 289, 293–294
  Korean War, 89, 104
  Vietnam War, 119, 123
  WWII, 54–55
US Army Air Corps, 2, 55
US Army Air Forces (USAAF), 36, 42, 48, 55–56, 75, 78–79, 128
US Central Command (CENTCOM), 257–258, 260–261, 265, 269, 272–273
US Congress, 108, 118, 123, 341
US European Command (USEUCOM), 246
US Marine Corps (USMC)
  Bosnian civil war, 217
  counterinsurgency doctrine, 195
  Desert Storm, 195
  Enduring Freedom, 258
  Iraqi Freedom, 280, 285–287, 289–290, 293–294
  Korean War, 104
  Vietnam War, 113, 116–117, 119
  WWII, 55, 59, 78
US Navy (USN)
  Allied Force, 240
  Enduring Freedom, 258
  Iraqi Freedom, 280, 285–286
  Korean War, 88
  nuclear weapons, 360
  Vietnam War, 110–111, 112–117, 118–120, 122–123, 340
  WWII in Europe, 35–36
  WWII in Pacific, 54–55, 56–59, 60–61, 69–70, 78, 79
US Strategic Bombing Survey of 1945-1946, 358–359
USAAF (US Army Air Forces), 36, 42, 48, 55–56, 75, 78–79, 128
USAF (US Air Force). *See* US Air Force (USAF)
USAFE (US Air Forces in Europe), 226–227, 231

Uzbekistan, 259

V-2 ballistic missiles, 155, 360, 375
Van Fleet, James, 333
vantage, timely, 378–379
Vautours, 131
VC-10s, 160, 161, 259
Verdun, Battle of, 11, 15, 24
Viet Minh, 336–337, 366
Vietnam War, 107–126
  background and overview, 81–82, 107–108, 338–340
  Linebacker I, 81–82, 117–123
  Linebacker II, 81–82, 118, 124–126
  North Vietnamese invasions of South Vietnam, 109–110, 118, 126
  peace talks, 109, 117, 123–124
  Rolling Thunder, 81–82, 108–117, 118–122, 381, 384
  US operations structure and resources, 111–113
  war's end, 126, 367
Vietnamese Air Force, South (VNAF), 339, 340
Villar, Jean, 16
Vincent, Daniel, 16–17
Vinh Linh, 116–117
VNAF (Vietnamese Air Force), 339–340
Vo Nguyen Giap, 109, 336
Vogt, John, 119, 120, 121
Voisin biplanes, 3–4, 6, 8, 11
Vojvodina, 205
Vucelic, Milorad, 228
Vulcan bombers, 83, 160, 161, 163–164, 165

Wade, James P., 282
Wake Island, 61, 62
Walker, Walton H., 90
Walleye glide bombs, 114
war doctrine. *See* doctrine, war
War in the Air, The (Wells), 3
War in the Twentieth Century (Robida), 3
War of 1812, 375
War of Attrition, 127, 136–141, 153–154
War of Independence, Israel, 128, 307
War Plan Orange, 57, 59
Warba, 179
Warden, John, 247, 362–363, 376
Warsaw, 356
Warsaw Pact, 140

Warthogs. *See* A-10 Warthogs
WCMD (wind-corrected munitions dispenser), 270
weapons of mass destruction (WMD), 27, 189–190
Wehrmacht, 355, 357, 358
Weir, William, 19, 23, 25
Weizman, Ezer, 132, 147
Wells, H.G., 3, 9–10, 372
Wessex helicopters, 160, 171, 172
West Bank, 128, 134
West Falkland, 168
Westmoreland, William, 112
Weygand, Maxime, 329
Weyland, Otto P., 101, 104
Wild Weasels, 113, 119, 120, 123, 125, 184
Wilhelm II, Kaiser, 9
wind-corrected munitions dispensers (WCMD), 270
Winograd, Eliyahu, 315
Winograd Commission, 304, 308, 315–316, 319
WMD (weapons of mass destruction), 27, 189–190
Woods, Kevin M., 198–199
Woodward, Sandy, 163, 164, 174
World War I, 6–25, 327, 351–353
    aerial bombardment, 6–11, 13–16
    aviation theories, 25
    national strategies and operations, 15–25 (*See also specific nations*)
    pursuit aviation, 8, 10–13, 15, 24–25
    reconnaissance aviation, 4–8, 11, 22
    summary, 24–25, 279
World War II, Europe, 27–52, 280
    antisubmarine campaign, 35–37
    Battle of Britain, 30–35, 357, 358, 381
    Eastern Front, 37–40
    effects of air warfare, 50–52, 353, 356–359

German air power, 354–359, 360, 366, 372
    pre-war expectations and planning, 27–30
    reconnaissance, 102–103
    rockets, 375
    Western Europe, 40–50
World War II, Pacific, 53–79
    Allied defensive-offensive phase, 65–70
    background and strategy, 53–60
    Japanese offensive phase, 60–65
    summary, 77–79, 87–88, 95
    US bombing offensive phase, 73–77
    war in Asia, 70–73
Wright brothers, 4, 372

Yadlin, Amos, 303
Yalu River, 94–99
Yamaguchi, Tamon, 65
Yamamoto, Isoroku, 54, 59, 60, 64, 68
Yediot, 369–370
Yemen, 130
Yen Vien rail yard, 115
Yom Kippur War, 82, 127, 130, 141–148, 154, 380
Yorktown, USS, 58, 63, 64–65
Yugoslav Air Force and Air Defense (RV i PVO), 232–235, 242, 243, 244
Yugoslavia, Federal Republic of (FRY), 204–205, 206. *See also* Bosnian civil war; Operation Allied Force
Yugoslavian National Army (JNA), 205, 216–217. *See also* Bosnian civil war

Zeppelin, Ferdinand von, 3
Zeppelins, 1, 3–7, 9, 13–14, 18
Zero fighters, 58, 59, 61–62, 69
Zhawar Kili, 263
zones of action (ZOA), 213, 221
Zuikaku, 63–64

BIOGRAPHICAL NOTES

Itai Brun is a brigadier general in the Israeli Air Force (IAF) and currently heads the Israel Defense Forces' (IDFs') Center for Interdisciplinary Military Studies. Prior to assuming that position in September 2006, he served as an analyst in the Israeli intelligence community, with special responsibility for political-strategic assessments and methodology. From 2001 to 2004, he was in charge of the Analysis Department in IAF Intelligence. In 1995–1996, he served as an assistant to the legal adviser in the Israeli Ministry of Defense; he was admitted to the Israeli bar in 1996. He has published various articles on intelligence and air power, gives lectures at conferences throughout Israel on military- and security-related issues, and contributes articles and essays to various publications on both the changing character of war and the role of intelligence in warfare. General Brun is a graduate of the IDF Command and Staff College; he also holds a bachelor's degree in law studies from the University of Haifa and a master's degree in political science from the University of Tel Aviv.

James S. Corum is the dean of the Baltic Defence College. From 1991 to 2004, he was a professor at the U.S. Air Force School of Advanced Air and Space Studies at Maxwell Air Force Base, Alabama; in 2005, he was a visiting fellow at All Souls College, Oxford, including a fellowship in the Levershulme Programme; and then an associate professor at the U.S. Army Command and General Staff College, Fort Leavenworth, Kansas. Professor Corum is the author of several books on military history, including *The Roots of Blitzkrieg: Hans von Seeckt and German Military Reform* (1992); *The Luftwaffe: Creating the Operational Air War 1918–1940* (1997); *The Luftwaffe's Way of War: German Air Doctrine, 1911–1945*, with Richard Muller (1998); *Airpower in Small Wars: Fighting Insurgents and Terrorists*, with Wray Johnson (2003); and *Fighting the War on Terror: A Counterinsurgency Strategy* (2007). He has also authored more than fifty book chapters and journal articles on a variety of subjects related to air power and military history, and he was one of the primary authors of *Field Manual 3–24*, the U.S. Army and U.S. Marine Corps' doctrine on counterinsurgency. Corum also served in Iraq in 2004 as a lieutenant colonel in the U.S. Army Reserve. He holds a master's degree from Brown University, a master of letters from Oxford University, and a Ph.D. from Queen's University, Canada.

Lawrence Freedman has been professor of war studies at King's College London since 1982 and was appointed vice principal (research) at King's in 2003. Before joining King's, he held research posts at Nuffield College, Oxford, the International Institute for Strategic Studies, and the Royal Institute of International Affairs. Elected a Fellow of the British Academy in 1995 and made a Commander of the British Empire in 1996, he was appointed official historian of the Falklands Campaign in 1997. Sir Freedman has written extensively on nuclear strategy and the Cold War, as well as commentating regularly on contemporary security issues. His more recent publications include *Kennedy's Wars: Berlin, Cuba, Laos and Vietnam* (2000); *The Cold War* (2001); *Super Terrorism* (2002); *The Evolution of Nuclear Strategy*, 3d edition (2003); *Deterrence* (2004); *Official History of the Falklands Campaign* (2005); and *A Choice of Enemies: America Confronts the Middle East* (2008). He was educated at the Universities of Manchester, York, and Oxford.

Shmuel L. Gordon entered the Israeli Air Force in 1964, served as a fighter pilot throughout his career, including three years as squadron commander, and retired with the rank of colonel as commander of the IAF's Command, Control, Communication, Computers, and Intelligence Center. In 1985, he became the director of a research team on the Future Battlefield at the Israeli National Defense College. From 1988 to 1991, he served as a senior analyst in doctrine and advanced systems at the RAND Corporation. Gordon has written extensively on Israel's national strategy and modern warfare, and is currently focusing on postmodern strategy and doctrine for counterterrorism air warfare. He has received the Carmon Prize for research in strategic studies, the Histadrut Prize for research in national defense, the Yizhak Sade Prize for security literature, and the IAF Silver Wings for twenty-five years of active operational flying. He has a bachelor's degree in general history, a master's degree in international relations from Tel Aviv University, and a Ph.D. in international relations and strategic studies from the Hebrew University of Jerusalem. He is a graduate of the Israeli National Defense College, Advanced Systems Program, Squadron Commanders Program, Flight Instructors School, and the Israeli Air Force Academy.

Richard P. Hallion holds a Ph.D. in history from the University of Maryland. He joined the National Air and Space Museum (NASM) in 1974, serving as curator of Science and Technology. In 1982, he went to work for the U.S. Air Force, where he was a senior issues and policy analyst for Secretary Donald Rice, and for eleven years, he was the Air Force historian. In 2006, Dr. Hallion retired from the Directorate for Security, Counterintelligence, and Special Programs Oversight as senior adviser for air and space issues, remaining as senior adviser for aerospace technology (hypersonics and global strike) to the Air Force chief scientist. Most recently, he served on a National Research Council committee surveying science, technology, engineering, and mathematics workforce needs. He has experience in a variety of aircraft, from biplanes to the F–15E. He has authored numerous works; teaches, lectures, and consults widely; and is on the Board of Advisers of the Royal Air Force Centre for Air Power Studies. Dr. Hallion has been a Daniel and Florence Guggenheim Fellow, held the H. K. Johnson Chair at the U.S. Army Military History Institute and the Charles Lindbergh Chair at the NASM, was Alfred Verville Fellow at the NASM, and is a Fellow of the Earthshine Institute and of the American Institute of Aeronautics and Astronautics. Hallion is the author of several books, including *Rise of Fighter Aircraft, 1914–1918* (1984), *Storm over Iraq: Air Power and the Gulf War* (1992), and *Strike from the Sky: The History of the Battlefield Air Attack, 1911–1945* (1998).

Benjamin S. Lambeth is a senior staff member at the RAND Corporation, Santa Monica, California. In 1989–1990, he directed RAND's International Security and Defense Policy Program. Before joining RAND in 1974, he served in the Office of National Estimates at the Central Intelligence Agency. A civil pilot, Dr. Lambeth has flown or flown in more than forty different combat aircraft types with the U.S. Air Force, Navy, and Marine Corps, as well as with the British Royal Air Force, Canadian Forces, Royal Australian Air Force, German Luftwaffe, Royal Netherlands Air Force, Royal Norwegian Air Force, and the Israeli Air Force. In December 1989, he became the first U.S. citizen to fly the Soviet MiG–29 fighter and the first Westerner invited to fly a combat aircraft of any type inside Soviet airspace since the end of World War II. In 2002, he was elected an Honorary Member of the Order of Daedalians, the national fraternity of U.S. military pilots. He holds a doctorate in political science from Harvard University and is the author of numerous books, including *Russia's Air Power at the Crossroads* (1996), *The Transformation of American Air Power* (2000), *NATO's Air War for Kosovo* (2001), and *Air Power Against Terror* (2005).

R. A. "Tony" Mason, Air Vice Marshal (Ret.) in the Royal Air Force (RAF), holds an Honorary Chair at the School of Social Sciences at the University of Birmingham. His academic field of specialization is the interaction of diplomacy and armed forces, with particular reference to air power. He has published several books, articles, and papers on air power and related defense subjects, including *Air Power in the Nuclear Age, 1945–1985* (1985) and *Air Power: A Centennial Appraisal* (1994). He has contributed to policy studies for the RAF, the U.S. Air Force, and the Australian, New Zealand, German, Swedish, Netherlands, Swiss, Norwegian, Omani, Indian, Thai, South Korean, and Republic of China Air Forces. Professor Mason is a graduate of the RAF Staff College and the U.S. Air Warfare College, and holds degrees from the Universities of St. Andrews, London, and Birmingham. His last RAF appointment was as Air Secretary from 1986 to 1989. He is a former director of the Centre for Studies in Security and Diplomacy at the University of Birmingham and specialist adviser to the United Kingdom House of Commons Defence Committee, as well as a frequent media commentator on defense issues. In 2007, he was appointed an Honorary Fellow of the Royal Aeronautical Society.

John H. Morrow Jr. is Franklin Professor of History at the University of Georgia, where he specializes in the history of modern Europe, warfare, and society. He is the author of *Building German Air Power, 1909–1914* (1976), *German Air Power in World War I* (1982), and *The Great War in the Air: Military Aviation from 1909 to 1921* (1993). Morrow has edited *A Yankee Ace in the RAF: The World War I Letters of Captain Bogart Rogers* (1996) and authored a chapter in *The Oxford Illustrated History of the First World War* (1998). His comprehensive history of the First World War, *The Great War: An Imperial History*, was published in 2004. In 1988–1989, Morrow was the Charles Lindbergh Visiting Professor at the National Air and Space Museum in Washington, D.C., where he consulted on the design of the present gallery on World War I aviation. He has lectured at the National War College, the Air War College, and the U.S. Military Academy at West Point, where he served as visiting professor in the spring of 2005. Morrow chaired the History Advisory Committee to the Secretary of the U.S. Air Force and has been a commentator on early air power in television documentaries. He has a Ph.D. from the University of Pennsylvania.

Richard R. Muller is professor of military history at the School of Advanced Air and Space Studies (SAASS). As a military historian specializing in the history of World War II and the development of air power, he teaches core courses in air power history, strategy, decision making, technology, and military innovation.

Prior to joining the SAASS faculty in June 2005, Muller spent fourteen years on the faculty at the U.S. Air Force Air Command and Staff College, where he served as course director, department chairman, and dean of education and curriculum. He is the author of *The German Air War in Russia* (1992); *The Luftwaffe's Way of War: German Air Force Doctrine, 1911–1945*, with James S. Corum (1998); *The Luftwaffe over Germany: Defense of the Reich*, with Donald L. Caldwell (2007); and many articles, book chapters, and reviews. Professor Muller received his BA in history from Franklin and Marshall College and his MA and Ph.D. in military history from the Ohio State University. He has held fellowship posts at Yale University and the National Air and Space Museum.

Williamson Murray graduated from Yale University in 1963. He then served five years as an officer in the U.S. Air Force, including a tour in Southeast Asia with the 314th Tactical Airlift Wing, before returning to Yale, where he received his Ph.D. in military-diplomatic history, working under Hans Gatzke and Donald Kagan. After teaching for two years he moved to the Ohio State University in 1977 and retired in 1995 as professor emeritus of history. Professor Murray has taught at a number of academic and military institutions, including the Air War College, the U.S. Military Academy at West Point, and the Naval War College. He is the author of *The Change in the European Balance of Power, 1938–1939: The Path to Ruin* (1984), *Luftwaffe* (1985), *German Military Effectiveness* (1992), *The Air War in the Persian Gulf* (1995), and *Air War, 1914–1945* (1999). Murray coauthored *The Iraq War: A Military History* (2003) and has edited a number of books and articles on military matters, held numerous fellowships and chairs, and lectured throughout the world. At present, he is a Senior Fellow at the Institute for Defense Analyses, where he has been working on the Iraqi Perspectives Project. He is also a visiting professor at the U.S. Naval Academy at Annapolis.

John Andreas Olsen is the dean of the Norwegian Defence University College, head of its division for strategic studies, and visiting professor of operational art and tactics at the Swedish National Defence College. An active-duty lieutenant colonel in the Norwegian Air Force, he is a graduate of the German Command and Staff College (2005). Recent assignments include tours as the Norwegian liaison officer to the German Operational Command in Potsdam, as the military assistant to the attaché in Berlin, and as a tutor and researcher at the Norwegian Air Force Academy. Olsen has a doctorate in history and international relations from De Montfort University, a master's degree in contemporary British literature and politics from the University of Warwick, and a master's degree in English and a bachelor's degree in engineering from the University of Trondheim. He is the author of *Strategic Air Power in Desert Storm* (2003) and *John Warden and the Renaissance of American Air Power* (2007), and the editor of several books, including *Asymmetric Warfare* (2002) and *On New Wars* (2006).

Richard Overy, educated at Gonville and Caius College, Cambridge, went on to teach at Queen's College, Cambridge, from 1972 to 1979, before moving to King's College London in 1980. He was appointed professor of modern history in 1994, and after twenty-four years at King's College he moved to the University of Exeter in 2004, where he is professor of history. He is a specialist in air power history and the history of the Second World War. His books include *Goering: The "Iron Man"* (1984); *Bomber Command 1939–1945* (1997); *The Battle of Britain* (2000); *The Air War 1939–1945*, 2d ed. (2006); and *Why the Allies Won*, 2d ed. (2006). His book *Dictators: Hitler's Germany and Stalin's Russia* (2004) won the Wolfson Prize and the Hessell-Tiltman Prize for history in 2005. He was awarded the Samuel Eliot Morison Prize of the Society for Military History in 2001 for his contribution to military history. He is currently preparing a history of the Second World War and a history of bombing in Europe. Professor Overy is a Fellow of the Royal Historical Society (1977), Fellow of the British Academy (2000), and Fellow of King's College London (2003). Professor Overy was also featured in the 2006 BBC documentary *Nuremberg: Nazis on Trial*.

Robert C. Owen is a professor in the Department of Aeronautical Science and director of Advanced Placement Programs for the College of Aviation at Embry–Riddle Aeronautical University. He teaches courses in aviation operations, law, and history, and serves as the director of the University's Aerospace Institutes. Professor Owen joined the Embry–Riddle faculty in 2002, following a twenty-eight-year career with the U.S. Air Force (USAF) and a brief career in private industry. His military career included a mix of operational, staff, and education assignments. Owen, a military command pilot, served on the Headquarters (HQ) Air Force Staff and the HQ Staff of the Air Mobility Command. His academic assignments include positions at the USAF Academy and the School for Advanced Air and Space Studies. While on the Air Staff, he wrote the *Chronology* volume of the *Gulf War Air Power Survey*. More recently, he directed and edited *Deliberate Force: A Case Study in Effective Air Campaigning*, and the Air Force History Center recently purchased the completed manuscript of his book, *The Rise of Global Airlift in the USAF*. Dr. Owen, who retired with the rank of colonel, also works as a military and national security commentator, and is an adjunct senior analyst with the RAND Corporation.

Alan Stephens is a visiting fellow at the University of New South Wales, Australian Defence Force Academy, where he teaches military history and strategy, with special reference to air power. His previous appointments include adviser on foreign affairs and defense in the Australian federal parliament, visiting fellow at the Strategic and Defence Studies Centre at the Australian National University, and official historian for the Royal Australian Air Force (RAAF). A pilot in the RAAF, Dr. Stephens is a graduate of the RAAF Staff College, the University of New England, the Australian National University, and the University of New South Wales. Dr. Stephens has lectured and published extensively, both internationally and nationally. He is the editor of *The War in the Air: 1914–1994* (1994) and *New Era Security* (1996) and has contributed to a range of air power seminars and various publications. Dr. Stephens is the author of *High Fliers: Leaders of the RAAF* (1996) and *The Australian Centenary History on Defence, Volume 2: The Royal Australian Air Force* (2001). His most recent book is *Making Sense of War: Strategy for the 21st Century* (2006).

Wayne Thompson earned his Ph.D. in history at the University of California, San Diego, in 1975. During the Vietnam War, he served at a U.S. Air Force (USAF) intelligence station in Taiwan. From 1990 to 2003, working at the USAF History Office at Bolling Air Force Base, he was the USAF history program's liaison with the Checkmate air campaign planning group in the Pentagon. Dr. Thompson was the senior historical adviser for the *Gulf War Air Power Survey*, a principal contributor to the survey's volume on *Operations*, and the coauthor of *Air War in the Persian Gulf* (1995). Dr. Thompson wrote the USAF's initial classified report on Operation Deliberate Force and contributed to *Silver Wings, Golden Valor: The USAF Remembers Korea* (2006). He is also the author of *To Hanoi and Back: The U.S. Air Force and North Vietnam, 1966–1973* (2000), which presents research based on twenty years of classified reports and covers Rolling Thunder, Linebacker I, and Linebacker II, in addition to the smaller air operations.

Martin van Creveld was born in the Netherlands but was raised and educated in Israel. After receiving his master's degree at the Hebrew University of Jerusalem, he obtained a Ph.D. in history at the London School of Economics and Political Science. Since 1971, he has been on the faculty of the History Department at the Hebrew University, where he is currently a professor. He is one of the world's leading experts on military history and strategy, with a special interest in the future of war. He has authored twenty books, including *Supplying War* (1978), *Command in War* (1985), *The Transformation of War* (1991), *The Rise and Decline of the State* (1999), *The Changing Face of War: Lessons of Combat, from* *the Marne to Iraq* (2006), and *The Culture of War* (2008). Professor van Creveld has been a consultant to the defense establishments of several countries and has taught or lectured at practically every defense college, both military and civilian, from Canada to New Zealand and from Norway to South Africa. He has also appeared on countless television and radio programs as well as written for, and been interviewed by, hundreds of papers and magazines around the world.